DOWN BEAT

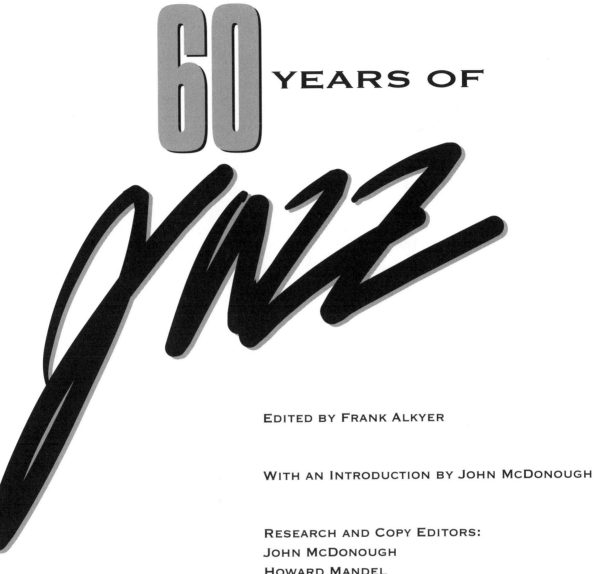

60 YEARS OF JAZZ

EDITED BY FRANK ALKYER

WITH AN INTRODUCTION BY JOHN MCDONOUGH

RESEARCH AND COPY EDITORS:
JOHN MCDONOUGH
HOWARD MANDEL
ED ENRIGHT
JOHN EPHLAND

HAL•LEONARD™
CORPORATION

7777 W. BLUEMOUND RD. P.O. BOX 13819 MILWAUKEE, WI 53213

Published by HAL LEONARD CORPORATION, 7777 W. Bluemound Road, Milwaukee, WI 53213
Printed in Winona, MN

ISBN 0-7935-3491-7

10 9 8 7 6 5 4 3 2 1

First Edition

TABLE OF CONTENTS

60 YEARS OF

INTRODUCTION
• • • • • • • • • • • • • • • • • •

6 0 Y E A R S O F

DOWN BEAT

By John McDonough

here are many roads to jazz, as any collection of fans will demonstrate. But for many of those fans, whose age today can fall anywhere between 10 and 80, that road has been paved with issues of *Down Beat* magazine.

Over the decades it has instructed, recommended, criticized, praised, condemned, advocated and, in the aggregate, honored the most dynamic American music of the twentieth century. Millions have been led to records and artists on the strength of a *Down Beat* review, news tip, or profile. It has shaped young tastes in need of guidance and challenged older ones in need of a wake-up call. In the 1930s, before any important book on jazz had yet been written, *Down Beat* collected the first important body of pre-1935 jazz history. It became a monthly, then semi-monthly, a diary of the swing era as it happened, then tracked the progression of bop, pop, rock, freedom, fusion, and nineties neoclassicism, all from the perspective of the musician. Hard to believe it began by selling insurance.

"YOU CAN'T SELL 'EM BOTH"

lbert J. Lipschultz was neither a full-time musician nor a professional journalist. He had no interest in leading a band, acquiring power, or editorializing on the affairs of the world.

Al Lipschultz had only one interest. That was selling insurance. After washing out as a saxophone player in Chicago during the years of World War I, he looked for better opportunities. Soon he found one that let him use his contacts in music. Starting in 1921, he began to cultivate an insurance clientele of working Chicago musicians. He took a special interest in

savings plans and annuities that promised musicians a monthly retirement income.

Lipschultz was not the only Chicagoan to take an interest in the welfare and financial security of musicians, however. There was James C. Petrillo, president of Local 10 of the American Federation of Musicians and one of the most commanding and aggressive—some would say reckless—figures in the American labor movement. The fact that the thirties was to be labor's moment at the moral center of American politics gave him even greater power. Anything that concerned musicians concerned Petrillo.

In the early thirties, as Lipschultz concentrated on building his insurance business, he began to see an opportunity that offered benefit to both himself and his customers. There was a need, he felt, for a musician's newspaper beyond the house organ of the AFM local. So in the summer of 1934, as the Century of Progress Exposition swung into its second season along Chicago's lakefront, Lipschultz took a small office on the eighth floor of the Woods Theater building on Clark and Dearborn, setting himself up as president of "Albert J. Lipschultz & Associates," publisher. He called his new magazine *Down Beat*, and it went on sale, all eight pages, in July 1934 for 10 cents an issue.

Adolph Bessman, an insurance associate of Lipschultz's, served as business manager. And three associate editors were hired to actually turn out the magazine. Of those three, only Glenn Burrs, a tall, balding ex-saxophone player, would stay with the publication.

By the second issue, *Down Beat* began listing band sidemen in orchestras playing around the Chicago area. Among the

hundreds of forgotten names, a few surprises leap out: Gene Krupa and Jess Stacey [sic] were working for scale and still unknown to the world. In September, *Down Beat* began running a musicians' directory. Among the 75 players listed, all within an easy ride of Chicago, was Woody Herman, then a sideman "at liberty," living on Third Street in Milwaukee. Benny Goodman's name appeared for the first time in *Down Beat* that issue; just a note that he was playing opposite Jerry Arlen at Rose's Music Hall in New York.

Jazz had not yet moved center-stage in American popular music. It was still marginalized and underground, hiding in the rank and file of the various sweet bands that made most of the music to which the country danced. The mainstream media rarely probed jazz. When *Fortune* magazine ran a major jazz article on Duke Ellington, Benny Goodman, and others in 1933, it was a rarity. Lipschultz held no brief for either form. He admitted to no partisanship, sweet or jazz. He was a salesman who felt arguments were bad for business. *Down Beat*'s raison d'etre was good will, not controversy. In 1934 the magazine ran no record reviews, no editorials, no music analysis, no criticism.

So, it must have taken Lipschultz by surprise when in the fall of 1934 he received a phone call from the formidable Petrillo. The union leader took a dim view of competition. He had seen the first issues of *Down Beat* and presumably had no particular argument with their content, which was thoroughly without provocation. What bothered Petrillo was Lipschultz himself, who seemed to be empire building. But in Chicago there was only one empire that counted, and that was Local 10. "You can sell my musicians insurance or you can sell them a magazine," Petrillo was reported to have said. "But you can't sell them both."

Lipschultz understood the situation immediately. He and Bessman withdrew their names from the

a sharp turn from being a parochial little news and gossip sheet to becoming a credible national publication with a solid musician orientation and a particularly

A former saxophone player, Glenn Burrs, second from left, bought *Down Beat* in 1935 for $1,500. He's pictured here with members of Duke Ellington's award-winning 1948 band. *From left:* Johnny Hodges, Burrs, Duke Ellington, Harry Carney, Lawrence Brown, and Billy Strayhorn.

masthead with the November issue. On November 28th Burrs purchased the magazine for a mere $1,500 and Lipschultz never again played a role.

By January 1935, the original associate editors were gone and the first record reviews began appearing, leading with Warren Scholl's enthusiastic praise for Duke Ellington's "latest composition, 'Solitude'," from Brunswick Records. Burrs took the official title of publisher and editor and hired a young free spirit named Carl Lynn Cons as associate editor and business manager, the latter title being something of a fiction. Cons had no head for business details. Nevertheless, the two soon became partners and co-owners. Burrs, a tall, extremely slender man in his late forties, was a back-slapping fellow who had a knack for being everybody's friend. His gregariousness made him a natural salesman, which in the magazine business means advertising. Cons came from Kansas City, where he had played piano professionally and dreamed of writing the Great American Novel. One associate called him "an editorial Barnum." He demanded bizarre headlines and lots of newspaper showmanship. Cons made the pages interesting, if not always entirely respectable.

During 1935 and 1936 *Down Beat* took

keen ear for jazz. Its timing couldn't have been more superb.

THERE WAS SUCH A MAN

Fresh forces stirred in popular music in the mid thirties, and where they were heading was not at first clear. Black bandleaders such as Fletcher Henderson, Duke Ellington, Chick Webb, and Bennie Moten may have been denied access to the prestige hotel venues and big money of the top commercial white bands. On the other hand, they were free of commercial constraints, too. The result was a kind of big band music that was the envy of the best, most creative musicians in America. It was only a matter of time before the music of musicians—jazz—mobilized for a vast breakout into the mainstream. What would be needed was someone who could put it into motion. Necessarily, he would have to be white, given the times. But he would also have to be a master virtuoso, a great jazz musician who understood the basic business structure of the music industry. He would have to be a man of iron discipline, enormous stamina, and ruthless determination to succeed.

In 1935 in New York there was such a man.

By the beginning of the year, *Down Beat*

was getting behind Benny Goodman in a big way. "Benny Goodman on Air in Amazing Program" a headline shouted in January. The Goodman orchestra pushed west, sometimes in the face of discouraging indifference, to keep its date with fate at the Palomar Ballroom in Los Angeles, where lightning finally struck and Goodman became a national sensation. In November, the band was back in Chicago at the Congress Hotel, four blocks from *Down Beat*'s Dearborn Street offices. Goodman stories filled the issues as his stay was extended into the spring of 1936. The music quickly acquired a name: "What Is Swing?" shouted a banner headline in April. "Here's the Answer." One of the answers was musicality. It was musicians' music, and *Down Beat* was a musician's magazine. As swing swept across the country, *Down Beat*'s fortunes rose with the tide.

The bylines of many writers who would one day emerge as the most-noted authorities on jazz first appeared in *Down Beat* as early as 1935. John Hammond appeared in June, calling Ray Noble's orchestra the "fizzle of the season." Helen Oakley, who worked as a producer for Irving Mills, wrote about Jack Teagarden. Marshall Stearns, president of the Yale Hot Club, praised Ellington. Leonard Feather, still living in London and appearing as "London correspondent" in October, wrote: "I was in New York for the first time last month and came away with the impression that, however dumb your great U.S. public may be, ours is even dumber." And Stanley Dance, another Londoner, received his first American byline in February 1936 when he took exception to a point in Stearns' article that suggested Ellington's "wah-wah" trumpets were old-fashioned.

The swing era was beginning. To the hip, the world was divided into us and them, meaning those who liked jazz and knew what was good, and everyone else. "An elect minority do really know what this jazz is all about," Feather wrote with the smug sense of superiority one feels when one is among the "elect" and everyone else is in the dark. *Down Beat* had both feet planted in the future.

The Woods Theater office was promptly shut down in the winter of 1935, and by June of that year *Down Beat* was set up at 608 South Dearborn Street. In the mid thirties it was a wonderful place for an entertainment magazine. A block away was the Dearborn Street Station at Polk Street, a rail crossroads of the continent where a reporter could easily catch celebrities for interviews as they killed time between the Santa Fe Super Chief and the Twentieth Century Limited.

Late in 1936, Burrs, who ran the business side of things, decided to take on a full-time advertising manager. *Down Beat*'s new location along the south Loop was only a few blocks from Lyon & Healy on Wabash, one of the largest music retailers in the country and a meeting place for local musicians. Among them was a 24-year-old trumpet player named Tom Herrick, who held down a day job at Shaw-Walker selling office equipment and jobbed in various groups on weekends. On Friday afternoons he would often take a long lunch and sit in at the Lyon & Healy jam sessions, usually held in the guitar department. Les Paul was among the regulars. Another was Sharon Pease, a *Down Beat* writer who specialized in piano. He was the one who brought Herrick into the *Down Beat* orbit, when he asked him to write a promotional piece called "The Book of Licks." Soon after, Burrs offered Herrick the ad manager's job for about $21.50 a week.

GREEN WITH ENVY

As *Down Beat*'s authority grew, the editors began to recognize the publicity value of a readers poll. Late in 1936, the first ballots were printed. *Down Beat* set up separate categories for swing and sweet bands, and asked readers, while they were at it, to nominate an "all-time corn band." The category was replaced the next year by simply "the king of corn," a crown that Spike Jones proceeded to win for the next 10 years, after which both his name and the category were retired. The "sweet" category ended after 1946, when Duke Ellington won in both sweet and swing, mocking the distinction and raising suspicions of ballot manipulations. As ad manager, however, Herrick recognized the poll's potential to expand the magazine's revenue base with "thank you" ads from musicians, agents, and other industry insiders. But there was one missed opportunity that left Burrs and Cons pounding their fists against the walls. "*Metronome* had also been running a readers poll," Herrick said, "and when the editor, George Simon, went to Victor

Records in 1939 with the idea of a recording session of *Metronome* All-Star poll winners, it was a real coup. We were green with envy."

Down Beat's early editor and co-owner Carl Cons, left, presents *Down Beat* Awards to Bob Crosby, Duke Ellington, and Glen Gray.

In 1938, Cons' lax attitude toward editorial deadlines began to catch up with him and the magazine. After selling hundreds of dollars of New Year's advertising, he took the page layouts home before Christmas to proof. Then he left town for a week and neglected to send them back to the office. Advertisers were not pleased when the special New Year's issue didn't come off the presses until mid January. The incident persuaded Cons and Burrs to hire experienced editorial help. The magazine had been receiving copy out of Kansas City from a 22-year-old unpaid stringer named David Dexter. He worked for the *Kansas City Journal-Post*, the smallest of the city's papers. Cons knew the paper was in financial trouble and that Dexter was looking about for other opportunities, preferably out of Kansas City. In the summer of 1938, he offered him $27.50 a week to work for *Down Beat*. Dexter accepted. Cons brought the staff to full strength when he hired Ted Toll as features editor. Toll was a drummer from Ohio who had actually recorded a half dozen jazz sides in London for Parlophone in 1936 (including an early version of "Christopher Columbus"). As an editor, Toll had a habit of jotting down catchy lines as they occurred to him, whether they

applied to a story or not. One he always wanted to use but facts never favored: BENNY KILLS THE CATS IN THE CATSKILLS. He finally bestowed it on altoist Pete Brown (July 1941) when he played the resort center.

By the late thirties, local Chicago bands had disappeared from *Down Beat*'s columns. The magazine concentrated on national names as records, radio, and movies forged a national culture. Nothing was important unless it had national potential. The swing bands were the biggest thing in music, and *Down Beat* had gotten in on the ground floor. It was not satisfied with being a "trade" magazine. There were millions of fans across the country who were as eager as anyone to know the inside stories of the music business. The more sensational, the better.

No one knew this better than Cons, who was to journalism what professional wrestling is to athletics. One day in 1939, he noticed Dexter working on a page layout. He walked into his office, looked over his shoulder, and eased him aside. "No, no," he said, taking up a pencil. "This is what I want to see." He outlined one-column pictures of Benny Goodman and Artie Shaw and scribbled a headline above: SHAW STABS GOODMAN WITH PARING KNIFE. "Or vice versa if you like," he told Dexter. "We have to have something sensational in every issue."

Cons' journalistic ethics were understandable, considering his real interests. He spent much of his time trying to write plays, none of which were ever published or staged. His office hours were sometimes pro forma. As for Burrs, who was a generation older, he seemed a bit lost in the changed music scene. He pressed his editors to do stories on pre-swing era orchestras such as Wayne King or sweet bands of the Joe Sanders-Orrin Tucker stripe. Dexter and Toll were polite, but largely brushed them off. "[They] were the ideal bosses," Dexter later wrote. "They left me alone."

Down Beat's location outside New York was no particular burden in the early years. Leonard Feather moved to America and began filing reports from New York by the end of the decade. In any case, all the important musicians came through Chicago. *Down Beat*'s people would be there, like everyone else, but with the valued privilege of access. When Harry James brought his new band into the Panther Room of the Sherman House, Dexter, Pease, and Toll showed up, pens in hand. Pease cornered Jack Gardner, James' pianist, while Dexter and Toll chatted with James' new singer, Frank Sinatra. Sinatra was flattered to be sought out by no less than *Down Beat*. He told them he had done only one other interview in his life, with George Simon of *Metronome*. The *Metronome* piece beat *Down Beat* by a month, Dexter later wrote, but they were the first two raves Sinatra received in the national press.

With Toll and Dexter on staff, the magazine began hitting the stand on schedule for the first time since its founding. Circulation climbed, along with ad revenues. George Hoefer, who began seriously collecting jazz records after seeing a Bob Crosby concert in Chicago, was invited to do a regular column on collecting. Herrick reviewed stock orchestrations put out by publishers to promote songs, in addition to managing ad sales. Bandleaders, or more accurately, their PR agents, began contributing articles.

The music world was a remarkably small place then, often with surprisingly little money to spread around. So writers on the jazz beat often worked both sides of the fence with an guileless insouciance. John Hammond produced sessions for Brunswick and later Columbia Records as he wrote about its artists. Oakley worked for agent Irving Mills, wrote for his house organ, *Melody News*, and produced many of Ellington's small-group sides, while contributing this and that to *Down Beat*. Feather was on Ellington's payroll as publicist for a period in the forties, produced records, and even wrote songs. *Down Beat* editor Dexter was producing

and annotating some of the first jazz reissues for Decca in 1941 for $35 a album. It was all quite open. Artists often would acknowledge a favor. Basie recorded an original Eddie Durham chart in 1941 that he named "Diggin' for Dex." And Jay McShann included "Dexter Blues" on his first Decca session.

CONTEMPT THAT JUMPED OFF THE PAGE

On the face of it, all this may flag conflict of interest. But it wasn't so. Beneath the appearances of slack journalistic ethics beat the hearts of pure jazz fans to the core, as devoted as any reader. Like a gathering of witnesses, they became, through *Down Beat*, what Whitney Balliett would later call jazz's first "cortege of critics." They wrote for love, rarely money. Their copy was seldom prejudiced by anything but honest excitement over great music, or indignation over corrupt commercialism. One of the virtues of amateurism is its incorruptibility.

Part of the fun of *Down Beat*'s early years was that its critics' opinions were rarely muddled with balance, nuance, or subtle elucidation. Typical was George Frazier, whose literary flair and arbitrary pot shots at the big shots won him a reputation for offbeat outrageousness. Frazier began writing for European music publications and for *Mademoiselle* while still at Harvard, where he also organized the Boston chapter of the United Hot Clubs, a network of local jazz fan clubs modeled on the organization of the United Hot Clubs of France. He became *Down Beat*'s ear in the Boston area in 1937 and wrote columns full of cranky, provocative copy the editors in Chicago loved.

Rather than play the booster, he blasted Boston's talent with a peevish contempt that, according to Charles Fountain, his biographer, "jumped off the page." To wit: "Any Boston band that plays in tune is a rarity." He hated all girl singers, except for his madonna, Lee Wiley. When all the world was beating a path to Benny Goodman's door, Frazier dismissed him as "world-weary and monotonous."

Frazier took more than a few of his musical cues from Eddie Condon. He rebelled by reflex against anything fashionable, unless, of course, it was something he made fashionable through his writing. But that was rare. He enjoyed

playing the outsider. Frazier later moved on to *Life* magazine and a place as one of jazz's first men of letters.

The other great intellectual Lone Ranger riding regularly through the pages of *Down Beat*'s early years was John Hammond, famous now as the career godfather behind Billie Holiday, Benny Goodman, Count Basie, Charlie Christian, Aretha Franklin, Bob Dylan, Bruce Springsteen, Stevie Ray Vaughan, and others. In the thirties Hammond was a product of exceptional wealth. He was the son of a prominent New York attorney of the same name and Emily Vanderbilt Sloane, whose name spoke for itself.

Hammond's passions regarding music and politics were equally fierce. He attacked racism at all levels of the music industry and beyond, anywhere he could, including the unofficial communist paper, *The New Masses*, where he wrote under the nom de plume Henry Johnson. *Down Beat*, on the other hand, while generally taking enlightened positions on such issues, was reluctant to jump on too many reform bandwagons. Nevertheless, Hammond often found ways to project ideology through his music pieces, sometimes ending up confusing art with propaganda and vice versa. In November 1935, he attacked Duke Ellington less for his music and more for shutting "his eyes to the abuses being heaped upon his race....He conscientiously keeps himself from thinking about such problems as those of the southern sharecroppers, the Scottsboro boys, intolerable working and relief conditions [sic] in the North and South....Consequently Ellington's music has become vapid and without guts." It was a curiously Stalinist view of the artist.

Among Hammond's most famous and influential *Down Beat* pieces were the raves he filed from the Reno Club in Kansas City in July 1936 about a new band led by Count Basie (though he had given the first scoop to *The New Masses* in March). Hammond was so excited and so eager to spread the word, he neglected to sign him to Brunswick Records, where he might have produced his first records. Instead, his raves in *Down Beat* brought Dave Kapp of Decca Records to Kansas City with a bargain-basement deal of his own, which the naive Basie promptly and unwisely accepted.

Legends were born in Hammond's *Down Beat* writings, none more enduring than the story he wrote in the fall of 1937 concerning the death of Bessie Smith in an auto crash. Hammond had heard through sources in the Chick Webb band that Smith had been refused admission to a nearby Memphis hospital and had died en route to another. He related the tale in a

John Hammond, right, one of Down Beat's legendary correspondents, with Count Basie.

Down Beat article headlined "Did Bessie Smith Bleed to Death While Waiting for Medical Aid?" He properly noted to readers that the account was unconfirmed, but added "I am prepared to believe almost anything [about Memphis] because its mayor and police chief publicly urged the use of violence against organizers of the CIO a few weeks ago," an observation that effectively neutralized his disclaimer about confirmation. The black press picked it up and gave it further credibility. A second *Down Beat* story a month later clarified the matter and said Smith had been taken directly to a black hospital in Clarksdale, Mississippi. But the first story had far more appeal—and, one could argue, mobilizing social value—as a rallying point for public opinion. In a time when far worse things routinely happened to black citizens in the South and when Congress could not even pass anti-lynching legislation in the face of southern opposition, the rumor had a larger validity that sustained it for decades and made it the basis of Edward Albee's 1960 play *The Death of Bessie Smith*.

Music criticism of jazz in *Down Beat* was, like jazz itself, young, arbitrary, and sometimes a bit immature. Reviewers evaluated single discs, rarely albums. They described the music and offered assessments, but analysis was thin and literary flair thinner still. Reviews were captives of a period jargon that would

sound quaint in a decade. Discographies notwithstanding, the first book-length history of jazz was still several years away.

The early outlines of that history began coming together in *Down Beat* in June 1936 when Marshall Stearns, the scholarly president of the Yale Hot Club, undertook a running "History of Swing" series, which ran more than 40 issues. It concluded with Jelly Roll Morton in March 1938. Twenty years later Stearns refined his early *Down Beat* history and published what remains today one of the more enduring jazz histories still in print, *The Story of Jazz*.

WRITERS ON A LONG LEASH

Of the three major jazz/big band publications in place by the late thirties, each had its reputation. *Orchestra World* was widely regarded as a bulletin board for PR agents. This left *Metronome*, whose history began in 1885 as a classical publication, and *Down Beat* to slug it out. *Metronome*, which was family-owned by Ned Bittner and edited by George Simon, emphasized the popular bands and current news. It was less concerned with jazz per se and its history. At *Down Beat*, Cons favored cheesecake and headlines that often promised more than they delivered. But he also gave his writers a long leash. Writers like Fred Ramsey, Paul Eduard Miller, Ahmet and Nesuhi Ertegun, and George Avakian, all of whom would one day make great

contributions, published their first national writing in *Down Beat*.

If *Down Beat* was the most important jazz publication, one would not have known it from its covers. Pursuant to Cons' notions of effective journalism, *Down Beat* covers were a mixture of celebrated musicians and anonymous models. Photos of sexy models in bathing suits and tight sweaters and aspiring starlets adorned every second or third cover. Generally, the less talent, the more skin. When a top bandleader was featured, it was often at the cost of considerable personal dignity. Gag shots were contrived by publicity agents or Cons himself: Woody Herman dressed as Santa Claus, Jimmy Dorsey dolled up as Father Time. Observant readers with an eye for little hypocrisies might have been amused when in the mid forties *Down Beat* ran an angry editorial criticizing "leaders who will sacrifice musical value for any funny hat routine."

Down Beat has been taken to task by some for the relatively few black faces on its covers in the early years. Indeed, Lester Young, Benny Carter, Charlie Christian, Ben Webster, Art Tatum, Charlie Parker, and Earl Hines, to name just a few, all had to wait until well into the fifties or sixties before they were on a cover. Was this racism?

Perhaps, though to assume so misses to some extent the point of a magazine cover in those days. It had only had one purpose: to flag attention and invite purchase. With rare exceptions, a picture on *Down Beat*'s cover had absolutely nothing to do with anything inside the magazine, save for a brief identifying caption in a small inside box. From July 1936 through 1952 *Down Beat* published about 375 covers, and fewer than 145 featured any important jazz figures. Woody Herman holds the cover record in those years with 11. Jimmy Dorsey and Duke Ellington are tied at second with 10 each. Benny Goodman is third with nine. Louis Armstrong, Peggy Lee, Frank Sinatra, Red Norvo, and Doris Day had six covers each. Gene Krupa and Stan Kenton were tied with five. Lionel Hampton, Cab Calloway, Sarah Vaughan, and Harry James had four. Nat Cole, Artie Shaw, and Glenn Miller had three each; Count Basie and Ella Fitzgerald, two. Billie Holiday never appeared on a *Down Beat* cover during this period. In total, black artists appeared on *Down Beat* covers nearly 60 times from 1936 to 1952.

But the admonition not to judge a book by its cover is quite literally true in the case of *Down Beat*. Inside, no music magazine of the period was more progressive or aggressive on the race issue, or in making sure that its readers understood the black innovators who lay behind swing. As early as September 1936, Stearns posed the basic question that has dominated discussions of jazz and its racial politics ever since: Did white musicians "borrow ideas from Negroes?" To Paul Eduard Miller, race was the music's central issue. "After more than 10 years of comparative analyses...of white and colored instrumentalists," he wrote, "I have come to the inevitable, and to me obvious, conclusion: Negroes are superior." Many black musicians who played a major role in the music—often ones whose names had fallen into obscurity, such as trombonist Jimmy Harrison or King Oliver—received proper recognition for their contributions in *Down Beat*.

In September 1939, *Down Beat's* monthly circulation brushed against 80,000. In October, the magazine became a semi-monthly, publishing on the first and fifteenth of every month, a move that, according to Dexter, increased the editors' work load about 60 percent and the revenues 100 percent. Dexter and Toll also found their salaries raised to $35 a week.

By the end of 1940, Cons was in a dilemma over *Down Beat's* New York presence. Leonard Feather, whose $8-a-week apartment on West 92nd Street had served as the magazine's New York news bureau since February, was "imprudently suggesting that $40 a month was not an adequate stipend," according to Feather. Cons disagreed. One reason was that Dexter had just told him he had received an offer from *Billboard* to go to New York as that magazine's music editor at a salary of $60 a week. Cons saw an opportunity to kill two birds with one stone: keep Dexter happy and continue a strong New York presence, though at Feather's expense. So he dropped Feather, matched the *Billboard* offer to Dexter, and sent him off to Manhattan. The New York *Down Beat* office moved to the Forrest Hotel, a musicians' residence, on 49th Street near 8th Avenue.

To cover the West Coast, *Down Beat* was sufficiently prosperous by 1940 to buy a small Los Angeles music publication called *Tempo: The Modern Musical Newsmagazine.* The acquisition brought its editor Charles Emge onto the *Down Beat* staff, with L.A. offices on Rampart Street near MacArthur Park. Over the years his columns would accumulate a wealth of information on the Hollywood studio scene and become a major source for film music historians.

Meanwhile, *Down Beat* had problems at the top. In November 1940, a little magazine called *Music and Rhythm* was launched in Chicago, with Paul Miller editing and most of the regular *Down Beat* byliners contributing articles. Other stories were written by (or ghostwritten for) top musicians and bandleaders. The orientation was features, not news. By all appearances, however, it was a sister publication of *Down Beat*, turned out by the Maher Printing Company, the same shop that produced *Down Beat*. The address on the *Music and Rhythm* masthead, 609 South Federal, was simply the rear entrance to the same building in which *Down Beat* was located at 608 South Dearborn. Even the phone numbers were the same, HAR-2706. In August 1941, Carl Cons, while still at *Down Beat*, replaced Miller as editor.

About the only *Down Beat* name not connected with *Music and Rhythm* was Glenn Burrs, who sat by and grew increasingly impatient with Cons' moonlighting while much work remained to be done on *Down Beat*. Finally, in March 1942, Cons sold his half interest in *Down Beat* to Burrs for a reported $50,000. He may have used part of the money to bolster the sagging fortunes of *Music and Rhythm*. Soon, though, additional financial reinforcements materialized when John Hammond joined Cons as co-editor that same month. With Hammond writing fighting editorials attacking racial discrimination in unions, recordings, and radio, the magazine's focus took an ideological tilt left.

The departure of Cons, which was announced in April 1942, meant more to *Down Beat* than just the loss of a founding editor. It meant that Hammond, who had taken leave of Columbia Records to devote attention to *Music and Rhythm*, would be taking his opinions elsewhere too. Most important, when he and Cons offered the post of managing editor to Dexter at $75 a week, it meant *Down Beat* would be losing its key New York editor.

Music and Rhythm was written and edited in New York by Hammond and Dexter, but dummied and printed in Chicago by Cons. The production arrangement was error-prone. By August 1942, it published its last issue. Cons went into the army and never returned to the music business or publishing. Dexter, after army duty himself, went on to one more stab at publishing: *Hollywood Note*, which featured such *Down Beat*-bred writers as George Frazier and George Hoefer but ran for only a few issues starting in March 1946. He had already begun working for Capitol Records, however, where he went on to a highly successful career.

THE CARNATION KID

Ned Williams, a veteran publicist who had edited a house magazine for Irving Mills' company and had done publicity for Cab Calloway and Duke Ellington, came over from the Hansen-Williams PR agency to become managing editor of *Down Beat* in Chicago. Mike Levin, who had been a stringer, was hired to replace Dexter in New York. Both men would dominate *Down Beat's* editorial content through the rest of the forties. Williams was a natty dresser who always wore a carnation in his lapel, carried a cane, and sported a turned up wisp of a mustache. Friends called him "the carnation kid." He was widely know and respected throughout the music business, and brought much good will to *Down Beat*. Levin was a superb writer with strong opinions and a nose for intelligent controversy. "He was extremely bright," says *Down Beat* colleague Jack Tracy, "and living evidence that the better the writer, the worse the speller. His copy was terrible to edit. You had to look at every word."

Within weeks, the look of the magazine changed too. During the early years there had been relatively minor adjustments in graphics. From the beginning, for example, the inside masthead had carried the line, "The Musicians' Newspaper." Later the editors perhaps decided that their success warranted a promotion. So, in May 1939, the line became "The Musicians' Bible," a claim that perhaps proved a bit overreaching. It quietly disappeared the following March. Meanwhile, color came to the cover for the first time in October 1939 when the magazine went to a semi-monthly schedule. This prompted the first in a series of redesigns of the cover logo. In July 1943, after eight years on South

Dearborn Street, *Down Beat* moved north to 203 North Wabash, a block from the Blackhawk and Fritzel's, two of Chicago's most celebrated celebrity hangouts, and a few hundred feet from the stage door of the Chicago Theater.

For *Down Beat* the war years meant lean years. Advertising shrank, though not because the instrument manufacturers lacked for sales. Quite the opposite. They were overwhelmed with war work and could sell anything they could make. Moreover, the War Production Board froze sales on new musical instruments. Marketing and advertising became unnecessary. All magazines felt the pinch. *Down Beat* began generating a stack of accounts payable at its printer.

The relationship between a magazine and its printer is like a marriage. Few things are closer or more interdependent. When a printer starts giving large credits to a struggling client magazine, it may be a sign that the printer may one day be going into the magazine business.

Such a printer was John Maher, who had entered *Down Beat* history in the summer of 1938 at age 39. At that time he bought Mead-Grade, a moderate-sized south-side print shop, and renamed it the John Maher Printing Company. The *Down Beat* account, which is believed to have been with Mead-Grade since 1936, went with the purchase. Maher had been a printer all his professional life. But he also had the cost control and financial instincts of an entrepreneur, attributes that Burrs lacked. In July 1943, after a six-year relationship, Burrs suddenly pulled *Down Beat* out of Maher Printing. As of August 1, the magazine began rolling off the Cuneo presses in Milwaukee, Wisconsin. The reasons for the shift are vague, but some say Maher was left holding a debt of undetermined size. Whatever the issues, the split would be temporary.

After the war, *Down Beat* began a long series of periodic "new eras" in its life. New, young writers began appearing. Ralph J. Gleason, who had been associate editor of a tiny magazine called *Jazz Information*, debuted with a guest editorial in January 1945. Herb Caen, still in the Air Corps, appeared in March. And Bill Gottlieb joined *Down Beat* after the war, bringing not only his typewriter but his camera. Yet *Down Beat* was slow to catch up. All its life the magazine had covered bands. Now it was slow to realize that that

era was passing. It reminisced increasingly. It seemed to assume that copycat leaders such as Tommy Reynolds and Jerry Wald, or even original ones like Jimmy Zito and Boyd Raeburn, would replace Goodman, Shaw, and Basie.

In January 1946, *Down Beat* went from a semi-monthly schedule (the first and fifteenth of every month) to a bi-weekly one (every other Monday), with plans to go weekly in the future. But it ran into a double whammy that included one of the sharpest inflationary spikes of the century and severe shortages. Costs rose; income didn't, despite a boost in the newsstand price from 20 to 25 cents. Among the most conspicuous of the early cost-saving shakeups was another switch in printers in July 1947. Burrs left Cuneo for an offset press in Dixon, Illinois. Suddenly, *Down Beat* appeared on a newsprint stock so coarse and cheap readers could practically pick splinters out of the fibers. The magazine looked awful. It was an appropriately unlucky way to celebrate a thirteenth anniversary. "With this issue," the magazine announced, "*Down Beat* begins a change over from a slick semi-monthly magazine type to a rugged trade weekly in better newspaper style." The editors did their best to put a good face on what was a discouraging situation.

The new *Down Beat* did indeed look rugged. But it promised quicker deadlines, bigger press runs, and expanded circulation. "You will notice many improvements in the new *Down Beat*," an editorial noted. But all readers noticed was the cheap paper and murky photos. They reacted quickly with a rush of "what's happened to *Down Beat*?" letters. Six weeks later, the editors 'fessed up with an apology and an explanation. "We don't like the present appearance of the sheet any better than you do," the magazine admitted. "As part of the general bitter struggle for survival these days, *Down Beat* was obliged to retrogress drastically. [We were] just as seriously affected by general economic conditions during the last year as many other publications." Burrs pressed on with the rugged look into 1948. Finally, on February 25, after seven months of offset type and newsprint, *Down Beat* returned to the John Maher Printing Company. With a smooth coated paper stock and letterpress printing, *Down Beat* looked like itself again.

FALLING WITH A TIDE

In the late forties, jazz seemed to be losing its cohesion. As the big band era ebbed and swing stars were dismissed as "has-beens," tradition and modernism fought for the privilege of defining jazz. Even the word "jazz" seemed curiously passé to some. So in July 1949 *Down Beat* took it upon itself to announce a contest for the best word to replace "jazz." The magazine offered to pay $1,000 in cash to the person "who coins a new word to describe the music from dixieland through bop," the headline said. Second and third prizes included the services of Charlie Barnet's orchestra and the Nat Cole Trio for one night in one's home. Even Norman Granz, whose Jazz at the Philharmonic tours were keeping a mass market interested in jazz, contributed $400 worth of prizes. In November came the word that the panel of judges deemed preferable to jazz: crewcut. Other alternatives included jarb, freestyle, mesmerrhythm, bix-e-bop, blip, schmoosic, and other equally contrived specimens.

The "let's rename jazz" contest was symptomatic of a larger challenge for *Down Beat* as the decade turned. The magazine had risen on the tide of big band swing, and now it seemed to be falling with it. Two of the top three big band winners in the magazine's 1949 poll (Barnet and Herman) disbanded before the results were announced. It was embarrassing and alarming. Everyone recognized the slump but no one could explain it, as if an explanation might lead to a solution. Critics, pundits, and industry types wrung their hands in *Down Beat* columns wondering how to "bring back the bands." But solutions of that kind were only slightly less likely than a solution to Burr's financial difficulties with *Down Beat*.

By 1950 he was falling deeper and deeper into the red on his printing bills. Maher waited and watched, not forgetting what had happened in 1943 when *Down Beat* shifted to the Cuneo Press under circumstances in which money may or may not have been owed him. He did not want it to happen again. To make financial matters worse, Burrs was undergoing a divorce, needed money, and may have feared the consequences of a property settlement with a major asset like *Down Beat* in the picture. With Maher anxious for his money and Burrs in need of liquidity, it was clear that each had something to gain by the sale of the magazine. In May 1950, the long-running tension between *Down Beat* and its printer finally came to an end, as Maher took over the magazine. Burrs' name disappeared from the masthead on

John Maher brought much-needed entrepreneurial ingenuity to *Down Beat* when he purchased it in 1950.

June 2, 1950, replaced by Tom Herrick, whom Burrs had originally hired in 1936 as advertising manager. Herrick had left in 1943, but had been contributing record reviews since the spring of 1948. Now he was publisher.

Other changes followed. As of 1951, Leonard Feather took over the New York office from Mike Levin, who joined the Roser-Reeves ad agency and in 1952 became a key player in the agency's work for Republican party during the Eisenhower campaign—the first time consumer advertising methods helped elect a president. More than personnel switches, though, there was a conscious effort at *Down Beat* to expand coverage outside the big band field. The magazine started radio and television columns and expanded pop and record coverage. It added a classical department (i.e., "longhair") and launched an annual classical critics poll in 1953. In October 1951 Maher, in his most effective cost-cutting move yet, shut down the

magazine's Wabash Avenue offices and shifted all editorial operations to the printing plant at 2001 South Calumet Avenue, where *Down Beat* shared a bullpen with several Spanish-language publications. In April 1952, Herrick left to take a job with the Seeburg Company, and Ned Williams, who liked to keep a bottle of whiskey in his desk for emergencies, was fired by Maher for having too many emergencies. A caretaker regime moved in. Harold English, a friend of Maher's who owned a press-and-type company, came in as publisher. And Hal Webman came over from *Billboard* as editor in chief, working out of New York. For the first time in *Down Beat*'s history the magazine was edited outside Chicago.

More stability arrived in October 1952 when Maher appointed Norman Weiser president and publisher. Weiser was originally from New York, where he had cultivated the music publishers and worked for a radio trade magazine. That brought him to *Billboard*, which sent him to Chicago as an ad salesman and writer. To Maher, who was actively seeking to grow *Down Beat*'s advertising base, Weiser may have looked like a rainmaker. As expected, he carried over many of his music publisher customers, though little else.

If advertising follows editorial, one of the more puzzling questions of *Down Beat*'s first 20 years was its failure to attract record advertising, save for small jazz labels such as H.R.S. This despite the fact that *Down Beat* had been reviewing records since 1935, and that the major retail outlets for records were the musical instrument stores. After the war, record coverage was even expanded. A four-step record-rating system of musical notes began with Mike Levin in May 1946. Four notes meant a top rating. This went on until January 1951, when the ratings were spread out to simple numbers from one (a dud) to 10 (a masterpiece). This lasted only 18 months, though, and was replaced in May 1952 with the five-step rating of stars, which continues today. Still, record ads remained rare. One reason was that companies used radio to do their advertising for them. They didn't know or care about consumer advertising. The recording business was also relatively small. As late as 1960, it was still dreaming of a $500 million industry gross.

But that was about to end. Technology would succeed where salesmanship had

failed. The LP began to change the marketing of records when it appeared in 1948, and revolutionized it after it became the industry standard by 1951. Norman Granz became a significant and loyal *Down Beat* advertiser, promoting his tours and record albums in big double-page layouts, even as he battled *Down Beat* critics who nit-picked his JATP concerts. Columbia Records launched its Benny Goodman Carnegie Hall Concert box set with a full-page *Down Beat* ad in January 1951, despite a near pan of the album in the same issue from Mike Levin.

One of Norm Weiser's first acts as 1953 began was to appoint Jack Tracy as editor. Tracy joined the *Down Beat* staff in March 1949 at $75 a week. "I had just graduated the University of Minnesota School of Journalism," Tracy recalls, "and that was one of the highest salaries of anyone in my class. I was 22." Another move Weiser made was to hire Chuck Suber as advertising manager. Suber was then a rising agent at General Artists Corporation, which had long-range plans for him that included Hollywood and the business side of TV. But Weiser's timing was good.

"I had just been offered a job at MCA," says Suber, "and that made me think: If they see anything in me that they want, then I want out [of the agency business]. MCA was the largest and most ruthless of all the talent agencies. You quickly learned when you worked there that your main competition was inside the company, not outside. It was company policy, and you did whatever you had to do. So when Norm offered me the *Down Beat* job, it was the alternative I needed."

The Suber-Tracy team would take *Down Beat* through the better part of the fifties and set it on the course that would spell survival. In the meantime, a new generation of noted jazz writers already had begun breaking into print through *Down Beat*: Bill Russo, John S. Wilson (from *PM* magazine), John Tynan, Nat Hentoff, and a bit later, Ira Gitler and Dan Morgenstern. In May 1952 Leonard Feather brought in a rising young TV personality, pianist, and composer in New York to write a weekly page-two column on the intrigues of song writing. The feature had to be discontinued in the summer of 1953, though, when the writer undertook a local late-night program on NBC called "Tonight." He was Steve Allen.

AFTER A DECADE OF DENIAL

In 1953, there was a slump. Suber remembers circulation dipping to below 40,000 and sinking. In broadening coverage, he recalls, the magazine had gone off in many directions and thus had no direction. As Nat Hentoff replaced Feather as New York editor in September, Weiser, Tracy, and Suber tackled the magazine's larger problems in Chicago. One strategy centered on annual issues devoted to special topics. The first annual combo issue and dance band directory appeared in 1953. They were successful enough with advertisers and readers so that ultimately there were annuals devoted to percussion, reeds, trumpet, keyboard, and other music categories. Another enduring annual ritual added in 1953 by Tracy: the *Down Beat* Jazz Critics Poll and the Hall of Fame.

In July 1954 came the first price increase since 1946, from 25 to 35 cents. To make it seem more palatable, the magazine was decked out in another graphic face-lift. It was getting to look so much like a magazine that early in 1955, after 21 years as a news tabloid in magazine's clothing, *Down Beat* finally crossed the Rubicon and converted to the standard 8½-inch by 11-inch format it maintains at this writing. The rationale was to gain greater newsstand distribution. The old newspaper look gave way in part to feature story pages. *Up Beat* and *Hi Fi* became regular supplements. The first in a 27-year line of *Down Beat* Year Books also began that year. And collections of *Down Beat* record reviews were collected in hard-cover editions in the late fifties. After Norm Weiser's departure in April 1956 to return to the music publishing business, where he became executive vice president of Chappell Music, Suber became publisher and proceeded to undertake the most radical remaking of the logo in the magazine's history. In September, the bold, all-cap look that had marked *Down Beat* graphics in various permutations from the beginning yielded to an all-lowercase look that (with periodic stylistic touch-ups) would stand for the next 34 years. In January 1957, Tracy began the *Down Beat* policy of listing complete personnels in record reviews. And in February 1958, he and Suber jettisoned the traditional news-style layout for a clean, egalitarian format inspired by *The New Yorker*.

With musicians increasingly marginalized from the center of pop music, the question at *Down Beat* was how to reach the audiences in which its traditional advertiser base would invest. One answer was to increase pop coverage at a time when pop music was at its most bland. *Down Beat* covers in the mid fifties featured show business types such as Patti Page, Maurice Chevalier, Jerry Lewis (a great big band fan and patron), and even Liberace. After 1956, *Down Beat* faced another question: how to deal with Elvis Presley. "Jack [Tracy] and I realized it couldn't be avoided," says Don Gold, then associate editor. "He was establishing a kind of new mainstream and we had to acknowledge it, though we never thought of him becoming a voice of rock and roll." Alas, neither Patti Page nor Elvis Presley would be the answer *Down Beat* was seeking. The real answer came one day from Brownsville, Texas.

In the spring of 1956, Tracy received an invitation to attend a festival of high school jazz bands in Brownsville. He was unable to attend but, he passed the invitation on to Suber, who was very interested in going. He went down to cover it as a story, and came back extremely excited by its implications. He had never seen anything like it. From then on he took a special interest in building a relationship between *Down Beat* and what he recognized as a growing movement. He helped organize clinics and rallied *Down Beat*'s major advertisers to co-sponsor clinics with musicians such as Louie Bellson, Clark Terry, and Buddy DeFranco, who had been endorsing their products for years.

After Tracy left to join Mercury Records in March 1958, and Gold, whom Tracy had hired in 1956, became editor, Suber began writing the First Chorus column. He used it often to press his theme of jazz education, which he and Maher were convinced did not have to stop at the high school level. In the late fifties he wrote a First Chorus in which he argued that the success of the high school festivals meant it was time to start a college one. "If anyone is interested," he said in effect, "call me." Someone did. Shortly thereafter, two young men from the University of Notre Dame were sitting in Suber's office, finding much to agree with Suber about. Soon all parties shook hands on a deal, and the Notre Dame Jazz Festival was born. Maher put up sponsorship money in the magazine's name with the proviso that *Down Beat* would have control over rules and procedures and would appoint the panel of judges.

The success of the Notre Dame program brought others into the field, including Stan Kenton, who became a major figure in the development of the clinic and music summer camps. His young musicians were keenly attuned to the idea of being a music faculty, and he also recognized the long-term business potential.

Jazz education turned out to be the strategy both *Down Beat* and its advertisers needed. The business justification was a straight and clear. The best way *Down Beat* could survive as a magazine was to serve musicians, particularly learning musicians. And jazz education provided the magazine an opportunity not only to write about music, but to help build it as well. "We had this burgeoning school jazz movement," says Suber, "with several hundred thousand kids and a generation of educators who came out of the swing band period. It was not only a growing audience. Most of our best circulation that the advertisers wanted to pay for came directly from this market." This pleased John Maher enormously; his support of jazz education would continue to be a major mission of *Down Beat* from then on. It pleased him that he could serve a good social purpose while at the same time helping to fortify the magazine's future.

COVER POWER

Maher generally respected editorial independence, and rarely crowded its prerogatives unless something profoundly offended him. He would become involved in editorial questions when he thought they had direct sales consequences—such as artists represented on the magazine's cover. He would look at newsstand sales, for example. If he saw a drop, common sense told him the problem was in the issue's cover power, or lack of it. He constantly weighed the selling merits of art vs. photos, of blue vs. red, of single subjects vs. groups, of knowns vs. unknowns. In the late fifties Tracy and later Gold began freshening up *Down Beat* covers with stylized, often slightly abstract illustrations. The days of leggy starlets were gone. When the magazine was preparing to move from South Calumet to 205 West Monroe in the Loop in the summer of 1959, Suber remembers he and

Gold standing ankle-deep in "band chicks" for two days as they emptied out the photo files.

In 1961, Gold commissioned David Stone Martin, whose work for Norman Granz had given Clef and Verve the most elegant album jackets in the industry, to produce 11 *Down Beat* covers. All were magnificent, especially a regal vision of Billie Holiday in February 1962. Maher authorized the unheard-of art budget of $200 each for one-time ownership.

The illustrated covers helped solve another nasty little problem, too. They helped make black artists look less black. Before drawing back in horror, however, and striking an attitude of moral outrage, one would do well to consider this matter in light of the racial zeitgeist that then prevailed. In the late fifties and early sixties, black access to many basic civil liberties was the most fiercely argued issue in American politics. The civil rights movement was underway, but nowhere near its crest. Even a staunchly liberal presidential candidate such as John Kennedy recognized the prudence of putting distance between himself and lunch counter sit-ins in the South rather than jeopardize his ambitions. Against these facts, some of the most dynamic figures in jazz were both youthful and black: Miles Davis, Ornette Coleman, John Coltrane, Charlie Mingus, Eric Dolphy, Cannonball Adderley, and many others. This put *Down Beat* in a unique dilemma. Maher became increasingly sensitive to frequent *Down Beat* covers featuring black artists. The ferocity of the controversy in America, generally, and *Down Beat*, in particular, was not something abstract, but palpable. Bundles of issues bearing black artists on a cover would be returned unopened from certain markets. In the early sixties the post-paid subscription cards in each issue started coming back blaring angry messages. About half had Jim Crow obscenities scrawled on them. The other half had Crow Jim. Maher finally approved their removal altogether. What had been a minor concern to an otherwise progressive magazine in the thirties, when race was a minor matter on the American agenda, now became a major issue. Today reservations about putting appropriate African-American subjects on magazine covers would properly be regarded as racism. But in 1960, it wasn't that simple. The hard fact of publishing life then was

that the only magazines to regularly feature black faces on their covers were members of the so-called black press, such as *Jet* and *Ebony*. Within *Down Beat,* Gold, and later Gene Lees, argued that *Down Beat* had little choice, since so many of the leading jazz artists were black. Maher was more cautious. "He never never leaned on me about it," says Gold, "only raised the question."

A BUSINESS, NOT A CAUSE

There were indeed advertisers who were unhappy about too many black faces on the cover," Suber recalled, "though nobody canceled his advertising." One of the reasons Maher listened to his advertisers was that he didn't see *Life, Look, Time, The Saturday Review, The Atlantic*, or other general-interest publications in any great hurry to put black subjects on their covers. As a jazz-oriented magazine, of course, *Down Beat* had special reason to disregard that. But Maher, who was known to take Oscar Peterson, Ray Brown, and other black acquaintances to the Union League Club without hesitation, was unwilling to take what he saw as risks with *Down Beat*'s future. He tried to balance inherently conflicting interests. He understood that the integrity of the magazine depended on editorial independence. "When I became editor," Dan Morgenstern recalls, "the first thing the Old Man said to me was, 'If you get any pressure from advertisers, let me know immediately.'" Yet, it was his nature to run the magazine as a business, not a cause. "He was neither a racist nor a reformer really," Suber recalled recently. "He was a businessman, and he responded to the things he felt affected the fundamentals of his business."

Suber may have felt less forgiving in April 1962, when Maher fired him. The two men had differences on a range of issues, and when Suber began saying publicly that he was thinking of starting a new magazine, Maher replaced him. (Suber would return in 1968, after Maher had suffered a heart attack. "I suspect he wanted someone in place who knew the magazine" in the event of his death, Suber recalled later. "Asking me back was probably a tough thing for the Old Man to swallow. But he did it graciously and willingly.")

Meanwhile, the magazine continued to grow under Don DeMicheal, an excellent

drummer and vibraphone player whom Gene Lees had brought to Chicago from Louisville, Kentucky, in 1961. DeMicheal was a superb editor who would see *Down Beat* through a time of impressive growth, as the guitar industry boomed along with the jazz education movement. He would also bring in many innovations. Layouts grew more interesting, color was added, and analytical pieces by LeRoi Jones probed social issues through music. Jazz became a vehicle for social and ideological protest in the sixties, and the black agenda moved to the center of American life—a fact that threw off the last shackles of any "cover quotas." In 1962, Ira Gitler moderated a two-part discussion on prejudice that drew more letters than any piece in a decade.

Down Beat continued to attract the finest writers. Gold had brought in Don Henahan, who later went on to become first-string classical critic for *The New York Times*. And Martin Williams had come to the magazine on Nat Hentoff's suggestion in the late fifties. But DeMicheal became the first to lure such prominent working musicians as Marian McPartland and Kenny Dorham to *Down Beat* as regular record reviewers—at $5 a review. When Atlantic brought out Ornette Coleman's album *Free Jazz* in 1961, DeMicheal recognized it as a landmark. He assigned it to two different reviewers, whose reactions polarized from no stars (John Tynan) to five (Pete Welding). Both the music and the polarization were a preview of things to come in jazz.

In the nearly seven years DeMicheal edited *Down Beat* (during which operations moved to 222 West Adams Street), he and Maher developed what one observer called a love-hate relationship. This over and above the expected tensions of any partnership between art and commerce. DeMicheal was a highly ethical man and a fighter. As Dan Morgenstern, who succeeded him at editor, has pointed out, DeMicheal would not compromise his principles. "That's why he and the Old Man may have had their fights, but they respected and even had affection for each other."

In the late summer of 1967, DeMicheal left *Down Beat*, and Morgenstern, who had first written for the magazine in the late fifties and had been associate editor in New York since the end of 1964, moved to Chicago, reluctantly, to take over. The next two years would be rocky ones. Maher suffered a heart attack complicated by emphysema late that year. At the end 1968 he died.

With Maher's death, the last remaining figure whose career went back almost to the beginning of the magazine passed from the scene. There was considerable concern for the future of *Down Beat*. Maher's will left everything to his wife. The magazine went into the hands of American National Bank as trustee, with instructions to sell it after 12 months. Neither Maher's widow, who served as titular president during the trust period, nor his two daughters had any interest in buying it themselves. But during the course of the year and at the suggestion of the bank, Maher's son Jack began to check in on *Down Beat*. The magazine was approaching profitability, and the music and record industry was on the threshold of an economic explosion. Maher decided to buy out his family's interests and continue *Down Beat* as a Maher publication. His decision was based on business, not sentiment. He frequently told friends, "The first responsibility of a business is to stay in business."

A FORCE TO BE RECKONED WITH

Before Jack Maher finally took over *Down Beat* in January 1971, he and Suber had a meeting. Maher was the owner and would take care of the business and money. Suber would take a salary and run the magazine. Both men re-emphasized the

magazine's franchise in the stage band movement and jazz education, which by then was booming.

So was rock. Its gravitational field affected almost every music being played in the post-Monterey-Pop years, from Bob Dylan to Miles Davis. *Down Beat* had to deal with it without submitting to it. "Jazz-blues-rock" became part of the cover logo, even as Morgenstern fought to moderate the magazine's

The *Down Beat* Readers Poll Winners Show in 1975. *From left:* James Newton, Bill Watrous, Freddie Hubbard, George Benson, Sonny Rollins, and Rahsaan Roland Kirk.

Jon Randolph

commitment to the pop sensibility. A compromise policy finally was reached. *Down Beat* would talk about rock acts such as the Who and Jefferson Airplane, but from the point of view of musicianship, not personality or their part in the "youth culture." There was balance. In 1972, Morgenstern invited Gary Giddins, then 22, to review jazz records, while Alan Heineman focused on rock.

By the seventies *Down Beat* had survived its old rival *Metronome* and numerous other jazz magazines that had come and gone. Now, however, there loomed *Rolling Stone*, which targeted a distinctly different readership but many of the same advertisers. Each magazine symbolized and reflected a part of the musical culture of its time. The difference was that *Down Beat* focused on the music; *Rolling Stone*

Jack Maher (shown here with his wife, Pat) purchased the magazine from his father's estate in 1971, continuing the magazine's focus on helping the learning musician.

concentrated on its attitude. Drugs were rampant in each magazine's venue. *Down Beat* had traditionally condemned their use or remained silent. *Rolling Stone* gave them the lure of myth.

Maher and Morgenstern recognized *Rolling Stone* as a force to be reckoned with. They talked about it. But in the end, the only way to directly fight back was to start another magazine. *Down Beat* could not become *Rolling Stone* without undermining its own heritage and its readership. And the prospects of succeeding at a new magazine were dim. First, Chicago was not the place to do it. But to go to L.A. or New York would take a huge investment. More important than money would be the right people. Jann Wenner was young and hungry when *Rolling Stone* appeared in November 1967. *Down Beat* was neither. "We felt jazz would not disappear, but recognized it might be in eclipse for quite a while," Suber says. "We had to just wait it out."

Down Beat did wait it out and prevailed. After Dan Morgenstern's departure to head the Institute for Jazz Studies at Rutgers University, Jack Maher took a strong editorial role as well as the title of editor for most of the next 11 years. One of his coups came on January 5, 1977, when the *Down Beat* Readers Poll became the focus of the PBS national music series, "Soundstage." Producer Ken Ehrlich had approached the magazine the previous summer with the idea of a *Down Beat* all-star program. The result was a remarkable snapshot of contemporary jazz in the seventies: Chick Corea, Stanley Clarke, George Benson, Jean-Luc Ponty, Sonny Fortune, Ron Carter, Bill Watrous, Billy Cobham, Thad Jones, Gary Burton, and others, with Quincy Jones as musical director. It was one of the most memorable jazz-on-TV events of the decade. Everybody won—jazz, *Down Beat*, PBS, and Chuck Mitchell, who left his post as associate editor of *Down Beat* and went to work in television.

In July 1979, *Down Beat* went to a monthly schedule for the first time since 1939. Circulation climbed steadily, though the appearance of country singer Merle Haggard on the cover in May 1980 cost *Down Beat* at least one outraged subscriber, Buddy Rich. A long line of editors and contributors helped put out the magazine in the seventies and eighties, of whom Larry Kart, Art Lange, John Litweiler, Howard Mandel, Robert Palmer, and Neil Tesser would establish reputations in the music world at *Down Beat* that have sustained and grown. Chuck Suber finally left in June 1982, after nearly 30 years with *Down Beat*, less six years in the sixties.

This cleared the way for a third generation of Maher men to join the company. John "Butch" Maher signed on in 1983 after a successful career in advertising sales with *The Chicago Tribune*. He ascended to publisher and continued the magazine's focus on music education by founding Musicfest, a national

who served as publisher of *Music Inc.* (a Maher-owned trade publication written for musical products retailers), assumed the role of publisher for both magazines. Frank Alkyer, who had signed on as editorial director in October 1989, was appointed editorial director/associate publisher. Those two, along with John Ephland, managing editor, and Edward Enright, associate editor, compose the editorial staff as of this writing. The success of their tenure is left to the magazine's future biographers.

In 60 years of covering jazz and related fields, *Down Beat* has distinguished itself in a way no other magazine of its kind has. It has survived, though not always in purity. "In the nineties," Howard Reich wrote in *The Chicago Tribune Magazine*, "[*Down Beat*] has annoyed and infuriated some fans by celebrating on its cover Lyle Lovett, Lou Reed, Kenny G, and Stevie Wonder. When covers such as these alternate with pieces on major jazz artists such as Wynton Marsalis, Dizzy Gillespie, and Miles Davis, *Down Beat* still gives the impression that it doesn't know exactly what it wants."

Reich may state the case of the occasionally frustrated reader. But the financial health of the magazine is at its peak. Its search for popular musicians to validate jazz is more a reflection of the splintered state of jazz. Gillespie and Davis unfortunately are dead, along with many of the other jazz legends who filled concert venues and sustained *Down Beat* during decades past. In between the boppers, who built their audiences in the fifties,

the insurgent generation devoted itself to experimentation and fusion with rock. *Down Beat* can only reflect that reality.

Through it all, however, *Down Beat* has always "kept the faith," in the words of Chuck Suber. "When it strayed from jazz, it never cut its tethers." Cons, Burrs, Herrick, Hentoff, Williams, Tracy, Emge, Suber, Feather, DeMicheal, Morgenstern, and many others all might take a measure of satisfaction in that.

But no one more than John Maher, who always carried a little piece of folded paper in his wallet and would from time to time show it to people with pride. On it were all the names of all the jazz publications that had started and folded since *Down Beat* came into being in 1934. Every time he could add a name to that list he was a very happy man. By the time he died, he was able to take considerable pleasure in the length of the list.

Today it continues to grow. ●

JOHN MCDONOUGH has been a contributing editor to *Down Beat* for 26 years. He has written numerous liner notes for albums and CDs, three of which have been nominated for Grammy Awards. His music writing appears regularly in *The Wall Street Journal,* and he has written for *American Scholar, American Heritage Magazine,* and *The Chicago Tribune* and has appeared on National Public Radio.

Current publisher Kevin Maher with Maynard Ferguson and Armand Zildjian, of Zildjian Cymbals. *Inset:* John "Butch" Maher.

student jazz festival that helped bring such young talents as Roy Hargrove and Joey DeFrancesco to the foreground.

In 1991, at the age of 43, Butch Maher lost a battle with cancer. His brother Kevin, an advertising sales professional

and Marsalis, who began building his in the eighties, is the lost generation of the sixties and seventies. For 20 years, as artists such as Stan Getz, Oscar Peterson, Gerry Mulligan, and Sonny Rollins slowly built careers and ascended to solid bankability,

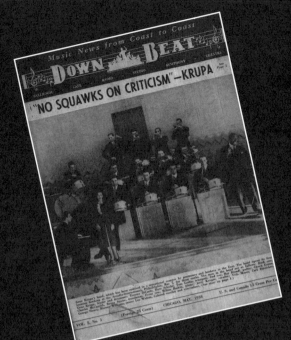

THE 1930s

INTRODUCTION

By John McDonough

I tell you," John Hammond wrote in his autobiography, "those were lovely times." He was talking about the 1930s, and he was not the only one to get sentimental over those desperate years. Historian Eric Goldman once called them "the most creative, warming, and downright exciting decade of the last century."

Today 91 percent of living Americans have no memories of that time. As you read this, the thirties are drifting with deliberate speed toward the outer frontiers of nostalgia into the unimpassioned objectivity of history, where judgments are not prejudiced by memory or longing. The decade began in the wreckage of Wall Street ("Brother Can You Spare a Dime") and ended in a streamlined vision of the future at Flushing Meadows ("Over the Rainbow"). Along the way, the twentieth century finally caught up with America.

Midway between the time markers of Wall Street and Flushing Meadows, *Down Beat* materialized in Chicago as a good-will gambit for an insurance salesman who sold to musicians.

The big band era was actually about 15 years old by 1934. If you were a musician, work was abundant. And was it work! Pre-swing dance bands thumped out fox trots like metronomes. The music and the dancing were bound in a rigid formality. A famous band could offer either a cloying sweetness (Guy Lombardo, Eddy Duchin) or an entertainer with a baton (Cab Calloway, Paul Whiteman). The real musicians were still in the rank and file and did what they were told.

The white big bands were still something of a commodity as *Down Beat* was born. In the hierarchy of the music business they were important as conduits for songs, which they were expected to play straight down the middle. This was because the chieftains of the industry power structure were the old-line music publishers of Tin Pan Alley. And the unifying product, the real source of wealth, in music was the song. In 1934 there were two ways to make money on it: selling sheet music and collecting performance royalties. With the growth of mass media and particularly radio, the second alternative set up a tremendous incentive to log as many public plays by as many bands as possible. A record made money only once. No one earned a cent when it was played at home. But a song copyright could grow money like a tree grows fruit. Thus, the trade monitored music through sheet music sales and radio plays. Records were such a minor factor; sales were not even tabulated during the thirties.

That began to change with the swing bands. Musicians who had sweated out the early thirties in so many mushy dance bands and radio orchestras revolted. Led by Benny Goodman and undergirded by the seminal writing of Fletcher Henderson, Edgar Sampson, Jimmy Mundy, and others, virtuosos began replacing baton twirlers in front of the best bands. In a decade reaching for social justice, there was a joyous sense of cultural justice in watching a mass audience respond to the pure power of truly extraordinary musicianship. As the decade slid into World War II, Count Basie, Artie Shaw, Tommy Dorsey, Harry James, Benny Carter, Lionel Hampton, Glenn Miller, and a long line of luminous soloists gave America the finest popular music it would ever know.

The musician-leaders put a unique and unforgettable signature on every record they made. It was no longer enough to have a record of "Begin the Beguine." One demanded Artie Shaw's "Begin the Beguine," Benny Goodman's "Sing Sing Sing," Count Basie's "Jumpin' at the Woodside," Glenn Miller's "In the Mood." Tunes became increasingly defined by a single version. Only Tommy Dorsey played "Song of India." Yet these were record-driven hits, not performance-driven ones. So the system didn't catch them. Today when you look at a log of Hit Parade titles, none of these anthems of the thirties appear.

Surely the most widely watched and written about event of the decade was Benny Goodman's 1938 Carnegie Hall concert. Many young intellectuals and writers who had taken up the cause of jazz were now eager to elevate perceptions of its social and artistic status to concert hall level. Perhaps it was a form of intellectual self-justification: "If I'm so smart, this stuff must really be great." In any case, the push for "legitimacy," in the European sense of the word, was off and running by the late thirties. Technique became the defining test. Virtuosity, of course, was one of several filters that classical music had used for centuries to identify and honor its master performers. Well, now in the thirties jazz suddenly had produced a generation of players who were, by any standard, virtuosos too. To any seeker of legitimacy, Goodman, Art Tatum, Teddy Wilson, Charlie Christian, Artie Shaw, Roy Eldridge, Harry James, and others became the trump cards in any argument over the parity of jazz and classical music.

For jazz the 1930s ended on a crest of consensus and unity it would never see again. There might be passing disputes over the merits of the small groups in 52nd Street vs. the big bands and tell-tale signs of commercialism. But Basie was leading the orchestra of his lifetime and Ellington had entered into the most magical years of his career. Buddy Rich and Artie Shaw were working miracles off the lobby of the Hotel Lincoln (now New York's Milford Plaza, for those who like to walk old battlefields), and Goodman had found Charlie Christian. If all that were not enough, in 1939 America made two choruses of "Body and Soul" by Coleman Hawkins a hit.

Hammond was right: "Those were lovely times." ●

GOODMAN'S PLAYING DEFIES ADEQUATE DESCRIPTION

By H.M. Oakley

AUGUST 1935

Benny Goodman played two nights in Milwaukee a couple of weeks ago. There was good attendance and the place was filled with musicians who had come up from Chicago and numerous other nearby towns. In Milwaukee they had all hired substitutes. The band was an unqualified success.

It was magnificent...two very pleasant surprises...Bunny Berigan and Jess Stacy both recently joined the

band...the one great disappointment being the absence of Toots Mondello who had stayed behind in New York. Toots has undoubtedly left a great gap in the band. It would be difficult to equal him at once—he would distinguish any reed section. The section sounds alright even now, but it lacks the beautiful airy tones and that feather-light phrasing peculiar to Toots. The saxophones have always closely resembled those in the best colored units, for lightness and swing—as a matter of fact, that statement applies to the whole band. He combines the best points of a colored band with the best of the white characteristics. This is due to a great extent to Fletcher Henderson's superb arrangements and also to Benny himself who has always shown an understanding and great appreciation of colored traits.

BERIGAN A REVELATION

Bunny Berigan was a revelation to me. Never having heard him in person before, even though well acquainted with his work on recordings, I was unprepared for such a tremendous thrill. The man is a master...he plays so well and at the same time I doubt if I ever heard a more forceful trumpet...unending ideas and possessed of that quality peculiar to both Teagarden and Armstrong, that of swinging the band as a whole at the outset and carrying it solidly along with him without a let up until the finish of his chorus. Bunny is, I believe, the only trumpeter today comparable to Louis. So much must be left unsaid, one feels stupid in attempting to evaluate Bunny's work on paper. A splendid thing all around has been Jess Stacy's addition to the band. Jess has many admirers both in this country and on the continent who will be delighted to realize that at last he has gained the proper setting, in that his work has been for the most part greatly unappreciated, and yet here is a musician who has really something to offer. Hugues Panassié considers him the greatest pianist of the white race. Judging from the point of view of swing and sincerity, Jess is a somebody that has to be listened to. He is shown to his best advantage on wax, so let us hope we'll hear a couple of piano choruses on future releases.

KRUPA UNDISPUTED KING

I had previously considered that John Hammond was overdoing it a little when he spoke of Gene Krupa's worth in the band but I am forced to tender apologies. Gene is invaluable. If not undisputed king, then certainly he is the next thing to it, and as far as the band is concerned he holds it in the palm of his hand. Everything and anything seems to be anticipated by Gene and in providing a background for a soloist he is a veritable source of inspiration. The only drawback as far as I am concerned is a purely personal one. I have a great dislike of showmanship, though granted this is a necessary and a valuable asset, and without a doubt at this Gene reigns supreme.

I can't understand why Helen Ward is not more generally appreciated. Her work is excellent, she phrases well, sings clean and with plenty of attack and knows how to swing. In this day and age when a girl vocalist is so often a thing of horror, I would think this miracle should be duly acknowledged. She sounds very swell to me.

One of the greatest things about the Goodman bunch is their arrangements . . . over two-hundred specials...any number by Henderson and some beauties by Spud Murphy and also Dean Kincaid. By the way, "Hundakola" is one of Kincaid's—and surely one of his best. I don't think the reviewer who called it "a rather stupid affair" and decidedly "Casa Lomaish" can have listened to it very carefully. There is a great deal of intricate and delightful scoring in the number and there isn't a doubt in the world but that it swings from start to close. The finish is really (in desperation I use the term) terrific.

And now Benny. A musician about whom one can very appropriately use the term "frightening." Benny plays so much clarinet. It is unbelievable...a proper leader for such a band...It would be difficult to equal his standard...Benny's work on the whole defies adequate description. The sole criticism might be that it is so easy for him to play clarinet and for this reason, there sometimes appears an added phrase or two which if it can not be labeled in bad taste must then more likely have been created in a satirical vein. I must consider the fact that Benny is playing to his public, which can be responsible for a lot of things. Tunes such as "Always," "Blue Skies," etc., must surely have been written just so that Benny might create masterpieces of them. As far as I am concerned the only bring down in the band is the work of Jack Lacey...I hate a quibbling trombone... Lacey never seems to get to the point... He lacks punch and from his recorded work, it would seem he lacks ideas, though his chorus on King Porter (Victor) is a finished trombonist but in this band he just doesn't measure up. Jo Harris, Ben Pollack's former trombone player, has joined the band chiefly in the capacity of vocalist. I hope Benny will see fit to let us hear some of his work on trombone; it would be a welcome change. Dick Clark's work has always sounded so lovely on the air, but the acoustics in a ballroom made it difficult to hear him.

HEARS JOHNSON

Benny heard LaVere Johnson singing and playing at the Lincoln Tavern and was favorably impressed. LaVere has a sensational voice and style which would be ideally suited to the Goodman way of doing things. It would be swell were LaVere to interpret vocals and Joe Harris to remain on trombone, where he is badly needed.

It had been suggested that I am putting things a little bit too strongly. I should add I did not think it necessary to state that Benny's band is immeasurably superior to any other outfit playing today, and is taking its place as the third greatest band this country has ever known, one which will probably have the greatest influence on future standards of dance music, the other two being the old Goldkette and the Pollack band of 1928. ●

"MY CHOPS WAS BEAT—BUT I'M DYIN' TO SWING AGAIN"

JUNE 1935

Louis Armstrong and his newly formed orchestra begin a tour of one-nighters, opening at Indianapolis the first week in July. Joe Glaser, Louis' newly acquired personal manager, is handling the details of the bookings.

Louis Armstrong, king of the trumpet, whose freak lip and "hot" solos have amazed and delighted musicians for 10 years, will definitely resume his career the first week in July.

"My chops was beat when I got back from Europe," said the leather-lipped and balloon-lunged Louis. "My manager worked me too hard, and I was so tired when I got back that I didn't even want to see the points of my horn. And 'pops,' he wouldn't even let the 'cats' come backstage to visit me, and you know I'm always glad to see everybody."

All musicians are "cats" to Armstrong. He usually addresses his acquaintances as "pops" or "gate."

Armstrong has been resting in the Chicago home of his mother-in-law waiting for his contract with manager Collins to expire.

His inactivity and seclusion has started a score of rumors that he had "lost his lip," that he had a split lip, that his former wife [Lil Hardin Armstrong], now leading her

own band, had tied up his earnings to satisfy the demands of her suit for alimony, and so on. Musicians all over the world wondered what the real truth was in Louis' "solitude."

"My chops is fine, now," Armstrong said, "and I'm dying to swing out again. They gave me a new trumpet over in Europe, and I've got a smaller mouthpiece than I had on my old horn. And my old first-trumpet man, Randolph, is making some swell arrangements. I'm all rested up and dying to get going again."

Asked what he thought of American dance bands after his two-year absence from the States, Louis said, "I think Benny Goodman and Casa Loma have mighty fine bands." His attention was called to Louis Prima, an Italian youth from his hometown of New Orleans, who is creating something of a sensation at the Famous Door in New York.

"I don't know Prima," Louis replied, "but his voice on phonograph records tells you that he's a mighty sweet boy. And say," Louis replied with a great deal of enthusiasm, "my old drummer, Zutty Singleton, has a nice little band right here in Chicago." Zutty plays nightly at the famous Three Deuces. ●

IMPRESSIONS OF ART TATUM AT THE GRAND PIANO

By George Duning

OCTOBER 1935

CHANGES OF KEY REMINISCENT OF BIX BEIDERBECKE'S BRAIN CHILDREN—PIANISSIMO PASSAGES THAT REMIND YOU OF A DEBUSSY NOCTURNE

Chicago, Ill.—The scene is "The Three Deuces," popular gathering place for the Chicago music profession. The tables are crowded and among the regular customers we see musicians and entertainers from the better known dance bands and radio studios. A sudden hush gathers over the room as a grand piano is rolled out upon the pocket size dance floor. A ripple of applause as Art Tatum, negro pianist extraordinary, calmly seats himself at his piano. There is no introduction, no ballyhoos—he simply starts to play—and the eyes of everyone, musician and layman alike, are trained intently upon this pianistic marvel. Sam Beers, genial host of "The Three Deuces," hovers in the background, and even Paul and Bill our pals the waiters, have stopped for a moment to listen to Tatum's meanderings over the keyboard. And there's a reason for all this rapt attention. Man! What rhythms, what harmonies, what beautiful techniques.

"In the Middle of a Kiss" for an opener—soft and sweet—a pianistic caress and a sigh, then a sudden "Swing Out! Gate" for a few bars, immediately followed by an expressive return to a "Sweet and Slow" interpretation.

HIS FLAT-FINGER TECHNIQUE

One of the first things apparent to the eye is the Tatum flat-finger technique. The backs of his hands are fat and pudgy, but the fingers are long and taper to slender tips. Instead of the customary high wrists and curved fingers of the "legit" pianist, Tatum's hand is almost perfectly horizontal, and his fingers seem to actuate around a horizontal line

drawn from wrist to finger tip. Even in the fastest scale passages, the fingers of his right hand barely seem to move but rather appear like a breath of wind through a wheat field. From "In the Middle of a Kiss" into a flashy, rhythmic arrangement of "Lulu's Back in Town." This Tatum is a showman and seems to know the meaning and value of change of pace. That rhythmic left hand is "sailing" and has every foot in the place tapping. The right hand is traveling like greased lightning, now playing measure after measure of scale and arpeggio work through black and white keys alike, then suddenly "swing out" into some octave passages of "licks" that brings inarticulate sounds of admiration from the "hot" men gathered around. There is no let-up in the one-in-a-bar tempo and swiftly the number comes to a flashy close....The applause has hardly died down and Tatum has made another change of pace by softly leading into "Sentimental Over You."

MARVELOUS "CHANGE OF PACE"

The person who doesn't raise "goose pimples" upon hearing Tatum's rendition of this favorite simply hasn't a heart. A beautiful soft legato touch—thrilling pianissimos—first chorus in tempo and melody—2nd chorus with a full harmony accompaniment in the left hand and an embellished melody in the right—3rd chorus, peculiar rhythms and more change of harmony structure with much elaboration on thematic material,

but you can still pick out the melody—4th chorus slightly Harlem and how he "takes off,"..."Tea for Two" and we are convinced that this boy is a real showman who knows how to pick his numbers. What amazing confidence. Tatum shows in his perfect hand and finger control. Scale passages and arpeggios clear cut and beautifully clean. More clever modulations and interesting harmonies....More of that excellent legato touch in "Chasing Shadows," A little comedy touch with the incongruous introduction of "Johnny Get Your Gun" themes at unexpected places....Now an improvisation that displays Tatum's ability to great advantage.

"RIGHT HAND FASTER THAN HINES"

It seems to us that his right hand is even faster and more interesting than that of the great "Father" Hines, which is saying a lot. But we think Hines' left hand is more versatile than Tatum's, who sticks to straight rhythm most of the time, whereas Hines goes in for those weird off-beat, out-of-tempo, left-hand accompaniments. But Tatum's right hand is something to behold.... "Moonglow" variations show a remarkably keen and active mind with a great conception of the possibilities of elaboration on thematic material....A novelty number suggestive of a Confrey solo, with an interesting left hand

"JUST WANT TO PLAY MODERN PIANO" SAYS TATUM

He has a black man's genius for improvising....And a white man's practiced technique.

He is a serious colored man. A fine artist in love with his instrument. And fascinated by its possibilities:

He doesn't rely on an instinctive flair for phrasing, or a "fine ear" but "hoes his row of chords" as carefully and as diligently as a gardener cultivating the soil.

Art Tatum, 26 years old this month, is unquestionably, one of the finest products that the musical melting pot of America has yet given forth.

Born in Toledo, Ohio, Art started studying piano at the age of 12 with Overton G. Ramey, under whose tutelage he continued for 6 years. then he organized a little band, and for 3 years, played in first one small club and then another. Since that time, he has devoted his efforts mostly to playing solo piano, composing, and recording.

Not usually known, however, is the fact that Tatum played violin a year and half before he took up piano. It was due to his father's wishes that he changed instruments. ●

accompaniment that sounds like the pizzicato of a full string section...."East of the Sun," with pianissimo passages that remind you of a Debussy nocturne. A chord passage that might have been taken from Stravinsky's "Firebird." Changes of key that are reminiscent of one of Bix Beiderbecke's brain children. Yet, through all of this, we can still hear and recognize "East of the Sun." And that's sumpin'. Did you hear that modulation? Cyril Scott would have admired that succession of chords.

TATUM A SHOWMAN ON KEYS

Tiger Rag" as a finale. This tune is one of our pet peeves, but Tatum makes us like it. Brother, you have never really heard "Tiger Rag" unless you have heard Tatum's version. A pianistic "Tiger" gone berserk with a vengeance. A fast chromatic passage in the left hand that is practically a realistic growl. A part of one of the famous Jimmy Dorsey sax choruses in the right hand. Listen to him go! A whirlwind finish and a great round of applause. For an encore, a soft sweet ballad. What a startling and effective contrast from "Tiger Rag." And there, friends, you have the great Art Tatum, pianist extraordinary—a fine musician and a clever showman. More power to you, Art. And here's hopin' you hit the top. You deserve it.

HE IS NOT BLIND!

Although Art has had trouble with he eyes since he was 9 years old, he is not blind. In his own words, he describes them as "not too good, but I can see enough to read and write and get around." For all fine writing, he uses a strong pair of glasses.

At the piano, Art never uses manuscripts nor reads music. In the privacy of his room, he works out the chords, and then experiments with the melody. When his "arrangement" of that melody is complete, he has mastered every conceivable chord relationship possible, and the theme has been so masterfully interwoven in intricate and pleasing rhythmic passages, and framed in the most colorful and brilliant minor and diminished chord formations that it takes your breath away.

Tatum is an architect of music with the artisan's impulse to create. He builds as confidently and with remarkable taste, structures in melodic beauty as surely as a craftsman builds a monument in steel and mortar.

MODESTY REFRESHING!

Though, Tatum knows he is a fine performer (and what artist doesn't), with him, it is not a question to be discussed; but to be dismissed at once with the thoughts of what he wants to do. Asked what his approach to music was, or to what his particular genius was due, he answered very frankly, "There's no technique or anything special about it. I just want to play modern piano! I just strive for something different; that's what the public wants."

His ambitions embrace a desire to have a band of his own some day, and to evolve a style of music, that the boys and girls of today will be playing 10 years from now.

HIS WIFE TO ASSIST HIM

Art is also in the process of teaching his wife Ruby to play the piano. He believes she will be an invaluable aid to him, when she can read the chords to him or more intricate compositions, and save him the difficulty with which he works now, with the assistance of powerful glasses.

The two people most generally admired by this wizard of the ivories is Horowitz for concert piano, and "Fats" Waller for the more popular brand of melodic outpourings. He is also very fond of Louie Armstrong.

Art has recorded for both Decca and Brunswick, the more popular of his releases being "The Shout," "After You've Gone," St. Louis Blues," "Tea For Two," "Sophisticated Lady" and "Star Dust."

He is now playing over NBC network mornings (except Sunday) from 9 to 9:15 Central Standard Time, over station WMAQ and appearing nightly at the 3 Deuces. ●

THE TRAGEDY OF DUKE ELLINGTON, THE "BLACK PRINCE OF JAZZ"

By John Hammond
NOVEMBER 1935

A MUSICIAN OF GREAT TALENT FORSAKES SIMPLICITY FOR PRETENSION

Of all our native popular composers Duke Ellington is probably the most gifted and original. For more than ten years, he has been producing, with the aid of the most accomplished orchestra in America, songs and arrangements quite unlike those of any other musician, black or white. His work has been received with international acclamation, in some cases, less than it deserved and in a few, considerable more.

Unlike so many of his contemporaries, Ellington is a hard-working, ambitious individual. Confronted with the undiscriminating praise of critics like Constant Lambert, he felt it necessary to go out and prove that he could write really important music, far removed from the simplicity and charm of his earlier tunes. "Daybreak Express," and "Rude Interlude." were the first signs of this, but even they could not prepare us for the pretension of his new 12-minute work, "Reminiscing," which Brunswick has just seen fit to release on two ten-inch records. The saddest part of the tale is that the composer considers it his most important contribution to the field of music.

The reasons for the complete sterility of this new opus are so numerous that it is difficult to know exactly where to begin. The most logical place would be with the Duke himself, since his life during the last eight years is almost the ideal example of what the modern composer, Negro or white should avoid at all costs.

As a person, Ellington is one of the most completely charming I have ever come across. His disposition is without rival among artists, for he has never been known to lose his temper or do conscious ill to anyone. He suffers abuse and exploitation with an Olympian calm and fortitude, never deigning to fight back or stand up for even his most elemental rights. Unpleasantness of any sort he flees from. He would greatly prefer not seeing the seamier side of existence and has spent most of his recent years in escaping from the harsh reality that faces even the most secure among negroes.

The Duke has been exploited in a way that is absolutely appalling to anyone not thoroughly conversant with the ethics of Broadway. Although he and his orchestra have earned between $5-and-$10 thousand a week consistently for the last eight years, he has received disgracefully little himself. His living habits are exceedingly modest for one in his position, and yet he has accumulated nothing.

Ellington is fully conscious of the fact that Broadway has not treated him fairly, knowing many of the sordid details. And yet, he did not lift a finger to protect himself because he has the completely defeatist outlook which chokes so many of the artists of his race.

It is easier to accept abuse without fighting back than to go through the unpleasantness of rows with associates. As a result, Duke has no time for rest and contemplation. He must be steadily on the run, hopping from one spot to the other in grinding out one night stands, picking up work when it can be had in theaters, and never getting down to any sustained labor. Since his music is losing the distinctive flavor it once had—both because of the fact he has added slick, un-negroid musicians to his band and because he himself is aping Tin Pan Alley composers for commercial reasons—he and his music are definitely losing favor with a once-idolatrous public. And unless there are definite changes very soon, he will be in a very precarious position.

SHUTS HIS EYES TO ABUSES

But the real trouble with Duke's music is the fact that he has purposely kept himself from any contact with the troubles of his people or mankind in general. It would probably take a Granville Hicks or Langston Hughes to describe the way he shuts his eyes to the abuses being heaped upon his race and his original class. He consciously keeps himself from thinking about such problems as those of the southern share croppers, the Scottsboro boys, intolerable working and relief conditions in the North and South—although, he is too intelligent not to know that these all do exist. He has very real fears as to his own future, and yet, he has never shown any desire of aligning himself with forces that are seeking to remove the causes of these disgraceful conditions.

Consequently, Ellington's music has become vapid and without the slightest semblance of guts. His newer stuff bears superficial resemblance to Debussy and Delius without any of the peculiar vitality that used to pervade his work. The Duke is afraid even to think about himself, his struggles and his disappointments, and that is why his "Reminiscing" is so formless and shallow a piece of music.

There is one extremely significant factor regardless of whatever worth there still exists in Ellington's orchestra. the majority of the musicians do not accept unfair dealings with the equanimity of their leader. Within the past year, they have struck together twice in my knowledge and won their demands from an unwilling manager. Even the most highly paid among Harlem musicians do not forget the fact that they come from a race that has been traditionally exploited and that a determined fight has to be waged to preserve even their present status. ●

PLENTY OF "SWING" TALENT HIDDEN IN CHICAGO

By John Hammond
MAY 1936

For many years, it has been the custom of Chicagoans to wail about the scarcity of good swing music in their city. Of course, Benny Goodman and Fletcher Henderson did give them a new lease on life, but it was still the custom of the day to say that these two inspired bands were the only good ones to be heard in that particular part of the country. As far as white bands are concerned these musical pessimists were entirely correct, but hidden away in murky spots around the South Side are joints which now do and always have featured a brand of music; which New Yorkers have never even heard about.

ISRAEL CROSBY INCOMPARABLE

A few months ago, I happened to go to an establishment run by one Mike deLisa far down on State Street. An unknown band led by Albert Ammons was playing there, and it's no exaggeration to say that I was plain knocked off my feet. In the East there just aren't any rhythm sections comparable to this one, and if there are any pianists more solid than Ammons I have yet to hear them. In many ways, the 16 year old bass player in the band, Israel Crosby, was incomparable, and the young drummer, Jimmy Hoskins, is the envy of Gene Krupa. In connection with Israel in Ammons' band I have to use the past tense, for Fletcher Henderson has been astute enough to grab him for his own orchestra. While Ammons produced by far the most compelling swing to be found on the South Side, the patrons of the deLisa, mostly colored, took him entirely for granted, and until a week or so ago the place has not even bothered to feature the name of the band in the ads.

ALBERT AMMONS ORCH. PLAYS BEST SWING IN CHICAGO

Right now Ammons' orchestra still swings more than any other I've heard in Chicago, even without Crosby. the new bass has exceptional technique but none of the rich tone his predecessor used to produce from his instrument. Guy Kelly, when he's not flying too high, plays the most soulful trumpet in the city, compensating for the flashy clarinet and alto of Dalbert Bright. The best feature of the group is that when they are feeling right, they will take a tune like the boogie woogie and play it for a half-hour, working themselves and the dancers into an emotional frenzy. but the orchestra is temperamental as hell; whole evenings go by when they are dull and lifeless. Perhaps their peculiarly bad working conditions have much to do with it.

MEADE LUX AND HIS CHIPS

There is still another place on the South Side which has music that is unquestionably greater than anything to be found in the neighborhood of New York. The place is run by Doc Huggins, who also specializes in beauty parlors, ward politics, and trucking, and the music is furnished by Lux and his Chips, which means that Meade Lux Lewis, of Honky Tonk Train Blues fame, is at the piano, assisted by an old-time trumpet and drummer. Benny Goodman, Johnny Mercer and I were there one night when Lux felt right and played some blues that must have made Pinetop sound like a member of Chicago's Four Hundred. One blues, which started out with the Jimmy Yancey bass, took more than fifty minutes, and the Honky Tonk ran on for more than half an hour. As a climax Lux whistled some blues to his own piano accompaniment which impressed Benny so much that he is getting him a Victor contract.

NEGROES EXCLUDED FROM CHICAGO UNION

If these two places are only a sample of what the South Side offers there must be more good music here than in any community outside of Kansas City. In New York, stiff license fees keep small joints from employing orchestras, and the union wage scale is so rigorously enforced that there are few spots in Harlem which can afford even a small band. but Mr. Petrillo's exclusion of Negroes from the regular Chicago local has made it possible for relatively prosperous places on the South Side to employ good bands at an average of fifteen dollars a man for a seventy hour week. The only blessing that this vicious system brings is informal and unlettered music with an almost primitive wallop. but if we once get started on the abuses Chicago's Negro musicians are forced to suffer we would consume at least sixteen of *Down Beat's* precious pages.

OVERWHELMED BY CHICAGO RHYTHM CONCERT

The concert staged by the Chicago Rhythm Club on Easter Sunday, featuring Benny Goodman's band and Teddy Wilson, is what lured me to Chicago. The success of the previous affairs had persuaded our New York Hot Club to sponsor a concert by Benny's band on the last Sunday in May, and I decided to run out to find just how these things were done. My expectations were of the highest, since Helen Oakley's organizational ability is practically legendary and the artists themselves about tops in the world of swing.

Although I had expected a large crowd, I was literally overwhelmed at the mob which attempted to jam its way into the Urban Room. My suspicion has been that the fee of a dollar and a half per seat and the fact that it was the third session would keep away most of those who had a superficial interest in improvised music;

but I was wrong, utterly wrong. My eye could spot only a small minority of musicians and all the faddists and would-be-society folk which could be collected on an Easter day.

BENNY PLAYS HENDERSON'S CREATIONS

Benny had made some rather revolutionary plans for the date. Instead of playing the bombastic Bugle Call Rags, he wanted to play the more subtle and quiet Henderson creations, omitting the usual vocal choruses. But in the first group it became obvious that what the crowd had come for was jive and strident brass, and in the middle of this Irving Berlin group he decided to cater to their whims. He interpolated about five or six songs featuring Helen Ward, finishing up with his most "sensational" arrangements. About the only place in the program where the accent was on sheer musicianship was during the trio playing of Benny, Teddy Wilson and Gene Krupa.

GOODMAN TRIO BEST IN COUNTRY TODAY

Perhaps I am prejudiced, but I do believe that this trio represents about the best ensemble playing in the country today. Wilson and Goodman have a way of cooperating and supplying each other with ideas that is almost unique in American music. Gene Krupa's drumming is usually very discreet, sometimes giving a fine lift to the others' work. When Wilson got up on the stand that Sunday, however, he seemed to sense the essential coldness of the crowd, with the result that he played with no assurance during the first set. But in the second, both Benny and he seemed entirely oblivious of the surroundings and played for their own enjoyment. the result was not so far from perfection. Wilson's own solos, however, were nothing to write home about. there was really no reason for him to feel that he had to show off his technique and play stuff like Waller's "Handful of Keys" and prestissimo "Liza."

As a consequence of the Chicago concert, the New York one has been canceled. ●

BASIE'S FINE MUSIC FROM ONE OF TOWN'S WORST DIVES

JUNE 1936

Kansas City, Mo.—While musicians and swing connoisseurs come away from a session with Basie talking to themselves with amazement, the bright business men who spend thousands of dollars to import name bands for Kansas City dancers, continue to pass up an opportunity to put the town on the musician map à la Coon-Sanders and the Nighthawks in 1921.

With a couple of years' seasoning, Count Basie's Orchestra will probably rank with any band in the country for top honors in the swing division. Hammond, Mills or some other music mogul will give them the push that should come from Kaysees hotel and restaurant big shots. Meanwhile, Basie's squad huddles together in the darkest corner of a dive known as the Reno Club, one of the town's most unsavory holes. There they swing some of the country's finest arrangements under the noses of pimps, bags and shipping clerks who may or may not appreciate them fully, but who, it is certain, cannot pay them a living wage.

BAND SWINGS OVER W9XBY

One can imagine lots more life in Basie's music than is evident at one of the Club Reno sittings. Perhaps the clean, pure air of W9XBY's studio brings the boys out of it when they broadcast. But even in the smoke-filled darkness of the rough 'n ready Reno one gets a tremendous boot listening to Basie's riders. His front rank men are Lester Young, who lackadaisically plays tenor sax 'til "who laid the chunk;" Clifford McTier, guitar; George Hunt, trombone; Walter Page, bass and Mack Washington, drums. The rhythms furnished by Basie, McTier, Washington, and Page are as solid as a booker's head, and give a rich, stimulating background to the solos.

Buster Smith, first alto sax, does the arranging, carrying out Basie's ideas with taste and finesse. It is a real pleasure to watch Basie's men play such arrangements as Savoy Stomp without even looking at the scores. They get in the groove together and work from memory without missing a note.

HIS OUTSTANDING MEN

Basie's own rating spots Young, Page, Mack Washington and Hunt as his outstanding men. The others, especially Buster Smith, rank far above the average colored musician in tone and execution. Full personnel of the band is as follows:

Count Bill Basie, piano and leader; Buster Smith, first sax and arranger; Jack Washington, third sax; Lester Young, first tenor; Slim Freeman, second tenor; Joe Keys, first trumpet; Dee Stewart, second trumpet; Carl Smith, third trumpet; George Hunt, trombone; Walter Page, bass; Mack Washington, drums; Clifford McTier, guitar; Alice Dickson, singer; and James Rushing, singer.

Basie was scheduled to leave the Reno early in June in order to rehearse his band for recording. His plans after that are uncertain at this writing, but he will doubtless be signed up by some astute booker for a good Eastern spot, while Kansas City goes smugly on its way, unconscious of the laxity of those who are supposed to bring its public real entertainment and music. ●

KANSAS CITY A HOTBED FOR FINE SWING MUSICIANS

By John Hammond

SEPTEMBER 1936

ANDY KIRK & COUNT BASIE'S ELEGANT MUSIC SPOILS CITY FOR OUT-OF-TOWN NAME BANDS

After months of yelling about Kansas City and its music, I finally got around to the place late in July. Immediately, I went to the Reno Club, where Count Basie plays; the Sunset, where the wonderful Pete Johnson and his swing band performs; and the Fairyland Park, where Andy Kirk's elegant orchestra plays nightly.

In Kansas City there are no less than 854 spots with night life of some kind, whether it be orchestras, piano players, or nickel phonographs. Descriptions of the place as the hotbed of American music are in every way justified, for there is no town in America, New Orleans perhaps excepted, that has produced so much excellent music—Negro, of course.

RENO CLUB NOT INFERIOR

But first, a few words about the Reno Club, which was so loudly razzed by some anonymous correspondent in July. If the place were any different in its clientele and management from thousands of other reasonably reputable spots in the country, perhaps last month's abusive language might have been justified. But the Reno Club is not only not inferior to comparable spots in Chicago and New York; it is infinitely preferable to them. It caters to the less privileged members of society, to be sure, but managers and bouncers, courteous ones for a change, are always on hand to see that nothing is pulled off on or away from the dance floor: the performers are promptly paid off every week (Ed Fox, please take notice), and Count Basie's band has an environment and audience properly appreciative of its miraculous music. The prices in the place are as low as the quality of liquor (ten cents for rye and gin, fifteen for Scotch, and no cover or minimum charge).

BASIE'S BAND HAS MAKINGS OF ONE OF THE FINEST

Hearing Count Basie's band is an experience I will never forget. The stage was all set for a complete disillusionment, for I had been plugging the band only from its radio work, sight unseen. I was almost scared to go near it, lest I might have to retract some of the raves I have been scattering about. but after spending only one night in the place I came away convinced that the band has the makings of the finest the country has ever known (it isn't so far from that state right now).

RHYTHM SECTION VERY VERSATILE

The first thing that flabbergasted me was the realization that all the music I had been hearing over W9XBY every night was from a mere 10-piece group: three rhythm, three saxes, four brass. The voicing of the arrangements is so deft that the band had sounded at least like a five brass four reed combination. Then there was the work of the rhythm section, with Walter Page on bass, Joe Jones, drums, and the Count on piano. the only section I have every heard even remotely comparable to it is the four-piece one of Albert Ammons in Chicago when Israel Crosby was still on bass, but even Ammons' doesn't begin to have the versatility that belongs to the Count's.

Page is one of the great bass players of the world, with a wonderful tone, flawless technique, and infinite experience. Jones, who is a recent replacement, is about as near perfection as the best drummers can come, and Count Basie on piano—well, there just aren't any words for him. He has all the solidity and endurance of Fats Waller, most of Teddy Wilson's technique and some of his taste, plus a style that is quite definitely his own. He actually swings a band that is already rocking more than any I have known.

BAND SHELL FLATTERS BRASS SECTION

As a section the brass is fine, although I would feel safer about my superlatives if I could hear it some place other than the excellent shell at the Reno, which would flatter any section. The trombone is not quite so assured as he had seemed over the air, and the trumpeter Lips Page was definitely at a disadvantage due to a temporarily wrenched leg. Outstanding in the reeds, of course, is Lester Young, who would be an asset to any band in the country on tenor. He is the kind of guy who just likes to make music, with the result that he is always to be found jamming in some unlikely joint. Buster Smith, the first alto and an important arranger, is no slouch either, for his technique is unlimited and his tone quite free from the cloying quality which colored alto men took over from the Lombardo tribe.

BASIE'S GROUP PLENTY OF ADMIRERS

Despite the fact that the Reno Club is "on the other side of the railroad tracks", it attracts many of the town's hinetier folk who are properly disgusted with the music at the Muehlebach and its high-class rivals. Basie's band has a group of fanatical admirers who are not unlike that strange eclectic group that used to follow the old Fletcher Henderson bunch from city to city. They are at a loss to understand why the Count has been allowed to remain in comparative obscurity while bands like Lunceford rise to the top.

Right now it looks as though the Eastern office of MCA will bestir themselves on Basie's behalf and exploit the band which Benny Goodman, Teddy Wilson and others consider unexcelled in the world of swing. The leader himself is a consummate natural showman, and his men have that infectious enthusiasm that inspires an audience. Whatever rough edges there still are can either be removed or made more jagged, preferably the latter.

MCA TO BOOK BASIE

Aug. 27—The above mentioned MCA office did get busy, and as a result Basie goes to work in a swell New York spot towards the end of the year. In the meantime, the band will have a chance to increase its library and make the necessary additions for a New York debut. Since I wrote the first paragraphs, I have returned to K.C. and retained all initial enthusiasm for the place.

KIRK'S BAND DESERVES A BETTER SPOT

Andy Kirk's is another band that is deserving of a far better fate than has been allotted to it. right now it is playing at a large amusement park, the Fairyland, where the customers properly appreciate it. When Mary Lou Williams does the tunes and the arrangements the band can hold its own with any in the country, because its ensemble is excellent and its rhythm section absolutely first class. Aside from Mary Lou the best of the soloists are Dick Wilson, the tenor man, and a fine trombone player whose name I continually forget. The trumpets are the weakest part of the band, but Kirk is planning on some changes, even if he has to raid Basie to do it.

THEY MAKE IT BAD FOR OUTSIDE BANDS

With the Kirk and Basie bands around to excite them, Kansas City folk are highly critical of outside orchestras who come in for one-night stands. Consequently Cab Calloway flopped dismally. Louis Armstrong's band made a bad impression, though Louis, of course, went over; and Fats Waller's group was viewed with something akin to horror. It is also ironic that K.C.'s only "class" spot, the Muehlebach Grill, should have foisted such

outrageous hands as Leon Belasco's, Buddy Fisher's, and the one I heard there in mid-July on a pretty "hep" audience. If the place had not been air-cooled, I hate to think what business would have resembled.

PETE JOHNSON A FINE BOOGIE WOOGIE PIANIST

Over at the Sunset Club, which is the town's class colored spot now that the Harlem is closed, there are two amazing personages, the blues singing Joe Turner, and the great Pete Johnson, whom Duke Ellington is said to consider the finest of the boogie woogie pianists. These two artists work perfectly together. Turner is a tremendous young guy with a powerful voice that makes him the best of an almost extinct species, the male blues singers. Pete's playing closely resembles that of Albert Ammons, and he has his full share of admirers in the town. Unfortunately his band is really sad, for which there would seem to be no excuse in a spot like that.

SHORT WAVE STATION W9XBY

W9XBY, the high fidelity broadcasting station, was another place that lived up to all of my expectations. Musically speaking, the station has the most advanced staff of any in the country. The announcers, program directors and supervisors not only appreciate the best in local music and put it on the air; they have collected a record library which I suspect to be unrivaled in the radio world. They have wires in the Sunset, Harlem, and Reno Clubs, and delight in broadcasting two hour and a half "spook" dances early Monday mornings form these joints. Not only have they all the Goodman and old Armstrong records, but also a sizable lot of race stuff which no other station in the country would consider playing. Next winter the station will have a power of five thousand watts, five times its present output. ●

A BLACK GENIUS IN A WHITE MAN'S WORLD

MUCH NONSENSE HAS BEEN WRITTEN ABOUT THE DUKE

A FRANK INTERVIEW REVEALING MANY UNHERETOFORE KNOWN FACTS ABOUT EDWARD KENNEDY ELLINGTON

By Carl Cons
JULY 1936

Editor's Note: **May it be to the white man's eternal credit, that a black man's genius is so universally recognized and acclaimed in a white man's world. The color line which has built so many racial barriers in the social world and other lines of endeavor have not corralled or subdued the Duke's great talent although it of course has influenced him. The following remarks are an honest attempt to get THE MAN on paper. The sketch is the result of an interview from midnight to sunup, and a search for the tangible is a brilliant talent. the key to understanding and appreciating fully his unusual compositions and his brilliant scoring, is to UNDERSTAND THE MAN. Because of the short acquaintance and the limited time to probe his genius necessarily this must be a portrait in miniature.**

THE DUKE IS A NEGRO!

He is a black man fully conscious of the extraordinary talents of his race AND PROUD BECAUSE HE IS A BLACK MAN.

He thinks and acts in Negroid ways. He is not a black edition of a white man, and he is not trying to imitate a white man as is the case with many negroes who prostitute their own fine talents trying to copy or emulate those of the white.

His inspiration comes from within and his music is written in what he calls the Negro idiom. Every race has its own characteristic feelings and ways of expressing them. For instance, the colored man makes love, dresses with different ideas, sings and pants, etc., quite differently than his white brother.

All these the Duke has grown up with and been a part of, and his genius is the first to translate in music all the rich color and personality of the American Negro. Their feelings of racial minority, their hopes and ideals, their tremendous vitality and good humor, their possibilities and their limitations.

Remember then that when a colored man is full of jive, he isn't always that way because he wants to be, but because when he is sincere he usually isn't taken seriously. Remember then when he is sad, that he still isn't completely free. Remember that he lives in a world that has boundary lines that he cannot cross. That when he gets out of line he may be trampled by the cruel fact of race hatred. Yes there are many overtones in negro music.

HIS EARLY LIFE—HOW HE GOT HIS START

Duke was born in Washington, D.C., as Edward Kennedy Ellington on the 29th day of April, 1899. He was a talented child and like many composers before him—it was a toss-up whether he would distinguish himself as a musician or as a painter. Duke majored in art in school, and won a scholarship in fine art at the Pratt Institute. At 14, he played piano by ear for his own amusement, and for house-rent parties. His first money was 75 cents from 8 p.m. to 1 a.m., and he was so elated that the moment the job was over he broke out for home with it.

His first real chance in fast company was the Abbott House as relief pianist for Doc Perry, and it brought an awakening to his first need for study. Duke comments jovially "that now I was recognized as a musician I had to live up to it—and protect that reputation." So he studied harmony with Henry Grant.

MARRIED AT 19

At 19, Duke got married. The world against 2 [World War II] gave him more of the fighting spirit. So he went into business for himself, took a big sized ad in the telephone directory and waited for the phone to ring. There were many parties in Washington then during the war, and between them and "these

Virginia gigs" Edward Kennedy did well. Well enough to buy a home. It was a four-piece band, that got so good, the horse-shows in the part of the country stopped hiring those 30-piece bands and hired Edward Kennedy. Bill Miller played banjo, Lloyd Stewart, drums: Duke on the piano and a fellow by the name of Tobin played C melody sax.

DESERTED THE "BARNYARD BLUES" FOR THE ROSARY

In 1923, Duke went to New York with Sonny & "Tobie" and Otoe Hardwick to join Wilbur Sweatman, a terrific clarinet player and the source of many of Ted Lewis' licks at that time. But they found they had just deserted the "Barnyard Blues" for three clarinets on the Rosary. So they Sunday concerted until the Biscuits called them back to Washington. Duke said "It was alright to be ragged, but it's bad to have your feet on the ground."

After they got fat, Elmer Snowden, banjo; Sonny Greer, drums; Art Whetsel on trumpet; and Otoe Hardwick on sax and clarinet; joined "Fats" Waller in New York. Sometime later, they sent word to Duke to join them to take "Fats" place on a vaudeville tour, and that everything was "ducky." Well, when the Duke arrived, they met him with a "Well

Ray Rising

lend me a quarter pal," and a story that bookings had been temporarily canceled. "We starved for five weeks," says Duke, "and once we split a hot-dog five ways.

WINS ON A 6-BALL GAME

Then we got a break, playing in an exclusive place in Montmartre, France, and after that worked three months in Barrens. Then five years in the Kentucky Club. "Sonny and I—we lived in the street," Duke went on. "We wouldn't eat those hot dogs anymore, so we would shoot up a '6-ball'—win $2 on a deuce, spend 75 cents each on dinner, tip the waiter 25 cents and keep 1 quarter to start in another game.

"In 1927, we opened the Cotton Club and in 1931 we closed it. And we have been on the road ever since. We sailed for Europe and the Blue Mills Rhythm Band came down and played 'Stormy Weather.' Yes, the world is full of jive, but we have never been bored."

HIS PHILOSOPHY

Duke is a Baptist and a Methodist. And believes in a hereafter. Definitely so. He is kind and forgiving and believes there is a leniency in the after world. And believe it or not Duke said, "I read the Bible every night before retiring whether I'm 'tight' or not. I got a lotta things to answer for." He also returns thanks before each meal.

There is a lot of the passive resignation of his race in the Duke. And an engaging modest charm, that amazes when you consider the amount of attention that has been showered upon him. He is a perfect gentleman, and leans backward in his efforts to be courteous and considerate. He will not even talk to a white woman without his manager. He knows too well, the inflammatory

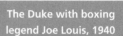

The Duke with boxing legend Joe Louis, 1940

moods of a dominant race.

REFUSED TO STUDY COMPOSITION

It is significant to know that Duke refused to study composition because he felt he had something essentially Negro to express in his muscle, and an intangible something he felt academic training would stifle rather than encourage. He does not like mathematical problems and avoids the mechanical in music.

Duke is highly imaginative and extremely sensitive to close and weirdly beautiful harmonies. He has a mirror type of mind that catches all the brilliant, colorful and vivid images of living and reflects them in tonal pictures. He is reflective rather than interpretive in that he is interested principally in reproducing all his experiences rather than accounting for them. He is a tone painter, that tries to catch all the warmth and color of a setting sun on his canvas keyboard, translating sight into sound, and using chords as his pigments.

HIS MUSICAL IDEAS

Many critics read a great deal of their own personalities into Duke's music when they start interpreting it for us—and usually miss the central ideas. This is regrettable, but a simple mistake that would not be made over and over again, if they understood one fundamental characteristic of the Duke. He is a narrator, and a describer. "Lightnin'" is the description of a train journey with all its excitement and variety of scenes and sounds. "Mood Indigo" is an innocent little girl longing—soliloquizing. "TOODLEO," the picture of an old Negro man broken down with hard work in the field coming up a road at sunset, his broken walk in rhythm.

One critic described his composition "Monkey" as an experimental exercise in whole tone scales, and a weaving of rhythmic and melodic patterns. Duke says "It's just a bunch of monkeys, that all; it

sounds like the jungle because it doesn't sound like anything else." And he received his inspiration one day at the zoo!!!

WHAT HE STRIVES FOR

I like to work alone, and to reach for intricate figures. I always figure cluster: never any of that single jive. and I always try to get a lift in my music—that part of rhythm that causes a bouncing, buoyant, terpsichorean urge. My idea of real Negro music is getting the different Negro idioms in cluster forms, and the distribution of those idioms in arrangement and still retain their Negroid quality.

"I don't like to trifle with another man's idea, unless I can finish it in the same manner and style that it was conceived. It's bad to interfere with another man because you interrupt his inspiration and spoil the flow of his thoughts.

"I stop writing when I stop feeling because if you continue after that you become an observer rather than the participator. Many of the boys in the band get good ideas and I always try to let them finish them out themselves unless I too can feel it, and can help them by suggesting.

HIS AMBITIONS

I have never caught a vine swinging in a forest, but I think that would be a real moment in musical literature when the gently swaying to and fro of that vine, and the rhythmic swish of the leaves as they were caressed by it, could be captured in orchestral sound."

Duke is living for the day when he can write an opera. He has already planned a suite of numbers depicting the history and accomplishments of his race from their origin in Africa to their present day status, catching all the violence, misery, torture, and the yearning of their trials and tribulations.

It is a gigantic task but one that challenges and inspires him and the type of thing that should interest and intrigue our more commercial white maestros into some genuine creative musical enterprise. ●

PREDICTED RACE RIOT FADES AS DALLAS APPLAUDS QUARTET!

By John Hammond
OCTOBER 1937

A minor revolution took place in deepest and darkest Dixie early in September when Benny Goodman's band invaded the South for the first time. Benny's boys were engaged for the purpose of pulling the Dallas Exposition out of the red, but the world at large was scared that if Benny attempted to foist Lionel Hampton and Teddy Wilson upon a typically Southern crowd, he would not only be a flop but would possibly goad the population to acts of violence.

On all sides Benny was advised to leave the two colored boys behind. White folks told him Southerners detested Negroes even as entertainers, and that they positively would not stand for Negroes being presented before their eyes on terms of complete equality with white performers. Even the colored press was skeptical; Porter Roberts, the Pegler of negro columnists, ventured to predict that Goodman would never dare bring them along, and it is a fact that Lionel and Teddy went to Texas with considerable misgivings.

All along I had the suspicion that if the trio and quartet made excellent music the crowd would swallow its prejudices and acclaim the artists. But just the same I made it my business to be in Dallas on the day of the opening just to see what would happen. After watching the parade that the Chamber of Commerce had organized to greet the so-called King of Swing, I made my way to the exposition ground and into the beautiful Casino which Jo Mielziner designed in one of his more inspired moments.

So that the point of this story might not be lost, I would like to explain that the

Casino puts on two shows a night, one at 8:15 p.m. and the other at 10:30 p.m.. The spectator must pay a separate admission and stiff minimum charge for each performance, with the room being completely cleared between each show.

The opening night Benny was a harried individual and neglected to find enough time to set up Lionel's vibes on the stand. The show ran a little longer than usual, and as a result Benny was forced to omit the trio and the quartet in the early part of the evening. When the crowd, many of whom had come hundreds of miles for the occasion, heard that they would not be able to hear Teddy and Lionel they were loud in their fury, and several of them even went so far as to demand a refund. After that, Benny knew that a Dallas audience was no different from any other in the country. Needless to say, when the quartet was presented at the later show it was an enormous success, and there was not even the slightest hint of a protest during the entire 11-day stay from anyone in the audience.

There is one interesting feature about this whole affair. Most of the middle- and upper-class Southerners I spoke to about the use of Negroes with white musicians assured me there would be no objection to the mixture as long as the music they produced was superlative. It was only a few Southern white musicians who said that Benny could never get away with it, and I suspect that a Marxist would have no difficulty in analyzing their wistful thinking.

MOVIE IS TYPICAL DULL LAVISH MUSICAL

Goodman spent a hectic two months in California, making another of those dull, lavish Warner Brothers musicals by day and smashing all records for the third and last time at the Palomar by night. The movie, which appeared to be badly directed by Busby Berkeley, unimaginatively photographed by Charlie Rosher, and appallingly written by one Jerry Wald, will do nothing to injure Benny's reputation, however. The recording was nothing less than perfection (Benny can thank Dave Forrest for this), and the trio, quartet, band all have good spots in the picture.

There was only one really unpleasant episode during the entire filming. Secretly one night after the band had left the set, the director photographed Johnny Davis, who has some comic part in the story which calls for him to play in the band, playing all of Harry James' choruses. Benny and the band found out about this by accident and made such violent protests that the Warner folk were forced to abandon the idea and destroy the film. But now that Benny has left Hollywood it would not surprise me at all to see Dick Powell playing Benny's clarinet choruses in the finished production. ●

Benny Goodman and Lionel Hampton, 1942

CARNEGIE HALL GETS FIRST TASTE OF SWING

By Annemarie Ewing

FEBRUARY 1938

BENNY'S CLARINET SOUNDS GOOD TO LORGNETTES—BAND A BIT SHAKY

The boys are nervous.

After all, it *was* Carnegie Hall and the pile of the red plush seats was still ruffled from contact with the devotees who had listened to the Beethoven Fourth Symphony and the Mozart Haffner Symphony and the violin of Georges Enesco playing the Saint Saens concerto that afternoon. Even the New York Philharmonic Symphony microphone still hung in austere silence twenty feet above the first rows of the orchestra.

And supposing you were Harry James or Gene Krupa or Babe Russin, with a nervous grin on your face and the knowledge of a vast concert hall filled with 3,900 people, more than a hundred of them sitting on the stage (at $2.20 a chair), and the space in the rear crowded with the dim shadows of people who had waited in line since 2 p.m. that afternoon for standing room to go on sale.

It isn't the same as playing for the crowd at the Manhattan Room, or even the hysterical audiences in the CBS Playhouse.

"Sure, I'm nervous," Harry James said. "You know, Carnegie Hall, after all."

Later he went out to take the first big band of the evening!

And "Sure, I'm nervous," said Gene. "But gee! I always get nervous. Every time we change hotels I get nervous!"

Then he went out to take the second big hand of the evening.

Babe Russin said he'd prepared himself with a half gallon of blackberry wine. And Gordon Griffin with lobster and whiskey.

Only the inscrutable Teddy Wilson, with a face like an East Indian deity, and Lionel Hampton, last arrival, shrugged as if to say, "It's only another performance after all."

Then all of them lost themselves, discussing degrees of nervousness with Ivy Anderson, who came down in a Persian lamb coat and her customary breezy camaraderie, to cheer the boys on.

"I guess this is the top," Ivy said. "Say, I was so nervous when I made my first movie, my knees knocked together!"

She demonstrated how her knees behaved in Hollywood.

"And on our first European tour—boy! was I nervous."

At this point, Sam, the major domo of backstage Philharmonic Symphony proceedings, warmed up to the whole business. Out of the vest pocket of his tuxedo, he produced the key to that holy of holies, the door marked with a plaque "For Members of the Philharmonic Symphony Society Only." Sam conducted a personal tour through the big club room where the Philharmonic Symphony musicians play chess, or smoke or gossip during intermissions. Gene and Teddy and Ivy and one of the Philharmonic violinists who had come over to see what all the shooting was for, looked around in awe, stretching their necks at the pictures on the wall.

Everybody was impressed with the Toscanini pictures—a photograph of him with the orchestra on its European tour, a portrait, and a drawing by a Philharmonic flutist, very moderne.

"I guess he's about the biggest musician of all," said Ivy.

"He's even considered greater than Stokowski," said Teddy, with amiable deference. Then seemed surprised to learn that Stokowski is at least fifty-five years old.

Sam showed them the old lithograph of Wagner's dream of "Tannhauser." They all recognized it—but Ivy called him "Vogner" to Philharmonic Sam's "Waggonner."

When the sacred door was again locked, we heard music seeping through the dressing room section of Carnegie Hall—rhythmic, pulsating music, not much like the kind that comes from concert meister's bow.

It came from the sanctum sanctorum of Philharmonic conductors, the chamber with ante room just to the right of the back stage stairway. And it was your swing man's cure for all evils—a jam session!

As I live and breathe, Jess Stacy started playing the piano back there. And it wasn't long before Benny himself—complete with that blue carnation, and not nervous (oh, no! except that those papers in his hands were trembling like the Lullaby of the Leaves!)—Benny who immediately got the point and set in with the clarinet. Pretty soon there was a trumpet or two. And a sax. And the feet of the artists of the evening, tapping with as many rhythms as there were feet.

By the time Martha Tilton skipped up the steps looking like a blushing version of Snow White in pale pink tulle, full and fresh as a little girl's first party dress, with pink roses in her blonde hair the jam session was going full tilt. Martha trucked into the same room in which Enesco, five hours earlier, had turned the famous violin which the Frenchman, Coll, made specially for him.

"Martha! Honey!" everybody shouted—showing that everybody was set.

"They just start playing," said the violinist who had come over to see what all the shooting was for, a little wistfully, "and it all synchronizes!"

Then, all of a sudden, it was 8:45 p.m. and Benny, pale as a ghost, was instructing everybody to go on together, and the boys pushing each other around in the wing space—about four square feet, filled with photographers, musicians, ticket holders with seats on the stage, a curly-headed usher, trying to be dignified, and the press. And all the boys refusing to be the first one out. And Gene asking if there was anybody in the house, and grinning. And Benny instructing his man Godfrey ("Benny calls me Godfrey, but mah name's Jimmie," he said later at the Savoy) to call the boys from Ellington's band and the boys from Basie's band as soon as he finished with "Sometimes I'm Happy." And Gordon Griffin finally being pushed out first. And the applause welling up. And nobody being able to forget the way "Godfrey" (or

Jimmie, as you will) leaned down and polished off the tips of Benny's shoes before he went on!

Much of what followed is by now, as the man says, history.

The unassuming way that American swing took the platform, plain and unadorned and panicking them. The way Bobby Hackett dreamed through the Beiderbecke chorus of "I'm Comin' Virginia." The way Benny took off Ted Lewis, even to the angle of the clarinet, with a nuance that said, louder than words, that he was playing a caricature. The way Harry Carney, Cootie, and Johnny Hodges made "Blue Reverie" everything that Duke Ellington had in mind when he created it.

The way Teddy grinned with appreciation when his audience lifted him on the palms of its applause after "Body and Soul." The way dignified, gray-haired gentlemen in the orchestra seats laughed as they have not laughed this side of a smoking car to hear Lionel Hampton's "Yeah! Yeah's!" in "Nobody's Baby Now" and "I Got Rhythm." The way the hush fell, more poignant than any of the Gershwin eulogies as Benny, unaccompanied, set into the opening phrase of "Man I Love."

Well, by the time they had polished off the program's jam session—with Benny sitting happily in the back row like one of the boys, and such artists as Lester Young, Buck Clayton, Johnny Hodges, Bobby Hackett, Harry Carney, Cootie Williams, and Count Basie himself giving performances that would surely have been approved by the master improvisers of a hundred years ago, by the man Beethoven himself—it was time to see what was going on out in front.

And don't get the idea that the audience was all jitter bug. There were lots of collegians or their equivalent, naturally. But there were also gray-haired gentlewomen in the Dress Circle whose white gloves clapped in time to the rhythm during "Bei Mir Bist du Schoen" like any debutante, of whom there were also plenty.

Not to mention the lady with the lorgnette to clap as hard as the little crippled boy whose father helped him up the steep steps to the balcony.

It was that lorgnette that made Whiteman's wire to Benny seem almost prophetic. The wire said simply, "Congratulations on your coronation! And remember, son, a clarinet sounds just as good to a lorgnette."

And don't forget Yella Pessl, the Viennese harpsichordist who has not yet got over the way Teddy Wilson plays Bach on her harpsichord, as well as swing. And who tells you, in a delightful Viennese accent, impossible to reproduce on paper, now Teddy comes to her house Friday nights and swings on her delicately classical instrument.

"Such a clarity of line," Miss Pessl says, "So much nicer to hear swing music well played than classical music played badly!"

And Rose Bampton, Metropolitan singing star who is so glad that these swing musicians can reach out to a new audience, the concert hall audience, and considers it a fine idea to preach swing to a brand new public.

Of course, there is Deems Taylor's opinion that jam sessions are only one long cadenza—and cadenzas bore him. But he will still admit that anything is worth trying once—and that a swing concert in Carnegie Hall may turn out to be more worthwhile than it seems on the surface to the Philharmonic broadcasting commentator.

One of the most interesting listeners was Shiraly, drummer with Shan-Kar, the Hindu dancer, Shiraly attracted some attention in the audience with his delicate brown profile and long, curling hair, as well as with his absorption in Krupa's playing.

"The man has a genius for rhythm," Shiraly said. "It's quite different from our Indian way of drumming, of course. He beats in multiples of two whereas we think of rhythm in multiples of three. But I am amazed to find that he makes almost a melodic instrument out of the drums. His variations are so intricate that they seem to have an absolute melodic line."

Shiraly's comment didn't differ very much from that of Sol Goodman, tympanist with the Philharmonic who was among the many Philharmonic musicians who dropped in back stage, near the end.

Sol Goodman is the man who took the pictures of Toscanini that appeared in *Life* a month or so ago. He made a special enlargement of one of his shots as a present to Benny, whose admiration for the great symphonic conductor Sol appreciates.

"There isn't a drummer I know that has the feeling for rhythm that Gene has," Sol said. "Even when he sets into a chorus cold, he seems to have some sub-conscious idea of a pattern that is perfect for what he's playing."

And perhaps some of the highest praise came from Nicholas Moldavan, viola player with the Coolidge String Quartet who were Benny's guests on his broadcast the Tuesday following the Carnegie Hall concert.

Benny played the Mozart Quintet with the Coolidge group and Mr. Moldavan.

"I consider Benny Goodman one of the great musicians of our time," Moldavan said.

With string music generally conceded to be the highest form of musical art because of its abstract purity—it's pretty hard to get higher praise than that!

But nobody is trying to insist that we make an honest woman of swing. It's enough for the moment that 3,900 people were made ostensibly joyous while a swing band made music in the nation's Number One concert hall, and still left the hall intact for the enjoyment of Beethoven, Tchaikovsky, Stravinsky, et al.

There was a little holy roller enthusiasm, certainly. There were intermittent shouts screams, and reckless hoop-la, of course. There was even sporadic trucking going on up in the Dress Circle as the boys got their teeth into "Sing, Sing, Sing."

But for the most part, the audience did just what the music indicated. When it was noisy, they were noisy. In fact, at one point, during "Bei Mir Bist du Schoen," they all began clapping in time to the music—even the woman with the long white gloves and the woman with the lorgnette. And because of the size of the hall, they were inevitably a little off the beat—a circumstance which filled the boys with momentary consternation, until Gene set in on all the drums he had, to drown them out and keep the rhythm intact.

And when the music lowered to a quiet passage, folks sat rapt and quiet, too. Sometimes it seemed almost as if Benny were directing the audience.

But the pay-off came when somebody asked Jimmy Mundy if he felt anything like George Gershwin, having his music played in Carnegie Hall. It might have been Whiteman's press agent, sitting on the stage, and remembering the famous "Rhapsody in Blue" concert.

But Mr. Mundy said, "No, I just feel like tapping mah feet!"

If that be musical treason, can anybody be blamed for wanting to make the most of it? ●

"I CREATED JAZZ IN 1902, NOT W.C. HANDY"

By Jelly Roll Morton
AUGUST & SEPTEMBER 1938

Dear Mr. Ripley:
For many years I have been a constant reader of your (Believe It or Not) cartoon. I have listened to your broadcast with keen interest. I frankly believe your work is a great contribution to natural science.

In your broadcast of March 26, 1938, you introduced W. C. Handy as the originator of jazz, stomps, and blues. By this announcement you have done me a great injustice, and you have also misled many of your fans.

It is evidently known, beyond contradiction, that New Orleans is the cradle of jazz, and I, myself, happened to be creator in the year 1902, many years before the Dixieland Band organized. Jazz music is a style, not compositions; any kind of music may be played in jazz, if one has the knowledge. The first stomp was written in 1906, namely "King Porter Stomp." "Georgia Swing" was the first to be named swing, in 1907.

You may be informed by leading recording companies. "New Orleans Blues" was written in 1905, the same year "Jelly Roll Blues" was mapped out, but not published at that time. New Orleans was the headquarters for the greatest ragtime musicians on earth. There was more work than musicians. Everyone had their individual style. My style seemed to be the attraction. I decided to travel, and tried Mississippi, Alabama, Florida, Tennessee, Kentucky, Illinois, and many other states during 1903 and 1904, and was accepted as sensational.

In the year of 1908, I was brought to Memphis by a small theatre owner, Fred Barasso, as a feature attraction and to be with his number-one company for his circuit, which consisted of four houses, namely Memphis, Tenn., Greenville, Vicksburg, and Jackson, Miss. That was the birth of the negro theatrical circuit in the U.S.A. It was that year I met Handy in Memphis. I learned that he had just arrived from his home town, Henderson, Ken. He was introduced to me as Professor Handy.

Who ever heard of anyone wearing the name of Professor advocate ragtime, jazz, stomps, blues, etc.? Of course, Handy could not play either of these types, and I can assure you he has never learned them as yet (meaning freak tunes, plenty of finger work in the groove of harmonies, great improvisations, accurate, exciting tempos with a kick). I know Mr. Handy's ability, and it is the type of folk songs, hymns, anthems, etc. If you believe I am wrong, challenge his ability.

Professor Handy and his band played several days a week at a colored amusement park in Memphis, namely, Dixie Park. Guy Williams, a guitarist, worked in the band in 1911. He had a blues tune he wrote, called "Jogo Blues." This tune was published by Pace and Handy

Frank Driggs Collection

under the same title, and was later changed to "St. Louis Blues." Williams had no copyright as yet. In 1912, I happened to be in Texas, and one of my fellow musicians brought me a number to play—"Memphis Blues." The minute I started playing it, I recognized it. I said to James Milles, the one who presented it to me (trombonist, still in Houston, playing with me at that time), "The first strain is a Black Butts' strain all "dressed up." Butts was strictly blues (or what they call a Boogie Woogie player). I said the second strain was mine. I practically assembled the tune. The last strain was Tony Jackson's strain, Whoa B-

Whoa. At that time, no one knew the meaning of the word jazz or stomps but me. This also added a new word to the dictionary, to which they gave the wrong definition.

The word blues was known to everyone. For instance, when I was eight or nine years of age, I heard blues tunes entitled "Alice Fields," "Isn't It Hard To Love," "Make Me A Palate On The Floor"—the latter which I played myself on my guitar. Handy also retitled his catalogue "Atlanta Blues." Mr. Handy cannot prove anything is music that he has created. He has possibly taken advantage of some unprotected material that sometimes floats around. I would like to know how a person could be an originator of anything, without being able to do at least some of what they created.

I still claim that jazz hasn't gotten to its peak as yet. I may be the only perfect specimen today in jazz that's living. I guess I am 100 years ahead of my time. Jazz is a style, not a type of composition.

Please do not misunderstand me. I do not claim any of the creation of the blues, although I have written many of them even before Mr. Handy had any blues published. I had heard them when I was knee-high to a duck. For instance, when I first started going to school, at different times I would visit some of my relatives per permission, in the Garden district. I used to hear a few of the following blues players, who could play nothing else—Buddie Canter, Josky Adams, Game Kid, Frank Richards, Sam Henry, and many more too numerous to mention—they were what we call "ragmen" in New Orleans. They can take a 10¢ Xmas horn, take the wooden mouthpiece off, having only the metal for mouthpiece, and play more blues with that instrument than any trumpeter I had ever met through the country imitating the New Orleans trumpeters.

I hope that this letter will familiarize you more with real facts. You may display this in the most conspicuous places, it matters not to me. I played all Berlin's tunes in jazz, which helped their possibilities greatly. I am enclosing you one of my many write-ups hoping this may help you in the authenticity of my statements. I am able to uphold all of my statements against any that may contradict. I barnstormed from coast to coast before Art Hickman made his first trip from San Francisco to New York. That was long before Handy's name was in the picture.

I think one should have conclusive proof before being able to claim a title. I also advocate much more rigid laws so thieves may get their just deserts. There are many who enjoy glory plus financial gain's abundance, even in the millions, who should be digging ditches or sweeping the streets.

My dear Mr. Ripley, I also ask you for conclusive proof, which I am sure that you will never be able to offer, due to the fact that the one who inveigled you into this announcement cannot give you any. He doesn't know anything about the foundation. New York itself is just beginning to get wise to jazz and all the decent dispensers either came from parts that I have educated or from tutors of the good New York musicians. Not until 1926 did they get a faint idea of real jazz, when I decided to live in New York. In spite of the fact that there were a few great dispensers—such as Sidney Bechet, clarinet and William Brand, bass—New York's idea of jazz was taken from the dictionary's definition—loud, blary, noise, discordant tones, etc., which really doesn't spell jazz music. Music is supposed to be soothing, not unbearable—which was a specialty with most of them.

It is great to have ability from extreme to extreme, but it is terrible to have this kind of ability without the correct knowledge of how to use it. Very often you could hear the New York (supposed-to-be) jazz bands with 12-to-15 men. They would blaze away with all volume that they had. Sometimes customers would have to hold their ears to protect their eardrums from a forced collision with their brains.

Later in the same tune, without notification, you could hear only drums and trumpet. Piano and guitar would be going but not heard. The others would be holding their instruments leisurely, talking, smoking reefers, chatting scandals, etc. Musicians of all nationalities watched the way I played; then soon I could hear my material everywhere I trod; but in an incorrect way, using figures behind a conglomeration of variations sometimes discordant, instead of hot swing melodies.

My contributions were many: First clown director, with witty sayings and flashily dressed, now called master of ceremonies; first glee club in orchestra; the first washboard was recorded by me; bass fiddle, drums—which was supposed to be impossible to record. I produced the fly swatter (they now call them brushes).

Of course many imitators arose after my being fired or quitting. I do not hold you responsible for this. I only give you facts that you may use for ammunition to force your pal to his rightful position in fair life.

Lord protect us from more Hitlers and Mussolinis.

Very truly yours,

Jelly Roll Morton
Originator of Jazz and Stomps
Victor Artist
World's greatest Hot Tune writer ●

"I WOULD NOT PLAY JAZZ IF I COULD"

By W.C. Handy
SEPTEMBER 1938

Gentlemen:
In looking over *Down Beat* I came across an article by Jelly Roll Morton captioned: "W.C. Handy is a Liar!" For your information, Ripley had me on his program "Believe It or Not," and Mr. Jelly Roll Morton wrote a similar article in the Baltimore Afro-American—a negro journal. In order to refute such statements by Jelly Roll Morton in the future, we obtained letters and statistics, etc., to make available to any newspaper that would carry such a scurrilous article.

When a paper like yours circulates lies of Jelly Roll's concoction to musicians and other professional people, it is doing me not only an injustice but an injury that is irreparable. If you want to be fair I am giving you material in this letter that you can assemble and use as a denial.

I feel perfectly sure of my position in the musical world and of my ability as a pioneer, creative musician, and composer. I brought a quartet from Alabama to Chicago for the World's Fair in 1893, which sang native songs of my arrangement. I traveled with Maharas' Minstrels, which had its headquarters at the Winterburn Show Printing Co. of Chicago in 1896, in which I arranged and played unusual unpublished Negro music. In 1897, I led the band that started from the same address, giving our first performance at Belvidere, Ill., on Aug. 4, 1896, and in Joliet, Ill., in 1897.

I was then arranging music for band, orchestra, and singers with my pen and later played Chicago at the Alhambra theatres, where some of Chicago's ablest musicians followed my band to hear us play original compositions like "Armour Avenue." This minstrel show traveled throughout the United States, Canada, Cuba, and Mexico. I had a great opportunity to hear what Negroes were playing in every city and hamlet. I lived and traveled all over the South and because

of a knowledge of Negro music, and because of my exceptional ability to write down the things peculiar to him, I created a new style of music which we now know as the "Blues," and no one contested in these 25 years my copyrights which I own, nor challenged my ability until this jealous man comes along 25 years later.

I am sending you a copy of the "Jogo Blues," which I as a musician and composer wrote, which was an instrumental following up the success of the "Memphis Blues," which I composed and wrote. In my early compositions I didn't allow anyone to dot an "I" or cross a "T" other than myself. Now, out of this "Jogo Blues" I took one strain and put words to it and composed the "St. Louis Blues." Wrote the words and music myself. Made the orchestration myself and, contrary to Mr. Morton's statement that I was playing for colored people at Dixie Park, I played this composition atop of the Falls Building in Memphis, at the Alaskan Roof Garden, which was an exclusive spot. My band played for the elite of Memphis and throughout the South. Almost every state in the South, every society affair. I did control the music at Dixie Park and played there on Sundays but substituted musicians for other days. The records of every steamboat, amusement park, dance hall, exclusive club in Memphis will reveal these facts. The Universities of Mississippi, Arkansas, Tennessee, Alabama, Georgia, Virginia, North Carolina, and Kentucky will also substantiate these claims.

Handy's band was a household word throughout the Southland because we could play this music that we now call jazz better than any competitor. Yes, I remember when Jelly Roll played for Barrasso in Memphis on what we call T.O.B.A. time. But we were too busy to take notice of his great musicianship. Guy Williams, to whom he refers as the originator of the "Jogo Blues," which I stole and called "St. Louis Blues," was the guitarist in my No. 2 band. I never heard

him create or play anything creative, and if I had heard him and plagiarized his idea, he himself would have sought satisfaction 25 years ago.

When A. & C. Bony, Inc., published my "Blues"—An Anthology, I was invited to St. Louis to the convention of the American Book Publishers and autographed 300 copies to guests. Guy Williams invited me to his home, where I spent one week with him and his family, which proved our friendly relationship. He always takes advantage of my visits to St. Louis, to extend such hospitality. Never once has he referred to my work other than original.

Morton says that up to 1925, "St. Louis Blues" was as dead as a doornail. I am sending you proof contradicting this statement in the form of a letter from Otto Zimmerman. He printed the first copies in 1914, and you will see that they printed 37,000 the first two years when I was down in Memphis. In 1921, the Dixieland Jazz Band recorded "St. Louis Blues" on the Victor records, and their first statement (which I am sending you) was 179,440 plus 25,521, plus their third statement of 5,243—records. That's almost a quarter of a million records in 1921 from one phonograph company. The Brunswick, in 1921, paid me for 39,981 records. In 1923, the Columbia Co. recorded 94,071 records by Ted Lewis. In 1924, the Brunswick recorded 30,472 records. In 1925 Columbia recorded 17,945; also in 1925, Columbia recorded 36,870 records by Bessie Smith. Add to these recordings on the Arto, Edison, Emerson, Pathe, Autophone, Grey Gull, Paramount, Pace Phonograph Co., Banner, Regal, Little Wonder, etc., and you will find that "St. Louis Blues" has had more recordings, sold more records, than any other American composition. With all these records being played in people's homes before 1925 and with our tremendous sales of sheet music from 1914 on, say nothing about the piano rolls and vaudeville artists singing it from coast to coast on every stage and in every cabaret, how could he say that "St. Louis Blues" was dead?

It was because of the popularity of "St. Louis Blues" that Mr. Melrose sent his representative, Henry Teller, to New York in an effort to acquire the dance orchestration rights only for "St. Louis Blues" for the existing term of its copyright, which expires in 1942. We reserved the symphonic rights and have

ready for publication now a symphonic suite in three movements for a standard symphony orchestra.

Mr. Melrose was kind enough to write us a letter that we could use with the Afro-American. He refuted Jelly Roll's statement, which we are sending you herewith attached. For the public's information, you must know that I own the copyright to "St. Louis Blues" but have permitted arrangements for piano, accordion, all kinds of guitars, organs, etc., to be made and sold by firms that specialize along these lines. But they do not own the copyright to "St. Louis Blues." I own that.

Jelly Roll Morton says I cannot play "jazz." I am 65 years old and would not play it if I could, but I did have the good sense to write down the laws of jazz and the music that lends itself to jazz and had vision enough to copyright and publish all the music I wrote so I don't have to go around saying I made up this piece and that piece in such and such a year like Jelly Roll and then say somebody swiped it. Nobody has swiped anything from me. And, if he is as good as he says he is, he should have copyrighted and published his music so that he could not be running down deserving composers.

If I didn't know him, I would think he is crazy and it is the act of a crazy man to attack such fine men who have done outstanding work like Paul Whiteman and Duke Ellington. He reminds me of Captain Higginson, who wrote articles for *The Saturday Evening Post*. He said in one of these articles: "There was an old negro on the Mississippi River who played the fiddle away back before the Civil War and played the 'Memphis Blues' and 'St. Louis Blues' before Handy was born," which of course was fiction.

I expect to hear such tirades as long as I am living, but I don't expect to see you print them and under such captions as the one in this issue. Jelly Roll Morton is running true to form. Booker Washington always told a story in which he likened negroes to crabs in a basket, when one was about to get out of the basket the other grabbed a hold of him and pulled him back.

Very truly yours,

W.C. Handy ●

CRITICS IN THE DOGHOUSE
BASIE EXAMINES BASIE

By Count Basie
(as told to Dave Dexter, Jr.)

JULY 1939

Criticizing one's own band isn't the easiest thing to do, and yet I welcome the opportunity. Sometimes, you know, we form snap judgments of bands on broadcasts, in theaters and even on one-night stands which are not quite fair. Unless the listener hears and studies a band seriously, there's a chance that he will form his own opinion of that organization's ability and worth. And sometimes that's not so good.

"TATE FITS IN OKAY"

Some of you know that our band features a "heavy" brass section. I guess the word "heavy" is okay in this instance, because our brass includes four trumpets and three trombones. Frankly, I think the brass is our problem, but—and I'm being just candid in my opinion—I also think we have that particular section just where we want it now. My problem, of course, is keeping it that way.

The saxes, four of them, are also phrasing the way I want them to phrase, and their intonation—which gave us a little trouble back in the days when the band was first organized—apparently is up to the par we set. Of course we were a little rough a few months ago when we made a change as a result of Herschel Evans' death, but George (Buddy) Tate caught on in a hurry and fits right in now.

"NO RHYTHM WORRIES"

I am sure that the rhythm section is right as it is. It's the one section that has given us no trouble at any time. And when I speak of the rhythm, I mean bass, drums and guitar. You can count me out.

Am I satisfied with the band today?

FOLLOWS HIS OLD IDEAS

Not by a long shot, Jack. I have a purpose in everything I try to do with the band. A few years ago I was using nine pieces in a little club called "The Reno" in Kansas City. We worked together a long while. We got so we coordinated every move, every solo, perfectly. That was how Walter Bales, John Schilling, Don Davis and a few other Kansas City cats found us playing; that's how we got to broadcast every night. It was nine pieces that saw Basie get his biggest break with Benny Goodman, John Hammond and Willard Alexander, as a result of that radio wire and the raves of the men I just mentioned.

Now—and this is the point I want understood most, if you don't mind—I want my 15-piece band today to work together just like those nine pieces did. I want 15 men to think and play the same way. I want those four trumpets and three trombones to bite with real guts. BUT I want that bite to be just a tasty and subtle as if it were the three bass I used to use. In fact, the only reason I enlarged the brass was to get a richer harmonic structure. The minute the brass gets out of hand and blares and screeches instead of making every note *mean something* there'll be some changes made.

"NOT TOO MUCH PIANO"

I, of course, wanted to play real jazz. When we play pop tunes, and naturally we must, I want those pops to kick! Not loud and fast, understand, but smoothly and with a definite punch. As for vocals, Jimmy Rushing and Helen Humes are handling them the way we feel they can best be handled. Earl Warren, who plays lead alto, also sings occasionally. That's all the comment I have on our purposes, style and our vocalists.

My piano?

Well, I don't want to "run it into the ground," as they say. I love to play, but this idea of one man taking one chorus after another is not wise, in my opinion. Therefore, I feed dancers my own piano in short doses, and when I come in for a solo, I do it unexpectedly, using a strong rhythm background behind me. That way, we figure the Count's piano isn't going to become monotonous.

EIGHT ORIGINAL MEN REMAIN

We get a lot of questions about personnel. It includes Earl Warren, alto; Lester Young, tenor; Jack Washington, alto and baritone, and George (Buddy) Tate, tenor; Ed Louis, Wilbur (Buck) Clayton, Shad Collins, and Harry Edison, trumpets, in that order; Benny Morton, Dickie Wells and Dan (Slamfoot) Minor, trombones in that order, and Jo Jones, drums; Walter Page, bass; Freddie Green, guitar, and Basie, piano. That's it. Of that number, Louis, Clayton, Washington, Young, Jones, Page, Minor and Jimmy Rushing all have been with me since the old Reno Club days in Kansas City. They are a great bunch, and any success we have had is due entirely to the grand spirit among us all.

MOST ARRANGEMENTS "ON SPOT"

We recently hired Lloyd Martin, an Indiana youth, who is turning out some good arrangements. Buck Clayton's are also used a lot. But with most of our arrangements, one of the boys or I will get an idea for a tune, like "Every Tub" for instance, and at rehearsal we just sorta start it off and the others fall in. Fist thing you know, we've got it. We don't use paper on a lot of our standards. In that way, we all have more freedom for improvisations.

That's about the best I can do as a reviewer, I'm afraid. I'd like it known that the band works hard—rehearsals three hours long as held three times a week, on the average—and that we get our kicks from playing. ●

THIS ISN'T BUNK; BUNK TAUGHT LOUIS

By Park Breck

JUNE 1939

So many articles have been written by phonies who claim they started jazz that I hesitate to reveal the truth.

Through an investigation which has been made with great care and thoroughness by eight "critics" and record collectors during the last six months, startling facts have been uncovered. The facts have been checked and rechecked and are as close to the truth as will ever be known.

The writer can only disclose the most important at this time.

LETTER TELLS ALL!

In a letter to William Russell, owner of the world's most complete record collection, Willie "Bunk" Johnson, the cornetist who taught Louis Armstrong his first music, tells the story:

"Now here is the list about that jazz playing: King Buddy Bolden was the first man that began playing jazz in the city of New Orleans, and his band had the whole of New Orleans real crazy and running wild behind it. Now that was all you could hear in New Orleans, that King Bolden's band, and I was with him. That was between 1895 and 1896, and we did not have any "Dixieland Jazz band" in those days. Now here is the thing that made King Bolden's band the first band to play jazz. It was because they could not read at all. I could fake like 500 myself, so you tell them that Bunk and King Bolden's bank were the first ones that started jazz in that city or any place else. And now you are able to go ahead with your book".

BUNK TAUGHT LOUIS!

Bunk has been acclaimed by many of the old time musicians as the greatest cornetist of his day. There were three great cornetists, they say — Buddy, Bunk and Louis. Their music was passed from one to the other. Bolden played a real "stomp trumpet," and Bunk added fast fingering, runs and high notes with a sweet tone. Then Louis combined the two styles with his own ideas to become the man who is recognized today as the greatest hot musician of all time.

The influence of King Oliver upon Louis has been exaggerated, but through no fault of those who claim that Oliver taught him. New facts now show that Louis had been playing for more than five years before he joined Oliver's band.

SATCHMO AGREES IT'S TRUE

Sidney Bechet, Luis Russell, Pops Foster, Clarence Williams, Lil Armstrong and Louis himself all recognize Bunk as the greatest pioneer in hot jazz in the early part of the century.

Said Louis: "Bunk, he's the man they

Bunk Johnson

ought to talk about. What a man! Just to hear him talk sends me. I used to hear him in Frankie Dusen's Eagle band in 1911. Did that band swing! How I used to follow him around. He could play funeral marches that made me cry."

I'll let Bunk tell you in his own words of his influence on Louis—facets which Louis himself has corroborated:

"When I would be playing with brass bands in the uptown section (of New Orleans), Louis would steal off from home and follow me. During that time, Louis started after me to show him how to blow my cornet. When the band would not be playing, I would let him carry it to please him. How he wanted me to teach him how to play the blues and 'Ball the Jack' and 'Animal Ball,' 'Circus Day, Take It Away' and 'Didn't He Ramble?,' and out of all those pieces he liked the blues the best.

BLUES CAME FIRST

I took a job playing in a tonk for Dago Tony on Perdido and Franklin street and Louis used to slip in there and get on the music stand behind the piano. He would fool around with my cornet every chance he got. I showed him just how to hold it and place it to his mouth, and he did so, and it wasn't long before he began getting a good tone out of my horn. Then I began showing him just how to start the

blues, and little by little he began to understand.

"Now here is the year Louis started. It was in the latter part of 1911 as close as I can think. Louis was about 11 years old. Now I've said a lot about my boy Louis and just how he started playing cornet. He started playing it by head."

Old-time musicians say that Louis' early records with King Oliver, Fletcher Henderson and blues singers were almost repetitions of the many licks he learned from Bunk. Bunk himself never recorded, and now I come to the sad part of his story

Bunk played his cornet in bands throughout the deep South until 1933. Then the merciless tragedy which every musician dreads struck him—a physical handicap, put an end to that glorious music which was his life and soul.

I am sorry that Louis doesn't play those old blues any more, and I'm sorry that King Bolden is stomping in the Angel Gabriel's band. But my heart goes out to the artist who sold his trumpet and went to work in the fields at $1.75 a day to keep his body clothed and his soul on this earth.

"We have work only when rice harvest in, and that over, things go real dead until cane harvest," Bunk wrote in a letter. "I drive a truck and trailer and that pays me $1.75 a day, and that does not last very long, I'm down and in real deep need.

"I made up my mind to work hard until I die as I have no one to tell my troubles to, and my children cannot help me out in this case. I've been trying to get me $150 for three years, and I cannot make that kind of money here. Now I haven't got any other way but to put my shoulder to the wheel and my nose to the grinding stone and put my music down for good, and work. I cannot blow any more."

But with the help of modern dentistry Bunk can play again. Many persons who have heard of his plight have volunteered to subscribe to a fund to help to get him back on his feet.

"I want to become able to play trumpet once more. I know I can really play stomp trumpet," he says.

Louis Armstrong is giving his old teacher a trumpet, and promises of jobs for Bunk have come from many sources. Perhaps soon we will all have the opportunity to hear the man to whom we owe an unpayable debt of gratitude—the man who taught Louis Armstrong and thereby indirectly influenced the whole scope of modern swing music—Bunk Johnson. ●

"BENNY SHOULD BE CONGRATULATED FOR HIS COURAGE"—JIMMY DORSEY

OCTOBER 15, 1939

How do American Band leaders and side men feel about Benny Goodman's adding Charlie Christian and Fletcher Henderson, negro instrumentalists, to his band?

That question aroused tremendous interest last month when Christian, following Henderson, was added. Goodman claims he wants to have the best band possible to assemble, and he chose Christian and Henderson because "they are the best on their respective instruments." In addition, Lionel Hampton is an outstanding member of the Goodman company.

JIMMY DORSEY FAVORS IT

Siding in with Benny was Jimmy Dorsey, among others. He said: "Frankly, I think Benny should be congratulated for his courage in adding negro musicians to his orchestra.

"I have a very good idea of the criticism to which he'll be subjected, for it will be remembered that for nearly a year we had June Richmond as vocalist with my band. I also think it would be presumptuous for any leader to tell Benny he is jeopardizing his professional future, for offhand I can't think of any leader doing better than Benny. To my mind, the question resolves itself to one of style. I feel my present instrumentation, without negro talent, expresses my style best. If Goodman feels he can better express his band's style with colored artists, more power to him. If anyone can make a mixed band acceptable to the public—Benny Goodman can!"

Woody Herman pointed out that "no orchestra has greater admiration and respect for negro musicians and their music than ours. Our devotion to the blues and to the blues idiom should be evidence enough of that fact. But in spite of the tremendous debt we owe negro musicians and composers for our style, we would not consider that the addition of one or more negroes would enhance that style, any

more than the addition of a white musician would improve Duke Ellington's orchestra....We have too much respect for the vitality and imagination of negro musicians to ask any one of them to sacrifice his integrity."

Woody, in making the statement, gathered his band around him and they drafted his quotation together. All felt the same way.

Other comments:

TEDDY WILSON—"I believe the hiring of colored musicians to play in white bands is an excellent idea. I think, musically speaking, it is of mutual benefit to both. The colored musician is the gainer where quality is concerned, and the white musicians are often further inspired by the rhythmic feeling of the negro. I feel that this sort of mixing is conducive to the production of a higher type of swing band. Charlie Christian is the

Woody Herman

finest guitar soloist I have ever heard and his addition to Benny's band music be musically effective. It is easy to understand that the arrangements of Fletcher Henderson must prove to be of great advantage to any musical organization."

ELLA FITZGERALD—"I believe the hiring of colored musicians in a white band is really mutually beneficial. Both races have a lot to offer each other. It would be hard to understand the advisability of racial distinction where artistry in musical advancement is concerned. The interchange of musical ideas between both races surely must be broadening in

influence."

ARTIE SHAW—"It's most unfortunate that there are still

Jimmy Dorsey

promoters who book bands on appearance. Every bandleader should be free to hire men on the basis of ability and ability alone. I'd put colored boys in the band in a minute if they had the talent—and a great deal of them have."

JACK JENNEY—"There should be no discrimination. Selection of men should be on ability basis."

SHEP FIELDS—"Have always regretted prejudice that forbids mixed bands. Hope to see it lived down in my generation."

CASPER REARDON—"Good for Benny! I'm for him. His ideas are like mine. If a negro is a better performer use him. One cannot hope to draw a color line in music or any other art."

VIDO MUSSO—"I think it's a terrific idea and I give Benny a lot of credit, but whether it's going to go over depends on the public's reaction. What do you suppose will happen if he ever goes down into Texas with the band? I not only admire Benny's musical taste in adding these men, I also think his using negroes is a smart promotional and business move to buck all these good swing bands that are coming along to crowd him out of the limelight. More power to Benny."

Asked for opinions, several other "big name" leaders and side men refused to be quoted. Interviews with the majority, however, indicate that great progress has been made in the last five years in regard to equality of races in the music field. Several leaders, in fact, said they believed that "within two or more years, use of colored artists in white bands will be accepted everywhere in the States."

All gave credit to Goodman for effecting the change. ●

SHOULD NEGRO MUSICIANS PLAY IN WHITE BANDS?

OCTOBER 15, 1939

Editor's Note: The following is an editorial that appeared in the same issue as the preceding article.

"No! Definitely No!" said many leaders and side men.

"But why?" asked *Down Beat*'s reporters. "It's professional suicide" said one, "but don't quote me. It's not fair for negroes to replace white musicians when there is so much unemployment." "The Union should forbid it!" said another.

"It will break down race lines," said a third. "But in music and art we thought there were no race lines," interposed *Down Beat*'s reporter. "Of course there aren't," replied the musician, "but dance music is a business, not an art. And we've got to make a living!"

Southern musicians were unanimous in denouncing it as a bad idea, full of trouble. "The north has spoiled the negro and success has made him insolent and overbearing!"

"I wouldn't have a negro in my band," said another, "for the simple reason that the musical ideas of the negro and white are too far apart for the best results. But I'll be damned if I'll tell anyone else what to do. If Benny wants 'em, Benny can have 'em."

"It's too bad," reflected one leader, "that this question can't be decided on pure musical ability. The negro has exceptional musical ability but unfortunately for him, there are social overtones involved which, although he is not to blame, still work against him.

"White people do not want to mix socially with negroes. It's not a question of equality, it's a matter of privacy. And, any uninvited trespassing of it is bitterly resented. There have been many instances of negro musicians making overtures to white women in cafes they were playing. That alone is enough to incense a white man against the colored race. But in an atmosphere of drinking, where normal restraints are gone—it's murder.

"You see, and it's too bad too, but music ability has damn little to do with it."

Another leader who had guts enough to express himself, but not be quoted, said "when a negro enters a white band, he loses his identity as a negro musician. I think the musical progress of all-negro groups such as Duke Ellington and Count Basie has been tremendous, and has contributed originality and freshness to American music we would never have if there were mixed bands.

"But after all it is really up to nobody else but John Q. Public. If the public wants negroes in its white bands, it'll get negroes in them. If it doesn't want them, well, the box office will always tell us what the answer will be."

And so they go!

Free expression of opinion—WHATEVER IT IS! in free America! Criticism, whether it be good or bad—WITHOUT FEAR OF ARREST OR PUNISHMENT.

The only regrettable thing confronted when the question was asked, "Should Negro Musicians Play in White Bands?" was the desire by most of the musicians who were critics NOT TO BE QUOTED.

If a man has a serious conviction that something is wrong or not good, HE SHOULD HAVE COURAGE TO EXPRESS THAT CONVICTION PUBLICLY.

Those musicians who either approved of Benny Goodman's using negro musicians or could see no harm in it, certainly did not mind being quoted.

Whether it is good or bad, in its final analysis, the editors of *Down Beat* frankly do not know. They are trying to encourage musicians to *think* about it instead of *feeling* about it.

And if promoting honest discussions about debatable issues can bring those issues into an atmosphere of "give and take," reasonableness, and impartiality, *Down Beat* will certainly open its columns.

One thing sure, we want to see a square deal. And any American, no matter what his race, his color, or his creed, is entitled to that. ●

"I'LL NEVER SING WITH A DANCE BAND AGAIN"—HOLIDAY

By Dave Dexter, Jr.

NOVEMBER 1, 1939

BILLIE FOR THE FIRST TIME TELLS WHY SHE LEFT SHAW & BASIE: "TOO MANY BAD KICKS"

Chicago—You sit with Billie Holiday and watch her smoke cigarets chain fashion. The first thing that strikes you is her frankness.

"I'll never sing with a dance band again," she tells you. "Because it never works out right for me. They wonder why I left Count Basie, and why I left Artie Shaw. Well I'll tell you why—and I've never told this before.

"Basie had too many managers—too many guys behind the scenes who told everybody what to do. The Count and I got along fine. And the boys in the band were wonderful all the time. But it was this and that, all the time, and I got fed up with it. Basie didn't fire me; I gave him my notice.

BAD KICKS WITH SHAW

Artie Shaw was a lot worse. I had known him a long time, when he was strictly from hunger around New York, long before he got a band. At first we worked together okay, then his managers started belly-aching. Pretty soon it got so I would sing just two numbers a night. When I wasn't singing, I had to stay backstage. Artie wouldn't let me sit out front with the band. Last year when we were at the Lincoln Hotel the hotel management told me I had to use the back door. That was all right. But I had to ride up and down in the freight elevators, and every night Artie made me stay upstairs in a little room without a radio or anything all the time.

"Finally it got so I would stay up there, all by myself, reading everything I could get my hands on, from 10 o'clock to nearly 2 in the morning, going downstairs to sing just one or two numbers. Then one night we had an airshot Artie said he couldn't let me sing. I was always given two shots on each program. The real trouble was this—

Shaw wanted to sign me to a five-year contract and when I refused, it burned him. He was jealous of the applause I got when I made one of my few appearances with the band each night."

NEVER PAID FOR RECORD

You ask Billie why she didn't make more records with Shaw. You remember that the only side she made, on Bluebird, was

a thing titled "Any Old Time" and was really wonderful.

"That's a laugh," she answers. "Artie never paid me for that record. Just before it came out I simply got enough of Artie's snooty, know-it-all mannerisms, and the outrageous behavior of his managers, and

left the band. I guess Artie forgot about 'Any Old Time.' I know he never paid me. With Basie I got $70 a week—with Artie I got $65. When I make my own records I get $150. That's another reason I left Shaw.

"One afternoon we were driving along in Artie's car to a one-night stand. We passed an old man on the road who had a beard. I asked Artie if he had ever worn a beard, and that I'd bet he sure'd look funny if he wore one.

"Chuck Petersen, George Arus, Les Jenkins, and a couple of other boys in the band were also in the car. So we were all surprised when Artie said 'I used to wear a beard all the time—when I was farming my own farm a few years back.' I asked Artie if he looked good or bad with a beard—and I was just joking, you know, to make conversation on a long drive.

"'Indeed I did look fine with a beard,' Artie said. 'I looked exactly like Jesus Christ did when he was young.'"

Billie slapped her pudgy thigh, lighted another cigaret, and continued.

GAVE HIM A NAME

You should have heard the boys and me roar at that. We got a bang out of it. Artie looked mad, because he had been serious. So I said, 'We'll just call you Jesus Christ, King of the Clarinet, and his Band.'

"Now here's the payoff—the story got out around Boston and even today, we hear a lot of the musicians refer to Artie as 'Jesus Christ and his Clarinet'."

You figure you've heard enough dirt about the pitfalls of a young girl with a dance band and you ask Billie to tell you something about herself. She comes through with the word that she is Baltimore born, and that she got her first job when she was 14 years old, after she and her mother moved to New York.

BILLIE GETS DESPERATE

This is the truth. Mother and I were starving. It was cold. Father had left us and remarried when I was 10. Mother was a housemaid and couldn't find work. I tried scrubbing floors, too, but I just couldn't do it.

"We lived on 145th Street near Seventh Avenue. One day we were so hungry we could barely breathe. I started out the door. It was cold as all-hell and I walked from 145th to 133rd down Seventh Avenue, going in every joint trying to find work. Finally, I got so desperate I stopped in the Log Cabin Club, run by Jerry Preston. I told him I wanted a drink. I didn't have a dime. But I ordered gin (it was my first drink—I didn't know gin from wine) and gulped it down. I asked Preston for a job…told him I was a dancer. He said to dance. I tried it. He said I stunk. I told him I could sing. He said sing. Over in the corner was an old guy playing a piano. He struck 'Travelin'' and I sang. The customers stopped drinking. They turned around and watched. The pianist, Dick Wilson, swung into 'Body and Soul.' Jeez, you should have seen those people—all of them started crying. Preston came over, shook his head and said 'Kid, you win.' That's how I got my start.

GOODMAN USES HER

First thing I did was get a sandwich. I gulped it down. Believe me—the crowd gave me $18 in tips. I ran out the door. Bought a whole chicken. Ran up Seventh Avenue to my home. Mother and I ate that night— and we have been eating pretty well since."

Benny Goodman used Billie on a record (Columbia) of "My Mother's Son in Law" when Teagarden, Krupa and others were in his recording band—before he really organized his present combo. The disc is an item today, not only because of the fine instrumental work, but because it was Holiday's first side. She was pretty lousy. You tell her so and she grins. "But I was only 15 then," she said, "And I was scared as the devil."

SHE DOESN'T SING

You tell Billie you think you've got enough dope for a little story, but that one thing worries you. That is—why does she sing like she does—what's behind it?

"Look Dex," Billie answers. "I don't think I'm singing. I feel like I am playing a horn. I try to improvise like Les Young, like Louie Armstrong, or someone else I admire. What comes out is what I feel. I hate straight singing. I have to change a tune to my own way of doing it. That's all I know."

SAD LOVE LIFE

You ask her one more thing, recalling how at various times Billie has been reported ready to marry. She shows her frankness again. "I've loved three men," she tells you. "One was a Marion Scott, when I was a kid. He works for the post office now. The other was Freddie Green, Basie's guitar man. But Freddie's first wife is dead and he has two children and somehow it didn't work out. The third was Sonny White, the pianist, but like me, he lives with his mother and our plans for marriage didn't jell. That's all."

Billie says she isn't satisfied now. She wants to get somewhere. Maybe on the stage. She wants to make money—a lot of it. She wants to buy a big home for her mother. She doesn't expect any happiness—she is used to taking hard knocks, tough breaks. And she admits she is envious of Maxine Sullivan and other colored singers who have gotten so much farther ahead than she. Someday, she thinks, she'll get a real break. But she's not very optimistic about it. Billie Holiday is convinced the future will be as unglamorous and unprofitable as her past. ●

SHAW DENIES IT

"Billie's claim of nonpayment for her record is ridiculous," said Artie Shaw, referring to Holiday's charges. "If it were true would she have waited a year before saying anything about it? She certainly was paid. Her charge is preposterous."●

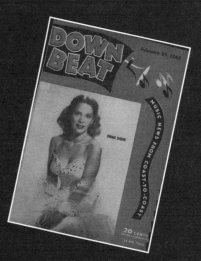

THE 1940s

INTRODUCTION

By John McDonough ···

Jazz entered the 1940s as a homogeneous music in the center of American popular music. It exited the decade a divided, quarrelsome, and squabbling lot of partisans, well on its way to becoming once again the underground cult music it had been in its pre-swing youth. Its original audience of Depression-era teens had met its "rendezvous with destiny" in World War II and grown into a vanguard of suburban-bound organization men and women. They would have a soft spot in their hearts for Glenn Miller until the day they died. But for now had no time for records or bobby socks.

Early in the decade two fights over money bounced back on their perpetrators with catastrophic consequences. When ASCAP pulled virtually the entire standard catalog of American popular songs off the air in 1941, the radio networks poured millions into building BMI, which quickly located new sources of music in such marginalized categories as country & western and rhythm & blues. ASCAP gave up by the end of the year. But neither the American Hit Parade nor ASCAP would ever be the same again.

The big bands were never the same again either, after James Petrillo took every musician in the country out on strike against the record industry in August 1942. It seemed like a good idea at the time, no doubt. But like the ASCAP fiasco, it left a clear track for newer voices to attend to an impatient public. By the time it ended in 1944, it was too late. The big bands had offended the golden goose and the singers were out of the bag.

By mid decade, babies were booming, bands were busting up, and jazz was going modern. When all is said and done, two men fundamentally changed the nature of jazz simultaneously in the forties: Charlie Parker and Norman Granz. One revolutionized the way it was played. The other revolutionized the way it was sold. Coincidentally, both men's names appeared for the first in separate *Down Beat* stories in the same issue, July 1, 1942.

"Charlie Parker offers inspired alto solos, using a minimum of notes in a fluid style with a somewhat thin tone but a wealth of pleasing ideas." So said *Down Beat*, reacting to its first encounter with the decade's most seminal figure as it considered the work of the Jay McShann orchestra. Parker's entrance upon the scene was assured, elegant, and well within the bounds of swing-era convention. Bop never was the frontal assault to tradition that history sometimes portrays it to have been. This was because it was a logical and incremental extension of the best mainstream swing. It rolled on the same 32-bar harmonic chassis on which Benny Goodman and Duke Ellington had built their repertoire: "I Got Rhythm," "Honeysuckle Rose," and naturally the blues. Though augmented with fiendishly difficult rhythmic and harmonic extras, it still swung mightily.

Bop was more tough-minded and unsentimental, though. It was all muscle and demanded as much of its listeners as it did of its players. Bop was the result of rising but unused reservoirs of virtuosity in search of problems to solve. The famous so-called cutting contests of the thirties had put constant pressure from within on the envelope of technique. Musicians always reached for the topper. Higher notes. Faster notes. More surprising notes. The vocabulary of possibilities grew with dynamic suddenness. The result was bop, which gave a field of structure to a mother lode of young virtuoso players.

But bebop had an attitude that resisted sustained commercialization. It had been nurtured in private in the intimate world of the after-hours jam session. Audiences were small and full of other musicians. Secret passwords of phraseology full of inside ironies and winks were passed around. Bop became defined by its "insideness." The hip were welcome. The squares were a draft.

Parker was a problematic role model for the new generation. Unlike Armstrong, Ellington, or Goodman, he was defined not only by a mastery of the alto saxophone so complete it remade the sound of all instruments, but also by a charisma that was as perverse as it was irresistible. His followers were so blinded by its incandescence, some confused creative genius with a profound failure of character. Jazz had seen it all before, of course, in Bix Beiderbecke, Bunny Berigan, and some lesser early figures. But their tragic flaws had not been contagious. Parker was different. Never had an outlaw lifestyle had such an impact on a contemporary generation of jazz musicians.

While the squares drew comfort from their numerical mass and seemed uninterested in bop's elitism, the hip cloistered together and fed on the sense of moral empowerment that fills the soul of every embattled minority. In the forties the jazz world plunged into a civil war of musical cultures. One wing went off in search of jazz's roots in the deep past. The modernists sneered at anything before 1942. The swing generation was, for a time, caught in the crossfire.

In the end, however, young musicians could not escape the knowledge Parker had given them. Bop won the civil war in jazz. But jazz lost the broad middle class that had once embraced swing. Perhaps in the long run this was best. It freed jazz to pursue its path toward art music in relative isolation, which is its natural habitat. Meanwhile, Dizzy Gillespie had a lot going for him, and he donated all of it to music. Uniquely blessed with a monumental endowment of talent and an ability to take neither himself nor the myths of bop seriously, he fought a rear-guard action of acceptance. Thoroughly fluent in the private codes of the culture, he made them seem not only unthreatening but even downright charming to outsiders. He was just about the cleverest ambassador there ever was. With his goatee, his twinkle, and his tilted trumpet, he became the most enduring symbol of the post-war jazz scene.

Speaking of symbols, the great bandleaders of the swing era were, of course, set for life. As the business infrastructure of the band era collapsed and tastes changed in the late forties, Ellington, Goodman, Basie, and a few others were beginning to find that their names had acquired the golden momentum of symbolism. In the years ahead it would prove sufficient to carry them into old age as tenured and treasured musical icons. Only two bands made lasting reputations during the middle and late forties: Woody Herman and Stan Kenton. Most of the new stars of popular music were the singers, many of whom had been nurtured in the bands: Sinatra, Como, Clooney, Patti Page, Jo Stafford, Doris Day.

The closest thing to a mass audience jazz saw in the forties was Jazz at the Philharmonic, which brings us the Norman Granz, who was to the marketing of jazz what Parker was to its musicology. In the same issue in which *Down Beat* first encountered the altoist, it also took note of a series of Sunday afternoon jam sessions in Los Angeles organized by Granz. To most fans, the jam session was jazz in a state of nature, where the music reached its highest and purest form in private. Granz opened that ritual to the public, first in small clubs in Los Angeles and ultimately concerts halls before thousands around the world. Granz was the first to strategically exploit the marketing synergy between recordings and touring. He was the first the use the concert stage as a recording studio. He was the first to consistently mobilize box office power in the cause desegregation. He was everywhere.

Through the forties *Down Beat*'s pages were smoldering with controversy. What is most ironic, however, is that a decade so torn by the heat of dispute should end on a note that was so prophetically cool. When Gil Evans, Miles Davis, Gerry Mulligan, Lee Konitz, and others recorded eight sides in the last year of the decade, they defined yet a third major jazz movement. With *Birth of the Cool*, jazz was well on its path to polycentrism. In 1940, it had a single center. By 1950, it had three. ●

"I DON'T WANT A JAZZ BAND" —GLENN MILLER

HE CLAIMS HARMONY, NOT A BEAT, IS WHAT COUNTS WITH THE PUBLIC

By Dave Dexter, Jr.

FEBRUARY 1, 1940

New York—"I haven't a great jazz band, and I don't want one."

Glenn Miller isn't one to waste words. And he doesn't waste any describing the music his band is playing these nights at the Hotel Pennsylvania here. Soft-spoken, sincere and earnest in his conversation, Miller is now finding himself at the top of the nation's long list of favorite maestri.

"We leaders are criticized for a lot of things," says Miller. "It's always true after a band gets up there and is recognized by the public. Some of the critics, *Down Beat's* among them, point their fingers at us and charge us with forsaking the real jazz. Maybe so. Maybe not. It's all in what you define as 'real jazz.' It happens that to our ears harmony comes first. A dozen colored bands have a better beat than mine.

"WE STRESS HARMONY"

Our band stresses harmony. Eight brass gives us a lot of leeway to put to use on scores of ideas we've had in mind for a long time. The years of serious study I've had with legitimate teachers finally is paying off in enabling me to write arrangements employing unusual, rich harmonies, many never before used in dance bands."

Glenn isn't fooling either. How he was the first to use a clarinet lead above four saxes is fairly old stuff at this late date. He went on from there to experiment with trombone-trumpet combinations to achieve entirely original ensemble effects. That's keeps the Miller band a step ahead of competition.

DID NOT GRIPE ABOUT CHESTER

In recent weeks reports blossomed forth that Miller, hearing Bob Chester's band, which employs a somewhat similar instrumental style, "hit the roof" and demanded that RCA-Victor drop the Chester band from its list of

recording combos. No report could be more untrue. Leonard Joy, Victor chieftain, denounced the rumor.

"Neither Glenn nor any member of his orchestra has ever approached RCA-Victor regarding the Chester band," said Joy.

Small talk irks Glenn. He's no tin god, and he has his faults like all of us, but he isn't the kind to bellyache about competition. He's had plenty of it, all down the line, and until eight months ago—when his platters started clicking and sent the band's stock up bullishly—he was a pretty sad and disillusioned guy.

"I thought I had swell ideas, and wonderful musicians," he recalls, "but the hell of it, no one else did."

THEN ALL OF A SUDDEN...

Then it happened. Glenn remembers the night, and so does his wife. "We were playing the Meadowbrook early last spring," he says, "and up front, all of a sudden, the band hit me. It was clicking. For the first time I knew it was playing like I wanted it to. It sounded wonderful. I didn't say anything—just drove home and told my wife. But I prayed it would last."

Later on, the second spurt hit the band

the same way.

"We were then at Glen Island Casino, and it hasn't been long ago," says Glenn. "Bang, again the boys hit me hard. They sounded wonderful, better than ever before, better than any band I had ever heard. When I drove home that night I knew we had hit the top. And believe me, from that night on everything broke right. My problem now is to keep it there. I don't expect any more bangs coming right off the stand at me."

Glenn thinks Benny Goodman is the hardest working leader in the business. His admiration for Benny, as a friend and as a clarinet-playing leader, isn't easy to restrain. Glenn today will do battle arguing that BG is the greatest clarinetist ever to lick a reed. The two get along great, and why not? They've known each other 15 years, shared rooms, split dimes to eat, and risen to fame.

Actually, this Miller man is a quiet sort of guy. He does little back slapping; employs less loud talk. When he discusses his band, you feel a subtle sarcasm behind his words, because for nearly two years he worked like a fool, borrowed money, traveled constantly, and fought like a wild man to keep his band—and his ideas on dance music—intact. He doesn't gloat about victory today. He's too big a man, and he is wise enough to know that a great group can slip fast in a hurry. He's proud that he has a band of virtual "unknown" kids in his crew; kids which he found himself and which he has taught personally. Most of them are in their early twenties; all of them have become professionals since Goodman made his historic rise.

TROUBLE WITH "STYLES"

I had a time with some of them," he declares. "Take Hal McIntyre on alto. He phrased, breathed and played in every respect like he was playing with Benny's band. I pointed out that *maybe* there was another way to play sax in a section, and we slowly worked out the style we use now. Sure it was tough, but all the boys know what I want and they're fast to learn."

Result? Miller's saxes are the most famous in the land today.

For the record, Miller was born March 1, 1905, in Clarinda, Iowa. But he didn't stay in corn country long. His parents moved to Denver, and out there, in the land of the Rockies and "tall" air, Glenn learned to play trombone. He was still a moppet when he started playing professionally.

ROSE FROM NOBLE BAND

Glenn first became prominent, nationally, while with Ray Noble's first American dance band five years ago in New York. It was a great outfit—Miller, Spivak, Mince, Cannon, Freeman, Irwin, Thornhill, D'Andrea, and a lot of other terrific musicians—all were members. And it was with Noble that Glenn worked out his early ideas on harmony. He also played with the Dorsey Brothers' band. His decision to form his own crew was somewhat sudden; he hadn't, as the storybooks say, "always dreamed" of leading his own outfit.

Glenn doesn't claim to be a star soloist on his horn. Not as long as Tommy Dorsey lives. Tommy to Glenn, plays the greatest tram in the business. But as a section man, Glenn Miller's on trombone don't bob up often. That's why Glenn chose to organize a band which stresses excellent musicianship and perfect ensembles rather than a band which gets by on one soloist jumping up after another to take hot choruses.

MEN ALL "GREAT" GUYS

The men in the Miller Band? Once he starts talking, Miller won't stop. They're all great. And they were "great" before last Christmas eve when they all got together, pooled their money, purchased a huge shiny new Buick Roadmaster for their boss, and presented it to him in the lobby of the Pennsylvania Hotel a few hours after the band had broken a 14-year attendance record up in Harlem at the Savoy Ballroom.

But Gordon (Tex) Beneke—the young and hungry tenor man whose name rhymes with "panicky" except for the "a" in the latter—is Glenn's fair-haired boy. Miller claims Tex, in another year, will be acclaimed by even the righteous guys as a great man as Hawkins. Already Glenn says Tex is the greatest white tenor alive.

HARMONY ABOVE RHYTHM

But back to the music....Glenn doesn't want a strict jazz band. Of course he likes the pure stuff himself, and he admits Louis Armstrong's old Hot Five and Hot Seven discs of the early 1920's have given him a lot of ideas which he used to advantage. "But the public has to understand music," he says. "By giving the public a rich and full melody, distinctly arranged and well played, all the time *creating* new tone colors and patterns, I feel we have a better chance of being successful. I want a kick to my band, but I don't want the rhythm to hog the spotlight."

Just one more slant on Glenn Miller's way of thinking. Smart? Not long back he pulled Tommy Mack out of the band to make him manager of the band. Tommy plays trombone. So when Glenn, rehearsing for a record date or a broadcast, wants to step into the control room to check balance, intonation and the like, Tommy drops back, sets up his sliphorn, and no time is lost. The band sounds exactly as it will sound with Glenn riding along with the other three trombones later.

REMEMBER WINCHELL'S ADVICE

Glenn Miller deserves every break he's gotten. Plenty of the big guys refused him help when he needed it. He's had to fight for every break. Now that he's at the top he can look back and grin, but he doesn't hold a peeve for anyone.

Meanwhile, he's working harder than ever. He remembers reading in Winchell's column a few years back that you meet the same people on the way down that you met on the way up. Some of those people Glenn doesn't want to mix up with again. ●

BERIGAN "CAN'T DO NO WRONG," SAYS ARMSTRONG

SEPTEMBER 1941

New York—Urged for several years by *Down Beat* reporters to "come on and tell us which trumpet players you like best," Louis Armstrong last week patiently and carefully typed out an answer between jumps on the road. From Huntington, W. Va., came the answer directly from Louie, who typed his words out on yellow stationery bearing the single word "Satchmo" in the upper left-hand corner:

"Now this question about my opinion about the trumpet players that I admire— that is actually asking an awful lot of me....Because there's so many trumpet players that I admire until there would not be room to mention them on this paper. And to name only six...well that is leaving me on the spot.

BERIGAN IS "HIS BOY"

But—as you wished—my friend, I'll do my damnedest so here goes. First, I'll name my boy Bunny Berigan. Now there's a boy whom I've always admired for his tone, soul, technique, his sense of 'phrasing' and all. To me Bunny can't do no wrong in music. Harry James is another youngster who won Ol' Satch' right along side a million other fans....His concertos, etc., make him in my estimation a grand trumpet man. And he can swing, too.

"Roy Eldridge is another youngster after my own heart. He has power and a pair of chops that's out of this man's world. And there's no use wondering how high Roy can go on his trumpet because he can go higher than that!

HEMPHILL GETS PRAISE

Now for a number one first chair man, and I have him right here in my own orchestra. And that man is none other than Shelton (Scad) Hemphill. Any time Scad holds down that first chair in your orchestra, just don't worry about a thing. Because any time, any phrasing, attacking, giving each note its full value, tone or hell, anything that a first chair man

Bunny Berigan

should have (which most of them don't have) Scad's got it. And believe me, Scad can see. What I mean by that is...he can read his what's his name off. Ha...Ha.

"And for real get-off men I have two youngsters right here in my orchestra and I personally think they will swing with the best of them. And they are Frank Galbreath and Jean Prince. Jean Prince played with me years ago and even in those days everybody said the same thing...meaning, I sure know how to pick 'em....And that Frank Galbreath. I defy anyone to say that he can't phrase or improvise and he has a sense of changes....My Gawd....And that tone is in there in person. Dig him some time.

"Well, I guess I've run my big mouth too much, eh? Of course I am expectin' a lot of this, that and the other about this article but as I told you once that I never let my mouth say nothing that my head can't stand. Ha, Ha....You dig?

"So I'll be like the little boy who sat on a block of ice and said MY TALE IS TOLD....Goodnight and God bless you, Mr. Joe Glaser and all my fans and my public.

"Am Redbeans and Ricely Yours,

"LOUIS ARMSTRONG" ●

Satchmo

"INSPIRATION WAS SATCHMO"— BERIGAN

By Julian B. Bach

Columbus, O.—Informed that Louis Armstrong had named him first among a group of his favorite trumpet men, Bunny Berigan commented to *Down Beat* here the other day:

"You can't imagine what a kick that is, especially when it comes from Satchmo, the king. All I can say is that Louis alone has been my inspiration, and whatever 'style' I play you can give Armstrong the credit.

"Why, when I was a kid back in Chicago, at night I used to sneak down to the Savoy, where Louis was playing, and listen to him night after night. Later, I got one of those crank-up phonograph jobs and would play Armstrong records by the hour." ●

ARE COLORED BANDS DOOMED AS BIG MONEY MAKERS?...

By R.L. Larkin

DECEMBER 1, 1940

"NEGRO LEADERS COULD MAKE MORE MONEY RUNNING A RIB JOINT"

New York—Is the era of big time colored bands over?

Are Negro dance bands doomed as money makers? Are there too many good bands kicking around? Has public turned to white schmaltz?

A trend in that direction appears obvious as the year nears an end. from the very top on down Negro bands are up against it. Apparently they are fighting a losing battle. There seem to be no exceptions.

Count Basie is in the middle of a high-powered war with his booker, MCA. Basie's band has not been working steadily. His men—and they are some of the world's finest—have had their paychecks chopped. At the moment there is no remedy in sight.

Duke Ellington, for 10 years tops in the sepia division, is struggling. Last month he and his band were idle not a couple of nights, but many. Rather than work for little money Duke elected to work not at all. But he can't go on doing that indefinitely.

HAWKINS A FAILURE

Coleman Hawkins' recent tour with a large band was not successful. The day it returned to New York in November the band dissolved. Now, Hawk is playing with five men in a little dimly-lit club on 52nd Street, where the pay is meager and the chances for becoming nationally prominent—with an uninterested public—negligible.

Cab Calloway, whose white tie and tails and silk hat, coupled with his shouting, and scatting, for several years in the 1930's drew top money at all theater box-offices, is a little better off. But Cab doesn't get the money he used to get, nor do his records sell as they once sold. Calloway knows the end of his career isn't far off. The buzzards are following his band.

ONE-NIGHTERS TOO MUCH

Andy Kirk is working. Joe Glaser miraculously keeps the Clouds busy with rarely an open night. But how long can Kirk, Mary Lou Williams and the boys continue jumping from 200 to 450 miles every night, night after night, year after year, without air time, without a location job, and without the rest they as human beings must have? There's a limit to that kind of work and Kirk knows it. Either the men will collapse or they'll leave and the band will fall apart.

Erskine Hawkins and Ella Fitzgerald are not safe. Neither is a big name yet—in the sense that Calloway was in 1933. Hawkins playing the Savoy Ballroom in Harlem and making his regular quota of wax is doing all right—but he isn't making a lot of money. The man on the street still has never heard of him and probably never will, judging by current conditions in the colored band field. Fitzgerald not only suffered heartbreaking personnel changes since Chick Webb's death, but she's also had it tough making sleeper jumps and working in holes-in-the-wall out in the sticks where on more than one occasion the operator has failed to pay off. Records remain her best bet. But she's miles behind the par set by Cab and Duke five years ago in theaters— where antes of $7,500 to $10,000 were not only possible—but almost monotonously regular. What's in it for her next year?

CARTER IN TOUGH STRAITS

Most poignant of all situations is Benny Carter's. On paper Carter should have the best of all colored bands. As a musician he is unsurpassed, playing alto, trumpet or clarinet. His arrangements are better than those used by Fitzgerald, Kirk, Erskine Hawkins, Coleman Hawkins, Calloway and in some cases—but just a few—the Duke and the Count. Yet Carter works so rarely that he can't keep a band intact. Handsome, personable and intelligent, Carter could be the best of all colored front men if conditions were identical with those of three, five or even seven years ago. As Berigan used to blow—he can't get started. Nor will he ever, unless the public changes its attitude.

Roy Eldridge's small band flopped. Roy sure as hell will end up as a sideman. As a leader he doesn't mean a thing.

Teddy Wilson is no better off. His big band was a commercial failure. His current band, a smaller group, is a so-so success at a swank east-side nitery here. Teddy had a terrific "in" with the spot's management and advisers. His band got the job. But Teddy—and he'll admit it—could be making a lot more money, and be free of a leader's worries, by playing with Benny Goodman as a sideman.

KIRBY BETTER OFF

John Kirby gets by because he plays a style which fits into locations ordinarily barred to colored organizations. But how fat are John's salary checks? He'll have to work a long time before he can retire.

Jelly Roll Morton, once a big name; Lips Page, Jimmie Noone, Ernie Fields, Harlan Leonard and dozens of others, with bands, don't work regularly. Some work not at all. And when they get a job it's scale. Plain scale. They could make more money running rib joints.

Jimmie Lunceford is in Kirk's boat. He's always working, but he jumps like a madman, and air time doesn't come his way often. He knows what a buzzard looks like.

Louis Armstrong left Chicago a couple of months ago for Los Angeles. When he opened at the Paramount Theater there he looked fine in his white suit, backed by his neatly-dressed musicians and shiny instruments. The customers out front didn't know that Louie and his men had traveled across the western half of the United States in a cold bus, beat and weary. And they couldn't see their paychecks—which would amount to about half of what a white musician receives, working under a leader as well known as Armstrong. They've got buzzards on the West Coast, too.

That's the story—and it's a sad one to anyone who ever listened to any of these bands beating it out as only Negro musicians can. Where do they go from here? What's in store for them? Will 1941 be better or worse? ●

Benny Carter

ARTIE: "SHOULD BE GREATEST DANCE COMBO EVER ASSEMBLED"

By Dave Dexter, Jr.
SEPTEMBER 1, 1941

New York—Artie Shaw isn't kidding. The band he has been rehearsing here since August 15 is made up of a million dollars worth of talent and once it gets under way, playing theaters and jazz concerts throughout the eastern section of the nation, it should shape up as the greatest dance combination ever assembled.

When Artie sent out a call to his old sidekicks, asking them to return and be cogs in his latest orchestral venture, not a single man brushed off his invitation. Les Robinson quit Willy Bradley. George Auld refused to accept big-money offers from others, and went without work six weeks until Shaw's rehearsals got under way. Lee Castaldo quit Bradley, too. And, Eddie McKinney toted his big bull-fiddle right off Tony Pastor's bandstand and into Artie's room. "Lips" Page, abandoned hopes to get his own jazz band clicking and made a beeline to Shaw's initial rehearsal. Mike Bryan fluffed Bob Chester to strum a guitar, even taking lessons to brush up on the electric box which Shaw frequently likes to feature.

Musicians never before headed a leader's call as these men headed Shaw's. Trombonist Ray Conniff junked his own band in preference to holding down a chair in the Shaw unit.

ARTIE WORKS ALL DAY!

Artie appears eager to get back in the game with a great band. During his recent rehearsals it has been a common sight to find him busy with the string section as early as 10 a.m. Along about 6 p.m., some eight hours later, he's still up there at Nola's working with the saxes, or brass.

"We hope it will be the finest outfit yet," Shaw told *Down Beat*. "The job ahead of us is tough and is going to take a hell of a lot of work on the part of every man. But I think we'll have something a little out of the ordinary to offer.

"The band is shaping up wonderfully so far," he said. "We'll be better

able to tell exactly what goes, and which men will be permanently set, a little later, after the kinks are ironed out."

SHOOTS NO DEATH RAYS

When Artie asks for something, he gets it. The guys who blow the horns like his way of doing things, his musicianship, and his ideas. Watching him rehearse is a revelation. Shaw gets discipline without ever asking for it; without flashing a "death ray" at the sidemen.

Artie will be in action with his new crew

MESS OF "STARS" IN SHAW BAND

New York—Artie Shaw's tentative lineup, subject to change, includes these prominent musicians:

"Lips" Page, Max Kaminsky, Lee Castaldo, trumpets; Georgie Auld, Mickey Folus, tenors; Les Robinson, Gene Kimsey, Art Baker, altos; Jack Jenny, Ray Conniff, Morey Samuel, trombones; Dave Tough, drums; Mike Bryan, guitar; Johnny Guarnieri, piano; Eddie McKinney, bass, and eight violinists, three viola and three 'cello players who are not yet definite.

Bonnie Lake, Jack Jenney's wife and sister of Ann Sothern of the screen, will be Shaw's girl singer. ●

very soon, playing theaters (at a reported price of $10,000 cash a week) and later, going on tour for his concerts. For the latter engagements he will augment his band about 20 pieces, bringing the full personnel up to about the 50 mark.

VICTOR RECORD DATE, TOO

Lips" Page was set for a trumpet chair with Shaw although there was talk, which no one could verify, that Henry (Red) Allen, Jr., also would be hired. Allen's band has had no work since leaving a Greenwich Village nitery Aug. 6.

Shaw will soon record six sides for Victor with his all-star group.

Dave Tough quit his drum-pounding assignment with Joe Marsala and joined Shaw. One of the best-liked rhythm masters in the business, Tough is making his debut as a tub-beater with Artie, most of his other big-band experience coming from Benny Goodman and Tommy Dorsey.

TO STRESS U.S. MUSIC

Artie will put much "new American music" in his books, including jazz arrangements of the blues and compositions by known and unknown American songwriters. It is his greatest ambition to make the public aware and appreciative of native music rather than European and Asiatic art which for years has been crammed down its throat. Music by Ellington, Handy, William Grant Still and other colored composers as well as the better music from the pens of Kern, Gershwin, Vernon Duke, Rodgers and Hart, De Rose and other top-notch writers will be emphasized by Artie as he swings around the nation on his first tour since he junked his other dance crew in November, 1939. ●

"YOU CAN HAVE KENTON, I'LL TAKE MUGGSY ANY DAY," GROWLS FRAZIER

By George Frazier
FEBRUARY 1, 1942

If 1941 accomplished nothing else, it at least witnessed the completion of Mike Vetrano's phone call to Woody Herman. That call had been a source of deep and abiding anxiety for me ever since Mike first tried to put it through and I could never quite rid myself of the terrifying suspicion that he would run out of nickels before he had finally made himself clear. But now it's in the can, as they say out on the Coast, and both Ted Lewis and I can be at ease. Everybody's happy.

That particular line is still busy, though. No sooner had Mike hung up the receiver than Carlos Gastel picked it up and another significant conversation was under way. Things being what they are these days, I can't promise a thing, but I'll try them again in twenty minutes and call you back. Carlos Gastel is a very busy man and it is not at all improbable that he will soon be an affluent one. That, at any rate, would seem to be in the books. Carlos has a band that shapes up as one of those sensations (and I don't mean Sonny Dunham). He has, for your dancing pleasure, Stan Kenton and his orchestra, with a slew of network shots and a flood of publicity and the kids out front eating it all up, and before you know it you've got another Miller, another Tommy, another Jimmy.

"I DON'T LIKE IT"

The Kenton band has everything. But I don't like it. It has singers and soloists and pretentious arrangements and Publix endings. But I don't like it. To me, it's terrific in a revolting way. It's the poor man's Whiteman, and has no Beiderbecke to race your pulse.

("The Kenton band has everything....I...like it. It has singers and soloists....I...like it. To me, it's terrific.... It's...Whiteman and...Beiderbecke to race your pulse." George Frazier in *Down Beat*.)

Now there is one thing I think we ought to understand: If what Kenton has to offer, if his particular brand of dance music, is what is going to put him up there with the big boys and make him a lot of money, then I say good. No one, except possible Peewee Russell, is in this business for his health. There is nothing tainted about being a smash hit, nothing disgraceful about being in the big money. If Lombardo and Kyser and Heidt and Kaye can reach the higher income brackets on the strength of the mediocrity they peddle, I say more power to Lombardo and Kyser and Heidt and Kaye. But a commercial success is of itself no guarantee of a *succes d'estime*. It is my own considered feeling that Stan Kenton is going to be a great big name one of these days—and by that I am not implying that his music is in the same lowly class with either Lombardo's or Kyser's or Heidt's or Kaye's. (In fairness to Kyser it should be noted that there are a lot worse bands around than his.) As bands go, Kenton's is a pretty good one, but not, it seems to me, the stirring affair that several of my knowing colleagues insist that it is.

"TOO PRETENTIOUS"

In the first place, I think, that it's too much out for significance rather than for simplicity and the natural flow of the music. In the second place, I don't care for its intonation. In the third place, I cannot stand performers who take themselves too seriously, and it is my impression that practically everyone in the

Kenton band owns a complete set of Aeschylus. Off the stand they may be

the sweetest characters on the face of God's green earth (and those who know them personally assure me that they're a swell bunch), but once they see a mike they're transformed into palpable hams. In the fourth place, I fail to find the soloists either eloquent or especially stirring. All of which means no more than that Kenton's band does not produce my sort of jazz. But like I'm telling you, it will probably be a sensation and if you're waiting to make a call, I suggest that you look for another booth. I have an idea that Carlos Gastel will have that line tied up for quite a while.

BUT MUGGSY'S BAND IS GOOD

If you would like to know my notion of a good white band, I suggest you listen to Muggsy Spanier's. It's simple, with the economy and the clean strength of the old Pollack band, but it is enormously exciting too. I like it because it's sincere, because its time is good and its soloists are imaginative and original and its intonations genuinely hot. I like it because, in many ways, it represents all the things that Stan Kenton's band very definitely does not represent.

SO IS CROSBY'S

And if you are still curious and would like to know my idea of another white band, I give you Bob Crosby. It is understandable, of course, that if you don't care for Dixieland you will probably have to be convinced. But

Dixieland or no Dixieland, it is a good band, one of very, very few absolutely first-rate white bands in the business today. It's not the faltering affair that had the Bob-o-Links (I haven't a thing against them personally, honest), but a band that is strictly barrelhouse for 20 minutes out of every half-hour broadcast. It has the time and the colossal soloists; it has the good tunes, the redolent tunes out of an earlier day and age and the modern classics on the order of "Take the 'A' Train"; and it never, never gets fancy. And it is versatile too. It can do a hot one, and that, in this age of specialization, is no mean accomplishment.

PRAISE FOR NEWTON

For the first time since the resonant nights of Bobby Hackett's apprenticeship at the old Theatrical Club, Boston has a really first-class small band in its midst. The band is Frankie Newton's and it came into the Savoy on Columbus Avenue Jan. 12 for at least six weeks. Newton, of course, us an admittedly exciting musician, but his band is no one-man affair. George Johnson on alto and Ike Quebec on tenor are superior performers, while Vic Dickerson, although not to these ears a magnificent soloist, plays some of the most exquisite trombone backgrounds imaginable. All in all, it's a swell little band and distinctly in the nature of a hypo for Boston's listless night life.

There is just one thing I should like to mention: This Buster Bailey is one hell of a clarinetist and don't let anyone tell you differently. The precise, intellectual Kirby scores don't always allow him sufficient latitude to display his gorgeous talents, but he appeared at a recent jam session in Providence and knocked the cover off the ball. It was one of the most breathtaking clarinet performances I have ever heard and, for my money, this Bailey is really something. ●

CHARLIE CHRISTIAN DIES IN NEW YORK

MARCH 15, 1942

New York—Musicians here are mourning the sudden, unexpected death of young Charlie Christian, who died of tuberculosis March 2 while a patient at the Seaview Hospital on Staten Island. The bespectacled, personable Christian succumbed a few days after physicians assured him he was making progress in his long fight against the dreaded illness.

Unmarried, Charlie's body was sent to Oklahoma for burial. He is survived by his mother, who handled all funeral arrangements herself, and a brother, also a musician-bandleader.

BORN IN TEXAS

Christian became prominent as a member of Benny Goodman's sextet, but for many years before he joined Goodman, Christian was highly regarded in the Southwest, not only as a guitarist, but also as a bass fiddle player. Born in Texas, Charlie was moved to Oklahoma City at age 2 , and from that time on considered the state capital his home.

Charlie's father was a guitar player, and when young Charlie at age 12 (after a bass teacher had unsuccessfully tried to make him a trumpeter) took his dad's two gitboxes, he was on his way. At 15, he was working professionally in a little Oklahoma City joint. Later, he worked with bands led by his own brother, Alphonso Trent (in this band he played bass) and Anna Mae Winburn. Tired of traveling the gopher-meadowlark circuit of the Midwest, Charlie organized his own little jump band and worked again in an Oklahoma City nitery.

A HAMMOND DISCOVERY

Came July, 1939, and John Hammond was driving madly across the nation to be present for the Goodman band's opening night at Victor Hugo's in Beverly Hills. Hammond, always on the lookout for colored talent, remembered that Teddy Wilson and Mary Lou Williams had often praised the

musicianship of a young guy in Oklahoma City. So he stopped in the nitery to dig Christian. Much impressed, Hammond continued on to the coast, sold Goodman the idea of hiring Charlie, and Benny then wired Christian to join him at Hugo's.

Christian made almost all the sextet records, most of them on the red Columbia label, and also a few big band sides with Goodman, among them "Honeysuckle Rose," in which he plays an excellent solo. In 1940, after more than a year with Goodman, during which time he became without question the favorite guitarist of all musicians, Charlie became ill. He had been ill off and on but this time, physicians advised him to give up music and take hospital treatment.

PLANNED TO JOIN COOTIE

Christian had since been reported "much improved" and only a few weeks before he died, was said to be progressing rapidly toward complete recovery. Like the late Dick Wilson, who died of T.B. last November, Christian was restless and eager to return to the bandstand when he took a sudden, inexplicable change for the worse.

Goodman and John Hammond, Charlie's closest friends, were especially grieved at Charlie's passing and personally handled details of sending the body to Oklahoma. They, too, helped Christian financially on the doctor and hospital expenses. Cootie Williams, a few weeks before Christian passed on, announced that Charlie would join Williams' new band as soon as he was released. But his plans — and Charlie's — never materialized. ●

"PUT FULL McSHANN ORK ON WAX"

By Bob Locke

JULY 1, 1942

DECCA IS FOOLING THE PUBLIC, IS WAIL OF JAZZ CRITIC

Chicago—Somebody, and I think it's Dave Kapp of Decca Records, has been fooling the public!

I'm sore, and so are a gob of other critics. And for good cause, since there's no reason on earth why the Jay McShann band, yeah, all sixteen pieces of it, shouldn't be on wax instead of hiding it behind the skirts of a blues singer, Walter Brown by name, and a rhythm quartet. (By the way, Walter, that "skirt" is only a figure of speech.)

WHY FOOL THE PUBLIC?

The McShann band played a one-nighter at the Savoy ballroom here last month. Did the patrons expect a full-sized powerhouse swing band, playing a wild earthy gutbucket style of jazz much in the fashion of the rough Basie band of a few years ago? No! They heard McShann on records, playing a piano background of "Confessin' the Blues," which has turned out to be massive hit on Decca's sepia series, and assumed he was a solo act, backed up by a pickup band. The reason was that sepia communities, and indeed many ofay communities, have been bilked too often in this fashion before. That they did get their money's worth this time is a point to be taken up later on. The point here is that it isn't good business to keep the entire band off wax, and that' it's not doing either Decca or McShann any good.

I don't know what Decca's idea is, but I imagine they figure that four musicians play for a cheaper price than sixteen and the profits are the same. But they're wrong, for the profits aren't the same in the long run. But enough of that.

Here is a band which is the greatest unrecognized band in the country. In the Midwest, it is a sock box office attraction. It went East last winter and took the Savoy by storm. And that isn't easy to do. Harlan Leonard's Kansas City Rockets lasted two weeks in New York. And don't let anybody kid you that Count Basie's band didn't flop all over the joint when it opened at Chicago's old Terrace several years ago, even if it did pull out of the spin and make good later on.

A KANSAS CITY OUTFIT

The band is mainly a Kansas City-grooved outfit, although McShann is an Oklahoma boy himself. McShann came to Kansas City about five years ago.

The original band with an oversized rhythm section proved to be the jumpiest outfit Kansas City had ever seen. South Siders flocked to Martin's, which soon became a hub of jive. The boys in the band were young, enthusiastic, full of musical ideas.

MANAGED BY JOHN TUMINO

Then, in December, 1939, John Tumino, general manager of Consolidated Orchestras, became manager of the band, I understand, and helped Jay build his outfit up to its present size. The going was tough; bookings were hard to get for a big band. But the band made it. They preemed at Kansas City's Century Room, went into Fairyland Park, moved to King's Ballroom, Lincoln and soon were making the whole middle west circuit.

Today, the band is a nation's sensation. And for once, I quite agree with the taste of the nation. Though, I still think you "ain't seen nothing" yet until the full band gets on wax.

It's a Basie-like band, concentrating on heavy rhythm and heated riffs. There's a five-way sax section which tends at times to be Luncefordian and five brass in number, all of whom share the solo books.

MCSHANN IS OUTSTANDING

McShann, of course, is the outstanding instrumentalist. He plays with a solid, well-developed left hand, using mostly 10ths, and any variety of licks and Teddy Wilson-like runs in the treble. His style is difficult to dissect. Sometimes, he sounds like Hines, more often like Mary Lou.

The remainder of the rhythm section is made up of bassist Gene Ramey, drummer Gus Johnson, and guitarist Leonard Enois.

Jay McShann

Charlie Parker offers inspired alto solos, using a minimum of notes in a fluid style with a somewhat thin tone but a wealth of pleasing ideas. Bob Mabane and Freddy Culliver (a former Harian Leonard man) split tenor sax specialties.

PRAISE FOR TRUMPETER

As for trumpets, Bob Merrill and Buddy Anderson seem to get the hot work but my tastes prefer the more delicate and well-controlled solo performances of Orville Minor, who also does well on much growl trumpet work. This lad needs only a couple of years to be one of the country's top-notchers, I think. His talent has been underestimated.

James Coe and Skippy Hall (he also arranges for Glenn Miller, remember) pen most of the arrangements, Coe taking most of the pop tunes. There are also a number of arrangements in the book by Shay Torrent, former Wichitan, who is now in the army at Fort Leavenworth. Torrent is white.

Vocals are by Walter Brown, who sings a nasal sort of blues, and by Albert Hibler, who is blind. Hibler's voice has a wide sensitive range and a deep feeling for blues and ballads.

The McShann band is currently touring the Middle West and will open at King's Ballroom, Lincoln, Neb., on July 14.

The complete personnel: Bob Merrill, Bernard Anderson, Orville Minor, trumpets; Bob Mabane, Charlie Parker, John Johnson, James Coe, Freddy Culliver, saxes; Joe Baird, Lawrence (Frog) Anderson, trombones; Leonard Enois, guitar; Gus Johnson, drums; Gene Ramsey, bass; Albert Hibler and Walter Brown, vocals, and Jay McShann, leader and director. ●

DUKE FUSES CLASSICAL AND JAZZ!

By Mike Levin
FEBRUARY 15, 1943

STUFF IS THERE, SAYS MIX, NEEDING DEVELOPMENT TO ATTAIN NEW ART FORM

New York—Duke Ellington has taught me a lesson I'll never forget—namely, never blow your top before the third time over lightly. Three weeks ago he and his band gave a concert in Carnegie Hall. It lasted for three hours, including a 48 minute work entitled *Black, Brown and Beige*. At three minutes to 12, an exhausted audience filed out of the hall, each excitedly asking the other what his opinion was.

It was obvious that most were a little confused, but in general delighted with the last half of the program. Of BBB, the more honest ones said, "I don't get it." Others vociferously liked certain portions; many, including ace musicians and writers, said it was a complete failure.

The critics said:

Robert Bagar (World-Telegram *):* "It is too long a piece....Mr. Ellington can make some two dozen brief, airtight compositions out of BBB. He should....It is far from being an *in toto* symphonic creation."

John Briggs (N.Y. Post *):* "Mr. Ellington was saying musically the same thing he had said earlier in the evening, only this time he took forty-five minutes to do it."

Paul Bowles (N.Y. Herald-Tribune *):* "Formless and meaningless....Nothing but a potpourri of tutti dance passages and solo virtuoso work. The dance part used some pretty corny riff too. Unprovoked modulations, a passage in 5/4, paraphrases on well-known tunes that were as trite as the tunes themselves, and recurrent climaxes that impeded the piece's progress. Between dance numbers there were "symphonic" bridges played out of tempo. This dangerous tendency to tamper with the tempo within the piece showed far too many times in the evening. If there is no regular beat, there can be no syncopation, and thus no tension, no jazz. The whole attempt to fuse jazz as a form with art music should be discouraged. The two exist at such distances that the listener cannot get them both into focus at the same time. The rhythms were never jumpy or breathless, and the saxes often played in unison, which eliminated the thick-sounding choir these instruments form in many bands."

*Henry Simon (*PM*):* "First movement all but falls to pieces…can't compare with the second movement…but there's no doubt of his importance to American music."

Abel Green (editor of Variety, *a theatrical fan magazine, who after devoting his lead paragraph to disapproving of the band's uniforms in strict hep jive, went on to say):* "A bit self-conscious, as these tone poems usually are…a bit fulsome.…"

Irving Kolodin (N.Y. Sun*):* "Brown and Beige *were the best sections.…*Black *needs a little trimming.…One can only conclude that the work would be much better if scored for full orchestra with solo parts as indicated by Ellington."

CRITICS UNFAMILIAR

And so on, much too far into the night.

With the exception of Kolodin, who wrote the program notes, none of these gentry know much about jazz and even less about Ellington, other than that his brass men make unusual noises now and then. Bagar and Simon are acquainted with the stuff, and did their honest best. Others, not quoted here, wrote greater literary epics.

Abel Green came up with this gem: "For a different reaction to the performance of the band and its soloists, it was interesting to watch the faces of noted musicians. As the outstanding instrumentalists took solos, the auditors' feelings were plainly evident."

Abel was given New York City's fence-sitting trophy last month.

Maybe it isn't ethical to make cracks about other scribes. But I honestly feel that they made fools out of themselves, and were unfair as hell to Duke in the process.

I know—I made the same mistake.

EVERYBODY HEDGING

Coming out of the concert, my first reaction was letdown. Too much music, too much intermission chattering. Everybody was looking for an opinion, so they could be sure of what to think themselves. The well-known tunes were "wonderful"— BBB had wonderful ideas mind you, but was "formless, don't you think, Jack?"

That night I had heard things I liked—also things I didn't like. I didn't dig at least half of *Black*, and parts of the rest of the suite. And I wasn't sure that I understood what Duke was trying to do with the rest of the program.

I talked to musicians, arrangers, critics, record fans, and just people. They disagreed violently on the second half of the concert, a series of Duke's best-known records. But they all seemed to agree BBB had pretty ideas and nothing else.

ALMOST LET HIM HAVE IT

So I oiled up the old portable and prepared to give Duke hell for betraying his public. Then I began to remember that the boss had never tried to pan a band without hearing it at least four times first. At that here was something much more complex musically than any dance band ever served up—which I was judging on one hearing at a jammed concert hall.

Brother, believe me, the gremlins had me but good. To pan the Duke, the most fertile figure in American music, or to duck the review completely. The boss wouldn't let me do the latter, and I hated like heck to do the former. The only answer was either that I had to write a pan, and a bad one at that, or prove my own opinion was wrong.

It was!

Danny James, Duke's manager, had a set of records made at the concert. Being a good guy, and also having a terrific laugh at the way I was squirming, he lent me the records. Since then, I have listened to that concert exactly six times over.

Anybody who says that BBB doesn't have form and continuity simply doesn't know what he's talking about. That's no question of opinion or anything

controversial. That's a question of musical fact, and is easily settled by listening enough times to the records. There are a lot of things about the form that I don't like. Duke has a habit of shifting tempos with solo instruments, and of throwing recaps right smack on top of a developing theme.

But the principal trouble was one of dynamics, rather than writing. The Ellington band is famous for its shadings and colorings. There were very few of these present in BBB. That is not the music's fault. That was a question of rehearsal, and familiarity with the score. Duke didn't really get it set until three weeks before the concert, and new parts and sections were added several days before the concert itself.

HARD TO DIG IDEAS

The abrupt shifts from loud to soft and back again with no shading, and the trick of either playing completely out of tempo, or "jumping" the particular groove hit, made it all but impossible to detect the various ideas moving in the score.

Therefore, when Duke read the unfavorable reviews the next morning and said, "Well, I guess they didn't dig it," and nothing more, he was perfectly correct. But it wasn't all the critics' fault. The band didn't give BBB the performance it should have had. It isn't perfect. But it is a tremendous step forward for music and for Ellington.

BLUES ARE WONDERFUL

The "Blues" section of *Brown*, sung wonderfully by Betty Roche, was an admirable example of this. Purists screamed because it wasn't strict blues in the old shouting fashion. No, but what you had was a woman singing about what was worrying her heart, backed by some powerful cadences similar to those used by Stravinsky in his pre-war stuff.

It was a synthesis of everything Duke has been able to learn from the history of music, his rich background and that of his men in the great Negro tradition, plus the personal virtuosities of the Ellington band.

Look to music like this for the first undeniable American expression I've heard in a concert hall. I played the discs for Red Norvo. When the blues came in, Norvo, an impeccable musician, said, "Those are the blues the way they hit me. *That's it.*" ●

HERMAN'S IS FINEST OFAY SWING BAND

By Frank Stacy

MARCH 1, 1945

New York—"Woody Herman has the greatest ofay swing band in the country—bar none!" That's what all the band popularity contests said this year and that's just the way I feel about it. Out of the 1,606 swing fans who named the Herman Herd their favorite dispenser of jive in *Down Beat*'s annual contest, undoubtedly some (the bobby-soxers) cast their votes that way because they go for the snappy corduroy jackets that Woody sports on the stand. Most fans, however, picked Woody's crew for its crack over-all musicianship, for its up-to-the-minute presentation of advanced big band orchestrations, for Woody's superior talents as an instrumentalist, singer, showmanly stick-waver, and, above all, for his grasp of the *right* band idea.

It's always been my contention that a great band demands a great leader. There may be exceptions to the rule but BG, the Duke, Basie, Artie Shaw and now Woody Herman are plenty of examples to prove its validity.

"NOTHING BUT TRUTH"

One of my first meetings with Woody took place when he was playing a network show and had hired a new press agent to exploit it. It happened that I was sitting nearby when the p.a. came up to ask Woody his slants on publicity. Were there any special angles to his bandleader life that he wanted stressed or covered up?

Woody thought a minute.

"No," he said finally. "There's nothing special…just so you stick to the truth."

That answer is not only refreshing coming from a man in the limelight, it's a clue to Woody's real character and accounts at second remove for the integrity of his whole band.

Shortly after that meeting, I spent a week on the road with Woody's band, playing one-nighters in New England and ending up with a stay at the Steel Pier in Atlantic City. If the overheard conversation between Woody and his publicist gave me insight into the bandleader's character, days spent with him in trains, autos, hotel dining rooms, one-arm lunches, and dance halls only strengthened the conviction that here was a remarkably rare species of the genius *big-time personality.*

BALANCED SHOWMAN

This is what I learned—Woody Herman is not a musical trickster. He's aware of his own musical capacities, realizes that he doesn't play the greatest clarinet or alto in the world nor sing the best blues, but plays his considerable talents to the hilt. Neither is he a show-off on the bandstand, though he has an expert conception of what sells, due perhaps to the fact that he spent his early, formative years as a vaudeville performer. He's a proud parent, a happy husband and a home lover. Most indicative of all, his sidemen not only respect him as a leader-musician, they like him as a friendly, amusing guy.

Beyond this, Woody gave me some candid opinions of his own which I'll record here briefly. He likes what he calls "modern" jazz; jazz that is matured; that reflects the temper of the times; that demands both creative ability and command of instrument on the part of the performer. In other words, though he pays proper tribute to the historic jazz musicians and bands of the past, he feels that the old style (as exemplified by the New Orleans, Dixieland and Chicago groups) has had its day, and that big band music is the logical musical art form of our day.

ADMIRES, NEVER IMITATES

He likes the Duke obviously enough from the number of Ellington-inspired arrangements in his book. He is not, however, a sedulous imitator of the Duke nor of any other bandleader. The

Arsene Studio

recent blast let loose by booker Joe Glaser which accused Woody of "stealing" ideas from Lionel Hampton was completely without basis. If Woody uses Dukish material it's only to give implicit credit and honor to Ellington and his matchless orchestra.

The man who leads the band that plays the blues was born, you may or may not know, in Milwaukee on May 16, 1915, which makes him twenty-nine years old. Like so many other jazzmen, he came from a musically-inclined family and started his own career at the usual early age of nine. Alto sax was his first instrument but when he was eleven, he started working on the clarinet as well.

After playing in vaudeville for a couple of years, Woody went to Marquette University, though he never completed college training. Out of school, he gave up his single act and began working with bands. His first name jobs were with Gus Arnheim, Harry Sosnick, Tom Gerun and finally Isham Jones, leader of one of the best outfits of his day. Woody sang with Jones' band, besides playing the reeds, and, all in all, displayed the stuff of which bandleaders are made. When Jones broke up his ork in 1937, Woody and several of the other sidemen stepped out with a cooperative crew of their own.

LONG, HARD STRUGGLE

Inevitably they had troubles. For one thing, the style of the band (a semi-Dixieland—gutty blues pattern) was out of step with current band favorites and it was some time before the distinctive theme "Blue Flame" became anything like a musical household word. Careful attention to booking engagements and plenty of hard work finally paid off, however, and there came a time when "Blues Upstairs," "Blues Downstairs," "Blues on Parade," "Fan It," "Golden Wedding," "Sorrento," and "Woodchopper's Ball" were best sellers on Decca, the disc firm for which Woody did most of his recording until his recent switch to Columbia.

The band developed other personalities besides its leader, though the war has cut into their ranks until only one member (Joe Bishop) of the old Herman Herd remains and even he doesn't play in the band anymore but does arranging exclusively. Drummer Frankie Carlson, bassist Walter Yoder, trumpeter Chuck Peterson, trombonist Neil Reid and all the other excellent members of the original Herd have packed their name band instruments away for the duration. With the addition of newer, younger sidemen, coupled with Woody's musical maturity, a new, unconventional Herman Herd has emerged.

HERMAN HERD ON NEW CREATIVE KICK

It wasn't until 1943 that Woody Herman began to hit his real musical stride, even though his band had found considerable success before then and had played considerable music of merit. With the beginning of World War II, Woody suffered the same losses and gained the same sense of insecurity that was affecting not only all bandleaders but everyone in every field. Undoubtedly, had an interviewer shortly after Pearl Harbor asked Woody what his plans were for the immediate future, he would have answered: "Are you kiddin'?"

Yet, oddly enough, if war can ever be held responsible for going good, it exercised a benign influence in the case of the Herman Herd. With the draft and other war-time problems, Woody started

losing his best men; the musicians he hired at first either couldn't play the old "blues" book well enough or they didn't like it enough to play it with feeling. Bookings became more of a problem and a thousand other restrictions arose to plague the bandleader. Like most leaders at the same time, Woody was forced to look for talent among younger, lesser-known musicians to replace sidemen who had become established stars in his band, but who now were either playing to a martial beat or hoisting a Garand.

It was this gradual influx of new talent that brought out latent possibilities as a musician and leader in Woody. It was the exciting contact with the "new right idea" that allowed him to let himself and his band go free musically. And it was the happy coincidence of sixteen or seventeen young talented musicians meeting in one band that led to the development of a big, white band where music was *created* and not merely played.

The fact that the Herman Herd is one for the few white bands now creating music not only seems to me undeniable but has brought me to the extreme conclusion that the Herd stands as one of the last exponents of what can only be called "good" swing music as approved to the watered-down, dull and repetitious routine of alternate "sweet and swing" numbers with which most name bands are giving out currently.

USE HEAD ARRANGEMENTS

Watching the Herman band in rehearsal and on the stand, I get the impression that here perhaps is the only ofay band in the business working in great part along the Ellington method of music creation. Many of the best numbers in Woody's book (like "Apple Honey," "Perdido," "Flying Home") are "head" arrangements, which means that they were not completely notated originally but grew up within the band by means of spontaneous contributions from different sidemen to form perfect solo and ensemble wholes. In effect, this is what the Ellington band does and the same kind of spontaneity in a white orchestra is not only precedent-making but gives Woody's band most of the interest it holds for anyone concerned with swing music phenomena. ●

NEW YORK JAZZ STINKS, CLAIMS COAST PROMOTER

By TAC
AUGUST 15, 1945

New York—"Jazz in New York stinks! Even the drummers on 52nd St. sound like Dizzy Gillespie!"

Thus spoke Norman Granz, West Coast expert and promoter in town to unearth some hot local talent and survey the general jazz scene. He earns the right to speak with his background as head of Vanguard Records, as the sponsor of twelve successful jazz concerts on the coast during the past year, and for his work as technical director of Warner Brothers' *Jammin' the Blues*.

"I can't tell you how disappointed I am in the quality of music here," Granz told *Down Beat*. "We keep getting great reports out west about the renaissance of jazz along 52nd St. but I'd like to know where it is. Literally, there isn't one trumpet player in any of the clubs with the exception of 'Lips' Page and he was blowing a mellophone the night I caught him. Maybe Gillespie was great but the 'advanced' group that Charlie Parker is fronting at the Three Deuces doesn't knock me out. It's too rigid and repetitive. Ben Webster wasn't playing anything when I heard him. And Billie Holiday…I'm sorry!

"I've heard two good things in the three weeks I've been in town. One was Woody Herman's band which is just as sensational as everyone's been saying it is. The other was Erroll Garner, whose piano is really wonderful. And I almost forgot, there's a young guitarist named Bill De Arango who plays fine.

"Otherwise, the West Coast may not be the happy hunting ground of modern jazz but, brother, neither is 52nd St. these days!" ●

Norman Granz

DELAUNAY ON FIRST VISIT TO AMERICA
COMPLETING FIFTH EDITION OF HOT DISCOGRAPHY

By Bill Gottlieb

AUGUST 26, 1946

New York—Charles Delaunay, visiting the U. S. for the first time to prepare the fifth edition of his epochal *Hot Discography*, has brought with him a Hollywood tale of the French Hot Clubs' role in the anti-Nazi underground.

Some typical episodes: The murder of the president of the Hot Club of Marseille in a German gas chamber….The same for Charles' own girl assistant….Using the Paris Hot Club as a regular contact point for parachuted British agents…. Confinement in dreaded Fresnes Prison but escaping deportation to Germany…. The banning of swing and the subsequent publication of the fourth edition of his discography under the noses of the occupying German forces. Also the changing of jazz titles from "St. Louis Blues" to "Tristesses De St. Louis" (Sadness of St. Louis) and from "I Got Rhythm" to its phonetical counterpart "Agate Rhythm" (Stone Rhythm).

Delaunay also brought news of an overwhelming burst of enthusiasm by Frenchmen for jazz, beginning with the fall of his country in 1940 and continuing to the present.

This 35-year-old Parisian, who became the greatest research scholar on American hot music without having crossed the Atlantic, also came with the lament that America, itself, had not produced a real jazz critic…certainly no one of the stature of his fellow countryman, Hugues Panassié (*Hot Jazz* and *The Real Jazz*).

FAILED TO GET TO U. S.

Following the surrender of the French army in August 1940, Charles received his discharge and lit out for southern France to avoid prison camp. After an unsuccessful attempt to get to America, he returned to German-occupied Paris and resumed his old role of Secretary General of the Hot Club of France.

By December, Delaunay had engineered the most brilliant Hot Club production given before or since. The Carnegie Hall of

Paris, Salle Pleyel, sold out its 2,500 seats so far ahead of opening day that a second concert was scheduled immediately following the first. Musicians flocked from distant French points to play or listen and arrangements were made to hold three such concerts a month, thereafter.

FRENZY ABOUT JAZZ

Frenchmen had suddenly taken to hot music. The frenzy was inexplicable," Delaunay relates. "Although isolated jazz events had caused a great stir in Paris before the war—notably the Duke Ellington triumph of 1933—typical affairs of the Hot Club, even Paris sessions featuring Django Reinhardt and Eddie South, drew only about 400 spectators. But after the fall of France, small towns of three or four thousand—like Martignes of Salon, just outside of Marseille—could draw a thousand enthusiasts at each monthly concert. With a mediocre French "star," a hot club in a town of a hundred thousand, like Bezed or Beziers, could top 2,000.

"A total of 70 French Hot Clubs sprang into being. And," added Delaunay, who is an executive of Swing Records, "discs that formerly sold 500 copies a month began to sell 3,000, even with inflated prices."

LECTURE JAZZ IN VILLAGES

Pre-war jazz fans were either musicians or the kind of analytical intellectuals who were also interested in surrealism and other novel ways of expression. "Yet by 1941," Charles pointed out, "I was able to lecture on hot music in farm villages."

Delaunay says that no one in France or in Belgium, which was similarly affected, can explain the sudden universal interest in hot music that took place after the Germans had taken over. Perhaps, some say, jazz is the music of despair. Perhaps it is a sedative.

Delaunay, himself, feels that jazz became the symbol of, or the last tie with, the outside, free world. All else was closed

off—movies, radio, magazines. There were, however, large stocks of American records that had been gathering dust in music shops. There was also a nucleus of American-inspired French jazz musicians who could make new records. (Synthetic "shellac" had been developed by the Germans and was available in reasonable quantities.)

PANASSIE'S INFLUENCE

The French seized upon hot music as upon a floating straw in a sea of doom. They chase jazz instead of sweet music because the original French enthusiasts, beginning with Panassié, had established a base in which only relative purists like Armstrong and Ellington could be found.

Fortunately for the fate of jazz in France, Delaunay had once read *Mein Kampf*. He suspected that as soon as the conquering Nazis had taken care of more urgent matters, they would ban swing because of its American-Jewish-Negro origins. On the other hand, he also knew Hitler encouraged a sense of pride among satellite nations in their own traditional cultures. Adding these two factors together, Delaunay set out from the very first concert of December, 1940, to make hot music appear to be a distinctively French matter, with French artists, composers and origins emphasized and with American elements falsified to appear French. Hot music was pretty much centralized in the Hot clubs; so any program of Delaunay's could be made to cover jazz activities throughout France.

First of all, what little France had contributed to jazz was inflated astronomically. Django Reinhardt's name was invoked in every other paragraph of every speech on the history and development of jazz. Panassié, giant that he actually is among jazz writers, was referred to as the Messiah.

METHODS USED

Another part of the program was the changing of titles. Ordinarily, French fans like to be snobbish and use only original English titles, just as many Americans prefer French on their dinner menus. But by 1941, titles became French, as in the illustrations given earlier. Above all, the word "swing" was never used, though "jazz," with its long-standing French usage, was acceptable. Because blues were easy to retitle ("Blues in C Sharp," etc.) they were heavily featured at concerts.

Composers' names were either omitted or, when necessary to satisfy copyright authorities, French musicians were given credit of authorship. At "record" sessions, the lecturers, in anticipation of snooping by Gestapo in the audience, pasted phony labels over the originals. Delaunay used Jean Sablon, for example, as a blind for Louis' Hot Five. He figured the German squares would never know the difference.

As Delaunay suspected, American swing eventually became *verboten*. But by then, the Hot Clubs had pretty well established jazz as an old French custom. The music itself was probably distasteful to Hitler, who was a complete esthetic corn-ball. But he played along as long as the French jazz men made as good a case for themselves as they did.

ESCAPADES WITH GESTAPO

In 1941, some months after the Germans occupied France, Charles Delaunay received permission to cross into the unoccupied zone on urgent, personal business. While away from Paris, the hot discographer came across an artist who had been his first employer, (Before jazz became all-confirming, Charles had been a painter. His father, Robert Delaunay, is the early cubist whose paintings hang in the Museum of Modern Art in New York.)

The ex-employer turned out to be the leader of one of the several French underground groups. He asked Delaunay for help and, as a result, Charles returned to Paris to establish the French Hot Clubs as message centers for the underground group led by the artist.

To better escape detection, the underground met at a different place each night. It was the duty of the Hot Club to inform the proper people, including Allied agents who had parachuted into France, of the whereabouts of each successive meeting place.

The Paris Hot Club, national headquarters for the Hot Clubs of France, is an old, three-story house. The cellar is a large, sound-proof rehearsal hall. Upstairs are various record rooms, Delaunay's office and a library with current magazines and books on jazz.

During the Occupation, hundreds of people milled about the building each day talking, listening to records, reading, or holding jam sessions. Strangers, including British soldiers disguised as Frenchmen, could mix freely with a minimum chance of detection. In fact, on nights when agents weren't busy making mayhem, they came to the Hot Club just to listen to the music.

In October 1943, the Germans "dug" the set-up and the Gestapo moved in, picking up British military men and Hot Club officials. They were dragged to the Fresnes Prison, a kick-off point for the German hell-camps. Madeline Gemaine, a Club secretary and a lieutenant of the artist who led their underground movement, was subsequently murdered in a gas chamber, as was the president of the Marseille club.

Delaunay was kept in Fresnes for a month. One day he was interrogated for five and one-half hours.

"It was my grandest day," Charles recalls. "They wanted to know where to find our leader. I was fortunate enough to understand enough of the German that was spoken preparatory to each question to have time to work out the best possible answers. Never have I talked so much or so well."

Much to everyone's surprise, Delaunay was released, though presumably so that he could be tailed to the hiding place of the leader. But the artist had secretly flown from France as soon as he learned the game was up. He is now a commercial artist in New York.

Even as Delaunay languished in jail, the galleys of the fourth (1943) edition of the *Hot Discography* were lying on his desk at the Hot Club, waiting to be proof read.

Delaunay had been prompted to undertake the new edition by some Belgian jazz fanatics who assured him they could get enough black market paper.

At the time, the Germans permitted the publication of scientific reference books, provided no more than 500 copies were run off. Delaunay needed, however, 2,500 copies, 1,000 of which had to go to the Belgians. He got around this obstacle by juggling with the numbering of the books. One set, for example, was marked from A-1 to A-500, others in italics and so on.

HELP FROM MANY SOURCES

Through contacts with Swedish and Swiss jazz groups, Delaunay was able to get a surprising number of additions to his previous edition. A German officer, Dietrich Schultz, who is now in a prisoner-of-war camp, also helped. He was an old jazz fan and was in constant contact with Scandinavian jazz publications.

The grapevine was sufficiently effective for Delaunay to learn the personnel of all the records made by Duke Ellington up through 1942! He had Armstrong, Goodman, Bechet and others covered through 1941.

He was also able to learn of important news events. He knew of Fats Waller's death within a month.

Relatively speaking, Charles Delaunay's fifth edition will be written under ideal conditions. Now in this country for the first time, Delaunay had to compile his first edition by carrying on voluminous overseas correspondence, by talking to a handful of American musicians who chanced to get to Europe and—most incredibly—by listening so long and so intently to records that he could identify who was playing lead trumpet and who second trumpet after hearing a bar or two of the music!

CHECK FIRST HAND HERE

In America, he'll be able to check, first hand, with musicians, record companies and the dozen or so discographers who have followed in his footsteps and expanded facets of the broad field that he first explored.

Since Delaunay does not consider himself a critic, he feels free to speak harshly of what he calls America's failure to produce one full-blown critic of its own distinctive art form, jazz.

"Instead of having a creative critic who can view the whole field of jazz with deep insight and clairvoyance, America has only a collection of superficial historians or narrowly biased partisans. Where there should be a broad discussion of the esthetics of hot music, there is only hair splitting.

Jazz Combines Extremes

Jazz is more than just dixieland or just re-bop. It's both of them and more."

Delaunay also feels that lack of real criticism is partly responsible for the lack of greatness in new bands. He feels they are not aware of a growing, developing course that art should follow. Instead, they move in hit or miss fashion, each by himself.

The whole situation makes Charles Delaunay shake his head. It makes those of us who know his work shake our heads, too. It's our art. Yet the two greatest students of jazz, Panassié and Delaunay, are Frenchmen! ●

George Evans

DIXIELAND NOWHERE, SAYS DAVE TOUGH

By Bill Gottlieb
SEPTEMBER 23, 1946

New York—"Dixieland jazz," Dave Tough told the *Beat*, "was once revolutionary stuff. But now it's just a straight-Republican-ticket kind of music. It's stuffy, musically limited and requested only by snobs who affect a 'pose'."

That was the beginning of a long string of invectives aimed at the variously titled Dixieland - New Orleans - Chicago - Nicksieland - "Ameri-condon" style of music that was the subject of the current "Posin'" column. So sharp and lengthy was Tough's answer, so authoritative the speaker and so pertinent the story, in light of the recent move at Condon's toward "modern" swing, that the *Beat* decided to turn Tough's answer into a separate article.

In direct answer to the "Posin'" question, "Why don't young musicians today play Dixieland music?" asked little David, who looks like John Carradine after a 50-day fast. "None of the kids take it up because the kids play what they first hear. New styles *fortunately* can easily be heard. Old styles *fortunately* can not easily be heard. Those playing the old style are going up a blind alley. They're completely limiting their music. It's silly. Like still saying 'twenty-three Skidoo!'"

THROUGH WITH CONDON'S MUSIC

Tough, the man who's currently playing both Condon's club and radio studios; the drummer who has played with Benny Goodman, Tommy Dorsey, Artie Shaw, and Woody Herman. In fact, the musician who has probably played with a greater number and greater variety of important bands than anyone else, says that he and the boys in the band think Condon is a great guy, but they're through with the music with which he's most generally associated.

At the time of the interview, Condon had been away a couple of weeks and the music was sounding less and less "Ameri-condon." But Dave insisted it wasn't just a matter of when the cat's away the mice will play.

"We've been getting away from the old music all along. When Max Kaminsky joined us, that finished the transition. The dyed-in-the-wool, old-time jazz men were all out of the band.

IGNORES THE CHANGE

Condon probably doesn't like the change," Tough continued, "but he doesn't say anything. Maybe he just doesn't notice what we're doing most of the time. He's not always on the stand. He's too busy with business. He comes up for a set and requests some Dixie tunes. We play 'em, but more in our style than the traditional way. Then the set's over and Condon goes with his friends or back to his office and gets lost."

With the sound of the band's "C-Jam Blues," "Whispering," "How High the Moon" and other Ellington and Gillespie specialties still in the air, Dave continued: "We're not exactly playing re-bop music; but we're playing plenty of re-bop tunes in our own way…just not as frantically as they do on the Street. When we play oldies like 'Riverboat Shuffle,' a few old Dixieland fans hardly recognize it. But the majority of listeners don't know the difference. They tell us that the old jazz is the only jazz. And when we play Dizzy's 'Whispering,' they clap like mad.

FITZGERALD CHARACTERS

Those Dixieland characters come here to live their youth over again. They like to think it's still prohibition and they're wild young cats up from Princeton for a hot time. All they need is a volume of F. Scott Fitzgerald sticking out of their pockets."

Then Dave Tough wound the thing up.

"This old music that you used to hear down here.…All it is is a bad copy of the music that white Chicago musicians played, who were in turn doing bad imitations of the music that they heard from the musicians who came from New Orleans. The end product was a music that was harmonically infantile, devoid of embellishments and interesting connecting chords and, all in all, scaled to the level of musicians with meager technique." ●

CONDON RAPS TOUGH FOR "RE-BOP SLOP"

By Bill Gottlieb
OCTOBER 7, 1946

Eddie Condon

New York—"If anyone but Dave Tough were perpetrating that Re-Bop Slop at my joint, I'd see how much my insurance would pay off and burn the club down."

That was Eddie Condon's opening shot in his reply to Dave Tough's statement in the last *Beat* that he and the boys in the band were through with dixieland music, even though Eddie didn't like it.

"Dave's been playing on too many sad kicks with big name bands (Herman, Dorsey, Goodman, Shaw). He's gotten into a negative frame of mind. No matter what he plays now, he says, 'I don't like it!' Which just furthers my contention that Dave should write—and I don't mean music. He has a writer's attitude and that should be his business, albeit the fact that he's the greatest drummer in the world.

SINGS KID ORY PARTS

In intellectual arguments, Dave changes his mind to fit a situation, like a chameleon changes his colors. If the guy Dave is talking to is an Elk, then Dave is an Elk, That goes for a Moose, K.C. and Odd Fellow, too. He says dixieland is nowhere; but I've heard him, after a few drinks, singing Kid Ory trombone parts."

Tough mentioned that Condon wasn't on the stand enough to really be bothered by what the rest of the boys played. "Unfortunately, that's not true," Eddie told the *Beat*. "I may be in my office or lost with friends, but I catch every note of that Ka-Lunk music. Believe me, every time I hear a chorus of "Whispering" or any other of Gillespie's Ka-Lunk specialties, I have to drown my sorrows. With each Ka-Lunk, I reach for a glass and down flow my profits."

JUST CAUGHT BEARDS

Eddie told of the changes that had come over his musicians while he was on vacation in Minneapolis. "I got back one night by plane and just had time to get over to the club an hour before closing. First thing I hear is that Re-Bop Slop, that Ka-Lunk. I figured the boys must be growing hedgework on their chins, just like Dizzy; and sure enough, when I rushed up to them, their beards were getting rough. I caught them just before it was too late."

Eddie continued: "Dave says my king of music is promoted by musicians with meager techniques. Let's go back to the very first records we made in 1929. The band was McKenzie and Condon's Chicagoans and we cut sides like 'Liza' and 'China Boy.' Here's a list of the men on that date who had such meager techniques: Bud Freeman, the late Frank Teschemacher, Joe Sullivan, Jimmy McPartland and Jim Lannigan, who now happens to be with a little unschooled jam band called the Chicago Symphony. Oh, yes, the drummer was some guy named Gene Krupa, who's nowhere with technique.

NEVER DICTATES STYLE

As for Tough saying that my king of music—assuming there is a special 'my kind'—is devoid of interesting 'chord connections,' he must have meant 'cord connections.' Probably was referring to a friend's operations.

ONLY PLAYED GOOD JAZZ

And let's get this 'dixieland' business straight," old Bow-Ties told the *Beat*. "Tough to the contrary, I've never had a Dixieland band…or a Chicago band…or a New Orleans band…or any other style band. All I'm aware of is good jazz and bad jazz. Good jazz is improvised music, with each man playing in his own particular way, maintaining, of course, a certain amount of cooperation with the others. That's what we've always played. I never dictate any style or any anything to may guys except to name a tune and state the key. They have no restrictions other than to be themselves. They not only play the way they like, they can wear red suspenders, drink on the stand and show up in paper hats. I don't make them buy uniforms and, in Tough's case, we even arranged an apartment for him just two blocks from his job."

"UNREHEARSED MISTAKES"

Condon pointed out that Re-Bop music was carefully planned or read and always played the same way. "at least when we make mistakes, they're not rehearsed.

"As for Dave saying our customers are snobs from Princeton who carry copies of F. Scott Fitzgerald in their pockets, a paltry percentage have attended Princeton…as customers at football games. And the only copy of Fitzgerald I've ever seen in the club was carried by Dave Tough." ●

TATUM CHANGED ANDRE PREVIN'S PIANO DESTINY

By Sharon A. Pease
FEBRUARY 26, 1947

I think this kid, André Previn, has a lot of talent and a hell of a good chance," said Frank Sinatra in a recent conversation with your writer. Sinatra's opinion is subscribed to by many musicians who have worked with this sensational 17-year-old pianist. In fact, some believe he is a genius destined to become one of the big names in American music. He has already fulfilled many important assignments in addition to his regular work, composing and arranging motion picture scores for Metro-Goldwyn-Mayer. These include record albums for Sunset and Victor and a number of guest appearances on Sinatra's radio show.

Previn is from a musical family. His father, Jack, is a concert pianist and teacher. His uncle, Charles Previn, now conductor of the orchestra at Radio City Music Hall, New York, was formerly musical director at Universal studios in Hollywood. André was born in Berlin, Germany, and began his musical training under the guidance of his father. The Previn's fled to Paris in 1937 and a year later proceeded to Hollywood. There André attended Selma Grammar School, John Burroughs Junior High and Beverly Hills High from which he was graduated last spring. He also continued his musical education studying with Mario [Castelnuovo-] Tedesco and the late Joseph Achron.

TATUM INFLUENCE

When 13, he played a series of classical concerts along the West Coast, winning the acclaim of audiences and critics. "At first I wasn't too much interested in American dance music," André recalls, "but that was because I wasn't hearing the right things. My attitude changed when I heard Art Tatum's recording of 'Sweet Lorraine'." Since that time he has been equally interested in jazz and the classics and has given much serious thought to the development of his dance style.

His knowledge of both fields is an asset to the Metro studios where he is called upon to compose, score and play music in either category. Among his assignments was the writing of the solo material which Jose Iturbi played in the motion picture *Holiday in Mexico.*

NO BE-BOP ADMIRER

Upon meeting André one is impressed with his keen mentality and mature judgment. Although still a youngster, who admits being in a formative stage, he has many set ideas, likes and dislikes concerning music. He is definitely antagonistic toward be-bop. Regarding Benny Goodman, he says, "I consider him the absolute giant of American Jazz."

Among contemporary piano stylists he admires the musical ideas of Art Tatum and Nat Cole. The works of these men have been most influential in the development of his own style.

André has chosen to illustrate his piano style through an original composition titled "Blues for Georgia." It is based on the traditional blues form and should be performed with a pronounced four-to-the-bar beat. The melodic inventions delve into the realm of modern tone poems, background and mood music.

The exploitation of whole tone harmonies (measure two of chorus) and chromatics (measure four of chorus) indicate his familiarity with the works of modern classicists. The tenth measure exemplifies the ease with which we can accept dissonance when it is properly prepared and resolved—The first C sharp is preparatory, next two C sharps are preparation with satisfying resolutions. Therefore, the extreme dissonance on the third count is readily acceptable, and the similar dissonance on the fourth count is practically unnoticed. ●

André Previn

THELONIOUS MONK—GENIUS OF BOP

By Bill Gottlieb
SEPTEMBER 24, 1947

ELUSIVE PIANIST FINALLY CAUGHT IN AN INTERVIEW

New York—I have interviewed Thelonious Sphere Monk.

It's not like having seen Pinetop spit blood or delivering the message to Garcia. But, on the other hand, it's at least equal to a scoop on the true identity of Benny Benzedrine or on who killed Cock Robin.

Thelonious, the George Washington of be-bop, is one elusive gent. There's been much talk about him—about his pioneering role at Minton's, where Bebop began...about his fantastic musical imagination...about his fine piano playing. But few have ever seen him; except for people like Diz and Mary Lou, I didn't know anyone else who had seen very much of him, either.

Come to think of it, I had seen him once, at the club where Dizzy's band was working some time ago. Even without his music, which was wonderful, you could recognize his cult from his be-bop uniform: goatee, beret and heavy shell glasses, only his were done half in gold.

I listened in fascination until he got up from the keyboard. "And who," I finally inquired, "was that bundle of bop?"

"Why, Thelonious Monk."

But by that time the quarry had disappeared.

MEETING IS ARRANGED

Finally, through the good offices of Mary Lou Williams, I was arranged with Thelonious. In order to take some pictures in the right setting, we went up to Minton's Playhouse at 208 W. 118th St.

In the taxi, on the way up, Thelonious spoke with singular modesty. He wouldn't go on record as insisting HE started be-bop; but, as the story books have long since related, he admitted he was at least one of the originators. Yes, he continued, verifying the oft told tale, it all began up at Minton's in early 1941.

Orchestra leader Teddy Hill had broken up his great orchestra because of problems brought on by the draft, poor transportation facilities and the like. He had bought into the tavern owned by Morris Milton (who had been the first colored delegate to the New York local of the musicians' union). Teddy eventually took over active management and instituted a policy of good music.

GUYS IN BAND

As a starter, Teddy called together some of the boys who had played in his last band, including John Birks Gillespie (by then with Calloway), and Joe Guy, trumpets, and Kenny Clarke, drums. There was also Nick Fenton on bass. Monday night was the big night at Minton's. Bandleaders like Goodman, Dorsey and Johnny Long would come in to visit. And practically every jazz man of merit in town sat in at one time or other. Charlie Parker, who had come to New York with the Jay McShann ork, appeared often and became a regular at Minton's.

"Be-bop wasn't developed in any deliberate way," continued Thelonious. "For my part, I'll say it was just the style of music I happened to play. We all contributed ideas, the men you know plus a fellow called Vic Couslen, who had been with Parker and Al Hibbler in the McShann band. Vic had a lot to do with our way of phrasing."

PIANO FOCAL POINT

If my own work had more importance than any others, it's because the piano is the key instrument in music. I think all styles are built around piano developments. The piano lays the chord foundation and the rhythm foundation, too. Along with bass and piano, I was always at the spot, and could keep working on the music. The rest, like Diz and Charlie, came in only from time to time, at first.

By the time we'd gotten that far, we had arrived at Minton's where Thelonious headed right for the piano. Roy Eldridge, Teddy Hill

and Howard McGhee dropped around. McGhee, fascinated, got Thelonious to dream up some trumpet passages and then conned Thelonious into writing them down on some score sheets that happened to be in the club.

HILL GIVES CREDIT

Teddy Hill began to talk. Looking at Thelonious Monk, he said:

"There, my good man, is the guy who deserves the most credit for starting be-bop. Though he won't admit it, I think he feels he got a bum break in not getting some of the glory that went to others. Rather than go out now and have people think he's just an imitator, Thelonious is thinking up new things. I believe he hopes one day to come out with something as far ahead of bop as bop is ahead of the music that went before it.

"He's so absorbed in his task he's become almost mysterious. Maybe he's on the way to meet you. An idea comes to him. He begins to work on it. Mop! Two days go by and he's still at it. He's forgotten all about you and everything else but that idea."

While he was at it, Teddy told me about Diz, who worked in his band following Roy Eldridge. Right off, John Birks G. showed up at rehearsal and began to play in an overcoat, hat and gloves! For a while, everyone was set against this wild maniac. Teddy nicknamed him Dizzy.

DIZZY LIKE A FOX

But he was Dizzy like a fox. When I took my band to Europe, some of the guys threatened not to go if the frantic one went, too. But it developed that youthful Dizzy, with all his eccentricities and practical jokes, was the most stable man of the group. He had unusually clean habits and was able to save so much money that he encouraged the others to borrow from him so that he'd have an income in case things got rough back in the states!" ●

From left: **Thelonious Monk, with Howard McGhee, Roy Eldridge, and Teddy Hill in front of Minton's Playhouse in 1948**

"BOP WILL KILL BUSINESS UNLESS IT KILLS ITSELF FIRST"—LOUIS ARMSTRONG

By Ernest Borneman
APRIL 7, 1948

At the end of the international jazz festival, correspondent Ernest Borneman spent the night in Louis Armstrong's room at the Negresco hotel in Nice, talking to Louis, Mezz Mezzrow, Barney Bigard, Big Sid Catlett and others about progress and tradition in jazz until the sun came up and it was time to catch the early morning plane for Paris. Others present were Velma Middleton, Louis' featured singer, and Honey Johnson, Rex Stewart's vocalist. Louis asked that some of the things said be considered "among friends." These parts of the conversation have therefore been kept off the record. A transcript of the remaining passages, mainly those of argument between Louis, Bigard and Mezz, is given below because it seems to cover nearly all the points of opinion that have recently divided the old school of jazz from the novelty school. The interview might also be considered as a fitting reply to Stan Kenton's statement that "Louis…plays without any scientific element" and that "all natural forms of inspiration in music have been exhausted." The actual text of Mike Levin's interview with Stan had of course not reached Louis yet at the time of the Nice festival, but some of Louis' statements sound almost telepathic in view of their direct relationship to the questions which Stan raised simultaneously in New York.)

Borneman: Well, now that it's all over, what do you think the verdict is going to be in the cold light of the morning after?

Mezzrow: If it proves anything, it shows that jazz is the greatest diplomat of them all. Did you dig those young French cats playing like Joe Oliver? Man, that's old Johnny Dodds on clarinet and Baby on woodblocks. And that's thirty years later and in another country. If that's not the great leveler, I don't know what is.

Bigard: You mean Claude Luter? You must be kidding.

Mezz: What do you mean kidding? Those

cats sound real good to me.

Bigard: They're out of tune so bad it hurts your ears.

Louis: What's that you're saying, man? Ain't you never played out of tune?

Bigard: Sure, man, but I try to do better. I learned a few things all those years since I was a kid in New Orleans. And if you blow wrong you try to keep it to yourself.

Louis: How about records? How about that thing you made with Duke, the one about the train?

Bigard: "Happy Go Lucky Local?" I didn't make that.

Louis: No, the other one. "Daybreak Express."

Bigard: That was the trumpet, and maybe they just cut him off in the end.

Louis: Yeah, maybe.

Bigard: And how about the one you made with the big band on "Struttin' With Some Barbecue?" How about that clarinet?

Louis: That was half a tone off, but it sold all right.

Bigard: Yeah, but you were satisfied with it?

Louis: It sold all right. Them cats know that a guy got to blow the way he feels and sometimes he hits them wrong. That's better than them young guys who won't blow for fear they'll be off.

Mezz: I'll tell you why he hit it wrong that time, Barney. The guy was playing tenor at the time and then switched to clarinet and his embouchure knocked him out.

Bigard: That's because you can take any kind of outfit and blow everyone else out of the room.

Louis: That's a fine band, pops. That little cornet player sounds just like Mutt Carey to me, I can hear all them pretty little things Mutt used to do when that boy gets up and plays. That's the real music, man.

Bigard: Real music! Who wants to play like those folds thirty years ago?

Louis: You see, pops, that's the kind of talk that's ruining the music. Everybody trying to do something new, no one trying to learn the fundamentals first. All them young cats playing them weird chords. And what happens? no one's working.

Bigard: But Louis, you got to do something different, you got to move along with the times.

Louis: I'm doing something different all the time, but I always think of them fine old cats way down in New Orleans—Joe and Bunk and Tio and Buddy Bolden—and

know that's not the way any good music ever got made. You got to like playing pretty things if you're ever going to be any good blowing your horn. These young cats want to make money first and the hell with the music. And then they want to carve everyone else because they're full of malice, and all they want to do is show you up, and any old way will do as long as it's different from the way you played it before. So you get all them weird chords which don't mean nothing, and first people get curious about it just because its new, but soon they get tired of it because it's really no good and you got no melody to remember and no beat to dance to. So they're all poor again and nobody is working, and that's what that modern malice done for you.

Mezz: Because they're full of frustration, full of neuroses, and then they blow their top 'cause they don't know where to go from here. All they know is that they want to be different, but that's not enough, you can't be negative all the time, you got to be positive about it, you can't just say all the time "That's old, that stinks, let's do something new, let's be different." Different what way? Go where? You

From left: Jack Teagarden, Louis Armstrong, Sid Catlett (drums), Barney Bigard, and Arvell Shaw (bass)

Bigard: Embouchure, huh! I was playing tenor too. I had two embouchures. For tenor on this side and for clarinet on that one so what about that?

Louis: That's not what we're talking about. You're always knocking somebody, pops. I say that little French band plays fine. I could take them youngsters up to the Savoy and bring the walls down with them any day.

when I play my music, that's what I'm listening to. The way they phrased so pretty and always on the melody, and none of that out-of-the-world music, that pipe-dream music, that whole modern malice.

Borneman: What do mean by that, Louis?

Louis: I mean all them young cats along the Street with their horns wrapped in a stocking and they say "Pay me first, pops, then I'll play a note for you," and you

can't take no for an answer all the time. You got to have a tradition. They lost it. Now they're like babes in the wood, crying for mammy. Poor little guys, and one after the other blows his top. They ought to see a psychoanalyst before they start playing music. We made a blues about it for King Jazz, and we called it "The Blues and Freud."

Bigard: But we're in a new age now, man.

It's a nervous age, you got to bring it out in your music.

Louis: When they're down, you gotta help them up, not push them in still deeper.

Bigard: You can say that because you're a genius. I'm just an average clarinet player.

Louis: Now none of that, pops, you're all right. You just got off the right track when you were playing with [*name withheld*]. All that soft-mike stuff that can't cut naturally through the brass. You just remember the way the boys used to play way down on Rampart Street and you'll kill the cats.

Bigard: You know who has the best band in America now? Kid Ory.

Mezz: Treason!

Bigard: And I'll tell you why. Because they got a full tone and they play in tune.

Mezz: An no mop-mops and be-bops.

Louis: Because they play together, not every prima donna for herself. And not like them cats who got too big for their boots when somebody gave them a chance to lead a band and now they can't play their instruments no longer. Look at [*name withheld*] starting off "West End blues" in the wrong key. He don't remember his own solo no more. I remember every note I ever played in my life.

Bigard: But that's what I was saying. It's all so easy for you to talk because you're an exception in everything. We others just got to keep scuffling, and if they want us to play bop, we gotta play bop. It don't matter if we like it or not.

Louis: No, that's because I got some respect for old folks who played trumpet before me. I'm not trying to carve them and do something different. That's the sure way to lose your style. They say to you "I got to be different. I got to develop a style of my own." And then all they do is try and not play like you do. That's not the way to do anything right. that's the sure way you'll never get any style of your own. Like I was telling you about [*name withheld*]. He had a style once because he played like the old timers did on their horns, and all he tries now is to play solos and not back up a band or a singer.

Bigard: That's because he was a leader, man, and he just got used to waving a stick.

Louis: Jack was a leader too. You were a leader. I've been a leader for some time now, but don't try and carve you when we play a passage together.

Mezz: That modern malice.

Louis: You see, pops, it's wonderful with the trumpet players because the trumpet is an instrument full of temptation. All the young cats want to kill papa, so they start forcing their tone. Did you listen to [*name withheld*] last night? He was trying to my piece, make fun of me. But did you hear his tone? 'Nuff said.

Bigard: I won't argue with that.

Louis: I'll tell you another. Remember Lunceford? Those first things he did, "White Heat Jazznocracy," why, that was wonderful work on reeds. And then the trumpets came in and that was the end. They killed it stone dead every time.

Bigard: That was Steve.

Louis: No, that wasn't Steve. Steve was all right. It was [*name withheld*]. And I'll tell you another one. You know [*name withheld*]? One day he told Braud I was playing 1918 trumpet and the hell with me. You know that was the wrong man to talk. Braud nearly killed him for it. Now they tell me he never said it, he loves me too much, but I know those cats. They want to play good trumpet, and they want to show off at the same time. But you can't have it both ways. You can play good trumpet with a pretty tone and a fine melody or you can play them weird chords. You can't do both at the same time and if you try, that's when you get unhappy and hate everybody and then you blow your top.

Bigard: That's right. I don't go for those guys who get so high they can't work and then come sucking around you looking for sympathy. Last night [*name withheld*] comes up to me and says he can't send money home to his wife because the French won't let him. So I say to him, "What were you doing when you were touring [*name withheld*] where they let you send money home? Who was buying all your drinks then?" That's the way they talk and all the time you know they get high just because they're fighting their horns.

Louis: This cat comes up to me last night and says: "Louis, don't you like me no more? You don't ever talk to me." I say "Pops, don't give me none of that Harlem jive," and I leave him standing there. I don't dig those cats.

Mezz: And [*name withheld*], how about [*name withheld*]?

Louis: Best white drummer I ever heard and can't hold a job and that's why he keeps knocking everybody in the business.

Mezz: That modern malice (*laughs*).

Louis: Pops, I'll tell you what it's all about. Just look at the Street today. Don't let me tell you nothing. Just look at the Street. They've thrown out the bands and put in a lot of chicks taking their clothes off. That's what the bop music has done for the business. And look at them young cats too proud to play their horns if you don't pay them more than the old timers. 'Cause if they play for fun they aren't king no more. So they're not working but once in a while and then they play one note and nobody knows if its the right note or just one of them weird things where you can always make like that was just the note you were trying to hit. And that's what they call science. Not play their horns the natural way. Not play the melody. And then they're surprised they get thrown out and have strippers put in their place.

Bigard: Well, I don't know.

Louis: Well, you oughta know, pops, you've been around long enough. Look at the legit composers always going back to folk tunes, the simple things, where it all comes from. So they'll come back to us when all the shouting about bop and science is over, because they can't make up their own tunes, and all they can do is embroider it so much you can't see the design no more.

Mezz: But it won't last.

Louis: It can't last. They always say "Jazz is dead" and then they always come back to jazz.

Enter Louis' valet dragging a trunk: We gotta pack, pops. (*Draws the curtain.*) It's daylight, boys. We gotta be at the airport in a hour.

Mezz: Well, let's scuffle.

Louis: It's always the same thing in all languages. You make a pretty tune and you play it well and you don't have to worry about nothing. If you swing it, that's fine, and if you don't, well look at Lombardo and Sinatra and they're still not going hungry. We'll be around when the others will be forgotten.

Mezz: They'll be cleaning the streets of the city when we eat lobster at Negresco. ●

NO BOP ROOTS IN JAZZ: PARKER

By Michael Levin and John S. Wilson

SEPTEMBER 9, 1949

Bop is no love-child of jazz," says Charlie Parker. The creator of bop, in a series of interviews that took more than two weeks, told us he felt that "bop is something entirely separate and apart" from the older tradition; that it drew little from jazz, has no roots in it. The chubby little alto man, who has made himself an international music name in the last five years, added that bop, for the most part, had to be played by small bands.

"Gillespie's playing has changed from being stuck in front of a big band. Anybody's does. He's a fine musician. The leopard coats and the wild hats are just another part of the managers' routines to make him box office. The same thing happened a couple of years ago when they stuck his name on some tunes of mine to give him a better commercial reputation."

Asked to define bop, after several evenings of arguing, Charlie still was not precise in his definition.

"It's just music," he said. "It's trying to play clean and looking for the pretty notes."

Pushed further, he said that a distinctive feature of bop is its strong feeling for beat.

"The beat in a bop band is with the music, against it, behind it," Charlie said. "It pushes it. It helps it. Help is the big thing. It has no continuity of beat, no steady chug-chug. Jazz has, and that's why bop is more flexible."

He admits the music eventually may be atonal. Parker himself is a devout admirer of Paul Hindemith, the German neo-classicist. He raves about his *Kammermusik* and Sonata for Viola and Cello. He insists, however, that bop is not moving in the same direction as modern classical. He feels that it will be more flexible, more emotional, more colorful.

He reiterates constantly that bop is only just beginning to form as a school, that it can barely label its present trends, much less make prognostications about the future.

The closest Parker

will come to an exact, technical description of what may happen is to say that he would like to emulate the precise, complex harmonic structures of Hindemith, but with an emotional coloring and dynamic shading that he feels modern classical lacks.

Parker's indifference to the revered jazz tradition certainly will leave some of his own devotees in a state of surprise. But, actually, he himself has no roots in traditional jazz. During the few years he worked with traditional jazzmen he wandered like a lost soul. In his formative years, he never heard any of the music which is traditionally supposed to inspire young jazzists—no Louis, no Bix, no Hawk, no Benny, no nothing. His first musical idol, the musician who so moved and inspired him that he went out and bought his first saxophone at the age of 11, was Rudy Vallee.

Tossed into the jazz world of the mid thirties with this kind of background, he had no familiar ground on which to stand. For three years he fumbled unhappily until he suddenly stumbled on the music which appealed to him, which had meaning to him. For Charlie insists, "Music is your own experience, your thoughts, your wisdom. If you don't live it, it won't come out of your horn."

Charlie's horn first came alive in a chili house on Seventh Avenue between 139th Street and 140th Street in December 1939. He was jamming there with a guitarist named Biddy Fleet. At the time, Charlie says, he was bored with the stereotyped changes being used then.

"I kept thinking there's bound to be something else," he recalls. "I could hear it sometimes, but I couldn't play it."

Working over "Cherokee" with Fleet, Charlie suddenly found that by using higher intervals of a chord as a melody line and backing them with appropriately related changes, he could play this thing he had been "hearing." Fleet picked it up behind him and bop was born.

Or, at least, it is reasonable to assume that this was the birth of bop. The closest Charlie will come to such a statement is, "I'm accused of having been one of the pioneers."

Did Dizzy also play differently from the rest during the same period?

"I don't think so," Charlie replied. Then, after a moment, he added, "I don't know. He could have been. Quote me as saying, 'Yeah'."

Dizzy himself has said that he wasn't aware of playing bop changes before 1942.

As for the accompanying gimmicks which, to many people, represent bop, Charlie views them with a cynical eye.

"Some guys said, 'Here's bop,'" he explains. "Wham! They said, 'Here's something we can make money on.' Wham! 'Here's a comedian.' Wham! 'Here's a guy who talks funny talk.'" Charlie shakes his head sadly.

Charlie himself has stayed away from a big band because the proper place for bop, he feels, is a small group. Big bands tend to get over scored, he says, and bop goes out the window. The only big band that managed to play bop in 1944, in Charlie's estimation, was Billy Eckstine's. Dizzy's present band, he says, plays bop, could be better with more settling down and less personnel shifting.

"That big band is a bad thing for Diz," he says. "A big band slows anybody down because you don't get a chance to play enough. Diz has an awful lot of ideas when he wants to, but if he stays with the big band he'll forget everything he ever played. He isn't repeating notes yet, but he is repeating patterns."

It was on a visit to New York, in late 1942 after he had worked out his basic approach to complex harmony, that Charlie heard Stravinsky for the first time when Ziggy Kelly played *Firebird* for him.

The only possibility for a big band, he feels, is to get really big, practically on a symphonic scale with loads of strings.

"This has more chance than the standard jazz instrumentation," he says. "You can pull away some of the harshness with the strings and get a variety of coloration."

Today, Charlie has come full-cycle. As he did in 1939, when he kicked off bop in the Seventh Avenue chili house, he's beginning to think there's bound to be something more. He's hearing things again, things that he can't play yet. Just what these new things are, Charlie isn't sure yet. But from the direction of his present musical interests—Hindemith, etc.—it seems likely he's heading toward atonality. Charlie protests when he is mentioned in the same sentence with Hindemith, but, despite their vastly different starting points, he admits he might be working toward the same end.

This doesn't mean Charlie is through with bop. He thinks bop still is far from perfection, looks on any further steps he may take as further developments of bop.

"They teach you there's a boundary line to music," he says. "But, man, there's no boundary line to art."

For the future, he'd like to go to the Academy of Music in Paris for a couple of years, then relax for a while and then write. The things he writes all will be concentrated toward one point: warmth. While he's writing, he also wants to play experimentally with small groups. Ideally, he'd like to spend six months a year in France and six months here.

"You've got to do it that way," he explains. "You've got to be here for the commercial things and in France for relaxing facilities."

Relaxation is something Charlie constantly has missed. Lack of relaxation, he thinks, has spoiled most of the records he has made. To hear him tell it, he has never cut a good side. Some of things he did on the Continental label he considers more relaxed than the rest. But every record he has made could stand improvement, he says. We tried to pin him down, to get him to name a few sides that were at least better than the rest.

"Suppose a guy came up to us," we said, "and said, 'I've got four bucks and I want to buy three Charlie Parker records. What'll I buy?' What should we tell him?"

Charlie laughed.

"Tell him to keep his money," he said. ●

By John S. Wilson
OCTOBER 7, 1949

The Bird is wrong about the relationship of bop and jazz, says Dizzy Gillespie. "Bop is an interpretation of jazz," Diz told the Beat. "It's all part of the same thing." Last month, Charlie Parker said that bop had no roots in jazz, was something entirely separate and apart from the older tradition. Parker identified the beat as the distinguishing factor of bop.

"It [bop] has no continuity of beat, no steady chug-chug," Parker said.

This lack of a steady beat, according to Dizzy, is what is wrong with bop today.

"Bop is part of jazz," Dizzy said, "And jazz music is to dance to. The trouble with bop as it's played now is that people can't dance to it. They don't hear those four beats. We'll never get bop across to a wide audience until they can dance to it. They're not particular about whether you're playing a flatted fifth or a ruptured 129th as long as they can dance."

The important characteristics of bop, Dizzy says, are the harmonics and the phrasing. Tossing in a variety of beats isn't essential.

These are conclusions which Dizzy has reached after dragging his big band around the country for more than a year. As a result, he's revising his book so as to turn his outfit into a band which can be danced to.

"We'll use the same harmonics," he said, "but with a beat, so that people can understand where the beat is. We'll use a lot of things which are in the book now, but we'll cut them and splice them together again like you would a movie so as to leave out the variations in beat.

"I'm not turning my back on bop. My band has a distinctive sound and I want to keep that. But I want to make bop bigger, get it a wider audience. I think [pianist]

George Shearing is the greatest thing that's happened to bop in the past year. He's the only one who has helped it along. He plays bop so the average person can understand it.

"Anybody can dance to Shearing's music. By doing that, he has made it easier for me and for everybody else who plays bop."

The main pressure on Dizzy to make the switch has come from his wife, Lorraine, a former dancer, and his manager, Willard Alexander. For the last year, Lorraine has circulated in the audience on his one-nighters, getting audience reaction and trying to impress him that a lot of his numbers were making the dancers unhappy.

From Alexander's point of view, the big hurdle with Dizzy's band, as it was, was scarcity of places where a big band which didn't draw dancers could be booked.

"We can't play small places that hold 100 or 200 persons," Dizzy pointed out. "We're playing big auditoriums that hold a couple of thousand, and you can't rely on the extremists to support you there."

Alexander says he isn't asking Dizzy to become commercial.

"Ellington has always made it as a dance band, and nobody accused him of being commercial," he said. "I don't want Dizzy's men to bastardize their instruments or be corny. But I think they should perform and not look bored. Unless bop is improved in the next six months, I think it will die. Shearing is the only thing that's holding it up now."

Under the new setup, Dizzy will carry a dance book, a concert book, and a theater book. New arrangements are being turned out for him by Garland Wilson and Buster Harding. J.J. Johnson has done a pair of medleys for him, each medley consisting of three standards and winding up with a current pop tune. As part of the switch, Dizzy has dropped singer Johnny Hartman and taken on a girl, Tiny Irvin, whom he found in Pittsburgh.

The first tryout of the new Gillespie dance book was made on a late August date in Mahoney City, Penn., a big mickey stronghold. The operator, who reluctantly set the date as a favor to Alexander, was so impressed with the results that he burned up the wires to New York with reports of Dizzy's "sensational" success.

"As long as they say I've got a great band," said Dizzy, "I don't care if they say it's bop or what." ●

Dizzy at the helm of his big band

THE 1950s

INTRODUCTION

By Nat Hentoff ••

During those years in the fifties when I was New York editor of *Down Beat*, I spent nearly every night in the clubs and many afternoons at rehearsals. It didn't seem like a job because jazz at that time was indeed "the sound of surprise."

So it was too in the next decade, but there was unusual ferment in the fifties. The historic rise of jazz festivals. The rapid diversification of modern jazz—from hard bop to largely white West Coast jazz. The breaking down of Jim Crow in auditoriums in the South and other places—due to the pioneering insistence of impresario Norman Granz, who was a promoter of civil rights as much as jazz.

Most exciting of all was the unexpected. One night, Oscar Pettiford was leading a combo at Cafe Bohemia in Greenwich Village. A very large young man carrying an alto saxophone—that seemed quite small against his girth — asked to sit in. Nobody knew who he was.

Oscar Pettiford motioned him to the stand and then set a startlingly fast tempo. He wasn't going to let this young man even warm up. The saxophonist flew through the tempo with stunning ease, strikingly cohesive ideas, and passion. All of us were exhilarated. Even Oscar was impressed. The young man was Julian "Cannonball" Adderley, a college music teacher from Florida. He was signed to a record contract the next day.

The practice—and challenge—of sitting in was still common in the fifties, and there were still jam sessions where younger players could learn how far they had to go.

The decline of after-hours sessions has been lamentable. These days one can major in jazz playing and composing at a growing number of colleges; but valuable as this training is, it does not help a young player find his voice as effectively as when Coleman Hawkins or Dizzy Gillespie came to town and accepted all comers in the small hours of the morning.

The fifties were also a time when some—not all—of the musicians were becoming aware that they didn't have to be exploited by booking agents and club owners. Contracts started to be read seriously. One afternoon I saw Dizzy Gillespie, smiling exuberantly, coming down Broadway in Manhattan. He had just come, he told me, from his booking agent, Billy Shaw.

"I told him," Dizzy said, "that I finally realized that I don't work for *him*. He works for *me*."

Issues of race began to emerge more in conversations and in the music. I went to the first rehearsal of The Jazz Messengers—a blazing, deeply swinging combo, co-directed by Art Blakey and Horace Silver. They were angry, they told me, because of the abundant publicity and more money being given the white jazz groups—Dave Brubeck, Gerry Mulligan, Shorty Rogers, et al. Many black musicians found that music, as I did, largely tepid and derivative. Derivative of black music sources.

So, the Jazz Messengers would be playing music that whites couldn't borrow—music that came from the roots of black musicians in black churches. The result was what could be called "soul jazz"—with songs like "The Preacher."

Miles Davis felt as strongly as they did about discrimination, and his music certainly came from black sources as well as others. However, he was to be criticized when he hired a white musician for his group. Miles' stinging answer was: "I don't care if a musician is green, white, black, or with purple polka dots—so long as he can play."

Miles had some bad years in the early fifties, and some said he would never come back to his old form and force. But he conquered his heroin habit, and he triumphed again at the 1955 Newport Jazz Festival. The value of a festival like Newport, covered by all of the music press and many other nonspecialized journalists, was that if something dramatic happened, millions of people would know about it. Not only in America, but around the world.

If Miles had played as compellingly and personally in a club as he did at Newport, only the people there that night, and their friends, would have known about it. But word of his dramatic return went from Newport to Japan, Latin America, and other lands.

Similarly, Duke Ellington and his orchestra had been in a slump for some time. He knew it but didn't know how to rise again. At Newport the next year, however, he called for one of his classic compositions, "Diminuendo and Crescendo in Blue," and was surprised when in the course of the performance, tenor saxophonist Paul Gonsalves—seized by the very spirit of jazz improvisation—took off on a chorus that seemed to last for hours but was too short for the ecstatic crowd. Duke was in demand again.

The fifties also saw the most authentic and magnetic jazz television program produced before or since. Whitney Balliett of *The New Yorker* and I were the musical advisers, and although this tribute to the show may seem self-serving, it was the musicians who deserved all the credit. Among them were: Count Basie, Thelonious Monk, Coleman Hawkins, Lester Young, Ben Webster, Gerry Mulligan, Henry "Red" Allen, Roy Eldridge, Rex Stewart, Pee Wee Russell, Doc Cheatham, and Billie Holiday.

There was no script on "The Sound of Jazz," except to announce the names of the players. The producer, Robert Herridge, the most original producer in television history, insisted that the program be "pure" jazz. The cameramen were told to improvise—just as the musicians did. The hour was "live," and so the electric excitement integral to jazz was heightened. No mistakes could be corrected.

At one point, Billie Holiday and Lester Young—who had not been speaking to each other for years—made loving, reminiscing contact when Pres, in Billie's set, played a spare, luminous blues as she nodded and smiled with understanding. That solo was the very definition of pure jazz.

In the control room, Herridge, the director, the engineer, and I had tears in our eyes.

Ornette Coleman did not get so warm a reception when he came to New York in the fifties. But then, neither had Charlie Parker years before. In the case of the uncatergorizable Coleman—who practically sang and spoke on the horn but in language not everybody could follow—there was a lot of confusion. And hostility. Roy Eldridge, for instance, came down to hear him and announced that this wasn't jazz and indeed wasn't even music.

But several critics and some musicians were intrigued by this singular music, and Ornette Coleman eventually found an audience.

Not only the so-called avant-garde players could surprise you in the fifties. The lure of jazz, as Bix Beiderbecke once told Jimmy McPartland, is "You never know what's coming next, do you, kid?"

One evening, I was in Basin Street East in New York, and Sonny Stitt came on. Sonny was a very consistent swinger who also shaped ballads that made you remember your own experiences, good and bad, with love or its illusion. I always enjoyed his playing, but this night, he made time stop.

During one number, Sonny's rhythm section laid out, and Sonny made his horn totally command the room. Everyone stopped drinking and talking and sat, transfixed, at the deeply personal power of the music. I remember thinking: "And some people say that jazz isn't 'serious' music."

What has turned out to be the longest-surviving unit in the history of jazz—the Modern Jazz Quartet—emerged in the fifties. Playing what could be called "chamber music" jazz, the MJQ essentially reflected the formal precision and the flowing lyricism of pianist John Lewis. A necessary—for jazz—complement to Lewis was vibist Milt Jackson, who is also lyrical but more of a spontaneous swinger.

One of the most remarkable and wholly independent jazz figures of the fifties and beyond was Thelonious Monk. Although he had been part of the birth of modern jazz in the forties, Monk, for years, was not taken seriously by many critics, and he had yet to attract a considerable audience.

His compositions—like his piano playing—were fascinating because they were like no one else's. No other player or composer had ever constructed such complicated designs that nevertheless sounded exhilaratingly inevitable.

One night, at the Five Spot in New York, John Coltrane, then playing with Monk, came off the stand looking very unhappy. "I was playing a solo," Coltrane told me, "and I lost my place. It was like falling down an elevator shaft."

As always, there were obituaries during the decade. Frankie Newton, an unusually sensitive trumpet player, had never gotten the recognition he merited, but he is still remembered by musicians as a player—and man—of integrity.

Clifford Brown was not only a trumpet player of fluent grace and invincible swing, but he was also a man of extraordinary generosity of spirit. I never heard him say anything invidious about anyone, nor did anyone ever backbite him.

Bird died laughing at a comedian on the Tommy Dorsey television show. Charlie Parker did for modern jazz what Louis Armstrong had done for the music in the twenties. Bird so changed conceptions, jazz time, harmonic textures, and turns of sound that every musician of his generation, and younger, incorporated Bird into their own playing. Trumpeters and drummers and trombonists, as well as alto saxophonists.

Charlie Parker became the doomed romantic self-destroyer of jazz lore. As a musician with whom he had stayed in New York later said, "I owed Bird everything, but who could afford him?"

Lester Young, who died in that decade, also became part of the jazz mythology of fallen heroes. Unlike Bird, however, Lester did not intrude on other people's lives. A gentle, ironic man, he was mostly a loner, and when he was in form, Pres (as Billie Holiday named him) improvised soliloquies that were unmatched in their seamless, subtle delight in surprising both the listener and himself.

Billie Holiday, who also died before the decade was out, was often astonishingly resilient. She'd known hard times, been in prison for drugs, and had bad luck in choosing lovers. But even toward the end, there were times—in her singing and in her conversation—when she could light up the room. Not long before her death, she and I were at a mutual friend's home, and Billie began to imitate—with sardonic exactness—some of the leading booking agents and managers. I'd had no idea she was a mimic. But I should have known, from her singing, how acute and critical an observer of the jazz life she was.

The most vivid event of the fifties concerned one of the most influential jazz musicians of all jazz time—Louis Armstrong. The civil rights movement was gathering momentum. There were dangerous freedom rides and sit-ins. And in Little Rock, Arkansas, a small, extraordinarily brave number of black youngsters were trying to attend a white school that had been integrated by court order.

Vicious, howling mobs of white adults were preventing the entrance of the black kids to the high school. Moreover, the governor of Arkansas, Orval Faubus (to whom Charles Mingus was later to dedicate a mockingly contemptuous song) had pledged that the schools there would never be integrated.

And the president of the United States, Dwight Eisenhower, did nothing. Meanwhile, Louis Armstrong, who had not been directly involved in any civil rights project, and who had in fact been sponsored by the State Department as a goodwill ambassador, was being called by some younger jazz musicians an "Uncle Tom."

To the astonishment of his booking office, headed by the terrible-tempered Joe Glaser, Louis Armstrong told the press what he thought of Dwight Eisenhower. It was a direct, unsparing attack on Eisenhower's character and integrity. No jazz musician had ever before so publicly eviscerated a president of the United States.

Enraged, Joe Glaser sent one of his assistants to tell Armstrong to shut up. Louis threw the assistant out of his dressing room.

It was a fitting prelude to jazz—and the rest of America—in the sixties. ●

NAT HENTOFF served as New York editor of Down Beat for a large portion of the 1950s. An internationally respected writer, Mr. Hentoff currently writes for The Village Voice and The Wall Street Journal, as well as numerous other publications.

LENNIE TRISTANO: WATERED-DOWN BOP DESTROYING JAZZ

Jan Persson

By John S. Wilson

OCTOBER 6, 1950

The efforts of such groups as the Shearing quintet and the Bird-with-strings combo to wean the public to bop by offering it in a commercialized form is producing the opposite effect, according to pianist Lennie Tristano. Lennie, one of jazz's most adamant iconoclasts, says such efforts are killing off the potential jazz audience and lousing up the musicians involved.

"If you give watered-down bop to the public," he says, "they'd rather hear that than the real thing. Has George Shearing helped jazz by making his bop a filling inside a sandwich of familiar melody? Obviously not, because there are fewer places where jazz can be played today than there were when George and his quintet started out.

"Look what happened to Charlie Parker. He made some records featuring the melody, and they sold, and he got to be a big thing with the general public. So they brought him into Birdland with strings to play the same things. And he played badly. Why? Because the psychological strain of playing in a vein which didn't interest him was too much for him. Things like that don't help Bird and they don't help jazz."

It is for this reason that Lennie has consistently turned a deaf ear to suggestions that he temper his esoteric style, that he play more in a manner that the public can understand in order to build a wider audience for the things he wants to play.

"It would be useless for me to play something I don't feel," he says. "I wouldn't be doing anything. If I played something that I'd have to impose on myself, I wouldn't be playing anything good."

Because he can make enough to live on by teaching, Lennie feels he can stick to what he wants to do even though this means he plays in public only once every couple of months at best. He is not at all surprised that there is a very limited market for his stuff today. This, he thinks, is a natural result of the psychological atmosphere in which we are living.

"Everybody in this country is very neurotic now," he says. "They're afraid to experience an intense emotion, the kind of intense emotion, for instance, that's brought on by good jazz. There's more vitality in jazz than in any other art form today. Vitality arises from an emotion that is free. But the people, being neurotic, are afraid of being affected by a free emotion and that's why they put down jazz.

"Since the last war we've been overwhelmed by a feeling of insecurity. To try to offset that insecurity, people are reaching back toward happier times. And we're in an era of nostalgia which is being inflicted on the younger people who have nothing to be nostalgic about.

"Nostalgia brings on anticipation because you know what's going to happen next. When people start to anticipate, they become intense, waiting for what they know is going to happen. And this tension feeds their neuroses.

"That's why there's such a small audience for what I'm doing. What I play is so unorthodox that when you first hear it, you don't try to anticipate. You just sit there. You have to be very relaxed to start with before you put on one of my records. Consequently, people don't want to hear my sides as often as, say, [Erroll] Garner's, because as a rule they won't be in a mood that's receptive to what I play.

"Personally, I make it a definite practice to listen to new music with a blank mind. When I first hear a new piece of music, I make no attempt to analyze it because analysis eliminates emotional reception."

Eventually, when the atmosphere becomes more relaxed, Lennie thinks people will pick up on jazz. But, conditions being what they are, he foresees as much as a decade of emotional tension that will keep jazz from gaining public acceptance again.

Meanwhile, he feels that everyone who is interested in jazz—musician, fan, and promoter alike—will have to mend his ways if jazz is to stay alive. One of the major factors that is driving jazz into a corner, he thinks, is the development of hidebound jazz cliques.

"Such groups as the New Jazz Society merely continue and stress the cliquishness that is killing jazz today. There ought to be one organization for all jazz fans."

The ideal way to present jazz to the public, according to Lennie, is to follow the format of the opening show at Birdland last winter. That show exhibited the major elements of jazz and included Max Kaminsky's dixie group, blues shouting à la Hot Lips Page, Lester Young's combo as a bow to the swing era, Charlie Parker's bop outfit, and Lennie and his Tristanos.

"That was a wonderful show until it got loused up by a word-happy emcee," Lennie recalls. "For the first few nights I was very happy. Before we opened I was afraid that some of the dixie fans might boo Parker or the boppers might put down Max, but everybody was very happy.

"Nobody on the stand or in the audience put anybody down, and everybody seemed glad to get together. I had some very good talks with Max and with George Wettling during those nights."

Lennie spends very little time listening to dixie now, but that doesn't mean that he fluffs it off or dismisses it as an inconsequential jazz element.

"I developed with dixie," he says. "I used to buy all the records. But it's like growing up. When you've spent 10 years with an art form, it's time to move on. I've listened to it all, and now I'm interested in other developments in jazz."

Many musicians, according to Lennie, are not helping jazz by their attitudes toward their work.

"Musicians could do more for jazz than they're doing," he says. "They could take a greater interest in what they're doing. I know that if I were hired to play in, say, Dizzy's band, I'd play my tail off." ●

NO MORE WHITE BANDS FOR ME, SAYS LITTLE JAZZ

By Leonard Feather

MAY 18, 1951

New York—Little Jazz is back in town. After a whole year's absence, Roy Eldridge planed into New York April 5. On Friday the 13th he opened at Birdland with a quintet featuring two of the three men who crossed the Atlantic with him last year as part of the Benny Goodman outfit, Zoot Sims and Ed Shaughnessy, plus Billy Taylor on piano and Clyde Lombardi on bass.

Presenting Miles Davis with his *Down Beat* plaque on Symphony's Sid's WJZ show from Birdland, Roy said: "I'm sure glad to be back. It's good to see the lights of Broadway again." Miles interrupted to say "Why don't you tell 'em what you were just telling *me*?" After a moment of embarrassed dead air, Sid tactfully changed the subject.

GREAT DETAIL

Later, in a lengthy and honest talk with this reporter, Roy went into great detail about his true feelings. Naturally, he is happy to be home with his wife and daughter, he said, and Birdland was a pleasant surprise—the conditions and the people there were very fine.

"But I know what I have to face," he added. "I've just made up my mind not to let anything bug me. I'm going to be real cool.

"One thing you can be sure of, though. As long as I'm in America, I'll never in my life work with a white band again!"

OVERSEAS, TOO

This drastic statement, uttered with great finality, aroused our curiosity. Would that apply to working with white bands overseas? "That's different. You don't even think in those terms over there."

How about having white musicians in his own band over here?

"Now, that's fine—I like that. Zoot's

playing real nice, too, and Shaughnessy's great."

TROUBLE WITH BENNY?

What was the trouble, then? Didn't he get along with Benny Goodman?

"Benny and I got along fine. The only run-in we had was right after our first date, in Copenhagen. I went over about twice as well as Benny at the concert, and naturally Benny didn't like that. He complained about my drinking—I wasn't juiced—but he told me to take the next plane back to New York.

"Anyway, I went along to Stockholm and all of us were real drug; nobody played good and Benny missed that last high note on 'World Is Waiting for the Sunrise.' I felt so bad I had to get some schnapps to make it. After that Benny said he didn't mind my drinking on the job. Everything went along fine. Later on I even had Benny dancing and scat-singing on stage; one time he handed me his clarinet and I blew a little. We had a ball."

DECISION

When did he decide not to go home with the band?

"That happened during a record date. We cut some sides for Vogue in Paris: Zoot, Dick Hyman, Shaughnessy, a French bass player, and me. Everyone was so relaxed—we made six sides in less than three hours, and no master-minds in the control booth were telling us what to do. It wasn't like any session I'd ever made.

"Charles Delaunay had already propositioned me to take some jobs in Paris, and I made up my mind to stay. I was in Paris until August, then I went to Tunis, North Africa, for a week at the Belvedere Casino. From then until April, when I wasn't in Paris I was playing various other French cities; went up to Scandinavia for a few concerts with Charlie Parker, then they invited me up again for a whole bunch of dates.

"I was in Germany once, too, in Frankfurt. The people there are crazy about jazz—it was amazing. And I never saw so many cameras clicking away in my life.

"A WONDERFUL YEAR"

It was a wonderful year. During that whole time I was never once reminded that I was colored—the only exception was when there were some visiting Americans out to make trouble. Did you read about how some sailors beat up James Moody in a bar in Paris a couple of weeks ago? You know they weren't French sailors."

BACK 10 YEARS

Was that the story behind his decision not to work for a white band?

"No, it goes back way before that. All the way back to 10 years ago this month, when I joined Gene Krupa's band. Until that time no colored musician had worked with a white band except as a separate attraction, like Teddy and Lionel with Benny Goodman.

"That was how I worked with Gene at first; I wasn't treated as a full member of the band. But very soon, I started sharing Shorty Sherock's book, and when he left the band I took over. It killed me to be accepted as a regular member of the band. But I knew I'd have to be awful cool; I knew all eyes were on me to see if I'd make time or do anything wrong.

"All the guys in the band were nice, and Gene was especially wonderful. That was at the Pennsylvania hotel. Then we headed west for some one-nighters, winding up in California. That was when the trouble began.

"We arrive in one town and the rest of the band checks in. I can't get into their hotel, so I keep my bags and start riding around looking for another place, where someone's supposed to have made a reservation for me. I get there and move all my bags in. Naturally, since we're going to be out on the coast several months, I have a heavy load—at least a dozen pieces of baggage.

"Then the clerk, when he sees that I'm the Mr. Eldridge the reservation was made for, suddenly discovers that one of their regular tenants just arrived and took the last available room. I lug that baggage back into the street and start looking around again.

"By the time that kind of thing has happened night after night, it begins to work on my mind; I can't think right, can't play right. When we finally got to the Palladium in Hollywood I had to watch who I could sit at the tables with. If they were movie stars who wanted me to come over, that was all right; if they were just the jitterbugs, no dice. And all the time the bouncer with his eye on me, just watching for a chance.

"On top of that, I had to live way out in Los Angeles while the rest of the guys stayed in Hollywood. It was a lonely life; I'd never been that far away from home before, and I didn't know anybody. I got to brooding.

THEN IT HAPPENED

Then it happened. One night the tension got so bad I flipped. I could feel it right up to my neck while I was playing 'Rockin' Chair;' I started trembling, ran off the stand, and threw up. They carried me to the doctor's. I had a 105 fever; my nerves were shot.

"When I went back to the Palladium a few nights later I heard that people were asking for their money back because they couldn't hear 'Let Me Off Uptown.' This time I was allowed to sit at the bar."

The farthest south the band played was Norfolk, Va., where Roy was not allowed into the washroom with the other men, but was handed a bucket of water. For "Let Me Off Uptown" he and Anita O'Day had to work on two separate microphones at opposite ends of the bandstand. Riding on the Norfolk ferry, he joined some of the musicians on the top deck and was informed "We don't allow no niggers up here." When a complaint was made to the captain, the captain said, "Well, if you can stand him it's all right with me."

"Just as if I had leprosy," said Roy.

TRAIN TROUBLE

There was trouble in the train, too—Virginia's Jim Crow laws were invoked to try to get him to ride in a separate car. Then in Youngstown, Ohio, when no arrangements had been made for a room for him, no good accommodations were available in the Negro neighborhood, and the restaurant next door to the theater wouldn't serve him, even Gene's offer to let him use one of the twin beds in his own room couldn't console him. He left town without even telling Gene, and it was a week before he could be talked into rejoining the band.

After Gene's band broke up it wasn't until the fall of 1944 that Roy again became the only Negro in a white band. He joined Artie Shaw, and again his real troubles began in California. "We got to Del Mar. I got in the hotel all right but couldn't eat in the dining room. Some of the guys who knew I liked Mexican food suggested that we go to a little Mexican joint. When they refused to serve me, all the other guys walked out with me, but it still started to put me in that mood again.

"I went to the place where we were supposed to play a dance and they wouldn't even let me in the place. "This is a white dance," they said, and there was my name right outside. Roy 'Little Jazz' Eldridge, and I told them who I was.

"When I finally did get in, I played that first set, trying to keep from crying. By the time I got through the set, the tears were rolling down my cheeks—I don't know how I made it. I went up to a dressing room and stood in a corner crying and saying to myself why the hell did I come out here again when I knew what would happen? Artie came in and he was real great. He made the guy apologize that wouldn't let me in, and got him fired.

"Ava Gardner was great, too. She's a very fine person, and she and Artie became real good friends to me. But finally I left the band in San Francisco after another thing where I couldn't get into the auditorium.

"Man, when you're on the stage you're great, but as soon as you come off, you're nothing. It's not worth the glory, not worth the money, not worth anything. It was the trip to Europe that made me really realize that and make up my mind for good. Never again!"

ON OWN

Roy's decision may be purely academic, since it seems unlikely he will have to work under any leader, white or colored; he's going to be doing pretty nicely as a leader himself. The Shaw office currently has him at Lindsay's Sky bar in Cleveland, with bookings to follow in Chicago and Milwaukee. Norman Granz has set him for Mercury records, and many of the excellent sides he cut in France and Sweden are due for release here on Discovery, Prestige, and other labels.

Little Jazz, who celebrated his 40th birthday in Stockholm recently, is embarking on a new phase of a long and brilliant career, a career to which improved social conditions in his native land and intelligent guidance of his bookings should bring a little taste of hard-won happiness. ●

CHARLIE MINGUS: A THINKING MUSICIAN

By Ralph J. Gleason
JUNE 1, 1951

San Francisco—The agile fingers of Charlie Mingus plucking the strings of his bass in the Red Norvo Trio were the wonder of musicians during the group's four-week stay at the Black Hawk—as they have been wherever he has played. The Mingus talent transcends that, however, and gets across to the drink-buying public, a feat many musicians feel impossible.

Musicians and public share one opinion regarding Charlie—he's the greatest bass player they have ever seen. Smiling and happy, playing unbelievable things with apparent ease, Charlie, after all these months with the beautiful Norvo trio, still knocks out Red and Tal every night.

WHO IS HE?

Everywhere musicians are wondering "Who is this guy Mingus?" Well, he's young, only 29. He's been with only two bands that traveled around the country very much. But to everyone who has gotten to know him, Charlie Mingus is not only one of the most impressive of the contemporary musicians, but one of the most impressive thinkers about music that jazz has produced.

I've been proud to call Charlie my friend for some time now, and it is my firm conviction that he may well become one of the most important musicians that jazz has produced because he has proven that there should be no segregation in music between classical and jazz and that it is possible to make classical musicians swing by *writing* it correctly for them.

For the record, Charlie was born in Nogales, Ariz., and came to Los Angeles when he was 5. While a student at high school he studied trombone, but put it down (Britt Woodman, an early friend, now trombonist with Duke, was too far ahead of him, Charlie says) and took up bass at Britt's suggestion.

He studied for several years with Red Callender and others in the Los Angeles area, worked in small bands, made numerous records, spent some time on the road with Louis Armstrong and Lionel Hampton, played with Alvino Rey and was, with Red, co-leader of a remarkable little band up here a couple of years back that featured two basses.

He got the tag "Baron" when he made records in L.A. (there was an Earl, a King, a Count, a Duke, why not a Baron?) but it has never really stuck.

After our first talk with Charlie, he wrote us a letter—a long letter, all about his ideas on music. "I don't think you could get as much from me in conversation," he wrote. "This way I didn't know what you would ask, so I am only quoting my beliefs."

SOME OF BELIEFS

Here are some of Charlie's beliefs. Take heed, because he's not only a player of music, but a thinker, too.

"How many jazz musicians realize that a musician classically trained, never having even listened to jazz, could sit in with a jazz group and read and swing the most?

"I don't mean reading jazz the way it is written now by notes alone, and then following the first man. I mean reading jazz that has been mathematically written—every phrase, dynamics, and notations. Write down the free flowing lines in a time with which the classically trained musician is familiar. For instance, write him in 12/8 while the band still swings in 4/4. It can be done. I've done it.

"And once it has been proven, how can anyone fail to see that all music is one? The only difference being that the trained jazz musician learns to *feel* naturally, through reading or improvisation, while the classical musician is trained to read only the conception written and no more.

BEHIND BIRD

This also gives answer to the question of 'How can violins swing behind Bird?' How can they, when Bird is playing all free phrasing naturally and the violins are reading plain eighth notes with none of the bowings that could swing them? Because arrangers have just given up and said, 'well violins! Violins just don't swing!'

"Why not try writing in a few dynamics and bowings that fit with what Bird blows? Put them in times with which the classical violinists are familiar and don't ask them to swing. Just play what's written—and man, violins will swing for the first time in history!

"Yet they will still basically be following familiar classical form. Those who have always separated the two into jazz and classical will finally see that it's all one music we're playing and what they've been buying is just the confusion out of the separation of the two. Then Kenton can play Carnegie, not as the representative of 'jazz,' but as a modern composer of American music.

JAZZ AN ART

True jazz is an art, and as with all the arts, is the individual's means of expressing his deepest and innermost feelings and emotions. What will live on past the arrested development of boogie-woogie, Dixieland, and bop remains to be seen. It may take 500 years for the average American audience to advance sufficiently out of the mental turmoil and anxiety of the atomic age to be able to concentrate more on the art of music and to understand and appreciate a musician's individual interpretation of a melody rather than only the composer's.

"At that point in the growth of jazz, it will no longer be necessary for a musician to jump up and down on a drum or to dance on the bandstand to receive recognition of his talent.

"Every musician must seek his own individual solution to the problem of making a living. Some leave jazz for other fields where they can advance without compromising their art. Some give up. Others continue, solving their frustrations temporarily (or so they believe) with dope or the old-fashioned way of preserving their talents in alcohol.

"But there is another solution for the musician who believes in his ability, and that is to reach the realization that he cannot alter the inevitability of time or destiny and there is no gain in destroying himself.

MANY POSSIBILITIES

There are innumerable possibilities and ways to advance in music by exploring further outlets for study and improvement on one's musical abilities. There is something to be learned from every score of the great composers, old and modern; each page bears evidence to the musical tight-rope walker that he has looked only at his own tiny rope, not realizing that men have not only walked ropes years before him, but tiny threads—perhaps the water. And can we not all learn one more step while restudying what might possibly aid us in walking the earth tomorrow?

"Is it possible that the world has convinced us that all artistic talent belongs to past centuries? Can't we look around us and see there is a wealth of talent and genius seeking to express itself? Charlie Parker is in his own inimitable way creating complete, clearly thought out compositions of melodic line every time he plays a solo, as surely as one was ever written down by Brahms or Chopin or Tchaikowsky.

"Kenton is just one of the multitude who is suffering while trying to show his country that music is *one*, now that jazz has advanced out of its 'by ear alone' stage.

NO STANDOUT RACE

Today musicians in all races are proving that no race is endowed with special abilities for any profession and that every musician has an equal chance if given the proper start and study needed for playing correctly. Once this is universally recognized, musicians like Buddy Collette (flute), Milton Hinton (bass), and Bill Douglas (drums), among countless others, will find their places in any symphony as competent musicians.

"Now these musicians find a color bar preventing their acceptance in symphonies and their qualifications are unknown except to myself and a few other musicians who have worked or studied with these thoroughly trained men whose reading, conception, and playing are beyond reproach.

"Can we send a potential Ravel, Debussy, or Stravinsky to his grave without affording him the chance to prove that music has advanced many steps and that many composers as great as any of the old are being forced to write background music for the slipping of Mabel's girdle, rather than the true emotions of his inner self?

"You can quote me as saying 'I'm only thinking.' Are you?"

Listen to what this guy says. Think about it a bit. It poses a terrific possibility—if, as Charlie says he has done, jazz can be *written* so classical cats can blow and sound *right* with their jazz brothers, it will be revolutionary. At one stroke it will remove the little badge of specialness all jazz musicians have been wearing for years. The one that reads "WE can swing."

Discovery may give Charlie a chance to put all this on record soon. Let's hope they do. He deserves it. ●

By Oscar Peterson
JANUARY 13, 1954

I have long been disturbed about what I've seen of the state of mind of the average young jazz musician around the country, especially in New York. The general mass of jazz musicians, for one thing, have become so ingrown with regard to the music they're playing and are associated with, that a very unhealthy atmosphere is being bred.

There are so many groups that are unhappy with what they're doing, that are unhappy with everything. They've gotten into an attitude where nothing means much any more. They have no outside interests. They're just musicians and know of nothing else. With some, it becomes so bad they know of nothing else except themselves.

I hear a young talent in a city I play, and almost invariably, I'll come back a few months later, and the talent's been washed away by a number of bad activities. So many things are going the wrong way; and so few the right way.

PARENTS' ATTITUDE CITED

I can remember when a lot of parents would go along with their children's interests in jazz, but since the recent newspaper stories and mishaps among musicians, jazz today isn't encouraged by the parents. The reason is that the parents feel that jazz is not a healthy enough a profession today. And many of the men in it have made it that way.

That applies to the whole jazz scene. If, God forbid, I should lose a man, it would be very hard to replace him. I'd have to find out whether a possible replacement was personally straight. I'd actually have to screen him. It wasn't like that years ago. There were always plenty of good musicians you could use, and you didn't have to go around and ask, "Is he straight?"

I don't enjoy discussing this, and I've always avoided talking about it in radio or magazine interviews, but I've come to realize that you can't just look the other way and hope it'll go away. These people

THE JAZZ SCENE TODAY

have created a monster they'll never destroy.

ENCOURAGED BY IMBECILES

And I should add that a lot of guys who have gone that way have been encouraged by the imbecilic cultists. I mean the ones who say that if one of their favorites blows well, he's always the greatest all the time. That's the biggest falsehood ever told.

That mistaken attitude leads to the fact that regardless of what a man has done to himself to destroy his talent, the cultist keeps saying that man is still the greatest. And so they keep on encouraging him in his self-destruction.

Speaking of the musicians themselves with regard to what caused this present-day scene, I would say that among the contributing factors have been too many false pedestals, biased opinions and staid minds. This false worship of one's self has been combined with the feeling that what is duly and rightfully owed one in terms of appreciation and recognition has been denied. It's hard to converse with them—they're always complaining.

APPRECIATES FEELING

I can appreciate the feeling of not being recognized, of one's work not being appreciated. But the answer is to work harder and fight to get recognition through your work. It's a matter of a half a loaf being better than none, especially when the none is self-destruction.

The healthy spirit of competition is gone. It has been replaced by animosity, envy, and slothfulness. There are so few jazz musicians left like Billy Taylor who are honestly eager to do something, who get a kick out of what they're doing, who are not biased in their attitudes.

A man's personality shows up in his music. If frustration has formed a cold attitude in a man, he plays that way. And he plays disjointedly—one way one night and another the next night. The way you play music is a tonal biography of yourself—your thoughts and feelings.

The other night Gerry Mulligan was telling me that our trio is the happiest group he's heard or seen for some time. Well, I don't see how you can project happiness in music unless you're happy yourself and happy with what you're doing, as we are.

HAPPINESS GONE

I honestly believe that a lot of the happiness that used to be so much a part of it has left jazz. Bands like Duke Ellington and Count Basie and the Benny Goodman quartet and sextet had an honesty and genuine fire you rarely hear in jazz today. And one reason modern music is so hard to sell for a lot of groups is that very coldness. Some musicians give the listeners the feeling: "Be glad you're here, that you've been allowed in."

They've slumped into the kind of low mental state that helps account for the high narcotic rate among the so-called intelligentsia of modern music.

And it's reflected not only in the attitude on stand, but also in the unpressed clothes, the unkempt appearance—and the worried relatives. A person like that can contribute nothing to music of any sort.

The present scene has affected me so that I would honestly like to bring my career, such as it is, to a successful close at the opportune time and just sort of forget some of the monsters I've seen in the business. When that time comes, I'd like to leave music and go into the field of photography and also sound.

ENJOYS WORK

When I say that, I don't mean I'll retire in the very near future. With me, it's a case of my enjoying the work I do now with the group and enjoying being with them outside of work.

So it's not my own group that bothers me; it's what I see around me.

I have never been so appalled with conditions in my life. And especially in New York which is why I have to play that city. It's unbelievable. I'll probably be asked why I single out New York as being so particularly bad. I think the reason is the city is so overcrowded with musicians.

It's so hard…for musicians there to establish themselves because so many of them are all on the scene at once, and so many of them can do the

Oscar Peterson

same kind of thing almost as well or as well as many other musicians. New York, therefore, is a frustrating place for the young musician who goes there with great aspirations.

GOTHAM OVERRATED

I think, too, that New York has been highly overrated as being a jazz mecca. In the last year or half year, I've heard so many new things and so many *good* things coming from the West Coast. A lot of musicians in New York have lost their feeling for experimentation or the cultivation of anything in the way of good sound or modern sound.

They've lost all kind of respect for the fact that if you're going to build a group, you don't just assemble all-stars and have somebody write a melody line. You have to nurture and cultivate a group like you would a baby.

That was the way big bands used to be regarded, too. One reason there are so few good big bands today is that attitude toward building has fallen so.

Take our trio as an illustration of what I mean by building a group. Here are three guys who, first of all, have respect for each other's talent and endeavors. All three have the desire to produce something that's good, and all of us realize how much work and preparation has to go into making a real unit. Yet we lead three happy lives on stand musically, and off stand personally.

CAN'T UNDERSTAND THEM

I can't understand other groups I've seen where each man comes in and leaves individually, and you don't see them together at intermissions. It ends up in the way they play—they very seldom do anything well together. In fact, among present-day musicians, there is so little conception left of how to live with one another.

All of us in the trio have other interests besides music. I'm a firm believer in diversified interests. I love music, believe me, but I couldn't spend 23 or 24 hours consecutively just in music. That's why I've gotten so much out of traveling—like with Norman Granz—and out of photography and other things.

When I first came down to the United States from Canada, I came with stars in my eyes. When you hear great artists, as I did on records, you inevitably build up a certain amount of personal respect for them. But when you see some of them, it's apt to be another thing altogether. Your dream is shattered and your respect washed away. How can you build respect for someone who doesn't hold respect for himself?

RESPECT FOR DIZZY

One man I do respect very much is Dizzy Gillespie. As much as he's been called a trend starter and the head of various cults, Diz is one of the straightest-thinking musicians I've come in contact with. He's one of the most level-headed men I've met. I know Dizzy has been one of the greatest inspirations in my life, speaking of modernists. And I know anyone who gets to know him will feel as I do.

In Dizzy there's a happiness projected in his music, a vibrant personality. I have seen him in front of a band, and that was one of the great moments in my life. He is one of the greatest bandleaders of them all, a man who can fire a whole orchestra. But he's one of the few in jazz today with that kind of fire.

If you stop to realize the great jazz things that preceded the period we're in now, this is a nightmare era. As a result, so much of the stuff today is way out of kilter. For example, I've heard so many bad records in recent months.

I used to be able to go out and buy close to $100 worth of jazz recordings, and I'd gotten something. But you can't do that today if you're a discerning person, unless a lot of it is reissues.

CAN'T SEE IT

As for the future of the jazz scene, people say things are getting better. But honestly and truthfully, from what I see, the way it's going, any real change seems to be far off. I don't think you can any longer help the condition in the mass, but *individuals* can be helped, and that in time may bear on the mass.

I hate to say this, but the majority seems to be on another tangent. The only way you can help bring them back in is by helping and encouraging the younger musicians who are straight and who are trying to do something.

The young musician today wonders where he's going from here, and sees no helping hand. It is these men who should be encouraged.

I know, for example, one fellow in Toronto who has one of the greatest groups

I've ever heard—Phil Nimmons, a young arranger and clarinet player and composer. He's organized a unit and is in the process of building it so successfully that I believe it will end up on records and create quite a stir in music circles in the States. He has a new approach, and you can feel the belief in his work and in the way he plays his work.

SILVER CITED

Horace Silver is another young musician who could stand a whole lot of encouragement because he has something to say.

I have five children who have, I hope, been brought up right, and I must admit that I have an inside fear that one of them might become a musician and become exposed thereby to the sort of thing I've been discussing.

I wouldn't discourage any of them who did want to go into music—my oldest daughter has already started studying—but I'll certainly try to instill enough self-confidence into them so that as long as their life span in music lasts, they won't fall into the destructive attitude which is so prevalent today.

The jazz scene as it stands today, if it continues the way it's going, is one that I don't want to be a part of very much longer. ●

THE MAMBO!! THEY SHAKE A-PLENTY WITH TITO PUENTE

By Nat Hentoff

OCTOBER 6, 1954

New York—Though the older pop vocalists still reign, music with a beat is relentlessly returning to national popularity. Evidences include the steadily widening audience for jazz and rhythm and blues—and the growth of the mambo!

Dance studios find a course in mambo these days is as essential on the time payment plan. And almost all dance halls and night clubs now require its bands to have at least some mambos in their sets. Columbia records, prodded by its distributors and district sales managers, has started a special series of mambo sessions. Victor, in answer to disc jockey requests for more mambo material, sent out a mambo kit with 25 of the label's most popular mambo sides. Significantly, many of those disc jockey requests came from the smaller towns as well as the major cities that already are confirmed mambo centers.

Although there are several major mambo leaders, Tito Puente (El Rey Del Timbale), particularly reflects in his success the many signs of the rise in mambo popularity. Tito who is featured on vibes and timbales and also plays piano, bongos, conga drum, and alto, starred recently in the first Mambo-Rhumba Festival tour. Covering 16 cities, the tour did better than even the more optimistic of its backers had hoped. Tito is also a major attraction of Tico Records, and his strong selling mambo sides are one of the chief reasons for that firm's sturdy growth in the past few years. These Puente records on Tico are used by Arthur Murray and many other dance studios around the country to teach the mambo.

Tito's career has paralleled the appearance of more and more night clubs that are solely devoted to the mambo and its polyrhythmic allies. The chief of these is Broadway's Palladium, a few doors up

from Birdland, and the head bandman at the Palladium is Tito Puente.

At these memorable Wednesday festivals, the $1.75 admission entitles the adventurous patron to mambo instructions early in the evening, plus an amateur contest for mambo dancers, plus a professional mambo show from 11 to 12, plus dancing to Tito and a relief band. The consensus of the clientele seems to be that this is far

Tito Puente   Popsie

better exercise than bowling or turning off the TV commercials.

Surveying this disarming spectacle of Broadway-turned-offbeat, Tito explains the rise of the mambo this way: "Rhythm is what you dance to, and the mambo is popular because its strong rhythms make for good dance music. What is making it even more successful is the combination of jazz elements with the mambo. Bop, for example, by itself has crazy sounds harmonically, but rhythmically, it is not easy to dance to. That's why bop bands are putting in conga drums and adding a mambo flavor to their work.

"Similarly, in my band, I use certain aspects of jazz. In our arranging, we use some of the modern sounds in the manner of Gillespie and Kenton, but we never lose the authenticity of the Latin rhythm." Tito confirmed that among the frequent famous

visitors at the Palladium to absorb his fusion of mambo and jazz are such jazz vanguardists as Kenton, Gillespie, Duke Ellington, and Woody Herman as well as innocent bystanders like Henry Fonda and Mel Ferrer.

"The popularity of the mambo," Tito believes, "is still in its early stages. All the major record companies will soon be organizing mambo sessions. More clubs and theaters will introduce special mambo evenings. Already the Savoy ballroom and the Apollo have Monday mambo nights. And the mambo itself is capable of more and more variations. Like the *Cha-Cha-Cha* we've been introducing. It came over from Cuba a little over a year ago and it's a mambo in a slow, rocking tempo.

"The mambo itself, you know," continued Professor Puente, "is basically a rhythm from Africa. Some of the slaves introduced it to Cuba and it became mingled with Cuban rhythms in the rituals and ceremonies that took place in the jungles of Cuba. The mambo became modified through the centuries in Cuba, and came to the United States about seven years ago, though its main rise has been within the past two years.

"The mambo," Puente explained, "differs, let's say, from the rhumba in that it concentrates more on the off beat, the after beat, like modern jazz whereas the rhumba is mostly on the beat. And the mambo has more syncopation in its melodic forms than the rhumba. Any person, I think, who digs jazz, will dig the mambo."

As the joyously waving bodies at the Palladium indicate, the essential reason for the mambo's popularity is that these particular musical ingredients make it so exhilarating to dance to. Or as a friend of Tito said one evening at the Palladium as he watched the swirling multitude, "The reason the mambo is tremendous is that it's a great exhibition dance—everybody who dances it is a star." ●

ELLA TELLS OF TROUBLE IN MIND CONCERNING DISCS, TELEVISION

By Nat Hentoff

FEBRUARY 23, 1955

New York—"We had a request to sing," Ella began over the applause—and suddenly she stopped. "You know," she grinned, "we really didn't have a request. This is just our next number." Ella had displayed again the candor that has been hers for 20 years in the music big leagues.

Yet, despite this open-hearted honesty, very little is known about what Ella really thinks on subjects closest to her career and emotions. For, except with intimate friends, Ella is one of the shyest people in the entertainment business.

Backstage one night at Basin Street, however, Ella relaxed and spoke openly of several things that long have troubled her.

POTENTIAL SCOPE

Ella, though she underrates herself, is conscious of the warm esteem in which she's held, and often revered, over much of the world. But she is also conscious of the potential scope of her vocal skill and warmth, a potential that never has been realized as fully as it deserves—for reasons that have nothing to do with her undeniable talent.

Take records, for example, Ella has in her repertoire an arrangement of "Teach Me Tonight," one of the current pop best-sellers, that is musically a delight and is as commercial as any direct expression of emotion (with close attention to the melody line) can be.

Yet she has not had a chance to record the number for Decca, nor does she often get a chance to record any really "hot" pop material for the label.

"And," Ella adds, "it's been so long since I've gotten a show tune to do, except for the album. Or a chance to do a tune like 'The Man That Got Away.' Frank Sinatra came into Basin Street often while he was at the Copa, and he asked for that song every time. And he also asked, 'How come, Ella, you don't have a number like *that* to record?'

"DON'T KNOW MYSELF"

I don't know why myself," Ella told him. "Yet I never do get a chance at the songs that have a chance. They give me something by

Ella with Steve Allen at Ella Fitzgerald night at Birdland in 1955

somebody that no one else has, and then they wonder why the record doesn't sell.

"I'm so heart-broken over it. Maybe it's me, but there are so many pretty songs I *could* sing on record. I need a record out. I know that, but I don't know what they're doing at the record company. There must be something I can make that people who buy records would like to hear.

"The album (*Ella*, Decca 12" LPDL 8068) was something I was pleased with. It got such wonderful write-ups, and I remember when I was on the coast it seemed like everybody was playing it. But the disc jockeys claimed that the company didn't give them the record. In fact, we had to go out and buy the record and give it to those disc jockeys that didn't have it.

WHAT'S MAIN INTEREST?

Now I don't like to say anything against anybody, but maybe it's because that record company is mainly interested in pictures now that they don't give as much attention to the records. But I sure would like to record with someone who would give me something to record."

Then there's the matter of Ella Fitzgerald and television. "Like every singer," Ella said, "my ambition for a long time has been to have a TV show of my own, but," she shook her head, "I don't like to think too far ahead. What I mean is I don't know anybody who has one. Do you understand what I'm trying to say?

"Sammy Davis, Jr., for example. He didn't get his show, and no one certainly could get tired of looking at *him* for 15 minutes. Do you remember how great he was on the "Colgate Comedy Hour"? And there's Lena Horne, Jimminy Crickets! If *Lena* doesn't have a show of her own! We have so many wonderful artists who deserve a TV show. But I don't know…the way things are.…

"SOMEDAY MAYBE"

I hope someday maybe," Ella continued, "somewhere I can get a TV show. Even if it were just a New York program. So I could stay home a little. It's not that I don't like the road, but traveling all the time, year in and year out, isn't as easy on a woman as it is on a man. And you've heard how guys complain about the road.

"I can dance, you know, if I get a show. I don't say I can read lines," she smiled again, "but for the kind of show I want to do, that wouldn't be so necessary, I'd like a program that was like inviting the audience into my home. The feeling that Peter Lind Hayes and Mary Healy had on their show. It would be informal.

"One evening, for example, we could do a song two ways, fast and slow, and see which turns out better. I could have guests drop in—people like Sarah or maybe a dancer. The routines wouldn't always have to be rehearsed, and if there were mistakes on the program, we'd just do the song or dance over again.

COMMERCIAL TWIST

I f the show turned out to be a commercial one," Ella animatedly went on, "instead of reading the same commercial every night, we could make up new words and change it every night. And as for talent, if the show wasn't on too late, we could even have somebody drop in with some talented kids from time to time.

"I'd even write music for the program," said ASCAP member Fitzgerald (whose credits include "A-Tisket, A-Tasket," "You Showed Me the Way" and "Rough Riding"). "Lately I've lost all my ambition for songwriting. Every once in a while, I do write a new song down and put it away some place, but when I go to find it, I don't know where it is. But if I had a TV show of my own, I'd be real eager to write some music for it.

"Oh, I have gobs and gobs of ideas, but…well, you dream things like that, and that's what these are, you know—my day dreams." ●

MILES: A TRUMPETER IN THE MIDST OF A BIG COMEBACK MAKES A VERY FRANK APPRAISAL OF TODAY'S JAZZ SCENE

By Nat Hentoff
NOVEMBER 2, 1955

A fter a time of confusion and what appeared to be a whirlpool of troubles, Miles Davis is moving rapidly again toward the forefront of the modern jazz scene. He has just signed a contract guaranteeing him 20 weeks a year in Birdland. He has been added to the three-and-a-half-week all-star Birdland tour, and there are reports—at present unconfirmed and denied by Prestige—that Miles may leave Prestige for one of the major record companies.

Miles already had shown clearly this year how important a jazz voice he still is by his July performance at the Newport festival, a performance that caused Jack Tracy to write: "Miles played thrillingly and indicated that his comeback is in full stride." A few weeks later, Miles surprised the international jazz audience by tying Dizzy for first place in the *Down Beat* Critics' poll.

But those listeners who had heard several of his Prestige records over the past year (particularly the "Walkin'—Blue N' Boogie" date with Lucky Thompson, J.J. Johnson, Kenny Clarke, Horace Silver, and Percy Heath) decided on second thought that there really should have been no cause for them to have been surprised.

So, Miles is now in the most advantageous position of his career. He has the bookings, the record outlet, and he has the group that he's been eager to assemble. As of this writing, on drums there's Philly Joe Jones, described by Miles as "the best drummer around today." On bass is the young Detroit musician, Paul Chambers, who's recently been working with George Wallington at the Bohemia and of whose ability Miles says only "Whew! He really drives a band. He never stops." On piano is Red Garland from Philadelphia. The tenor is Sonny Rollins, for whom Miles has deep respect. Miles has been trying to

convince Sonny to leave Chicago and go on the road with him and finally, to Miles' great delight, he has succeeded.

"I want this group," says Miles, "to sound the way Sonny plays the way all of the men in it play individually—different from anyone else in jazz today. We've got that quality individually; now we have to work on getting the group to sound that way collectively. As we get to work regularly, something will form up and we'll get a style."

As for records, Miles is dissatisfied with most of his recent output, since his standards call for constant growth and change, and his criteria for judging his own works are harsh. "The only date of mine I liked in the last couple of years was the "Walkin'" session. And the one with Sonny Rollins. The rest sounded too much alike."

Of the records he made in the years before, Miles looks back with most satisfaction to the set with J.J. Johnson that included "Kelo" and "Tempus Fugit," the earlier albums with Rollins and the 1949–50 Capitol sides with Gerry Mulligan, Lee Konitz, Al Haig, Max Roach, J.J. Johnson, John Lewis, and Kenny Clarke. He remembers, however, how tense those Capitol sessions were, and wishes he had a chance to do a similar date, only with a full brass section and with writing that would be comfortable for all.

Miles, as his sharply perceptive "Blindfold Test" (*Down Beat*, Sept. 21, 1954) indicated, is an unusually knowledgeable observer of the jazz scene. In a recent, characteristically frank conversation, he presented his views about several key figures and trends in contemporary jazz. This is a record of his conversation:

THE WEST COAST:

T hey do have some nice arrangements. Jimmy Giuffre plays

real good and Shelly is good, but I don't care too much for the other soloists. Carl Perkins, though, is an exception—he plays very good piano, but he doesn't record enough. I wish I could get him to work with me. You know, that man can play bass notes with his elbows!

"My general feeling about what's happening on the coast is like what Max Roach was saying the other night. He said he'd rather hear a guy miss a couple of notes than hear the same old cliches all the time. Often when a man misses, it at least shows he's trying to think of something new to play. But the music on the coast gets pretty monotonous even if it's skillfully done. The musicians out there don't give me a thrill the way Sonny Rollins, Dizzy, and Philly Jo Jones do. I like musicians like Dizzy because I can always learn something from him; he's always playing new progressions, etc. Kenny Clarke, too, is always experimenting.

BRUBECK:

Well, Dave made one record I liked— 'Don't Worry 'bout Me.' Do I think he swings? He doesn't know how. Desmond doesn't swing, either, though I think he'd play different with another rhythm section. Frankly, I'd rather hear Lennie. Or for that matter, I'd rather hear Dizzy play the piano than Brubeck, because Dizzy knows how to touch the piano and he doesn't play too much. A lot of guys are so conscious of the fact that the piano has 88 keys they try to do too much. Tatum is the only man who plays with a whole lot of technique *and* the feeling too. Along with Bud Powell, he's my favorite pianist.

"Getting back to Brubeck, I'd say first he ought to change his drums. Another thing is that if Brubeck could play the piano like that pianist in Sweden—Bengt Halberg— in combination with the way he himself already thinks, he would please a lot of musicians. Brubeck has wonderful harmonic ideas, but I sure don't like the way he touches, the way he plays the piano.

TRISTANO AND KONITZ:

Lennie has a different problem. He's wonderful by himself. He invents all the time, and as a result, when he works with a group, the bass player generally doesn't know what Lennie's going

to do. I don't think, therefore that Lennie can be tied down to writing one bass line. He should write three or four bass lines, so that the bassist can choose.

"As for Lee Konitz, I like the way he plays. With a different rhythm section, he swings—in his way. Sure, there are different ways of swinging. You can break phrases and you can play 7- or 11-note phrases like Lee does, and they swing, but you can't do it all the time.

BIRD:

Bird used to play 40 different styles. He was never content to remain the same. I remember how at times he used to turn the rhythm section around when he and I, Max, and Duke Jordan were playing together. Like we'd be playing the blues, and Bird would start on the 11th bar, and as the rhythm sections stayed where they were and Bird played where he was, it sounded as if the rhythm section was on one and three instead of two and four. Every time that would happen. Max used to scream at Duke not to follow Bird but to stay where he was. Then eventually, it came around as Bird had planned and we were together again. Bird used to make me play, try to play. He used to lead me on the bandstand. I used to quit every night. The tempo was so up, the challenge was so great.

"Of the new altoists, Cannonball plays real good. He swings and has real drive, but he doesn't know the chord progressions Bird knew. Bird used to play things like Tatum. But if Cannonball gets with the right musicians—men like Sonny Rollins—he'll learn.

MJQ:

I was talking about small groups before. I can't omit the Modern Jazz Quartet—that's the best group out. That piece, 'Django,' is one of the greatest things written in a long time. You know, John Lewis teaches everyone all the music in that group.

MAX ROACH-CLIFFORD BROWN:

I don't like their current group too much because there's too much going on. I mean, for example, that Richie Powell plays too much comp. Max needs a piano player that doesn't play

much in the background. Actually, Brownie and Max are the whole group. You don't need anybody but those two. They can go out on-stage by themselves. What happens is that the band gets in Brownie's way the way it is now.

WRITING:

With regard to big bands, I liked some of the arrangements this last Stan Kenton band had at Birdland, and, of course, Count Basie sounds good, but that's just swinging. I also admire the big band writing Billy Strayhorn does. Do you know the best thing I've heard in a long time? Alex North's music for *Streetcar Named Desire*. That's a wild record— especially the part Benny Carter plays. If anybody is going to be able to write for strings in the jazz idiom or something near to it, it'll be North. I'd recommend everyone hearing that music.

"Now as for Kenton, I can't think of anything he did original. Everything he did, everybody else did before. Kenton is nowhere in the class with somebody like Duke. Duke has done more for jazz than anyone I could name. He takes in almost everything when he writes, he and Billy.

"You can really tell how a man writes when he writes for a large band. But funny things happen, too. Like if it weren't for Neal Hefti, the Basie band wouldn't sound as good as it does. But Neal's band can't play those same arrangements nearly as well. Ernie Wilkins, on the other hand, writes good, but the Basie band plays Neal's arrangements better.

"About the kind of things Charlie Mingus and Teo Macero are writing for small groups, well, some of them are like tired modern pictures. Some of them are depressing. And Mingus can write better than that. 'The Mingus Fingers' he did for Lionel Hampton is one of the best big band records I ever heard, but he won't write like he did on that number any more. For one thing, in his present writing, he's using the wrong instrumentation to get it over. If he had a section of low horns, for example, that would cut down on some of the dissonance, he could get it over better. I heard one of Teo's works at Newport, but I don't remember it. And if I didn't remember it, I didn't like it.

"My favorite writer has been Gil Evans. He's doing commercial things now, but if you remember, he did the ensemble on 'Boplicity' and several other fine things around that time. In answer to that critic who recently asked why a song like 'Boplicity' isn't played by modern groups, it isn't played because the top line isn't interesting. The harmonization is, but not the tune itself.

"Other writers I like are Gigi Gryce—there were several nice things in the last date he did with Art Farmer—and Gerry Mulligan is a great writer, one of my favorites. Bill Russo is interesting, too—like the way he closes the harmony up. He sure loves trombones. He uses the brass section well.

"A lot of musicians and writers don't get the full value out of a tune. Tatum does and Frank Sinatra always does. Listen to the way Nelson Riddle writes for Sinatra, the way he gives him enough room, and doesn't clutter it up. Can you imagine how it would sound if Mingus were writing for Sinatra? But I think Mingus will settle down; he can write good music. But about Riddle, his backgrounds are so right that sometimes you can't tell if they're conducted. Billy Eckstine needs somebody like Sinatra, by the way, to tell him what kind of tunes to sing and what kind of background to use.

INSTRUMENTALISTS:

There are other musicians I like. Stan Getz is a wonderful musician, and Bobby Brookmeyer is real good. The man I like very much is J.J. Johnson, because he doesn't play the same way all the time. And he's a fine writer. If J.J. would only write for a big band, then you'd hear something. The best small band arrangements I've heard in a long time are the ones J.J. writes for the Jay and Kai

group, and that's only two horns. I liked, too, what he wrote for me on the Blue Note session. J.J. doesn't clutter it up. He tries to set the mood. He has the quality Gil Evans has, the quality I hope Gerry Mulligan doesn't lose.

"As for trumpets, Brownie plays real good. Yes, he plays fast, but when you're playing with Max, you play real fast almost all the time, like the time I was with Bird. Art Farmer is real good, but he has to get his tone together. Thad Jones, if he ever gets out of the Basie band, then you'll really hear him. Playing in a big

band makes you stiff. It doesn't do a horn man good to stay in a band too long. Conte Candoli, for example, told me he hasn't been the same since Kenton. He can't keep a flowing line going. His lips tighten up and he has to play something high even though he doesn't like to play like that. I told him to lay off three weeks and start over again. Dizzy had to do the

same thing after he had the big band. Part of that stiffness comes from playing the same arrangement again and again. The only horn players a big band didn't tie down were Bird and Lester.

"Now about drummers, my five favorites are Max, Kenny Clarke, Philly Joe Jones, Art Blakey, and Roy Haynes. Roy though has almost destroyed himself working with Sarah so long. He's lost some of his touch, but he could pick up again if he had a chance to play more freely. Elvin Jones, the brother of Thad and Hank, is another drummer who plays real good. Elvin comes from the Detroit area which is producing some very good musicians.

Tradition and Swinging:

Bird and Hawkins made horn players realize they could play fuller progressions, play more of the chord, and still swing. I saw Stan Getz making fun of Hawkins one night and I said to Getz, 'If it weren't for Hawkins, you probably wouldn't be playing as you are!' Coleman plays just as well as anybody you can name. Why, I learned how to play ballads by listening to Coleman. I don't go for putting down a man just because he's older. Like some guys were once looking at a modern car, and they said, 'A young guy must have designed that car!' Why does he have to have been a young guy?

"On clarinet, I only like Benny Goodman very much. I don't like Buddy DeFranco at all, because he plays a lot of cliches and is very cold. Tony Scott plays good, but not like Benny, because Benny used to swing so much. No matter what form jazz takes—Lennie or Stan or Bird or Duke—jazz has to swing.

"What's swinging in words? If a guy makes you pat your foot and if you feel it down your back, you don't have to ask anybody if that's good music or not. You can always feel it." ●

AN OPEN LETTER TO MILES DAVIS

By Charlie Mingus

NOVEMBER 30, 1955

Four editions of *Down Beat* come to my mind's eye—Bird's "Blindfold Test," mine, Miles', and Miles' recent "comeback story"—as I sit down and attempt to honestly write my thoughts in an open letter to Miles Davis. (I discarded numerous "mental" letters before this writing, but one final letter formed last night as I looked through some pictures of Bird that Bob Parent had taken at a Village session.) If a picture needs to go with this story, it should be this picture of Bird, standing and looking down at Monk with more love than I think we'll ever find in this jazz business!…

Bird's love, so warmly obvious in this picture, was again demonstrated in his "Blindfold Test." But dig Miles' "Test"! As a matter of fact, dig my own "Blindfold Test"! See what I mean? And more recently, dig Miles' comeback story. How is Miles going to act when he *gets* back and gets going again? Will it be like a gig in Brooklyn not too long ago with Max, Monk, and me when he kept telling Monk to "lay out" because his chords were all wrong? Or even at a more recent record date when he cursed, laid out, argued, and threatened Monk and asked Bob Weinstock why he hired such a nonmusician and would Monk lay out on his trumpet solos? What's happening to us disciples of Bird? Or would Miles think I'm presuming too much to include myself as one?

It seems so hard for some of us to grow up mentally just enough to realize that there are other persons of flesh and bone, just like us, on this great, big earth. And if they don't ever stand still, move, or "swing," they are as right as we are, even if they are as wrong as hell by our standards. Yes, Miles, I am apologizing for my stupid "Blindfold Test." I can do it gladly because I'm learning a little something. No matter how much they try to say that Brubeck doesn't swing—or whatever else they're stewing or whoever else they're brewing—it's factually unimportant.

Not because Dave made *Time* magazine—and a dollar—but mainly because Dave honestly thinks he's swinging. He feels a certain pulse and plays a certain pulse which gives him pleasure and a sense of exaltation because he's sincerely doing something the way he, Dave Brubeck, feels like doing it. And as you said in your story, Miles, "if a guy makes you pat your foot, and if you feel it down your back, etc.," then Dave is the swingingest *by your own definition*, Miles, because at Newport and elsewhere Dave had the whole house patting its feet and even clapping its hands.…

Miles, don't you remember that "Mingus Fingers" was written in 1945 when I was a youngster, 22 years of age, who was studying and doing his damnedest to write in the Ellington tradition? Miles, that was 10 years ago when I weighed 185. Those clothes are worn and don't fit me any more. I'm a man; I weigh 215; I think my *own way*. I don't think like you and my music isn't meant just for the patting of feet and going down backs. When and if I feel gay and carefree, I write or play that way. When I feel angry I write or play that way—or when I'm happy, *or depressed, even*.

Just because I'm playing jazz I don't forget about *me*. I play or write *me*, the way I feel, through jazz, or whatever. Music is, or was, a language of the emotions. If someone has been escaping reality, I don't expect him to dig my music, and I would begin to worry about my writing if such a person began to really like it. My music is alive and it's about the living and the dead, about good and evil. It's angry, yet it's real because it *knows* it's angry.

I know you're making a comeback, Miles, and I'm with you more than you know. You're playing the greatest *Miles* I've ever heard, and I'm sure you already know that you're one of America's truly great jazz stylists. You're often fresh in a creative sense and, if anything, you underevaluate yourself—on the outside—and so with other associates in the art. Truly, Miles, I love you and want you to know you're needed here, but you're too important a person in jazz to be less than extra careful about what you say about other musicians who are *also trying* to create.…

Remember me, Miles? I'm Charles. Yeah, Mingus! You read third trumpet on my California record dates 11 years ago on the recommendation of Lucky Thompson. So easy, young man. Easy on those stepping stones.…

If you should get around to answering this open letter, Miles, there is one thing I would like to know concerning what you said to Nat Hentoff about all the tunes you've recorded in the last two years. Why did you continue to record, session after session, when you now say you don't like them except for two LPs? I wonder if you forgot the names of *those* tunes; also, how a true artist can allow all this music, which even he himself doesn't like, to be sold to the jazz public. Or even accept payment for a job which you yourself say wasn't well done.

Good luck on your comeback, Miles. ●

PRES: ONE OF JAZZDOM'S GREATS REMINISCES, EVALUATES, AND CHATS

By Nat Hentoff

MARCH 7, 1956

On a recent Saturday afternoon at his home in St. Albans, Long Island, Lester Young was alternately watching television and answering questions. Eight-year-old Lester Young Jr. had gone to the movies. The pet of the house, a 7-year-old Spitz named Concert ("We got him on the day of a concert") was in quizzical attendance. Making coffee was Mary, Lester's wife; also present was the astute, outspoken Charlie Carpenter, Lester's long-time friend who has been with him since 1946 and has been his manager since 1948.

Lester had recently recovered from an illness. He looked to be in good health, was much more relaxed than he usually is in interviews, and his answers were lucid and carefully thought out before delivered. A few days after this interview, Lester made a record session for Norman Granz with Vic Dickenson, Roy Eldridge, Teddy Wilson, Gene Ramey, Freddie Green, and Jo Jones. He played so well that Granz delayed his departure from New York so that he could record Pres again, this time with Wilson, Ramey, and Jones. In both his current conversation and music, then, Lester indicates that he is finding some of the inner peace and confidence for which he's been searching a long time. These are some of the subjects Lester talked about:

Autobiography:

I was born in Woodville, Miss., not New Orleans. The family moved to New Orleans after I was born and stayed there until I was 10. I remember I liked to hear the music in New Orleans. I remember there were trucks advertising dances and I'd follow them all around. I don't remember the names of all the musicians I heard then.

"I was raised up in a carnival, a week in each town. I liked it, but in the wintertime, my father, who was in charge of the band, wanted to go down south. I didn't like the idea and I'd run away.

"I've been playing music ever since I was 10. I started on the drums, but it was too much trouble to carry the traps. So I switched to alto. Frankie Trumbauer and Jimmy Dorsey were battling for honors in those days, and I finally found out that I liked Trumbauer. Trumbauer was my idol. When I had just started to play, I used to buy all his records. I imagine I can still play all those solos off the record. He played the C melody saxophone. I tried to get the sound of a C melody on a tenor. That's why I don't sound like other people. Trumbauer always told a little story. And I liked the way he slurred the notes. He'd play the melody first and then after that, he'd play around the melody. I did like Bud Freeman very much. Nobody played like him. That's what knocked me out. I remember when he was with Benny Goodman.

"I played in my father's band until I joined the Bostonians, an outfit from Salina, Kan. My father could swing. He liked to play. He taught and could play all the instruments. I was with the Bostonians for about two or three years when I was around 16 and 17. We played through North and South Dakota and Minnesota. Sometimes, I used to go back to my father's band.

"The first instrument I played was alto. The way I switched to tenor is that when I was with the Bostonians, the tenor player kept grandstanding all the time. So I told the leader, if you buy a tenor for me, I'll play it. You see, the regular tenor was a boy from a well-to-do family. He didn't have to play. I remember we'd go by his house sometimes and beg him to play. I got sick of it.

"After the Bostonians, I played with King Oliver. He had a very nice band and I worked regularly with him for one or two years around Kansas and Missouri mostly. He had three brass, three reeds, and four rhythm. He was playing well. He was old then and didn't play all night, but his

Lester Young

tone was full when he played. He was the star of the show and played one or two songs each set. The blues. He could play some nice blues. He was a very nice fellow, a gay old fellow. He was crazy about all the boys, and it wasn't a drag playing for him at all.

"As for how I went with Basie, I was playing at the Cotton club in Minneapolis.

I used to hear the Count on his broadcasts when I was off from work. I used to hear his tenor and I knew they needed a tenor player. Everything was fine with the band but the tenor player. I sent Basie a telegram and asked him if he could use a tenor player. I was in my twenties by this time. He'd heard of me because people had gone up to Minneapolis for various shows, and Minneapolis was the winter quarters for the band I was with.

"So I joined Basie. It was very nice. Just like I thought it was going to be. Jo Jones came into the band after I did. I've always liked his drumming. He did a lot of things then that the modern drummers do now. Would I compare the Basie band then with the way it is now? It was different from today's, a different style, so I wouldn't compare them. But the band he has now is very nice.

"I remember Buster Smith. I played with him in the 13 Original Blue Devils led by Walter Page. They came to Minneapolis while I was there and they had a sad tenor, too, so I joined them. Buster used to write all the arrangements and he could play crazy alto and clarinet. Oh, he could blow.

"I played with Fletcher Henderson for a short time when Coleman Hawkins left. I had a lot of trouble there. The whole band was buzzing on me because I had taken Hawk's place. I didn't have the same kind of sound he had. I was rooming at the Henderson's house, and Leora Henderson would wake me early in the morning and play Hawkins' records for me so I could play like he did. I wanted to play my own way, but I just listened. I didn't want to hurt her feelings. Finally I left and went to Kansas City. I had in my mind what I wanted to play, and I was going to play that way. That's the only time that ever happened, someone telling me to play differently from the way I wanted to.

TENORS, ETC.:

Herschel Evans was a Hawk man. That was the difference between the way we played. He played well, but his man was Hawk like my man at the beginning was Trumbauer. As for Coleman Hawkins, I used to ride in Hawk's car. He plays fine. He was the first to really start playing tenor. I thought Chu Berry played nice, too. He was on a Coleman Hawkins style. I think he got the job with Henderson after I left. Ben Webster had a taste of it, too. I think Ben plays fine, too.

"Of the newer tenors, I like all them little youngsters. I like to hear them play. About the finest I heard them play is on that "Four Brothers" record. Do I hear my influence in what they play? Yes, I hear a lot of little things from what I play, but I never say anything. I mean I hear a lot of little riffs and things that I've done. But I don't want it to sound like I think I influenced everybody."

(At this point Charlie Carpenter told the story of the night Lester and Paul Quinichette, who are good friends, were leading units on alternate sets at Birdland: "Lester came off the bandstand and said: 'I don't know whether to play like me or like Lady Q, because he's playing so much like me.' He wasn't putting Paul down. Why, Paul is the only man I've ever known him lend a tenor to. But that night, Paul sounded so much like Lester that Lester was at loose ends as to what to do.")

"Have any of the young tenors," Lester echoed a question, "come up to me and said anything about my having influenced them? No, none have.

"I liked a lot of the younger hornmen. I've heard more of Miles than most, and I like him. And Jessie Drakes who has been playing trumpet with me since 1949. I like him because he plays his own way and doesn't try to imitate nobody. We've been playing together so long I just call a number and we're gone. Things like that mean a lot.

"I thought Bird was a genius. The way he knew his instrument he'd be a hard man to cap. We did a little jamming mostly when I was out in California in the forties. He was a very nice person, well-educated. He loved that instrument. The people woke up very quickly to his playing.

THE FUNCTIONS OF A RHYTHM SECTION:

The piano should play little fill-ins. Just nice little full chords behind the horn. I don't get in his way, and I let him play, and he shouldn't get in mine. Otherwise, your mind gets twisted. That's why I always let my little kiddies play solos. That way they don't bother me when I solo. In fact, sometimes I get bawled out by people who want to hear me play more, but I believe if you're paying a man to play, and if that man is on the bandstand and can play, he should get a chance to tell his story.

"An example of the kind of pianist I like is Gildo Mahones, who plays with me a lot. He never gets in your way. Some pianists just run all over the piano when you're playing, and that's a drag. I like John Lewis' playing very much. The Modern Jazz Quartet, I think, is very nice, but they have to play some place where it's quiet so you can hear them. The little things they play are their own. It's something new. I've never heard anybody play like that but them.

"A bass should play nice, four-beat rhythm that can be heard, but no slapping. I can't stand bass players when they slap the strings. I love bowed work. It's very nice on ballads. But not all bass players can play good with a bow, and yet it's so nice to have one who can in a small group. I like Johnny Ore, who has worked with me a lot.

"On drumming, I don't go for the bombs. I want the drummer to be straight with the section. He's messing with the rhythm when he drops those bombs. In small groups, I like the drummer to play a little tinkety-boom on that one cymbal, four-beats on the pedal. Just little simple things, but no bombs.

"The Basie rhythm section was good because they played together and everybody in it was playing rhythm. They played for you to play when you were taking a solo. They weren't playing solos behind you.

"On a date, I play a variety of tempos. I set my own tempos and I take my time. I wish jazz were played more often for dancing. I have a lot of fun playing for dances because I like to dance too. The rhythm of the dancers comes back to you when you're playing. When you're playing for dancing, it all adds up to playing the right tempo. After three or four tempos, you find the tempos they like. What they like changes from dance date to dance date.

THE CLARINET:

I never could find the one I wanted. I used a metal clarinet on those Kansas City Six records for Commodore, but I never could find one like that one afterwards. I got a tone on that metal one like I wanted. I'd like to pick it up this year if I could find one. Of the newer clarinetists, I'm going to pick up Jimmy Giuffre's records. I think he was the one I heard being played on the radio. He sure plays me, especially in the low tones. About clarinetists, I have to put it right on Benny Goodman always, him and Artie Shaw.

HONKING TENORS:

Those tenors who stay on one note, I don't go for that. I like to see a person stand flat-footed and play the instrument. When I'm on the stage with honking going on I never pay it no mind. I don't but that no kind of way when a person gets on one note for an hour. But they sell it like hot cakes. Yet it's dying out, if you notice. I wouldn't go to see nothing like that.

ADVICE TO YOUNG MUSICIANS:

A musician should know the lyrics of the songs he plays, too. That completes it. Then you can go for yourself and you know what you're doing. A lot of musicians that play nowadays don't know the lyrics of the songs. That way they're just playing the changes. That's why I like records by singers when I'm listening at home…I pick up the words right from there.

"Every musician should be a stylist. I played like Trumbauer when I was starting out. But then there's a time when you have to go out for yourself and tell your story. Your influence has already told his.

"You have to have a nice rhythm section. When you get a rhythm section that doesn't swing, you can't do what you want to do.

"A good way to learn is jamming with records. Find somebody you like and play his records. That's the way I started. That way you can stop the record and repeat it. If it isn't in the key you like, you can slow it down. Some of the records I used to play

with were 'Singing the Blues,' 'A Good Man Is Hard to Find,' and 'Way Down Yonder in New Orleans.' I have great big eyes for Bix. I used to be confused between him and Red Nichols, but finally had to put Bix on top.

DREAMS:

If I could put together exactly the kind of band I wanted, it wouldn't be a great big band. I'd have a guitar that just played rhythm—like Freddie Greene. I'd have three more rhythm, a trumpet, trombone, baritone, and myself. Frank Sinatra would be the singer. But that's kind of way out. That'll never happen. As for arrangements, there are a lot of people I'd like, but I'd have to think about it.

"I'd also like to make some records with strings, some soft ballads. And if we did jump tunes with strings, the strings would play some whole tunes in the background. I was supposed to make some records with strings in California. It still might happen. I'd maybe also like to make some more records with Billie, but that would be left up to her. Those records we made with Billie and Teddy Wilson were mostly heads, you know. He'd always have some little guide to go by, just a little sketch. I remember the well—like 'Sailboat in the Moonlight,' 'Mean to Me,' and 'This Year's Kisses.'

RECORDS:

I usually hear records over the radio and the TV, but I also collect some. I like to get records with singing. Really my man is Frank Sinatra. And I like Lady Day, Ella, Sarah, and others like that. I forgot Al Hibbler. He registers on me very greatly. He sure did break through, didn't he? Most of the time I spend in listening to singers and getting the lyrics to different songs.

"I feel funny listening to my own records. I think I enjoy them too well. I might repeat them when I play so I don't

like to listen to them over and over. If I listened to them too much, I'd be thinking about them when I'm playing or recording new ones instead of creating. Among those of mine I like the best are 'Lester Leaps In,' 'Clap Hands,' 'Here Comes Charlie,' 'Every Tub,' 'Swing the Blues,' 'One O'Clock Jump,' and 'Shoe Shine Boy,' the first record I made.

CONCLUSIONS:

I think they'll all be finally coming back to swinging and to dancing to music again. A lot of the things now are just novelties. For me, the music has to swing first.

"I'd like to hear nice big bands with a variety of music that people can dance to and good soloists. I myself though wouldn't like to play in a big band. You don't get a chance to play. You walk to the mike for your eight bars or 16 bars and then you sit down. You're just sitting here and reading the music. There are no kicks for me that way.

"After all these years, there's still kicks for me in music. I don't practice because I think I've been playing long enough. But I love to play.

"Let me ask *you* something," Lester said at the door. "Do you like Dixieland?"

"Yes, if it's good," I said.

"Same with me," said Lester.

"The only thing in music he can't stand," Charlie Carpenter pointed to Lester, "is hillbilly music."

Lester nodded.

"And radio and TV jingles?" I added.

"Yes, indeed," Lester laughed. "Those and hillbilly music." ●

SWEE'PEA...IS STILL AMAZED AT FREEDOM ALLOWED IN WRITING FOR ELLINGTON ORCHESTRA

MAY 30, 1956

Freedom is the key to Billy Strayhorn's long and happy association with Duke Ellington.

"There are no restrictions on my writing," he said in Boston where the band played Storyville. "There are no restrictions either on material or on length. That's why I like working with Duke.

"I've always written what I wanted how I wanted for Duke. Sometimes I turn in things; other times we have a conference." Billy said occasional disagreements pop up between him and Duke. "We carp at each other all the time. Sometimes he wins out; sometimes I do."

The chief arranger for the Ellington band since 1939 admits that the Duke has been an influence in his writing. "I'm certain Duke has influenced me. He says I've influenced him, but I don't know...I'm not even sure he knows."

Ask the Duke, and Ellington laughs, "That's inevitable. We've been together so long. We discuss things, but I find that if I'm going to do the arrangement, it's about the same as if he had done it. That happens even when we may not agree on things."

Strayhorn, who stands just 5 feet, 2 inches off the ground but is heads and shoulders above the crowd in musicianship, is a study in alertness. He appears to be noticing everything going on as he walks or rides.

Even while carrying on a conversation or paying the cashier in a restaurant, Billy is busy noticing what the headlines say in a newspaper lying on the counter or craning his neck to check on new construction work going on down the street.

His capacity for work is amazing. During the bands stay in Boston, Strayhorn was busy adding to the book and reworking some of the numbers already part of the book. "The Duke says we need some new stuff. We seem to have recorded just about everything in the book," he chuckled.

Strayhorn was working on "eight or nine new things." He had completed four pieces before the band came into town. A few weeks earlier he scored 13 pieces in two days for an album of songs Rosemary Clooney cut with the Ellington band.

"The thing about that album that got me was everything was in a hurry," Billy laughed. "Duke called me one Friday morning at six o'clock. Told me I had a reservation on a plane for California Monday. I didn't find out until I saw him that night that we were going to do this album with Rosemary Clooney—*Blue Rose*, they called it.

"I had to make the trip because I didn't know her keys or anything. It turned

out we put the thing together in practically no time."

Among the songs Rosemary sang with the band are "Mood Indigo," "I Let a Song Go Out of My Heart," "It Don't Mean a Thing If It Ain't Got That Swing," "Sophisticated Lady," "If You Were in My Place," "I'm Checkin' Out," "Goodbye," and "Grievin' and Sittin' and Rockin'."

Strayhorn's alertness finds its way into the titles of many of his pieces. "Titles are important," he said. "Some pieces are program music, you know, the tune tells a story—like Duke's 'Tattooed Bride' and 'Harlem Airshaft'."

Some titles describe the music, and Billy pointed to his "Flippant Flurry." "Duke named that one," he said "and it tells you perfectly what the piece is. It's a flippant sort of thing. It's agitated, all up in the air.

"Here's the funny thing. 'Jack the Bear' was originally called 'Take It Away.' Duke originally wrote the thing as an experiment. He had big chords working against a melodic thing," and Billy described with his hands and vocal cords the way the band chords worked against the melody.

"It didn't work out, and the piece just dropped. Then Jimmy Blanton came into the band, and Duke wanted to feature him as a solo man. We needed some material quickly, so I reworked

From left: **Duke Ellington, Billy Strayhorn, and Timmie Rogers**

'Take It Away' as a showpiece for Blanton's bass."

When asked if long-playing records had given him more freedom in composing, Billy shook his head. "'Take A Train,'" he said. "The little version the way it was on the Victor 78, that was exactly as I wrote it. It just happened to come out to three minutes.

"The long version, the one we play now, evolved from the fact that Duke likes to get some variety into the band's playing. The lyric came from a movie.

"It used to be we'd go into a record session with new stuff, all too long. We'd just cut the material down to three minutes." Billy threw back his head and laughed aloud. "Most of the time, the cuts improved the pieces."

Strayhorn is enthusiastic and colorful, but there are times when the bright eyes behind the heavy horn-rimmed glasses can become serious.

"Funny thing," he said. "You have to really go abroad to gain some perspective. Some Americans going abroad think of it as if they were going camping. But they find Europe has everything we have over here—except jazz. They haven't really got it. They play at it, but they don't quite make it.

But the European people think of jazz musicians as artists and too often here a musician is thought of as an eccentric or a dope fiend or worse. That's not universally true, understand, but it does exist.

"Maybe it's because this music is right under our noses. You remember that thing about not seeing the trees for the woods?

"But I'm happy to see that jazz is finally coming into its own in this country. I mean it's becoming a part of our cultural picture. There are concert seasons which feature a jazz presentation. I know of two, one in Des Moines and the other in Toledo. They have civic concerts there, not to make a profit or anything like that, but backed by bankers and people interested in presenting a well-rounded musical season.

"It used to be that an artist had to go to Europe and come back again with recognition to be anybody. That's changing here. Look at the Metropolitan Opera. It's working that way in jazz, too.

"Jazz is being recognized as a part of the American musical culture, and these people are making it part of their concert season so the picture will be complete musically." •

A TRIBUTE TO BROWNIE

By Quincy Jones
AUGUST 22, 1956

To me, the name of Clifford Brown will always remain synonymous with the very essence of musical and moral maturity. This name will stand as a symbol of the ideals every young jazz musician should strive to attain.

This name also represents a musician who had intelligent understanding and awareness of social, moral, and economic problems which constantly confuse the jazz musician, sometimes to the point of hopeless rebellion.

In the summer of 1953, while I was working with the Lionel Hampton band in Wildwood, N.J., I begged Hamp to hire three of the musicians from Tadd Dameron's band, which was nearing the end of its Atlantic City engagement—Gigi Gryce, Benny Golson, and Clifford Brown. They were all hired and then began an association that I'll always be grateful to Lionel for.

Brownie stayed on to go to Europe with this band and became closely associated with several other young musicians who were of growing importance in the jazz world, such as Art Farmer, Anthony Ortega, Jimmy Cleveland, Alan Dawson, and George Wallington. Although this band never played in the states together, I think it was one of the best Hamp ever had.

By means of an extensive recording schedule abroad, Brownie came first to the eyes and ears of the French and Swedish jazzmen and a new thoroughbred was on the jazz scene. The uniting of Clifford Brown with the trumpet must have been declared from above. For seldom does a musical vehicle prove to be so completely gratifying as the trumpet was to Clifford.

Here was the perfect amalgamation of natural creative ability, and the proper amount of technical training, enabling him to contribute precious moments of musical and emotional expression. This inventiveness placed him in a class far beyond that of most of his poll-winning contemporaries. Clifford's self-assuredness in his playing reflected the mind and soul of a blossoming young artist who would have rightfully taken his place next to Charlie Parker, Dizzy Gillespie, Miles Davis, and other leaders in jazz.

In this generation where some well-respected and important pioneers condemn the young for going ahead, Brownie had a very hard job. He constantly struggled to associate jazz, it's shepherds, and it's sheep, with a cleaner element, and held no room in his heart for bitterness about the publicity-made popularity and success of some of his pseudo-jazz giant brothers, who were sometimes very misleading morally and musically. As a man and a musician, he stood for a perfect example and the rewards of self-discipline.

It is really a shame that in this day of such modern

From left: **Sonny Rollins, Clifford Brown, Richie Powell, Max Roach, and George Morrow**

techniques of publicity, booking, promoting, and what have you, a properly-backed chimpanzee can be a success after the big treatment. Why can't just one-tenth of these efforts be placed on something that is well-respected, loved, and supported in every country in the world but it's own?

Except for a very chosen few, the American music business man and the majority of the public (the Elvis Depressley followers specifically) have made an orphan out of jazz, banishing its creators and true followers and adopting idiots that could be popular no place else in the universe. I'll go so far as to bet that the salaries of Liberace, Cheeta, and Lassie alone could pay the yearly cost of booking every jazzman in the country.

This is why it's such a shame that Clifford Brown, Charlie Parker, Fats Navarro, and others have to leave the world so unappreciated except for a small jazz circle. I hope some of us live to see a drastic change.

In June, 1950, Clifford Brown's career was threatened by an auto accident while he was with the Chris Powell band, which kept him from his horn for a whole year. Exactly six years later, by the same means of an auto accident, death took its toll of Clifford Brown, along with his pianist Richard Powell (brother of Bud Powell), and Richard's wife.

Clifford, at 25, was at the beginning of showing capabilities parallel only to those of Charlie Parker. There was nothing he would stop at to make each performance sound as if it were his last. But there will never be an ending performance for him, because his constant desire was to make every musical moment one of sincere warmth and beauty; this lives on forever. This would be a better world today if we had more people who believed in what Clifford Brown stood for as a man and a musician. Jazz will always be grateful for his few precious moments; I know I will. ●

THE FRANK SINATRA I KNOW

By Sammy Davis, Jr.
AUGUST 22, 1956

I first met Frank in the early forties, about three months before he left Tommy Dorsey to go out as a single. The band was playing Detroit, and a unit called Tip, Tap, and Toe was to open with them, but the unit was hung up in Canada. So they put us in for three days on the same bill as the band.

My first impressions of him were that he was a very nice warm guy, but I was close to Buddy Rich then because I wanted to learn drums. One thing I do remember is that Frank had the lapels taken off one of his jackets because he couldn't afford a cardigan.

We next met in 1945. I'd just gotten out of the army. He was doing the "Old Gold" and "The Hit Parade" shows from Hollywood at the time. I stood for tickets in the servicemen's line with my uniform on. I went backstage. He came out the stage door, and they rushed him to a car, and I yelled, "Hi, Frank."

I went two weeks in a row, and one day I caught him going into a rehearsal and asked him to sign my book. "You've been here a couple of weeks," he said. Seeing my discharge emblem, he asked why I wore the uniform in line, and I told him it was because I couldn't get tickets otherwise. Frank turned to one of his men and said, "See that there are tickets there for Sam from now on."

My dad, uncle, and I were laying off around this time so I used to go to both of his shows every week. I came to be known as the kid who hung around Frank. Frank was an inquisitive guy if he liked you, and he'd do little considerate things like once at the beginning of a rehearsal asking me if I

wanted some coffee. I said, "Yuh," shaking a little and with my palms sweating.

"You're in show business?" he asked.

"Yeah."

"You work with your uncle and father?" And he asked about our act and what we were doing.

I didn't see him for a year and when we met, he said he was going into the Capitol theater. I told him it would be great for us to get that kind of date. He said "Yuh."

Without our knowing it, he went on to pitch us to Sid Piermont, head of Loew's booking agency. Sidney didn't know who we were, and by this time, we'd left town. All he knew was that I was a kid named

Frank Sinatra

Sam with a father and an uncle. He finally found us through AGVA.

We were a $300-a-week act then. "We can save on the budget," Sid told Frank.

"No," said Sinatra, "give them $1,000."

"But we can get the Nicholas Brothers for that."

"No," said Frank, "I want the kid."

That was our first major break. At that time I was doing just a six-minute hoofing act. Frank had a Thanksgiving party at the Capitol where I got up and sang. He told me I had a good voice and should sing. "You sound too much like me, but you should sing," is what he said.

After that, we became very close. I used

to go to his home in California, and he'd ask how my career was going. I'd see him about once in every six months. This was in the late forties and early fifties. I was getting a hold in the business. Every time I saw him it was a real breath of spring. No matter which of his own troubles and problems he was involved with then, he always had time to talk to me about my career. He'd advise me what to do and whom to watch out for.

Frank next saw our act in 1952, the act with the impressions, etc., in it, and he flipped. "This is it," he said. "Now why don't you make records?"

"I have no style of my own," I said.

"Find one."

"Well, they tell me I sound too much like you."

"Well," said Frank, "that's not the worst thing in the world. You could sound like Dick Todd. But sing more of yourself and go for yourself. One day you'll get your future together."

Our friendship has progressed beautifully since then as we've become more and more close. After my accident, for example, he had me at his home in Palm Springs recuperating for two weeks. Our friendship now is at the point where we expect nothing of each other except the friendship itself. He's likely to call up in the middle of the night, as he did once, and claim to be the house detective.

Frank is also the man for whom I'm starting my film career. My first picture will be *The Jazz Train* for his own company. It'll start in the spring. The show has been a very popular one in England. Frank will play an army captain, and I'll be his buddy. Don Maguire, who directed Frank's *Johnny Concho*, will direct *The Jazz Train*, too.

Another film project Frank has asked me to do with him is *The Harold Arlen Story*, to be produced by Sol Siegel for MGM. The title probably will be changed to one of Arlen's hits. I'll be the guy, a college friend of Arlen, who first takes him to the Cotton club in Harlem and introduces him to the blues and blues-influenced music. My role then calls for me to go to work at the Cotton club as a sort of composite of Cab Calloway and Bill Robinson, and Arlen will be depicted as writing material for me.

About *The Jazz Train*, Sinatra got me a lot of loot for the film, plus 25 percent of the picture. He personally made the deal for me, and that's just another indication of his generosity.

Frank is the type of man every guy from a truck driver to a Hollywood producer would be proud to call "my friend." And it's not because of his position. It would be the same thing if he were a cabbie. The man stands for everything that is good in a human being and like a human being, he makes mistakes. But he never really hurt anyone else, only himself. Sure, he's made a lot of mistakes. But there's only been one perfect being. Frank oughtn't to be condemned for having made mistakes.

I'm very proud to be considered a friend of this man. He has ways of doing things that are unbelievable. Like when *Confidential* came out with its story on me, Disneyland opened about the same time. I went to the Disneyland opening with Frank and his three kids. Millions of people saw it on television. That was his way of refuting *Confidential* without ever mentioning it.

Frank is now in an enviable position—he can record whatever he wants, and he makes a lot of records. As for being influenced by him, as one guy said, "It's good sense to sound like Sinatra because he sounds better than any other singer."

I have a complete collection of Sinatra. On the coast when we get together, I take a Dorsey record from the forties and contrast it with one of his current releases. Even then you can see the beginning of what he has now.

He's painstaking about his recordings. Nelson Riddle doesn't write a note that Frank doesn't eventually change one way or another. He'll do 20 takes if he feels it isn't the way he wants it. He'll say all day to get *one* ready. There was a session for "Wee Small Hours." It was 3 a.m., and he was still going over certain things, listening to the playback, and shaking his head, saying, "No."

He was there until dawn until he got what he wanted. He hears the smallest detail. It's not that he doesn't trust Riddle, but there are certain things he wants done his way. It was Frank, incidentally, who selected Nelson for his dates. Riddle had

always been sort of a free-lance artist. Nelson started doing things for Nat Cole, and Frank heard them. That's the way I think it happened.

As for whether Frank is a jazz singer, he certainly has a feeling for jazz. Remember the swinging thing he did for Dorsey, "Oh, Look at Me Now" and all the others since? Look, if I were to be around Laurence Olivier and John Gielgud for 30 years, some Shakespearean knowledge would have to rub off on me if I were a good student and listener. Now Frank was with James and Dorsey in the years when they had bands, that had jazz soloists and a jazz feel, and it would be impossible for a lot of that not to have rubbed off.

Buddy Rich for example, was an influence. Of course, he was also a target once, too. Frank didn't like the way Buddy would beat the drums sometimes when he was singing. Once in Detroit Frank was singing "This Love of Mine," and Buddy was talking in the back of the bandstand. "Sh-sh-sh," went Frank.

"What did he go 'sh' about?" asked Rich.

Dorsey said at this point, "Keep it quiet, Buddy."

So Rich paradiddled instead. Frank went into the wings and from there on to the back of the stand, and he knocked Buddy off the drums. But they're very good friends now, and it was Frank who financed Buddy's first band.

So to sum up Frank as a singer, I would say Frank has the musical integrity to do what he feels like doing, and he does it all so very well that he's the musical end. ●

Sammy Davis, Jr

SONNY ROLLINS

By Nat Hentoff

NOVEMBER 28, 1956

Sonny Rollins is the first major influence on a significant number of young tenors since the Stan Getz of the late forties and early fifties. Unlike the mesmeric Getz of that period, Sonny's approach is far from cool, and he is seldom lyrical. Sonny's style is hot, driving, deeply pulsating, and is rooted in Charlie Parker and before Bird, Coleman Hawkins.

In an intriguing genealogical chart at the end of an essay on Rollins by Ira Gitler for Prestige, Gitler points out that Charlie Rouse, the contemporary Allen Eager, J.R. Monterose, Hank Mobley, John Coltrane, Dexter Gordon, and Phil Urso have all been shaped in part in the forge of Rollins' style. Scores of lesser-known tenors throughout the country and now abroad also have been marked by Rollins.

Sonny is currently with Max Roach's quintet, and is an important factor in the climbing excitement generated by that unit. The position with Roach is Sonny's first regular gig in some time and represents an important stage in what has been up to now a rather disorganized career.

Theodore Walter Rollins was born in New York on Sept. 7, 1930. He recalls "there was always some kind of music going on in the house." An older brother was a violinist good enough to be considered for the Pittsburgh Symphony orchestra, but he finally chose medicine instead.

When he was 8 or 9, Sonny took a few piano lessons at the behest of his parents, but his first self-propelled instrument was the alto on which he took lessons both privately and at Benjamin Franklin High School where drummer Sonny Payne and tenor Percy France were among his contemporaries. Rollins' first influence was the virile Louis Jordan and his Tympani Five. "He opened me up to really listening more and finding out musicians' names,…" he says.

Then there was Coleman Hawkins—"his conception, the way he was able to play changes." Hearing Hawkins and Lester Young was one factor in Sonny's switch to tenor in 1946. He had played a few gigs around the city as well as in school on alto, and he found the number of jobs increased after the change of horn.

Sonny finds in retrospect no clash in having been influenced by *both* Hawkins and Young. "The things that were alike about them were more important than their differences. As for Lester's tone, I never thought it was a bad tone. The saxophone, after all, is a very young instrument, and people are still finding criteria by which to judge its players. There are still a lot of different ways a person can sound and still have acceptable tone. To me Lester had a very big sound. Hawk's was diff-erent because he played with a bigger vibrato."

By the time he was graduated from high school where he had majored in music, Sonny had got to the point "where I could handle a gig." His music major had introduced him to elementary theory, and he first planned to go to the Manhattan School of Music. He didn't, not yet convinced that music was to be his career.

"I don't think I ever did decide," he says. "I seemed to mold myself into it. I'm fortunate that I'm making a living at it now because I'm not equipped to do anything else. As the years went by, music was the only thing I was doing."

After high school, Rollins gigged around New York and New Jersey. Among the youngsters coming up with him were Jackie McLean and the late Richie Powell. The next and most searing major influence had also struck Sonny by this time.

"I heard Bird first on record and then I began to see him in the early forties at a lot of sessions on 52nd St. and at others around town like the Lincoln Square center on 61st St. Bird seemed to combine all the things I'd heard so far and liked. What he was doing seemed all new when I first heard it because I didn't really understand it.

"After I understood what he was doing, I realized it was a combination of everything up to that point, plus himself. He added something without taking away from what had come before.

"I got to know him, not as well as I would have liked to. We'd talk about music, and he'd always encourage me quite a bit. I remember asking once about some changes, whether they were right for a certain song. Bird answered that whatever I heard was right. What he meant was that if you can hear at all, you should be able to hear what's right; and if you can't hear, you won't make it anyway. He was telling me to keep the freedom to try things and not to limit myself.

"Bird befriended quite a few guys. Sonny Stitt before me. With us and a few other cats, especially saxophone players, it was like a father thing. When we were hung up personally, we went just to talk to him, just to see him. There was one time at a record

House of Moorhead

date for Prestige in 1952 or '53. It was Miles' date. Bird and I both played tenor. It's never been released. It was a great honor to play with him. I was so scared and nervous.

"At that time," Rollins continues, "I was going through a mixed-up personal period. A lot of things I was doing because I figured they were the things to be done because a lot of my idols did them. But Bird never encouraged me to do anything that would prove wrong for myself. And on that record date, he really told me what to do so far as music and my life was concerned.

"He asked me how I had been doing because he knew I was a young wild kid running around and not knowing what was happening. That day he showed me the thing he wanted me to do and the thing he stood for. The purpose of his whole existence was music and he showed me that music was the paramount thing and anything that interfered with it, I should stay away from. Later on I was able to take advantage of his advice, but he died before I had a chance to see him and tell him I had.

"Bird made a deep impression on me on tenor. I heard him play it very seldom, but his ideas, his drive, the way he could create moved me very much. As soon as he started to play on tenor or alto, he'd create the complete mood and would carry everyone, including the rhythm section, along with him. That's the mark of a true soloist. He was very sure and definite."

Sonny cut back to the years just before that key talk with Bird. His first record date had been in 1948 with Babs Gonzales for Capitol. ("I was just a kid. I didn't know anything.") There had been the help of Bud Powell. ("I was fortunate in knowing him very well. He lived around the corner from me, and I used to go by his house a lot. He'd show me a lot of things.") And Sonny recorded with Bud and Fats Navarro on Blue Note.

Thelonious Monk began to be an influence, when Sonny rehearsed with him for a few months in 1948, and he has continued to be. ("Monk is a teacher with a different way of playing and of voicing chords.") Sonny also is indebted to J.J. Johnson, with whom he had a few record dates on Savoy. ("He, too, was a very great help. He tried to show me how to read, and encouraged me. He was the first to record something I'd written.")

While leading the intermission trio at the 845 club in New York's Bronx, Sonny played opposite Davis. Miles was impressed, and for about three years off and on from 1951, Sonny worked with Miles, who turned into another considerable aid and influence. ("Anything I play now which might sound individual is excerpted from what I learned from all those great people. If my mind had been more settled, I would have really gotten serious about music *then*.")

Rollins was in Chicago to work at the Beehive in late 1954 and stayed until November, 1955. He was intent then on completing his musical studies and started at the University of Chicago. ("I didn't have the money for tuition so had to leave. But because I'd made a few records, I was fortunate to come into contact with teachers who were willing to instruct me. I wanted to get a thorough foundation because I was very depressed about the records I'd made. I knew now that music was sacred to me.")

He took a day job as a manual laborer while studying. Max Roach and Clifford Brown came through a couple of times, and Sonny would go down to see them and sit in.

"I'd always admired the group," Sonny says, "and what they stood for, not only musically but the personal conduct of the band, too. They were something that was needed at that time. At least I needed to see a group of musicians who could really play and who also could command respect by the way they conducted themselves."

When Harold Land, the tenor with Max and Clifford, returned to the West Coast, Rollins joined for what was to be only a week or two. Rollins recalls working alongside Brown with wonder:

"It was a pleasure. There was never any kind of conflict at all. In fact, at times I wished there was something I could be mad at him for—he blew so much. But there was nothing. He was perfect all the way around. We were just starting to achieve a sound when the accident happened." (Rollins was referring to the car crash in which Brown and the group's pianist, Richie Powell, died.)

"On the last job we played together, all of a sudden we both heard it. We were phrasing, attacking, breathing together.

That's a very difficult thing for two horns to make in unison playing. It's easier playing harmony. In unison, for one thing, the intonation of both has to be exactly the same. That's why I really think all groups that are together should *stay* together. It's the only way for them to achieve what they want to."

Rollins said he intends to stay with Roach indefinitely although eventually he'd like a combo of his own. But school still remains an obsession.

"Next year I may take some time off, go back to school, and stay away from the scene completely until I'm finished. I've continued studying off and on by myself and with teachers. I've just started. I've just scratched the surface. That's an honest appraisal of myself, so I don't dig this being an influence. I'm not trying to put myself down or anything. Being considered an influenced admittedly is more of a challenge because people look for me to produce. But that bugs me, too, because I really don't feel I'm as great as they think I am. Being considered that good creates a mental thing, too. Honestly, what I am is because I've been lucky enough to have been with the best people. I've got a lot of work still to do, a lot of work.

"I've been really serious about music for about two years. Music is the main thing now. It's a commitment—that's stronger than a decision—to make it a career. I want to learn as much as I can about music and be as sincere as I can be in every respect concerning it."

Rollins says he doesn't think he should be "on any kind of a pedestal" because "I don't have the background to be looked up to."

He says young musicians should get as much academic knowledge and as much practical experience in sessions and big bands as they can "because all these things will come up later on.

"I didn't have all that experience and background," Sonny adds. "I was thrown into making records without the kind of background I should have had. I'm not satisfied with anything about my playing. I know what I want. I can hear it. But it will take time and study to get it." ●

THE BIRTH OF THE COOL

By Nat Hentoff

MAY 2, 1957

Among Jazzmen, particularly player-writers, Gil Evans is uniquely admired.

"For my taste," Miles Davis says, "he's the best. I haven't heard anything that knocks me out as consistently as he does since I first heard Charlie Parker."

Coincident with Miles' recent tribute, Capitol released a few weeks ago the first complete collection of those 1949–50 Davis combo sides which were to influence deeply one important direction of modern chamber jazz—*Birth of the Cool.*

Evans was perhaps the primary background factor in making these sessions happen, and he wrote the arrangements for "Moon Dreams" and "Boplicity."

"Boplicity" is listed as the work of "Cleo Henry," a nom-de-date for Davis, who wrote the melody after which Evans scored the written ensembles. "'Boplicity,'" declares André Hodeir in *Jazz: Its Evolution and Essence*, "is enough to make Gil Evans qualify as one of jazz's greatest arranger-composers."

Despite these and other endorsements from impressive jazz figures, Evans is just a name to most jazz listeners. In the last few years, he has written comparatively little in the jazz field; but his influence on modern jazz writing through the effect of his work for the Claude Thornhill band of the forties and the Davis sides has remained persistent.

"Not many people really heard Gil," Gerry Mulligan explains. "Those who did, those who came up through the Thornhill band, were tremendously affected, and they in turn affected others."

Gil has now decided to return to more active jazz participation and is writing all arrangements for a Davis big band Columbia LP to be recorded at the end of April. He's also become more interested in creating original material, an area he's largely avoided up to now.

Evans once again is at a crossing point of his career.

He was born Ian Gilmore Green in Toronto, Canada, on May 13, 1912, and took his stepfather's name. Gil is self-taught and says, "I've always learned through practical work. I didn't learn any theory except through the practical use of it; and in fact, I started in music with a little band that could play the music as soon as I'd write it."

Evans first learned about music through jazz and popular records and radio broadcasts of bands. Since he had no traditional European background either in studying or listening, he built his style entirely on his pragmatic approach to jazz and pop material.

Sound itself was his first motivation. "Before I ever attached sound to notes in my mind, *sound* attracted me," he says. "When I was a kid, I could tell what kind of car was coming with my back turned."

Later, "it was the sound of Louis' horn, the people in Red Nichols' units like Jack Teagarden and Benny Goodman, Duke's band, the McKinney Cotton Pickers, Don Redman. Redman's Brunswick records ought to be

Gil Evans

reissued. The band swung, but the voicings also gave the band a compact sound. I also

was interested in popular bands. Like the Casa Loma approach to ballads. Gene Gifford broke up the instrumentation more imaginatively than was usual at the time."

Gil led his own band in Stockton, Calif., from 1933 - to - 1938, playing accompaniment-rhythm piano and scoring a book of pop songs and some jazz tunes. When the band was taken over by Skinnay Ennis, Gil remained as arranger until 1941.

"I was also beginning to get an introduction to show music and the entertainment end of the business," Evans recalls. "We used to play for acts on Sunday nights at Victor Hugo's in Beverly Hills, and the chance to write for vaudeville routines gave me another look at the whole picture."

Thornhill had also joined the Ennis arranging staff, and the two wrote for the Bob Hope radio show while the Ennis band was on the series. The radio assignments gave Evans more pragmatic experience in yet another medium.

"Even then," Evans remembers, "Claude had a unique way with a dance band. He'd use the trombones, for example, with the woodwinds in a way that gave them a horn sound."

In 1939, Claude decided to form his own band. Evans recommended the band for a summer job at Balboa, and he notes that Claude was then developing his sound, a sound based on the horns playing without vibrato except for specific places where Thornhill would indicate vibrato was to be used for expressive purposes.

"I think," Gil adds, "he was the first among the pop or jazz bands to evolve that sound. Someone once said, by the way, that Claude was the only man who could play the piano without vibrato.

"Claude's band," continues Evans, "was always very popular with players. The Benny Goodman band style was beginning to pall and had gotten to be commercial. I haunted Claude until he hired me as an arranger in 1941. I enjoyed it all, as did the men.

"The sound of the band didn't

necessarily restrict the soloists," Gil points out. "Most of his soloists had an individual style. The sound of the band may have calmed down the over-all mood, but that made everyone feel very relaxed."

Evans went on to examine the Thornhill sound more specifically: "Even before Claude added French horns, the band began to sound like a French horn band. The trombones and trumpets began to take on that character, began to play in derby hats without a vibrato.

"Claude added the French horns in 1941. He had written an obbligato for them to a Fazola solo to surprise Fats. Fazola got up to play; Claude signaled the French horns at the other end of the room to come up to the bandstand; and that was the first time Fazola knew they were to be added to the band.

"Claude was the first leader to use French horns as a functioning part of a dance band. That distant, haunting, no-vibrato sound came to be blended with the reed and brass sections in various combinations.

"When I first heard the Thornhill band," Gil continued, "it sounded, with regard to the registers in which the sections played, a little like Glenn Miller, but it soon became evident that Claude's use of no-vibrato demanded that the registers be lowered. Actually, the natural range of the French horn helped cause the lowering of the registers. In addition, I was constantly experimenting with varying combinations and intensities of instruments that were in the same register.

"A characteristic voicing for the Thornhill band was what often happened on ballads. There was a French horn lead, one and sometimes two French horns playing in unison or a duet depending on the character of the melody. The clarinet doubled the melody, also playing lead. Below were two altos, a tenor, and a baritone, or two altos and two tenors. The bottom was normally a double on the melody by the baritone or tenor. The reed section sometimes went very low with the saxes being forced to play in a subtone and very soft.

"In essence," Evans clarifies, "at first, the sound of the band was almost a reduction to an inactivity of music, to a stillness. Everything—melody, harmony, rhythm—was moving at a minimum speed. The melody was very slow, static; the rhythm was nothing much faster than quarter notes and a minimum of syncopation. Everything was lowered to create a sound, and nothing was to be used to distract from that sound. The sound hung like a cloud.

"I should add, incidentally, that Claude's desire was to avoid unnecessary activity even extended to the correction of mistakes. There was a minimum of discussion of the music. He hated to correct an error. 'Find it yourself,' was his attitude. If a guy was out of tune, Claude would touch the fellow's note as he was passing through the harmony part on the piano, to show him the way it should be played instead of telling him.

"But once this stationary effect, this sound, was created, it was ready to have other things added to it. The sound itself can only hold interest for a certain length of time. Then you have to make certain changes within that sound; you have to make personal use of harmonies rather than work with the traditional ones; there has to be more movement in the melody; more dynamics; more syncopation; speeding up of the rhythms.

"For me, I had to make those changes, those additions, to sustain *my* interest in the band, and I started to as soon as I joined. I began to add from my background in jazz, and that's where the jazz influence began to be intensified."

The next addition Thornhill made in modern band instrumentation was the tuba.

"In the old days," Gil explains, "the tuba had been used mainly as a rhythm instrument. The new concept with Thornhill started when Bill Barber joined the band, around the middle of 1947 or in 1948. Claude deserves credit, too, for the character of the sound with tuba added."

Gil returned to the jazz aspects of his work with Thornhill, saying, "I wrote arrangements of three of Bird's originals, "Anthropology," "Yardbird Suite," and "Donna Lee." And I also got to know Charlie well. We were personal friends, and were roommates for a year or so. Months after we had become friends and roommates, he had never heard my music, and it was a long time before he did."

(Gerry Mulligan explains: "What attracted Bird to Gil was Gil's musical *attitude*. How would I describe that attitude? 'Proving' is the most accurate word I can think of.")

"When Bird did hear my music," Gil continued, "he liked it very much. Unfortunately, by the time he was ready to use me, I wasn't ready to write for him. I was going through another period of learning by then.

"As it turned out, Miles, who was playing with Bird then, was attracted to me and my music. He did what Charlie might

Bill Gottlieb | Claude Thornhill

have done if at that time Charlie had been ready to use himself as a voice, as part of an overall picture, instead of a straight soloist."

Gil's influence worked in other ways as a corollary to the Davis Capitol sessions and to his writing for Thornhill. "I was always interested in other musicians, I was hungry for musical companionship, because I hadn't had much of it before. Like bull sessions in musical theory. Since I hadn't gone to school, I hadn't had that before.

"I got to know a lot of the writers, and I used to recommend my musical friends to Claude as arrangers—men like Gerry Mulligan, Johnny Carisi, Gene Roland, and Tom Merriman."

It was during this '46–'48 period, incidentally, that among Thornhill's sidemen were Lee Konitz, Red Rodney, Rusty Dedrick, Roland, Louis Mucci, and Jake Koven, whom Evans describes as "a very good trumpet player in the Louis Armstrong tradition with his own voice—there aren't many of those left."

Evans asked what he thought his influence had been on the development of Mulligan.

I don't really know," Gil replied. "We got together often; we were musically attracted to each other. Gerry, John Brooks, John Carisi, and George Russell, and I. The way we influenced each other was not of much importance. I feel we kept our own individuality through having each other as musical colleagues, rather than by having a common platform or working alone.

"As for the influence of Claude's band,

its sound and writers, I would say that the sound was made ready to be used by other forces in music. I did more or less match up with the sound the different movements by people like Lester, Charlie, and Dizzy in which I was interested. It was their rhythmic and harmonic revolutions that had influenced me. I liked both aspects and put them together. Of course, I'm not the only one who has done that. Those elements were around, looking for each other.

"Jazz musicians had arrived at a time when they needed a sound vehicle for ensembles, for working with larger bands, in addition to the unison playing between solo work to which they were accustomed.

"The point was," Evans went on "that an interdependence of modern thought and its expression was needed. If you express new thoughts and ideas in old ways, you take the vigor and excitement out of the new thoughts.

"For example, Miles couldn't play like Louis because the sound would interfere with his thoughts. Miles had to start almost with no sound and then develop one as he went along, a sound suitable for the ideas he wanted to express. He couldn't afford to trust those thoughts to an old means of expression. If you remember, his sound now is much more highly developed than it was at first.

"The idea of Miles' little band for the Capitol session came, I think, from Claude's band in the sound sense. Miles had liked some of what Gerry and I had written for Claude. The instrumentation for the Miles session was caused by the fact that this was the smallest number of instruments that could get the sound and still express all the harmonies the Thornhill band used. Miles wanted to play his idiom with that kind of sound.

"Miles, by the way, was the complete leader for those Capitol sides. He organized the band, sold it for the record contract, and for the Royal Roost where we played.

"I remember," Gil says grinning, "that original Miles band during the two weeks we played at the Royal Roost. There was a sign outside—'Arrangements by Gerry Mulligan, Gil Evans, and John Lewis.' Miles had it put in front; no one before had ever done that, given credit that way to arrangers.

"Those records by Miles indicate," Gil said, "what voicing can do, how it can give intensity and relaxation. Consider the six horns Miles had in a nine-piece band. When they played together, they could be a single voice playing a single line. One-part writing, in a way. But that sound could be altered and modified in many ways by the various juxtapositions of instruments. If the trombone played a high second part to the trumpet, for instance, there would be more intensity because he'd find it harder to play the notes. But you have to work these things out. I never know until I can hear it.

"After those records, what we had done seemed to appeal to other arrangers. There was, for one thing, a lot of tuba-type bands. I'm glad for Barber's sake, but I think it was overdone. It was done sometimes without any definite meaning except to be 'traditional.' It got to be traditional awfully fast to do a date with French horn and tuba." ●

DAVE BRUBECK: "THEY SAID I WAS TOO FAR OUT"

● ● ● ● ● ● ● ● ● ● ● ● ● ● ● ●

By Ralph Gleason
AUGUST 8, 1957

David Warren Brubeck, at the age of 36, is a successful man in his chosen profession, a man who has designed his life to suit his own taste and despite the rigors of a high-pressure business, manages to spend more time at home with his wife and five children than can almost anyone in a comparable position.

During the year 1956, Brubeck spent only 180 days on the road. He frequently flew back to Oakland, Calif., for a week with his family. Perhaps it was for only one or two days. And during the time, he was off the road, much of it was devoted to digging and raking and shoveling on the mountaintop he owns in the residential district of Oakland.

He was born in 1921 in Concord, Calif., a small town inland about 30 miles from San Francisco. His father was a cattleman, buyer of herd beef and manager of cattle ranches. His mother was the daughter of a stage coach operator who ran a regular passenger and mail coach from Concord over the hills to Oakland.

Mrs. Brubeck, however, was an unusual woman. In a society where—except for those who had struck it rich—there was little opportunity to inquire into the arts because the business of scraping out a living was too time-consuming, she managed to become a musician and even in later years, after her children were reared, returned to college and resumed studies.

The Brubecks moved from Concord when Dave was 8 to a ranch in Ione, a California mountain town, where his father had been made manager of a ranch, but Dave's memories of the Concord home are still vivid:

"I remember that house yet. It was built for strictly music. Pianos were in four different rooms there, and they were going all day long. My mother was teaching or my brothers were practicing. The first thing I heard in the morning was her teacher or them practicing. And the last thing at night. We didn't even have a radio in Concord."

Dave's mother was his first, and actually his only, teacher of any importance until he studied with Milhaud, and she gave Dave his first piano lessons.

"It was apparent right from the beginning," he says, "that I would be a composer. I was always improvising from the time I was 4 and 5. And I refused to study! My mother saw this and taught me completely different from Howard, who is about as schooled a musician as I can think of. She didn't force me to practice, and she didn't force me to play serious music, but she gave me a lot of theory, ear training, harmony. From the time I was very small, it was impossible to make me play any of the classical pieces except when I'd sit down and play them by ear. So I developed differently from my brothers."

Through high school and college, Brubeck was working in bands in the California mountain country. He began appearing professionally with pianist Bob Skinner, who has been a great influence on Dave and who introduced him, via records, to jazz. Skinner and Brubeck had a tap-dance-ukulele-piano team when they were 6.

"We were giggin'!" exclaims Brubeck. "Lions Clubs and socials. We could be hired for as little as getting out of school to $5 apiece!"

Later when he became more proficient on piano, he played with cowboy and hillbilly swing bands in California.

Even after he switched in college to studying music, Brubeck says, he was a

Dave Brubeck with sons Mike and Darry and Fantasyans Max and Sol Weiss

Bob Willoughby/Fantasy Records

poor student.

"But I absorbed, almost through osmosis, from all my teachers, which is the real reason why you study, not for grades," Dave recalls. "I was NEVER a good student except in this way—I found that I had the ability to do something most students don't have. When I learned something, I could use it that day or that night. I found that if we were in counterpoint and we were going over two-part inventions, well, that night my piano playing would be two lines. Or if somebody had mentioned Darius Milhaud using two tonalities, on the job that night I'd be using two tonalities."

Brubeck's experimentation with the material from the classroom on the job at night prompted the usual reaction from the men he worked with. He remembers:

"The reaction has gone on ever since I was a kid: *What the hell is he doing?* And it's a common experience for me. I was always experimenting on the job. Most musicians don't like that. I was always doing some-thing where I'd just *have* to say to the bass man or the guitar man, 'Just stay in the key you're in, and I'll superimpose this on you.' Or I'd say to the drummer, 'Just play the beat you're playing; what I'm going to do won't disturb you as long as you do what you're always used to.'

"And from the beginning, I've always tried to superimpose on the known and what's going on around me. And when I started using polytonality in jazz (some people say I used it before I heard of Milhaud—*I* think that maybe I was influenced by Milhaud, Dave says with a wry smile), I always figured you weren't stepping on the other musicians' toes if you were superimposing something that wouldn't clash—either polyrhythmic or polytonal. That's really been the styles you could identify me with. And it started, I would say, when I was 18 years old.

Fundamentally it's the style I'm using now."

When Brubeck is criticized for not having his roots in the mainstream of jazz, it is important to remember that aside from the records he heard as a youth—Teddy Wilson, Fats Waller, Duke Ellington, Benny Goodman—he heard very little if any jazz at first and until he was in college.

"I had little opportunity to listen to much music in jazz after I moved to Ione," Brubeck says, "and our family didn't listen to much jazz on the radio. Occasionally, I could get the Benny Goodman show on Saturday night. That's one of the things I can look back on and remember having had an opportunity to listen to.

"But as to records, I had only this one Fats Waller record, which I still have—I bought it in Sacramento when I was about 14. It was 'Honey on the Moon Tonight' and 'Close as Fingers in a Glove.' Of course, I imitated that when I was a kid, but I never saw Fats. That's another thing about being raised in the West. These people weren't available to you much.

"I remember we had to drive cattle usually all summer, and we'd be out on the roads from, oh, four in the morning to six at night, and cars would come through on their way up into the mountains—vacationers.

"I used to *dream* about maybe Benny Goodman was going come down this road. All day I'd dream, as we drove the cattle, about how Goodman would have to come through the cattle—going from Stockton to Sacramento for a one-nighter—and I wouldn't let him through unless he's let me on the band bus, and there'd bound to be a piano on the bus, and everybody'd be jamming and somebody would get to hear me play!"

Once in awhile, when Brubeck was at the College of the Pacific in Stockton in the early forties, he'd catch a band on a one-nighter.

"At the time," Dave recalls, "if I stood in front of a band, and somebody looked up at me or somebody would stop and talk, I was so thrilled it was fantastic. Now, when I see these guys all the time, especially Duke or Stan, I always think of the time I walked out of Duke's dressing room afraid to say hello to him!"

Despite the isolation from the mainstream of jazz in the early days, Brubeck branched out when attending College of the Pacific. He made frequent trips to San Francisco, where Skinner was beginning to emerge as one of the best jazz pianists, and sat in with such musicians as Jerome Richardson, Johnny Cooper, Vernon Alley, Bob Barfield, and Wilburt Barranco. Then, while he was doubling from classes at COP to night jobs in Stockton joints, he worked opposite Cleo Brown.

"She was a tremendous influence on me because of her left hand," he says. "She had a tremendous left hand, and she played boogie woogie faster than anybody. God, she could go! If she'd had a right hand like her left, she'd have given anybody a lot of competition."

In 1942, Brubeck enlisted in the army. Dave says, "I went right into the army. No traveling bands. This is important, I'd never ever been in L.A. until I went into the army."

When Brubeck went into the army, he enlisted in a band which was supposed to be a permanent unit and was stationed at Camp Haan near Los Angeles. His reception there, he remembers bitterly, was the same as it had been when he first got to Stockton. The musicians put him down.

At Stockton when he first wanted to play, he went up to two musicians and announced that he was a jazz pianist. Dave recalls, "They turned around and said, 'Where you from?' I said, 'Ione.' They just turned around again and didn't say anything. I had to walk away! Later when they found me playing at the ballroom, they couldn't believe it. 'Aren't you the guy from Ione?' they said."

At Camp Haan it was the same thing. Brubeck was the kid from Stockton, the equivalent of coming to Stockton from Ione.

There were several bands at the camp, and the personnel was from the Hollywood studios mainly. It was three weeks before Brubeck got to play, but when he did, he says, "I shocked everybody. This was the first inkling I had that I would be accepted and allowed in the inner circle.

"I was 21 then and I was amazed. All the guys in these bands were wonderful musicians and very competent, but I was shocking everyone. I don't know of a pianist who's ever come along that has shocked the accepted guys like that. They just completely wigged over me there were so many new ideas.

"And, of course, they all thought I was too radical. The first time I wrote an arrangement for the band nobody would play it. So I took it to Kenton in L.A. Stan said, 'Bring it back in 10 years!' It was my first big-band arrangement, and I wouldn't be ashamed for Stan to play it today.

"I would say it predated a lot of things. It didn't have a tremendous jazz, swinging feeling, but it was very polytonal and harmonically it was tremendously advanced, and it had a message you don't usually find in jazz.

"I wanted to use jazz for something much more serious than most people wanted to. At an early age I thought this was a medium to express deeper emotion. Kenton said, 'What is this? A dirge? Where did you ever hear chords like this?'"

Brubeck spent 18 months at Haan. He began writing small-combo arrangements there, and "those were very similar to how I would arrange now. And here again I wasn't accepted. Only by the furthest-out jazzmen in the band."

Then the army broke up the four 28-man bands at Haan. Brubeck was shipped to the infantry. He got into Normandy, France, about 90 days after D-Day and eventually was sent to the front, near Metz, as a rifle replacement. "It was just the worst possible place to be," Dave recalls, "because the Germans were really wiping them out."

At the last depot, Brubeck volunteered as a pianist during a Red Cross show, and because that was the moment when the area commandant had decided to have a band, he was selected to lead it. He missed going to the front by a matter of minutes.

After the German capitulation, Brubeck led his band accompanying USO tours throughout France and Germany. In 1946, he was discharged and went directly to Mills college in Oakland to study with Milhaud.

"I had taken a couple of lessons from Milhaud before I went into the army," he says, and one of his brothers was Milhaud's assistant at that time.

"When I went back to study under Milhaud, to be honest, I was going to give up jazz because of all the hassle I had had, even in the army, to get the musicians to play my stuff. And I recalled even Kenton thought I was too far out. So I figured jazz wouldn't be the place to present the ideas I wanted to. It was too narrow. So I thought composition would be the answer.

"It turned out that Milhaud was the one

who convinced me to go back, saying I couldn't possibly give up jazz, that it was in me and if I wanted to represent the culture, jazz was such an important part. He said it was more important to express the culture and not gain the technique. And he pointed out that every great composer had expressed his culture in which he was familiar and was completely familiar with the folk idiom and jazz was the folk idiom of America. He talked me back into it. It took a period of six months, I guess, and then I became interested in jazz again."

During the time he was at Mills, Brubeck also played in and around the San Francisco area.

When he was working at the Geary Cellar, a small club in the theater district, Desmond began to sit in regularly with him. Norman Bates was the bassist, Frances Lynne (later with Gene Krupa and Charlie Barnet) was the vocalist, and Darryl Cutler was the tenor, doubling on cocktail drums.

The Geary Cellar became the No. 1 spot for visiting musicians, Jack Egan, then an advance man for bands, wrote a piece about it for *Down Beat*, becoming the first to mention Brubeck in a national publication.

One night Benny Goodman dropped in.

"I'll never forget that night," Brubeck recalls. "I had been playing for about 10 minutes, and I wondered why Cutler didn't play. So I looked over at him—he used to play sock cymbal standing up with the tenor around his neck—and he was just looking at the sock cymbals. And I said, 'Play,' and he said, 'No, man, no!'

"So pretty quick I looked right in front of me, and there's Goodman! I quick turned away! Bobby Ross was always around there, and he says 'Whatsamatter with you, you seen a ghost?' And so I said, 'No, Goodman's sitting there, man,' and I tried to keep playing, and I was just panicked because here at last was Goodman. And Ross said, 'Aw what's the matter with you? Why should that make you nervous?' And I said, 'If you're not nervous get up and sing, because I *can't* play and Cutler *won't* play. So right away Bobby Ross comes running around the piano, and he starts singing 'Body and Soul,' and to this day he won't admit he left out two bars!"

Then in the spring of 1949, the Brubeck octet was presented in a concert at the Marines Memorial Theater in San Francisco by Ray Gorham.

The octet had been a rehearsal band all along and never actually a working unit until several years later when it played a series of Sunday afternoon sessions at the Black Hawk. At the Marines concert, disc jockey Jimmy Lyons heard the group and flipped.

The next morning he went in to the office of the KNBC program director and talked him into a new program, "The Lyons' Busy," to start that fall featuring Lyons and a trio led by Brubeck. It was the first live modern jazz show on radio in the West.

Brubeck, in addition to the Lyons' show, began teaching a course in jazz history at the University of California extension school. At this time also, his two articles on jazz appeared in *Down Beat*, reprinted from the Local 6 *Music News*. The fall of 1949 was very important for Brubeck. Not only did his trio start its first regular job— at the Burma lounge in Oakland, where they were to stay until April, 1950—but they also were heard regularly on KNBC and cut their first records, for trombonist Jack Sheedy's label, Coronet (later changed to Koronet).

Lyons arranged for the record date, and later when the Sheedy firm had difficulties, an arrangement was worked out which begat Fantasy. Sheedy had pressed his records at Circle Record Co., the only custom record-pressing plant in the area. Sol and Max Weiss, the proprietors, took over the Brubeck masters and started Fantasy with Brubeck as a partner in his own sides.

He never owned Fantasy nor was he involved in the recording of any other artists. In fact, the original plan was for Fantasy to record only Brubeck.

In August, 1950, the group made its first appearance outside of town—a date at Salt Lake City for disc jockey John Brophy— and then returned to the Black Hawk in San Francisco. All this time, Lyons on his nightly radio show was plugging Brubeck and the Fantasy records heavily. The KNBC signal is 50,000 watts, clear channel, and soon an audience for Brubeck rose throughout the West.

In the spring of 1951 Brubeck broke up the trio, which then included Jack Weeks and Cal Tjader. Dave's next step was to form a quartet with Paul Desmond, who, meanwhile, had been playing with Alvino Rey at the St. Francis hotel. This was the

group which, on its eastern tour later that year, was so successful.

By the beginning of 1954, the jazz boom had caught the attention of the major record companies. Brubeck was bombarded with offers to depart from Fantasy. One company offered as high as $5,000 an album, and another offered guarantees of concerts totaling $30,000. *The Jazz at Oberlin* and *Jazz at the College of the Pacific* Fantasy LPs had created a national stir in the record business, and everyone wanted in.

Brubeck signed with Columbia, and his first two LPs for that label, *Jazz Goes to College* and *Brubeck at Storyville*, were hits. Then came the *Time* magazine cover and his coast-to-coast tour with Gerry Mulligan, Stan Getz, and Duke Ellington.

But before the days of plenty, there were days of famine during which the group played for scale and the Brubeck family traveled on the road with him, living in trailer courts and furnished rooms. Later, when the money came, there were compensations, but it was still a grind, sometimes with jumps of 1,000 miles a night on the college tours.

Is Brubeck surprised that he has made it so big? He replies:

"I remember telling my wife when we were discussing how I would make a living at jazz in 1946, that I could be one of the outstanding pianists in the country if I were in New York or some place where I could be heard. That's how I felt."

On the other hand, Dave now says, "For years I thought only in terms of wishing I could get a job for scale. And if I had it all to do over again, that's all I'd want. I can truthfully say that.

"The tremendous strain I had to put my wife and family and myself and the kids under to arrive where I am, it's too much. I think that anybody who arrives in jazz has to have more courage per unit of success than in any other profession.

"I would prefer to be a part of one community, accepted, and with a job in a joint and not have to put the emotional strain on myself and my family that this has taken. I would prefer not the feast or the famine, but to be an average part of society." ●

AARON COPLAND

THE WELL-KNOWN AMERICAN COMPOSER FINDS VIRTUES AND FLAWS IN JAZZ

By Don Gold

MAY 1, 1958

What does jazz mean to you?"
Aaron Copland smiled, paused, and replied:

"It means several things....A whole period in my career when it seemed to be an exciting source material for serious music. And today, the more progressive versions always seem very tempting to me. I'd like to take a month off and hear the latest manifestations.

"The phase that interests me most is the marriage—the fact that the young jazzmen are composers, often bridging the gap between fields. And they have the same trouble getting a big audience we have.

"I think of jazz as a special area of music, with great attractiveness, but with serious limitations. Dixieland, when it's good, seems to me to be quite complete within its sphere. One can be fascinated by the contrapuntal relationships, relationships an academic musician wouldn't think of."

The 52-year-old, Brooklyn-born composer has been a vital part of the development of American music since his first compositions were presented in 1924. In co-operation with Roger Sessions, he organized the Copland-Sessions concerts, to present American music, during the years 1928-to-1931. He was the first director of the American Festival of Contemporary Music at Yaddo in Saratoga Springs, N.Y. In 1941 and 1947, he toured Latin America, as pianist, conductor, and lecturer, in concerts of American music. He has taught, lectured, presented concerts, performed, directed, composed, and written books on music.

His work has been influenced by American life and it reflects his concern for native music, from his ballets: *Billy the Kid*, *Rodeo*, and *Appalachian Spring*, to his clarinet concerto, commissioned by Benny Goodman, to his full-length opera, *The Tender Land*.

For many years he has watched the development of jazz in America. He is particularly concerned with contemporary jazz. Recently, he visited Northwestern University to conduct a performance of *The Tender Land*, among other assignments. He discussed jazz in a faculty member's office.

"Progressive jazz has been freed of harmonic limitations," he said. "Now its main trouble is a lack of unity in expressive content, by failing to drive home a unified idea. Progressive jazz composers don't always know, expressively, what they're trying to do. They seem to be distracted by amusing things along the way.

"The commercial aspect may influence this but shouldn't if it is thought of as a work of art.

"I heard Charlie Mingus' piece at Brandeis—he builds up a sense of excitement and freedom. I found it difficult to differentiate between the writing and improvised portions of his work. He was incredible. Another of my favorites is Tristano, who knows how to unify a piece. He sticks to the point without being dull.

"Erudition in jazz often has a phony sound," he noted. "Often, the ones who sound off are pretentious, as if they have to make something of jazz with fancy explanations."

Copland said he feels that America has produced its own music and that jazz will play a role in the continued development of that music.

"I think there is a type of American music," he said. "All good music written here doesn't fit into that type, however. There is a robust, straightforward music, with much counterpoint and long lines, that is American.

"I don't think jazz will be a direct influence on composers from the other side of the fence. Now, however, there will be an interest in jazz, instead of an unconscious borrowing from it. Composers, I hope, will grow up with jazz and use it."

Copland noted that he had been influenced by jazz in his own works and explained:

" A movement called "Dance," in *Music for the Theater*, written in 1925....I was thinking very much about the use of jazz. It was an attempt to make jazz even more exciting. The "Dance" movement is in 5/8 time, so it wasn't a literal use.

"In 1926, when I wrote the piano

concerto, there was a conscious attempt to whip it up. I was listening to jazz in those years. Oddly, I had heard jazz in Europe during my student days and had Milhaud's *Creation of the World* in mind. I had written a few short pieces as a 17-year-old in Brooklyn, but I could never play jazz. I didn't have the capabilities."

In 1948 he wrote *Four Piano Blues* and the concerto for Goodman.

"The *Blues* is more of a blues mood," he noted. "It's not a blues in structure but in quality. Writing the concerto for Goodman naturally made me think of jazz; the second part of it is part jazz-influenced and part Latin-American."

Copland next considered the plight of the jazz composer, and said.

"I don't think these men are stuck with their side as I am with mine. They don't have to contribute to contemporary classical music. The two fields will continue to borrow and perhaps eventually will overlap. But I don't feel that there ever will be one form.

"However, if I were giving a course in composition regularly, I'd always bring to my students happenings in the jazz field— for the freedom of invention present. The difficulty, of course, is that jazz often slips. An entire day of listening to jazz might be depressing. There's something limited about it. I know it has more than the two moods I attributed to it in 1926, but there's something about it that makes it difficult to live with exclusively."

Copland noted that jazz can be employed effectively by the contemporary classical composer, and said that it doesn't mean necessarily using the 12-bar blues form, "but then some composers might do this. I can hear myself reflecting the moods of jazz. Oddly enough, the closer the jazzmen come to our field, the less we can get from them. The wildness of jazz attracts me—the mood stuff and the colorful stuff. The let-loose quality is rarely found in 'serious' music."

Certain jazzmen create with definite appeal, Copland emphasized, and added that his knowledge isn't wide in this subject but that some such musicians had crossed his path.

"Tristano was the first," he said. "I like his sense of harmonic freedom and his ability to write a piece on one expressive thing without being dull. It seems like real composition to me, not happenstance.

"I like what I've heard of Teo Macero's, too. He's one who, once in a while, must reduce his tone to make it salable. I thought his "Fusion" was lots of fun. He has a keen sense of sound and sound combinations.

"Actually, the jazz field is full of arrangers posing as composers."

But getting back to individuals, Jimmy Giuffre has things every once in a while that are "very striking," according to Copland. And Duke Ellington is "an old admiration of mine. The originality of his work! There's something to think about. He has a real personality.

"I like some of Shelly Manne's work, too," he added....."In a way, I realize that Louis Armstrong's work is terrific, but I don't miss it....George Russell's material is fine, but a little on the arranger's side....My complete knowledge of Charlie Mingus is confined to his work at Brandeis. After I heard it, I felt it would be worthwhile to go out and buy his records.

"Stan Kenton, for orchestral excitement, appealed to me in the old days.

"And there's nothing in 'serious' music quite like the down-in-the-mouth aspect of the cool jazz and that guy Davis."

Copland recalled a final anecdote:

"I once took Serge Koussevitzky to 52nd St. to hear jazz. He listened carefully, then said, 'It's just like the gypsies; it's just like the gypsies.' And it is. Like the wild, impassioned, improvised music of the Russian gypsy." ●

'TRANE ON THE TRACK

By Ira Gitler
OCTOBER 16, 1958

Asked about being termed an "angry young tenor" in this publication's coverage of the 1958 Newport Jazz festival, John Coltrane said, "If it is interpreted as angry, it is taken wrong. The only one I'm angry at is myself when I don't make what I'm trying to play."

The 32-year-old native of Hamlet, N.C., has had his melancholy moments, but he feels that they belong to a disjointed, frustrating past. The crucial point in his development came after he joined Dizzy Gillespie's band in 1951.

Prior to that, he had studied music and worked in Philadelphia, assuming many of the fashionable nuances of the Charlie Parker-directed groups. When the offer to join the Gillespie band came, Coltrane felt ready.

The feeling turned out to be illusory.

"What I didn't know with Diz was that what I had to do was really express myself," Coltrane remembered. "I was playing cliches and trying to learn tunes that were hip, so I could play with the guys who played them.

"Earlier, when I had first heard Bird, I wanted to be identified with him...to be consumed by him. But underneath I really wanted to be myself.

"You can only play so much of another man."

Dejected and dissatisfied with his own efforts, Coltrane left Gillespie and returned to Philadelphia in search of a musical ideal and the accompanying integrity. Temporarily, he attempted to find escape in work.

"I just took gigs," he said. "You didn't have to play anything. The less you played, the better it was."

Plagued by economic difficulties, he searched for a steady job. In 1952, he found one, with a group led by Earl Bostic, whom he admires as a saxophonist even though he disliked the rhythm-and-blues realm the band dwelt in. But this job did not demolish the disillusion and lethargy that had captured him.

"Any time you play your horn, it helps you," he said. "If you get down, you can help yourself even in a rock 'n' roll band. But I didn't help myself."

A more productive step was made in 1953, when Coltrane joined a group headed by Johnny Hodges.

"We played honest music in this band," he recalled. "It was my education to the older generation."

Gradually, Coltrane rationalized the desire to work regularly with the aim of creating forcefully. In 1955, he returned to Philadelphia and, working with a group led by conga drummer Bill Carney, took a stride toward achieving his goal. As he recalled. "We were too musical for certain rooms."

In late 1955, Miles Davis beckoned. Davis had noted Coltrane's playing and wanted him in a new quintet he was forming. He encouraged Coltrane; this encouragement gradually opened adventurous paths for Coltrane. Other musicians and listeners began to pay close attention to him. When Davis disbanded in 1957, Coltrane joined Thelonious Monk's quartet.

Coltrane will not forget the role Davis and Monk played in assisting his development.

"Miles and Monk are my two musicians," he said. "Miles is the No. I influence over most of the modern musicians now. There isn't much harmonic ground he hasn't broken. Just listening to the beauty of his playing opens up doors. By the time I run up on something, I find Miles or Monk has done it already.

"Some things I learn directly from them. Miles has shown me possibilities in choosing substitutions within a chord and also new progressions."

Enveloped in the productive atmosphere of both the Davis and Monk groups, Coltrane emerged more an individualist than ever before. In early '58, he rejoined Davis. In the months since he did so, he has become more of an influence on other jazz instrumentalists. His recordings, on Prestige, Blue Note, and with Davis on Columbia, often are matters for passionate debate.

Yet, there is no denying his influence. There are traces of his playing in that of Junior Cook, with Horace Silver's group, and in Benny Golson, previously a Don Byas-Lucky-Thompson-out-of-Hawkins tenor man.

Coltrane's teammate in the Davis sextet, Cannonball Adderley, recently said, "Coltrane and Sonny Rollins are introducing us to some new music, each in his own way. I think Monk's acceptance, after all this time, is giving musicians courage to keep playing their original ideas, come what may."

When the jazz audience first heard Coltrane, with Davis in 1955 and '56, he was less an individualist. His style derived from those of Dexter Gordon (vintage mid forties), Sonny Stitt, Sonny Rollins (the Rollins of that time and slightly before). Stan Getz (certain facets of sound), and an essence of generalized Charlie Parker.

R. Howard

As he learned harmonically from Davis and Monk, and developed his mechanical skills, a new more confident Coltrane emerged. He has used long lines and multinoted figures within these lines, but in 1958 he started playing sections that might be termed "sheets of sound."

When these efforts are successful, they have a cumulative emotional impact, a residual harmonic effect. When they fail, they sound like nothing more than elliptically phrased scales.

This approach, basic to Coltrane's playing today, is not the result of a conscious effort to produce something "new." He has noted that it has developed spontaneously.

"Now it is not a thing of beauty, and the only way it would be justified is if it becomes that," he said. "If I can't work it through, I will drop it."

Although he is satisfied with the progress he's made during the last three years, Coltrane continues to be critical of his own work. Dejection is no longer a major part of this self-criticism. Now, he seeks to improve, knowing he can do so.

"I have more work to do on my tone and articulation," he said. "I must study more general technique and smooth out some harmonic kinks. Sometimes, while playing, I discover two ideas, and instead of working on one, I work on two simultaneously and lose the continuity."

Assured that the vast frustration he felt in the early fifties is gone, Coltrane attempts to behave in terms of a broad code, which he outlined:

"Keep listening. Never become so self-important that you can't listen to other players. Live cleanly....Do right....You can improve as a player by improving as a person. It's a duty we owe to ourselves."

A married man, with an eight-year-old daughter, Coltrane hopes to meet the responsibilities of his music and his life without bitterness, for "music is the means of expression with strong emotional content. Jazz used to be happy and joyous. I'd like to play happy and joyous." ●

MORE MAN THAN MYTH, MONK HAS EMERGED FROM THE SHADOWS

By Frank London Brown

OCTOBER 30, 1958

Thelonious Sphere Monk finally has been discovered.

For years a mystery man of modern jazz, Monk now has emerged from a six-year involuntary absence from New York's night-club circuit to win first place in the *Down Beat* Critics' Poll, surpassing such men as Duke Ellington, Erroll Garner, Oscar Peterson, Dave Brubeck. In the year since his return to the jazz clubs, Monk has received rave reviews in *The New York Times* for his Randalls Island jazz festival appearance, offers to compose for French films, and notice in magazines that customarily ignore jazz.

How did this taciturn creator of far-out music get that way? What made him different? What has he done in music that others haven't?

Mrs. Nellie Monk, his articulate wife, said about his complex personality:

"Thelonious was never like ordinary people, not even as a child. He always knew who he was. Sometimes when he plays the blues, he goes way back to the real old-time pianists, like Jelly-Roll Morton and James P. Johnson. I'm always amazed, because I know he hasn't spent a lot of time listening to these pianists—yet it's there in his music.

"He has smaller hands than most pianists, so he had to develop a different style of playing to fully express himself."

Bobby Barnes, a singer, and Baron Bennerson, a bartender, leaned on the bar in New York City's Green Gables, one of the two W. 62nd St. bars that Monk occasionally goes to. They spoke of him, mingling awe with admiration.

"Monk's mother always catered to him," Bennerson said. "He was the first guy in the neighborhood to wear peg pants. We all laughed at him then. But he said, 'You guys'll soon be wearing them yourselves!' Right after that, pegs became *the thing*. We looked up to Monk from then on."

Bennerson remembered another anecdote:

"Monk has a '56 Buick Special. Not long ago I bought a '56 Buick Roadmaster. When Monk saw my car, he tried to tell me that his Buick Special was a better car than my Roadmaster. In fact, he said that *his* car is the best in the *world*! He *thinks* that way."

Harry Colomby, Monk's youthful, schoolteacher manager, offered what perhaps constitutes the most reverent description of this almost legendary figure:

"Sometimes I feel like I'm breaking into his world. He never engages in any kind of conversation he doesn't like.... He disconnects sometimes—then all of a sudden he comes up with a statement that is so profound it scares you.

"He's always been like that. Monk has the kind of personal freedom that very few people have. He can keep his inner self apart from outside influences. I once spent the night at his house, and when I woke up, I saw Monk at the piano composing while the radio on the top of the piano was blasting away, playing hillbilly music."

Lawrence Shustak

To say that Monk is doggedly individual becomes something of an understatement when one considers the whole man. He is singular in the strict sense of the word.

One phase of the interview for this story took place while Monk was in bed. It was 4:30 p.m. "Often Monk doesn't go right to bed after coming home from work," Mrs. Monk explained. "He talks, writes or sometimes just lies in the bed without closing his eyes. Sometimes it's daylight before he goes to sleep."

He is a tall, rugged-appearing man, a 200-pounder, and "when he walks into a room, he dominates it," according to Colomby. "The force of Monk's personality intimidates you." The manager cited an incident that occurred on the set of the "Stars of Jazz" television show.

"Monk was supposed to play a number on the show—one-two-three, like that, no more," Colomby said. "But while Monk was doodling around with the piano during a coffee break, the stagehands, cameramen, and everybody who could hear him, wandered over to the piano. Then in came Count Basie and Billie Holiday, and Lester Young—all the stars! They gathered around the piano and stared as though they'd been hypnotized, as though it was the first time they'd ever heard anything like that.

"The director was so impressed by the expressions on their faces that he had Billie and Count and the rest of them stand at the piano when the show went on the air, just so he could televise their reactions while Monk played."

Monk himself said of his power of concentration, "I've even composed while sitting in my son's wagon in front of the house."

Monk Jr.'s red wagon figured in a dispute Monk Sr. had with Riverside Records, his current recording company, over the cover of the *Monk's Music* album.

"They wanted me to pose in a monk's habit, on a pulpit, holding a glass of whiskey," the pianist said. "I told them no."

Then with a wry smile, Monk added, "Monks don't even stand in pulpits.

"Then they wanted to dress me in evening clothes, white tie and all. I told them I would pose in a wagon, because I have actually composed while sitting in my kid's wagon on the front sidewalk."

And that is the way it was.

Monk is clothes conscious, for all his indifference to the usual worldly affairs. Nellie Monk, referring to her husband's clothes at a time when work was scarce and money scarcer, said, "He was always neat, no matter how hard times got."

Then she elaborated:

"Monk is a proud man. He doesn't suffer on the surface. He never let people know how bad off he was, even when he couldn't find work. Not even when he was sick in the hospital. He's like a rock. I think that's why people admire him. He proves that one can keep his integrity under the worst circumstances. It's interesting that some of the letters Monk gets thank him for just being himself. He couldn't be any other way."

Monk's integrity has led him into a lot of trouble, according to his manager.

"Monk lost his work permit for six years," Colomby said, "because he refused to inform on a friend. He couldn't work in any New York club. Yet he wouldn't tell, and he wouldn't leave New York. 'This is my city,' Monk would say. This was a low point in Monk's life. He had an unfavorable contract with another recording company. They didn't push his records, and he got very little money for his work. His only work consisted of a concert now and then, a little from records, and an occasional out-of-town job.

"He could have got more out-of-town work except for the fact that he wouldn't work under scale. He would say, 'If I do, those guys will get used to it and want to make the other musicians work cheap, too.'

"Monk is always aware of the problems of other musicians. He used to promote concerts himself. Sometimes he'd let his two children sit on the stage while he played.

"A lot of Monk's troubles arise from the fact that he has a sharp business eye. He hates matinees, calls that an extra day. He has an uncanny ability to tell how much a club is making. Booking agencies didn't like this about him, and so a lot of strange rumors about Monk's undependability began to come out of nowhere and scare off the club owners. No one has a greater sense of business responsibility than Monk."

Monk received his New York City police work permit only a year ago, and things have been happening nonstop ever since. He not only has kept pace in his field but also has continued to contribute new concepts upon which many established musicians rely.

Monk's secret is that he has pushed ahead in the study of musical problems which have not yet been thoroughly investigated. In making a study of specific concrete musical problems, Monk has been able to rely upon his own findings and not on the general truths that attract and satisfy the large majority of today's modern jazz musicians. Monk said of his technique:

"Everything I play is different. Different melody, different harmony, different structure. Each piece is different from the other one. I have a standard, and when the song tells a story, when it gets a certain *sound*, then it's thorough…completed."

Monk's playing ability frequently has been a matter for discussion, particularly since his Critics Poll designation as the No. 1 jazz pianist.

Seldom does one hear the flashy, long, single-line runs that characterize so many refugees from Bach, Bud Powell, and Art Tatum. The avoidance of this technique, more than anything else, has offended the tradition-conditioned ears of today's modern-jazz listeners.

Monk *can* make these runs. I recently heard him do it at the Five Spot. He did it so adeptly that he stopped all conversation for the rest of the set.

The controversial father of an 8-year-old boy and a 4-year-old girl continues to live in the rear apartment of an old tenement building on E. 63rd St., surrounded by housing projects and warehouses.

Monk's tan, polished baby grand piano stands like a throne in the same room in which there is also the kitchen sink, an icebox, and a small kitchen table. The living room and bedroom are not much larger than a good-sized closet.

That this cramped space is orderly and attractive is a tribute to Mrs. Monk. Several pieces of new furniture indicate the slowly changing fortunes of the Monk family.

But there is another reason: The old furniture, including Monk's piano and some of his uncopyrighted music, was destroyed by a fire that burned out the apartment. Everything went—clothes, letters, precious clippings. Mrs. Monk had removed most of her husband's music to the one shelf in the house that escaped the flames.

Part of the resentment some modern-jazz musicians feel toward Monk may stem from the fear of inevitable public recognition of Monk as the procreator of musical advances for which they have received credit. The contributions of Monk now are being recognized as the sources they are. And they fast are becoming the mainstream of modern jazz. Listen to Monk's influence in the work of Mal Waldron, Horace Silver, Cecil Taylor, Randy Weston, Kenny Drew, Martial Solal, Dave Brubeck. Even Duke Ellington pays his tribute to Thelonious in his introductory solo in the *Ellington at Newport* recording.

One interview or 10 cannot shatter the protective wall Thelonious Monk has built around himself. His answers to questions are guarded, cryptic, and even defensive, yet they are honest, intelligent responses when it is considered that he has been cuffed about a good deal and that much of this has resulted only because he will be different.

"I want to achieve happiness in life, in music—the same thing," he said. "My influences? I am influenced by everything and everybody. There used to be a time when I would go around joints where there would be just piano players and you played piano by yourself, no rhythm section....A lot of piano players would be playing. You know people have tried to put me off as being crazy. Sometimes it's to your advantage for people to think you're crazy. A person should do the thing he likes best, the way it pleases him."

When asked where he thinks modern jazz is going, he replied (to the exasperation of his wife):

"I don't know where it's going. Maybe it's going to hell. You can't make anything go anywhere; it just happens."

At this point, Mrs. Monk, slightly piqued by Monk's reticence, exclaimed, "You must know how you feel. Are you satisfied with where it's going? Is it going on the right direction?"

Monk glanced at the foot of the bed, where she sat, and said, "I don't know where it's going. Where is it going?"

Mrs. Monk, not to be defeated, countered, "Do you think anything can be done to educate the coming generation? So that they know quality when they hear it, so that they have discriminating taste? Are they listening to the right sounds except for yourself? Are you satisfied with what you are presenting to the public?"

Monk answered, "Are they doing something about it? I don't know how people are listening."

By this time, Monk appeared to be undergoing a third degree in a precinct back room. The microphone of a tape recorder sat on his night stand. I sat in a chair near the night stand, his niece and wife sat on the edge of the bed, and Monk lay propped on a pillow, his chest rising and falling rapidly, perspiration ridging his brow. But his hands were calm, twisting his goatee.

Monk's niece tried to amplify the question:

"Do you think the people are being educated properly?"

"Well, they've got schools," he said.

His niece, an impertinent teenager, snapped:

"Unk, are they learning anything in the schools?"

Smiling, he replied:

"I haven't been in the schools."

At the outset, his wife had told Monk, "Thelonious, you can open your mouth when you speak."

He had answered, "I talk so plain a deaf and dumb man can hear me."

Nellie then had settled down to a nice, relaxed interview.

"Why don't you do some of those *corny* jokes down at the Five Spot like you did in Philadelphia?" she asked her husband.

Then to me, she said, "He would make remarks that were so timely that you would have to laugh. He doesn't even have a mike at the Five-Spot because he wants to keep the singers away."

Here Monk protested.

"That's [the mike's absence] because the horn would be playing into the mike," he said. "It would be too loud."

Mrs. Monk added, "Most of the people have never seen that [joking] side of him. He won't do it down there. Like last year he did a dance…during the solos."

Monk's comments on various subjects are always revealing:

"My music is not a social comment on discrimination or poverty or the like. I would have written the same way even if I had not been a Negro."

(Manager Colomby said, "Monk once told me that, 'when I was a kid, some of the guys would try to get me to hate white people for what they've been doing to Negroes, and for a while I tried real hard. But every time I got to hating them, some white guy would come along and mess the whole thing up.'")

Monk is definitely aware of the racial conflicts throughout the world, but even this has not penetrated his world of music.

On the sudden prominence of Sonny Rollins, John Coltrane, Frank Foster,

Wilbur Ware, Johnny Griffin after each had become associated with him, the pianist said:

"I have noticed that with a lot of musicians."

Then, with a wry smile, "I don't know why it happens."

About the records he listens to:

"I listen to everything."

About a Charlie Parker-Dizzy Gillespie-Monk recording session:

"Just another session."

About a Miles Davis-Milt Jackson-Monk session:

"They're all just sessions."

About how he met his wife?

"Mental telepathy."

Mrs. Monk confirmed this, explaining, "I was playing in a playground, and we had heard about each other. One day he passed the playground, and our eyes met, and I knew him, and he knew me. We didn't speak then, and we didn't actually meet until six months later. Years later he could tell me what I wore that day."

The world now seems to be "ready" for Thelonious Sphere Monk.

"Why are people afraid of me?" he asked. "I've been robbed three times; they must not be afraid of me."

He has been through disappointments, malicious rumors, exile, sickness, and a destructive fire.

Now, his bandwagon seems to be rolling. The onetime skeptics are hopping on.

Monk has withstood failure. Now the question is: Can he withstand success? ●

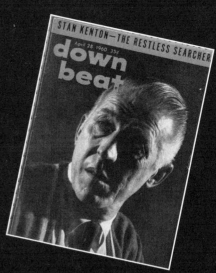

THE 1960s

INTRODUCTION

By John Ephland ···

It was impossible to think of jazz in the sixties and not think of *Down Beat*. Despite the fact that *Down Beat* was and is "just" a magazine, what set it apart from others were the same elements that set *Sports Illustrated* apart: when you weren't playing or listening to the music (or at the ball park playing or watching), reading about it was the next best thing to being there.

Both magazines had a profound influence on my early years as a reader. (In fact, *Down Beat* was the first magazine I ever took out a subscription to.) No wonder—both asserted their influence on a generation of school kids growing up on the new technologies of radio, television, and audio equipment, not to mention our greater access to music instruction and organized sports.

I can still remember summer afternoons reading both *DB* and *SI* cover to cover on my folks' back porch, ads included.

My introduction to *Down Beat* came via a local music retail store where my dad would buy sheet music for the piano that was such an important part of his life. Attracted to his love of music, specifically jazz, I found myself joining him on his occasional trip to Northwest Music in the Chicago suburb of Park Ridge. It was there that I also was exposed—big-time—to musical instruments: pianos, horns, guitars, and, especially, drums. I eventually experienced the urge to play and take lessons (in that order). In a way, it was like that scene in *Easter Parade*, where Fred Astaire goes wild in a toy/music shop. Accompanied by a little boy, Fred dances, sings, and especially plays the various drums and cymbals strewn throughout the store, all to the notes and rhythms of Irving Berlin's "Drum Crazy."

But back to *Down Beat*. The music store had *DB* in a prominent location. The way musicians were illustrated on the cover served as bait for further exploration (not unlike baseball cards). To me, *Down Beat* represented a calling card to another cultural universe separate from the often sterile one I usually inhabited. After all,

what did Stan Getz, Louie Bellson, and Cannonball Adderley have to do with fire drills, Ed Sullivan, and manicured lawns? Even Elvis, the heartthrob of both of my older sisters, seemed somehow square, unhip, cartoonish by comparison. *Down Beat* had 'em all covered, including Elvis.

It wasn't like I wanted to *not* fit in, with jazz somehow being this music of escape and rebellion—after all, my *parents* liked it. No, it just turned out that way. Enjoying jazz wasn't your typical adolescent type of activity. That's unless the music was something like Vince Guaraldi's "Cast Your Fate to the Wind" (a hit on the AM radio pop charts) or, later on, Ramsey Lewis' "The In Crowd" (another AM hit). Otherwise, listening to records, gradually listening and playing along (my parents made it possible for me to play my drums in the basement), or actually going to see and hear the music live—sometimes getting to meet musicians in the process—was a solo or parent/son activity, mostly devoid of peer accompaniment.

All along the way, *DB* was bearing witness to the ongoing changing climate in jazz, with the occasional nod to blues music, classical, and other forms. Somehow, *DB*'s wider palette for music made the magazine seem more trustworthy, as if the Gospel of Jazz wasn't the only game in town, and that, maybe, jazz had something to do with other musics. So it wasn't like going to church and taking this music called jazz any more seriously than it already was. After all, the perception of jazz on the part of my friends was of this "serious" music you couldn't understand. Like the line in the sixties pop song "Rock & Roll Music": "I got no kicks against modern jazz/Unless they try and play it too darn fast/It starts to lose the beauty of the melody/And starts soundin' like a symphony!" Taking the eclectic approach, I found *DB* honest as well as informative and enjoyable. No genuflects to "Chinese music," thank you.

I guess you could say reading *DB* felt

like checking in on a community of lovers, a community of searchers where the script was sincere and damn well-written. I mean, I was reading Martin Williams, Don DeMicheal, and Nat Hentoff all while I was learning my math tables and digging monsters like Frankenstein, the Werewolf, and Dracula. Come to think of it, my "self-education" in the English language came mostly from reading *DB*! It was here, spurred on by great and entertaining writing, filled with interesting ideas and notions that didn't exist anywhere else (certainly not in school!), that I came to appreciate the written word and the power behind it. What better way to learn a language than through subject matter that draws you in, that takes you for a ride down roads you didn't know existed. For example, *DB*'s 1963 coverage of racial prejudice in jazz (e.g., a cover story, "The Need for Racial Unity in Jazz"—April 11, 1963) was an eye-opener for someone growing up in a relatively sheltered environment. Sure, it wasn't an essay or conventional interview with a writer's perspective. Instead, what I got was a variety of perspectives from not only writers but musicians, too.

Which gets back to this notion of community I've been speaking of. For me, jazz wasn't so much about being cool or countercultural as it was about sharing. And *DB* faithfully shared on a bi-weekly basis. The people chronicled in the interviews, news stories, record, book, and concert reviews were real people; people whose lives were taken seriously without being morose about it. It wasn't tabloid/exposé journalism, but stories and reports on people who were *DB*'s lifeblood. The stories about Miles Davis and his run-ins with the law; an appreciation of legends like Charlie Parker and Bud Powell, who lived tragic yet triumphant lives; the occasional story on an expatriate like Dexter Gordon or Johnny Griffin—all these were items (and people) that helped form my childhood. Ultimately, *DB* was about putting a face on the music, bringing people to life, acknowledging and celebrating that music is made by real people. For me, this was a radical concept, light years beyond *Teen Beat*.

But *DB* was even more. It introduced me to people who I might never have heard of. As I got older, I started to pay attention to the club listings, looking for musicians I read about and wanted to see, sometimes dragging my mom and dad along (it felt like that, anyway). Maybe I would've been interested without reading about him in *DB*, but I still credit the magazine with helping me make the connection with Ed Thigpen at the London House when he was drumming with Oscar Peterson and Ray Brown. Having read about him, I also had the courage to seek him out between sets at a particular engagement. (Even though he doesn't remember, I'll never forget him giving me a broken drumstick from the previous set.) There were others that *DB* helped fill out the picture on: seeing and hearing Ella and Duke live, with the Oscar Peterson Trio as a part of Norman Granz's Jazz at the Philharmonic in Chicago's Opera House; or Chick Corea with Stan Getz before Corea joined Miles—*DB* complemented their musical lives in ways that helped me maintain the sweetness of these greats. The music I'd heard them talk about in interviews, the records my parents bought that were reviewed in the magazine, and concerts I'd read about that were part of the same tours—I can't imagine having experienced jazz as a kid any other way. It was like the program to a concert, but with much more, since the copy wasn't promotional and the opinions of readers (in the "Chords & Discords" column), musicians, and critics were lively and sometimes controversial. The rough, wild side of Stan Getz, for example, was only hinted at in a Blindfold Test (Feb. 27, 1964), as he zinged the first batch of tunes played to him by Leonard Feather. My first encounter with Getz a few years later filled out the picture, showing me he could be a real bastard. My parents and I had front-row seats to see his group at the London House one night. During one of Getz's choruses, he accidentally knocked his sheet music off his stand. My dad simply had to reach over to pick it up and held it up for Stan to "read." What looked like a favor to

us was received as an insult by the sweet-sounding tenor of all those bossa nova hits as he grabbed the music from my dad with a sneer.

On the lighter side, there were the cartoons of Jules Feiffer, the much-anticipated poll issues and instrument-featured issues (especially drums and percussion!), and even the ads were groovy as they illustrated musicians playing or posing with their instruments in color or black and white. Along with record companies and the names of musicians, I learned the names of manufacturers—years before I saw Ludwig on Ringo Starr's bass drum or Gretsch on Charlie Watts'. And, as mentioned above, the Blindfold Test, still the most popular column in the magazine, was a gas. I mean, where else in music journalism could you find musicians in a game-like situation as they tried to figure out who was playing what and read some pretty wild commentary in the process? Then there were significant sixties entries on people like Henry Mancini, Louis Jordan, Frank Zappa and The Mothers of Invention, and Howlin' Wolf—damn straight! If a magazine could do them in the context of jazz, they definitely were the next best thing to being there. And, before I forget, those delicious record reviews were my guide when it came to picking which albums to buy. But the reviews themselves, apart from providing consumer information, were many times a work of art, if not worth a laugh or two. For example, here are some excerpts—from Martin Williams' review of Robert Johnson's *King of the Delta Blues Singers* (May 24, 1962): "I might [also] say that his work is a stark lesson to anyone who thinks that jazz and its progenitors are 'fun' music or a kind of people's vaudeville"; Larry Kart's analysis of *Miles in the Sky* (October 3, 1968): "This record…shows the effect of the Coleman-Coltrane revolution even as Miles [Davis] denies it, for their assault on the popular song has pushed Miles along the only path that seems open to him, an increasingly ironic detachment from sentiment and prettiness"; Alan Heineman's no-star review of Chick Corea's *Now He Sings, Now He Sobs* (May 29, 1969): "Well. Quite clearly, I'm going mad"; the hilarious one-star review of Ornette Coleman's *This*

Is Our Music by Don DeMicheal (May 11, 1961): "I do not understand the babblings of my two-year-old daughter. Does this make those sounds profound? Hardly."

Free-jazz, via *DB* (pans notwithstanding), prepared me for the oftentimes tumultuous late-sixties music scene. As much as *DB* was about stage and marching bands, big bands, music education, the business of music, and maintaining the music's center of gravity, *DB* has also written about the changes in jazz—changes that many times were not welcome. When veteran scribe Nat Hentoff interviewed free-jazz pioneer Albert Ayler (with brother Donald) in the Nov. 11, 1966, issue, for me, it was like affirming Ayler's legitimacy as a player within the jazz tradition even as his playing drew livid responses from lovers of Louis and Duke. The wild music of rock 'n' roll that was entering its first flush of renewal in the wake of Elvis' fade was tame, if not lame, when heard next to Coltrane, Shepp, and Sun Ra.

The next best thing to being there, finally, and ultimately, was driven home by the fact that *DB* was letting the musicians literally speak for themselves with their own articles. A few influential examples from the sixties of this 60-year tradition must suffice: Steve Lacy's "The Land of Monk" (Oct. 10, 1963), Ornette Coleman's "To Whom It May Concern" (June 1, 1967), and Wayne Shorter on "Creativity and Change" (Dec. 12, 1968).

By decade's end, *Down Beat*, with Dan Morgenstern at the helm, was offering copies of Bob Dylan's five-star *Nashville Skyline* in its subscription offer. To some, this was blasphemy. To others, it reflected a magazine in touch with the world of music–the next best thing to being there. ●

JOHN EPHLAND began working for *Down Beat* as associate editor in 1987. He has served as managing editor since 1988. During his career, Ephland has served as an educator, editor, critic, feature writer, and part owner of a music retail shop.

ORNETTE: THE FIRST BEGINNING

In the recent fuss and furor over Ornette Coleman, a good many persons have been making hasty leaps for the tailgate of what might turn out to be a bandwagon. But as Ralph Gleason pointed out recently in the *San Francisco Chronicle*, Coleman, at the early stages of his career, had one lone champion among those who write on the subject of jazz: *Down Beat*'s West Coast editor, John Tynan.

Tynan was praising Coleman when the esotericists of jazz were ignoring him—if, in fact, they had ever even heard of him.

Recently, Tynan was asked to write his own account of Coleman's early days. By inclination and training, Tynan is opposed to personalized journalism. But at last he acceded, producing the following report. It is defective in that it underplays Tynan's own role as Coleman's first critical champion. But it is an oddly moving story, and it helps put Ornette Coleman in perspective as what, at base, he is: a human being.

By John Tynan
JULY 21, 1960

Few artists in recent years have provoked such a tempest of controversy as has 30-year-old alto saxophonist Ornette Coleman. In less than two brief years his highly individualistic playing has drawn from musicians and laymen cries ranging from "fraud…!" and "unbearable nonsense…" to "genius…" and "another Bird." From a hungry and virtually unemployable unknown, Coleman has become one of the most promising record "properties" in jazz and today need have few worries about working steadily with his group in clubs or at festivals.

To Coleman, this radical shift in economic status must seem rather ironic. The slim, reserved young Texan has never asked anything but opportunity to write and play his horn. This was denied him at open sessions; most musicians he sat in with in Los Angeles couldn't tolerate playing with him and often left the stand rather than do so.

Coleman followed a lonely course. He wrote and played at home because "most musicians didn't take to me; they said I didn't know the changes and was out of tune." Daytimes he held down a job as elevator operator in a Los Angeles department store where he would park on the 10th floor and study harmony. When the store introduced self-operating elevators, Ornette was out of a job.

Despite the economic bite, Coleman kept writing. By now he was beginning to attract a coterie from the ranks of the Young Turks on the Los Angeles jazz scene. Three who were among his earliest cohorts were trumpeter Don Cherry, bass player Don Payne, and a drummer still in his teens at the time, Billy Higgins. They felt they understood Ornette's aim; they felt a surge of almost overpowering emotional force in his expressionist blowing; they were wild about his writing. When they couldn't find a club to sit in with Coleman, they'd play in one of their homes.

Coleman was no longer ignored in his art, but to the jazz world at large he remained unknown and unsung. Whenever he tried auditioning for a clubowner he was dismissed in derision. Deaf to the beauty of his original writing, the club operators winced and howled for mercy when he played.

Howard Rumsey, bass playing leader of the jazz group at the well known Lighthouse cafe in Hermosa Beach, Calif., recalled the first time Coleman sat in there.

"He played here one Monday night when I wasn't working. The off night. The boss thought he was nuts!"

Reminiscing, Rumsey went on, "Everybody—the musicians, I mean—would panic when you'd mention Ornette. People would laugh when his name was brought up."

But if Coleman wasn't permitted personally to express himself for pay to audiences of cash customers, he had his missionaries. Possibly his chief evangelist was bassist Payne. In August, 1957, Payne,

Cherry, Higgins and Texas tenor man James Clay worked a fortnight at the Cellar in Vancouver, B.C. Much of the music they played during the engagement was written by Ornette.

When the group returned to Los Angeles, Payne called the *Down Beat* office one afternoon. He told me about the job in Vancouver and said, "Look, we made some tapes up there. I'd like you to hear them because I really think you'll dig the charts. Some of them are Ornette Coleman's and, John, they're just too much."

That, I believe, was the first time I had heard the name, Ornette Coleman.

Unable to resist Payne's enthusiasm, I drove up to his apartment of Hollywood's Beachwood Drive. What I heard that afternoon in 1957 convinced me that in Coleman jazz had birthed an important *writer*. I had yet to hear him play.

In *Down Beat*, Sept. 5, 1957, I termed the group that worked in Vancouver a "neo-bop quartet." I only bring this up to clarify an important point. While Coleman worked independently at first, forging his personal concept of jazz which today has emerged as possibly an important force, it would be a mistake to conclude he that was fountainhead of an avant garde movement. His mission was personal; he served his own bright muse. But the new, vital life-force stemming from the assertion by Negro musicians of their own musical-cultural birthright made it possible for Coleman's music to be appreciated by his fellows and for it to be recorded.

Perhaps the point is more clearly seen if put this way: "The "discovery" of Ornette Coleman had to await the demise of the tutti-frutti intellectualism of the "West Coast jazz" of the early 1950s. Coleman first arrived in Los Angeles—center of the new experimentation—in 1951. He didn't trek west from Fort Worth by choice: he was left there high and dry by Pee Wee Crayton's rhythm and blues outfit, which he had joined in his home town. Ruefully, Coleman has said, "He (Crayton) didn't understand what I was trying to do, and it got so he was paying me not to play."

Such was the hostility of most Los

Ornette Coleman and Don Cherry

Angeles musicians whenever Coleman showed up at a session, the altoist quickly got the message that sunny Southern Cal was giving him the freeze and returned to Fort Worth before the end of 1952. He wasn't to view the Pacific again for more than 18 months.

The jazz climate in Los Angeles at the time of Ornette's first trip west was such that general professional acceptance of his music was totally out of the question. He rejected the then prevalent slavish imitation of a living Charlie Parker though the root of his musical thought was buried in Bird; he was completely alien esthetically to the experiments of the white sophisticates.

By 1957, a virile new current was detectable in jazz on the West Coast. A new generation was reaching for a jazz mode of expression in which it could find fulfillment; most of the youngsters of this generation turned their faces east to the "hard boppers" and drew inspiration from Rollins, Coltrane, et al. Personifying the new stirring in the west were the young acolytes who turned to Coleman's music. Ornette was waiting for them.

New altoist Ornet Coleman may do an album (very, very avant garde) for Contemporary Records...."

I ran the item in *Down Beat*, Feb. 20, 1958, at the outset of a year that was to mark Coleman's breakthrough. Behind those 15 words and the misspelled first name hides a story as gratifying as any of the happier tales of jazz.

Bass players, like guitarists, are a breed prone to seek out one another, to compare notes on their craft and to play together. Here's an illustration: During one brief period in 1958 both the Modern Jazz Quartet and the Oscar Peterson Trio happened to be in Los Angeles at the same time. Ray Brown was staying at Hollywood's Knickerbocker hotel and before you could say *soundpost* Percy Heath, Leroy Vinnegar and Don Payne were jamming in Ray's room in one of the wildest bass sessions in history. It continued all afternoon and its spirit was caught on still film by singer Don Nelson. To the bass players there was nothing unusual about the get-together. It just figured.

When Don Payne found himself living near Red Mitchell that year in Hollywood it also figured they would see much of one another. Mitchell, a musician of incurable esthetic curiosity and apparently ceaseless development as an artist, was quite conversant with the new directions being sought by younger jazzmen. For a time, in fact, he led a short-lived quartet that featured James Clay's tenor sax and flute.

One day in Payne's apartment Mitchell heard a Coleman original. He was quite impressed and told Ornette, who was present together with Don Cherry, Billy Higgins and pianist Walter Norris, that he should take the music to Lester Koenig, owner of Contemporary Records. Ornette agreed.

Coleman's first visit to Contemporary is not without a touch of comedy.

"He came in alone one day when I was very busy," Koenig recalled. "I asked him to come back in a few days. When he returned the following Friday, he said he had some music he wanted to sell and mentioned Red Mitchell had suggested he come see me.

"I took him to the piano and asked him to play the tunes. Ornette then said he couldn't *play* the piano.

"Then I asked him, 'How did you hope to play your tunes for me if you can't play piano?'

"So he took out his plastic alto and began to play."

Koenig liked the tunes, but, said he, "I liked the way he played the alto, too."

He spoke to Coleman about recording and when Ornette told him he'd been playing with Cherry, Norris, Payne, and Higgins, Koenig arranged for the entire group to play an audition.

Payne remembers that audition. "Red Mitchell sat with Les through the whole thing," he said. "The group played a few charts of Ornette's and next thing we knew we had an album date."

Ironically, as Koenig noted, "Ornette had no intention of recording when he came to see me. He needed some money and came in to sell me some tunes."

Coleman recorded two LPs for Contemporary, *Something Else! The Music of Ornette Coleman* (C3551) and *Tomorrow is the Question* (M 3569) and after he moved to New York, switched to Atlantic Records, his present affiliation. Koenig was extremely sorry to lose him and makes no bones about it.

"We just couldn't support him here in Los Angeles," he said. "There was no place for the group to work and when Ornette and Don got the chance to go back east, they had to take it.

"When Ornette was going through a period of development and experiment here, we stood by him and gave him encouragement and money when he needed it. At least we helped all we could in that period."

I first heard Ornette play when Don Payne brought a test pressing of *Something Else!* to the *Down Beat* office. My first impression was one of complete shock. But I felt the power and experienced a curious sense of elation at the absolute lack of inhibition in his playing. Key words and phrases flitted through my head, rather than fully formed thoughts. "Vitality...furious passion...what was *that?*...the guy's crazy...where is he?...what the hell is he doing?...power...force...freedom."

After that baptism of Ornette's fire, I couldn't wait to hear him play in person.

One night Payne told me he was coming to sit in at an open session after hours in a beer-and-coffee joint called Terry Lester's Jazz Cellar. Coleman had been dropping in occasionally possibly because of the frequent presence of another sax man, Joe Maini, an unabashed admirer of Ornette.

As Payne and I sat at a table by the wall, Ornette joined the four or five other musicians on the section of floor space that constituted the "bandstand." He held his fire until other horn men had had their way, then he blasted loose with the fiercest, weirdest, most abandoned utterance I had heard in more than 15 years of listening to jazz. It was almost literally stunning. As Maini beamed a satanic approval, Coleman carried, through chorus after chorus of the tune being played, a message so intensely personal and emotionally raw as to be rather frightening. Here was naked emotional power, all right; here was something that defied clinical analysis. Here was an originality never before experienced in jazz.

Apparently others felt as I. Payne invited Percy Heath and Connie Kay to the after hours session at the Cellar. They came, heard Coleman, and a few nights later brought John Lewis to hear him, too.

Lewis' excitement over Coleman resolved into determination to help the bearded revolutionist whose humble and completely unassuming manner was at such variance with his alto playing. The leader of the MJQ arranged for Coleman and Cherry to attend the annual School of Jazz at Lenox, Mass., that summer. That was the second beginning.

In the fall of 1958 I urged Jimmy Lyons, general manager of the Monterey Jazz festival, to get Coleman and Cherry on the program. It was too late; Lyons had already filled the bill. The following year, however, they made it. Critical reaction to their performance may be found in the journals.

Since the beginning of this "Ornette Coleman controversy" I have bowed to its predictability but have been rather bored by it. And I'm sure Coleman by now must be bored stiff with all the hullabaloo. Ornette is heart and soul an artist following the star of his own musical and esthetic convictions. Let him just put pen to paper. Let him blow his little plastic saxophone. ●

BILL EVANS

By Don Nelson
SEPTEMBER 1, 1960

It may distress believers in the jazzman legend, but the truth is that Bill Evans has become one of the most creative modern jazz musicians without benefit of a miserable childhood. With candor, he said:

"I was very happy and secure until I went into the army. Then I started to feel there was something I should know that I didn't know."

If the 31-year-old pianist upsets a few cherished illusions about the origins of jazz musicians, he demolishes another held by many jazzmen themselves and fondly nurtured by the hippy fringe: that a jazzman must be interested only in jazz.

Evans is no such intellectual provincial. For one thing, he does not believe that jazz—or even music as a whole—necessarily holds the key to the "something" he began searching for in the army. His basic attitude is that music is not the end most jazzmen make it. It is only a means.

A glance into Evans' library provides an indication of what his mind is up to. The diversity of titles shows how many avenues he has explored to reach his "something"—Freud, Whitehead, Voltaire, Margaret Meade, Santayana, and Mohammed are here, and, of course, Zen. With Zen, is Evans guilty of intellectual fadism, since everyone knows that Kerouac, Ginsberg & Co. holds the American franchise on Oriental philosophy? Evans waved a hand in resignation and said:

"I was interested in Zen long before the big boom. I found out about it just after I got out of the army in 1954. A friend of mine had met Aldous Huxley while crossing from England, and Huxley told him that Zen was worth investigating. I'd been looking into philosophy generally so I decided to see what Zen had to say. But literature on it was almost impossible to find. Finally, I was able to locate some material at the Philosophical Library in Manhattan. Now you can get the stuff in

any drugstore.

"Actually, I'm not interested in Zen that much, as a philosophy, nor in joining any movements. I don't pretend to understand it. I just find it comforting. And very similar to jazz. Like jazz, you can't explain it to anyone without losing the experience. It's got to be experienced, because it's feeling, not words. Words are the children of reason and, therefore, can't explain it. They really can't translate feeling because they're not part of it. That's why it bugs me when people try to analyze jazz as an intellectual theorem. It's not. It's feeling."

Such a manifesto may pain the academicians of jazz, but Evans is no pedant with a B-plus critical faculty. He is an intellectual in the true spirit of the word: an intelligent inquirer. His flights into philosophy and letters spring not from the joy of scholarly exercise but from the fierce need to comprehend himself. It is this need, whipped by surging inner tensions, that has driven him to Plato, Freud, Thomas Merton, and Sartre. It is responsible for his artistry on the one hand and his erudition on the other. The former has enabled him to catharize his emotions; the latter has given him the opportunity to understand them. Hence his great emphasis on feeling as the basis of art.

Undoubtedly, the four years he lived in New Orleans and attending Southeastern Louisiana College had much to do with shaping this emphasis. It certainly exerted a powerful influence on his personality and playing. He himself admits it was the happiest period of his life.

"It was the happiest," he said, "because I had just turned 17, and it was the first time I was on my own. It's an age when everything makes a big impression, and Louisiana impressed me big. Maybe it's the way people live. The tempo and pace is slow. I always felt very relaxed and peaceful. Nobody ever pushed you to do this or say that.

"Perhaps it's due to a little looser feeling about life down there. Things just lope along, and there's a certain inexplicable indifference about the way people face their existence. I remember one time I was working in a little town right near the Mississippi border. Actually, it wasn't a town. It was a roadhouse with a few tourist cabins out back and another roadhouse about a half-mile up the highway. There didn't seem to be much law there. Gambling was open and thriving. I worked at the first place for months, and I never saw any police. Well, the night after I had left to take a job in the saloon up the road, a man walked in and pointed a .45 at another fellow. As I heard it from a friend, all he said was, 'Buddy, I hear you're foolin' around' with my wife,' and Bang! That was all. The second guy fell dead. As far as I know, nobody ever gave it another thought, and nothing was ever done.

"Still, there was a kind of freedom there, different from anything in the north. The intercourse between Negro and white was friendly, even intimate. There was no hypocrisy, and that's important to me. I told this to Miles (Davis) when I was working with him and asked him if he understood what I meant. He said he did. I don't mean that the official attitude is sympathetic or anything like that. Some very horrible things go on down there. But there are some good things, too, and the *feel* of the country is one of them."

Bill absorbed this feel not only by living there but also by gigging around New Orleans and the rural areas almost nightly. One job took him and his fellow Casuals (the name of the band suited these collegiate artistes to a man) far into the country. After turning off the main highway, they headed up a road, which appeared to have been paved with the contents of vacuum cleaner bags. Small tornadoes of choking grit swirled around them as they pushed along. Each time another car passed, the windows were closed tight to fend off suffocation. They were beginning to taste the *Grapes of Wrath* in their dust-parched throats when they sighted their target after about an hour.

"It was a church in the middle of a field," Evans recalled. "A boxlike structure about 40 x 20 with nondescript paint on

the outside and none on the inside. It was more like a rough clubhouse than a church. I think they built it themselves."

"Themselves" were the 70-odd folk who had hired the Casuals to play for their outdoor do. "You wondered where the hell they came from because you couldn't see any houses around," Evans said.

The bandstand where they were to play was one of those little round summer pavilions you see in films like *Meet Me in St. Louis* when the town band plays concerts in the park. This one was fenced around with chicken wire.

"It was a dance job," the pianist said. "We played three or four tunes for them, and then blew one for ourselves. They didn't seem to mind. Everyone had a ball. The women cooked the food—It was jambalaya—and served it from big boards. Everything was free and relaxed. Experiences like these have got to affect your music."

Apparently they have affected Bill's, and

all to the good, because his playing has caused much nodding of heads among musicians, critics, and fans for the last couple of years. Yet he scoffs at people who claim to hear two or three specific influences in a musician's playing.

"A guy is influenced by hundreds of people and things," he said, "and all show up in his work. To fasten on any one or two is ridiculous. I will say one thing, though. Lennie Tristano's early records impressed me tremendously. Tunes like "Tautology," "Marshmallow," and "Fishin' Around." I heard the fellows in his group building their lines with a design and general structure that was different from anything I'd ever heard in jazz. I think I was impressed by Lee (Konitz) and Warne (Marsh) more than by Lennie, although he was probably the germinal influence. I guess it was the way Lee and Warne put things together that impressed me."

It was the way Evans put things together that brought him to the attention of his fellow craftsmen. In New York less than five years, he has worked with such as Charles Mingus and Miles Davis, who pick their bandstand associates with care and discrimination. Obviously, Evans has the touch. But he is still not satisfied with his playing and, because he is an artist, it is doubtful that he ever will be.

"I once heard this trumpet player in New Orleans who used to put down his horn and comp at the piano," he said. "When he did, he got that deep, moving feeling I've always wanted, and it dragged me because I couldn't reach it. I think I've progressed toward it, but I'm always looking to reflect something that's deeper than what I've been doing."

What he is seeking to reflect came out in

a conversation about William Blake, the 18th century poet, painter, and mystic. Evans had found that Blake's poetry was a sort of intellectual orgasm. Bill, in describing Blake's art, defined what he was looking for in his own:

"He's almost like a folk poet, but he reaches heights of art because of his simplicity. The simple things, the essences, are the great things, but our way of expressing them can be incredibly complex. It's the same thing with technique in music. You try to express a simple emotion—love, excitement, sadness—and often your technique gets in the way. It becomes an end in itself when it should really be only the funnel through which your feelings and ideas are communicated. The great artist gets right to the heart of the matter. His technique is so natural it's invisible or unhearable. I've always had good facility, and that worries me. I hope it doesn't get in the way."

Even a cursory hearing will indicate that the Evans struggle for simple beauty is not without its triumphs. When he plays, it is like Hemingway telling a story. Extraneous phrases are rare. The tale is told with the strictest economy, and when it is over, you are tempted to say, "Of course. It's so simple. Why didn't I think of that?" He is, in essence, a synecdochist, an artist who implies as much as he plays. And moving all his music, coloring every note, is that deep, rhythmic, almost religious feeling that is the seminal force of jazz.

It was perhaps these qualities that recommended Evans to Miles Davis after the trumpeter lost the services of Red Garland. The move was somewhat of a departure for Miles. Indeed, there were rumbles in some quarters that the color of Bill's skin automatically depreciated his value to the group. But Davis knew what he was doing. The association was a successful one for both.

Bill worked with Miles for about eight months and quit. Just why has mystified a good many persons in the jazz arena. He was playing with one of the most respected musicians in jazz and getting a $200 a week salary. The job meant not only inestimable prestige but a rare opportunity to improve artistically. Bill's explanation of the parting is, like his music, a simple statement of how he felt:

"At the time I thought I was inadequate. I wanted to play more so that I could see where I was going. I felt exhausted in every way—physically, mentally, and spiritually. I don't know why. Maybe it was the road. But I think the time I worked with Miles was probably the most beneficial I've spent in years, not only musically but personally. It did me a lot of good."

Upon leaving the Davis group, he flew to Ormond Beach, Fla., to see his parents. "And think," he said. He stayed there three weeks, mostly relaxing and playing golf, which he had learned as a boy in Plainfield, N.J., where he was born and schooled. His father, now retired, owned a driving range, and Bill and his brother, Harry, were frequent customers and ball shaggers. According to Bill, Harry was good enough to be a pro—he played in the 70s—but music pulled him as strongly as it did his brother. Harry still lives in Baton Rouge, not too far from where he and Bill went to college together, teaching music in public school and playing three or four gigs a week.

The Florida retreat was a productive one. By the time Bill was ready to return to New York in November of 1958, he had cleared some of the fog from his brain and shot a 41 on his last nine holes. Both accomplishments brought him a certain measure of satisfaction, and he came back to grapple with his music problems.

His method of doing this is a familiar one to artists whether they are musicians, writers, painters, or mathematicians. He concentrates on his stone wall intensely and when he breaks through, he explores the new terrain beyond for about six months. Then he gets bored and, as new problems are born, he abandons it to go through the same process.

"I wish it were easier," he said.

For the man who wishes to create, however, there can be no other way. He may hate the time he spends at it and fear that he may not be able to succeed; he may give up in disgust a hundred times, but he goes through with it anyway, because, in the summing up, nothing slakes the artistic thirst except the satisfaction of its own work well done. Yet Evans has some reservations concerning the sustained intensity with which an art should be pursued.

"Sometimes it can happen that you see everything in terms of music," he said. "It's like a fixation. You can't help it. I get that way every time I'm trying to work something out. But it's bad if you can't pull out of it. Nothing should be that dominating. If it is, it is perverted."

Because he respects his craft so deeply, he abhors those who would degrade it through a distorted loyalty. He looks with fascinated horror upon the hippies who try to live something they aren't.

"They live their full lives on the fringe of jazz and yet miss its essence entirely," he said. "They take the neuroses that are integral in every art and blow them up to where they're the whole thing. Do you remember the Platonic dialog in which Socrates argues the definition of wisdom with Hippocrates? As far as I'm concerned, Hippocrates was the first hippy, a guy who was smug because he thought he knew something. Socrates *was* wise because he realized how little he knew."

Bill's way of life is consonant with his anti-hipster philosophy. Jazz jargon constitutes a small factor in his lexicon. "Dig" and "man" he uses frequently, but over-indulgence in hip talk, to him, is an "excuse for thinking." His clothes are just about what's in fashion, he shaves every morning, and his Manhattan apartment is an ordinary three-room affair.

A bed, a few chairs, and a kitchen table is the furniture complement, all of it thoroughly bourgeois. A piano takes up half the living room. There is a hi-fi set and a television set, the latter of which he sits before almost every afternoon to apprise himself of the sports scene. He has some 50 books in two bookcases, but only two paintings decorate his walls. One, by Gwyneth Motian, wife of his drummer, Paul Motian, is a small but extremely effective abstraction. The other, by himself, is an attempt at design. It's terrible, but this has not stopped him. He continues to paint with this as his credo: "I can be as good as Klee at least."

His view of his piano playing is more in accord with reality. He is no longer the confused youngster whose feelings about music were badly shaken by the military psychology of the army.

"I took everything personally, because I thought *I* was wrong," he said. "I was attacked by some guys for what I believed and by musicians who claimed I should play like this pianist or that. Pretty soon I lost the confidence I had as a kid. I began to think that everything I did was wrong. Now I'm back to where I was before I went in the army. I don't give much of a damn now what anybody thinks. I'll do what I think should be done."

He is doing it with his own trio, featuring Motian and bassist Scott LeFaro. So far, he is fairly happy with the results and said, "If there is any dissatisfaction with the group, it's only with myself."

The question of whether a group of musicians who play together continually tend to become stale and/or rigid in their attitudes is one of individual capacity, Bill said.

"As a leader, it's my role to give direction to the group," he said, "and Paul and Scott have indicated that they are more comfortable in the trio than anywhere else. Does a group get stale? It all depends on whether there is continuing stimulation, whether all the musicians concerned want to share each other's progress. As for myself, I want to grow, but I don't want to force it. I want to play as *good* as I can, not necessarily as *different*. I am not interested in consciously changing the essence of my music. I would rather have it reveal itself progressively as I play. Ultimately, what counts is its essential quality, anyway, and differences vanish in a short time.

"What is most important is not the style itself but how you are developing that style and how well you can play within it. You can definitely be more creative exploring specific things within a style. Sometimes, Paul, Scott, and I play the same tune over and over again. Occasionally, everything falls in right, and we think it's sensational. Of course, it may not mean much to a listener at the time, but, then, most people in clubs don't listen closely anyway."

Up until now, the trio has been a unit for many months and acceptance is, in general, high. The fellows are not playing as many gigs as they might wish, but they are not starving. Evans himself puts no restrictions on the type of club they'll work.

"We'll play anywhere that people will listen," he said.

That should be just about everywhere. ●

COLTRANE ON COLTRANE

By John Coltrane
in collaboration with Don DeMicheal
SEPTEMBER 29, 1960

I've been listening to jazzmen, especially saxophonists, since the time of the early Count Basie records, which featured Lester Young. Pres was my first real influence, but the first horn I got was an alto, not a tenor. I wanted a tenor, but some friends of my mother advised her to buy me an alto because it was a smaller horn and easier for a youngster to handle. This was 1943.

Johnny Hodges became my first main influence on alto, and he still kills me. I stayed with alto through 1947, and by then I'd come under the influence of Charlie Parker. The first time I heard Bird play, it hit me right between the eyes. Before I switched from alto in that year, it had been strictly a Bird thing with me, but when I bought a tenor to go with Eddie Vinson's band, a wider area of listening opened up for me.

I found I was able to be more varied in my musical interests. On alto, Bird had been my whole influence, but on tenor I found there was no one man whose ideas were so dominant as Charlie's were on alto. Therefore, I drew from all the men I heard during this period. I have listened to about all the good tenor men, beginning with Lester, and believe me, I've picked up something from them all, including several who have never recorded.

The reason I liked Lester so was that I could feel that line, that simplicity. My phrasing was very much in Lester's vein at this time.

I found out about Coleman Hawkins after I learned of Lester. There were a lot of things that Hawkins was doing that I knew I'd have to learn somewhere along the line. I felt the same way about Ben Webster. There were many things that people like Hawk, Ben, and Tab Smith were doing in the forties that I didn't understand but that I felt emotionally.

The first time I heard Hawk, I was fascinated by his arpeggios and the way he played. I got a copy of his "Body and Soul" and listened real hard to what he was doing. And even though I dug Pres, as I grew musically, I appreciated Hawk more and more.

As far as musical influences, aside from saxophonists, are concerned, I think I was first awakened to musical exploration by Dizzy Gillespie and Bird. It was through their work that I began to learn about musical structures and the more theoretical aspects of music.

Also, I had met Jimmy Heath, who, besides being a wonderful saxophonist, understood a lot about musical construction. I joined his group in Philadelphia in 1948. We were very much alike in our feeling, phrasing, and a whole lot of ways. Our musical appetites were the same. We used to practice together, and he would write out some of the things we were interested in. We would take things from records and digest them. In this way we learned about the techniques being used by writers and arrangers.

Another friend and I learned together in Philly—Calvin Massey, a trumpeter and composer who now lives in Brooklyn. His musical ideas and mine often run parallel, and we've collaborated quite often. We helped each other advance musically by exchanging knowledge and ideas.

I first met Miles Davis about 1947 and played a few jobs with him and Sonny Rollins at the Audubon ballroom in Manhattan. During this period he was coming into his own, and I could see him extending the boundaries of jazz even further. I felt I wanted to work with him. But for the time being, we went our separate ways.

I went with Dizzy's big band in 1949. I stayed with Diz through the breakup of the big band and played in the small group he organized later.

Afterwards, I went with Earl Bostic, who I consider a very gifted musician. He showed me a lot of things on my horn. He has fabulous technical facilities on his instrument and knows many a trick.

Then I worked with one of my first loves, Johnny Hodges. I really enjoyed that job. I liked every tune in the book. Nothing was superficial. It all had meaning, and it all swung. And the confidence with which Rabbit plays! I wish

I could play with the confidence that he does.

But besides enjoying my stay with Johnny musically, I also enjoyed it because I was getting first-hand information about things that happened way before my time. I'm very interested in the past, and even though there's a I don't know about it, I tend to go back and find out. I'm back to Sid Bechet already.

Take Art Tatum, for instance. I was coming up, the musicians around with were listening to Powell, and I didn't listen too much to Tatum. That is, until one night I happened to run into him in Cleveland. There were Art and Slam Stewart Oscar Peterson and Ray Brown at a private session in some lady's attic. played from 2:30 in the morning 8:30—just whatever they felt like playing. I've never heard so much music.

In 1955, I joined Miles on a regular basis and worked with him 'til the middle of 1957. I went with Thelonious Monk for the remainder of that year.

Working with Monk brought me close to a musical architect of the highest order. I felt I learned from him in every way—through the senses, theoretically, technically. I would talk to Monk about musical problems, and he would sit at the piano and show me the answers just by playing them. I could watch him play and find out the things I wanted to know. Also, I could see a lot of things that I didn't know about at all.

Monk was one of the first to show me how to make two or three notes at one time on tenor. (John Glenn, a tenor man in Philly, also showed me how to do this. He can play a triad and move notes inside it— like passing tones!) It's done by false fingering and adjusting your lip. If everything goes right, you can get triads. Monk just looked at my horn and "felt" the mechanics of what had to be done to get this effect.

I think Monk is one of the true greats of all time. He's a real musical thinker— there's not many like him. I feel myself fortunate to have had the opportunity to work with him. If a guy needs a little spark, a boost, he can just be around Monk, and Monk will give it to him.

After leaving Monk, I went back to another great musical artist, Miles.

On returning, this time to stay until I formed my own group a few months ago, I found Miles in the midst of another stage of his musical development. There was one time in his past that he devoted to multichorded structures. He was interested in chords for their own sake. But now it seemed that he was moving in the opposite direction to the use of fewer and fewer chord changes in songs. He used tunes with free-flowing lines and chordal

R. Howard

direction. This approach allowed the soloist the choice of playing chordally (vertically) or melodically (horizontally).

In fact, due to the direct and free-flowing lines in his music, I found it easy to apply the harmonic ideas that I had. I could stack up chords—say, on a C7, I sometimes superimposed an E^-7, up to an F^-7, down to an F. That way I could play three chords on one. But on the other hand, if I wanted to, I could play melodically. Miles' music gave me plenty of freedom. It's a beautiful approach.

About this time, I was trying for a sweeping sound. I started experimenting because I was striving for more individual development. I even tried long, rapid lines that Ira Gitler termed "sheets of sound" at the time. But actually, I was beginning to apply the three-on-one chord approach, and at that time the tendency was to play the entire scale of each chord. Therefore, they were usually played fast and sometimes sounded like glasses.

I found there were a certain number of chord progressions to play in a given time, and sometimes what I played didn't work out in eighth notes, 16th notes, or triplets. I had to put the notes in uneven groups like fives and sevens in order to get them all in.

I thought in groups of notes, not of one note at a time. I tried to place these groups on the accents and emphasize the strong beats—maybe on 2 here and on 4 over at the end. I would set up the line and drop groups of notes—a long line with accents dropped as I moved along. Sometimes what I was doing clashed harmonically with the piano—especially if the pianist wasn't familiar with what I was doing—so a lot of times I just strolled with bass and drums.

I haven't completely abandoned this approach, but it wasn't broad enough. I'm trying to play these progressions in a more flexible manner now.

Last February, I bought a soprano saxophone. I like the sound of it, but I'm not playing with the body, the bigness of tone, that I want yet. I haven't had too much trouble playing it in tune, but I've had a lot of trouble getting a good quality of tone in the upper register. It comes out sort of puny sometimes. I've had to adopt a slightly different approach than the one I use for tenor, but it helps me get away—let's me take another look at improvisation. It's like having another hand.

I'm using it with my present group, McCoy Tyner, piano; Steve Davis, bass, and Pete LaRoca, drums. The quarter is coming along nicely. We know basically what we're trying for, and we leave room for individual development. Individual contributions are put in night by night.

One of my aims is to build as good a repertoire as I can for a band. What size, I couldn't say, but it'll probably be a quartet or quintet. I want to get the material first. Right now, I'm on a material search.

From a technical viewpoint, I have certain things I'd like to present in my solos. To do this, I have to get the right material. It has to swing, and it has to be varied. (I'm inclined not to be too varied.) I want it to cover as many forms of music as I can put into a jazz context and play on my instruments. I like Eastern music; Yusef Lateef has been using this in his playing for some time. And Ornette Coleman sometimes plays music with a Spanish content as well as other exotic-flavored music. In these approaches there's something I can draw on and use in the way I like to play.

I've been writing some things for the quartet—if you call lines and sketches writing. I'd like to write more after I learn more—after I find out what kind of material I can present best, what kind will carry my musical techniques best. Then I'll know better what kind of writing is best for me.

I've been devoting quite a bit of my time to harmonic studies on my own, in libraries and places like that. I've found you've got to look back at the old things and see them in a new light. I'm not finished with these studies because I haven't assimilated everything into my playing. I want to progress, but I don't want to go so far out that I can't see what others are doing.

I want to broaden my outlook in order to come out with a fuller means of expression. I want to be more flexible where rhythm is concerned. I feel I have to study rhythm some more. I haven't experimented too much with time; most of my experimenting has been in a harmonic form. I put time and rhythms to one side, in the past.

But I've got to keep experimenting. I feel that I'm just beginning. I have part of what I'm looking for in my grasp but not all.

I'm very happy devoting all my time to music, and I'm glad to be one of the many who are striving for fuller development as musicians. Considering the great heritage in music that we have, the work of giants of the past, the present, and the promise of those who are to come, I feel that we have every reason to face the future optimistically. ●

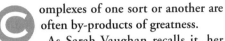

SARAH VAUGHAN

By Barbara Gardner
MARCH 2, 1961

Complexes of one sort or another are often by-products of greatness.

As Sarah Vaughan recalls it, her life began with a devastating, unutterable resentment of being dark skinned and unattractive.

"I often wished I was a medium-brown skin color," she once said. "I imagined people that color were regarded more highly than I. To most persons who knew me, I thought, I was just another little black girl for whom the future was just as dark as it was for thousands of others like me."

As a child, Miss Vaughan remembers, she had dreams of being rescued by a fairy prince—only to be shoved from his horse when he discovered she was dark.

Even then, she wanted to sing. She dreamed of winning great acclaim. But in the midst of her triumph, a light-skinned girl would start calling her names.

Too young to understand the social shame inherent in race prejudice, the young Sarah Vaughan shifted the responsibility of the rejection and injustice she suffered to herself and her color. As she grew older, understanding came. But nothing could ever repair completely the emotional and psychological hurts she had suffered.

Not all her nightmares happened when she was asleep. Some were real, the kind you can't wake up from, and they have contributed to her tendency to minimize herself. Despite the fame, glamour, commercial success, and acclaim she has achieved, she still says simply and quietly, "I don't feel like a big star."

And how does she think a great star should feel?

"I don't know," she admits. "I just feel like me, plain Sarah Vaughan."

During most of her life, that description was painfully accurate. Sarah Vaughan was just that—plain. "I was nothing much to look at," she says.

Even after she had begun to sing professionally, her looks were a cross she bore gravely. In the mid-1940s, a New York writer cut her to the heart when he wrote:

"She is not exactly handsome to look at, having a toothy face with a flattened, ski-jump nose, almost oriental eyes, and a low forehead oppressed by a pile of black hair."

The shy, defensive, bucktoothed girl who was to become world-renowned for her lyrical presentation, vocal flexibility, and remarkable harmonic sense, was the only child of Mr. and Mrs. Asbury Vaughan. She was born in Newark, N.J., March 27, 1924.

Her father was a carpenter whose hobby was playing guitar and singing Negro folk tunes. Her mother, Ada, sang spirituals and hymns in the church choir in Newark. The Vaughan home was always filled with music. "Not the kind of music I sing," Sarah adds. "They sang the music of God."

It was the first music to influence her. As she grew, she sang bits of the tunes her parents sang. When she was 8, she began studying piano and organ. One of the proudest moments of her mother's life came one Sunday when Sarah, then about 12, became the church organist. Her ambition at the time: to become a good choir director.

The Vaughans, deeply religious, encouraged their daughter's dedication to the church. And although Sarah had begun to wander from that direction early in her teens—by playing piano in the high school orchestra and singing popular songs at parties—she had turned 19 before the decision to become a professional entertainer was taken. Friends persuaded her to enter the amateur contest at New York's Apollo theater. She sang "Body and Soul" and won first prize. Her career was born.

But her family wasn't entirely happy about it. "My mother was a little disappointed in me," she said recently. "She wanted me to go on in school and become a teacher or a choir director or something 'respectable'."

But whether she admitted it to her mother or not, Sarah had always wanted to be in show business, though not necessarily as a singer. In fact, she had been preparing herself for it by tirelessly studying piano and organ for eight years. There are musicians today who remember that Sarah was once a *very* good pianist.

Even after the Apollo victory, Sarah wasn't at ease. She had a gnawing suspicion that she would never make it.

The winsome singer with the bright smile who, beautifully gowned, graces the stage today, is actually a composite put together by her two husbands.

Her first husband was George Treadwell, a trumpeter who later became her manager. Treadwell was prompted to begin her metamorphosis by an experience she had at the Chicago Theater some 10 years ago.

Waiting in the wings, the duckling had not yet become a swan and was going through great inner struggles. But Dave Garroway was the emcee, and the glowing terms with which he introduced the new star dissolved much of her fear. Suddenly she was no longer just an unattractive little girl, but someone special, and she loved the feeling. She glided onstage and stood before the audience ready to pour out this newfound confidence and affection in music. Then she saw a streak in the air, felt a sharp pain in her head, and saw red stains spreading down her white dress.

"I've been shot!" was her first terrified thought. But the bullets were tomatoes, and they kept raining on the stage as the frightened singer stood petrified. Young bigots in the balcony did their damage and scurried away.

Garroway was livid with rage. He delivered an infuriated statement against bigotry while the confused, humiliated singer huddled in the wings with her husband.

From the audience came thunderous applause for the singer, and a demand that she return. She went back to the microphone in tears, and looked out into what she felt was the last audience she would ever face. She tried to sing. She could not utter a sound.

After several futile starts, she left the stage, positive she would never sing again. But so sympathetic was public response to the incident, and so immediate was it, that she was persuaded not to give up her career.

Treadwell decided something must be done to give her confidence. He invested all the money he had, about $8,000, in the building of a star. He arranged for nose-thinning plastic surgery on her face and the straightening of her teeth and sent her to a beauty salon to have her figure streamlined. He paid for special arrangements and elocution lessons, and personally selected and bought becoming clothes for her.

It worked. So transformed and elated was she that he gave her a nickname. That's how she came be known as "Sassy."

Yet Miss Vaughan today doesn't like to talk about her first marriage. "I want to forget that," she said. "I never want to think about that again."

Asked directly whether she thinks Treadwell should be given credit for guiding her to stardom, she revealed her tendency to rely on things current.

"No, my second husband did that," she said.

"All George ever did for me," she maintained, "was really for himself. You know, nobody wants to print that, but it's the truth, and I wish people would understand that."

Miss Vaughan's second husband is C.B. Atkins, a Chicago businessman and taxicab company owner whom she married in the summer of 1958 after a whirlwind courtship.

The marriage was regarded in some quarters first with amusement and then with alarm. Few persons felt there could be anything serious between the imaginative artist and the shrewd, resolute businessman.

Shortly after the wedding, Atkins took control of the Vaughan organization, and the amused ones stopped laughing, and the alarmed ones grew more so. Within months, parasites, hangers-on, and even more legitimate acquaintances found that to get to the singer they had to get past Atkins first.

Not everyone disapproved, however. "Sarah needed somebody strong," one associate says. "She needed somebody to do the hard, dirty work in this business. C.B. isn't going to let anybody take advantage of her."

Today, Atkins devotes most of his time to personal management. He manages Max Roach, the MJT + 3, and several younger singers. His chief client, of course, is his wife.

He, in turn, is the center of her universe. This is not surprising to those who know her. Basically, she is still a lonely woman, one who has to be in love.

Extremely defensive and sensitive offstage, Miss Vaughan allows almost no one to penetrate the shell of polite disinterest into which she has withdrawn. Outside her immediate family, she has only one female friend.

Her reticence leaves reporters and other interviewers nonplussed. After talking to her for hours, they will come away shaking their heads, utterly bewildered. She, for her part, hates interviews. She consents to them only when Atkins insists.

"They always ask the same questions," she complained. "Where was I born? When did I start singing? Who have I worked with?

"I don't understand why they can't just talk to me without all that question bit. I just freeze."

And freeze she does. So cautious is she, so fearful of being misquoted or misunderstood, that natural responses are choked at the source. All that comes out is a rush of colorless, harmless, impotent words.

As a result, there is a widespread belief that she is a shallow woman, with no more to her than meets the eye. Nothing could be more inaccurate. When she is comfortable in a familiar environment, she emerges as a dynamic and powerful woman with a sharp sense of humor—and, at times, a sharp tongue.

Recently she sat in a club with acquaintances, silently watching her husband send a stream of bills across the bar as he bought drinks for friends. A merrymaker said that, at this rate, the party could go on all night.

Freezing the grin from the woman's face with a cold stare, Sarah snapped:

"Not hardly. When the time comes for us to go, we'll go. You can believe that, honey!"

Within the hour, she and her husband left the club.

Miss Vaughan has developed her stony

stare to perfection. When she uses it, however, it's "because somebody is really dragging me," she said. "Usually, it's somebody who walks up to me and calls me Sarah. They don't know me, and they should say Miss Vaughan, or Mrs. Atkins, or something. That's what I would do. So I just keep walking."

The lighter side of

Charles Stewart

Sarah Vaughan is something few people see, except when she feels particularly frisky onstage.

She is, in private life, a mimic and comedienne of no mean skill who can keep friends entertained for hours, re-creating scenes and situations from her travels. These are situations she observed with poker face and apparent disinterest.

There is another myth about Miss Vaughan that deserves exploding—the idea that she is a "natural" singer with little knowledge of music. It is an assumption made by people who don't know about her years of piano studies.

While it is true that she was a professional singer before her first husband induced her to take voice lessons, she has, from the beginning, been equipped with an excellent knowledge of the mechanics of music. She credits much of it to training she received at Newark's Arts High School.

"While I was playing piano in the school band," she said, "I learned to take music apart and analyze the notes and put it back together again. By doing this, I learned to sing differently from all the other singers."

That is probably the nearest thing to an analysis of her style as you are likely to get from her. Beyond this, she simply says that she sings songs a different way each time because she would get bored singing them the same way.

Her skillful, natural, and frequent changes of key and her use of improbable intervals give each of her performances a freshness and originality unmatched by any other singer. With her, enunciation is completely subservient to music.

Miss Vaughan doesn't waste her singing. She loves to sing but does so only for a purpose. She must have an audience she cares about. It need not be large. Once, reportedly, she sang for an audience of one. Shortly after her engagement to Atkins, she called him in Chicago from New York and sang one of her best-known ballads, "Tenderly."

There are, in fact, times when it seems everyone wants to sing but Sarah.

Once, in 1960, she made the alarming discovery that her husband, her maid, and her pianist all felt the magnetic pull of the spotlight. A member of her accompanying trio recalls, "Man, those trips in the car from one gig to the other were something else. We had great singing contests, and we tried to get Sarah to be the judge. Each one of us would sing his or her best number. It was too much, now that I think about it. Everybody was singing but Sarah.

"She was just sitting in the corner, wishing everybody would shut up so she could get some sleep."

Most of the early fears are conquered now. In their place have come problems of adjustment, and some new fears.

But Mrs. Atkins has never looked healthier or happier. She makes no decision regarding either her career or her personal schedule without her husband's approval. She is openly adoring of him, and obedient to the point of subservience. Often she sits quietly, watching him, hanging onto every word. If he asks her to do anything, she is off like a shot.

She is almost childlike in her anxiety not to displease him. If in his absence she goes for a moment against his wishes, she is almost instantly contrite, hoping he will never find out what she has done.

"I guess I'm too sensitive," she admits. "But I'm so afraid of being hurt. I've been hurt so much."

Onstage, she alternates between revealing herself as the pixie-ish Sassy and the sedate Miss Vaughan. At those moments when the old fears and nightmares peek through, it is the little church organist from Newark who stands there with the cloth of her skirt between her fingers, holding on tightly. It is then that she wants to slow the pace and spend more time as Mrs. Atkins.

"What's the use of having a home if you can't enjoy it?" she asked. "Of course, I want to keep singing as long as anybody will listen. But I want to spend more time at home?"

She is tired of the public demands on her and, although she remains gracious when she is talking to them, she resents autograph hounds and pushy people generally.

When her husband reminded her recently that this was a part of her responsibility as a star, she replied, a little pathetically:

"Honey, I'm tired of all this. Let me just be Mrs. Atkins, and *you* be Sarah Vaughan." ●

HAWK TALK

By Stanley Dance

FEBRUARY 1, 1962

It's surprising that a musician with his knowledge and experience should take time out to listen to younger musicians, but then his thinking isn't limited by the past." Lockjaw Davis was talking about Coleman Hawkins, a senior he holds in high regard. "And he doesn't just listen to saxophones. He listens to all instruments. He always retains his personal flavor, but you find young musicians on his dates, and he's just as comfortable with them as with the older guys."

Hawkins' perennial freshness is echoed by Johnny Hodges: "The older he gets, the better he gets. If ever you think he's through, you find he's just gone right on ahead again."

Paul Gonsalves, himself one of the formidable technicians of the tenor saxophone, never hesitates to express admiration.

"Coleman Hawkins is more than a stylist. He is a great stylist, of course, but he is also a very, very good musician. He plays jazz, and he also plays the instrument the way it should be played. I'm sure he could take a place among symphony musicians and command their respect. You might say that the secret of his success has been that he had a natural gift and that he took trouble to develop it, just like Duke. You can't rely on natural talent alone in today's competitive music world. There certainly aren't many guys around with talent like Hawk's, and there are even fewer with what I'd call the humility to recognize any need for developing that talent."

The subject of these perceptive comments is a jazz phenomenon. In terms of durable artistic accomplishment and growth, the only parallel to Hawkins' career is provided by that of Duke Ellington. Hawkins has been challenged by different stylists several times in his long career, but his supremacy has soon been reasserted. Basic to this, and to his ability to go on adding creatively, is his sound.

Discussing "the wide range of tonal approaches" to the tenor saxophone in *The Book of Jazz*, Leonard Feather refers to the "manly sonorities of a Coleman Hawkins." There have been many approaches, but for the majority of musicians and listeners, the Hawkins tone has consistently represented the ultimate. The tones of some others have been appealing, permissible deviations, though they often have suggested loyalties split between alto and tenor. Others again have sought to match Hawkins tone, but they have never quite attained its full, rounded power and authority.

Despite his strong convictions about tone, Hawkins' appreciation of another musician's ideas is unaffected by a different tonal approach.

"I like most music unless it's wrong," he said. "I liked Lester Young the first time I heard him, and I always got along very well with him. We were on a lot of tours together, and I spent a lot of time with him, talking and drinking, in hotel rooms and places like that. People forget that Chu Berry's sound wasn't like mine either.

"As for mine, sometimes when people think I'm blowing harder or softer, I'm really blowing with just the same power, but the difference is due to the reed. I like my reed to speak. It's supposed to sound just like a voice. On records, the engineering can do things, too—make the sound harder or sharper. I dropped the buzz a long time ago and just play with a clear tone now."

His attitude toward contemporary activities is unambiguous.

"I've got all that current scene," he said. "If I play with you, I've got you. Coltrane, Lockjaw, Charlie Rouse, Paul Gonsalves, Johnny Griffin—I hear what they're doing, and I've played with all of them. And…I nearly forgot Sonny Rollins. He's a favorite of mine."

He kids the members of the quintet he and Roy Eldridge lead jointly: "Last night you had Coltrane. Tonight you're going to get plenty of Ornette!"

On his nocturnal rounds and in record studios he hears plenty of jazz, but at home the records he plays are almost entirely classical.

"I love all the operas," he said. "I like Stravinsky when I'm listening to Stravinsky, Bach when I'm listening to Bach, and Beethoven when I'm listening to Beethoven. I have no prejudices. I think Tchaikovsky was a great composer, but I guess his music became too popular to be chic.

"You see this sheet music here—*Deux Arabesques* by Debussy? I must have bought it 10 times, but I always seem to lose it. I play it on piano and on my horn.

"I'd been telling Roy for a year that I'd write out the melody of "I Mean You" for him, the number I did with Fats Navarro. Well, today I decided to do it, and I went out and bought some music paper and a couple of pencils, and there was this piece lying in the store right under my nose."

Almost every night, between sets, wherever Hawkins happens to be playing, the length of his career becomes the subject for discussion.

The talk may at first sound unkind, even malicious, but with familiarity the outlines of a kind of gang emerge, the object being to prove Hawkins older than he really is. (According to *The Encyclopedia of Jazz*, he was born in St. Joseph, Mo., on Nov. 21, 1904). The players do not expect to win. Their pleasure lies rather in seeing how he will extricate himself from the traps they set or how their arguments will be refuted. Two notably talented players of this game are Sonny Stitt and Roy Eldridge.

"Yeah?" someone says. "Then how about the time when you were working with Mamie Smith?"

"That was somebody else using my name," Hawkins replies with crushing finality.

"I can remember you, a grown man, playing with Fletcher Henderson when I was still a child," says some swing-era veteran.

Reminiscences flood in. Hawkins himself talks with more animation, to give the impression that his guard is down. Then:

"I don't think," he says, suddenly and airily, "that I ever was a child!"

When the Eldridge-Hawkins Quintet was playing the Heublein Lounge in Hartford, Conn., recently, an 8-year-old girl insisted on getting the autograph of Hawkins—and only his.

"How is it, Roy," Hawkins asked afterwards, "that all your fans are *old* people? They come in here with canes and crutches. They must be anywhere from 58 to 108. But my fans are all young, from 8 to 58 years old!"

"That little girl thought you were Santa Claus," said drummer Eddie Locke.

"Is that so? Well, who's got more fans than Santa Claus?"

An often-cited example of Hawkins' mischievous and sometimes macabre sense of humor goes back to the early Jazz at the Philharmonic tours. Several musicians on the tour were unaccustomed to flying and fearful of it. On this occasion, the plane took off uneventfully. No sooner were safety belts unloosed, however, than Hawkins was on his feet, slowly pacing the aisle, his head behind an opened tabloid, the big black headlines of which proclaimed the number dead in a catastrophic air crash.

Unsentimental about the past, he prefers to talk about today—and tomorrow. For instance, of Jimmy Harrison, one of the great pace-setters on trombone, with whom he had a close friendship, he will simply say:

"Yes, Jimmy and I were real tight. He

Herb Snitzer

could play. He had a good beat, and he could swing."

Although he prefers not to talk too much about the past, Hawkins remembers the time when bands were hired by clubs for long-run engagements. He said he feels that the current club policy of hiring groups for short periods of time has hurt the music business.

"They have a different group in their place every week, or every two weeks," he said. "You don't get to know the people, and they don't get to know you. They don't get into the *habit* of coming to hear you. They may like what you're doing, but when they come back, they find a totally different group and music. You take when Red Allen was at the Metropole all those years. People liked him and knew he was there and kept on coming back. Same thing with Wilbur DeParis at Ryan's. Engagements used to be much longer, and then you had a chance to build up a following. The combo would be identified with the place and the place with the combo."

Hawkins' ability to construct solos of

depth, especially on ballads, has been noted by many critics. This sensitivity to emotion in music was reflected when he said:

"I think a solo should tell a story, but to most people that's as much a matter of shape as of what the story is about. Romanticism and sorrow and greed—they can all be put into music. I can definitely recognize greed. I know when a man is playing for money. And, good gracious, there's plenty of that going on right now!

"Tempo is important, too, of course. Tempo should go according to the piece. Certain pieces are writing so that the right tempo—fast, medium, slow—is really quite clear. If you play a slow ballad fast, you lose everything. There's plenty of that going on, too!"

Then the tenor saxophonist reminisced a bit about his career.

"Some of my biggest moments," he said, "have been in jam sessions, but I don't want to talk about them. There were always other people involved.

"A big kick of another kind was when I opened at the Palladium in London with Jack Kylton [in 1934]. It was my first experience of an audience in Europe. And it was a huge stage. Just to walk out there was something! And then I was very well received.

"London and Paris were great metropolitan cities when I first went there," he reflected. "If you were good or if you were bad, you were treated accordingly, and that was that. But since those days, New York has become a very cosmopolitan city, too.

"When I came back here the first time [July, 1939], I was disappointed with what had happened in the music. Charlie Parker and Dizzy were getting started, but they needed help. What they were doing was 'far out' to a lot of people, but it was just music to me. Joe Guy was playing their way when he started with me in 1939.

"Another kick was when I opened with my own big band at the Golden Gate in

1940. They wouldn't let us off the stand. I enjoyed that period very much, and being leader didn't worry me. The band was very good—too good in some ways. We had fine arrangements by Andy Gibson, Buster Tolliver, and Buster Harding. And every now and then I wrote one.

"I always used to write when I felt like it. I remember writing an arrangement of "Singin' in the Rain" for Fletcher Henderson when that song was popular. I don't think Smack was recording then, because we never made a record of it. I also wrote a theme for him. We didn't give it a name, but it was written for the saxes and rhythm, including tuba.

"Since my own band broke up, I haven't worked regularly with a big band, and I like blowing with a big band just as much as with a small combo. I don't know how it is, but I never have played with Duke's band. I'd like to. I hope I can record with him some day.

"A date I did in November was one I'll remember. Benny Carter came into New York to do some work with Basie before going on to Europe again, and we recorded together for Impulse with the same instrumentation we used on a session in Paris in 1937, the one where we made "Crazy Rhythm" and "Honeysuckle Rose." We made those titles again, but this time we had Phil Woods and Charlie Rouse. They can play, those two, and read!

Hawkins has said, "Nobody likes home town." Sometimes it rings true in Hawkins' case. He doesn't seem to be appreciated adequately in his own country. He is, after all, one of the greatest musicians jazz has produced and an aristocrat in his profession. In club after club he stands, detached, serene, distinguished, listening with a slightly benign smile as others play, a figure of evident intelligence and sophistication.

Then he begins to blow. Sometimes the audience listens appreciatively, and sometimes it doesn't. Sometimes it continues its unknowing babble and ignores the quality of the music. A poor audience deserves a poor performance, but it doesn't get it. Eyes closed, Hawk is immediately in flight. ●

ELVIN JONES: THE SIXTH MAN

By Don DeMicheal
MARCH 28, 1963

In the last 20 years there has emerged a relatively small number of influential jazz musicians—this despite the overall excellence displayed by men playing jazz. Among drummers during these years there have been five who have been of utmost importance: Kenny Clarke, Shelly Manne, and Max Roach in the forties; Art Blakey and Philly Joe Jones in the fifties. Listing these five does not deny the contributions made by such men as Roy Haynes, Tiny Kahn, and Joe Morello, to name just three; but it was to Clarke, Manne, Roach, Blakey, and Jones that most young percussionists of the period turned as patterns.

There is now a sixth name to add to this list of dominant drummers: Elvin Jones.

Just as the five who preceded him into prominence developed new drummer roles, so Elvin has been doing by his work with John Coltrane, with whom he's played for the last two years or so. And just as Charlie Parker's playing was one of the crucial factors in the development of Roach, for example, so Coltrane's has been to Elvin's—Parker's approach demanded new drummer concepts and so does Coltrane's. In Parker's case the demand generally was for division of the time by two (eighth and 16th notes, or duple meter); Coltrane's present work most often gives rise to a feeling of three (various forms of triplets, use of triple meters such as 3/4, 6/4, 6/8).

But like all manners of playing jazz, Jones' approach to the drummer's role has roots in what preceded it.

"It isn't something I developed deliberately," he said recently. "It's more or less a natural step, a natural thing to do. It was a step from staying *away* from the soloist, staying in the background, staying with the form of the composition without joining the soloist in his improvisation— the conventional way of playing."

He pointed out that drummers in the forties, like Clarke, began to play more figures in their supportive roles than did their immediate predecessors, such as Jo Jones and Sid Catlett, but they still "kept their distance" from the soloists. Though his approach places the drummer in much closer contract with the soloist, "it must be done with a great deal of discretion and feeling for what the soloist is doing," he said. "And I always realize I'm not the soloist, that John is, and I'm merely the support for him.

"It may sound like a duet or duel at times, but it's still a support I'm lending him, a complementary thing. It's being done in the same context of the earlier style, only this is just another step forward in the relationship between the rhythm section and the soloist. It's much freer— John realizes he has this close support, and, therefore, he can move further ahead; he can venture out as far as he wants without worrying about getting away from everybody and having the feeling he's out in the middle of a lake by himself."

To give this close support, Jones has loosed himself from some of restrictions jazz drummers sometimes place on themselves.

For example, why must the sock cymbals [*two cymbals mounted on a device that allows the cymbals to be brought together by depressing a pedal with the foot*] always be closed sharply on the second and fourth beats of every bar of 4/4 time? Most drummers would answer something about its being necessary to swinging. But not Jones; he often plays the sock on the first and third beats, something most drummers—and other musicians— consider the antithesis of swinging.

In explaining why he turns the sock-cymbal rhythm around occasionally, Jones talked about what he calls the "sound balance," that is the blending of sock cymbals, snare drum, bass drum, top cymbals, tom toms with the other instruments in the group.

"One thing can't be dominant over the other," he said. "For instance the bass drum can't be too loud or too consistent [*played on every beat of the bar*] or your sock too sharp or heavy.

"As to playing the sock one and three, I do that to make more variety. The sound balance can't be maintained in a uniform manner if you have the consistency of rhythm with the sock coming on two and four all the time. It's akin to playing all four beats on the bass drum; it's the same kind of restrictive force. It can be varied without throwing the soloist off, as far as the meter goes. The over-all picture of the composition comes off fine with the sock on one and three. It works....

"And sometimes John gets on one and three; I go right along with him to let him know he's not alone. It lends sort of a moral and physical support to whatever he wants to do. It knits the whole thing a little tighter and makes it flow more smoothly, keeping in mind, as far as the rhythmic picture is concerned, where you're at all the time."

Jones contributes more than just support to a performance by the Coltrane group; he has an ability to construct drum solos of sometimes-amazing complexity and rhythmic daring that, nonetheless, retain form, and form is the ingredient often missing from most drummers' solos.

"I follow the improvisation the soloist has taken," he said regarding his solos, "and when he's through I pick up the last phrase he's played and use this as the beginning to my improvisation on the melodic pattern of the composition. It can be very simple or very complicated, and you can get unlimited rhythmic and polyrhythmic patterns and phrases. Actually, a lot of solos I have taken have drum and rhythmic phrases, just as a saxophonist or trumpeter will play phrases with his instrument...drums have to breathe too."

And breathing is not always regularly paced, nor is most other human behavior.

It would seem, then, that a jazz performance, since it is to a great extent a reflection of life, need not always be restricted to one, steady tempo. There has been some probing of jazz in free tempo and some experimentation with purposely speeded and slowed tempos within a performance. There has not been much of this but enough to lead one to wonder why a performance must be in only one tempo and why a tempo shouldn't change if this enhances the

Lawrence Shustak

artistic merit of the music.

"The trend I see taking place in this music," Jones said, upon reflection, "it doesn't have to be in one tempo—not with a solo. It's reverting in a sense....That is, there are movements in classical compositions, and it's natural to change the tempo when you get to a new movement. In jazz there haven't been so many tempo changes as metric changes—where you might go from duple into triple meter, though there usually is some connection—for instance, a quarter note in

4/4 equals a dotted quarter in 6/8.

"Sometimes I've used accelerandos and decelerandos in my solos. It seems a natural thing to do because it's a *solo*. And a solo can take any form the artist chooses; he can use any form he wants within the framework of the composition. it goes back to getting away from the rigidity that jazz had to face when it was primarily dance music."

There are times in the heat of a Coltrane quarter performance when the leader's adventurous improvisations and the support offered by Jones, with both cast in bold relief by a repeated figure played by McCoy Tyner on piano and Jimmy Garrison on bass, is reminiscent of Ravi Shankar's performance of Indian music— Shankar, playing the sitar (a guitarlike instrument), solos and is given close support by the tabla (two small drums) player, who also serves as sort of a foil to the soloist, and both play over a drone set up by the player of the tamboura, another stringed instrument.

Jones agreed that there is at times an Indian flavor to the quartet's work, that there is a definite link. But though he has tried his hand at playing tabla a little, he said he feels it would take too long to master the style.

"I have enough to do without trying to step over into something I know so little about," he said. "But this, like anything else, you can borrow from, a little here and there. You don't always do this consciously, of course.

"But I think even Indian music has its origins in the African art form. You can see the influences. Whatever we do, it can be traced back to some of the African forms— there are so many. It's like the languages; there might be a thousand dialects in one section of Africa, and the music has as many, if not more, dialects, you might say.

"When we recorded the *Africa Brass* album, I was trying to think in terms of the African interpretation as much as I was capable. But that was the only time I tried consciously to put African drumming into modern American jazz drumming. I don't know enough about it to say, 'I can do this, I can do that,' but I'll use whatever interpretation I feel appropriate for a particular composition."

Jones expressed strong feelings on the playing of drums.

"For any student who wants to play drums," the 35-year-old drummer said, "the most important thing is to learn the instrument thoroughly. After he has the facility, he has the knowledge and ability to play any kind of music he wants. But first he has to learn the instrument."

How to learn the instrument?

"I don't think rudiments, as such, will ever be out of date," he answered. "It's necessary to learn them for control, for developing your hands. But the emphasis shouldn't be placed only on them in instruction books. Rudiments are like scales, but you're not going to play scales on, say, a clarinet all your life. There's another step: the uses rudiments should be put to…to get into *music*.

"The control of the sticks is the most important thing to get; when you control the sticks, that's the first step toward controlling the instrument. You have to have the sticks under control before you can touch the instrument—and I mean *touch*, not beat on it. The drum is supposed to be *played*."

He went to point out that it's important for a drummer to know the melodic line of a tune, that this gives him more insight into how to follow and complement the soloists and serves as an invaluable guide as far as tempo consistency is concerned. "It gives him more of a belonging to a unit, to know that he's right," he remarked. "It isn't necessary to follow chord by chord but he should know the melody so that when the improvisation begins he knows too. That way the song can be played as a unit, not just two or three people carrying the whole thing and the drummer sitting back there just keeping time. This can become very boring and depressing to the listener *and* the drummer. The drummer becomes uninterested because he doesn't know what he's doing—this affects the listener in the same way."

No one could ever say that about Elvin Jones. ●

THREE IN THE AFTERNOON

The following discussion took place on a Sunday afternoon in Count Basie's dressing room during the recent Jazz Supports the Symphony concert at Chicago's Civic Opera House.

The conversation began while Basie and his band were on stage, and Jack Teagarden (who also was featured at the concert), Maynard Ferguson (whose band was playing in Chicago that night), and members of the *Down Beat* staff waited for the bandleader.

After much good-natured bantering, the conversation turned to the problems brass players have with their teeth.

Teagarden: Whenever anybody asks me how I keep my hair, I ask them how they keep their teeth. Because I don't have any teeth, you know.

Ferguson: That's all right, man. I don't have mine either. I deteriorate faster, that's all.

Down Beat: *Could you play better when you had your own teeth, Jack?*

Teagarden: No, I don't think so. I've got a better range now. Maybe I've lost a little thing in one way and gained it in another. But I don't think I've suffered from it really at all. I swore it wasn't going to become a mental block to me. It's just like you find a new ball bat, and you just pick it up and slug with it instead of figuring out how you're going to hold the thing.

Ferguson: I think a lot of guys got a lot of fear of that.

Teagarden: I did at first until they got the teeth out, and I put my horn up….

Down Beat: *Are all of them false?*

Teagarden: I don't have a tooth in my head, not a one.

Ferguson: Fantastic.

Teagarden: I had a disease called pyorrhea, which is hereditary, I guess, in my family. I never had a toothache 'til I was 36, and I never had a cavity, but they just got loose and fell out….But it didn't stop me for a week even. I went right on.

Down Beat: *How are your teeth, Maynard?*

Ferguson: Mine are fine. I went through the same thing, except I was full of theories which said let's not bother trying to re-create the faults in my own teeth. You know, the space between the front ones and—everything like that. It's all like you yourself trying to go into the instrument rather than trying to pull the instrument into your mouth—that's my theory. So I had all these magnificent theories down so cleverly that I couldn't miss. Within four days they had filed down all my front teeth, put caps on, and I went right to work. It was fine the first weekend because I felt that I wasn't supposed to be able to play at all, so, therefore, the fact that I could play adequately was just fine. But the next week….

You know every time you go in there they shoot you with Novocain, and you get those scars on your gums. My gums were swollen, and I had a lot of problems for about a week and a half. I started to get nervous about it, and I started thinking maybe this isn't going to work—I think that's where a lot of guys make a choice between whether they're going to get mentally hung up on "I will never be able to play such and such a way again" or else they're just going to say, "It will take care of itself." Now it's turned out to be better.

(Count Basie enters.)

Basie: Jack, I've been looking for you.

Teagarden: Ah…I waved at you when I came in….

(Confusion of greetings all around.)

Band Boy: Two more numbers—then you're back on.

Basie: Right.

Teagarden: Our paths don't cross too often. I think the last time I saw you was at the *Playboy* festival. Then once in France.

Basie: Oh, Lord, that was so….Yeah.

Teagarden: Have you seen Louis lately?

Basie: No, I haven't seen Pops in a long time.

Teagarden: I miss him by hours sometimes.

Basie: We're either ahead of him—or behind him, which is the wrong way to be, behind him, you know. But we worked seven, eight days down in the place in Washington together. Boy, that was great. That was the greatest thing I ever did. Man, we just play eight bars of that theme and nothing is going to happen in the next three minutes.

Teagarden: That's right. Nothing but applause....

Down Beat: *Count, why did you keep a big band going, when it became increasingly difficult to keep bands going?*

Basie: 'Cause I was simple. There's nothing else I could do. I can't play in a small group because you have to play too much. And, then, I guess I'm simple—I just like that sound, that's all. Excuse me, gentlemen.

(Teagarden and Basie leave to go on stage for finale; 10 minutes later, they return.)

Down Beat: *Count, you've had a band since the middle thirties. When you came up within the so-called big-band era, people were dancing, right?*

Basie: Absolutely.

Down Beat: *Was business good then?*

Basie: Well, that was the dance era.

Down Beat: *Now, today, there are just a handful of big bands—two of the best being yours and Maynard's. How does today differ from the thirties as far as people dancing? Do people come to hear the band more than they come to dance? Do you play more concerts than you do dances? Just how is it different?*

Basie: I think we play more concerts. I know we do, and we get to play a few dances, mostly at the universities, colleges, and things. But as far as our dance career is concerned, it's been kind of beat. But for the last year or so it seems as though it's picking up a bit. That's mainly due, I guess, to the wonderful work the disc jockeys have been doing on instrumentals throughout the country.

Down Beat: *Can you call your band a jazz band and be a dance band at the same time?*

Basie: I think you can.

Down Beat: *Why?*

Basie: I don't know, but I think you can.

Ferguson: Basie's band always sounds like a jazz band to me—if I may insert that—and I know what Basie's doing when he plays an arrangement for dancing and when he chooses certain numbers when he's on the concert stage. At times he will play numbers for dancing that he wouldn't play on the concert stage. But many of

them overlap. It's not like the old saying "he has two separate books." I don't know if anyone ever really had two separate books—I think that was just a phrase.

Down Beat: *Maynard, do you play more concerts than dances?*

Ferguson: Yes, I would say so, if we are to include jazz clubs as concerts.

Down Beat: *When both of you play dances, are some of the kids hard to get on the floor? In other words, Count, do you have to play different now than you did in the thirties to get people dancing?*

Basie: If we're playing a dance, we find that slower melodies fill

From left: **Jack Teagarden, Count Basie, and Maynard Ferguson.**

the dance floor. It's still more of a listening audience that we have, especially if we have the teenagers, but if we do have the older people, naturally they're not going to dance so much, because their dancing has become cut in half too—unless you play a little slower so they can get together and reminisce a little.

Down Beat: *In the thirties....*

Basie: They were doing the Lindy Hop in those days. Sometimes you couldn't play too fast. That's when they were really doing the Lindy.

Ferguson: Basie, did you see that again in Sweden?

Basie: Yes, yes, I did.

Ferguson: You know, when we played the

dances in Sweden—the first night I played nothing above a medium tempo, and I thought, "Gee, they dance to that awful easy." And then I started getting into these faster things that really are the things we play in the jazz clubs. They are melody dancers in Sweden. If you play well-known jazz standards, and you play them fast, they'll just start walking around the floor, and they all do it like puppets—they all do it together.

Down Beat: *What do you mean melody dancers?*

Ferguson: They love American jazz standards. By that I mean, I would have been a smash hit if I would have had "Honeysuckle Rose" in the book. I was speaking about

the commercial dance public, for which you could play very hip music.

Down Beat: *The average age of your band, Maynard, is about 26?*

Ferguson: Right.

Down Beat: *And, Count, the average age of your band is....*

Basie: Don't say it!

Down Beat: *But what can be said about the youth of Maynard's band as opposed to the polish and massive musicianship of your own band—men who have played longer?*

Basie: You just said it. They just played longer, not that they played any better, they just played longer....Let me tell you something—we haven't been old all these years. Like the teenagers now—well, we were playing to their parents, and they were young then. I mean, like we haven't *always* been 90 years old. Twenty years ago, remember, I was 20 years younger too.

Down Beat: *If you and Basie have to play more concerts and dances than you do jazz clubs, do you think this compromises you as jazz musicians leading big jazz bands?*

Ferguson: One of the greatest things to do is to try and always find out how you can be happy in what you do, and one of the things I spend a lot of time on is seeing how I can play jazz at a dance. And I think that in Jack Teagarden's day he did a great job—days when you could have just played the melody and they could have danced. Instead, you figured "I'll start off with the melody, then I'll go from there and do my own scene."

Teagarden: Start my melody first. I've given this a lot of thought because I've lived through this whole generation. I'm almost 58. I think if the television and radios would have more programs like this ["International Hour: American Jazz"]....For instance, this will be talked about for several weeks—like when they had the Timex programs, the great shows that they had about once every six months—there was a lot of comment, but there was nothing solid. The have to keep it up, have some live music on television, and it'll make people come back to listen to music again—they just don't get to hear enough music.

Then, I think a lot of the fault of where the dancing went was the musicians themselves. Now, I'm not criticizing us. We're all a little bit of a ham in a way, which I guess is true in any business. But you just can't go out there and play every number fast to show off your technique. You've got to play some numbers for the dancers....Dancing is a romantic recreation. Play four tunes for the public and one for yourself; "Star Dust" and a lot of pretty things...it's real beautiful for romantic dancing—and then let them all ride.

Basie: You sneak one in.

Teagarden: You sneak one in.

Ferguson: Jack, one thing I've always felt, when you play at a university...when Count Basie or Maynard Ferguson play for a prom, where we won't have as many esthetic kicks, shall we say; nonetheless,

the whole student body comes to that dance. And I'm sure Basie puts on a jazz concert for them in the middle of the evening just as I do, and what happens is that you gain a lot more new fans for jazz in general as well as for yourself at the dance than you do at the concert.

Teagarden: Suppose a person comes up to you and tells you, "You know, I proposed to my girl, who's my wife now—we've been happy for 30 years—at a dance you were playing and you played a certain waltz. Would you play that for us again?" I never ignore requests like that. Play a waltz, play a rhumba, or anything that a person would ask for, and I think you make more friends that way and will make dancing be a pleasure again.

Down Beat: *Stan Kenton has said that the future of the large jazz bands as opposed to dance bands lies in the colleges. Maynard, you were touching on this when you were talking about North Texas State and the high-school bands. Kenton holds that the colleges will be the places where musical progress will be made because there's no economic pressures. They don't have to worry about where they're going to be working tomorrow and how to keep the band together. Is this valid or will the greatest things still be done by the working bands?*

Ferguson: I believe the greatest things will be done by the working bands. You're going to get those little young geniuses out of college....I don't mean that. I just can't tell you how impressed I was with the North Texas State band-lab setups—I mean all the bands. I heard five bands in a row, and they were all about 18 men, 22 men, whatever size they wanted. Here's an example of the teaching that went on there:

Johnny Richards had done an album for Kenton, *Adventures in Time*. They played the arrangements from that whole album, and they played almost flawlessly. Sure, there were little weaknesses here and there, and it is true that they had had the whole semester to work on this music, but it was just astounding to me how great it sounded....The way these kids would fight over who was going to play with what band!

All this interest is going to spread....

We do have a problem in the big-band field today: everybody wants to blow and

everybody wants to be a soloist. The day of the fifth trumpet player is gone, in terms of a guy being happy to do it. He may be happy to do it while he is developing. But supposing I, as a bandleader, want a *great* fifth trumpet player. I want a guy who's really going to play those parts and isn't going to be saying, "Well, isn't it a drag that I don't get to solo." It's a thing that has always kept me from adding more men to my band; I feel that I can keep 12 young guys happy in my band, and I'm really not convinced that I can keep 20 of them happy.

Down Beat: *Do you call this a problem, Count?*

Basie: I agree heartily with Maynard. No comment on this because he's telling the absolute truth.

Down Beat: *Returning to an earlier question, can a big jazz band call itself that if it has to depend somewhat on dances in order to exist?*

Basie: As far as I'm concerned, I only have one book of things to play. I don't have anything arranged for concerts. I play the same type things for dances as I do for concerts. I don't know how Maynard has his....I *do*, too—Maynard has a real mixed book, you understand what I mean? But we aren't smart yet or something like that or we just haven't gotten into it; you understand? Now Ellington and these guys have really got concert bands. They play wonderfully for dancing too. But we—the guys will say, "Well, look, Basie, what are you gonna play?" and I say, "The same old beef stew."

Teagarden: This thing has got to start from the top. It has to be that fellows who are sincere at radio stations play it so it can be heard, not just put it on the shelf. And if it's played and it's heard, then it creates more demand for music, more interest. Otherwise it's an uphill pull all the way. If you make a record and it never gets played, then you don't draw a crowd; the guy goes out of business, and then we all flop.

Basie: I guarantee one thing, what you need is a record—if, you can get a record, it helps an *awful* lot. ●

MARY LOU WILLIAMS: INTO THE SUN

By Marian McPartland

AUGUST 27, 1964

Her early records are collectors' items. Her writing and playing have become part of the pattern of jazz history. She has transcended the difficulties experienced by women in the music field and through several decades has held a position of eminence as one of jazz's most original and creative pianists. She speaks softly: "Anything *you* are shows up in your music—jazz is whatever you are playing yourself, being yourself, letting your thoughts come through."

Her voice has the ring of authority, and well it may, for Mary Lou Williams' career, dating back to her childhood in Pittsburgh, Pa., and her Kansas City days with the Andy Kirk Orchestra, has always been one of consistent musical integrity.

Mary Lou's playing is real. Earthy. Running through all the emotions, it speaks volumes, for there is much in its creator that comes out in the music, a part of herself she cannot help revealing, so that at times one has the feeling almost of intruding on her thoughts, of hearing secrets not meant to be shared, of being able to probe the recesses of her mind. Sometimes Mary Lou's mood is dark, brooding—like a pearl diver, she searches along the depths of the lower register of the piano and then, as if triumphant at a sudden discovery, she shifts to the treble, launching into a series of light, pulsating, chordal figures.

She possesses a natural ability to generate a swinging feeling—an infallible time sense—an original harmonic concept, a way of voicing chords that is only hers. She doesn't veer far from the blues. Whatever her mood, whatever the tempo, she weaves a pattern, a design, faint at first, like a rubbed drawing, but then appearing more strongly, until it breaks into a kaleidoscope of color.

Mary Lou has found the way to put her emotions, thoughts, and feelings to good use. They come out powerfully, and sometimes prayerfully, for the spiritual side of the blues is always strong in her work. Yet there is a mysterious air, an enigmatic, slightly feline quality about her, which contrasts strangely with her direct, down-to-earth way of speaking.

One senses the inner fires, the inner tensions, and though she keeps her voice low, at times there is in it a note of bitterness. She has none of the typical trappings of show business. She seems almost indifferent to her appearance, her hair brushed casually, her dress plain and unassuming, her only jewelry a gold cross on a chain. But Mary Lou Williams is not a plain woman; with her high cheek bones, reminiscent of the Mayans, she is beautiful. When she becomes involved in her music, her face will set in masklike concentration, her eyes closed, giving an impression of stillness, of being lost to the world, even though her foot is tapping and her strong hands are moving swiftly and surely over the keys. Then suddenly she opens her eyes and smiles, and her face lights up and reflects her spirit, her gaiety, and her lively sense of humor.

A religious woman, Miss Williams was introduced to Roman Catholicism several years ago, along with Dizzy Gillespie's wife, Lorraine, (the Gillespies have long been her staunch friends), and it has evidently given her new strength and courage and a fresh purpose. Mary Lou is ready to do battle with the specters of the past. Strong in her faith, strong in her beliefs, a woman with a cause, a crusader, she rails against the injustices of a materialistic world and deplores musicians who talk against each other more than they help each other. Yet she seems to have had difficulty finding herself, too. In a sense, she is like a child who dreams of a good and perfect world and cannot quite tolerate the fact that it isn't that way.

At the Hickory House, where she has been ensconced for the last several months, the room casts a haze over her intricately voiced harmonies and, at times, blurs the impact of her changes in dynamics and clouds the clarity of her attack. But there are choice seats around the bar close to the piano where one can almost shut out the noise of the room and concentrate on Mary Lou and her trio. She sits at the piano with a certain dignity, playing with pride and a sureness of touch. Here is a natural showmanship, complete involvement with the music that speaks for her. But still one must listen closely to get the message.

"Anything you are shows up in your music.…"

Here is a woman who is conscientious, introspective, sensitive, a woman who, with her quiet manner and at times almost brusque, noncommittal way of speaking, has been misunderstood, thought to be lacking in warmth and compassion. The reverse is true. She feels keenly the various factions, contradictions, inequalities of the music business, wants to help people, to give of herself. A woman vulnerable. A woman hurt so many times she tends to withdraw from, and be suspicious of, others, unless she knows them well. She has an uncanny way of stripping them of any facade, of cutting through the deceit and shallowness of the sycophants. In many ways she is still confused, still searching, still figuring things out for herself, and in this she has been helped a great deal by her friend, the Reverend Anthony Woods.

"She has the beauty of being simple without any affectation—simplicity with her is a very deep thing," Father Woods said. "I have heard her discuss the esthetics of music with great penetration. She seems to have an understanding of what is good, of what is beautiful. She thinks that jazz is becoming superficial, that it's losing its spiritual feeling. She seems to be aware of a great deal of falsity and affectation, that people are not telling the truth, not saying what they really mean. In her uncomplicated way, she can't understand how anybody can't be sincere.

"To me, she is one of the greatest persons I have ever met—really a very great soul. She has exquisite taste, and where there is goodness, she gravitates to it naturally. But she is an emotional thinker, a disorganized thinker, and sometimes she has to sort out her ideas, and that's where I come in. She's simple and direct, primitive in a very good sense, and not spoiled by the sophistication around her. I don't believe that Mary is capable of producing anything except what is good."

Mary Lou has little business ability and scant knowledge of how to correlate, to direct, her ideas and plans. But her dreams and wishes for the betterment of musicians are logical and sound, and now some of them are just beginning to come true.

Several years ago, she started a thrift shop, the proceeds from which go into her Bel Canto Foundation, which she established to help needy musicians. Now more and more people have begun to hear about it and are giving her gifts of clothing and other donations. Besides these activities, much of Mary Lou's time is taken up with writing and arranging, plus her daily attendance at mass and care of her sister's little boy, who usually has the run of her apartment.

Being so busy does not seem to faze her, but it has been a long time since she has "come out" to play in public. She has made a few sporadic appearances in the last few years— twice at New York City's Wells' Supper Club and once each at the Embers and the Composer (where I worked opposite her), plus the Palace Hotel in San Francisco. These engagements have been of short duration and have not been too satisfying to her. She seems to feel the pressures of a musician's life keenly, to become disillusioned, and then, as she expresses it, "goes back in"—back to her other world, to her apartment, to write, teach, and pray.

During her long stays at home, Mary Lou's talent certainly has not been lying fallow. She has composed a poignant minor blues she calls "Dirge Blues," which she wrote at the time of President John F. Kennedy's assassination. She is skillful in creating a mood—the feeling of this piece is tragic and gloomy. In its simplicity, it is very touching. She has put out an extended-play record on her own label, Mary records, consisting of three tunes,

arranged for 16 voices and her trio: "Summertime," "The Devil," and "St. Martin de Porres." The last tune, with a lyric by Father Woods, achieves an airy, ethereal quality by its voice blending. She has made a single, also on her own label, of "My Blue Heaven." She makes this warhorse like

new again, with a light, witty, Latin-based treatment. Obviously she has lost none of her powers of inventiveness. One has only to listen to her recordings of years ago, "Froggy Bottom," "Roll 'Em," and "Cloudy," to realize how her style has evolved with the years and how she has kept her playing and her thinking contemporary.

She composed one of the first (if not the first) jazz waltzes—"Mary's Waltz"—many years ago, yet she has never got the proper credit or recognition for this or for any of her several innovations that have been brought to the fore later by other musicians. Her importance, her influence, cannot be denied. She has written many beautiful tunes that are seldom heard, seldom recorded.

It has been said of Mary Lou Williams

that she plays in cliches, but she has so much to offer of her own that I feel that her occasional use of cliché is more tongue-in-cheek commentary than lack of inventiveness. She has been labeled by some a fanatic. To others, she is only an extremely dedicated musician. Yet perhaps there *is* something of the fanatic in her, as seen in her constant search for musicians with whom she can be compatible—in a way, she reminds one of a mother with her children, alternately scolding or praising them, trying to teach them, trying to instill her beliefs in them, expecting great things of them. Yet it is said too that she is a hard taskmistress, demanding and intolerant.

"Anything you are shows up in your music...."

Her feelings about the new freedom in jazz cannot quite be concealed, though she tries to be noncommittal.

"I just haven't got it figured out," she said. "To each his own, I guess, but if I can't hear chords...some sort of melody...well, if they think they're giving out a good sound, that's their business. Maybe they think we're squares? Or else it's some sort of protest? Take a guy like Coltrane: He knows what he's doing. But these people without a knowledge of music, it's like—well, it's a very neurotic world. People are nervous. Seems like everyone I know is nervous. It must be the pressures of the world. Musicians are very sensitive, and they really don't know what to do about it. I don't mean they're nervous about playing, but in their lives. I try to act relaxed because that's been my training, but I'm more nervous than anyone you ever knew—inside. Oh, I get mad, sometimes, but I expel it, get it out right away."

When one is discussing Mary Lou with other musicians, her sense of time always prompts admiration.

"I've heard her a few times at the Hickory House, and I'm amazed at her rhythmic approach more than anything else," said fellow pianist Billy Taylor. "She has the most consistent way of swinging; even with a rhythm section that isn't quite hanging together, she can make it swing, and this is really remarkable. It seems that no matter what's going on around her, she can get this thing going. When in doubt—swing! As a pianist, I naturally listen a lot to the rhythm section, and sometimes I'll notice that they're not together, and I'll think to myself, 'Come on!—let's give her some support,' but she'll be making it anyway. Not as many jazz pianists have this ability as do other instrumentalists. I mean this rhythmic propulsion. She's not like an Erroll Garner or an Oscar Peterson, who overpower the rhythm section. On the contrary, she plays so subtly she seems to be able to isolate herself and swing, though the others may not be. Considering all the psychological things that go into swinging, she's even more remarkable. You could wake her up out of a dead sleep, and she'd start swinging without even thinking about it.

"Mary Lou is looking for perfection. On the rare occasions when she had this chemical thing going that can happen between three people, she's been so excited by it that she wants it all the time. Swinging is so natural to her that she can't understand why it isn't necessarily natural to everybody all the time. She figures that they can do it, but they won't; she thinks to herself, 'Anybody I hire should be able to do this, so why don't they?' Most people associate the verb 'to swing' with the degree of loudness that they attain, but she refutes it—she'll take something pianissimo and swing just as hard as if it were double forte. She's one of the very few people I know that can do this, consistently swing in any context."

"Anything you are shows up in your music...."

"She lives in a world all her own, a dream world, and she doesn't want anything to spoil it," said her longtime friend and admirer, Hickory House press agent Joe Morgan. "She inspires a great devotion in people—she has many followers, but there are just as many people who look at her askance because they cannot understand her high artistic level. She is so dedicated, and the fact that her standards are high makes her very hard to please. In her accompaniment she wants to hear certain changes behind her, certain lines, certain rhythms, and it's difficult for a strongly individualistic bass player or drummer, with ideas of his own, to conform to her standards. But her motive,

her burning desire is for creation. In a way, she's like a little child with a doll house, setting up house in the piano, like a little girl on her own chair, not even thinking about what is going on around her. Sometimes she doesn't hear what you're saying—doesn't even see you—because her mind is a million miles away. People don't understand that if she doesn't speak to them, she doesn't mean to be rude...."

Mary Lou herself said, "When people tell me that I'm playing good, and I don't think I am, I want to run away from them, not speak to them."

Being so intensely self-critical, she has scant regard for musicians who, in her opinion, lack sufficient dedication to their instruments.

"So many musicians nowadays push too hard, spread themselves too thin, doing all kinds of things when they should be home practicing," she said. "People who push that hard never really get anywhere, but if you know your instrument, well, you can lay back and let someone pick you out. If you're doing too many things, there's no chance for your creativeness to come through.

"When the rhythm section starts composing things on the stand, they'll push me into composing. But if they are not together, you must let them walk, let them play by themselves, to find out where they are. Then when they're really tight, you come in and play. But if they're still not making it, then play another tune, play a ballad. When you hear me play chimes, it's because the rhythm isn't right, and you've got to bring a section together to let them hear themselves. But if, after this, they still don't make it, then I'll start cussing!

"Now that I'm out here, I'm beginning to like it. I haven't been late for the job, and I haven't wanted to leave, and that's unusual for me. Sometimes in the past, I've got fed up, and I would walk out and say, 'You better get yourself another piano player.' But this time it's fun for me. Sometimes I'm tired, but I haven't had that feeling of wanting to give up....I think this time that I'm out here to stay."

It is almost as if she sees herself emerging from darkness into the sunlight, to bask in the warmth of feeling generated by friends, admirers and family. Gazing out over the piano, her pleasure in playing comes through clearly. ●

HERBIE HANCOCK: WATERMELON MAN

By Don Heckman
OCTOBER 21, 1965

T he tenuous line between jazz-as-art and jazz-as-popular-entertainment is one that few jazz artists have successfully bridged. It is all the more unusual, therefore, that pianist Herbie Hancock, at 25, already has gathered fruits of both worlds.

It comes as no news to anyone that Hancock's "Watermelon Man" has been extensively recorded and widely received. But "Watermelon Man" is only one element in a burgeoning musical career. Since his arrival from Chicago in 1961, Hancock has been one of the most sought-after New York sidemen, first with Donald Byrd's group and later as a regular participant in rhythm sections for Blue Note records; occasionally with Jackie McLean, J.J. Johnson and the Clark Terry-Bob Brookmeyer Quintet; and from June 1963 as pianist for Miles Davis.

Hancock has had a long playing experience. The son of a Chicago government inspector, he began taking piano lessons when he was seven, focusing, as do most beginning students, on the traditional classical fare. An awareness of jazz came later.

"Jazz first made an impression on me when I was in high school in about 1954," he said. "When I was younger, I listened to rhythm 'n' blues. I remember turning on a rhythm 'n' blues station, and there was one record they played that I liked. I couldn't understand it, but I liked it, and I knew it was jazz. "Moonlight in Vermont," by Johnny Smith. I couldn't understand it for the world. It sounded pretty, but it didn't make any real sense to me. It sounded like it just kept moving.

"The first *real* impression jazz made on me was when I went to a variety program at my high school. There was a trio there, and a guy in my class was playing some music in a way that I could tell he knew what he was doing. I had thought jazz was for old men—I thought you had to really be 'down' musically to play jazz—and here's this guy my age playing it, and I was wondering how he could do that. So I became good friends with him. We hung out together during the rest of my two years in high school. His idol was George Shearing, so he was using all the block chord stuff. I didn't understand that either, but it was farther out than Johnny Smith."

The friend showed him some basic chords and bass lines.

"As soon as I could play the blues in one key," Hancock recalled, "I was playing for dances. I couldn't take any solos, and *forget* the right hand. I could just play chords. After Shearing, I dug Erroll Garner, then the West Coast people—Dave Brubeck, Stan Kenton, Pete Jolly. I still didn't know what I was listening to, but everyone interested in jazz that I knew liked certain people, and so I just followed the pack. From there I went to Oscar Peterson.

"Meanwhile, everyone was telling me they didn't like hard bop, so of course I didn't like hard bop either, even though I didn't know what hard bop was....Then one day I saw a record, and its title was *Hard Bop*. Maybe this is what they're talking about, I thought, and I bought the record and I liked it. From then on I went over to the East Coast, mentally."

Despite the gradually acquired interest in jazz, Hancock was not particularly eager to pursue a career in music. At Grinnell College in Iowa—a highly regarded liberal arts school—he started engineering, changed to music, and graduated with a bachelor of arts degree.

"I wasn't really quite sure of what I wanted to be," he said, "an engineer, a psychologist, or what. I promised my mother I wouldn't be a musician—promised myself too. But I had to break my promise. Even though my mother was against it, she didn't try to hold me back when I decided to be a musician. She's always been my biggest supporter."

Listening to Hancock's music, one can only be pleased that the promise was broken. His interests, his views—both musical and personal—reflect the attitude of a person who knows what he is about and where he is going. His comments on "Watermelon Man" reveal this. Hancock outlined its sources:

"At the time "Watermelon Man" was written, I had a dual purpose in mind. The first was to help sell the album, but I didn't want to prostitute myself to do that. I also wanted to write something that was actually authentic, something that I knew something about."

The most salable commodity at the time was soul music, so Hancock went into his own "personal American Negro background," to find within himself what he had gone through that could be projected musically.

"I've never been in jail," he said, "so I can't write about chain gangs or cotton fields. Then I remembered when I was in Chicago and the watermelon man used to go through the alley—a couple of times a day—and he had a little song, 'Wah tee mee lo-w.' There were cobblestone alleys, and the first idea I got was to try to make some kind of rhythmic sound like a soulful wagon going over the cobblestones, with the horse's hooves and everything. For the melody I started thinking, Suppose somebody were calling the watermelon man—what would they say? They'd say, 'Hey, watermelon man.' So I tried to write a melody that sounded like that. And even before the lyrics came out, any time anybody joked with me about "Watermelon Man," they'd sing, 'Hey, watermelon man,' to the first melodic phrase, even though they didn't know I had this in mind. I guess the melody sounds so strongly like it that you automatically get that kind of verbal image."

"Watermelon Man" has given Hancock access to an audience far wider than that reached by most jazzmen. Recently he was asked to write a song for Lena Horne, and other opportunities in pop music seem to be opening up. Characteristically, Hancock recognizes that "popular" does not have to mean "tasteless" or "shoddy." Like a number of other observers, he recognizes the significant changes taking place in pop music.

"My sister Jean loves rhythm 'n' blues, and she's been playing a lot of these things," he said. "At first I didn't pay any attention to it. But once she had a record on by somebody, I think Dionne Warwick, and I was just passing through the living room when all of a sudden I said, 'Wait a minute. What is this?' I heard some strange chords being played and different kinds of phrases—three-bar phrases and five-bar phrases and 19-bar tunes. And pretty soon I began listening to these things. Through the technical interest that was stirred up in me, I finally got back to the emotional thing which is actually the basis for rhythm 'n' blues. It just happens that certain tunes have 19 bars or have three-bar phrases. I think it's becoming very artful, as a matter of fact. The Beatles, for example: some of their songs are very artful. And Dionne Warwick, James Brown, Mary Wells, Smoky and the Miracles, the Supremes—I even know the names now."

Two-and-a-half years have passed since Hancock joined the Miles Davis Quintet. In that time, his work with bassist Ron Carter and drummer Tony Williams in the trumpeter's group has set a standard of inventive and progressive rhythm section playing. Yet the manner in which Hancock was added to the Davis group in June 1952 was hardly calculated to inspire a young musician's confidence.

"I heard that Miles' old group had been disbanded and he was looking for a new group," he recalled. "A couple of guys told me he was trying to get in touch with me. At the time I didn't believe it....Then I got a call from Tony Williams, and he told me that Miles was going to call and ask me to come over to his house to play. Next day, or maybe it was the same day, Miles called me up. He asked me if I was busy, if I was working. I was at the time, but I told him no; so he asked me if I would come over to his house the next day. I told him sure, but he hung up without giving me his address or anything. Luckily I had gotten it from Tony.

"Next day I went over. Tony was there with Ron and [tenor saxophonist] George Coleman. We ran over some things while Miles walked around and listened. Philly Joe Jones stopped by too. Then Miles called up Gil Evans. He said, 'Hey, Gil, I want you to hear my new drummer.' Because Tony really knocked him out.

"After we rehearsed the next day, he told us we were going to do a record in two days. I was wondering what was going on—he hadn't even told me whether I was in the group or not. So I didn't say anything, and we did the record—*Seven Steps*. Then we had another rehearsal, and he mentioned a job at Bowdoin College. I said, 'Wait a minute, Miles. You haven't even told me if I'm in the group or what.' And he said, 'You made the record, didn't you?' So I said, 'Yeah, okay.' That was fine. I was jumping through hoops."

Today Hancock gives serious consideration to his own music and his own developing artistic sensibilities.

"I'm trying to collect different kinds of musical experiences," he explained. "I guess I went naturally through the post-bebop and the late post-bebop thing, the impressionistic thing of Bill Evans, and now I've started to open my mind and my ears up a little more to other kinds of sounds, the so-called avant garde. I did an album with Tony Williams recently, and as far as the level is concerned, it's probably the farthest-out thing I've done that I've been satisfied with. I wouldn't say that the album is necessarily as far out as Grachan Moncur's *Some Other Stuff*, but I'm more satisfied with my own playing on Tony's record. Young as he is, Tony has really helped open my ears up to some of the new things."

Valerie Wilmer

Does Hancock, then, consider himself a participant in the avant garde?

"I have a certain concept of freedom," he answered. "At my best, I'd like to consider myself a free player. By freedom I mean I'd like to be able to play the music of my moods. And if I want to play rhythm 'n' blues all night, I'm still a free player. Or if I want to play rhythm 'n' blues for one number, and the next number play on the strings of the piano, or even if I'm playing bebop all night, I'm still a free player. No matter what I play, I just want to be able to recreate my moods or at least have my mind open enough so that I can do what I want, so that I can hear or conceive of what I want, even if I can't reproduce it. This is my freedom."

Nor does he pull punches in his estimate of avant-garde activities:

"Some of the sounds of the musicians I like, some I don't. Some I like sometimes. I have a feeling that there are a few musicians that have concepts about music that I can't agree with, for one reason or another. Some guys aren't ready to do a certain thing. Being a practicing musician is not for everybody. Even if you're musically talented, talent comes in degrees depending on a whole bunch of factors. Quite often some people just will not be prepared to do certain things."

Hancock feels there are three different ways in which he approaches his playing.

The first he calls the "mental approach"; in the second, he lets his fingers play "what they want to play"; in the third, he plays what he hears.

"I'm pretty sure that when I perform," he said, "there's sort of a subconscious thing that happens in which I use all three of these different techniques, at different times with different combinations of each. Sometimes I just let my fingers do what they want to do—whichever impulse is the strongest. If what I hear is stronger than what my fingers are doing, then I'll try to play what I hear. It depends on the situation, and it's hard work. Playing the piano is hard work, but I'd rather do it this way because it's the way I feel the most satisfied—even if it doesn't always come out."

Much of this is evident in the remarkably intuitive interaction that takes place between Hancock and the other members of the rhythm section. His conception of the musical relationship allows that if another member plays something stronger than what Hancock has in mind, he will react to the other player's urgency.

"I think all human beings are related in certain ways," he noted. "There are some things about you that are exactly like me, or directly related to me. It's like a common denominator. If you hang around with somebody long enough, you find the common denominator, musically. It's a subconscious thing. You don't *try* to do it. It's something that just happens. And when it does, it knocks me off my feet. Sometimes Tony and I get into a thing where we hit a particular kind of a groove or rhythm that becomes so strong, so hypnotic, that it almost throws me off the piano.

"I try to stay with it, you know, just trying to stay in there, to keep my balance, but it almost throws me off. It's really strange."

A relationship between the new jazz of the sixties and the social revolution now taking place in the United States has been noted by a number of observers. Hancock finds influences and inspiration from his youthful environment, but he seems always to be an artist first.

"I don't feel that I hate white people," he said. "It's like the shoe being put on the other foot—you change the label from white people hating black people to the other way around. Since I don't feel the hate-white thing, I don't identify with it. I understand what those who *do* are talking about, and to a certain extent I can see a partial validity to what they say, but that extremist thing I can't

go for. I can't hate the people who feel that way, but I'm just sorry that they believe in that sort of thing."

Hancock's plans for the future include a wide range of activities—from pop music to electronic sounds: "I like all kinds of music, and there are certain types that are directly related to me. Rhythm 'n' blues is part of my own personal background, not just from being a teenager during the time rhythm and blues first started, but because I'm a Negro; and as far as pop music is concerned, it is probably basic to everybody's listening. The next album I do for Blue Note is going to be a rhythm 'n' blues album."

With a smile, Hancock explained that it would not be a jazz version of rhythm 'n' blues, but a real rhythm 'n' blues album ("straight down the line"). "I want to see," he went on, "if I can do it, if I can produce authentic rhythm 'n' blues with that particular essence that makes it good."

Hancock has an equal fascination for a number of figures in the world of classical music:

Karlheinz Stockhausen, the German avant-gardist, whom Hancock credits with first interesting him in electronic music through his *Gesang der Jünglinge*. The pianist said he feels a jazz musician should have a different kind of feeling for that type of music, "probably a little less mathematical an approach."

Igor Stravinsky, whose *Rite of Spring* Hancock said he still hasn't got over and whose *Firebird Suite* also is a favorite of his, because "I like the sounds Stravinsky gets out of the instruments."

Lili Boulanger, a 1920s French composer of unquestioned talent and promise and sister of the world-famed conductor and teacher, Nadia Boulanger. "She was more modern than the Impressionists," Hancock said. "She died when she was 24, but the Everest recording of her works is one of the most beautiful records I've ever heard in my life."

The list can go on—the music of Robert Farnon (a special taste for a number of jazzmen), Béla Bartók, Ustad Ali Akbar Khan, among others—describing the tastes of a perceptive musical intelligence.

Explaining the effect of this catholicity of interests upon his music, Hancock said, "The sky's the limit. "I'm interested in music as a whole, including classical music as well as jazz. I want to study more; I want to do so much. I guess I'm still a kid at heart wanting to chase fire engines." ●

ROLAND KIRK: TELLING IT LIKE IT IS

By Bill McLarney

MAY 18, 1966

Since Roland Kirk first burst on the national jazz scene in 1960, he has been the subject of controversy. Most musicians and critics have come to accept his odd instruments and his playing two or three horns simultaneously. But in a world that pigeonholes artists, he has defined categorization.

His first recordings seemed to place him in the "soul" bag. Some of his later efforts brought him acclaim by adherents of the jazz avant garde. The music he has recorded ranges from rock 'n' roll hits to bop tunes to classical pieces by such composers as Saint-Saens and Villa-Lobos.

A conversation with Kirk on musical styles can quickly turn into a free-wheeling discussion of the ills of jazz and the music business today.

Bill McLarney: *Do you think the current crop of avant-garde or "new thing" players has contributed anything really new to jazz, and, if so, what?*

Roland Kirk: All I've heard is a new approach. Take Illinois Jacquet—the way he extended the range of the tenor. That was new. I've always accepted Illinois Jacquet. How can you put people like that down and still go along with what's happening today? You should accept the fact that people have done these things. Of course, these things are new to some young people and critics who never took time to listen to them. Fortunately, I took the time. The only new thing I've heard is harmonics. But even that….Listen! [*Lester Young's recording of "Afternoon of a Basie-ite" was on the turntable.*] Lester does something like that. Hear? He takes a C and makes it in two different positions to get sounds from that one note. I call it "squeeze saxophone."

BM: *At a session the other night, some saxophone players were startled by your breath control, the way you could play without taking a breath, and were questioning you about it. Do you consider that a new technique?*

RK: It's been done before but not the way I'm doing it. It can extend a saxophonist.

He has the freedom to play beyond the bar line. I've heard people write this way, but I never heard them play this way, because they had to take a breath. I came upon this by listening to all the sax players from Don Byas on down and up. Take Johnny Griffin. He's so fast. I thought, "If he were a piano player, he wouldn't have to take a breath—he'd just go on and on." If he was really conscious of this breath thing, he could play more.

BM: *Is playing two or three horns at once new in jazz?*

RK: There might be some guy in the woods somewhere who we never heard of who did it before me. I do know I'm the first to bring it to the public. I'd get more credit for it, but it's too simple. It's like the man who invented chewing gum. He was really into something. But it's so simple nobody wants to say it's something. They just overlook it. But I think that it will last through all kinds of music and will be recognized some day as a real contribution. I just hope that when the era comes that people are playing two and three horns, they'll point back at me.

BM: *How do you feel about the "freedom" school of jazz?*

RK: I sat in with one of those groups in New York, and it was the first time I've ever been ashamed of being a musician. I felt like pulling my coat up over my head so no one would take my picture when I came off the stand.

People talk about freedom, but the blues is still one of the freest things you can play. If you know the changes, you can take them anywhere you want to go. I don't say all of them, but I knew a lot of them can't play a melody for you. I'll sit in with people, and we'll play "freedom," and then I'll say, "Well, let's play a tune," and they can't even get through the time.

A person can't appreciate freedom unless he's been in prison. How can you know what it is to be free if you haven't gone through all the changes of being unfree? A guy can't tell me at 20 years of age that he's going to be "free" when he hasn't been through half the things I've been through as far as trying to play music—playing the

blues, the torment of people telling you to get off the bandstand, telling you you shouldn't do this or that. How can anyone be free from this when he hasn't suffered through it? But guys go downtown, buy a horn, and say, "I'm going to be free." And it's worse in New York than anywhere. I've seen guys who don't even know the scale, who wouldn't make it in some small town in the Midwest, come to New York, get on a record, and be an overnight success. New York is a very gullible place.

BM: *As a nonmusician, I can't separate the guys who bought the horn yesterday from the experienced players when they play "free." How do you evaluate them? How do you tell the good players from the bad?*

RK: Nobody can give you an answer. I can let my 2-year-old son play the piano, and that's free. When I pass out the whistles at the club, that's freedom. [*When Kirk plays "Here Comes the Whistle Man" at clubs, he passes out wooden whistles to the customers and invites them to participate.*] But if I ask the people are they musicians, they say, "No." They can't really play the whistles. But if freedom is your standard, then it's valid. They're doing what they feel.

BM: *Do you think the attitude of many young musicians, not necessarily just the freedom players, is not what it should be with respect to older forms?*

RK: There's not enough respect for the older players, and it's getting worse. I call older musicians I've respected "sir," and people think I want a favor from them. And I try to give older musicians credit. A lot of young guys feel if you give someone credit, you're being phony. Take Roy Haynes. Most all of the young drummers have copied him, but they don't want to acknowledge his name. That's what hurts, when you go out and pay your dues, and nobody wants to accept you.

BM: *Are some young musicians deficient in listening?*

RK: Yes. One night I went down to Eddie Condon's, and after the set somebody came over and said, "Say, aren't you Roland Kirk?" I told him I was, and he said, "What are you doing here?" I said, "Stealing." Most of the young musicians don't think they can hear anything down there. But I think that's the beauty of being in New York. I mean that's why I moved to New York—to be near *all* the music. I didn't go to be put in a box. Musicians and listeners tend to categorize themselves. One set of guys listen to one kind of thing. People come to my house, and they think they're going to see nothing but new jazz records. But they see classical music, Indian music, Japanese music, polkas, ragtime music, all kinds of music, and they're surprised. I like all kinds of music.

Don Schlitten

BM: *Young musicians have said they don't listen to certain things or to other people on their instrument because they're afraid of being brainwashed or overly influenced. What do you think of that?*

RK: If a musician doesn't listen to other guys, it shows his lack of sureness. If you know something about stride, boogie, and all of these things, it opens your mind up.

BM: *Do you feel that many musicians today are reluctant or even hostile when it comes to participating in sessions?*

RK: Yes. Long time ago, guys used to get together and try to outwit each other on their instruments. This doesn't happen any more. Now if you suggest this to some guy, he thinks you're trying to test him, and maybe he's not strong enough to be tested, so he rebels. It's good for me to be tested on my instrument now and then. If I don't have it, I'll go home and practice and get it together. Or if somebody sits in at the club and you call a fast tempo, he thinks it's out of malice. But it's not—it's for his own good. Speaking of fast tempos, I used to listen to 33-rpm records at 78. It put my ear at a different level.

BM: *Do you deliberately try to communicate with your audience or do you just hope they'll get the point?*

RK: I think it's wrong not to try to reach out to your audience. I've been on the bill with big-name groups that people want to come out and spend their money to see, and the leader didn't even announce the names of the guys in the group. I'd hear people at a table saying, "I wonder if that's so-and-so on bass," and I'd tell them, "Yes, it is." I feel that when people spend their money to come out, we owe them at least this much. A musician who puts this down is wrong.

BM: *You've been compared, both by your fans and your detractors, to Dizzy Gillespie, in that you dance and tell jokes and try to entertain your audience. Why do you do this?*

RK: I'm just being myself. I don't tell my musicians they've got to entertain. They don't have to smile if they don't want to, although I think it's going to reflect on them in the long run. But I don't think they should feel a draft if I'm laughing and talking. I have had people with me who think I shouldn't do this. But I'm going to be myself, and I'm not going to have no musician with me who feels a draft about what I do as long as it doesn't affect his playing.

BM: *You have certain tunes, either pop tunes like "Walk on By" or originals like "Whistle Man," that are sure crowd-pleasers. Do you feel that playing these tunes helps bring the people into your music?*

RK: Definitely. If you play two numbers in the set to get the house, no matter what you play the rest of the set, that house will be with you.

BM: *What do you want the audience to get out of your music?*

RK: I would hope you'd get some kind of laugh out of my music, some kind of joy. I think music should bring happiness—and sadness, too. Anybody who thinks it should be strictly an intellectual thing—I guess that's the way he was brought up. But when you're working in a club, those people don't come out to be no intellectual, unless they're told that's what it is in front. But I don't think you should tell a customer that, that he's got to come in the club and be cool. That ruins the whole thing. The customer should come in to feel how he wants to feel. If he gets too loud, I think the bandleader should be strong enough to make him feel so bad he won't talk any more.

BM: *Do you believe, as some of the new musicians claim, that music can or should be used for propaganda purposes? In other words, do you feel music should be used to further certain political beliefs or to bring about social change?*

RK: Anything I've got to say I would like to say out of my lips rather than to get you to believe this is what I'm playing in a song. When you hear the song, I'll leave it up to you to get whatever you hear from it. I wouldn't want to tell you you're wrong if you don't hear what I wrote. I write tunes about different things and situations, but this doesn't say you have to hear the same thing.

BM: *Do you prefer clubs or concerts?*

RK: We need both. People should relax in concerts as well as clubs. They should feel they're at your house and you're entertaining them. Trouble is, you can't get as loose at a concert. I might feel different about it 10 years from now. I'm not old enough yet to play one set and feel that's sufficient.

BM: *Do you have any particular complaints about clubs or any part of the business side of jazz?*

RK: For one thing, everybody thinks he knows what the musician should do. People should give the musician some credit for what he's doing with his art instead of dictating to him. And clubowners shouldn't complain if a guy goes over five minutes on a set. He's giving the people more music, and he's being true to his art.

Then there're prices. I feel embarrassed when I'm sitting next to someone's table and hear their bill is $20 and they've stayed one set. I don't charge the owner that much that he should set the prices like that.

And people don't want to give jazz any credit. Look at Las Vegas. They say they don't like jazz there, yet they have hardcore jazz out there—Basie, Woody Herman, Buddy Rich. But they don't call it jazz. Then when some jazz group doesn't draw, they say, "Jazz doesn't draw." Let anything bad happen and they say, "Jazz." People in other kinds of music are coming in late, smoking pot, and falling off the bandstand. But when it's a jazz musician, they want to make it an example.…You know, any kind of write-up that's got anything to do with dope—if there's a musician involved, they say he's a jazz musician when he might not be.

BM: *Has irresponsible behavior become such a part of the stereotype of the jazz musician that some clubowners and promoters expect it?*

RK: Yes. They seem to like it—like torture. I don't be late just to be weird, but they like that. The more you do that's detrimental to the music, the more they like it, especially in New York. There they can get headlines for it.

BM: *Where do you think the future of jazz lies? Musically, I mean.*

RK: I wouldn't be willing to speak for anybody else, but for me I think I'd like to get into electronic music more. [*Kirk used electronic sounds on two numbers on his album, "Rip Rig" and "Panic."*] Electronics is all around, but the average musician doesn't observe it. Like, take the telephone. When I was in Columbus, Ohio, if I wanted to know what key I was in, I could pick up the phone and the dial tone would be B-flat.

Edgar Varèse has been doing these things since the thirties, but it hasn't been adopted too much in jazz. I met Varèse in the Village, and he told me that Charlie Parker wanted to study with him. They really wanted to exchange ideas. But by the time they were supposed to get together, Bird had died or he couldn't find him or something.

BM: *Besides exploring electronic music, what are your plans?*

RK: I just want to play. I'd like to think I could work opposite Sinatra, B.B. King, the Beatles, or a polka band, and people would dig it. ●

WES MONTGOMERY BLINDFOLD TEST

Veryl Oakland

By Leonard Feather

JUNE 29, 1967

1 GEORGE BENSON. "Benny's Back" (from *The George Benson Cookbook*, Columbia). Bennie Green, trombone; Lonnie Smith, organ; Benson, guitar, composer; no bass listed.

It has a fresh sound.…The organ seems like it's in the background—doesn't seem like it's up front with the other instruments. Seems like it lost a little bit of fire at the end. But naturally, the guitar solo was out of sight! It sounded like George Benson. I think it rates three stars, anyway.

Sounded like Al Grey on trombone, but I'm not sure. The group sounded like it was baritone, organ, trombone, guitar, electric bass, and drums. You know, I think the electric bass is getting more popular; it's moving out of rock 'n' roll into jazz.

I liked the line very much—it sounded fresh, excited. Sounded like Georgie Benson's line—probably his tune.

2 ROLAND KIRK. "Making Love Afterhours" (from *Here Comes the Whistleman*, Atlantic). Kirk, flute, tenor saxophone, manzello, and strich.

Wow! First, it sounded like Roland Kirk and his group.…I don't know the personnel.

It's a funny thing about Roland Kirk—if you had two other men, with two horns identical like he's playing, and let the two men play the same parts he's playing, and let him play the two horns, it's still a different sound. It's a different approach even with the horns. It's amazing.

Anyway, I see he's got him one to go for the pop market. It's good, very good, but I think if you're speaking of jazz, you have to rate it as such, and it's not that jazzy. So therefore, I'll have to mark him down for three stars. It's a good track, but it appeals to the current market, which I'll give him credit for doing. He's still getting into it, even in that direction. So I think it deserves three.

3 JOE PASS. "Sometime Ago" (from *Simplicity*, World Pacific). Pass, guitar; S. Mihanovich, composer.

I don't know who that was…but it was beautiful. In fact, I couldn't concentrate on who it might be because of listening to it! It's beautiful. I like all of it—I like the lines, I like the phrases, the guitar player has beautiful tone, he phrases good, and everybody's sort of, like, together.

It's really together; I'd give that four stars, right away.

4 GRANT GREEN. "Brazil" (from *The Latin Bit*, Blue Note). Green, guitar; Johnnie Acea, piano.

Of course, from the style, right away I can tell it was Grant Green.…The piano player sounded like, had a taste of, Horace Parlan—I'm not sure. I don't know the other fellows.

The fire the tune started out with—I don't think the background came up to it. It was lacking fire in the middle section—I mean, to compete with Grant. Other than that, they picked a nice tune, nice rhythm for it, so I would give it three stars.

5 STANLEY TURRENTINE. "A Taste of Honey" (from *Jay Ride*, Blue Note). Turrentine, tenor saxophone; Kenny Burrell, guitar; Oliver Nelson, arranger, conductor.

Sounded like Stanley Turrentine with an Oliver Nelson arrangement to me—which is the current thing that's happening now, begun to be the bag: big band and soloist. And for that, I think it's a good arrangement. Nice direction, nice rhythm, exciting.

It's on the blues side, though. For that, I'd take Joe Henderson. I dig his kind of bag, because it's in the more jazz-er bag. Stanley's in the sort of more blues-er type bag. Which you can understand—it's selling records.

I have to give them three stars for effort.…I didn't see anything wrong with the band.…Still sounded like Oliver Nelson.

6 GABOR SZABO. "Walk on By" (from *Gypsy '66*, Impulse). Szabo, guitars.

That's Gabor Gabor…Gabor Gabo…Gabor Szabo—which one is it? I can tell right away. He's got a unique style. It's different.…Of course, I didn't think that particular number was too exciting. I've heard him a lot more exciting. The rhythm section didn't have enough bottom in it, and it seemed like there was drive missing.

For the soloist, Gabor, I would give him three stars, or maybe 3½, but I would put down two for this particular side. The tune? Yeah! "Walk on By."

7 HOWARD ROBERTS. "Cute" (from *Something's Cookin'*, Capitol). Roberts, guitar, arranger; Jack Marshall, co-arranger.

I think that was Howard Roberts on guitar. Very good arrangement. I don't know who the arranger was, but it sounded good—just wasn't long enough. The arrangement has a point of building up, like it's going to stretch out, but it doesn't.

That was a nice cut, very nice cut. I think it deserves four stars.

How could I tell it was Howard Roberts? By the runs he makes. He makes a lot of clean runs. Not only because they're clean, but they have a little different texture. And he sort of mixes it up: He'll play a subtle line, then the next line will be a double line, come back to subtle line, then he'll mix the chords next. It's a nice pattern.

LF: *Can you think of any albums you'd give five stars to?*

WM: Guitar records? Or any records at all? Well, I've heard a couple of things, but I don't know what the names of the albums are or the artists on them. That's pretty weird—can't think of any five-star records!

Oh, this new thing by Miles, *Miles Smiles*? Now that's a beautiful thing. He's beginning to change his things all the time, but he hasn't gone all out, and Wayne Shorter's playing a little different.…It's nice.

Joe Henderson's got a thing I think would be five stars too. I think it's *Mode for Joe*—he and McCoy Tyner, Elvin Jones, and Richard Davis. ●

HOWLIN' WOLF: I SING FOR THE PEOPLE

By Pete Welding
DECEMBER 16, 1967

With his fellow Mississippians, Muddy Waters, Elmore James, and John Lee Hooker, singer-guitarist-harmonica player Howlin' Wolf—born Chester Burnett—has had great impact upon the course of blues in the years following World War II. His early recordings—often derived from the work of older musicians of the Mississippi delta region—possessed an almost overwhelming power. That force is evident in the numerous recordings he has made since moving to Chicago in 1952, where he established himself as an individual and powerful performer in the modern rhythm 'n' blues style.

Howlin' Wolf's music has worn well. It seems less affected by the exigencies of the commercial record world than that of any of his peers, and it retains to this day much of the dark, burning force of his early recordings. Wolf has been notably reluctant to discuss his early, formative years in Mississippi. The few interviews with him that have been published have revealed him as guarded, even mistrustful. It was with this in mind that I approached him in his Chicago home. I was to find pleasantly that his guard was down. Perhaps Wolf has mellowed in recent years; in any event, I found him friendly, cooperative, and helpful. His candid recollections—unencumbered by exaggerations, fancies, and outright distortions that so many older blues men give out—follow.

I was born in West Point, near Tupelo, in Monroe County, Miss., on June 10 in 1910, and I left there in 1923 when I came to the Mississippi delta, around Ruleville, Miss.

I didn't start to fooling with guitar until about 1928, however, and I started on account of on the plantation—Young and Mara's plantation, where our family was living—there was a guy at that time playing the guitar. He was called Charlie Patton. It was he who got me interested.

He was a nice guy, but he just loved the bottle—like all the rest of the musicians.

He was a great drinker. I never did know him to do no gambling or anything like that…but *drink*! I did know him to play good, and everybody liked him. He was a mixed-breed fellow, a light-skinned guy. He looked kinda like a Puerto Rican. He was from Will Dockery's place—that's a plantation out from Ruleville. He had been up north somewhere and cut some records for some company at that time [*Patton's first recording session took place in June 1929.*] and then had come back down there in the fall of the year, in the harvest time—you know, when people're picking the cotton—to play for the folks. He'd go from place to place around there. He was playing by himself when I heard him. I don't know if he played with any other fellows because he was a grown man then, and I was a kid, and my mama didn't allow me out at night. I couldn't go; I'd have to slip off.

That was the first I heard him, and I liked it, so from then on I went to thinking about music. I remember he was playing the tune "Hook Up My Pony And Saddle Up My Old Black Mare" and also "High Water Everywhere," "Spoonful" "and "Banty Rooster"—oh, lots of tunes. I done forgot most of them, but at one time I could play his music. After all, he done taught me. I don't play it now much, but I *can* play it.

It was he who started me off to playing. He showed me things on the guitar, because after we got through picking cotton at night, we'd go and hang around him, listen at him play. He took a liking to me, and I asked him would he learn me, and at night, after I'd get off work, I'd go and hang around.

He used to play out on the plantations, at different one's homes out there. They'd give a supper—call it a Saturday night hop or something like that. There weren't no clubs like nowadays. Mostly on weekends they'd have them. He'd play different spots—he'd be playing here tonight and somewhere else the next night, and so on.

He mostly worked by himself because his way of playing was kind of obvious—

different—from other people's. It took a good musician to play behind him, because it was kind of off-beat and off-time; but it had a good sound the way he played. I never did work with him because he was a traveling man. In the spring of the year he'd be gone; he never came in until the fall.

He was a real showman. When he played his guitar, he would turn it over backwards and forwards, and throw it around over his shoulders, between his legs, throw it up in the sky. He was more a clown than he was a musician, it seems. But I never did hear nobody else playing like him—playing that bass, patting on the guitar—nobody mocking and using his patterns much.

He mostly played his songs the same way all the time. It was only when he'd get to "Spoonful" that he might change the background he'd play, and on "Banty Rooster," too. He played in regular [E-A-D-G-B-E] and in Spanish—that's open-G [D-G-D-G-B-D], we called it cross-guitar—tunings, but he mostly played in straight tuning, standard. He taught me in all of them—straight and cross, open-G. I never did hear him play anything in open-E.

Now, people around there didn't consider him the best musician. No. There was a group come up from around there called the Mississippi Sheiks. [*This popular group consisted of the Chatman brothers, Bo, Sam, and Lonnie; and Walter Vinson; and occasionally Sam Hill. The Sheiks enjoyed great commercial success on record in the period 1930–1935.*] They had a beat to their music. I think they were about number one around that part of the country. They played all around, but I never did get with them because I was farming at that time, and I really wasn't sure of myself about getting out and taking music up.

In those days I preferred the Sheiks to Charlie's music because the Sheiks had an up-tempo beat. They were a little more modern. Charlie's music was what you would call nowadays old-fashioned folk singing, stuff like that. But there weren't any people could play that old stuff like Charlie.

Up around Drew I remember there were two fellows—Dick Bankston and Jim Holloway. They stayed on the plantations around there, north and west of Ruleville. Bankston was a brown-skinned fellow; he worked at the compress, while Jim farmed. They were older than me, but they were right along there behind Patton in age, a little younger than him. But they couldn't play that sound like Charlie could, because

Charlie would strum his guitar and would kinda drum on it with the back of his hand.

Dick Bankston and them played nice, but they just couldn't put the strum in it. Now I don't know where Bankston or Holloway were from; I just met them in Drew, Miss. They lived there and just played music on weekends. I think he used to play a tune called "Bye and Bye, Baby, Bye and Bye"—something like that. I don't know for sure, 'cause I didn't fool around with them like I did Charlie and the Sheiks. I run into them often.

The last time I saw Charlie was at Cleveland, Miss., and it wasn't long before somebody cut him, and after that, it wasn't long before he taken the consumption and died. I think he's buried at Holly Ridge, near Lula.

I felt like I got the most from Charlie Patton and Lemon Jefferson—from his records, that is. He came through Mississippi—in different areas—but I never did see him. What I liked about Lemon's music most was that he made a clear chord. He didn't stumble in his music like a lot of people do—*plink*. No, he made clear chords on his guitar; his strings sounded clearly. The positions he was playing in—that made his strings sound clear. There wasn't a smothered sound to his chords.

As a kid I also heard records by Lonnie Johnson, Tampa Red, and Blind Blake—they played nice guitar. I heard tell of Tommy Johnson, too, but never did see him and also ran into Tommy McClennan later.

After Charlie started showing me guitar, I came along slow. I didn't really pick up my time—didn't get that right—until somewhere in the forties. I got my first guitar in 1928. My father bought it for me before we left Ruleville. We were living out there on the Quiver River, on Boosey's plantation—well, Boosey was the rider [overseer], but young man Morrow was the boss. He stayed in Winona, Miss. At that time I was working on the farm with my father, baling hay and driving tractors, fixing fences, picking cotton and pulling corn.

There was a lot of music around there. Work songs. Some of the fellows was making songs like "I worked old Maude, and I worked old Belle"—things like that. They'd just get out there and sing as they worked. Plowing songs, songs to call mules by. They'd get out there mornings and get to plowing and get to hollering and singing. They'd make these songs up as they go along.

See, people make their music just like you

think about what you want to do. They make their sound and their music just like they feel, and they sing like they feel. They made up the work songs as they felt. If they felt they was…somebody had taken something from them, that's what they sang about—however they felt. But you take myself: I never did have no ups and downs. I came from a good family, and I come up on a good plantation, and I was treated like a man.

It was in the late 1920s when I decided to go out on my own, to go for myself. I just went running 'round through the country playing, like Charlie and them did. The places I'd hit—I'd go to Greenwood, Winona, and back to my home, West Point, Miss., and go to Columbus, and then I'd go to Indianola and Greenville, Miss. Then I'd come over to the Arkansas side of the river around West Memphis and Parking and Pine Bluff and Brinkley, Ark. Just all through the cottonbelt country, and mostly by myself. I didn't start using other musicians with me until 1948.

I run across lots of good musicians. I was just playing blues and stuff like that. Some of the first things I learned how to play was "How Many More Years?" and "Smokestack Lightnin'," just common songs you heard down there. But, "How Many More Years?"—now, that's an original of mine. When I started to playing guitar and blowing my harp, anything come to mind I'd just sing it and rhyme it up and make me a song out of it. Mostly I'd just take things I heard from people around there. I don't think I got any of my music from church because, well, I never did go to church much. I just picked up music, just playing guitar. Of course, it might be from the church, but that's just the way I was brought up to play.

I mostly just stayed in the country. I never did get to Memphis until about 1933, when my father moved from the Mississippi to the Arkansas side of the river. Then I began to meet different musicians, but I didn't know too much about them. I'd just see them, speak to them, keep on going. I remember seeing different little bands—jug bands—play in Memphis at the square on Beale Street, but I never played in one. Stayed in the country farming.

It was Sonny Boy Williamson—the second one, Rice Miller—who learnt me harmonica. He married my sister Mary in the thirties. That's when I met him; he was just loafing around, blowing his harp. He could *blow*, though. But he lived too fast—he was drinking a lot of whisky, and that whisky killed him.

Sonny Boy showed me how to play. I used to strum guitar for him. See, he used to come there and sit up half the night and blow the harp to Mary. I liked the harp, so I'd fool around, and while he's kissing Mary, I'd try to get him to show me something, you know. He'd grab the harp and then he'd show me a couple of chords. I'd go 'round the house then, and I'd work on it.

It was somewhere around this time that I met Robert Johnson. Me and him played together, and me and him and Sonny Boy—Rice Miller—played together awhile. I met Robert in Robinsonville, Miss.; his mother and father stayed out there in Robinsonville. I don't know what happened to them, but I know what happened to *him*. He got poisoned by a woman down there. I think he was getting too many girls and didn't pay her too much attention. This took place somewhere around Greenwood, Miss., out there somewhere. I don't know exactly when— it's been so long I've forgotten what year it was. It was in the thirties, though.

At that time Robert wasn't more than about 21 or 22. He never did talk about his past life no more than the time he said that he and Sonny Boy, Rice Miller, was supposed to cut some records for the Diamond people, I think, down there in Jackson, Miss. I did hear him say he was going down there to cut some record. [*The details of such a recording session, if ever held, are unknown to discographers.*]

Robert was a little brown-skinned, slender fellow, weighed about 160 or 170 pounds. He was about 6 feet tall, maybe 6-3. The first record he put out was called the "Terraplane Blues"; he also did the "Cross Road Blues" and other different numbers. He was another fellow who played his songs near about the same way all the time. He had his own patterns and stuck with them.

I worked a little while with him around through the country; we was playing around Greenwood, Itta Bena and Moorhead. We didn't stay together too long because I would go back and forth to my father and help him in the farming. 'Cause I really wasn't ready for it—the music, you know.

At that time I couldn't play near as well as he could; I'd be just hanging around trying to catch onto something. Rice, though, he could play with him. We took turns performing our own tunes. If I played lead and sang, they'd back me up, see, 'cause at that time I wasn't good enough to back them up. But such as I did know, they'd back me up in them.

I hung around with Robert about two years, off and on. He traveled a lot. Last time me and him was together we was coming out of Memphis. I was going my way to Robinsonville, and he was on his way to Greenwood. But his mother and father lived out there from Robinsonville on Lake Cormorant, on the Mississippi River.

Robert had a nice personality. He was a nice-looking guy, and the women went for him. So that's why he got messed up by that woman who poisoned him. He was a nice person, but he was just wild amongst women, you know?

I don't know how long Robert had been playing when I met him, but at that time he was playing pretty nice. I never did ask Robert where he learned, 'cause we was just young and would just run in and meet one another at those parties and suppers, play and jam awhile, and take off. I never did ask him too much about his life.

I believe Son House mostly taught him because Son and Willie Brown…I used to play a little with them. Willie was the better musician 'cause Son House always played his guitar with that thing [bottleneck] on his hand. But Willie Brown, he fingered his, and could play all the way out. He knew more about the instrument; he didn't have to play it in open chords all the time. Now, Willie, he was a good singer, too. He didn't cut nearly as many records as Son did because—I don't know—he just left Son House and come back to the farming. Son House, he just kept a-going. See, Willie had a wife back down there—I can't recall her name—he came back and stayed around Robinsonville and Lake Cormorant. That's where I got acquainted with him.

I worked with the two of them at some of those Saturday night hops. I'd happen up on them at different places, and I'd jump in and play a tune or two with them. They was playing music for dancing mostly, fast numbers to dance to. According to what position [key] you want to sing in, you can sing and play in uptempo or in slow tempo. Well, most of the older people they preferred the slower tempo, but when you were playing for the teenagers, why, you had to jump it. They had the dances every weekend. That's the only time those people would have a chance to enjoy themselves—on a Saturday night or a Sunday—'cause those landlords would want them to work any other time.

Son and Willie worked well together; they teamed up pretty good. See, Willie Brown would play and follow Son House with his guitar. Mostly Son House would lead out, no matter which of them was singing, 'cause Willie kept in the background with the bass.

When I'd go out on them plantations to play, the people played me *so* hard; they look for you to play from seven o'clock in the evening until seven o'clock of the next morning. That's too rough! I was getting about a dollar-and-a-half, and that was too much playing by myself. People would yell, "Come on, play a little, baby!" A bunch would come in, and they was ready to play and dance. So I decided I would get a band, get two or three more fellows to help me out—but I didn't do that until 1948. Some of the jobs I had taken was 50 cents a night,

George Gilmore

back in Hoover's days. Seven in the evening 'til seven the next morning—and I was too glad to get it in those days?

I was calling myself Howlin' Wolf then. They also called me Foot. I don't know for sure how that name started—just because they say I had big feet. And some of them called me the Bull Cow. They just give me different names. But I just stuck to the Wolf. I got that from my grandfather. He used to tell me stories about the wolves in that part of the country, how they used to do way back in the days before they cleaned up this country.

He was one of them away-back guys, an old guy, whiskers way down to there. When those old folks first came to that country, there was a lot of game—wolves and cats—in the forest. So he used to sit down and tell me about it, and I would get frightened. Also, I was bad about getting my grandmother's little chicks. Every time I'd get one I didn't have enough sense to just hold him—I'd squeeze him and kill him. So I got so bad about it they told me they was going to have to put the wolf on me. Scared me up like that. So everybody else went to calling me the Wolf. I was real young.

[*Wolf continued this life of farming and occasionally performing until he was inducted into the Army in 1941. He remained in the service for the duration of the war, spending much of his tour stationed in Seattle, Wash. He returned to Mississippi in 1945.*]

After the war, I had gone back to farming, back to my father in Arkansas, out on the plantation they call Phillips' plantation—that's about 16 miles north of Parkin, Ark., on the St. Francis River. I stayed out there until after I figured I was grown enough to go for myself, and then I left there and went to Penten, Miss., and did some farming of my own for two years. I made two crops there, and then I moved to West Memphis, Ark.

It was there, in 1948, when I formed my first band and began to follow Johnson and M.T. Murphy, Junior Parker on harp, a piano player who was called Destruction—he was from Memphis—and I had a drummer called Willie Steele. We played all through the states of Arkansas, Alabama, Mississippi, and Missouri. The band was using all electric, amplified instruments at that time. After I had come to West Memphis, I had gotten me an electric guitar. I had one before I went into the Army, and when I came out I bought another one.

I was broadcasting, too, on a radio station in West Memphis, KWM. I went to a Helena station a time or two in Sonny Boy's place—Rice Miller. When he had to be away, he'd get me to blow harp with his little outfit. But I had a steady job on KWM. It came on at three o'clock in the evening [afternoon]. It was in '49 that I started to broadcast. I had been lucky enough to get a spot on KWM. I produced the show myself, went around and spoke to store owners to sponsor it, and I advertised shopping goods. Soon I commenced advertising grain, different seeds such as corn, oats, wheat, then tractors, tools and plows. Sold the advertising myself, got my own sponsors. Had that show for five years.

It was during this time that I started recording. The first record I cut, "Saddle My Pony" and "Worried All the Time," I made it for the Sun label through Ike Turner. I believe that at that time Leonard Chess was backing this fellow in Memphis who ran the Sun label, a guy named Phillips. So when I made the record, they sent it to Chess. It was done through two or three fellows, because I was a farmer, and I didn't know what was happening. Was glad to get a sound out, you know. This was in 1948.

Ike Turner had me do some recording soon after, for a label in California. He was a talent scout for them. RPM records. We cut them in Memphis, though he had come from California to cut them. See, something had gone wrong between Sun and Ike, so he switched around and put me with RPM. I cut a batch of numbers for RPM, all at the same time. Now, both of the records came out at about the same time—on Chess and RPM. Well, Chess, he jumped up and sent a man down there to catch me before I messed up again. I was fixing to get ready and cut for somebody else, but Chess signed me, put me under contract. I stayed down there and made my second recordings for Chess, but the next ones were made in Chicago. I came here in the winter of '52, before Christmas. I came here to cut the records, and I've been going ever since in the business.

I left the other guys in West Memphis and came up to Chicago by myself—they was afraid to take the chance. I went back down there a year later and picked up some of them, brought them back with me. But at first I was using guys that Chess furnished, the studio band that I recorded with—bassist Willie Dixon, guitarist Robert Lockwood Jr. and so on. A little later I got guitarist Hubert Sumlin; I sent back down south and got him. He was just a young man then. And I also

got Willie Johnson, one of the first guitar players I had in the South. In West Memphis I had been using Willie Steele on drums, but he didn't come up here; at the time I sent for him he had to go into the Army, and he decided to make a career of it. He's still in the Army.

After moving to Chicago, I found it easy to get into those clubs, playing my music, 'cause the people had heard about me before I come: The records were out before I came to Chicago. Right off, I started playing at a place at 13th and Ashland. Muddy Waters had been playing there at that time, and they put me in there. Then I went to stretching out all across town. After people found I was there, they commenced giving me jobs. I only played at one house-rent party here. They tore up all of my instruments, and I said to myself that I wasn't ever gonna play for no more of them.

When I first got here, a lot of these jazz musicians, they wouldn't even look around at me because I was playing blues: "Who's that, a blues singer? I don't like no blues." But things have changed a whole lot: More people go for blues nowadays than they do for jazz, it seems.

It's just that people's tastes change. I don't know why this has happened, but it does look like the blues are getting bigger from what they used to be. The reason is hard to say. It's just in the people's minds—what they want. People get these different ideas. Now, take you and me, we might want to hear "How High the Moon," "Sunny Side of the Street" or "It Ain't Gonna Rain No More." Here's a bunch over here, want to hear "Hey Baby, Where'd You Stay Last Night?" It's just in people's minds, their taste, what they want to hear. Now, me, I just like blues because to me it sounds good.

People ask me what the blues are. I think the blues is problems: when a man doesn't have no money and no job and has a family to look after and connections don't meet right for him. So that's what I call blues—when you don't have good connections for yourself. But singing about them doesn't really make things easier, I think—it just takes your mind off it. Your singing ain't gonna help you none; the problem is still there.

Now, I don't consider myself a professional musician. I couldn't say I'm a professional 'cause I don't know too much about music. I'm just an entertainer; I can entertain pretty well in my way of doing. There's some good musicians out there, way better than I, got better sound than I have, perhaps. Of course, I have my own sound.

But if you are a musician and you're going out to play music, you have to make up a song. It wouldn't sound right if you sat up all night and played and didn't sing nothing. People wouldn't be interested in it; I don't care how pretty music it is. It needs a song in it to make it blend. You got to fit your words into your music without any spots and spaces.

When I go out, I sing for the people. Before I became an entertainer, though, I sang for myself. Anything I set up and figured was good, I made up a song about it. I just watch people, their ways. I play by the movement of the people, the way they live. Probably, over there at that house there might be people—I don't think they're living right, they do things not becoming. You see, everything that I sing is a story. The songs have to tell a story. See, if you don't put a story in there, people won't want to listen to it, because people mostly have been through the same emotions. Since I'm an entertainer, that's what I have to give the people who come to hear me, buy my records. But me, myself, I just like music, period, regardless of what kind it is. If it's played right, got a good sound, and pleases my ear, and isn't too loud, I listen to it.

Now, I don't think my music has changed much over the years. Not much, really; but, of course, I did have to step up with the tempo. I used to play very slow, but I had to come up with the tempo of today. I went to school for my chords and positions on guitar after I got here. See, I didn't know my positions when I was playing those slow blues, but over the last few years I went to the Chicago Music School, and they taught me my positions.

On those early records, even the ones for RPM, I was the one told the guys what to play, how the music was to go. Now, the bass patterns on those records, they are mine— that's my bass. Some of those numbers are just on one chord; there's no changes to them. That's something I got from the old music. But the music, the songs, the sound— they are mine all the way out, from coming up playing guitar.

I always tried to play a different sound from the other fellow. Well, now, near about everybody got that rocking sound. Well, I just tried to make mine short and have a good sound, to play something different. My music. ●

CHICK COREA: THE CHICK COREA FILE

By Larry Kart
APRIL 3, 1969

I'm always hassling with people…who ask for biographies. They want to know when you were born and who you've played with. What good is that going to do anyone to know? I'd rather provoke someone's mind by saying something ridiculous, rather than giving them a bunch of details. Nonsense is more fun to me.

—Armando Anthony (Chick) Corea

My expression is very serious; when I laugh it is unintentional, and I always apologize very politely.

—Erik Satie

Born:

Yes. (6/12/41)

Name of Present Employer:

Miles Dewey Davis Jr.

Working Conditions:

My first conversation with Miles was over the phone. I was supposed to call him back to tell him whether I could do the gig, because Tony (Williams) had called me to do it. I told him I could, and I mentioned that I had looked at some of Wayne Shorter's music that I didn't know and that it looked interesting and open to a lot of different ways of being played. He said, "Yeah, it should remain that way." Then there was a little silence and he said, "I don't know what else to tell you except that we'll go and play, but whatever *you* think it is, that's what it is." That really inspired me and stuck with me, because that's the whole feeling of the way the band approaches music—whatever anybody feels that it is, that's the way it becomes.

When Tony had called me for the gig, he said that he thought Miles was more interested in an accompanist than a soloist, but the first few weeks I hardly comped at all. I didn't know what to comp. Previously, I had started to play in a very unharmonic atmosphere, using harmonies as sounds and textures rather than as voice leadings in song-like fashion. But when I got on the band, the things that Miles and Wayne were playing were so harmonically oriented (single notes they would hang onto would imply so much harmonically) that I was at a loss for what to do. Also there was the shadow of Herbie (Hancock) and what he had done hanging over the band. I couldn't do what Herbie had done, not that I particularly wanted to, and I didn't have anything else either, so I didn't play at all until Miles told me, "Whatever you have, just drop it in." So I began doing that.

Whenever I would have something, rather than hesitating because it might conflict, I would play it, and what started to happen (maybe just to my own ears) was that Miles and Wayne began to play all inside what I would put down. It would seem so apropos all the time that there was nothing that could be played which was "wrong." Whatever is presented always seems to fit. That really makes it very relaxed.

Also, I think the Fender piano I'm using has a lot to do with it, because the problem in clubs was that the piano was always too soft to be heard. I could never develop anything, get anything out. I would be at the mercy of the acoustics, having to play in between things. Now, with the Fender, I can set something out front by turning the volume up. I don't basically like the electronic feeling, but the problem that it solves really makes me feel like part of the band. If I could have a big Steinway on every gig there would be no need of an electric piano. Either that or a baby grand with some amplification equipment that would carry the true sound out.

Miles has a discipline, but it's unspoken. It's a magical thing that you hardly see anymore—the way family units used to be. The father would inspire the rest of the family, and they would try to become like him. The people that play with Miles respect him so much, and, knowing that he knows, they humbly put themselves at his disposal and learn from him.

When I saw [Wayne] Horowitz on TV last night, I thought, "Why isn't Miles received like that?" He has much more to tell us. Horowitz is a great performer, but the last piece on his program was something he had written himself, an arrangement of some gypsy songs, and it sounded like it was written in 1800. It was very pianistic and flashy, nice and entertaining, but it didn't show you anything about what's actually going on.

I wish people who have no means of abstract expression would realize how much artists are needed to show them what it's about. Scientists can look at small areas and find out what's happening, and then they have conventions to try and put it all together. Meanwhile, the artist, who doesn't particularly know about the details of any of these sciences, has the ability to put it all together and see what's going to happen.

OTHER MUSICIANS:

Wayne is carrying the music to someplace else. He really gets in the middle of things, in the tiny little crevices. He plays the saxophone so sensitively. Sometimes, when he and Dave [Holland] play alone, he'll play at a whisper, but be playing *fast*, doing all kinds of things.

Herbie and I have a similar kind of search. I hear a lot of things he's working with that strike a chord in myself. I heard the little track from *Speak Like a Child*, and that was a very humble effort. The harmonies were very subtle, and they do sensuous things to your ears, like Ravel's harmonies. On Tony's *Spring* album they do a free-form piece, and towards the end everybody stops and Herbie tacks on a little thing that's beautiful. I asked Tony about it, and he said that he'd written that part. I thought it was improvised. I'm sure what Tony meant was that he had indicated a melody or a chord or two and Herbie did the rest.

I made a tape collage from my record collection, and at first it was just snatches of things that I liked best. Then the transitions between one thing and another started to be interesting. There was one passage by Cecil Taylor and it spliced immediately into Art Tatum playing a fast stride version of a classical piece, and you couldn't tell the difference for a couple of seconds. Tatum was so harmonically advanced. You can only take harmonies so far; after that they become sounds.

I've heard the Beatles' records, which I like, but there's one album that Dave [Holland] has, an in-concert record of Cream. The fact that it's in concert enables them to stretch out, put in a middle section where they improvise. They're really good musicians, and the tunes are extraordinary. It's a helluva record.

RECORDING:

My recording contact with Solid State came about when I played a concert with Thad Jones, Mel Lewis and Richard Davis at the Eastman School of Music. Manny Albam was conducting an arranging course there, and at the end of the term they gave a concert featuring the students' works. We came up, and Thad brought some of his big band arrangements with him which we played with the Eastman band.

Manny Albam had some kind of connection with Solid State, and he introduced me to Sonny Lester when I got back to New York. At first I was very defensive about it, because a lot of people had approached me about recording before, but it was always with some kind of catch. I had to do some specific thing. Herbie Mann was always on me about "Do you want to record?" and he would say, "Get some timbales and a conga drum," which is nice, but....So I was defensive when Sonny Lester talked to me. He said, "Manny Albam, etc., etc., and your playing, and we'd like to sign you with Solid State." I said, "Wait a minute. Before we go any further, if I'm to do this, I'd like the freedom to record anything, absolutely anything. From what you might call commercial music to the strangest things you're ever heard, even without me playing piano or writing. Just so I know I can make an honest effort." He said, "That's our policy—to let the artist have freedom." I was amazed.

The first date (with Miroslav Vitous and Roy Haynes) turned out that way. They let me do what I wanted. I went to Steinway & Sons and spent a couple of hours choosing a piano for the date. I was like a little kid in a mountain of ice cream, jumping from Steinway to Steinway. When we got to the date they just turned the tape on—there was no take 1 and take 2—and we just played.

CLUBS:

When I'm sitting by myself between sets, the club is so dimly lit that sometimes my eyes will relax, so that they're not focusing on anything, and a whole world of shapes and forms starts happening. Just something to entertain myself, I guess. We entertain the people when we get up and play, but the other times we've got to entertain ourselves, let the people entertain us.

What's really funny is that the management at the door have a roll of money in their hands, a big wad of bills, and as soon as the people come in they pounce on them for the $2.50 before they even get their coats off. It's *freezing* out,

Joseph L. Johnson

and you want to get inside, *anything*, but just get inside to feel warm. They pounce, and you have to open your coat in the doorway and search for the money. It sets up the wrong kind of atmosphere.

Why aren't club owners ever interested in music? Very few of them are. Max Gordon (of New York's Village Vanguard) is one, and Lennie Sogoloff (of Boston's Lennie's On the Turnpike) is another. Max hires the groups he likes—the music he likes to listen to.

AUDIENCES:

Some people (probably the majority) want to be entertained by what they know will please them. They don't want to become involved in someone's search for where it's at, because that takes too much out of them.

I don't think there's ever been an honest

music made where the players were too wrapped up in what the audience thought of the music. Some of the older musicians who talk about being aware of the audience—those musicians are more entertainers than creators.

I've worked a few engagements with Sarah Vaughan that proved to be creative experiences. She reminds me of Miles a lot. The way she takes those standard tunes and condenses them, does different things with them. She'd sing "Misty" every night on every show, and sing the hell out of it every time.

PRACTICAL PHILOSOPHY:

I'm hanging between two things in the performance of music—concentrating on the subtleties of the music as opposed to letting it all out. There's some kind of median that I haven't found yet, but I know that it's possible. I've been involved in some situations where the music has taken itself into letting it all out, just playing whatever may be at hand rather than trying to create "gems of music." It's another kind of feeling, yet I feel some of both ways.

One time I was playing in a quartet with Pete LaRoca, and we had rehearsed and rehearsed. There was so much love involved that the rehearsals were like seances. We had no gigs except one weekend at the Vanguard. Playing there, I got the feeling that I had left my body and was watching myself and everything that was going on with great glee, not knowing what was happening and not really caring, but just seeing that it was wondrous. I was watching my fingers move over the piano and saying, "How did I do that?…That was wild!…That little thing was nice." It inspired my life and made everything new again.

To me, music is a key. It's a key because there's something I get snatches of from time to time that I want to know. It's like a white light that I catch glimpses of, and I know I'm very attracted to it. If it would stay shining long enough, I feel I could locate it, go into it, and come out the other side. Music is the key, because through music I can keep the light burning for longer periods of time.

I know that there is a point beyond which you would no longer need the arts. You get to a certain point in your own art where it has done what it has to do, which is show you where that light is. Once

you've passed that point, you don't need the means anymore, you can just *live.*

I went through a thing of trying to discipline myself, trying to level my life off by all the standards that I thought were good ones. It turned out to be a very unnatural process, and I had to let it all go and put my foot in everything, let it come out wrong if necessary. Whether it comes out wrong or not, something has been experienced that will color whatever else happens, rather than sitting and waiting.

You can get an idea that appeals to you, and start weighing it and end up with a long list of pros and cons. To me, it's just a labyrinth off from reality. It's like playing chess. When it's your move, you can find out all the possibilities and sit for years, but the point comes where you have to move. What seems to happen then is that your hand does it rather than your brain. You may have gone through all the analysis, but finally there's some kind of energy on the table, just from the way the pieces are sitting. Your hand approaches the table with an idea about which piece has to go where, and the hand does it and that's it. You're relieved of all guilt!

LIFE STYLE:

The idea of forming a musical community has been popping up a lot between me and my friends. Buying some land in upstate New York, where musicians of similar temperaments and moods could live with their families, relax and get some music together. What record companies should really do, if they want to get the best out of the people they record, is give them a month's freedom to go someplace comfortable and secluded with the people they want to make their music with, and *then* record.

I'm glad I don't have any money, because if I did I'd probably withdraw from everything. At least this way the wind forces me into relations with the outer world, which I guess is needed.

Often, when I live in a hotel room I get involved with sketching things. I buy some paper and some Pentels or crayons and hang what I sketch on the walls. Or I buy colored paper and make collages over the doors. Then just leave it there. That's a nice feeling—to leave something behind. ●

MILES DAVIS: AND IN THIS CORNER, THE SIDEWALK KID

By Don DeMicheal
DECEMBER 11, 1969

A little man scurries down the dark staircase of the dingy old building on Chicago's 63rd Street.

"Is Johnny Coulon's Physical Training Club upstairs?" I ask him.

"Third floor," he pipes.

"Miles Davis up there?"

"Oh, yes. You just missed seeing him box. Knocked a fellow down twice."

On the third floor, Miles Davis the boxer is busy skipping rope before a full-length mirror.…*Dittle-e-dop, dittle-e-dop, dittle-e-dop.* His feet dance lightly over the rope and across the floor. There isn't an ounce of fat on him.

"Hey, Don," he says, not missing a skip. "You should have seen me box."

Dittle-e-dop, dittle-e-dop.…

"A man just told me you knocked a guy down twice."

Dittle-e-dop.…

"Naw, man"…*dittle-e…*"We"…*dop…* "just sparred a little."

He drops the rope and goes over to a punching bag suspended at head height by ropes connected to the ceiling and floor.

He tries some combinations and jabs on the bag, dodging it as it bounces toward him. A heavy-set man comes up to him and starts sparring lightly, giving advance as Miles tries unsuccessfully to land a light blow. Miles stops and listens to the man, who is Kid Carson, a trainer. He tries what Carson tells him, finds it works, and smiles.

Miles introduces me to Carson, John Coulon (the little man on the stairs) and his eldest son, Gregory, up from East St. Louis, Davis' home town, for a visit.

"Greg won three titles while he was in the Army," says the young man's obviously proud father. "Plays drums, too."

"Can you beat your old man?" I ask, but the son is noncommittal, and the father chuckles.

"Hey, try to lift Johnny," Miles says with

an impish glint in his eye.

This didn't seem to be a problem, since Johnny Coulon, who was bantamweight champion many, many years ago, weighs about 90 pounds. So I lifted him.

"Now try it again," Miles says, suppressing a laugh.

Coulon cannot be budged.

"Ain't nobody ever lifted him when he didn't want 'em to," Davis says. "Show him your pictures, Johnny."

Coulon conducts his standard visitor's tour among fading photos of such boxers as Braddock, Dempsey, Carnera, Tunney, Louis, Clay—all trying to lift the little man.

In the middle of Coulon's reminiscences, Miles walks up in a white terry-cloth robe.

"Hey, man," he whispers gleefully, "keep your cool, but dig when I turn around."

There in that cloth script one has seen on hundreds of boxers' robes is inscribed "Miles Davis." Miles looks over his shoulder and flashes that beautiful smile of his. Miles Davis, boxer, seems a happier man than Miles Davis, musician.

After Miles had dressed, we climbed into his Volkswagen bus (used to haul his quintet's electric piano) and headed for Floogie's Restaurant, one of his favorite eating places in Chicago.

"Turn on your recorder," he said. "We can talk while I drive." And we did, while Miles dodged the traffic.

The obvious question was first:

Don DeMicheal: *Why do you box?*

Miles Davis: It gives you a lot of strength. It's good for your wind. I mean, when I go to play something that I know is kind of impossible to play, I have that strength, that wind. And it blows the smoke out of your lungs from last night.

DD: *Do you work out every day?*

MD: Uh-huh. Like, today I did about seven rounds, boxed four and worked out about three.

DD: *Did you ever think about boxing a bout somewhere?*

MD: It didn't go that way with me, 'cause I always could box, you know? Anybody'd I'd box as a kid I could beat. It's just a natural thing. But I like to go up against trainers like Carson to find out what they know. Carson trains Eddie Perkins. Eddie's the welterweight champ. I boxed Eddie yesterday, four rounds. He's so slick, can't even touch him.

DD: *How long have you been doing it?*

MD: All my life.

DD: *I mean working out in a gym.*

MD: I started about 10 years ago.

DD: *Anybody ever try to start some trouble with you? Say, in the club where you're playing?*

MD: I'd kill a man in the club.

DD: *I mean, does it ever happen?*

MD: Uh-huh. If they start it, I just tell 'em, you know? I just say point blank, "Y'wanna fight?" or "What's happening?" A man in the street is no contest against what I can drop on him. Even if he hits me three or four times, he'll be tired. I don't get tired. I just tell him, "Go sit down and enjoy yourself." A guy who doesn't know how to fight is the one who always wants to fight. They think it's a big deal to fight, but it's the easiest thing in the world to whip somebody like that. Can scratch their eyes out, kick 'em in the groin, and then they say that's not fighting fair. But a fight is a fight. Ain't nobody gonna stand up to me and say watch the Marquis of Queensbury's rules. If I get in a fight, I'm choking the mother. I just box on account it makes you graceful, and it shapes the body nice.

DD: *To play music you have to be in good physical shape.*

MD: You can say that again. And the way I play...I play from my legs. You ever notice?

DD: *Yeah, I've noticed how you bend your knees.*

MD: That's to keep from breaking the embouchure.

DD: *How does that keep you from breaking your embouchure?*

MD: You see, when I play....You notice guys when they play—and this is some

Giuseppe G. Pino

corny stuff—they play and they breathe in the regular spots; so, therefore, they play the regular thing.

DD: *You're talking about two- and four-bar phrases, things like that?*

MD: Yeah. But if you keep your embouchure up there and breathe out of your nose—or whatever comes natural—you can play different things. But don't drop your hands. [*Sings broken-rhythm phrases to show what can be done by not dropping hands.*] See, it'll fall in different spots. [*Sings short, jerky phrases.*]

DD: *You break the flow.*

MD: You break the flow, and it's the same thing. You're playing in a pattern. Especially if the time is getting mucked up, and you're playing in a pattern, it's going to get more mucked up 'cause you're going to start dropping the time when you drop your horn down, 'cause whoever is playing behind you will say, "Well, he's resting." You never let a guy know when your gonna rest. Like in boxing, if I jab a guy, I won't relax, 'cause if I jab him, that's a point for me. If I jab him, then I'm gonna do something else. I mean, you've got to keep something going on all the time.

DD: *If when you move, you break your embouchure, why move at all?*

MD: You keep getting your balance. You keep getting your balance back. Certain things jerk you. Say, like last night I was playing triplets against a fast 4/4. Jack [DeJohnette, his drummer] was playing [*Miles taps his fingers at a fast tempo against the dashboard*], and I'm playing like [*sings quarter-note triplets as he moves slowly up and down*]; it's got to break....

DD: *You mean different muscles, different pressures, to get the notes?*

MD: Yeah. So you got to keep getting your balance and...I mean you just got to keep in time [with the body] so it'll swing, or so it'll sort of stay connected. It's according to how you think. When you box, you gotta watch a guy. You understand? You gotta watch him, anticipate him…you gotta say if he jabs, I'm gonna stop it with my left hand. All this stuff has to be like this: [*snaps fingers*].

DD: *Then you're saying the same thing's true in music?*

MD: The things of music you just finish. When you play, you carry them through till you think they're finished or until the rhythm dictates that it's finished, and then you do something else. But you also connect what you finished with what you're going to do next. So it don't sound like a pattern. So when you learn that, you got a good band, and when your band learns that, it's a good band.

DD: *A lot of times you'll let, say, eight bars go by during a solo without playing anything.*

MD: Yeah.

DD: *Doesn't that break the flow you talked about?*

MD: It doesn't break the flow because the rhythm section is doing the same thing they were doing before.

DD: *In other words, you're letting the tension grow in there?*

MD: No, I'm letting it go off. Whatever's been happening has been happening too long; if it dies out, you can start a whole different thing.

DD: *As a listener, though, I feel there is another kind of tension in those places, of anticipation of when you're going to come back in, of what's going to happen. So that in that space, I feel a tension growing.…*

MD: Yeah.

DD: *So when you come in,* then *the release comes?*

MD: Sometimes if you do the same thing, it hits the spot.

DD: *You mean, do the same thing you ended with?*

MD: Yeah. It'd be mellow, you know? [*He turns to go into the parking lot.*]

You're not going to believe this…. [*Drives up the sidewalk and turns into a parking place.*] Screw it.

DD: *Say, you came driving* out *on the sidewalk the other day.*

MD: Right…the Sidewalk Kid. ●

FRANK ZAPPA: THE MOTHER OF US ALL

By Larry Kart
OCTOBER 3, 1969

A sage I invented once said, "The only event which might merit the term 'progress' would be an increase in the percentage of intelligent human beings." And he added, "Those who work toward this goal are known, variously, as fools, clowns and prophets."

For purposes of economic gain and protective coloration, Frank Zappa and the Mothers of Invention have promoted themselves as a group of truly weird people. Well, the Mothers may have their eccentricities, but no more than other musicians I have met, and Zappa himself is a man of striking sobriety. Sometimes, he even made me feel frivolous.

Zappa is standing onstage in front of 10,000 or so people, most of them under 21, at an open-air concert last summer. He says to the audience, "We've just had a request for 'Caravan' with a drum solo" (the fruit of their routine on *America Drinks & Goes Home*). Laughter. Shouts of "yeah!" "Now we may play 'Caravan' with a drum solo, or we might refuse to play 'Caravan' with a drum solo. Which will it be? We think we'll let you decide." (All of this is delivered in a light, mocking tone of voice.) An applause-meter type test indicates that the crowd does not want "Caravan" with a drum solo. "All right, we'll play 'Wipeout'" (the nadir of early-sixties schlock). Which they proceed to do, in three tempos at once. The mindless riff of "Wipeout" melts like plastic.

Consider this scenario. A bright young boy is attending a Southern California high school. It is 1955. We've just "won" the Korean War. The boy is prey to all the adolescent agonies—acne, young love, cars, dumb teachers, the rigid status system of the American high school, et. al. He doesn't particularly want to grow up and be a successful anything. There is a music called rock 'n' roll that expresses his condition. He likes the music, maybe loves

it. Since he is musically talented he begins to play it.

But soon several things disturb him. First, he is musically curious, so he begins to explore other kinds of music—jazz perhaps, certainly the 20th century classical avant garde. After this, the musical limitations of rock 'n' roll seem obvious. Second, he sees that popular music, and rock in particular, serves its consumers in ways they would never recognize. It diverts their anxious energy into rhythmic response and lulls their sorrows with romantic fantasy. It helps to render them harmless, or at least controllable. And behind all this there is a chain of promoters, DJs, record company executives, and on up who are making a living on the music. This makes the boy angry. He resents being used and manipulated. And his intelligence tells him that this is an insidious form of propaganda (definition: propaganda is not designed to change opinions, but to move men to action, or inaction). Perhaps he eventually resolves to do something about it.

On every Mothers' album, aside from *Ruben and the Jets*, this statement is printed on the sleeve: "The present-day composer refuses to die! Edgar Varèse, July 1921" (on *Ruben and the Jets* it reads: "The present-day Pachuco refuses to die! Ruben Sano, June 1955").

Varèse was born in Paris in 1885 and settled in New York in 1916. His distinction as a composer lies in his acceptance of the harsh sonic environment of the modern city as his musical material. Out of this "noise," with a scientist's precision, he created a musical order. Although Varèse's music can be violent, it is never programmatic or sentimental. He masters his environment on its own terms.

Zappa begins the second half of the concert by saying, "Ian Underwood will now play for you the Mozart Piano Sonata in B flat." Underwood begins to play the first movement of a Mozart piano sonata (K. 281, I think). He plays it very well.

I asked Zappa about his run-in at the London School of Economics, and he said, "I was invited to speak at the London School of Economics. So I went over there and asked, 'What do you want me to say?' So here's a bunch of youthful British leftists who take the same youthful leftist view that is popular the world over. It's like belonging to a car club. The whole leftist mentality—'We want to burn the…world down and start all over and go back to nature.' Basing their principles on Marxist doctrine this and Mao Tse Tung that and all these cliches that they've read in their classes. And they think that's the basis for conducting a revolution that's going to liberate the common man. Meanwhile, they don't even know any common men. With their mod clothes, either that or their Che Guevara khakis. It's a…game.

"I do not think they will acquire the power to do what they want to do, because I'm positive that most of them don't really believe what they're saying. I told them that what they were into was just the equivalent of this year's flower power. A couple of years before those same shmucks were wandering around with incense and bells in the park…because they heard that that was what was happening in San Francisco. The first thing they asked me was what was going on at Berkeley. I was thinking to myself. 'What, you guys want to copy that too?'…It's really depressing to sit in front of a large number of people and have them all be that stupid, all at once. And they're in college."

Zappa introduces the first piece on the concert as "a chamber piece for electric piano and drums." The title, I believe, was "Moderato." A chamber piece is exactly what it is.

The drum part takes typical rock rhythms (wham-wham-awhamma-bam-bam) and stretches the space between beats. The result is a series of percussive timbres suspended over a void.

The music verges on the Hollywood-sinister (background for some awful, invisible monster) but the close interaction between the two players (at times each seems to be imitating the other's part) gives the piece an extravagant formal vigor.

Zappa, like most moralists, is pessimistic about people in the mass. Perhaps he even

wants to punish them. The rest of the group seems considerably more optimistic, and occasionally there are good-natured clashes of will.

Frank Zappa: All those mediocre groups reap a huge profit, because people really like what they do. The more mediocre your music is, the more accessible it is to a larger number of people in the United States. That's where the market is. You're not selling to a bunch of jazz esthetes in Europe. You're selling to Americans, who really hate music and love entertainment, so the closer your product is to mindless entertainment material, escapist material, the better off you're going to be. People will dump a lot of money into a bunch of young pretty boys who are ready to make music of limited artistic merit so long as they can sell a lot of it.

Larry Kart: *What about your gestures of contempt towards your audience?*

FZ: I don't think the typical rock fan is smart enough to know he's been dumped on, so it doesn't make any difference….Those kids wouldn't know music if it came up and bit 'em on the ass. Especially in terms of a live concert where the main element is visual. Kids go to see their favorite acts, not to hear them….We work on the premise that nobody really hears what we do anyway, so it doesn't make any difference if we play a place that's got ugly acoustics. The best responses we get from an audience are when we do our worst material.

Don Preston: Oh, how can you say that?

FZ: It's true, man. "Louie, Louie" brings down the house every time.

DP: People were booing the last time you played that. One guy wanted "Louie, Louie," so you said, "OK, we'll play 'Louie, Louie'."…Booo!

FZ: Maybe they were booing because we didn't play "Midnight Hour" instead.

LK: *Isn't it difficult to function as musicians when you feel that no one is listening?*

DP: I don't feel that way.

FZ: I think most of the members of the group are very optimistic that everybody hears and adores what they do on stage. I can't take that point of view. I get really bummed out about it. Because I've talked to them [the audiences] and I know how dumb they are. It's pathetic.

DP: But they do scream for more when we do a good show.

FZ: They scream for more and more because they paid X amount of dollars to get in, and they want the maximum amount of entertainment for their money. It's got nothing whatever to do with what you play. Stick any group on there and let them play to the end of the show.

LK: *Do you have a solution to this situation?*

FZ: Yeah. I'm not going to tour anymore.

Then I asked some questions which amounted to, "Will rock survive?"

FZ: Rock won't die. It will go through some changes, but it ain't going to die. They predicted it too many times in the past. Remember—"the limbo is coming in, rock and roll is dead." There've even been some concerted efforts to kill it…but it will survive because there'll always be several very smart producers and record companies who are interested in giving people what they want instead of what they need.

During the concert the Mothers play several long numbers where everybody gets a chance to blow. Since several of the players have extensive jazz backgrounds (Preston, the Gardner brothers, and Underwood), their playing in this context clarifies the differences between jazz and rock improvisation.

An essential quality of the jazz solo is the sense it conveys of forward movement through time, which is the result, I think, of the jazz soloist's role in even the simplest contexts—establishing and revealing his identity. In the typical rock solo this kind of forward movement rarely occurs. Instead there is an amount of space to be decorated, with the emotional curve (excitement to ecstasy) a foregone conclusion. That's why many jazz listeners find rock solos boring, no matter how well played. They're like someone brought up on Beethoven who listens to a raga and says, "I dig the rhythm, but we're going around in circles. Where's the development?"

In many rock solos, guitar solos especially, there is a theatrical relation between the player and what he's playing, and the most "exciting" parts occur when it sounds as if what he's playing has got the upper hand. The drama is that he's conjured up a screaming musical monster, supposedly, and now the beast threatens to overcome him. The "excitement" comes from watching him master the "beast," surrender to it, or get even altogether and smash or burn the instrument. When someone like Jimi Hendrix presents this sexual fantasy, it can be Wagnerian.

The Mothers undercut this setup quite neatly. The soloists go through the outward motions of getting hot, but their precision of accent and the care they give to motivic development prevent any "loss of control" effect.

The reaction of the audience to this was curious. Zappa would stomp off a number that had "Watch Out! Explosion Ahead!" written all over it, and the people around me would murmur, "Yeah", and a blank look of anticipated ecstasy would settle on their faces. By the end of the piece no explosion had occurred, and they looked vaguely bewildered, although they applauded, of course.

The Mothers have made six albums, and *Absolutely Free*, *We're Only In It For the Money*, and *Uncle Meat* are worthy of anyone's attention. Their first album, *Freak Out*, is interesting but unformed compared to the others; *Mothermania* is an anthology, and *Ruben and the Jets*, an extreme parody of fifties rock 'n' roll, doesn't mean much to me, since I never got to that music the first time around.

Listening to all the albums in one sitting reveals an interesting facet of Zappa's musical procedure—in the pieces with lyrics the often elaborate rhythmic and melodic patterns are tied directly to the words (one beat and one note to each syllable, with few large melodic intervals). This effect carries over into the instrumental pieces, where the tight rhythmic-melodic motifs expand and contract as if they had a life of their own. It's an airy, bracing music, and the play of intelligence in it is so prominent that one must respond in kind.

Zappa thinks that *Uncle Meat* is "the best album in terms of overall quality," but his favorite music is on *Lumpy Gravy*, the album where he directs a large orchestra. It's hard for me to tell why he thinks so, since what comes through is a collage of rock and classical parodies that are disconnected by any standards. Perhaps he has in mind the album *Lumpy*

Gravy might have been, since both he and Bunk Gardner mentioned that the Los Angeles studio men on the date were unable to cope with some of the music and played without much spirit on what they did manage to record.

Frank Zappa might be described as a cultural guerrilla. He sees that the popular arts are propagandistic in the broad sense—even when they masquerade as rebellion they lull us into fantasy and homogenize our responses. So he infiltrates the machine and attempts to make the popular forms defeat their traditional ends—his music doesn't lull, it tries to make you think.

Obviously, he's balanced on a narrow edge. On the one hand, he's faced with an audience whose need for homogeneous response is so great that they can make his creations fit their desires. On the other, he must in some way reach a mass audience or his efforts are useless. And, of course, there's money, too. He's only human.

But, whatever the outcome, there is still the music, and if any of us are around in 20 years, I think we'll be listening to it. ●

Frank Zappa *(front row, second from left)* **and The Mothers of Invention**

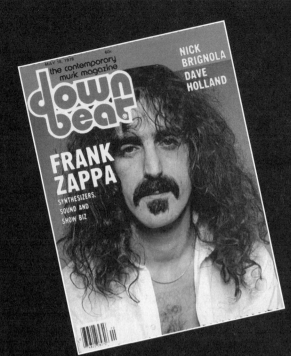

THE 1970s

INTRODUCTION

By Howard Mandel ....

For jazz, and for *Down Beat*, the 1970s were a time of transition and consolidation, a decade of production that was hotly debated, often misunderstood, and only now in the 1990s is being considered for re-evaluation.

Inevitably, the seventies took their toll on the great masters of the first American jazz century—including Louis Armstrong, Duke Ellington, Coleman Hawkins, Johnny Hodges, Stan Kenton, Rahsaan Roland Kirk, and Charles Mingus, to cite just a few. With the demise of some of the most enduring jazz giants and their lesser-known, if no less distinguished, professional colleagues, traditional forms of jazz such as dixieland and the big swing dance band sound suffered neglect to the point of seemingly irreversible decline.

Early in the decade, innovative developments in rock and soul music had a shock effect on jazz and its commercial outlets, overshadowing both tried-and-true styles and the progressive directions explored by daring young jazzbos. As the Baby Boom generation attained its age of consumer maturity, music for sale rather than for purely esthetic satisfaction was promoted by both the recording industry and new high-tech instrument makers. The increased availability of home recording equipment, synthesizers, and drum machines nurtured a newborn "jazz-rock," which in turn begat fusion and radio formats that resulted in new configurations of pop jazz spreading throughout our land (and beyond).

Still, there was no one dominant jazz form in the seventies. Rather, avid listeners were confronted by a plethora of possibilities and more questions than answers. Besides witnessing the release of richly bedded and detailed jazz studio sessions (remember Creed Taylor's flamboyant CTI hits?), the seventies was the decade of the scrappy artist-produced recording; intriguing, original works by stubbornly independent if little-known artists packed the racks of the national chain record stores that mushroomed in every new suburban mall. East Coast bop, West Coast mellow, Midwest avant garde, New Orleans rhythm 'n' blues, reissues galore, and efforts from overseas—Africa, Brazil, Cuba, Europe—abounded. Jazz thrived like a plant gone wild, green shoots extending where once there were none, aburst with buds. Innovators of the sixties and even earlier decades became ever more firmly established in the seventies. We think of Ornette, Coltrane, Miles Davis, Sun Ra, Cecil Taylor, Steve Lacy, founding members of the AACM (Muhal Richard Abrams, the Art Ensemble, Air, Anthony Braxton), BAG (Julius Hemphill and Oliver Lake, who established the World Saxophone Quartet), JCOA (Carla Bley, Michael Manler), and the Creative Music Studio (Karl Berger et al.)—as well as Gil Evans, George Russell, Paul Bley, and a Woodstock-sized population of electric guitarists and keyboard players—as creating the era's soundtrack.

Urban bluesmen such as Muddy Waters, Howlin' Wolf, B.B. King, and Bobby "Blue" Bland continued to impress upon us the stamina and rootedness of their expression. Country and cowboy improv styles such as bluegrass and western swing were reinvigorated through the efforts of mandolinist David Grisman, for instance, and Bob Wills' acolytes like Asleep at the Wheel. Latin dance jazz—salsa—enjoyed its Golden Era, through the efforts of Ray Barretto, Willie Colon, Celia Cruz, Larry Harlow, Johnny Pacheco, and Charlie and Eddie Palmieri. Musicians of every description scrambled to define, defend, and disseminate their work through ever more demanding schedules of performances and recordings at home and ever farther abroad.

Just where home and abroad *was* changed for many jazz musicians. It wasn't that the number of American expatriates exploded; indeed, the seventies heralded the return of Stan Getz, Johnny Griffin, Dexter Gordon, and Phil Woods, among others who'd taken refuge in Europe during the lean late sixties. But credible jazz musicians (and modernist improvisors) emerged in great numbers from Eastern Europe, Asia, the Caribbean, Canada, and other way stations out there. Maybe it seemed at the time that there was audience resistance to straight-ahead jazz and an entertainment economy in recession—but with hindsight we recall that New York City jazz lofts served as community centers. An ad hoc international network of fans, clubs, and presenters flourished. Collegiate jazz education became commonplace. Television as well as radio flirted with new prospects for jazz broadcasting.

As artist-run record companies and distribution services celebrated a startling array of non-commercial (anyway, non-conventional) music, Western Europe opened the stages of its state-supported music fests to cross-genre experimentalists and free improvisers, embracing with special enthusiasm Americans from Defunkt to James White and the Blacks who wed free play to funk. Yet there was also a contrasting new cool; Manfred Eicher's ECM label proposed a popular, influential music based on a reverence for stillness and reverberant ambiance, giving us Jack DeJohnette, Jan Garbarek, Egberto Gismonti, Keith Jarrett, Pat Metheny, and the group Oregon as leading exponents. Straight-ahead veterans and progressives including Art Blakey, the pianist Bill Evans, Dizzy Gillespie, Art Pepper, and Woody Shaw kept touring, recording, discovering, and influencing the future generations, greeted everywhere with the respect they deserved as devoted artists.

The U.S. government at long last recognized and determined to support jazz as an art form by funding composers, performers, and institutions through the National Endowment for the Arts. During the bicentennial Fourth of July, President Jimmy Carter sang "Salt Peanuts" with trumpeter Gillespie among the distinguished, panstylistic jazz guests on the White House lawn. Millions of Americans listened to the broadcast over National Public Radio's "Jazz Alive!" Local civic administrations in Chicago, Atlanta, and Detroit joined the movement, funding the expansion of fan-launched jazz festivals, the better to attract corporate support and tourist dollars to their towns.

Eventually, the excesses of the seventies—and let's 'fess up, there were some—subsided. The over-amped and highly contrived indulgences of those who imitated Miles Davis, Tony Williams' Lifetime, the Brecker Brothers, and the Mahavishnu Orchestra have been consigned to the back browser boxes of stores that still sell used vinyl. What endures from the infusion of electronics into jazz is not a desire to amass arena-filling audiences, but a willingness to access modern technology—these days reaching to MIDI, digital audio editing, and computers with CD-ROM applications.

Guitarists, particularly, gained ground as leading jazz voices in seventies: among them, John Abercrombie, George Benson, Larry Coryell, Mick Goodrick, Earl Klugh, John McLaughlin, Pat Metheny, John Scofield, and don't forget Frank Zappa came to the decade with depths of personal experience and humility in their regard for jazz past, while flashmasters such as Al Di Meola, Carlos Santana, and Eddie Hazel drew on pure pop energies. If keyboardists (Chick Corea, Keith Jarrett, Herbie Hancock, and Josef Zawinul) and drummers (those who tangled with loops and sequencers) were either liberated or enslaved by new technology, the final outcome of their struggles hasn't been decided—and likely won't be for eons. What's indisputable is that advances in electronic media brought the whole world's music within hearing. If you sought a sound, now you could find it. The modal classicism and also the rhythmic complexity of India (through Shakti's Zakir Hussain and Miles' sideman Badal Roy), the rebellious spirit as well as the deep bass anchor of Jamaican reggae, the pre-blues hum of West Africa and the highlife

doowop of South Africa, the Argentine tango, Brazilian bossa nova, Mexican mariachi, and Balinese gamelan, and gutteral chants of Tibetan monks all vied for their influence in jazz's global mix.

During the early and mid seventies, *Down Beat* suffered its mid-life identity crisis, dressing up in gaudy color layouts, identifying with flamboyant chops and pop stars, noting frequent changes in its editorial staff. By the time the seventies came to a close, *Down Beat* had reasserted itself as a monthly publication with muted but attractive graphics, increased space for longer features, and renewed interest in jazz of all forms. News pages were crammed with items of jazz resurgence, and candor regarding the workings of the real world again informed the magazine's most ambitious articles.

Like jazz itself, *Down Beat* in the seventies became aware that musical ideas were related without necessarily logical regard for generic social or historic distinctions. The magazine aimed to help its readers identify the values and standards of jazz, the tensile strength of America's adopted Western cultural tradition, and the true appeal of unapologetic pop. Then *Down Beat* directed the musicians and listeners who picked up toward a better, fuller appreciation of musical similarities and differences, transcending the barriers and divisions of commerce. That's the course the magazine pursued in the eighties and to which it hews today. ●

HOWARD MANDEL first wrote for *Down Beat* in 1975, and was associate editor during the late seventies and early eighties. Mandel is an award-winning columnist, features writer, and reviewer (with credits including *The New York Times Book Review*, *The Village Voice*, *Ear*, *Swing Journal*, and *The Wire*). He also serves as a reporter-commentator on National Public Radio's "Morning Edition."

LEE MORGAN: JAZZ CAN BE SOLD

By Joe Gallagher
FEBRUARY 9, 1970

The first rock 'n' roll group I was in—me and Archie Shepp, and Reggie Workman for a while, too—was Carl Holmes and the Jolly Rompers." Thirty-one year-old trumpeter Lee Morgan—at 18 a member of Dizzy Gillespie's State Department band, long-associated with Art Blakey's Jazz Messengers, writer of "The Sidewinder" and leader of his own quintet—was illustrating a point.

"Music is coming so close together," he said. "Everybody's using a little bit of everybody else. A tremendous amount of beautiful material is coming from rock musicians, from Burt Bacharach, from Broadway musicals and motion pictures.

"Now you hear rock tunes with beautiful changes. You'll see now that, as soon as a tune comes out—especially if it's a nice one—just about every form will adopt it. You might hear strings, or somebody singing it, or a guitar, or a jazz group will put an arrangement on it. That means everybody experiences more."

When Morgan was coming up, he recalled, he played bar mitzvahs and Polish weddings. At Mastbaum High School for the Arts in Philadelphia, he majored in music and half his day was spent in some form of music—composition, harmony, solfeggio. There was a concert orchestra, a concert band, a dance band, a marching band.

"I've been through all that, besides the jazz—and rock 'n' roll," he observed.

One could almost feel the backbeat as Morgan reminisced by singing a bit of the Jolly Rompers' version of "Things Ain't What They Used to Be."

"All that is beautiful experience," he said. "It's all our music. Jazz, rhythm-and-blues, spirituals. Look at Aretha Franklin, Sam Cooke. They came out of churches.

"I don't like labels. If you can play, you

can play with everybody. Look at Coleman Hawkins, Joe Henderson. Whatever you prefer, you'll find sufficient quantities of talented musicians who prefer the same. But you should never limit your mind. With the new thing coming in, I'm one of those who prefer to swing a lot. But I've experimented with free forms, like on Grachan Moncur's "Evolution" and Andrew Hill's "Grass Roots"—playing without the rhythm, against the rhythm, disregarding it—the whole freedom thing....The avant-garde organist who plays with Tony Williams—Larry Young. I made an album with him, and the next week one with Lonnie Smith, a whole different thing. Then Reuben Williams had me and George Coleman, and we did some pretty show tunes, things by Burt Bacharach."

But with regard strictly to jazz, Morgan expressed a view nurtured in anger over its treatment.

"For one thing, if they gave our music a chance on television and AM radio," he said, "you'd be surprised how many people would be listening to it.

"The people who control the media work on a low level. 'East Side/West Side' showed things, like interracial marriage, drug addiction, things that mean something to people. It was halfway good, so they took it off. 'Green Acres' and 'The Beverly Hillbillies' stay on. They insult us. They try to make you feel that your whole life is going to be straight if you use this deodorant. The guy's marriage is falling apart, and all this is because he ain't tried Listerine.

"I'm sure that if they exposed jazz and all the other arts, the people would go for it. But they don't want to because once people start thinking, they'll do more and more of it. Jazz is a true thing, and it's got to be surrounded by truth. And they don't want to get into truth—not when they can do something else and make just as much money.

"I really can't understand why they don't get behind it. They could make their money from it. You know, if they can get on television and sell Playtex girdles...and tell you about midriff bulge and all that, they damn sure can sell some music if they

want to. They say, 'Jazz is too hard to sell.' They've sold the Maharishi Yoga and Ravi Shankar playing sitars and everything. They can sell anything and make it packageable, make it commercial."

Jazzmen wouldn't have to be on the air all the time, in Morgan's view, but perhaps it would be nice to turn on the TV set once or twice every few months and see "maybe a concert by Duke Ellington's band or even an hour in color featuring the Miles Davis Quintet.

"They do show you a few concerts by the New York Philharmonic with Leonard Bernstein explaining to the kids," Morgan noted, "but this (jazz) is the only thing America has that's really ours. Television makes you think jazz is Herb Alpert and the Tijuana Brass or Louis Armstrong singing "Hello, Dolly." Louis Armstrong is a true jazz musician, but television won't show you. When I was with the Messengers, the Japanese and the English did television features on us. Everybody but our own people. The only exception was Steve Allen, but Steve's a musician himself.

"If a guy comes into a record company and says, 'Look, give me $1,000 for publicity for the Fifth Dimension'—it could be any of those rock groups—solid. You come in and ask for $200 to pay for two 30-second spots to advertise a jazz record, and they look at you like you're crazy. They just don't want to spend any money.

"It's almost like a conspiracy. It would help them to advertise. Everybody could make money from the music, but everybody is happy to keep the level of AM daytime listening in a trash bag."

The U.S. Information Agency makes propaganda specials, Morgan said, pointing out that last spring there was one featuring Nipsey Russell, with Billy Eckstine, Joe Carroll, Etta Jones, "and a guy from the Metropolitan Opera." Morgan was on it, too, with a big band.

"It'll be shown all over the world to foster good relations with our government," he said, but added, ruefully, "probably nobody here will ever see it."

"Even superstars like Miles Davis and Duke Ellington don't get the exposure of Leonard Bernstein and the New York Philharmonic," he said. "Maybe this music of ours isn't meant for the masses. But he's held as a great conductor, and he lives in a penthouse, and he's rich, and he conducts the New York Philharmonic in Lincoln Center. And Coltrane had to be playing in Slugs'. That's the difference.

"See, Leonard Bernstein plays to a minority audience, too, because everybody can't like symphony orchestras. But symphony orchestras are subsidized. And jazz should be subsidized. This is the only thing from America. The United States ain't got nothing else but what we gave it, man. And that seems to be the reason it gets the short end of the stick of everything."

Though angry about the mass media, Morgan is happy about the young people of today.

"Thanks to them," he said, "music has gotten much better. And when I was a kid, white people had one way of dancing and we had another. Now everybody dances the same. Rock and jazz—it's all good music. Now, you go over to Europe, and you might be on a concert or a TV show opposite The Doors, and it would be very successful. The ones in charge in the United States don't want to do this. Like I said before, jazz is still a thing that's dominated by blacks. At first there was blues and rhythm-and-blues, and then the white man got a hold of it, and it was rock. Rock didn't start in Liverpool with the Beatles. All that long hair and stuff came later. But most of the whites got the most money from it."

Noting that the work of some successful rock groups has an intricacy comparable to jazz, Morgan observed that even with its new hipness, rock "is selling millions. So I don't want to hear that stuff about they can't sell jazz, because the music's gotten so now that rock guys are playing sitars and using hip forms, and Miles is using electric pianos. Music's gotten close. There are no natural barriers. It's all music. It's either hip or it ain't." ●

J.J. JOHNSON: JAZZ WILL SURVIVE

By Thomas Tolnay

MAY 28, 1970

Jazz is a public art in the truest sense, a form that is most true to itself and to its audience when being created while people look on. For this reason, the world of jazz almost always accords its highest honors, rewards and recognition to those practitioners who—in addition to being first-rate musicians—remain active on the live scene, playing clubs and concerts in full view of their audiences. In this respect, J.J. Johnson is an exception.

For the past three years, the trombonist has been almost totally absent from the public arena of jazz. He quit the club scene entirely, steered clear of concerts, and has participated only in rare workshop-type sessions, combining lecturing with some playing. In spite of this, Johnson continues to be regarded by critics and, more significantly, by the average fan, as the most accomplished and swinging trombone player in the world.

Part of the reason Johnson has remained so omnipresent in the minds of jazz folk, without actually facing them, is that he has remained very active on the recording scene. Over the past three years, he did several albums with long-time sidekick Kai Winding. He also put together an album or two for himself, as he might say. In the recording studio, at least, he has been as active as ever.

In 1968 and 1969, the reunited J&K recorded two clean-cut, diversified albums for A&M Records, *Betwixt and Between* and *Israel*. The personnel, material and arrangements display the kind of range in musical thought and discipline that aware listeners have come to expect from Johnson. As always, the trombonist's warm tone and easy invention are very much in evidence.

Somewhat earlier, RCA brought out *The Total J.J. Johnson.* This album—boasting such excellent company as Benny Powell, Art Farmer, Jerome Richardson, Hank Jones, Ron Carter, Grady Tate, and others—consists of solid, straight-head jazz, the kind of music that pleases its creator most, not to mention the listener. Another album with Winding will be released soon.

So new records have been cut with regularity, and jazz lovers have been keeping in touch with J.J. that way. However, recorded jazz, valuable as it may be, is trapped, unchanging. Some immediacy, even if only occasional, is necessary to remain close to a musical form that depends on improvisation for its life force. Change is basic to jazz.

"Jazz has been in trouble quite awhile," J.J. agreed, "but don't count it out. Not by a long shot. As a matter of fact, I believe that in the long run—as far as the quality and integrity of the music is concerned—this low period will prove to be a good thing for jazz.

"Several years ago," J.J. explained, "there appeared on the scene a number of musicians who looked upon themselves as the saviors of jazz. These players went around shooting off about 'way out this' and 'avant garde that,' but in the end they didn't fool anyone but themselves.

"Once the public had a chance to really tune in, to see what they were all about, it didn't take them long to tune out. That's when the live jazz gates and record sales began to fall off. The public had caught on. As it turned out, instead of helping jazz, those so-called saviors nearly killed the music.

"That's what I've always admired about jazz listeners," J.J. said. "They can't be fooled. They're broad-minded enough to want to hear innovation. At the same time, they're too hip to be taken in by false prophets. Not only do jazz people love their music, but they know it too.

"The fans, in the way they know best, have shown the jazz world that they are not going to be taken in. In other words, musicians are going to have to get back to good music, to true innovation, if they want to be heard—live or on record. The jazz fans have forced their hand. That's why I called this low period good for the music.

"More and more people are beginning to talk about jazz again, to become interested in this vital form, and it's largely because the jazz fan has outlasted the jazz fake." To restate his important point, the trombonist credited the average jazz listener—through his knowledge and love of the music—with having saved the music.

The proof that the jazz public knew what it was doing all along, according to J.J., is that "the true innovators of the music are still being listened to regularly and carefully. Miles Davis, Dizzy Gillespie and Duke Ellington can't go out of style with the fans," he pointed out, "for these musicians do not represent a fad—they are the heart of the music, and jazz people understand this."

Although Johnson feels strongly about imitators and false prophets in jazz, he was careful to state very plainly that he is not opposed to "new jazz." "I've been a Coltrane man from the very beginning and still am today. Innovation always has been—always will be—a crucial part of jazz. The heart and soul of the music has always been embodied in its innovators.

"But change in art, as in life itself, ought not to be simply for the sake of change. New music or new painting or new poetry must be the result of an accompanying change in the world. If and when the next musical tributary develops in jazz, it will evolve out of the minds and hearts of the artists, not the opportunists.

"To be frank," he continued, "the blame cannot be laid only at the feet of the musicians who grind out notes merely to attract attention. Equally damaging are those who perpetuate this kind of music in print and on the air. The coverage afforded by the jazz press and radio to these fake innovators has been totally out of proportion to the significance of the contribution—if any.

"Naturally if it's new, it's news. But when you are dealing with an art form, there ought to be some objective consideration of what's really being created. There ought to be time to digest the new sounds before there's any fanfare. The fact that something sounds 'different' does not mean it is worthwhile—or even new for that matter.

"Just as guilty as the media on this score are the promotion people, booking agents and managers. I realize, of course, that the nature of their business is to do well by their clients. They want to survive, like all of us. But this is where the music—not the business—that must prevail in the end.

"The press and the promotion corps really jumped on the 'avant garde' bandwagon, but they jumped so hard they broke down the entire gig. If that 'way out' music had been given some time, it might have been able to find itself—it might have meant something. The exaggerated notice precluded this possibility. So jazz *has* been at a standstill—businesswise. But not in the way that it really counts—*creatively*.

"Through it all," J.J. said, "the class of the field has continued to play sensitively and intelligently, and the jazz fan has continued to respond to these musicians. When the Modern Jazz Quartet or Thelonious Monk or Sonny Rollins gives a concert, jazz people click off their radios and TV sets, and cool off their phonographs. They come out to hear their music in the act of being created.

"To me this is very encouraging and satisfying, for it shows how far the average jazz listener has come in terms of musical knowledge and taste. The fan has developed with the music. Today they are more selective, more aware than ever, and they have given notice that they will not harbor any false god that wields a horn."

J.J. is exactly the kind of musician that the jazz faithful would turn out to see. Over the years his playing has remained consistently interesting and inventive. And now, there's a better than even chance that the trombonist will soon again perform in public.

Recently J.J. resigned from MBA Music in New York and has established himself in Los Angeles where he is operating as a free-lance composer and arranger. But the change is not merely geographical. "In the not-too-distant future I am going to seriously consider moving into live performing," he said. "For one thing, I believe that jazz is just coming out of the doldrums. Interest in the music is on the increase. And if I can, I would like to contribute to this rebirth through playing as well as writing."

I asked him whether he would make the club rounds again. "I probably won't delve into that scene much," he said, "though an occasional date is not out of the question. I really got tired of the traveling, and if you want to play the clubs, 'wheels and wings' are unavoidable. Mainly I will concentrate on concert hall and college dates—one-shot deals. Perhaps that way I can both have my cake and eat it," he grinned.

What kind of music will J.J. offer when he does become publicly active? "I've been giving that question a great deal of thought lately. Frankly, I'm still not sure if I should realign my approach to groove with today's music, or if I will simply rely on straight-ahead jazz."

J.J. Johnson takes pride that his musical heritage sketches far beyond the realm of jazz. "I am a jazz man—first, last, always. But I feel that I must draw on all music to consider myself a complete musician." He practices what he preaches. His musical interests include classical, pop, rock, even country & western (he has an enormous record collection).

"Lately, like everyone else, I've been listening to a lot of rock. Some because it is interesting, some simply because I want to know what's happening. Musically speaking, a lot of the rock being ground out today is not particularly interesting to me. At the same time, some rock groups are really making sense, and I listen to them live and on record.

"Not long ago, I went down to the Fillmore East to tune in to Blood, Sweat & Tears. I think this is a beautiful group. Not because some critics have likened them to jazz. I like them because the music they play adds up. Their arrangements are carefully thought out, and they create a sound that you want to hear more than once.

"While I feel that today's rock musicians have something to learn from jazz players, I'm also well aware that jazz has something to pick up from rock—the good rock." That concluding statement may have been a hint that when J.J. finally does announce plans for his new group, still taking shape in his head, he may lean toward something totally different from what he's done in the past.

If so, few of his fans will be surprised. J.J. has long been among the great innovators—one of those dedicated musicians who have enabled the music to survive the rocky period. And you can be sure that jazz listeners will forget television when the number one trombone returns to the firing line. ●

WEATHER REPORT: OUTLOOK BRIGHT AND SUNNY

By Dan Morgenstern
MAY 27, 1971

WEATHER REPORT (Columbia)—*Milky Way; Umbrellas; Seventh Arrow; Orange Lady; Morning Lake; Waterfall; Tears; Eurydice.*

Personnel: Wayne Shorter, tenor and soprano saxophones; Joe Zawinul, electric and acoustic piano; Miroslav Vitous, electric and acoustic bass; Al Mouzon, drums, voice; Airto Moirera, Barbara Burton, percussion.

Rating: ★ ★ ★ ★ ★

An extraordinary new group merits an extraordinary review of its debut album. This, in fact, is more than a review. It is an introduction to Weather Report and a discussion of the music on the group's album by the musicians themselves, with parenthetical comments by this writer.

GENESIS

The musicians who make up Weather Report, an incorporated, co-operative group, came together early this year when all found themselves free to engage in a new venture.

Wayne Shorter and Joe Zawinul had worked together on Miles Davis' *Bitches Brew*, and, according to the pianist, "it was a fantastic cooperation kind of feeling." Not long thereafter, Shorter left Miles and was doing some freelance recording and thinking about forming a group of his own. He was trying to obtain the services of bassist Miroslav Vitous, then with Herbie Mann, for a record date, but the band was off for Japan.

Some time later, Vitous called Shorter and told him: "I'm free!" Wayne thought at first he meant for recording purposes, but Vitous explained he no longer belonged to any band. Meanwhile, Zawinul had decided to leave Cannonball Adderley and get into his own thing. He had used Vitous on an album of his own, and the two men had discussed the possibility of working together. In one afternoon, Miroslav called Wayne, Wayne called Joe, and, the pianist says, "all three of us found that we were free—so there was the band."

They wanted to find out how it would feel and sound, so they called drummer Billy Cobham (Al Mouzon, who'd recorded with Wayne, wasn't in town, though they had already talked about getting him) and rented a studio for the afternoon. "That was really an experience," says Joe. "We decided that we were going to need some fantastic management, because the quality of the music was very high," he continued. "So we got Sid Bernstein (who, as everyone knows, brought the Beatles to the U.S.). Then, I was supposed to do some independent producing at Columbia, and when they heard we had a band, the machine started rolling.

"Then we needed a drummer, and Al was the first choice, and when he started working with us in rehearsal it was really fantastic—he sings and all that. And then Airto—we'd tried another percussionist but he didn't have that individualism, and that's what we really are aiming for—individuals all, but playing together. So we called Airto and he fit right in.

"We rehearsed three weeks—or rather, we took a month and rehearsed four days a week—and then we went in the studio and did the record in three days. Rehearsing was quite something—every day when we got home we'd be exhausted, there was so much music going on."

The week the album is released, Columbia will present the group in a private concert—the first live performance by Weather Report—and a European tour is set for June.

THE MUSIC

Shorter: "Milky Way" was originally conceived by Josef Zawinul. (*Laughter*) He had an idea. We just did it with two instruments.

Zawinul: Horn and acoustic piano—no electronics whatsoever. But I think it's a new way of doing something with the pedals and with the saxophone. And what it really represents is that "Milky Way" is everything.

Shorter: We had to start somewhere before we got to the idea of weather and atmosphere and all that, so we thought of coming from a vacuum—nothing into something—and then we thought about our galaxy—we're on the outer edges of the milky way. So we thought of ourselves as seen from some all-seeing, mythical perspective, and then panning in and coming in closer, into the next cut and to humanization and reality.

Vitous: It would be almost as if you were sitting in a space ship, watching meteors flying by, and then a change into chords, like you see that and you see this....

Shorter: So instead of opening the album with a tune and everything that implies, from Tin Pan Alley to a classical concept, we decided on no concept at all except just as much of the universe as you can see. No matter how small you think you are, everybody's got a share in it. So we use sound to convey that idea; like all right, let's begin here.

Zawinul: A preparation for the rest of it. It's like a soundtrack to your mind. You can put yourself where you want; there's enough room in space.

This brought up the name of the group and its implications.

Zawinul: What the music does to people is also what the weather does to people. It doesn't really make that much difference to me if it rains or the sun shines, I can be happy either way; but most people, I think, make up their way of living by what's happening out there when they look out the window in the morning—or even by the report at night.

The people who've heard our music, it really does something to their heads. Instead of thinking, yes, here F7, and there this—it's nothing like that. Even the musicians who've heard it don't listen to it that way (i.e., analytically); they just sit back and get all kinds of thoughts....

Vitous: It's very difficult to analyze....

Shorter: Yes, and it's not like what do you use here, and so on. The only question was about "Milky Way"—what is that? Is that an electronic machine? And we'd say no, and that's the end of that.

Zawinul: Next is "Umbrellas." The first

piece Wayne and I did together. The second, Miroslav wrote the melody and we did a little background and fit it together. And it really gives you the feeling of different kinds of rain. Human behavior in different degrees of rain. The people—you can actually feel that in the tune. I can hear the little kids running with their mamas holding the umbrellas and getting a little wet on the side.

Shorter: Some people carry their umbrellas closed even when it rains—they refuse to open them. And then, when it really starts pouring—they open inside out. And some carry umbrellas when the sun is shining—in London.

If you hear anything in the album that sounds at all bluesy, it's like a blues upside down, with the downward part of the blues facing the oxygen of the good intent in life...like, you can do anything you

Early Weather Report. *From left:* **Miroslav Vitous, Wayne Shorter, Joe Zawinul.**

want to do; the blues doesn't control you, you control the blues.

I'm trying to get the feeling of playing upward, and if there's anything sad, we take that sadness under our wings and say, OK, come on, be sad—but that won't last too long. So each bent note that you hear, you can take it in that way, dig?

Zawinul: The next thing is the "Seventh Arrow," which Miroslav wrote. What can you say about it...it's a masterpiece.

Vitous: It's a continuous composition; in other words, we don't just play one motive and then something on that. It's first one motive and then comes another, almost like another song, and all these motives are written, so it never really is improvisation. Actually, the piece is two songs, two of my songs which we decided to put together—it reminded me of an arrow.

Shorter: He's a Sagittarian—it has that energy and speed. It's swift....

Zawinul: And it's a constant interplay of motives. There are three main lines and they appear in constant interplay. It's like a conversation. On the middle part, I use a ring modulator, to get a whirring sound. My wife used to teach archery in school, and when you stand on the side and hear those arrows flying by, that's what it's like.

I wrote "Orange Lady" thinking mainly of my wife, but also of most ladies who

have children and are stuck in a big city. There's a certain sadness in it. In my case, in order to really make my wife happy, and make myself happy by making her happy, I'll take her out somewhere in the country—that's what the middle part is about—and then that changes the whole attitude and you can go on being happy for a while again, and then you come back to New York and it's like the same thing all over again—it's like a constant change from a certain sadness....

Shorter: It's funny—Joe described that like a blues feeling, but he didn't use the word having the blues, and that's indicative of the change in what we're doing...we can't, we cannot play—we dig the blues and all that stuff, conceptionwise—but we cannot play something that's been played before, because the change is calling to us. It's a necessity....

Zawinul: So that's the first side. The second side starts with "Morning Lake," which was written by Miroslav, and which will create the feeling in you of being somewhere very early in the morning on a nice day, maybe in spring, and it's still a bit cold—a mountain lake....

Vitous: You can see that the water is cold, because you can see through it so well that it has to be cold....

Zawinul: And now and then a fish comes out, and you can walk and just breathe the fresh air; you hear the birds and there's that very peaceful feeling that you get early in the morning—lots of space, which gives you time to put your thoughts in there....

Vitous: And there'll be a duck swimming on the lake, with a little current behind it....The next piece—those two tunes are connected—is "Waterfall," which was written by Joe and the lake turns into a waterfall, with the water coming down at different speeds, and then it disappears into a big river....

Zawinul: You'll hear a lot in the upper register of the piano...it's kind of impressionistic. And after that comes a tune written by Wayne: "Tears."

Shorter: In a sense, the colors I see in that are maroon, purple; dark purple, and dark blue—and some deep yellows, which means it has a hint of the bluish kind of feeling, but not really like that. It's grounded, like in the earth; it has a firm pedestal. Pedestal meaning it's kind of earthy, in a sense, but there's a regal quality there. Maybe a hint of sadness, but carry whatever sadness you have with pride. The image I get is human: tears, blood, skin—a human being. The voice came out of that, the human voice, Al's voice—because we'd been through inanimate objects, objects of nature, water, the milky way, so at some point, we get to the molding of a human being....

Zawinul: The way that moves around, from C to A flat, that's very interesting the way it moves, and out of that come some real pretty notes....

Shorter: The color of the ruby, big flashes of emerald; but above all, this regal quality that is in every human being, no matter what they have to face in life....Al's voice was used in this without any literary message, just as an instrument, and he was given time to figure out how he wanted to do that...there's not much more to be said about that, except dig it.

Zawinul: The next tune is also by Wayne—a fantastic song, "Eurydice"—which is more traditional in the way of playing. It's more in the jazz tradition.

Vitous: Swing in 4/4 time....

Zawinul: Very hip swing...and this is really the only track where we solo a little bit, 'cause on all the other tunes, we don't solo; we just play with one another—like an orchestra. See, we want to use our little band...on this first album, we didn't use all our instruments. I have a synthesizer I'm working with, and several things attached on the electric piano. Except for my using the ring modulator on the bridge to "Seventh Arrow," we didn't use any of that, but next time we will. But only in a musical context, not to show everybody, here, we got this and we got that. We just want to use it for the music...we're taking advantage of everything, but we just try to make music....

Vitous: Each instrument as an extension of your mind.

Shorter: In "Eurydice," I was thinking of my horn in the sense of a woman. There's an Eurydice in every man's life, and she's elusive; like if you look back, she might be gone...and she's wearing something transparent. So the horn, to me, became the garment with the woman inside, very elusive, but floating around in everybody's life. Womanhood is opening up even more today, and that male private thing—art, music, this is *ours*—I tried to get to the woman thing without that overbearing sexual symbolism. You know, everybody is OK—sometimes (*laughter*)—most of the time....

THE FUTURE

Vitous: So that's the entire album. And in a way, we've set up a communication system between all of us, and the next time we'll use everything there is to be used, because we've established our basic thing and we can go from there....

Zawinul: Wherever we go, we'll have our own sound system, so we can always sound like we want to. It will be like having our own recording studio on the road. The equipment is all custom-built and really fantastic...we'll have a full panel with all kinds of settings, etc....

Shorter: But none of this will be used (as gadgetry) but for musical ends, and if something breaks down, no need to panic. We'll find a way of using what goes wrong, too...we'll have our own ESP.

Zawinul: About Airto—he has the most uncanny ability to hear what you want. He doesn't even have to rehearse with us. He didn't. He just comes in and hears the music and he knows what to pick, where to come in. He's incredible; he's a natural talent and we love him and whenever he can work with us, great."

POSTSCRIPT

The music of Weather Report is music beyond category. All I can add to what has been said by the men who made it is that it seems to me music unlike any other I've heard, music that is very contemporary but also very warm, very human, and very beautiful. I don't want to discuss it in detail, but I would be amiss if I didn't mention that there is, on "Orange Lady," a unison melody statement played by Shorter and Vitous in which the bassist bows in a manner quite beyond description. And that's just one of the many remarkable things Weather Report has to offer the listener. The forecast, if there is justice, must be clear skies and sunny days for these four creative men and their associates. ●

RON CARTER AND RICHARD DAVIS

● ●

By Tom Tolnay

MAY 11, 1972

The following dialog is not so much between musician and interviewer as between musician and musician. For this exchange of ideas, two of the most widely accomplished bassists were brought together. Richard Davis and Ron Carter placed first and third respectively in *Down Beat*'s 1971 Critics and Readers Polls. Obviously, the instrument itself provided an important focal point for their conversation. However, their comments were by no means limited to the art and care of the bass.

RELATIONSHIP WITH BASS

Davis: The bass is a personal instrument, a very personal part of my life. To me it's like having a person with you. The relationship is very different from other instruments.

Carter: If I have a different relationship with the bass, it's only in the sense that I play it differently than anybody else.

Davis: The instrument, of course, is associated with a woman—because of its shape and because the player theoretically has his arms around it. Bassists are very tender to their instrument, and they seem to caress the instrument when they play. Women in the audience especially notice this. In one sense, it's practically grounds for divorce! Every musician's wife knows that his instrument comes first. And having to live with that can be a chore.

Carter: Personally, I don't think of the bass as a woman, or anything else. To me it's just a vehicle of self-expression, and I let it go at that. If it were shaped like a lamp, and if it could do what I wanted it to do, I'd be a lamp player. Simple as that. I don't think of it in ethereal terms. Naturally I'm aware of the comments that people make about the instrument—how it must feel for a bass player to hold something shaped like that. Such thoughts, however, are not included among mine.

CARE OF INSTRUMENT

Davis: It's important to take care of the instrument well—the way you do with anything you love. A bassist is constantly wiping the instrument down. You want it to look right as well as sound right. I'm always very conscious of the temperament of the wood. Wood reacts to weather conditions, so I use a meter which registers the humidity in the air. Humidity causes cracks; I try to keep the humidity of the room just right.

Carter: As far as general care and maintenance are concerned, any workman—no matter what he does—makes sure his tools are in order. Again, to be less than ethereal, the bass is my work tool. I make sure it is in tip-top shape at all times so that I can get out of it what I want.

Davis: Traveling with a bass can be a problem. You're actually more concerned about the bass than yourself. In fact, most bass players prefer to buy a half-price ticket on the plane just to make sure that it comes out all right. That way you can protect it with pillows, strap it down, and so on. The bass can be a worry when carried outside too. You may make a mistake in judgment when going through a door, or someone swinging an attaché case may knock against it.

Carter: I've accepted the bulk of the instrument as an occupational hazard. And I feel it won't get where I'm going safely unless I am the one who is responsible. I've accepted *that* part of it too.

Davis: A bass will last through the years if it's cared for properly. The instrument can be almost completely destroyed and still be put back together by a good repair man. But there is a limited number of good old basses around, so you have to be careful.

PLAYING THE BASS

Davis: It takes a lot of stamina to play the bass. For example, it usually takes me half an hour just to warm up. It takes time to loosen up my fingers, to blend them in with the strings.

Carter: Warm-ups are important to me if I'm playing an outdoor concert—especially during the fall. When I stand around waiting outdoors, my hands get cold. And like an athlete's, my muscles have to be loose before I can perform. Generally speaking, though, it's usually not necessary for me to warm up. My mind is warmed up. In other words, I try to have a proper attitude that's geared to what I'm going to do musically. When you're outside, as I said, it's a whole new bag—it could be cold, damp, maybe even raining. Then it's imperative for me to play some scales. It gives my hands a chance to become acclimated to the weather.

Davis: You have to practice the bass constantly, because there is so much space between the notes. The measurement between a whole step has many variant pitches—even a half step has about five different pitches you can blend in.

DEVELOPMENT OF THE INSTRUMENT

Carter: The bass does have great range, but it has taken time to develop this range. Over the past 10 years or so, however, more changes probably have occurred on the bass than on any other instrument.

Davis: The bass has been one of the slowest-developing instruments, particularly in jazz. It was always considered cumbersome, and has always been placed in particular roles in music. Not much was expected of the bassist. The image of the jazz bass began to change between 1937 and 1939. Bass players stopped playing typical tuba parts. You know, boom, boom, boom, boom. Musicians like Jimmy Blanton and Milt Hinton came along—studied players who made the bass a solo instrument.

Carter: Nowadays the music is demanding that the bass line be an integral part of the general sound structure. Also, players are getting involved in different concepts of the instrument. They are no longer able to sit back and just be smothered by the drums. They know that sometime during the course of the night, and often more than once, the bassist will take a solo on his instrument.

Davis: That's right, the bass is expected to play almost as many solos as any other

instrument today. And the solos have to be played with a lot of facility, creativity, imagination, lyricism. There are so many different fingerings and techniques that have been developed on the bass, and most of it has developed from the expression point. I mean, a guy wants to say something, and the only way to do it is by finding a way technically to get it out.

Carter: These changes are turning things around, making people a bit more aware of the instrument. The public doesn't know much about any instrument, and maybe even less about the bass.

Davis: The bass has so many different qualities of sound and tone and concept that there is a real problem in educating listeners about the instrument.

ROLE OF THE BASS

Carter: It's not only the listeners. Some musicians don't know much about it, either. One attitude among musicians toward the bass is that it's a workhorse. I dislike that term. A workhorse is nothing but a horse that pulls a plow, and which doesn't do anything but go straight ahead no matter what happens. Bass players have always been beyond that stage of development, and especially today. "Workhorse" is an uncomplimentary compliment. People who use the word mean well, but it's the wrong meaning.

Davis: I've always had a chip on my shoulder about the bass. One of my classmates in high school—a non-music student—mocked my wanting to play the bass. Whenever he saw me he'd say: Boom, boom, boom, boom. That was the first time I felt I had to prove the bass was more than that. I played many recitals in Chicago (which is where I'm from) just to make the point that the bass is a melodic instrument. In a way I was trying to educate each audience I played before. Some of them had never heard the bass played solo with anything close to a melody. At the same time I educated myself, too, for I found it was possible to do much more on the bass than I had previously realized.

SETTINGS FOR THE BASS

Carter: I used to prefer small groups, because you couldn't hear the bass in the big band. With the advent of adequate bass pick-ups that amplify the

sound, I don't mind playing with any size group or type of instrumentation. As long as the bass can be heard, I'm happy to be playing.

Davis: One of the problems of the string bass, especially in recording, has been that certain notes are not as strong as others—as with any instrument—so that the orchestration sometimes covers them. Lately, as Ron mentioned, they've been putting an electric pick-up on the string bass to get all the notes. But it's still basically the string bass, with all its sound quality.

Carter: If you're working with a quintet, and the two horns are listening to what you're doing as you try to assist them, it's just as satisfying as working in a trio when you *have* to listen to each other.

Davis: I like working with small groups rather than big bands because they are more flexible—there's more freedom, and you end up playing more solos. Also, in a small unit there's less chance of falling into a pattern or habit. With a big band there is so much that is planned that it cuts down the freedom. Besides, the small unit, with its limited variety of instrumentation, needs the change of pace that the bass can provide. This makes playing more interesting for the bassist.

Carter: I have to feel that everybody in the band—large or small—is listening to everybody else. I have to feel that the soloist is taking into consideration what I'm playing—just as I do with what he's playing—so that there is a real rapport.

Davis: I like the traditional instrumentation: basic rhythm section, saxophone and trumpet. Quintet—or six pieces, with a trombone. Working with a guitar is good too. Probably the best, though, is working close to the piano. There's something about the blending of the piano and bass that can't be matched by anything else. It's one of those basic combinations that has given jazz its staying power. ●

FAT CATS AT LUNCH
AN INTERVIEW WITH DIZZY GILLESPIE

By Mike Bourne

MAY 11, 1972

D izzy Gillespie hardly requires an introduction. We spoke during his nightly-packed, eight-day stand at Gourmet Rendezvous in St. Louis. We had lunch at Kemoll's: Dizzy with beef tips and noodles, me with pepperoni-stuffed calzoni, both of us fatties deluding ourselves that the calories from the ice cream and cake wouldn't count if we ate fast and no one we knew saw us....

MB: *When you all first began bop, were you conscious you were being revolutionary?*

DG: Not necessarily; it was just trying to get a new image of the music—not necessarily revolutionary, but *evolutionary*. The music, it's got to evolve, and somebody's got to do it. I don't think there was an awareness of the fact of trying to do something new, because there's not too much new anyway. But to have a new *conception*, that's where it is. We didn't know what it was going to evolve into, but we knew that we had something that was a little different.

MB: *Were you surprised that such a great change came out of it all, that such a focus came upon you?*

DG: We were aware of the fact that we had a new concept of the music by no other means than the enmity amongst the musicians: The old musicians who didn't want to go through a change. When you have a lot of static, you know you must be on the right track, 'cause if it's easy it's not worth it.

MB: *Did it happen gradually?*

DG: Yes, just gradually, and all of a sudden we were into the throes of this new music.

MB: *When you finally became aware of bop as this new music, how did bop differ from what had been before?*

DG: It was only a *style*, really, what we were doing. All of us were aware of the contributions of each of the individuals that had something to do with it; I'm sure that Charlie Parker was aware of his contribution to what was happening. But it wasn't the idea of trying to revolutionize, but only trying to see yourself, to get within yourself. And then if somebody copied it, okay! I'm the same way now. Music, retrospectively I look at it now, music is *One*—and therefore it's just an evolution of what has gone before. And if you miss that, if you don't know the fundamentals of the music that has gone before, you can get into serious trouble, 'cause it can go right out into space. If you think that you've created something and don't have any basic background to it, you're in there and all of a sudden you find yourself—Boom!—you fall off a cliff. But when you are based on what has gone before, you're on solid ground, so therefore you can build on that and *you* know how to go about building on that. 'Cause I used to try to copy Roy Eldridge, and I learned a lot from Red Allen, Rex Stewart, Louis Armstrong, Hot Lips Page, Bill Dillard, Harold Baker; there are a lot of things you get from these different guys as you progress in your music.

MB: *How have you changed since then?*

DG: I'm constantly in a state of flux, because that's the only way you can keep up with what's happening today.

MB: *Your music is international.*

DG: Yes, it's universal. See, the basic thing about our music is rhythm, and the basic type of rhythm we play, Western hemisphere musicians play, is basic African. Harmonically, Africans are into about the third grade or something like that. But we took European harmonies and merged it with African rhythms, with the soul of the slaves, the blues, the spirituals, and we melded all of this into jazz. Boy, some soulful music, the gospel music! These new guys doing rock 'n' roll now, they are thoroughly into gospel, and they do things with notes that you just can't write—I wish I could play like that myself! And that was a mistake when I was a kid, that I didn't go into the sanctified church; I used to listen, though. But the music is such a virile force and it lends itself to all kinds of improvisation; it's gonna be around, 'cause it ain't going nowhere but forward!

MB: *Do you feel music is a religious experience?*

DG: It is. Baha'u'llah is the head of my religious faith—I am Bahai, it's a relatively new thing, it's only 127 years old—he said music is a form of worship. I believe it, because in this music you must rid yourself of the hangups of racialism and things like that. You're on the bandstand and you're a white guy and you're looking at a colored guy playing—if you're going to get into the music, you gonna have to forget all about that white guy that he's white or that guy's colored and really get into the music, 'cause it won't click with all that stuff in there.

MB: *According to Mickey Roker, what he learns from you the most is the* authentic; *how you seek the authentic forms and rhythms of cultural musics or whatever when you adapt them to your own music?*

DG: Yes, I use my own conception of what I hear that they do. I'm not playing *exactly*, like I'm not playing exactly like the West Indians or Afro-Cuban music, but it goes with it. I put my own personal feeling into the music, of Brazil or wherever. It takes someone to understand those things rhythmically, 'cause you got to be very broad nowadays, a drummer, because the music is so closely entwined, you gotta be at home everywhere.

But that's my stick: rhythm! I have created a lot of harmonies that guys have used, that stuck to the music, but my real thing is rhythm. And all the drummers know it; I taught all the drummers, from Max, Art Blakey, on down, and they're doing things I showed them now. Like that 6/8 time: I copied a 6/8 rhythm from Chano Pozo and I adapted it to the drums and I showed it to Charlie Persip, and Charlie Persip showed it to everybody. And now, anytime they say go into 6/8, they play my lick!—everybody, I don't care where you go, in Europe, everywhere, because it was actually an authentic reproduction of what to do on the conga drums. And I play the conga drum myself. Last night, the guy on the radio played an old "Swing Low Sweet Cadillac" of mine that I don't even remember, and the conga player, I was explaining to him while the record was playing, I said: "Now there's the greatest in the world, this guy has the *sound* of the conga drums!—and I come to find out that it was I who was playing! I was so ashamed, I was saying: "Please forgive me, Chano Pozo, up there on the high concourse!" But you see, the evolution of music in another sense is like the evolution of religion. You see, I don't

believe in sticking in one place, because we're becoming more *perceptive*. If you got a message, if you got something to say, then get on with it!

MB: *Even in the most avant music, you can hear what's gone before; in Don Cherry you can hear you.*

DG: Of course! You gotta! You can't just turn your back on nothing, because you've got to have a foundation of whatever you create—if you don't, you'll just disappear! And the truth is the truth in any age. You see, *the truth is indestructible*, absolutely; it is the truth then and it's true now. But it's relative—you have to swing with it.

MB: *Mickey Roker impressed upon me that one of your main points is your discipline of yourself and your musicians.*

DG: That's the only way you're going to advance, is with discipline—you can't just let yourself go. There's so many little things in our music, I guess there are thousands of little things that help, rules that I go by; and I never break those rules, so I'm hipping the younger guys to it. There are iron-clad rules in our music, and I don't care what you're playing, it's true.

MB: *You're going to teach now, right?*

DG: Yeah, they need me, because the things that I know are getting lost, and you can't lose these things from my experience. See, when we first came out there were musicians who would copy me that had no idea why I did what I was doing! So now I think it should be told—because there must be a reason for everything. There's a wealth of information, like things that Charlie Parker did. (Dizzy demonstrated how he changed musical aspects of several songs, like "All the Things You Are," "'Round Midnight," "Now's The Time," "Salt Peanuts," and how other musicians copied his ideas wrongly or copied without realizing what he had done.)

MB: *You're saying, if you have the rudiments you can do anything.*

DG: Yeah, if you know where it is.

MB: *One great characteristic of your music is that you're such a complete performer.*

DG: I believe in it, if you want to entertain somebody. Your creation is on records, that's where your creativity comes in the music, without people looking at you. But we're in an age now where you look, you

see and you hear at the same time—so you better get with it. I always was a showman—I like to perform. I'm an actor, too!

MB: *Where did songs like "Ool Ya Koo" come from?*

DG: That came from the words like bebop: that's the way that our music sounds. The words don't mean nothing—that's what the music is doing; you're only humming the lick. How do you think the word *bebop* came into being? We'd be on the stand on 52nd Street—we had a lot of weird compositions; it was weird for those times anyway—and I'd say "Max is Makin' Wax," the title of the tune. They wouldn't even know what I was talking about! So what I'd do, I'd say: *be-op-a-dop-a-doo-doo-de-be-bop*, and they knew exactly what I'm gonna play. Most of the things we played ended on *bebop* or something like that when you hum it. So the people started coming up asking: "Hey, play that song!"—"What song?"—"That song that goes *bebop*?" And they just picked it up from there, and then the writers started saying that we're playing "be-bop music."

MB: *You still play "A Night in Tunisia" and that standard repertoire, yet it all still sounds new.*

DG: People ask for it—but you know, Billy Daniels still sings "Old Black Magic!" But I don't believe in going back in the past.

MB: *Do you believe that music must be happy?*

DG: That's right, it's gotta be!

MB: *You've obviously left a legacy in music; we can hear it. But could you crystallize a thought you'd like to leave?*

DG: I have to say something that was stolen from somebody else, but it's really my thing. I'm not too concerned with always being right, but I do always want to be *fair*. That's my creed; 'cause you're human, you err. But when you don't seek justice, that's the wrong attitude. The truth, I just want to always seek the truth! *True Believer* is exactly what I am! ●

DEXTER GORDON: TRANSCONTINENTAL TENORIST

By Jenny Armstrong

JUNE 22, 1972

Jørgen Bo

When Dexter Gordon won the 1971 *Down Beat* Critics Poll, the honor could hardly be considered premature. The tenorist, who celebrated his 49th birthday last Feb. 17, is one of the great voices in modern jazz and has been a professional musician since the age of 17, when he joined Lionel Hampton's band. After a stint with Louis Armstrong, he became a charter member of Billy Eckstine's famed big band, with which he made his mark.

For nearly a decade, the tall, debonair tenorman has made his home in Copenhagen, Denmark, where this interview took place. From time to time, he visits the U.S., to perform (he appeared at the 1970 Newport Jazz Festival), visit with friends and relatives, check out the scene, and record. (His 1969 and 1970 visits yielded an extraordinary series of albums for Prestige, all produced by Don Schlitten: *The Tower of Power, More Power, The Panther,* and *The Jumping Blues*—the latter reviewed in this issue.)

JA: *Why do you think you won the poll?*

DG: Because I'm the world's greatest tenor saxophonist, ha, ha, ha! No, I really don't know.

JA: *Was it a surprise?*

DG: Yes, I would say so. I hadn't really thought about it, you know....I was always kind of curious to peek at the results, but it has never been a really big thing for me.

JA: *In what way can it be of importance to you?*

DG: Well, first of all, recognition—to have a little recognition, that is very nice, you dig. It is good for the ego, for the psyche. A recognition of what I've been trying to do for years—it's certainly not just a spot opinion; I mean, it's something that obviously has been building up for years. Of course, it is also very good for publicity, and it is the kind of recognition that maybe will help financially, also.

JA: *Do you think that these polls mirror the reality of what is happening in the music world?*

DG: You know, there are two kinds of polls. There's the critics poll, and then there's another poll where the readers write in. But one would say that the first is the, of course, more critical poll, because it's supposed to be music critics who are voting. But it doesn't necessarily reflect your popularity or name value.

JA: *Do you think that critics are able to judge who's best?*

DG: Well, it's an individual thing, but we must assume that if they are music critics, then they must know something about music. They spend a lot of time listening—they must know something about music in order to be able to write half way intelligently about it. So you have to assume that they do know something about it.

JA: *Do you think that music can be criticized?*

DG: I think so, but it should always be kept in mind that it is also a personal opinion. I mean, there's always a certain amount of prejudice, pre-judgment, in anybody's opinion—about anything, you know.

JA: *So what would you say the critics have to go by?*

DG: Part of it must be comparison.

JA: *If you had lived in the States, would winning the poll have meant more when it comes to jobs and money?*

DG: Hmm—yes, I think so. But since this has happened, I've had all kinds of interviews for radio and the papers and all of this is very good.

JA: *What has it meant musically to live in Europe?*

DG: Well, for me, it has been very good because my whole lifestyle is much calmer, much more relaxed. I can devote more time to music, and I think it is beginning to show. It's not that everyday scuffle, and I'm able to concentrate more on studying. Of course, the music scene is more competitive in the States. I think it would be very easy for an American jazz musician to come over here and just relax and play by rote, so to speak, but I think that's very rare, 'cause, you know, if a man is a musician he is interested in music and he is going to play as much and study as much as possible. And I think most of the guys who have come over here have improved—there are some very good musicians over here.

JA: *What's the difference between audiences here and in the States?*

DG: I think the European audience has a more intellectual approach to the music, and in the states they're more demonstrative—the whistles and all that.

JA: *You go back to the States frequently. Is that to keep up with the music scene, with what's going on there?*

DG: In part, but also a lot of times I go back to record and to make a tour, but of course I'm very happy to do it, because it gives me an opportunity to dig and hear what's going on. After all, it's still the center—the new trends are coming from there.

JA: *What do you prefer to call your music—jazz or black music?*

DG: What I'm doing—I prefer to call that jazz, because to me it's not a dirty word. To me, it is a beautiful word—I love it. And, I mean, if I were to call it black music that would be untrue, because there are a lot of other influences in there. In jazz, there is a lot of European influence harmonically. Many of the harmonic structures of bebop come from Stravinsky, from Handel and Bartók, so to say "black music"—I don't know what that is, unless it would be some African drums or something. ●

LARRY CORYELL: MORE TO COME

By Harry Stamataky

NOVEMBER 9, 1972

Often, people of little or no musical ability receive wide public acclaim. This, in fact, may apply to the majority of pop musicians today: The status they have attained is largely due to slick public relations hype. Of course, this victimizes musicians who are truly talented and consistently produce music of the highest caliber.

One such victim is the great guitarist and composer Larry Coryell. For some time now, Coryell has been releasing jazz-rock albums that in my opinion outclass everybody else's attempts in the field. His music is compositionally intricate and complex and technically flawless. He can play demanding material so fast and with such finesse that it sounds (and looks) deceptively easy. All his notes are crystal clear and are not marred by the overdone electronics that have recently become fashionable among guitars. Coupled with this, Coryell has what might best be described as natural musical feeling.

During this year, Coryell has frequently played in New York City jazz clubs. It was at the Gaslight Au Go Go that I saw him for the first time. Larry was playing with his current group, made up of long-time musical friends: Steve Marcus on soprano saxophone; Mike Mandel on electric piano; Harry Wilkinson on drums, and, in place of bassist Mervin Bronson, who had temporarily left the group, John Miller, who fit into the group surprisingly well despite a completely different style from Bronson.

Two days later, when I entered the very cluttered office of the Gaslight, Larry, his wife Julie, and some friends were already engaged in conversation. The topic soon turned to John McLaughlin, Larry's friend (and possibly rival). A few years ago, Larry and Julie Coryell started practicing yoga with McLaughlin and his wife, Eve, under the tutelage of Sri Chinmoy, who is still McLaughlin's yogi.

"My wife had just had a baby. She was depressed and we were both unhappy.

When we were trying to be disciples, John, myself, Eve, and Julie were all very close. We saw each other almost every day. We meditated together; we made music together; we ate together; and we played Scrabble together. We had a great time and were the best of friends," Coryell said.

This relationship lasted about a year, but the Coryells found that the yoga teachings were in direct conflict with certain basic principles and ideas they did not wish to change.

"I spent a year and a half trying to conform to the kind of person John McLaughlin's guru wanted me to be, and I couldn't. First of all, I found that I couldn't love my wife the way I wanted to."

Musically speaking, Coryell does not consider this brief sojourn into mysticism fruitless. He wrote many songs during the period and is still happy with them.

"The last time I saw Sri Chinmoy, I wrote what I consider to be my greatest piece. It's called "The Meditation Of November 8th," and it's on *Offering*. The entire composition is nothing but peace and solitude and quiet. It's the best thing I ever wrote."

McLaughlin and Coryell remain friends. Concerning McLaughlin's current playing, Coryell has both positive and negative opinions.

"Let me first say that John McLaughlin is the only guitar player in the world beside myself who can play music that nobody else can play. He is one of the most gifted musicians on earth. The real positive virtues of *The Inner Mounting Flame* are its compositional aspects. All it really shows is what a good writer John is. It does *not* show what kind of player he is. I'm disappointed in that record because I know how great he can play. I feel that my album, *Spaces*, captured the true John McLaughlin. Listen to his solo on 'Wrong Is Right' or 'Spaces' or 'Rene's Theme,' and you'll hear one of the greatest guitar players in the world."

With Coryell and McLaughlin on guitars on "Spaces" are Miroslav Vitous,

Chick Corea, and Billy Cobham—all musicians to conjure with.

"The best I ever heard Billy Cobham was when he played on 'Spaces.' That's true, honest, artistic music. My wife wrote the music for that album, and it is to me one of the greatest records of our generation. People will be waking up to that years from now. We sat down, looked at the music, turned on the tapes, and we played it."

Coryell has high esteem for Vitous' associates in Weather Report. "Let me say that the musicians in Weather Report had a profound influence on my music. I respect those musicians about as much as anybody."

I asked Coryell about Jimi Hendrix. "Jimi Hendrix is the greatest musician who ever lived, as far as I'm concerned. The stuff I saw him do in person in jam sessions was some of the heaviest jazz music I ever heard. He is the greatest musician I've ever met." Hendrix and Coryell were going in the same musical direction in the sixties but Hendrix, it seems, was a split second ahead. "I hate him because he took everything away from me that was mine. I wanted to play just like that at the time. I knew that would be *the* sound. He took my stuff, man. I've never been so jealous of a cat in my life."

How does Coryell view his relatively obscure status in rock music circles?

"I want to be a star and make a lot of money," he said. "I have a large family and a lot of debts to pay off. I would like to be recognized, not as the greatest, but as one of the greatest guitar players in the world. My time will come. I'm not worried about it." He is, however, very pleased with being his own musician, not indebted to hype.

"When I get up there, either in a recording studio or on stage, I play my guitar the best I can. If you like it, that's fine, and if you don't, that's fine too, because I receive the full benefits of complete artistic integrity and freedom. As long as I continue with that philosophy, I can take care of all the obligations and responsibilities that are delineated to me."

Alain Bettex

It was time for the guitarist to go on, and I continued the conversation with his wife, who plays an integral part in her husband's music. It is almost impossible to talk about one Coryell without considering the other. Julie has temporarily stopped singing with the group because she is expecting, and she said she probably won't sing for a while to come in order to spend more time with the children. Working in clubs does not appeal to her.

"I hate clubs. I feel Larry's band plays much better in a larger audience situation where the artist plays for an hour, or so. In clubs, you have to play a lot of sets, and as the night progresses, the musicians get tired and the music deteriorates. The only reason for playing the clubs is survival, and keeping a band working.

The set under way now was even more explosive than the one I had witnessed a few days earlier, though I found that possibility hard to entertain. After the set, Larry was in a state of bliss. The group had sounded great, and they knew it even better than the audience. They weren't completely satisfied, though. The sound system had been too loud.

Steve Marcus explained: "It's a matter of dynamics. The loudness of the music can turn against you. On one level, it can enhance it, but a little more, and it will be ruined. You have to be aware at all times of the power of the changing volume. When you start loud, you can't get louder."

Nothing but praise for the group comes from Coryell's lips. Marcus, a remarkable saxophonist, "is, to me, the greatest living reed player…he took a giant step that Coltrane never took. He went into the rock bag and played from the jazz consciousness and spirit and played great rock and roll. He does for me what John Coltrane never did for me.…"

Mike Mandel, the blind keyboard player whom Larry has known since the age of 14, he calls his inspiration. "I got the greatest piano player, man. Bill Evans once asked to sit in, but I said, 'No, man, because I've got the greatest piano player in the world'."

Coryell said he was finishing a new album, his eighth, which will feature the current group. It will be a rock album, completely different from *Offering*, a jazz album. His first single, a vocal, will be released simultaneously with the album, probably in January.

On *Offering*, Coryell's group proves it can play high-quality jazz. The yet to be released rock album should provide an interesting basis for comparison in style and content. The group may yet successfully bridge the gap between jazz and rock.

But Coryell still faces his old nemesis: lack of publicity. That may change soon, however. "We haven't had a manager until now," Julie said. "But we do now, and he's a very good manager. John McLaughlin got a manager a year ago, and from that time on his career has soared."

Coryell is planning a tour of colleges that should open new ears to his talents. In my opinion, this man is one of the great musicians of our time. If you don't believe me, listen to *Spaces* or *Coryell* or *Offering*. Or even better, catch Larry Coryell live. You'll see (or hear) the light. ●

EUBIE BLAKE BLINDFOLD TEST

By Leonard Feather
MAY 24, 1973

There are two remarkable things about the double pocket album on Columbia entitled *The Eighty Six Years of Eubie Blake*. One is that the subject treats us to a unique guided tour through a career that has spanned virtually the entire history of jazz. The second is that the title is four years out of date.

When interviewers flatteringly refer to Blake as 90 years young, he bridles, "No," he says, "I'm 90 years *old* and proud of it."

Never content to lean on his age as a crutch, the amazing Mr. Blake continues to work, travel extensively (without benefit of plane) and even compose new works. One of the latter, "Rhapsody in Ragtime," was introduced when, a few weeks ago, he took the train to Los Angeles for a recital at the Wilshire Ebell Theatre.

After a busy week of promotional appearances, among them a spot on the Tonight Show, Blake charmed his audience at the theater with his new "Classical Rag," his James P. Johnson medley, a highly personalized version of "Mood Indigo," and of course the early hits that established him as a big man in ASCAP—"I'm Just Wild About Harry" (1921) and "Memories of You" (1930). The former was a product of *Shuffle Along*, the first real black Broadway musical, with words by Eubie's longtime partner Noble Sissle.

For this, his first Blindfold Test, I played mainly records by pianists who, in one way or another, represent the music of his era.

1 **WILLIE THE LION SMITH.** "Memories of You" (from *Music on My Mind*, Saba). Eubie Blake, composer; Smith, piano.

Fine. I couldn't say otherwise. No, not because it's my tune. His bass was always there. The fellers don't play much bass now, you see. He plays chords perfectly. Is that Tatum? No? One thing in there sounded like Willie The Lion Smith.

Willie is 75 now, and he was about 17 or 18 when I first knew him in New York.

Skinny!…looked like he'd had nothin' to eat. And he could play the piano. He played some trick rhythms, if he'd ever seen them written down, he'd have said "Oh, I couldn't play that," but he played them! I'd give him four stars.

2 ART TATUM — BUDDY DeFRANCO. "Memories of You" (ARS). Eubie Blake, composer; Tatum, piano; DeFranco, clarinet.

That one record is going to make me ashamed to play that tune any more! Oh, the changes. It's a shame that the people don't hear the different things—they only *think* they hear. Boy, great. I don't know how I'm going out to play it any more.

I *really* liked that piano player…and the clarinet player. The clarinet did not cross his changes, he was in the same chords doing variations on the changes that that feller put in there. Beautiful, beautiful! He goes up half a tone, then comes right back the way he went up. That's the right way to do it. Say, for instance, you're in key of F, then you go into F#, then into G, then back to F# and F…that's the correct way to do it.

I'm pretty sure that the piano was Tatum. Nobody plays quite like him. His left hand is perfect. Now the clarinetist sounded like Benny Goodman to me. Anyway, five stars. I wish there were six I could give it.

3 EARL HINES. "Bye Bye Baby" (from *The Mighty Fatha*, Flying Dutchman). Hines, piano; Richard Davis, bass; Elvin Jones, drums.

That's very good, but I don't know who it is. It's a good rhythmic number; he held his tempo. That's what a lot of players don't do. They start out in tempo and either increase or diminish it. I liked that rhythm section. Who's that on bass? I'd give that four stars.
LF: *It's Earl Hines.*
EB: Knew him when he was 17. I met him in Pittsburgh. He was playing at a place called Homestead. A feller named Gus Greenley said to me, 'You want to hear a guy play piano?' I said yes, so I got in the car with him and went there, and this guy's playing the piano. So I said to him. 'What are you doing playing in a place like this?' And he could play just the same then as he does now. He said. 'Oh, man, I get $18 a week.' I told him that if he came to New York he'd get $18 a night, twice that much

a night. But he never did come. He went with Jimmy Noone in Chicago, then to the Grand Terrace Hotel—with a big band.

You know that guy's a good showman. He can emcee a show…he's got a number he plays on one key. You know, nobody should ever play "St. Louis Blues" behind Earl Hines: no band should ever play "St. Louis Blues" behind Noble Sissle's band. When I first heard Earl Hines, he had no drums or nothing with him.

4 DICK HYMAN. "Harlem Strut" (from *Dick Hyman, Piano Solo*, Project 3). James P. Johnson, composer.

You just can't play that way, that's all there is to it! Boy! That's *vivace.*…That's James P. Johnson's composition, but I've *never* heard it played like that before!

I've never heard *anything* like that; the technique! And that tempo…that was the speed of *vivace.* That's the fastest possible, but still got the feeling of the tune; you heard the melody all the time. Five stars. I wish I could give it six for technique, dexterity.

5 DUKE ELLINGTON. "In A Sentimental Mood" (from *Piano Reflections*, Capitol). Piano solo, with Butch Ballard, drums; Wendell Marshall, bass.

Very good playing. I don't know who it is, but I know the tune.…Duke Ellington wrote it, but I don't know the name of it.

Some of the arpeggios were a little muddy; I guess on the pedals. You know those three pedals on there? The man didn't put them on there for nothing, you know. He could have saved all that money. If you play something and you've got an arpeggio, that chord is still playing if you hold that pedal down. So that makes it muddy. Now that wasn't bad, but some of the arpeggios were a little muddy. And that can happen to anybody if they don't understand that pedal. So four stars, because that feller can play.

6 FATS WALLER. "Smashing Thirds" (from *Smashing Thirds*, RCA). Waller, piano, composer.

Tops, tops, tops. Fats Waller, wasn't it? You know why I can tell? Solid bass! He plays a solid bass, boy. I knew him when he was a kid. He had on short pants when I first knew him. Fats used to play at the Lincoln Theatre on 135th St. He's the only man made me like the organ, the pipe organ. He used to set that place crazy

playing pipe organ.

(*Hums*)…he's playing all that stuff with the right hand, but still held the melody in the bass. That's hard to do. When a person knows what's going on, the public hears, but they don't know what's happening. What he was doing…you hit a note and you want that note sustained, and he's playing counter melody. That's five stars. I wish again I had six for them.

7 OSCAR PETERSON. "Tristeza" (from *Tristeza*, BASF). Sam Jones, bass; Bob Durham, drums.

Well, you talk about a technician, there was a technician. In both hands, that's very intricate to do. He was playing here and here, and I know he can't stretch that far because there's an octave between. So he must have been playing parallel lines with both hands.

Veryl Oakland

Now the tune, it was over my head, so I can't criticize the tune. All I can say is that what he was playing was perfect, but it was kinda over my head, like rock 'n' roll is over my head. I don't knock—I don't knock anything. But I'd have to give him five stars.

That bass player and the drummer I liked. Now I'm listening to the chords, and it's hard to get the tonic until he stops some place, then I can get the tonic, then I can tell whether the bass is on. Because it was so fast…he was in tune *each* time, in the chords.

I did rate that, didn't I? Five stars, and I'm rating on my opinion, and my opinion doesn't have to be right, but you asked my opinion and I'm giving it. ●

THAD JONES AND MEL LEWIS

By Jim Schaeffer
JULY 19, 1973

Four-four swing"—a lot of musicians today consider it old-fashioned. Thad Jones and Mel Lewis agree that 4/4 is the most basic thing to do. This, however, is not all they play or want to play, but they believe swing is the foundation for all time signatures.

As Mel says, "I believe that 4/4 should be happening first. The other thing, odd meters, should be placed as a change of pace and not as a steady diet. But, I have heard bands use 4/4 as a change of pace."

Thad adds, "That's the advantage of learning how to swing first because, if you can swing, you can do the other thing."

While we were discussing the use of odd meters, Mel started to talk about Don Ellis' band and their use of odd meters. Mel felt since this was a sensitive subject he did not want to be quoted, but he relented. And the interview begins at this point.

ML: I'm going to say something that I don't want on tape.

TJ/JS: Say it, man, say it!

ML: It has to do with that engagement we did in New York opposite Ellis' band. They came into town with all that electronic equipment. The band was new at the time but they played the hell out of that stuff. Steve Bohanan, I thought, was very much at home with it. He played it very smoothly, almost effortlessly. But, talking to some of the guys, they were all saying "man, you've got to concentrate. If you lose your place, you're dead. There's no one to help you. You've had it. You've got to count, count, count." We knew that. You could hear it. They played one tune that night—it was a blues thing—in four and nothing happened. It sounded terrible. No feeling at all. With all the electronic excitement they had going with odd meter, they had nothing going on a straight-ahead blues arrangement—4/4. They just couldn't get off the ground at all. It was such a shock. All that noise, then all of a sudden the most purist form of jazz—the blues—when they are suppose to be swinging, they just went plop on their fanny. Nothing happened.

I guess this could be in there. I'm not putting the band down. They did what they had to do very well.

Thad and I are involved in education and we see kids who don't know the most basic thing in jazz which is swing. They can't do it. They just don't know how because they are not concentrating on it, first. Swing should be the first thing they should go after.

JS: *Who do you think is at fault? The educators?*

ML: Well, it has to be whoever is directing. I think their ideas about what's really happening in music, in jazz,…

TJ: I think it's been pointed out to them that this is the direction and, there is some merit to it, because it boils down to getting rhythmic. It's gone harmonically just about as far as the ear can stand. So, it has to be rhythmic but at the same time there has to be some coherency—something that you can really relate to rhythmically and not just for musicians. I mean the general public. The people buying the records. They have to have something they can say, "Yes, I can dig that." It gets back to the same thing—if it's rhythmic, then why can't it swing? This is one direction that music education is bound to get into. Like in most things involving progress, sometimes the cart is a little bit before the horse.

JS: *You think it's more technical than feeling?*

TJ: No.

JS: *Then, what?*

TJ: I think it's another direction. It's all technical. Feeling is something that's a basic characteristic in people and that can be very involved, but the surface mechanics sort of open the door to feelings. To me, mechanics of execution is the minor technical part. You have to learn a lot, but your feelings are enormous. Like, I don't think you'll ever learn enough to express them all.

JS: *Do you think a lot of the young kids are getting into only playing their feelings and not taking the time to do the technical part? They are coming off sounding as if they only listened to the recent Miles, but didn't go*

back to see what he was doing in the fifties.

TJ: I was discussing that with a fellow today. I said, "It's surprising to me how people can listen to a simple phrase, say like, Ben Webster plays a simple melody, and not realize how much time he spent learning how to express himself musically." They think, "I can do that." But, when they pick up a horn and try to express what he expressed—his feelings and part of his emotional makeup—nobody else is going do it like him. You know, Freddie Hubbard's expression and technique have to run hand-in-hand. If his fingers run ahead of his mind or his feelings, nothing's going to happen. His feelings and techniques have to run together. So, you try to develop a technique that covers your feelings.

ML: When you hear a guy who plays simply, nine times out of 10, that's where that man's technique is at.

TJ: That's the way he's thinking. He's thinking of very simple phrases.

ML: He thinks that way and it works. You've heard guys with a lot of technique, play a lot of notes, and they can do that. But, it depends on who you are, where you are, how you think, and what you want to be. Since I've been doing quite a bit of drum teaching, I find too many drummers have gotten into this thing of wanting to play fast. Now, they can't play slow and they can't play soft, and they can't swing. They have forgotten it. The point is, they don't realize they are still young. I can play faster now then I could when I was young, and effortlessly and I never worked at it. It's just a matter of knowledge and growth. I used to die when somebody beat off a fast tempo. I'd say, "Here we go." I'd last three choruses and then start worrying about it, and the more you think about it, the worse it gets. Now, I don't let it even bother me. Things happen much easier now because I learned the basics and the simple way of doing things and of thinking simply. It just works and it grows. I really feel for these kids who think excitement comes from speed. They think the word "technique" means speed. The word "technique" just means the way you do something, that's all.

TJ: That's funny because I used to play awfully fast. But as the years rolled along, I've sort of gotten out of it because playing fast really doesn't have the meaning for me now that it had then. Your musical views change and are not necessarily centered on what's happening today. That's what makes music so important. As Mel said, "Your mind is constantly gathering new information and what you leave you leave off on this side you accumulate on the other side."

JS: *Have you thought what could happen tomorrow?*

TJ: Well, I haven't given it too much thought because, to get very practical, we've been trying to dig a couple of dollars out of the ground. We want to keep the band as busy as possible. But, I think the direction groups like Mahavishnu are into is a combination of the elements of feeling and technique. They are now whole musicians. That's very important. You get the feeling of tremendous force when you listen to Chick Corea, Herbie Hancock, etc. It seems to be happening more in the smaller groups and I'm sure eventually, with the knowledge they have to offer, they'll want to expand it and bring larger groups of people into it. But until that happens, I think they are on the right track—and it swings.

ML: My only complaint right now about any of it is that nobody is really thinking about dynamics, yet, and most of the groups are a little bit too loud. I'd like to hear a little more dynamics from some of those groups because they're playing some great things.

TJ: They'd have to hire somebody to…

ML: They'd have to get somebody to actually work controls. That's the electronic thing.

TJ: Electronics! I imagine that's what you were hinting at a little while ago. Electronics definitely has a place. I don't know whether or not it's going to completely take over but I don't think anything can take the place of the human element.

ML: I really don't think it will. It certainly should be a part of it. If you start turning everything electronic, what are we here for?

TJ: You know, good music has always had that perfect balance from the classics to now.

ML: Yeah. I think there's room for

everything, man. I think you have to extend things but when that gets too heavy into one direction, then it tends to be a drag.

JS: *In what sense? Monotony?*

ML: Yeah. Well, a lot of it is monotonous. There's room for every kind of music. It's a great pleasure to listen to a good symphony and that

Veryl Oakland

music is still here. There have been attempts to avant-garde classical music but it hasn't replaced the old masters.

JS: *It's just an extension.*

ML: It just comes in. And with jazz it's the same thing. I think there's a tendency towards overdoing it. For instance, if one group comes out and is working with electronics and is successful, immediately you've got ten more groups jumping in doing the same thing. That's what gets me.

TJ: Carrying along that same thought, I think musicians do have a tendency to sort of copy and get on the bandwagon instead of accepting one thing for what it is and realizing that it's another area of progress. They immediately want to emulate. Music is a very personal thing. It's strictly an individual thing. This one tenor player comes to mind who played like another player. He just tried to play every note exactly the same. He might have been sincere in his love for the musician but it didn't turn out that way. Eventually, he just went right down and like you never heard of him again. He was a very competent musician but it's just like my uncle always said, "There's only one thing that keeps us all from being rich and if we knew what that was, everybody would have a million,"

and that's probably the thing the tenor player didn't realize—copying was just another form of saying the other man was great. You just extend more adulation and acclaim or whatever to the other guy.

ML: Even our band. We've read and heard people say we really remind them of Ellington or Basie. Well, there may have been an influence of some kind, naturally. But, when you sit down with your record collection and put one of our records on after one of theirs, I don't hear it at all. If you listen, we have our own sound and our own feel. We don't sound like Ellington or Basie and they don't sound like us. We sound like the Thad Jones/Mel Lewis band. We have our own rhythm feel, which has to do with the human part of the guys who are playing, and with the way the music is written. Thad's arrangement and voicings are not like anyone else's and you've got to listen a little closer and you'll see, "no, it is different." It is individual. It's something else.

What about the time that great record that had Ellington and Basie bands playing together—Thad was on that. In fact, he wrote a thing for it. Well, you put the two bands together, depending on who wrote the charts, you had all the same guys from two different bands playing together, it worked. Everybody knew what to do. It's all part of the whole thing, interpretation and the experience of the players.

TJ: It goes back to experience. You accumulate knowledge as you go along, put it into your vision, or whatever you want. Maybe that's what develops into a style. I'm sure Ellington listened to quite a few classics, and it's evident that he learned quite a bit from them because his band, and his arrangements are very classic. They have the depth, the extension, and the real form—the classic structure.

JS: *A, B, A, B.*

TJ: Yeah. It's beautiful to hear. He recorded an album some years ago, oh, it must have been about twenty years ago, Ellington masterpieces and only four tunes on it: "Sophisticated Lady", "Solitude", "Tattoo Bride" and "Blue Indigo". He completely revised all the arrangements from the original. They are masterpieces.

ML: I remember one time, when I was doing the Monterey Jazz Festival, Ornette Coleman was on the show. Ornette was a student then and had a working relationship at the time with Gunther and John Lewis. I remember he brought in a piece he wrote, something that he felt, with no bar signs, nothing, and he wanted Gunther to look at it. It was an experiment and he said, "I think I wrote an absolute free-form piece." Gunther took it, and in no time at all subdivided the whole thing into meters and showed it to Ornette, and said, "You did?" "Well, here it is with meters. It's not free." Ornette thought he had something different, but it still boiled down to the same thing. It can all be divided up into bars and notes so it can be played by anybody.

TJ: I once wrote a piece in ten-bar phrases. There were no bar lines. It broke down to ten-bar phrases and nobody had any problem in reading it.

ML: No. Because you wrote notes and you play the notes with their values. It comes out anyway.

TJ: If you write the time, and write the time for the drummer, there's no question about it. As long as he's back there doing this you know you've got something going.

ML: And really some of those early things Ornette Coleman did, which I really liked, were very nice and different. He had straight-ahead rhythm section and they sounded good.

TJ: Ornette came out of Bird, too. So, what he's doing now may sound mysterious to the uninitiated, but he is a straight swinger from way back. Ornette Coleman can play.

ML: Right. I think so. Chico Hamilton, I think, made a remark I saw in *Down Beat* or some place. He made a very true remark about free-form drumming. He said, "How free is it?" "It's free from the point you hit something here until the point you hit something there, it's a meter." "It's a meter of some kind", he said. It's not really free if the drummer goes da-da da-da da-da, that can be written out. That's not free. It's in order. You just play a series of notes, so that's not free. How free can you be when you're playing things. Free would be, to me, to take a mallet on a cymbal and roll, and roll for any extension of time, now you've got something. You just never stop—infinity. All right, now, you've got free form. But when you're taking sticks or brushes you're playing patterns. Those patterns can be notated in some kind of way. So why talk about it, just do it and enjoy and hope it all works out. I still like it when it swings. ●

BOY WONDER GROWS UP

By Lee Underwood
SEPTEMBER 12, 1974

A t age 24, Stevie Wonder has reached a height of popular and critical success that few recording artists attain in a lifetime.

At his recent birthday party held at L.A.'s Speakeasy Club, Motown's president, Ewart Abner, presented him with a gold pendant and still another gold single. "Higher Ground" brings the complete total to 13 gold singles, two gold albums (*Innervisions*, *Music of My Mind*), and two platinum records (*Talking Book* and *Superstition*).

At this year's Grammies, Stevie won four awards, including Best Album of the Year for *Innervisions*. Best Male Pop Vocal Performance for "You Are The Sunshine Of My Life," and Best R & B Vocal for "Superstition."

In *Down Beat's* 38th Annual Readers Poll, Wonder placed in no less than five categories. He won the Pop Musician of the Year honor, had two albums in the Pop Album of the Year section (*Talking Book* and *Innervisions*), placed third in the Best Male Singer slot, and was also recognized for both his Wonderlove back-up group and his talents as a composer.

Sitting behind his desk at Motown Records, Stevie Wonder, blind since birth, danced his fingertips across the control board of the massive Sony TC 850 tape recorder. He punched the rewind buttons, and the old tape spun down. Stevie removed it, took a new ten-inch reel out of the box and threaded it up. We were about to listen to his new album, *Fulfillingness' First Finale*, the final mix completed only the night before. This was the first hearing outside of the studio.

"It's very important that you concentrate on the lyrics," he said. "I feel very peaceful inside for the first time."

He leaned forward and smiled. The scars from his car accident a year ago were smooth. Only a bump remained above his right eyebrow, with a few smaller scars on his right cheek.

"Things change when you meet someone that is very positive and gives you peace and understanding far better than any relationship in the past."

Finale burst from the speakers and swirled throughout the room with joy, anger, compassion, new love, new dreams, new hope, and a lot of downright *filthy* funk.

Earlier, Stevie's friend, confidant, and publicist, Ira Tucker, said, "*Fulfillingness' First Finale* is almost an anthology of *Music of My Mind*, *Talking Book,* and *Innervisions*. But the new material since the accident takes you to that *other level* no one thinks he can reach after *Innervisions*. But he has. You can feel the difference. That's his genius."

The accident, before and after. The pivot point, the reference point, an inescapable landmark in the life of Stevie Wonder.

August 6, 1973: while traveling north from Greenville, S.C. to Raleigh on a two-lane road, driver John Harris, Stevie's cousin, tried to pass the logging truck that was weaving from lane to lane in front of them. The trucker suddenly slammed his brakes and stopped right in front of John. The logs from the truck fell off and crashed through the windshield on Stevie's side of the car. Stevie was in a coma for three days, a semi-coma for seven more.

"My outlook on life has gotten a little deeper—closer to me," Stevie said, his voice almost a whisper. "I learned who loved me—like Abner, president of Motown, stuck with me all the way. And I learned about those who just said, 'Is he gonna be able to work again?'

"I also see that God was telling me to slow down, to take it easy. I still feel I'm here to do something for Him, to please people, to turn my world into music for Him, to make it possible for people to communicate with each other better. And that's what I'll do. If you go by your feelings, your first impressions, they'll almost never lead you wrong. That's what I didn't do before."

Born May 13, 1950, in Saginaw, Michigan, he is the third of six children. Stevie's uncle gave him a four-hole, key-chain harmonica at age five, and Stevie was off and running. He began piano lessons at six and started playing the drums at eight. He was just about ready.

When Ronnie White of the Miracles introduced him to Brian Holland of the Holland-Dozier-Holland Motown writing team, Holland took him to Berry Gordy Jr., top gun at Motown. Gordy signed him, changed his name to Wonder, and a superstar was born.

Because he was a 10-year-old minor, Stevie could not have a writer's contract. He had an artist's contract in which Jobete Publishing (Motown's main house) got 100% of the royalties. This condition changed dramatically when Stevie re-negotiated at age 21.

Stevie praises the excellent job Motown did in setting up his legal guardian, a Detroit lawyer, and establishing his trust fund. When he turned 21, he went through the courts and the judges, and was completely satisfied with the accuracy and honesty with which that trust fund was handled.

There were no alterations or bendings of the Michigan statutes regarding minors performing in public places. "The laws protected him," Tucker explained. "First of all, he did not play clubs. He played large halls. That's where his first hit, "Fingertips, Part 2," was recorded. When he turned 18, he could play some places where alcohol was served—New York, Detroit, etc.

"And by law, Stevie had to have a teacher—not a tutor, but a teacher. He had to put in a certain number of hours every day with that teacher, even if he was traveling and working, like with the Motortown Review (a Detroit-based show). He would do one or two shows at night and then have to go to school on the bus or the airplane afterwards. But he went to school."

When Stevie was 13, Motown suggested he attend the Michigan School For The Blind in Lansing, from which he graduated. "They taught me all the usual things," Stevie says, "But what I liked was the swimming pool and the wrestling team. They had a music department, too, and that exposed me to all those classical dudes, like Bach and Chopin. You can hear some of that on "They Won't Go When I Go" on the new album."

When Stevie turned 21, he battled for months with that patriarchal giant, Motown Records: the formula sound, the iron-fist controller of royalties, publications, production, publicity and

direction.

Stevie slashed loose and established an unprecedented Motown deal. He emerged with his own publishing company, Black Bull Music; his own production company, Taurus Productions; 50% of the royalties; the right to record whenever and however he chooses; and, just recently, the power to decide which album cuts will be released as singles.

"He had enough insight to see what he needed to sustain Stevie Wonder as an individual, not just as a product of a record company," Ira explains. "It's kind of awesome. I tend to think he had it all figured out from the time he was 14. Basically, God manages Stevie, and Stevie manages himself."

"That's right," Stevie says, toying with the gold pendant Abner gave him. "'Uptight' was the first thing I wrote, along with Sylvia Moy and Henry Cosby, but the first thing I recorded was 'Mother Thank You,' originally called, 'You Made a Vow.' Nothin' really happened, though, until 'Fingertips.' I was 13," he said, leaning across the desk, smiling saying. "I was 13, but they said I was just 12. Ha!

"And the first *released* thing I produced was 'Signed, Sealed, Delivered.' My mother helped me write it. So did Lee Garrett, another blind cat. He's recording for Warner Brothers now.

"I also produced the Spinners' 'It's A

Shame,' and the follow-up, 'We'll Have It Made.' I did an unreleased thing with Martha, 'Hey, Look At Me,' and a David Ruffin piece, 'Lovin' You's Been So Wonderful.' Oh, lots of people. Now my ex-wife Syreeta's second album just came out. I produced both of her albums, too, and wrote a lot of the stuff."

LU: *How long were you married?*

SW: A year and a half.

LU: *Was one problem a clash of artistic wills?*

SW: No, man. We're just better as friends. We still write things together.

LU: *Were you runnin' around, Stevie?*

SW: (*Laughs.*) I wasn't runnin' around. (*Laughs again.*) No, she's a Leo, and I'm a Taurus. They're two fixed signs, and I'm awful stubborn.

LU: *What are your sleeping dreams like?*

SW: My dreams are my life. It's the same feeling. I've been blind since birth, so there's no difference in my dreams. You're used to seeing things and hearing things. But do you ever experience smell in dreams? I do. And touch and sound—everything except sight, and for me that's everything.

LU: *When you were 17, there was a lull between* Where I'm Comin' From *and* Music of My Mind. *How come?*

SW: I just needed some time away from recording. But I was working—playing, writing, playing, writing all the time.

LU: *Even though you're only 24, you've been a pro for 14 years. That's a long time. You ever worry about burning out?*

SW: Well, it's something I think about. You have to always keep putting wood in the fire, you know. *Fulfillingness' First Finale* was going to be a double album, but instead we're going to release it in two parts, and I might wait a long time, maybe more than a year after the second record, before I release another album. The title indicates that this is the last of this kind of stuff that I'll be doing—different songs and essentially the same instrumentation. I think my next thing might be a large orchestral thing. A long piece.

LU: *In "Bird of Beauty," on* Finale, *you speak of resting and of letting your mind find the answers to things you always wanted to know, of taking a furlough, of recreation, having fun, of mind excursions and traveling. Are you finally going to take that trip to Africa you've been talking about for so long?*

SW: Yeah, in September. There's gonna be a festival for the Ali-Foreman fight in Zaire, Africa. I'm going to do one show there. Through Taurus Productions, I'm also contracting other acts for the festival, and we're going to film it all for a TV special. We're gonna donate all the money to the African drought areas.

LU: *Sounds like work to me. Fun work, but work.*

SW: Well, yeah. But after that, we're going to tour—Ghana, Nigeria, Tanzania, all over. It's not only that. I was to start a foundation to find a way to restore the eyes of people blinded by a fungus carried by flies that goes to the cornea of the eye at eats it away. Some 40 percent of the people in Ethiopia are blind because of that fly.

LU: *What kind of fly?*

SW: I don't know the exact name of it.

LU: *What do people think of your going to Africa?*

SW: It hurts me that a lot of American blacks think I'm turning my back on this country. It's not that I dislike America. It's that I want to experience Africa

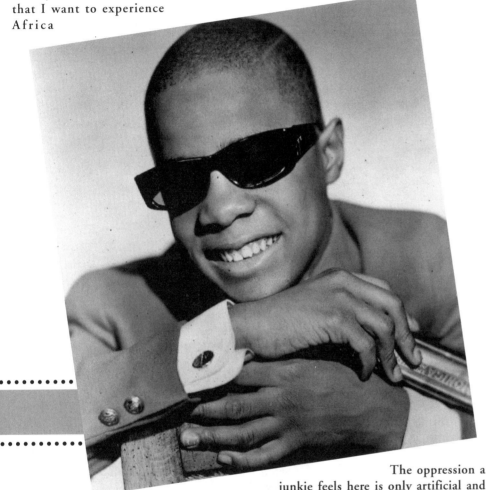

and help out as much as I can.

LU: *Do you feel your roots are there?*

SW: As a culture, as a motherland, I've always hoped to go there. And the culture of America has also given a lot. But in Africa there's not really a conception of time. Things are slowed down, and you have a chance to let your mind grow. To just think and to observe…the outdoors, insects, living off the land. "Feeding off the love of the land," like in a song I wrote.

LU: *Someplace you said you wanted to go to Africa to feel the oppression and the pain, and to bring it into your music.*

SW: Well, I think that there has been a great deal of oppression in this country,

but definitely not as much as has been, and is being experienced in Africa.

LU: *The SLA might take issue with that, not to mention the thousands of less radical militants. There's so much oppression here to experience, how could you want to go anywhere else?*

SW: African people feel we're living a great deal better. The massacres there are just not happening here.

The oppression a junkie feels here is only artificial and superficial—it's not real. He's lost, and his mind is not working properly.

LU: *And after Africa?*

SW: I learn off of life—knowledge is my firewood, you know? So I'll read, travel, listen to the music of different cultures and different people from far away and near.

In "Bird Of Beauty," I say life is gonna be what it is. "Cause what is/is gonna stay/till the heart of time/decides to change." And I really believe that. You have to do something with the time Father is giving you.

Sometimes I feel when I write lyrics that the Supreme Being is speaking to me. And I'd like to feel He is speaking *through* me. It's a very special thing to me to write a

word, to express how I feel.

LU: *In many of your songs you tell people to live up to the best in themselves—that's a hard demand, almost a cruel demand to make, isn't it?*

SW: If you're angry inside, why not turn it around the other way, do things to make it go away? I can't control what you do, but I *can* control what *I* do.

LU: *Turn negative energy into positive energy?*

SW: "Let God's love shine within to save our evil souls."

LU: *When you were a little kid, a junior deacon in the Whitestone Baptist Church, why did they throw you out, man?*

SW: 'Cause I was singin' rock 'n' roll! (*Laughs.*)

LU: *You've been influenced by a lot of white musicians, haven't you?*

SW: I like a lot of people. I've liked Bacharach since Chuck Jackson's recording of "I Wake Up Crying." Dylan, Simon and Garfunkel, Crosby, Stills, Nash and Young. I like the way the Beatles used their voices and echo on "For the Benefit of Mr. Kite."

LU: *Who else?*

SW: Well, I like Roberta Flack, and I've always liked Jesse Belvin. He's dead now, but he recorded for RCA. He's a very, very warm person. I like the sound of his voice. Listening to his singing, I felt if I ever met him, his character would be the same as mine. Not the lyric exactly, but the *spirit* of his music.

LU: *Did you ever do any formal vocal studying?*

SW: With an L.A. teacher, Seth Riggs, for about three months. He taught me how to sing without straining my throat.

LU: *What have you done since the accident besides the record?*

SW: Mostly cooled out. But I've also done four shows since then, three of them benefits. We did Madison Square Garden and donated the money to Mini-Sink Town House, an organization to send the children of Harlem to summer camp. We also did two shows at the Rainbow Theater in London, and a benefit for Shaw University, a black school in North Carolina.

LU: *Was the Stones tour a rough one for you?*

SW: Not as rough as everybody thinks. I mean, I used to do gigs, ride 500 or 1,000 miles in a bus, play another gig, then do it all over again. But the Stones tour was a good one because it was instrumental in exposing my music to a huge audience, and they loved it. When you write this, you let the public know I really love them back, won't you?

LU: *You just expressed it. But one of the major criticisms is that your music is rock and roll.*

SW: That's by people who hear only the singles, who never really get into the albums, and who don't really know that my music is a progression of my being. It grows the way I grow. I not only play the ARP and the Moog synthesizers, which a lot of people attack as being white, but I turn right around and put 'em in "Superstition" and just kill 'em!

LU: *And the clavinet, the string bass, the drums, the piano—everything. Is* Fulfillingness' First Finale *all yours?*

SW: I wrote all the lyrics except for "They Won't Go When I Go"—Yvonne Wright did those. I had the idea in my head, but she put it all together.

LU: *And the music?*

SW: Yes, the music. And I arranged all the horns and the voices and I played almost all the instruments.

LU: *Who are the other voices?*

SW: I used the Jackson 5 on "You Haven't Done Nothin'," and The Persuasions on "Please Don't Go."

LU: *What about the remark Miles Davis recently made about you in* Down Beat *(July 18) regarding your old bass player, Michael Henderson?*

SW: What remark was that?

LU: *Well, Miles refused to see Mick Jagger, and when he was asked why Jagger wanted to see him in the first place, Miles said, "One of his friends was trying to impress him by saying he knew me. Stevie Wonder, now there's a sad motherfucker. He thinks I stole Michael Henderson from him, but Michael came to me, I never did anybody like that in my life."*

SW: Oh really? Did he say that? He shouldn't have said that.

LU: *So, what happened?*

SW: Michael went and did a session with him...for Miles to say that...I think for Michael to go with him was an expansion.

LU: *So you don't think that Miles did steal him.*

SW: No. Maybe Miles did, I can't really say. But never did I feel that Miles stole my bass player....I didn't know he said that....I don't even have any reply. I think it's ignorant, really. Why would he fix his mouth to even say that?

LU: *Were you trying to impress Mick Jagger that you know Miles?*

SW: That's really...that's...I mean, I'm somewhat shocked at what he said. I've always admired Miles' music and his talent, but you can dilute your talent by having a character like that....That's really horrible, man. "A sad motherfucker." (Hurt laughter) Wow! You know? How can he even do that? Just hold the tape just one second, I have to regroup....I'll say one thing: Miles is smart enough to get young musicians, 'cause he *lost* it. It's *cruel* for him to say that. Why would I want to tell Mick Jagger I know Miles? I mean, I'm not into gossip. I prefer being alone.

LU: *You once said you didn't think you'd paid a lot of dues. You still feel that way?*

SW: I have not paid as many dues as, say, some of the musicians with Duke Ellington or Count Basie. I've been on the bus and rode for 14 hours and had to change out back somewhere and had to sing through mikes made of cardboard. But I'm very, very lucky and have to thank everyone my success has come early. I thank God and all the people who've made it possible....I...I don't see how Miles could say that, man.

LU: *Your soul is beautiful, Stevie....One last question: Do you listen to electronic music composers, people like Berio, Subotnick, Xenakis, to help you learn more about the synthesizer?*

SW: Some. The great thing about electronic music is you can make things larger than life. You can choose colors, and you can make the sounds of an instrument that does not exist.

But I feel you have to stay on the ground, that you can go too far and you lose the people—for me, anyway.

You listen to "They Won't Go When I Go." That'll tell you where I'm going—away from sorrow and hate, up to joy and laughter.

I feel *everyone* should be able to grasp what you're doing. I shouldn't be so complicated that it's beyond everyone's capabilities, nor should it be so simple that you cannot use your mind to think about it.

I would like to feel that as my albums change, my people—meaning all people—will come *with* me, that we will grow together. Everything that I experience is in the songs that I write. You see, my music is my way of giving back love. ●

JACO PASTORIUS: THE FLORIDA FLASH

By Neil Tesser

JANUARY 27, 1977

There's a real rhythm in Florida," Jaco Pastorius says in a voice saturated in matter-of-fact. "Because of the ocean. There's something about the Caribbean Ocean, it's why all that music from down there sounds like that. I can't explain it, but I know what it is." He pauses to unclasp his hands, like gangly sandcrabs, and drop his lanky arms to the sides of his lanky body. "I can feel it when I'm there."

The concept of Florida is not a constant among Americans. Some people think of Miami Beach, others warm to the less hectic conjuration of Ft. Lauderdale or sleepy St. Petersburg; for some it is the gateway to the new frontier represented by Cape Canaveral, for others the far older frontier that is the Everglades. Still others revel in the broad paradox of a mecca for retirees on the site of Ponce de Leon's Fountain of Youth, or the full-circle irony of a land discovered by Spaniards being gradually inundated by the Spanish-speaking. But *no one* thinks of Florida as a source of American music. No one thinks of it for jazz.

"The water in the Caribbean is much different from other oceans," Jaco says. "It's a little bit calmer down there; we don't have waves in Florida, all that much. Unless there's a hurricane. But when a hurricane comes, look out, it's more ferocious there than anywhere else. And a lot of music from down there is like that, the pulse is smooth even if the rhythms are angular, and the pulse will take you before you know it. All of a sudden, you're swept away."

The corresponding hurricane of music that has been unleashed by Florida on a hardly expectant world goes by the unlikely name of Jaco Pastorius, the 25-year-old, man-child of the Caribbean who popped up in early 1976 on a startling debut album of his own design, simultaneously replaced Alphonso Johnson in the fusion music showcase Weather Report—whose music he had never listened to before joining the band—and at once began to redefine the conception and connotations of the electric bass guitar. Jaco's playing is nothing less than revolutionary. In fact, he has almost single-handedly opened a heretofore unimagined world of resources for the instrument, forging in ultrasuede sound that at once encompasses the tonal characteristics and phrasing idiosyncrasies of amplified guitar and bass fiddle. In his extraordinary control and imaginative usage of the electric bass' harmonics alone, he has sketched a stylistic device of sizable potential.

But more than that, he has burst upon the scene with a wholly mature and wildly successful compositional ability that draws in varying doses upon jazz, modern rhythm and blues, the classics and the music of the by now familiar Caribbean, from the reggae riffs of Kingston Town to the steel drum bands of Trinidad. "I consider myself as much a writer as a bass player," says Jaco, who avoids boasting but never slights what he perceives as his real assets. I've always done both. The people at Epic (which released his first album, *Jaco Pastorius*) probably got a little more than they bargained for when they signed me. They knew they had some guy who could play a lot of bass, but they didn't know they had a *writer* as well."

Neither did his father, a drummer and singer in Norristown, Penn., when John Francis Pastorius III was born on Dec. 1, 1951. "He didn't want anyone calling me Jack, like everyone else named John, so he started calling me Jaco. And when we moved to Ft. Lauderdale, in 1958, that's how it got the spelling I use (Jaco substitutes a *t* for the *d* in Lauderdale), because that's how the guys from Cuba and Jamaica would spell it." His father provided the influence and the example, but there were never any lessons. Jaco developed his unique approaches to both performing and composing completely on his own, based on what he heard. And what he heard consisted mainly of the

handful of jazz musicians—Ira Sullivan was one of them—in the area, as well as the bands and musical shows that toured the state and the Afro-Cuban rhythms that filtered up from the relatively nearby Islands. But Jaco owned few records and listened to them infrequently, opting most often for the flesh-and-blood performance.

"I've just always had big ears," he shrugs to explain his self-taught talents. "I never had any money, so I had to work, and I caught on quick."

He actually caught on to a multitude of instruments before he eventually settled on the bass guitar. He also worked out on drums, piano, saxophone and guitar, and eventually started playing piano or bass behind many of the concert headliners that came through Florida: Wayne Cochran and the C.C. Riders, the Temptations, the Supremes, Nancy Wilson, and Charo, of all people, among others.

"I was playing like five instruments, and I was pretty good on all of them, but I wasn't *really* good on any of them. I mean, there's no way you can play that many instruments at a time. I had to concentrate on just one.

"That's not to say I was wasting time," he quickly continues. "I mean, I'm glad I fooled around with all of them, like for writing and stuff; I can write as fast as I can think for all those instruments. I'm not hung up on different keys or anything like that," a situation that facilitated his early big band charts for the University of Miami stage band and Ira Sullivan's Baker's Dozen. The precocious youngster was still in his teens. "But I finally realized that in order to do something really well, I'd have to settle on one instrument."

The impetus for that decision was the steady persistence of his daughter Mary—whose birth was imminent. Just 18, Jaco was already married, his wife Tracy was pregnant with the first of their two children, and he was working at a car wash, which he frankly admits "wasn't much fun. We needed money, and so I had to ask myself, 'OK, what do you really want to play?' and I decided to work on the bass.

"The truth is that I couldn't physically play the bass—at least, not like I play now—until was 18 anyway. I had been injured playing football when I was 13,

and my right arm had never healed correctly. It was sort of dead." As a result, Jaco had to give up his first dream—to follow in his father's steps as a drummer. "Finally, when I was 17, I figured I had to go see the doctor. It took about a year after the operation before I was strong enough to really *play* the bass. I could get by on it before then—I could play 'Soul Man' and 'Funky Broadway,' play reggae lines and walk a jazz line in four/four—but I couldn't solo. I couldn't have played 'Donna Lee'," he says, alluding to the stunning and audacious version of the Charlie Parker tune that opens his album.

"So it was really the influence of my family that got me to play. I had to be pragmatic about it, and they inspired me to actually get down to doing things. That's why I call my music Family Music. There's so much more involved than just playing the notes. I mean, a chimpanzee could learn to do what I do—physically. But it goes way beyond that. When you play, you play life. And my family is the main influence on my life. They're the main influence on my music."

Jaco relates a story to underscore the importance of his wife and children. "When my daughter was born, I had about $700 saved up to pay for all the hospital bills and all. This was about a month before she was born. And I went out and spent it on an amplifier instead. I needed it; we needed it. Playing was my life, and if I didn't have a good amp, I realized no one was going to hear me. And by the time she was born, I had already earned about $500 back, working with that amp. It was a decision forced on me by the realities of the situation.

"And something happened to me when my daughter was born. I stopped listening to records, reading *Down Beat*, things like that, because I didn't have the time anymore. That wasn't bad—that's why my sound is different. But there was something else. A new personality being born made me see that it was time for my musical personality to be born; there was no need for me to listen to records. I knew music, I had the *makings* of a musician; now I had to *become* one. My daughter made me see all this, because she was depending on me. I wasn't going to let her down."

The sound that Jaco was developing is indeed "different." In some respects, it is even unique, all the more so since the bass guitar is not an instrument that easily lends itself to a great range of individual expression. At least it didn't before Jaco, with a few notable exceptions such as Stanley Clarke, Alphonso Johnson, and especially Steve Swallow, whose style is the closest thing to an antecedent that one could find for Jaco's playing.

To begin with, Jaco conceptualizes the instrument as a guitar—which, of course, it essentially is. But whereas others have treated the instrument specifically as an *electric* guitar, Jaco somehow urges the rounded tone and fluidity more commonly associated with the amplified acoustic guitar, the hollow-body instrument favored in mainstream jazz. Very smooth, deeply resonant, Jaco's tone is a confluence of three important instruments: his left and right hands, and the Fender fretless electric bass.

"It sings," says Jaco in explaining the preference for the fretless instrument. "I've been playing it for about six years. It's all in the hands; in order to get that sound, you have to know exactly where to touch the strings, exactly how much pressure to apply. You have to learn to *feel* it. And then it just sings." Jaco's sound has come to embody a sometimes bewildering array of chord clusters, nearly tangible overtone qualities, swift improvisatory lines that retain a surprising tonal depth and a penchant for using the instrument's harmonics in both melodic and percussive senses. Quite simply, never has so catholic an imagination been applied to the bass guitar.

Still, there is one added dimension to Jaco's musical persona, as it is conveyed through the bass guitar: Its uncanny ability to sound, in its sonorous tonality and innovative phrasing, as much like an acoustic bass fiddle as it does a guitar. The nature of the instrument is not always clear to even the most experienced listeners. When Weather Report's Joe Zawinul first heard a tape of "Continuum," which

appears on Jaco's album, he drank in the velvety richness of Jaco's bass lead, then turned to the young musician and asked him if he also played the bass guitar. Which, of course, was what Joe had been listening to.

Jaco himself can present the clearest analysis of his technique: "I felt that I

Tom Copi

had never heard anyone clearly outline a tune on the bass. Maybe someone has done it before, I don't know because I don't listen to that many records, but I had never heard it before. I had never heard someone take a tune like 'Donna Lee,' and play it on the bass without a piano player so that you always could hear the changes as well as the melody. It's a question of learning to reflect the original chord in just the line. Players like Wayne Shorter, Sonny Rollins, Herbie Hancock, Ira Sullivan can do that. I wanted to be able to do it, too."

Choosing to display this on his record with a dazzlingly fresh version was no accident. Bebop was his self-imposed theory class. "The first jazz record I heard

was a Max Roach quarter date," he says, "with Kenny Dorham and Hank Mobley; I don't even know who the bassist was. The record was old, and shot, and I couldn't hear the bass player at all. The only thing I could hear was these lines. So I just worked them all out on the bass, without thinking anything of it. And at 15, I already knew how to play most of Bird's tunes. I couldn't play them very fast, because of my arm, but I studied them, and I knew how they worked. Just the heads. I didn't mess with the solos, man; I figured that was personal."

Jaco left the formal educational process after one semester at the University of Miami. He was never enrolled there: he taught bass in the music school. His dissatisfaction with high school—"I should've quit when I was 10; the schools in Florida didn't have much to offer"—was reflected in his decision not to go to college. Although he had excelled in art as well as music during his high school years, Jaco never had a second thought about which medium to pursue.

"I could draw real well, but it's just not spontaneous. You gotta buy material, you gotta have all this stuff....But music; I mean, the best musicians are singers. they can go to the beach, they don't need to take anything with them, they can go swimming and be making music. That's where it's at. Or like Hubert Laws, who played piccolo on my album. That thing is eight inches long, he can stick it in his back pocket, and yet he can make all that music from it. That's what I like about music. It's always there."

It was at about this time that Jaco, who had been exposed to the eclectic blend of Caribbean music that infused Florida during his entire lifetime, began to explore that heritage in a more first-hand manner. He became a show musician on the tourist cruise ships that would set off from the southern tip of Florida for a week at a time.

"These were hip little jaunts," he recalls, "not musically—the music we had to play was even below the normal show band thing—but we would sail all around. We'd go to Mexico for a couple of days, or to

Jamaica, the Bahamas, Haiti. We'd go out for a week, get back on a Saturday about noon, and then leave again a few hours later.

"So when we were docked, I'd just hang out, hit the streets. I got close to some guys in the Wailers. When I got back to Florida, and I left the tours, I played country & western music. Or soul. Or reggae that got up onto the mainland. You see, coming up in Florida, there was nobody really to hang out with. I mean, I had friends who were into music; but there was no one with a national reputation to hang out around. There weren't even that many of my friends that I could share this stuff with. There weren't any cliques of young musicians, like you'd find in New York for instance. And they're all talking so much, feeding off each other...for me, that wouldn't have been good. The diversity that I've developed came from me just being in Florida, just growing up and liking whatever I heard. No one convinced me if something was cool, or not cool. I was into the Beatles, the Stones, the Wailers, Sam and Dave, along with Max Roach."

Jaco's abilities, as well as his emergence onto the national scene, remained one of Florida's best-kept secrets for several years. He made brief and generally unnoticed inroads: during his time at the University of Miami, he had met Chicago guitarist Ross Traut, then enrolled there, and Traut introduced Jaco to Paul Bley, with whom he played a few dates. Also at the University, Jaco came into contact with the guitarist Pat Metheny, with whom he would occasionally play in Pat's home town of Boston, and on whose album for ECM he appeared.

During this time, Jaco played frequently with reedman-trumpet legend Ira Sullivan, and kept body and soul together by playing in the house band at Ft. Lauderdale's Bachelors III club. In the middle of 1975, Blood, Sweat and Tears were booked into the club for a short engagement, and Jaco met Bobby Colomby, the BS&T drummer, guiding light, and soon-to-be producer of Jaco's as yet unanticipated album.

"My wife was working at the club at the time," says Jaco, "and she, along with all the help, the maitre d's, the light men, everyone at the club who knew me, had been telling Colomby about me. His reaction, predictably, was 'Oh, big deal.' He had met my wife, and he knew that she was married to this guy everyone was talking about. Then one night, I dropped in just to see my wife—I didn't even know that BS&T were working there—and I saw Colomby, and we started to talk. We talked about an hour and a half, about all kinds of things, and then my wife came by and kissed me. Colomby said, 'you're Jaco'—I hadn't even introduced myself. And he asked me if I'd like a record date.

"I figured he was just talking—I mean, he hadn't even heard me play, we had just talked—but then, in about a week, he called me up, and within two months I was in New York. I went in with Bobby to see the big brass at Epic, just me and my bass, and I played solo for them. And they said, 'OK. You got it'."

While at work on the material for his own album, a rousing success that nonetheless only skims the surface of Jaco's diverse approach to modern music, he again came across for Zawinul, who was at work on the new Weather Report album (*Black Market*). Zawinul was in the midst of recording "Cannonball," his tribute to the late Julian Adderley who, like Jaco, was an emigrant from Florida. "Joe said he wanted that Florida sound," says Jaco. "So I recorded that tune, and one other, strictly as a sideman. Alphonso Johnson had already left the band, and even though I didn't realize it, Joe was auditioning bass players." They hit it off and, on April 1, 1976, Jaco joined Weather Report.

Since then, he has consistently been a focal point of the band's performances, no easy matter in a group boasting Zawinul and Wayne Shorter. His album, which enlisted the talents of Herbie Hancock, Don Alias, Michael Gibbs, Shorter, and Hubert Laws, almost immediately became an underground sensation and an above-ground debut of unusual success. At work on a second album, as well as touring with Weather Report, Jaco's major problem at this point is time—time to spend with his family at his quiet home in Ft. Lauderdale. There he listens to no music, does little if any playing, and keeps in touch with his personal founts of youth and inspiration: his wife, his children, and the mysterious rhythms of the Caribbean. ●

PHIL WOODS: WORKING MORE AND ENJOYING IT, NO LESS

By Jerry De Muth

JANUARY 11, 1979

D o you want some orange juice, glass of milk?" asked altoist Phil Woods as he and this writer settled down for an interview in a suite in Chicago's Lake Shore Drive Holiday Inn. Sixteen floors below was Rick's Cafe Americain, where he was appearing with his quartet for the second time in less than a year.

"Want a vitamin? We've got everything here."

Woods pointed past the table in front of us, where a bowl of sunflower seeds sat, to a table near the wall with a cluster of small plastic bottles holding a variety of vitamins.

Although Woods still plays with intense passion, he has mellowed. He has, at last, found success as both a soloist and a group leader back in the States, after living in Europe—where "everything became clearer"—from March 1968 to December 1972.

In the States he has fronted the same quartet for the past five years, and after some three years of only scattered work the group now turns down job offers. Woods has collected three Grammys, his home town of Springfield, Mass., held a Phil Woods Day—"A great day for my folks and relatives"—and his solo on Billy Joel's hit "I Love You Just the Way You Are" has propelled the 47-year-old altoist to even wider popularity.

"As a result of Billy Joel I could probably spend the next year backing up singers," he commented. Although Woods wants to avoid such a move—he gave up studio

Joseph L. Johnson

work in 1973—he probably will do a project with Frankie Laine which the singer proposed.

Woods' main concerns today are his quartet—"I'm putting all my energy into the group at the moment and doing fewer things on my own"—and bringing their music to a wider audience. "Right now we have to hit it pretty hard," he said, his voice reflecting enthusiasm more than determination.

"It's important to help open up these newer rooms and play the festivals. It's basically a new audience we're getting. It's great to see folks out. I've played for years to a dozen people. It's nice to draw. That means you can keep going."

Often when Woods isn't playing with the quartet, he is at schools, conducting jazz education sessions or serving as artist-in-residence, although he is doing less of this "as a matter of choice." But he admitted, "I've always been interested in education."

If Woods appears to be compulsive about playing across the country—from Massachusetts to Southern California and from Seattle to Florida—it's because, he explained, "I've always liked being busy and I wasn't busy when I was in my twenties and thirties."

Woods also has the satisfaction of seeing interest increase in the type of jazz he and the quartet play, which he describes as "acoustic improvised American music," after years in which electronic sounds dominated the jazz scene. During that time Woods himself, for a ten-month period in California after his return from Europe, was "using a ring modulator and a wah-wah pedal," an experience that was far from satisfying for him.

Woods now plays alto and soprano saxes without any electronic hookups, just as bassist Steve Gilmore and pianist Mike Nelillo stick to acoustic instruments with firm dedication. (Drummer Bill Goodwin completes the quartet.) The acoustic instruments fit their preference for "American songs, everything from Cole Porter to Tadd Dameron."

"That's kind of neglected material that we all think is important—and it sure is fun to play," Woods stressed. "It doesn't feel old fashioned to us and I think the kids are getting off on that. It's all fresh to them.

"I did my share of going out, working with a local rhythm section," he related, tension entering his voice as he leaned forward in his plush chair. "I don't think I'd ever do that again. If I couldn't sustain a group I think I'd go teach. I couldn't make it by myself…'Perdido' every night with a different group.

"Otherwise you carry around a little library and you have a rehearsal and it never gets off the ground. That would be such a bringdown after having my own rhythm section. I don't think I could stand it. Played 'Stella By Starlight' enough to last me a lifetime."

Woods lit up what has become almost as much of a trademark for him as his small flat cap, a long thin dark brown cigarette, and leaned back in the chair to reflect on the growing number of jazzmen who have abandoned traveling as a single to tour with a regular group. He mentioned Clark Terry, Woody Shaw, Dexter Gordon, Johnny Griffin and the tenor sax-trombone duo of Jimmy Forrest and Al Grey.

"More and more musicians have their own groups as it becomes economically feasible," he said. "But some musicians don't want to bother with that, and it doesn't hurt Zoot Sims. A great player will always be a great player, I don't care how lame the rhythm section is."

Still, for Philip Wells Woods, having their own group means being able to create something a little extra.

"I think it's better artistically if you have your own group and if it's better artistically it's got to be better commercially because the music will be better," he began spinning out his reasoning without pause. "And if the music is better you should make more money at it. Plus you can get a real identity with your own group."

As anyone who has heard Woods can testify, he almost always sounds damn good, even on that first set of the night, even opening night. The quartet gets up on the stand and with only a few words between them they start to play, usually an old standard that Woods tears into.

"We try to get hot right in front," Woods responded with a confidence that contained a hint of doubt as to whether he really was as successful at "getting hot" as he tried to be. "But I still feel our second sets are better than our first sets. But I think our first sets are above average. Sometimes we get to work and it's magic all the way through. It depends on the room. Sometimes it's hard to get going. It's like…." He paused to get his analogy correct, then smiled and waved his arms in a breast stroke as he continued, "…plowing through a sea of Mars bars. But if people are responsive, the band responds to that."

The five years Woods spent living in Europe and leading what was to be his first truly full-time band, the European Rhythm Machine which is represented on six albums, obviously had a maturing influence on the man, helping him develop as a musician, as a leader and as a businessman as well as an individual.

"I've always had a band of some sort," he reflected, casual softness in his voice, "but never on a regular basis. I never could learn about the business because Gene Quill and I didn't work that much. Or I had local quartets that were a local, easy type thing to manage—work a week and then have three months off."

Woods, after studying with the late Lennie Tristano and at the Manhattan School of Music and then for a full four years at Juilliard, began his professional career in 1954. Before the fifties came to an end, he had served with, among others, Richard Hayman, Charlie Barnet, Jimmy Raney, George Wallington, Friedrich Guida, Dizzy Gillespie, Gene Quill, Buddy Rich and Quincy Jones, with whom he remained for two years, besides his musical ally of long standing, Oliver Nelson. Then came a tour with Benny Goodman and a return to Gillespie, followed by much studio work until his departure for Europe in 1968 and residency in France.

He still has a farm outside Paris, and he with covivant and business manager Jill Goodwin, sister of his drummer, Bill, get there at least for part of every summer. He also keeps the place as a "touchstone for the kids."

"I want that to stay in the family," he explained. His son, Garth, now 19 and a professional photographer, spends much time there. Last fall he used it as a base while working on a photo essay on the wheat harvest.

"Garth is more French than American, a true Francophile," Woods related. "He thinks in French. I have a love affair with France myself, but you can't just sustain yourself on what I do in France."

Phil Woods is, at last, sustaining himself in jazz now. Not only has he said goodbye to studio work but he and the quartet are able to turn down job offers, including some they would have accepted only two or three years ago when they still were not working regularly. Now they will refuse an engagement if they don't like the room or if it's too far from their last or next gig. They even try to avoid traveling on a working day.

"We all make the decision whether to take a job," Woods explained the quartet's working relationship. The four function as a cooperative, whether they are deciding to accept a job (Woods as leader gets two votes) or dividing up earnings.

"I'm the leader and I should get a little more money, but not that much more money," he interjected with a touch of self deprecation. "It should be as equitable as possible. That way you get the best performance."

For traveling, the four musicians generally rent a van and try to keep dates within easy driving distance.

"Airlines can kill you," Woods said, touches of anger and frustration in his voice, "and they're a pain in the ass. They don't like the acoustic bass. They don't know what to do with it.

"We give the airlines a lot of money but when it comes to 20% of what you're making, that's too much. It's much more reasonable to rent a van. We try to keep travel down to 300 miles at top; 100 or 200 is nice between jobs. Then we do it on what we call a traveling day. We're not out to outdo Kenton or Basie. We've all done that when we were younger.

"I'm turning jobs down when they're impossible. I don't even take a vote on those. I'm the leader," he smiled, "and so I take the prerogative of saying 'no' to those.

"We're trying to space it out so we're not out on the road quite so long. We're trying to get more money in a shorter period of time.

"We can be choosier today," he added. "But we'll take a chance just because we feel it's important to open up new territory and out of the last two tours we've only had one bummer where we said, 'Oh God, I'm not going back to that one again'."

Woods stresses the importance of opening up "new territory" for the quartet, and for jazz in general.

"We've gotten to the Northwest—Bellingham, Seattle—where we'd never performed before," he commented. "Most of the places we play are new rooms and some are not just jazz rooms. They're all kinds of things. There's a lot of new places for music now—places in Amarillo, Austin, Buffalo.

"The best way to build an audience is to play for one; record companies can't do that for you," he explained, drawing on a recording experience of more than two decades that has involved more than two dozen different labels. "If you play to 100 people a night and play 40 weeks a year that insures the existence of the group."

Although Woods and the other three members of the group have been busy recording in recent years—and Woods has those Grammys to his credit—the saxophonist apologetically admits, "We don't have one quartet record out."

The Grammy winning two-record set on RCA, *Live from the Showboat*, and the direct-to-disc *Song of Sisyphus* feature the group in its year-and-a-half long incarnation as a quintet with guitarist Harry Leahey. (For *Showboat*, percussionist Alyrio Lima was added, making it the Phil Woods Six.) The quartet also was augmented for a still unreleased album cut in London which consists of a series of portraits of deceased jazzmen including Gary McFarland and Julian "Cannonball" Adderley. And Woods appears as soloist on an album RCA will soon release, *The Seven Deadly Sins*, for which he did some of the writing. ("Different composers each took a sin.")

Woods is presently involved in a contractual dispute which further delays any change of a recording by the quartet alone. Although obviously annoyed by this situation, he is resigned to the fact.

"The records out do show where we're at," he felt. "They give a pretty fair indication, although not instrumentation-wise. Musically they're not at variance with what the quartet is doing. And there is some quartet on *The New Phil Woods Album* (RCA).

That night at Rick's the crowd was small, and comprised mostly of unattentive—to the music at least—businessmen who wandered in for a drink. Woods was more puzzled than angered by this audience. Less than a year earlier, during a week-long snow storm in the middle of one of Chicago's worst winters on record, enthusiastic crowds had filled the room, and lined up waiting to get in for late sets, even on weekday nights.

"I'm older so I guess there should be a bit of inner peace in a way," he shrugged, "but I don't feel very different. I go to the gig. I take a shower. I get on the bandstand and we play music. I get a bite to eat. I watch television. I've been doing it for so long.

"I like to think I'm getting better but I'm not so sure. Maybe I'm dropping a step. Sometimes I feel I'm slowing up a bit. You're always questioning your playing. Some nights I don't believe how rotten I sound.

"I'm still looking for perfection. I want the perfect reed; I want the mikes right. I want the sound to sing.

"I think it might be easier when you're 27 and not 47. There's got to be some physiological shifting, but in general I feel pretty good about it."

As Woods sees the age of 50 approaching, he thinks it might be time to take things a bit easier.

"I'll be playing as long as I live but I want to moderate it some. I want," he added with the relaxed air of a satisfied and successful businessman, "to spend some time on the house, build a model airplane again which I haven't done in a long time.

"I don't want to stay out here forever. I do see a couple more years of active traveling. After that…who knows? Maybe I'll work six months and do something else for the other six months. By 50, I want to take a year off by myself. I think 50 is a good age to do that. After that I don't know. Teach somewhere, be an artist-in-residence.

"So that's my immediate plan and it's a silly one—as if there's something magical about the number 50. But it's a convenient time to reevaluate.

"I've been around jazz a long time, and I know you can't stay on the road forever. If you do, you usually end up dying alone and that's very sad.

"If it becomes a chore, if it becomes laborious to go to work, then it's time to call it quits. You're entitled to a slump but if it's that way all the time.…"

Woods shrugged. Then, his spirit back up, he exclaimed:

"Right now I just want to go out and play, play my best and play the music that I believe in.

"I want to play all the towns and all the rooms. I want to see what's going on out there. There's obviously an audience out there for what we're doing. I want to see it through. I think the work is important. There's a certain importance to playing this music, getting to young people who wouldn't be aware of some of this stuff." ●

RICH + TORME = WILD REPARTEE

By Mel Tormé

FEBRUARY 9, 1978

This interview with drummer and bandleader Buddy Rich was conducted by singer and composer/arranger Mel Tormé. The varied activities of both men make it impossible to sum up their careers with one or two adjectives.

Mel Tormé began his entertainment career in 1929 at the age of four, singing with the Coon-Sanders Orchestra. He began studying drums at age seven, and at the mellow age of nine began acting in radio soap operas. Since the end of World War II, Tormé has been a major singer, composing and arranging most of his material. He has consistently received recognition as a singer in the *Down Beat* polls, and is much admired by other musicians, most particularly for his talents as an arranger. Additionally, he has functioned as a drummer, pianist, producer, and as a writer of books and critical forays in these pages.

Buddy Rich nips Tormé in the child prodigy competition: *his* career began with his parents' vaudeville act at the age of 18 months. At age six he toured Australia as a solo act, managed by his parents. His jazz career started in 1938, and included work with Bunny Berigan, Artie Shaw, Tommy Dorsey (several times), Benny Carter, JATP, Harry James, and his own groups and big bands. Probably best known to the silent majority for his acid tongue and blips on "The Tonight Show," Rich several times briefly abandoned his drumming to perform as a singer, acted in TV in the late fifties, and is an accomplished tap dancer. Today, he is probably at the height of his popularity.

Rich and Tormé have been friends for years, and appear to have a certain love-hate relationship. When we contacted Tormé about the possibility of an interview between these two Renaissance men, he quickly accepted, and the next thing we knew the tape appeared in the morning mail. The interview will be used by Tormé in a forthcoming biography of Rich.

Tormé: *Can you define what the difference is between the way you play currently and the way you played in the days with Shaw and Dorsey, when you used to back soloists, mainly with hi-hats. The idea of playing on a top cymbal or a ride cymbal to back a tenor or trumpet was virtually unknown in those days. You didn't do it 'cause I heard a lot you played. You played a lot of snare drum.*

Rich: Yes.

Tormé: *On things like "Swing High," you would play snare drum.*

Rich: Yes. I played a five stroke plus roll.

Tormé: *Why is that changed?*

Rich: I can't do a five stroke plus roll any longer.

Tormé: *I see. Has the modern trend influenced you?*

Rich: Oh greatly, greatly.

Tormé: *Have you influenced it?*

Rich: No, I think that it has greatly influenced my playing.

Tormé: *The progressive jazz?*

Rich: Yes, I've determined to play the way I've always played. Why are we talking about the old days?

Tormé: *Because I want to get to the new days and what's different. I have a lot of questions here about what's going on now.*

Rich: Oh, I see. I'm sorry to interrupt you.

Tormé: *Let's talk about the way you've changed the playing. I've seen some old films that you did with Shaw and Dorsey. And when we saw them together, you were astounded at the radical angle of your snare drum, and how low and deeply tilted it was. You don't set up that way any more.*

Rich: No, that was the Shaw set up. I was using a 26" bass drum at the time, and consequently I had to sit two inches higher and I had to bring the snare drum up that high. I'd be playing above the drum, instead of my hands falling on top of the drum, they'd be above, and I'd be wasting all of this energy. I couldn't very well keep the drum at a flat angle and be down low. So the only way that I could hit a rim shot would be to have the drum below me, about the position that it's in today, except that it was tilted down, so that I could hit the rim easier. No way of hitting it if the drum was flat.

You have to play awhile to figure out exactly what is most comfortable, for you. When you're very young you make changes. Sitting high might be difficult for your foot on the bass drum, or tilting it one way might be beneficial to one hand or not.

So gradually, after about a year with Artie's band, I changed the set up, and I started sitting a little lower, and bringing the snare drum down a little bit so that it was in about the same area as the 9 by 13 tom tom. By not having to raise your hand to play the drum you can get around the drum because everything is on the same level as your hands.

Tormé: *More the economy of motion?*

Rich: That's the idea of playing. The idea of maintaining some kind of stamina is to be able to get around the drum with the least motion. And that's the way you do it. You have everything so that instead of having to play out everything, everything is just exactly where your hands would automatically be. It's the same as having dinner, with a knife and fork in front of you. The position is everything.

Tormé: *Once in Vegas, I asked you a dumb question about what's the key to mastering technique with drums, and you told me that if you can master a roll, both closed and open, that was the center—the core of playing. Why?*

Rich: If you can do single strokes and if you do them at an incredible speed, it automatically closes down to a closed roll. And if you lighten up on the speed, you pull back a little and you automatically have an open roll. One roll will take you back to single strokes. The single strokes will give you the flexibility to create rhythmical ideas, rhythmical patterns off of single strokes, and then you gradually follow that into triplets off the left hand, triplets off the right hand, back and forth going into a roll again. Most drummers who can't roll really don't have any techniques with the hands. You must have the ability to control your wrist to a point where you can make your roll sound like you're tearing a piece of sandpaper.

Tormé: *And not being able to tell the difference between the left and the right hand?*

Rich: That's exactly right. Most teachers teach kids today too that there is a definite way of playing: you start with the right hand, or you start a particular pattern with the left hand. But that's wrong. You are to play at the position your hands are, the way they automatically fall. Not left or right, or right or left, but whatever happens, as long as you have the technical control and ability to play what you have

• •

Buddy Rich

• •

in mind. That's the whole idea.

Tormé: *You're always in great physical condition. One of the things that people notice most about you is your pure stamina. If you're going to do an extremely long solo on, say, "Channel One" or "West Side," or whatever, rather than a diminishing of power, strength and thrust, it gets stronger and stronger until at the end, it's extraordinary. That is like a great Olympic runner, a great athlete....*

Rich: I was going to say that. It's exactly the same thing. All solos should be paced. You start with an idea. I like to think of my solos as telling a story. You tell the beginning of a story and you build up to a punch line. But if you tell a story and tell the punch line first, where are you going? That's it, you got your laugh.

The same thing applies to almost any instrument. If you are telling a story, if you are playing a beautiful piano solo, first tell about how you met. In terms of romance: how you met, what happened after that, until you finally jump on the bones. Isn't

that romantic, folks? That's the way I play—according to my moods, and stamina is automatically there.

Tormé: *You set parameters*

Joseph L. Johnson

for yourself?

Rich: Yeah, I know exactly what I want to do and where I want to go. I don't want to be the first guy there and not have anybody else in sight. I want to beat you by ten yards, not by a mile. I pace myself to where I know that at the very end of my solo, I'm going to play a roll or I'm going to knock some cymbals around or whatever I decide to do. But I know that I must conserve that much energy to get me through the ending.

Tormé: *Isn't it also the application of the way you play, manipulating the sticks?*

Rich: I don't use my body. It's all wrists. The only reason you raise your arms is to hit a cymbal or reach behind you to hit a tom tom or something. But the actual playing all takes place down here, so that you're not breathing heavily because you're just using your wrists.

Tormé: *Conserving your strength, really.*

Rich: Right.

Tormé: *I used to hear you with the old*

bands. *With Artie Shaw and Tommy Dorsey, principally, I watched you play hi hat cymbals, you played cross-handed, and you used to hunch your right shoulder up a little bit to come down on the cymbal. But I was always particularly moved by the Shaw band more than the Dorsey band. I think no other drummer ever got the kind of semi-closed choked sound out of the cymbal that you did when you played with the Shaw band. A very good example of it is on "Carioca," which is very rapid, and which has that very marvelous choked sound.*

Rich: In those days I used a much smaller, 11" hi hat. And both cymbals were thin, as opposed to today, where the bottom cymbal is heavy. Both were the same weight, medium thin. We only had three trumpets, two trombones and four saxophones in the Shaw band, so I didn't need the overwhelming sound of large cymbals and open hi hat to cover up five saxophones and eight brass. So the whole concept was different. You try to get a hi-hat sound, and at the same time make it definite enough for the band to hear where to and four would come. I always played so that I managed to hit two cymbals at one time. I never played the top of the hi hat. I always liked to hear both cymbals. Consequently I would play underhand so that I could hit both edges at the same time. Instead of just playing the top cymbal which gives you that "te, te, bah, te, te, bah." This way you get thw, thw, thw, thw, thw, thw. Just let the cymbal raise just a little bit. And the only way you can do that is to hit both cymbals at the same time.

Tormé: *Tell me that you still play cross-hand once in awhile.*

Rich: I do it once in a while if we're playing something that calls for it. We don't do too many things that calls for that sound. The book is totally different. So I play a lot of ride-cymbal and top cymbal, but in the rhythm section things, sometimes I get caught in the hi-hat thing. It has a very mellow sound. But it's still a throwback to the days of only hi hats, and it's very simple.

Tormé: *What about the lever action of your right hand when you play the cymbal?*

Rich: I don't know how to explain it. I don't play with my fingers for one. You don't get a sound with the fingers. Louie Bellson and Joe Morello are the true exponents of what they call finger control. But your fingers don't control the stick, your hand controls the stick, and if you can't use the wrist action then you don't have stamina and power to play *any* given tempo for any length of time. You must have the benefit of your whole hand. That's the same as walking—if you don't use your ankles you limp quite a bit. The same flexibility applies. You use the leverage of your ankle for the pedal, and you use your wrist, not your fingers, to control all of the motion for the stick.

Tormé: *Going back to your early days as a tap dancer....*

Rich: Yes, the early days of 1971.

Tormé: *Come on, wait a minute, we'll get to all the new stuff, but I wanted to ask you this.*

Chick Webb, Ray Baduc, Gene Krupa, Ray McKinley—all those guys—were superior drummers in their own ways, but none of them were very daring. They didn't incorporate bass drum and snare drum as alternate sounds. You're the first guy that ever did that, I think. Do you feel that your tap dancing talents are the reason that you're able to communicate between bass drum and snare drum, and tom toms and the rest of them, better than other drummers?

Rich: Tap dancing in the true sense is rhythmical dancing, right? I hate to say that you have to be born with it, but you don't *learn* how to be a jazz tap dancer. Baby Laurence was the daddy of jazz tap dancers. The Conners brothers, Bunny Briggs, Buck and Bubbles, Bill Robinson—I would bet that if that they wanted to and picked up a pair of sticks, they could have been outstanding drummers. It's that kind of feeling, that time thing.

Some of the best drummers I ever heard had no technique at all. Some of the show drummers. There used to be a guy in Chicago named Red Saunders. I remember that whenever I played Chicago on Saturday nights they used to have a breakfast show for the various entertainers. They always had a line of 16 girls, like the Apollo Theater in New York. I used to go only because Red Saunders was the greatest show drummer that ever lived. He had a

10-piece band, playing all these outside jazz things for the girls to dance to. He was a cue drummer; he would catch every step the girls did. He would catch comics, catch their lines. He had things with the band that were just impossible to know. You just have to instinctively know that this is the way to play. As far as technique was concerned, he couldn't play a roll if they slipped him a jar of butter. He had no technique, but he had the innate ability to play drums. He wouldn't astound you by playing a solo. He couldn't play a solo, probably.

I was very into that kind of playing, the show-type drumming. And I had a great feeling for Billy Gladstone. He used to play snare drum at Radio City Music Hall in New York. I used to go to see him and I used to sit in the last row in the balcony, in the back, only because I wanted to hear his roll. He built his own drum.

Tormé: *He had the Gretsch Gladstone drum.*

Rich: It was about a 6½ or 7" deep.

Tormé: *It had a great throw off.*

Rich: Just touch it and it would fall right down. In other words, completely away from the bottom head, so there was no rattle when you had the tom tom. He used a combination of gut and wire snares. And I would sit in the last row in the balcony, and without the slightest bit of motion he could almost shatter your eardrum. He had that kind of technique. When he played a roll you couldn't tell if it was a roll or if he had only one stick on the drum. It was that pure. That was the other kind of technique that I admired.

Of course Chick Webb was one of the great jazz drummers. And his technique was minimal, but he had enough technique to get around, and still have the other thing going for him. He put the creativity of what a jazz dancer would have danced into drumming.

I want to talk about Chick Webb. And Davie Tough, and Sid Catlett, and Ray Baduc, and Moe Purtill, and Cliff Leeman, and, of course, Jo Jones. We should mention Jo Jones before we mention anyone else. You can sit and listen to records and know exactly what drummer was playing. Every drummer had a particular sound and style. You could not mistake him. You could not say, "Well, I think that's Krupa, or I think that's Chick

Webb." You knew automatically. Every drummer had a different sound.

Tormé: *Every drummer? I don't believe that.*

Rich: Absolutely. Absolutely.

Tormé: *I think probably one of the greatest examples you can cite is Davie Tough when he played with Benny Goodman and Davie Tough when he played with Woody Herman. He virtually made his style fit the playing of the band.*

Rich: But dig how good he sounded in both bands. He sounded great with Benny. And when he did the sextet things with Benny he sounded *great*. Woody had a different approach. Woody was much more aggressive than Benny, so Davie had to exert an extra pound or two of his 98 pounds. But Davie Tough had those hands. Davie took to swinging a band with a pair of brushes like no other drummer.

Tormé: *Except you.*

Rich: Well, we're not talking about me; we're talking about guys that I admired. I have great respect for those guys.

Tormé: *Of all those guys that you just mentioned, what guys did you really admire tremendously? You said Red Saunders, and I agree with you there. You said Chick, and I'm sure you admire Gene for his innovations alone....*

Rich: Of course I admire Gene. I admire Gene from the standpoint of what he did to put the drummer in another light. The drummer finally got to be more than just the guy who sat down behind the rest of the band and played all night long. There used to be an old joke, "How many men in your band?" "I have 16 musicians and a drummer." Which is a really dumb joke, because you can get the best band in the world, and if you put a bad drummer behind it you have one drummer and 16 bad musicians. Let's really be honest about that shit. You take the Rams—if they don't have a good quarterback, they can have the best defensive line in the world. But if you don't have a guy calling the signals back there, you got nothing.

Tormé: *How much were you making with Shaw?*

Rich: With Shaw I was making $500 and I'm not talking about the money thing. The offer was $500.

Tormé: *Yeah, but you made $500 for sure. Which was, incidentally, a hell of a lot of money in those days, wasn't it?*

Rich: Well, when you consider what an

average salary in those days was, the high-priced guy was probably getting two and a quarter. Two and a half would be outrageously high for 1940. You know, so getting $500 was....

Tormé: *With all the money you made with Shaw, how come you didn't get commensurate billing?*

Rich: Well, maybe because I was stupid at the time and I didn't really believe billing was all that important. I had never really thought about stardom before.

Tormé: *But you were a star. As a child performer.*

Rich: That was another Buddy Rich entirely, I don't want to even talk about that. You're talking about Traps.

Tormé: *I don't want to get into it either, but you did understand about billing?*

Rich: No, I didn't. What you can understand about billing when you're four years old.

Tormé: *I'm talking about the fact that you did vaudeville units....*

Rich: Yes, I did vaudeville.

Tormé: *When you became 14 or 15 you stopped playing drums to become an MC.*

Rich: That's right. I never thought about billing after that, because that was something that agents and my parents thought about. I didn't think about billing, understand? That was that.

Tormé: *If you didn't think about billing, why did you insist on that huge billing with Tommy Dorsey when you joined him?*

Rich: Wait! Wait!

Tormé: *Ahh! Ahh!*

Rich: You're talking about Shaw, right? With Shaw it was a different thing, Helen Forrest was the featured lady singer and Tony Pastor was the featured tenor saxophone and singer. And I was very happy being featured with the band. So that was good for me. When I left the band I was starting to know just where I stood, or where I was about to stand in music. So when I said that I would fly to Chicago, I said to Bobby Burns that I'm coming to hear the band, not to join the band, because I didn't like the band. He asked me to fly out anyhow. He sent me a first class ticket, and I flew to Chicago. The band was appearing at the Empire Room of the Palmer House. It was an unlucky thing for me. I came in and I caught the dinner set when a band would play from 7 to 9 p.m.,

whatever.

Tormé: *Who was playing drums?*

Rich: I think Cliff Leeman. Anyhow, I heard the band and they were buying dinner and all that nonsense, and I finally met Mr. Dorsey, who had one of those "Oh, yeah, a little kid" attitudes. He went to his dressing room, or his suite, and they asked me to stick around until the ten o'clock set to play a tune with the band. I played a tune with the band, and I came off....

Tormé: *What was it, do you remember?*

Rich: It was a dance thing. Just something to play some time behind. Because the only time you did anything to show the band off was like a show thing. You just say for the next 15 minutes we're going to play some B.S., right? I played a couple of tunes with the band. I came off the bandstand and they offered me the job, and I said "No way, that's not my kind of band, I don't like what the band plays, it's the dixieland band, the ballad band." I went through the whole rap, and I left.

I went back to New York, and I got called again. They asked me to fly back to Chicago. I flew back to Chicago, because they told me that they were changing the style of the band, and that Sy Oliver was coming in to write and did I know who Sy Oliver was? Of course I knew who Sy Oliver was. Tommy was going to change the band into kind of a white Lunceford band. When I heard that, I was interested and the first couple tunes that Sy wrote were exciting for those days. He wrote a thing called "Losers Weepers," which was the first thing I ever recorded for the Dorsey band. I got 50% billing and $750 a week. I got $750 for about nine months and decided I was worth a little bit more than that. So I asked for $1,000 and they turned it down. I said that I would have to leave and they said goodbye; after two weeks he said $1,000, and I said okay. I stayed for years after that. When I left, I was getting $1,500. And my price went up after that. ●

ART ENSEMBLE OF CHICAGO:

15 YEARS OF GREAT BLACK MUSIC

By Larry Birnbaum

MAY 3, 1979

They have been called "the premier avant garde free improvisational ensemble of the day," (John Rockwell, *The New York Times*) although their music is highly structured and notated. Their style has been dubbed "guerrilla jazz" (Gary Giddins, *Village Voice*) although they reject the term "jazz" and deny that their work is politically motivated. They have been likened to such modern classicists as Webern and Stockhausen, but they claim that the Western academic tradition is foreign to their mentality. More eclectic than any "fusion" band, they have nothing in common with that popular electric school. Through periods of acclaim and obscurity, they have doggedly followed their own muse, unmindful of commercial and revisionist trends. After some 15 years of stubborn perseverance, they may at last be standing on the brink of wider acceptance with the issuance of an ECM album, *Nice Guys*, as the musical genre which they helped set in motion gradually comes to be recognized as the legitimate heir to the tradition of black art music. How then to describe the Art Ensemble of Chicago, who have pushed the heritage of Great Black Music, as they call it, to new frontiers of creativity? Perhaps a bit of history is in order.

In a recent *Down Beat* interview, Archie Shepp cited Lester Young as the first self-conscious art musician in the Afro-American tradition; yet Pres remained a popular figure, idolized in the black community. Charlie Parker transformed the music irrevocably into a listener's idiom, leaving the dancing audience uncomprehendingly behind. In the following decade, musicians like Miles Davis struggled to win respect for their art on a par with classical music, while retaining a considerable following of "sophisticates." Then in the sixties, Ornette Coleman and his followers abandoned what remained of convention to explore a visionary realm of pure artistic experimentation. Many listeners turned away in bafflement, and by the end of the decade pundits and industry executives were proclaiming the demise of jazz.

Nonetheless, the late sixties constituted a period of creative ferment perhaps unparalleled in the history of the music, the achievements of which have yet to be fully acknowledged. It was during those years that the Chicago cooperative known as the Association for the Advancement of Creative Musicians (AACM) was founded, whence sprang many of today's most original and creative voices. While the New York scene foundered on the shoals of commercial rivalry or spent itself in endless diluted Coltrane imitations, the Chicagoans, for lack of commercial outlets, turned to one another for support and kept their music vital and innovative.

Among the earliest and most accomplished units to emerge from the Association for the Advancement of Creative Musicians (AACM) was the Art Ensemble of Chicago. First in Chicago, then in Europe and back in the States, the Art Ensemble members were the point men of the AACM, exposing the music to new audiences and opening doors for their brethren to follow. They expanded traditional concepts of performance with a spectacle of aural and visual effects—employing arsenals of gongs, chimes, whistles, kazoos, all manner of exotic percussion, face paint, elaborate Third World costumes, poetry, dance, comedy, mime, and multi-media effects—fashioning an organic cross-cultural theater unique in modern music.

Ornette, replying to his critics, maintained that he was drawing on the inspiration of the early New Orleans musicians. The Art Ensemble took him at his word, then went a step further. Reviving the tradition of the multi-instrumentalist, reedmen Roscoe Mitchell and Joseph Jarman resurrected the entire saxophone family, from the ungainly bass sax to the tiny sopranino, as well as oboes, bassoons, piccolos, and other instruments unseen in the jazz world for half a century. St. Louis bred trumpeter Lester Bowie reached back to Armstrong and beyond to evoke the vocalisms and animal imitations of minstrelsy. The tradition of parody that had extended from vaudeville through Fats Waller was resuscitated with a mocking wit

unique in contemporary music.

Unique, too, was the group's expansion of the timbral spectrum to include sonorities not previously considered musical. Mitchell pioneered the use of "little instruments," comprising everything from rattles and klaxon horns to half-filled water buckets, to produce uncanny tonal effects. The others followed suit, accumulating a huge battery of unusual sonic devices that grew to envelop them onstage like a theater set. Conventional instruments, too, were deployed outside of their normal timbral ranges to achieve an amazing variety of original voicings.

Members of the group had been playing together since 1961, but it was not until 1968 that the Roscoe Mitchell Art Ensemble made its official debut with Mitchell, Bowie, bassist Malachi Favors and drummer Phillip Wilson, who soon defected to the Paul Butterfield Blues Band. The group continued as a drummerless quartet with the addition of Jarman, an early colleague of Mitchell and Favors whose own band had disintegrated with the tragic deaths of pianist Christopher Baddy and bassist Charles Clark.

Although they made occasional out-of-town forays, the Art Ensemble remained largely unknown outside their South Side home base, where they frequently performed in the environs of the University of Chicago. There, in a climate of political and cultural upheaval, they developed their revolutionary brand of conceptual theater, parading around and even outside of halls, once scheduling a concert at a specified location and performing at another. Another time listeners were given paper bags to wear over their heads. Audiences were attentive but small, and many people were bewildered or intimidated by the band's bizarre antics, costumes, and paraphernalia. In June of '69, the group pulled up stakes and set off for Paris with the parting words to a concert audience, "America is in your hands now."

In France, the Art Ensemble created an immediate sensation. They recorded 11 albums and three film scores, made dozens of TV and radio appearances, and played hundreds of government sponsored concerts in large halls and opera houses throughout Western Europe. Also in Paris they acquired drummer Don Moye, who had met Jarman at an artists' workshop in Detroit before embarking for Europe with

a quartet called Detroit Free Jazz. For all their notoriety there, the group felt that their music was actually less well understood in Europe than at home. Unpaid for their recordings, they were penniless by the time they returned to the States in April of '71 to renew their inspiration at its source.

Back in America, the Art Ensemble again took a cue from Ornette and demanded a fee commensurate with their critically heralded talents. Consequently, the next two years were lean ones, spent mainly in rehearsing, although they "managed to work out two or three gigs a year right along," according to Moye.

"We damn near died," said Bowie. Gradually, interest picked up; government grants and university workshops provided sustenance until, in 1975, the group played an extended engagement at the Five Spot in New York, followed by another triumph at Ali's Alley and a ravingly received West Coast tour.

Between widely scattered gigs, the members of the unit have undertaken an ambitious series of individual projects, including solo and duet recordings and collaborations with AACM and like-minded musicians. Jarman, who has recorded with Anthony Braxton, Muhal

Richard Abrams and Frank Lowe, returned to Europe for an extended stay. Mitchell has expanded the concept of the solo saxophonist with performances and recordings in the U.S. and Europe. Favors and Moye have also recorded solo sessions, and have worked behind many units—AACM and otherwise—in New York and Chicago. Bowie lived for a time in Jamaica, and is presently involved as featured soloist with the new Directions band of drummer Jack DeJohnette, a transplanted Chicagoan who was active in the early days of the AACM.

All five musicians have won critical acclaim as masters of their respective instruments.

Jarman and Mitchell have been slighted in the polls simply because they defy categorization; from alto each has developed equal facility on all saxophones, not to mention flutes, woodwinds and miscellaneous percussion. Their styles, while related, are quite distinct. Both draw on the models of Ornette and others of the new wave, especially Albert Ayler, but each has developed a unique, original voice imitative of no one. Mitchell admired Wayne Shorter and met Ayler in the Army; his compositions combine complex abstraction with an expressive, angular lyricism, and his breathtaking technique embraces the entire spectrum of possible reed intonations. Jarman will tackle any instrument from a Theremin to a kazoo. Verbally as well as musically articulate, Jarman publishes and recites poetry, and his delicate, shakuhachi-like flute shadings are as striking as his emotive, throaty sax work.

Favors, who has added the surname Magoustous, is virtually without peer in the

Tom Copi

contemporary bass idiom. A Wilbur Ware protegé, he couples his mentor's resplendently resonant tone with an uncanny sense of timing and harmony, plucking eerily hypnotic ostinatos or creating fantastic arco overtone structures.

Famoudou Don Moye is a fiery speed demon on percussion, a smoke-curdling soloist as well as a sensitive accompanist who is equally adept on traps, congas and marimbas. Each player is strong enough to front his own group; together they join in a continuous, five-sided dialogue of equals, and after some 15 years together their empathy is virtually telepathic.

Onstage, the Art Ensemble presents a spectacle unlike anything in the world. Jarman, Favors, and Moye bedeck themselves in African-style face paint, flowing robes, batiked pantaloons, coolie hats, and bracelets of bells at wrists and ankles. Bowie generally appears in a long white lab coat and railroad cap, with optional bow tie. Mitchell, by contrast, favors faded Levis and pullover shirts. Framing them on every side are walls of equipment—their patented and much-copied gong racks festooned with tintinnabula of all dimensions; shelves of whistles, clappers, school bells, calabashes, ballophones, xylophones, and log drums combine to form a sonic joss house, often fuming with aromatic incense.

Their music is as exotic and variegated as their appearance. Bowing their heads in prayer, the Art Ensemble commences with an extended clattering of little instruments, setting the tone and drawing the audience into their world. From there they embark on an unbroken series of structured episodes (not "free jazz"), including tightly charted passages, long stretches of group and solo improvisation, and a great many interludes of half-notated, half-impromptu interplay. They span the emotional spectrum, expressing rage, joy, melancholy, humor, tenderness, sarcasm, exultation. Sound and silence are weighted equally—furious outpourings alternate with periods of quiet reflection, players leap passionately into the fray, then lay out and observe. Recordings hardly do them justice—how does one tape a pantomime routine.

Their musical sources are equally eclectic. The entire "jazz" tradition is central, but gospel, blues, African, Oriental, Mid Eastern, and even classical influences abound, although Jarman specifically disavowed the latter in a recent interview. They have recorded examples of dixieland, r&b, rock, bebop, gospel, baroque, waltz, and even march music, sometimes in seriousness, often in lampoon form.

Their treatment of rock on the hilarious "Rock Out," from *Message to Our Folks*, is particularly devastating. An electric guitar squawks out a trivial little vamp with tedious monotony, punctuated by the irreverent tweakings of a bike horn, until at length the musicians abandon the effort and begin to blow for real, as though this music were beneath even parody. Some jokes do not survive on wax. At one concert the ensemble concluded a passage on a somber and dignified note; then, with great unction, Joseph and Roscoe harnessed themselves to a pair of huge bass saxophones and paused portentiously. The mood of hushed expectation was rudely shattered as a great flatulent raspberry issued from the twin behemoths, much to the disconcertion of the audience.

The currents of African and Eastern spiritualism figure heavily in the group's world outlook. The African attitude that music is inseparable from life and nature is evident in the mimicry of environmental sounds—bird calls, insects, forest sounds, train whistles—which infuses their music. The African derivation of music from vocal effects is manifest in the many spoken, shouted, or chanted interjections, as well as in the vocalized inflections of the horns. The percussive sense is pervasive through drums, horns and bass alike. The Eastern conception of the mystical unity of all being is reflected in the organic unity with which the group integrates its disparate influences, in the ebb and flow of their seamless programs, and more directly in their thrushlike flutings, clacking woodblocks, and sonorous gongs. The total effect is hypnotic, ethereal—one is lifted out of mundane reality onto a higher plane.

Evidently their name reflects prestige on company rosters, for despite their uncompromisingly anti-commercial stance, the Art Ensemble has been well represented on vinyl, with a score of group sessions and as many individual albums to their credit. Beginning with such independent Chicago outfits as Delmark and Nessa, they have been featured on American and European labels both large and small, including Atlantic, Prestige, Arista, and now ECM (*Nice Guys* promises to be a radical departure from producer Manfred Eicher's impressionistic "Euro-jazz" sound).

Delmark recently issued a tour de force, *Live at Mandel Hall* (University of Chicago), recorded at a triumphant concert appearance in 1972.

Still more recently, the Art Ensemble has released the debut package of their own AECO line, including solo albums by each member and a live ensemble recording at the 1974 Montreux Jazz Festival with featured guest Muhal Richard Abrams. Although they have no plans to abandon other outlets, the group is allowed under the AECO label unprecedented freedom in the presentation, promotion, and packaging of their own product.

It was with some trepidation that I approached the Art Ensemble for an interview. At the AACM's tenth anniversary celebration, Jarman had acknowledged the intimidating effect the group seems to have on onlookers. Ultra-hip trappings aside, the musicians have an adamant aversion to being categorized, defined or pinned down. Like that other "devout musician," Charlie Parker, they are apt to turn questions aside with other questions or witticisms. When I mentioned some comments by AACM violinist Leroy Jenkins in a British publication, they responded that "everyone is entitled to his own opinion," and that such "gossip questions" were of no interest to them. Nor were they eager to discuss the meager houses they have drawn at recent Chicago appearances, dismissing the issue as "political."

Another "political" question concerned the predominantly white audiences for an art form associated from its inception with black nationalist causes. "America is predominantly white," replied Lester, "and in any audience we've ever had, the proportions are about the same as those of the population in that particular location."

"If you play at Harlem University, you get a black audience," added Moye, "and if you play at NYU, most of the people will be white."

The group was more inclined to talk about the AECO label and their current recording activity.

"It's nothing new for us to be putting out our own label," said Moye. "Actually, the label has been in existence for about six years, at least on paper. We've been compiling cataloguing our music ever since we've been together, but it's only now that we've been able to pull together all the necessary factors, the economic factor, the time element, etc. It's nothing really new—other people are doing it, too. It's a reaction to the situation, to the climate out there in the business world. But we're not trying to compete with the larger companies—we're just working toward getting our music out to a wider audience. Part of that is having a working relationship with the larger companies, and at the same time producing our own things without any kind of pressure.

"People are beginning to deal with this music more. All the major labels are checking out the music and making little ploys. Columbia signed Arthur Blythe; people like Braxton, Oliver Lake, Henry Threadgill all have contracts of one form or another with various companies. It's all part of the growing trend for the music to get wider acceptance by the business establishment. For us to be with ECM is just a reflection of that, and it's going to continue in the years to come."

"ECM is trying to expand its market, its whole product line," said Jarman. "Manfred has produced quite a few records and he's just bored. He wants to get into different things."

Added Moye: "One of the advantages of maintaining your position over a period of time is that gradually it becomes apparent that you are the people who are occupying that position. Now we are the people who are in that position, because we have held on in the face of obstacles. It's hard to keep a group together—everybody knows what that's about—so as time goes by people begin to realize and appreciate what our music is really about."

"We aren't concerned with what's selling in the market," Lester went on. "They can sell tomatoes in the market; they can sell meat in the market; they can sell all kinds of things in the market. But we have our product, we have the music that we make, and what they sell is their business. We've learned, through all of these years, that we can survive doing what we're doing, and we don't have to care. We don't have to change our music, put a disco beat behind it to sell. What we do is what we're going to be doing, whether or not disco is in this year, or zipsco, or flipsky. We'll live—pretty well, too—and we'll have a lot of fun. But we don't mean to say that we do what we do and we shut off everything else. We feed off of life—that's why we have to work in a situation where we can live and grow." ●

JONI MITCHELL MAKES MINGUS SING

• •

By Leonard Feather

SEPTEMBER 6, 1979

The career of vocalist and songwriter Joni Mitchell has, within the last year, developed to emphasize her associations with jazz music, which have been evident at least since Tom Scott's L.A. Express joined her on *Court and Spark*. *Mingus*, her acclaimed collaboration with the late bassist/composer, and her *Playboy* Jazz Festival performance with Herbie Hancock, Don Alias, Gene Perla, and Randy Brecker are indicative of her latest direction. In conversation, Joni states her longtime involvement with jazz—the sound of Annie Ross is clearly discernible in some of Joni's phrasing, and sure enough—Lambert, Hendricks & Ross was an early favorite.

Born in McLeod, Alberta, Canada, Joni Mitchell enrolled at an art school in Alberta but soon drifted into folk singing. She took an increasing interest in songwriting, gradually from ukulele to acoustic guitar, and after working at coffee houses in Toronto, moved to Detroit in 1966.

Her career moved into top gear after she signed with Reprise Records in 1967. During the years that followed, her own personal success as a singer was at times partially subjugated to the impact of others' versions of her songs ("Both Sides Now" provided a hit for Joni and a gold record for Judy Collins). Since 1972 Mitchell has been with Asylum Records.

A natural musician rather than a schooled one, over the years her close association with sophisticated musicians has led to an ever more sensitive awareness of the fundamentals of jazz.

Last year, it became known that she was embarking on an album in collaboration with the ailing Mingus, the sidemen including Wayne Shorter, Jaco Pastorius, Peter Erskine and Herbie Hancock.

By late April, the project had been finally mixed and the album was previewed at a private party. The interview below took place a few days later, when Mitchell still had not decided on a final title, which she discusses here.

The art work consists of three paintings by Mitchell of Mingus. It was to this that I made reference in my opening comment.

Feather: *I like what you put outside the album almost as much as what you put in…it's a beautiful cover.*

Mitchell: Thank you. I like the cover myself. I've always done much more commercial covers—by that, I mean to distinguish it from my very personal, private painting. It's the first time I decided to put that out because it seemed to suit the music. The music is very painterly as well, I think, a lot of white canvas, and very brash, strokey interaction, especially on the things that were done with Wayne and Jaco, and Peter and Herbie.

Feather: *Had you ever considered making that your career?*

Mitchell: All my life I've painted. All through school it was my intention to go on to study art. It was a very academic culture that I came out of. Our parents had come up through the Depression, and insisted that we all have a very good education. I wasn't academically oriented and I was growing up just at the time before arts were included as a part of education. Four years later there were fully developed art departments and music departments in the high schools that I attended. But at that time I was kind of a freak.

Feather: *Music education was very limited then, too.*

Mitchell: Well, now, even though they've included that in the program, both the art and the music education are still limited. But they have access to a lot of fantastic equipment, and at least it is included in the curriculum.

At that point in my education, when they discovered on an aptitude test that I had musical abilities, they wanted me to join a glee club, which was pretty corny music; it wasn't too challenging. So I didn't join.

Feather: *Well, you couldn't learn the kind of music you later became involved with.*

Mitchell: No; it was all exposure to people who moved me, that's how it came. It came really from the street, going into a club and hearing somebody hanging out with somebody. Not so much playing with people like jazz musicians, but just observing.

Feather: *What was the first exposure you had?*

Mitchell: When I was in high school—like I say, I wasn't too swift academically, but I did a lot of extracurricular drawing. I did backdrops for school plays, drawings of mathematicians for my math teacher and biology charts of life for my biology teacher. That was a way of appeasing them for being so disinterested in the academic aspect. One year I did a Christmas card for a fellow who was a school leader, and he gave me a present of some Miles Davis albums and about that time my only musical interest, actively, was in rock 'n' roll—Chuck Berry, and this was at the level of dance. I loved to dance. I think my time developed from that love. Going to two, three or as many dances as were available to go to a week.

Anyway, by my doing this card, he introduced me to some jazz. Then I heard, at a party, Lambert, Hendricks & Ross, *The Hottest New Sound in Jazz*, which at that time was out of issue up in that part of the country, in Canada. So I literally saved up and bought it at a bootleg price, and in a way I've always considered that album to be my Beatles, because I learned every song off it. "Cloudburst" I couldn't sing, because of some of the very fast scatting on it; but I still to this day know every song on that album. I don't think there's another album that I know every song on, including my own!

I loved that album, the spirit of it. And like I say, it came at a time when rock 'n' roll was winding down, just before the Beatles came along and revitalized it. And during that ebb, that's when folk music came into its full power.

Feather: *What were the Miles Davis albums?*

Mitchell: *Sketches of Spain*…I must admit that it was much later that Miles really grabbed my attention…and *Nefertiti* and *In a Silent Way* became my all-time favorite records in just any field of music. They were my private music; that was what I loved to put on and listen to—for many years now. Somehow or other I kept that quite separate from my own music. I never thought of making that kind of music. I only thought of it as something sacred and unattainable. So this year was very exciting to play with the players that I did.

Feather: *You did let your hair down one time when you did* Twisted.

Mitchell: Right—and *Centerpiece*, I also did that. One by one I've been unearthing the songs from that Lambert, Hendricks & Ross album.

Feather: *But there's no seeming relationship between the two worlds.…*

Mitchell: Which two worlds are you referring to?

Feather: *The world of music you recorded and the jazz world.*

Mitchell: All the time that I've been a musician, I've always been a bit of an oddball. When I was considered a folk musician, people would always tell me that I was playing the wrong chords, traditionally speaking. When I fell into a circle of rock 'n' roll musicians and began to look for a band, they told me I'd better get jazz musicians to play with me, because my rhythmic sense and my harmonic sense were more expansive. The voicings were broader; the songs were deceptively simple. And when a drummer wouldn't notice where the feel changed, or where the accent on the beat would change, and they would just march through it in the rock 'n' roll tradition, I would be very disappointed and say, "Didn't you notice there was a pressure point here," or "Here we change," and they just would tell me, "Joni, you better start playing with jazz musicians."

Then, when I began to play with studio jazz musicians, whose hearts were in jazz but who could play anything, they began to tell me that I wasn't playing the root of the chord. So all the way along, no matter who I played with, I seemed to be a bit of an oddball. I feel more natural in the company that I'm keeping now, because we talk more metaphorically about music. There's less talk and more play.

Feather: *You've been associating with jazz studio musicians for how long?*

Mitchell: Four years. I made *Court and Spark* five albums ago.

Feather: Did that come about by design or

by accident?

Mitchell: The songs were written and I was still looking for a band intact, rather than having to piece a band together myself. Prior to that album, I had done a few things with Tom Scott, mostly doubling of existing guitar lines. I wanted it to be a repetition or gilding of existing notes within my structure. So through him, I was introduced to that band. I went down to hear them at the Baked Potato in Studio City and that's how all that came about.

They all found it extremely difficult at first, hearing the music just played and sung by one person; it sounded very frail and delicate, and there were some very eggshelly early sessions where they were afraid they would squash it, whereas I had all the confidence in the world that if they played strongly, I would play more strongly.

Feather: *So from that point on you worked with the L.A. Express?*

Mitchell: We worked together for a couple of years, in the studio and on the road.

Feather: *Did that expand your knowledge, being around them so much?*

Mitchell: Not really, not in an academic sense. It gave me the opportunity to play with a band and to discover what that was like. But I still was illiterate in that I not only couldn't read, but I didn't know—and don't to this day—what key I'm playing in, or the names of my chords. I don't know the numbers, letters or the staff. I approach it very paintingly, metaphorically: so I rely on someone that I'm playing with, or the players themselves, to sketch out the chart of the changes. I would prefer that we all just jumped on it and really listened.

Miles always gave very little direction, as I understand. It was just "Play it. If you don't know the chord there, don't play there," and that system served him well. It was a natural editing system. It created a lot of space and a lot of tension, because everybody had to be incredibly alert and trust their ears. And I think that's maybe why I loved that music as much as I did, because it seemed very alert and *very* sensual and very unwritten.

Feather: *And you, in turn, trusted your own ears.*

Mitchell: I do trust my own ears. Even for things that seem too outside. For instance, sometimes I'm told that So-and-So in the band, if I hadn't already noticed, was playing outside the chord. I see that there's a harmonic dissonance created; but I also think that the line that he's created, the arc of it, bears some relationship to something else that's being played, therefore it's valid. So in my ignorance there's definitely a kind of bliss. I don't have to be concerned with some knowledge that irritates other people.

Feather: *"Outside" is only a comparative term, anyway.*

Mitchell: Outside the harmony…but still, as a painter, if the actual contour of the phrase is, like I say, related to an existing contour that someone is playing, then it has validity. Like, if you look at a painting, there seem to be some brush strokes that seem to be veering off, or the color may be clashing, but something in the shape or form of it relates to something that exists; therefore it's beautiful.

I see music very graphically in my head—in my own graph, not in the existing systemized graph—and I, in a way, analyze it or interpret it, or evaluate it in terms of a visual abstraction inside my mind's eye.

Feather: *Where did you first hear about Mingus?*

Mitchell: I remember some years ago, John Guerin played "Pork Pie Hat" for me, which is one of the songs that I've done on this new album; and it was that same version. But it was premature; he played it for me at a time when it kind of went in one ear and out the other. I probably said "hmm-hmm," and it wasn't until I began to learn the piece that I really saw the beauty of it.

Mingus, of course, was a legend. Folk and jazz in the cellars of New York were overlapping, so I'd heard of Mingus by name for some time. As a matter of fact, I'd heard that name as far back as when I was listening to Lambert, Hendricks & Ross in Canada. I was in high school then, but my friends in the university spoke of these legendary people. That was in the early sixties.

Feather: *When did you actually get to meet him?*

Mitchell: I got word through a friend of a friend that Charles had something in mind for me to do, and this came down the grapevine to me. Apparently he had tried through normal channels to get hold of me; but there's a very strong filtering system here and for one reason or another it never reached me. So it came in this circular way, and I called him up to see what it was about, and at that time he had an idea to make a piece of music based on T.S. Eliot's *Quartet* [*Four Quartets*] and he wanted to do it with—this is how he described it—a full orchestra playing one kind of music, and overlaid on that would be bass and guitar playing another kind of music; over that there was to be a reader reading excerpts from *Quartet* in a very formal literary voice; and interspersed with that he wanted me to distill T.S. Eliot down into street language, and sing it mixed in with the reader.

It was an interesting idea; I like textures. I think of music in a textural collage way myself, so it fascinated me. I bought the book that contained the *Quartet* and read it; and I felt it was like turning a symphony into a tune. I could see the essence of what he was saying, but his expansion was like expanding a theme in the classical symphonic sense, and I just felt I couldn't do it. So I called Charles back and told him I couldn't do it; it seemed kind of like a sacrilege.

So some time went by and I got another call from him saying that he'd written six songs for me and he wanted me to sing them and write the words for them. That was April of last year, and I went out to visit him and I liked him immediately; and he was devilishly challenging.

He played me one piece of music—an older piece, I don't know the title of it—because we figured it was going to take eight songs to make an album: the six new ones and two old ones. So we began searching through this material, and he said, "This one has five different melodies," and I said, "And you want me to write five different sets of lyrics at once," and he said "Yes."

He put it on and it was the *fastest* boogieingest thing I'd ever heard, and it was impossible. So this was like a joke on me. He was testing and teasing me; but it was in good fun. I enjoyed the time I spent with him very much.

Feather: *How sick was he then?*

Mitchell: He was in a wheelchair. I never knew him when he was well, and I never heard him play; he was paralyzed then.

Feather: *How much contact did you have, actually working together?*

Mitchell: There were several visits to the house; the better part of an afternoon listening to old music; discussing the themes and his lyrical intent on the new melodies. Then he and Sue [Mingus] went to Mexico, to a faith healer down there, and during the time they were in Mexico I went and spent ten days with them. By that time his speech had severely deteriorated. Every night he would say to me, "I want to talk to you about the music," and every day it would be too difficult. It was hard for him to speak.

So some of what he had to tell me remained a mystery. But Sue gave me a lot of tapes of interviews with him and they were thrilling to me, because so much of what he felt and described was so kindred to my own feelings; he articulated lessons that were laid on him by people like Fats Navarro and others. So he was definitely a teacher of mine.

Feather: *What in your work had attracted him to you and caused him to get in touch with you?*

Mitchell: Somebody played him some of my records. Now, this is a story that came to me—there's a piece of music of mine called "Paprika Plains" which was done in sections. The middle of it is about seven minutes of improvisational playing, which I had somebody else orchestrate for me. And then stuck on to each end of it is a song that I wrote later around it. It was improvised off of a theme; then I abandoned the theme and just left the improvisational part which I cut together. It's a modern technological way of composing.

It was recorded in January, and the piano was tuned many, many times, so by August when I played the verses, which were born much later, the piano had slightly changed. So when it was orchestrated, it's in tune for a while, but then it hits that splice where it goes from the January piano to the August piano. With a fine ear you can notice this. So somebody was playing this piece for Charles, and Charles is a stickler for true pitch and time, and he kept saying, "It's out of tune, it's out of tune." But when the piece was over he said that I had a lot of balls!

So something about it—whatever it was he didn't like, he also saw some strength and certainly an adventuresome spirit, because I'd been pushing the limits of what constitutes a song for years; I keep trying to expand it—with an instrumental in the middle or with no known or prescribed length, but just as long as my own interest will hold out. And I presume that if it will hold my interest that long that it will at least hold the interest of a minority.

So, as near as I can tell, that was part of it, that he felt that I had a sense of adventure. ●

At the Berkeley Jazz Festival, 1979. *From left:* **Don Alias, Jaco Pastorius, Tony Williams, Joni Mitchell, and Herbie Hancock.**

Tom Copi

THE 1980s

INTRODUCTION

By Art Lange

I t was the best of times, it was the worst of times...." Well, maybe the eighties weren't quite so dramatic, in Dickensian terms, but they were an energetic, exhilarating decade. It was a great time to be working at *Down Beat*—and, hopefully, to be reading it, too—because music seemed to be everywhere; every day brought a new name, a new recording, new ideas to be experienced, discussed, evaluated, enjoyed. It was a time when many listeners were learning about the past as well as the present, and especially perceptive musicians were using the lessons of tradition to create a view of the future. It was...but maybe I'm getting ahead of the story. Let's start at the beginning.

In *DB*'s first issue of the new decade, former editor Dan Morgenstern gave a typically fair, detailed overview of the past 10 years and made one seemingly obvious, soon to be controversial, particularly far-reaching point in his summary—he included "the significant discoveries of the sixties" in his discussion of the music's imperishable, influential tradition. Why controversial and far-reaching? Why begin a consideration of the 1980s with the idea of innovations from the sixties? Because this was to fuel the most fiery argument of the eighties. What were these significant discoveries? They were the explorations of musical time and structure by the various members of the AACM, such as Roscoe Mitchell, Anthony Braxton, Muhal Richard Abrams, and, collectively, the Art Ensemble of Chicago; the extremes of timbre and ensemble interaction of free jazz, with proponents as different and dynamic as Albert Ayler, Sun Ra, and the late-period John Coltrane; the radical use of electric instruments and musical sources from around the world (from African drum polyphony and Stockhausen's layers of unrelated involvement to funky James Brown bass lines) in Miles Davis' *Bitches Brew*; and the various individual approaches to expanded form and personal expression proposed by Cecil Taylor, Ornette Coleman, and other avant-gardists

identified with them.

By the 1980s all of these advances had influenced jazz—as well as rock and other uncategorizable styles—enormously, with practitioners all around the world. But a backlash developed, claiming such innovations were not a part of the jazz tradition, that they distorted the true meaning of jazz as created and passed along by Louis Armstrong, Duke Ellington, and, ironically, the Miles Davis of an earlier age. Surprisingly, it wasn't the critics who came up with this neo-conservative definition of jazz (at least not at first, though a few did jump on the bandwagon fairly quickly), but a new generation of musicians, whose spokesman was a highly talented, highly opinionated trumpeter named Wynton Marsalis.

When Wynton was profiled in the January '82 issue of *DB*, none of us had the slightest suspicion that this would turn out to be the Marsalis Decade. We were too busy basking in the recent return of Miles Davis, after his six-year hibernation, and even though Miles' chops didn't seem quite up to par, and he had an over-amplified rock guitarist in the band, and the music had little of the dazzling complexity and audacious ambition of his post-*Bitches Brew* concoctions, well, it was still Miles, and he was just as charismatic and more friendly than ever, waving at audiences and even giving interviews again. But as it turned out, for the rest of the decade Wynton and Miles were to be on opposite sides of the Firing Line, one representing a return to conservative values and a "purer," if narrower, definition of jazz, the other representing the ability of jazz to evolve into many musics.

Wynton's popularity grew quickly, and he brought with him not only a new, sizable audience for mainstream jazz, but an entire generation of young musicians who admired his taste in clothes, his serious demeanor, and his alternately seductive and explosive swing. This new wave of neo-cons were proud of their heritage and looked to the near past for

their role models. Pianists listened once more to Wynton Kelly and Oscar Peterson for guidance; trumpeters memorized Miles' fifties licks; bassists rediscovered Paul Chambers and Wilbur Ware; drummers idolized Philly Joe Jones and Art Blakey. Not that these back-to-the-future types invented the controversy, though; remember, a few years earlier, the critical debate over saxophonist Scott Hamilton, cornetist Warren Vaché, Jr., and others who adopted Swing Era styles as the basis of their creative philosophy? Audiences, however, embraced Wynton to their heart in much greater numbers, and as his record sales increased the controversy raged anew.

Neo-con musicians were only part of the story, however; time and circumstances were right for a large-scale rediscovery of jazz's past. The new technology had a lot to do with it. By mid decade, the proliferation of CDs was so great that listeners were buying up all the discs they could carry out of the stores, replacing their favorite classic, dusty LP sides with shiny new clear-sounding CDs. To keep up with the demand, record companies pumped out session after session of reissued material, some classic and some not-so-classic. Of course, the reissue boom actually started earlier in the decade, even before the spread of digital technology, when conglomerates figured out it was cheaper to reissue an old session than to pay for a new recording and began buying up small independent historic jazz labels and putting out lots of product from the jazz past—RCA/Bluebird, MCA/Decca, and Fantasy's trend-setting Original Jazz Classics series were among the early leaders in marketing the jazz tradition and introducing it to a new audience. By the time CDs became the rage, there was a flood of reissues all but squeezing new releases out of the stores. Soon labels like Verve, Columbia, and Blue Note went into their vaults for previously unissued historic sessions—a practice that continues today.

Though jazz reissues continue to flow into the stores at a steady pace, we've still only uncovered the tip of the iceberg. But there is undoubtedly more of jazz's complete past available on disc than at any other time in its history. The effect of so much tradition at our fingertips meant that audiences had more opportunity to learn about the past than about the present, and that musicians had a greater supply of research documents at their disposal than ever before. For one thing, this not only led to audiences finding they had a built-in appreciation for younger musicians working within what was a now-familiar style, but it also allowed for renewed attention to be brought to deserving artists in that style. The eighties were a giant career boost for artists like Clifford Jordan, Gil Evans, Jimmy Giuffre, J.J. Johnson, Tommy Flanagan, and Dexter Gordon—especially Dex, who became a star to even non-jazz audiences with his appearance in the film 'Round Midnight.

Nevertheless, for all the attention paid to the jazz mainstream, the eighties were a decade of amazing diversity. Though hardcore jazz-rock fusion, so popular in the seventies, had faded, any number of new hybrids had developed. Still-surviving electric bands like Weather Report and Spyro Gyra were influenced by "world musics" arriving from Africa, Brazil, and the Caribbean. New bands popped up every day, and each one seemed to put a new slant on some aspect of our ever-inflating cultural interests. Jazz musicians formed bands like the reggae-influenced Jump Up and the R&B-oriented Defunkt to play in dance clubs. Adventurous types like guitarist James "Blood" Ulmer and drummer Ronald Shannon Jackson formed electric bands that mixed Ornette Coleman's Prime Time harmolodics with more popular grooves (and Pat Metheny hooked up with Ornette himself). Even post-punks had ambitious groups like James White & The Blacks (later The Contortions) and the Lounge Lizards on the fringe of jazz.

With so many jazz musicians looking for creative crossover possibilities, it was natural for an audience who enjoyed, say, John Scofield or Bill Frisell to also be interested in rock bands like Talking Heads or the Police—and when Sting left the latter trio and put together a band with Kenny Kirkland, Omar Hakim, and Branford Marsalis, both jazz and pop audiences were willing to listen to what they had to say. I remember being in a soccer stadium in Perugia, Italy, listening to Sting sing accompanied by jazz charts by the incomparable Gil Evans and his Orchestra, and thinking that this new fusion of sophisticated pop and undiluted jazz had real promise. Other such attempts at bringing jazz credibility to non-jazz artists found Linda Ronstadt singing standards arranged by Nelson Riddle, and British pop star Joe Jackson revisiting the jump band craze of Louis Jordan. None of them lasted long, but somehow they seemed more fun at the time than the blandly commercial chart-topping pop-jazz of George Benson, Earl Klugh, Grover Washington, Jr., or David Sanborn.

Some of the trends that emerged in the eighties were satisfying and long-deserved. The arrival of so many exceptional women musicians, like Jane Ira Bloom, Marilyn Crispell, Emily Remler, Geri Allen, and Michele Rosewoman, and the recognition they and others like them received, was gratifying. By paying more serious attention to European musicians we discovered that, from free improvisers to big band conceptualists, they were no longer to be considered imitators, but innovators. In fact, a host of terrific large ensembles came from Europe—from the Vienna Art Orchestra to the George Gruntz Concert Jazz Band, Pierre Dorge's New Jungle Orchestra, the Willem Breuker Kollektief, and many more—and combined with such American large and mid-sized bands as those of Muhal Richard Abrams, David Murray, Henry Threadgill, Anthony Braxton, and Charlie Haden's revitalized Liberation Music Orchestra, proved that there's still spirit and imagination in the big band idiom. And avant-renegades like John Zorn, who, in addition to his polystylistic constructions and Looney Tune collages, pillaged the past and redesigned hard-bop blowing tunes and Ornette's anthems in his own zany, icon-smashing fashion, provided a vibrant alternative to the studied demeanor of the post-Marsalis minions.

Another trend in the eighties was not so welcome. We lost a painful number of important and heartwarming artists, including some who originated crucial styles of playing, like Eubie Blake, Earl Hines, Count Basie, Thelonious Monk, Roy Eldridge, Jo Jones, and Kenny Clarke; others who synthesized key developments, like Benny Goodman, Mary Lou Williams, Bill Evans, Gil Evans, Sonny Stitt, Art Pepper, Philly Joe Jones, and Zoot Sims; and those unclassifiable practitioners who enriched the character of the music so much, like Warne Marsh, Jimmy Lyons, Chet Baker, Dick Wellstood, Lockjaw Davis, Buddy Rich, Pepper Adams, Thad Jones, and Charlie Rouse. If jazz is the home of the individual, the repository of the unique, and personal expression is to be prized above all else, the music lost a measure of authenticity that will be hard to replace. To make sure that the music itself did not disappear, the concept of repertory bands grew during this period. From big bands like the American Jazz Orchestra (led by John Lewis) and those sponsored by Lincoln Center and the Smithsonian Institution, to small groups like Mingus Dynasty and Sphere, the best of them explored ways of using the material and idioms of the past to express creative options and not just echo their originators.

The eighties are still so close to us in so many ways that it's difficult to determine what "significant discoveries" of the decade will become part of our tradition, the one that will inspire and inform the musicians of the next century. Personally, all I can say is that it really felt like there was a world of music out there, and I felt fortunate to be able to experience so much of it, and in turn help pass it along to the readers of *Down Beat*. ●

ART LANGE served as editor of *Down Beat* magazine during the 1980s. He has authored hundreds of essays, reviews, articles, and interviews on music and poetry, both in the U.S. and in Europe. Lange has written five books of poetry and recently co-edited *Moment's Notice: Jazz in Poetry in Prose* (Coffee House Press, 1993) with Nathaniel Mackey. He is currently serving as president of the Jazz Journalists Association.

MAX ROACH AND CECIL TAYLOR

By Lee Jeske

APRIL 1980

Maxwell Roach is the most melodic of jazz drummers. Cecil Percival Taylor is the most percussive of jazz pianists. Max Roach plays the jazz trap set with the touch of an angel while Cecil Taylor frequently plays the piano with his fists, palms and elbows. Roach has always been open to innovation, moving easily from bebop, which he helped pioneer, to hard bop to free improvisation. Taylor, on the other hand, has been almost xenophobic, playing his own conceptually two-fisted piano, frequently devoid of obvious harmonic and melodic structures, with a small coterie of musicians—including saxophonist Jimmy Lyons, a 20-year member of his unit, and drummer Andrew Cyrille, a 15-year member.

When it was announced that Messrs. Roach and Taylor would be meeting for two performances of duets at Columbia University, the New York jazz community buzzed with anticipation. The names "Max" and "Cecil" were bandied about as if they were two beloved, elderly uncles. Would Cecil Taylor, the infamous iconoclast of jazz piano, actually collaborate with Roach, or would the adaptive Roach be left to fend for himself under a barrage of pianistics?

If there is a currently discernible trend for jazz in the eighties, this embracing of the music's tradition is it. And when two masters of different styles, if not eras, meet for a concert of duets to close the decade, it is cause for rejoicing, especially when the two players are Max Roach and Cecil Taylor, and especially when the two performances are as successful as were the two on Dec. 15, 1979.

The first reaction to the pairing of Cecil Taylor and Max Roach was one of surprise, but after a moment's thought the idea didn't seem that farfetched at all. In the past several years Taylor has opened his deeply personal musical contexts to new ideas, however cautiously. On April 17, 1977, Carnegie Hall was the site of a concert entitled "Mary Lou Williams and Cecil Taylor: A Concert of New Music for

Two Pianos Exploring the History of Jazz with Love." Shortened, the concert was called "Mary Lou Williams and Cecil Taylor: Embrace." A still better title would have been "Mary Lou Williams *versus* Cecil Taylor"; that attraction was like two heavyweight prizefighters ferociously maintaining their individual styles for 15 rounds. After the final bell, the battle was declared a draw (it can be reviewed on Pablo's two disc documentation).

Early in '79, Tony Williams' *Joy of Flying* LP (Columbia) featured an intriguing duet between the drummer and Cecil Taylor; later in the year somebody came up with the idea of pairing Mikhail Baryshnikov with the pianist. This idea seemed to be on slightly better footing—Taylor has always emphasized the influence of dance on his music, and Baby Laurence is one of his few idols. The results of the pairing were mixed, according to those who caught one of the three performances in Chicago, Hollywood or Philadelphia. *Down Beat's* associate editor Howard Mandel, after seeing the debut performance in Chicago, found "no particular communication between them. Stylistically it didn't seem to correspond."

Max Roach, on the other hand, has been embracing the newer innovations of jazz for the past three decades. Rather than resting on his bebop laurels, Roach quickly formed one of the most influential hard bop bands in the fifties, co-billing himself with the young Clifford Brown. He was, perhaps, the most influential drummer of the sixties avant garde—Ed Blackwell, Dennis Charles and Sunny Murray all acknowledge their debt to Max Roach's melodic methods on a trap set. During the seventies Roach was at the helm of a quartet which was playing lengthy pieces with few harmonic restrictions, and in the late seventies Max Roach recorded duet albums with Archie Shepp (in Italy), Anthony Braxton (in France) and Dollar Brand (in Japan).

"But the one with Cecil was the one I looked forward to," says Roach. "That one was on my mind *all* the time. I've known Cecil and we've always said hello and I'd

say, 'Cecil, I hope someday we'll do something together.' And he'd say, 'Well, I'm looking forward to it.'"

When Max mentioned this desire on the airwaves of Columbia University's radio station WKCR-FM, Bill Goldberg, the interviewer, contacted Jim Silverman, Cecil's manager, agent and go-between, and the details were ironed out. Max and Cecil would receive a flat fee for the concert, Cecil would get to bring along the 96-key, $60,000 Bösendorfer concert grand piano which he endorses, and the two musicians would privately finance a tape of the performances which they could auction off to the highest bidder. The date was set, the hall was set and the tickets went on sale. Two of the liveliest masters of jazz, a mere eight years apart in age, would collaborate for two concerts on Oct. 11— and then one of those masters ended up in the hospital with a pinched nerve. On Oct. 9, the concerts were postponed.

"Max and I have been to the hospital to visit Cecil," said Jim Silverman, "and his doctors won't let him do it. But you should see Cecil and Max together. Cecil is so wound up and Max is so cool." But Cecil was wound up in two ways, since he was spending six hours a day in traction.

The concerts were rescheduled for Saturday, Dec. 15 and, again, the speculation began.

A rehearsal and sound check were scheduled for noon the day of the performances—there were to be two shows at 8 and 11 p.m. Bill Goldberg and WKCR were sponsoring the event so the venue was Columbia University's McMillin Theatre, a 1,200-seat shabby box on 116th St. and Broadway. Tickets were selling slowly, but steadily.

When I arrived early in the afternoon, Cecil Taylor and Jim Silverman were supervising the unwrapping and placement of the nine-foot Bösendorfer. The piano, which has an extra eight notes in the bass, is endorsed by only two artists in the jazz realm—Cecil Taylor and Oscar Peterson (I hope Bösendorfer won't one day come up with the perverse idea of pairing their endorsers). Watching five workmen juggle the piano is a chilling experience. Finally, after much huffing, sweating and swearing the instrument was on the stage.

Cecil was jittery when we spoke. His feet were shifting and he was rubbing his hands together. "I couldn't find this place," he barked to Goldberg. "Why the hell aren't there signs out there?" Cecil sashayed around the piano, singing to himself as Silverman buzzed about like a gnat, "Where's Max? Where are the soundmen?"

As he and Goldberg went sniffing, I sat myself in the center of the auditorium and Cecil sat himself at the piano. Dressed in brown pants tucked into knee-high boots, a bulky, blue parka, dark glasses and topped off with a green hat pulled over his eyes. Cecil began to spin chords and phrases from the piano. Sitting in the middle of the empty house and listening to Cecil Taylor slowly work himself into a froth, I felt like William Powell playing Flo Ziegfeld. His playing was bluesy and melodic and it was easy to hear the Horace Silver influence that Cecil claims. He ran up and down scales, slowly becoming as one with the instrument. Occasionally, Silverman would come in and say something to Taylor, who would nod or grunt without looking up from the keyboard. Soon he was playing hand-over-hand, his arms and fingers becoming a blur as they pursued each other over the keys. For one solid hour, Cecil played at a fever pitch. Then Max Roach showed up.

"Bösendorfer," cried Max from across the room. "Hey Boss," yelled the drummer jumping on the stage. "Hey, I'm sorry I'm late, CT." Taylor got up, greeted Max, and sat back down at the piano, where he would remain for the rest of the afternoon—furiously working over the entire length of the keyboard, including that voluminous, roaring bass octave.

In the meantime Roach, dressed in white sweater and dark pants and looking as if he just walked off the golf course, began setting up his drums. "I want to look right at Cecil." The drums were set up so that Max's left side faced the audience and his head was pointed right at Taylor. Soon Max was bombarding away. Cecil was thrashing the piano and Max was pummeling the drums. Cecil was in a fervor, never once looking up at Max, who

was exploding all over his kit. At one point Max asked, "Can Cecil be heard when I play really hard?" Told that he couldn't, Max shrugged and said, "I'm not going to play that hard, anyway."

There was no question that there were going to be fireworks that night, but Cecil Taylor gave no indication of paying any attention to his partner. When Cecil finally stopped playing to pose for some photos, he told Max, "Let's try for a wave of sound."

After some juggling of the piano and drums, Cecil wanted the piano toward the back of the stage. "But CT," Max patiently explained, "they won't be able to see you on the sides of the room." "Okay, but just move it a little," the pianist said, shuffling his feet like a cross between Muhammad Ali and John Travolta. "Enough," he growled after about six inches. "But CT," said Max. "Okay,

Enid Farber **Cecil Taylor and Max Roach**

just a little," snapped Cecil.

The difference in the two men was quite apparent. During the photo session, Max stood firmly at the piano with a Buster Keaton deadpan on his face. Cecil jumped and squirmed. It was going to be an interesting concert.

At one point during the rehearsal, Max Roach sat down at the piano and began playing a gentle, sing-song melody. All of a sudden, Max became Cecil Taylor—traveling up the keyboard, one hand over the other.

"He used to play drums," said Max, "and my first instrument was piano, gospel

piano in a church. Crazy!"

Not really crazy. Cecil Taylor is a kind of percussionist. In her book *As Serious as Your Life*, British jazz critic Valerie Wilmer suggests that every time Cecil Taylor sits down at the piano he is playing "88 tuned drums." Wilmer continues, "Cecil Taylor is different. He has often performed in a solo context but he *needs* drums, he *likes* drums. His collaboration with the percussionist is and Afro-American collaboration, an interweaving of polyrhythms." Cecil himself told Wilmer, "We in black music think of the piano as a percussive instrument: we beat the keyboard, we get inside the instrument."

Max Roach, on the other hand, is the most melodic of drummers. In *The Sound of Surprise*, a collection of his *New Yorker* pieces, Whitney Balliett wrote, "Though perfectly executed, his solos are made up of so many contradicting rhythms and disconnected, rapidly rising and falling pyramids of sound that the beat, which they are supposed to be embroidering, disappears. Indeed, it is not unusual to find oneself hypnotized by the lightning concatenation of sounds in a Roach solo, and then, astonishingly, to discover that it has been managed wholly without imparting rhythm." Max even has tunable Italian tom-toms made by Hi Percussion. "You just switch with the pedal and you try to create designs and patterns," he says.

McMillin Theatre was about three-quarters full for the first show. The crowd was filled with jazz critics and musicians and everybody was purring—there was an extremely high level of intensity in the audience, which spread through the room like a visible glow. Poet Bill Gunn made the introduction and Max Roach was out first.

Max seated himself at his kit, which was surrounded by various percussion instruments and a huge gong, and immediately began the most basic of rhythms—a heartbeat with the *lub* on the bass and the *dub* on the hi-hat. *One-two, one-two* in a steady dirge tempo, which produced an eerie tension throughout the five-minute solo. Max built his solo from the snare, sending off little flutters to start and then, working towards the cymbals and floor tom, sending a barrage of rhythms into the air, always pausing to reassert the boom-tick of the heartbeat. Soon Max was rolling over his set, producing little polyrhythms that were frequently only suggested, as was the consistent heartbeat. The piece developed into a flood of rimshots and ended with a bass drum bomb.

Max then departed, stage left, and Cecil entered, stage right. He seated himself quickly and began his solo with a quiet peck at the treble, accompanied by a thundering rumble in the bass. Cecil started weaving a melodic, Debussyish piece: blissful and quiet with a repeated staccato theme in the bass and a touching lyrical strain in the middle range. Cecil ended with a ringing bass note.

Before the concert Max told me that they would be playing a piece that was "spontaneous on some kind of melodic/harmonic form."

It began with Max using mallets on his Chinese gong. Cecil was still melodic, but was starting to slowly work himself into a frenzied state. Soon Cecil began to pull away from Max, who had begun concentrating on the rims and head of his snare. Max began catching up after a couple of minutes; Cecil was all over the piano's upper octaves—stabbing, stabbing, stabbing. Max was revving up, but still kept on the snare, with bass and hi-hat accents. Cecil was palming the piano like mad, sounding like windchimes in a hurricane. Max was keeping the tension and flying—his phrases on cymbals and toms were short and hot while Cecil wreaked hell on the Bösendorfer's upper octave.

Max tried a slight shift in tempo, letting out the string and trying to bring the piece down, but Cecil wasn't ready yet—he relentlessly pounded, with an occasional pause for a quick *one-two-three* in bass octaves. Max was quickly back to rolling and crashing on the full set. Max had, earlier, said that he wanted to watch Cecil's face to "pick up some of those good vibes," and Max was intent on Cecil's face—Cecil, however, had yet to look up once, as if he was propelled by the sheer force of the

collective energy which threatened a meltdown on stage.

Suddenly, 20 minutes into the piece, Cecil stared right as Max and began to subside into a more melodic and searching sound. Max began working only on the hi-hat, clearly and unashamedly showing his debt to Jo Jones. Cecil began fluttering in the sonorous bass as Max altered the texture by sticking to the hi-hat. Cecil again began playing hand-over-hand, once or twice pulling himself off the bench, but this time it seemed as if he was listening to and following the drummer. In unison, the two men started to build—faster and faster. Max noodled on his tunable floor toms for a minute and then—crash—Max was playing bebop on his ride cymbal. Cecil was flying again and the sound that was created was so intense and so powerful that at times it seemed the audience would explode from tension and excitement.

About half an hour into the work Cecil began to bring it down, as Max moved over to his percussion table, perhaps for a rest from the solid powerhouse display. Max picked up a piece of equipment and began to *whoop-whoop*. Cecil was playing a jagged, rhythmic section in response. Max began knocking and clapping and shaking with various devices on the table and Cecil responded with a rattling in the treble. Max ended his off-kit foray on the gong.

Cecil, ears and eyes open, was hunting and pecking now, using lots of triplets in the treble and working out a definite, single-note melody in the bass. Max returned to the traps on brushes—mixing and swirling right with Cecil. The tension, which had been sustained for a remarkable 45 minutes, began to dissipate. Max was playing a heavy *thud-thud* rhythm and, for a moment, the players began to drift.

Then, quietly, the two players become one. Taylor became playful and teased Max with single-note fragments. Together they began to dip and flow. Cecil, staring into Max's eyes, laid out for a moment and then began mimicking Max's patterns, on the piano. The two pawed at each other gently and respectfully.

Max let Cecil go it alone and the pianist was ethereal and gentle—quietly, easily winding down. "*Bwa-dee-duh,*" played Cecil and then quiet.

Max picked it up and began playing

"*one-two*-and and-*two*-and, *one-two*-and and-*two*-and," adding polyrhythmic patterns which began to boil and pop. There were gasps and "Whews" from the assemblage as Roach played beautiful patterns that sounded like a dozen drum geniuses together.

Cecil began to spray gentle dissonance in between Max's patterns and soon the two were playing percussive Parcheesi. Then it was back to the early segments, but this time the two men were truly playing *together*. They started to build momentum—Cecil twirling over the keyboard like an entranced dervish and Max just pushing and kicking on the traps. After one hour and a quarter, the energy of the two players was stunning—Cecil was palming the piano in opposite directions from the middle octave, his right and left hands like two repellent magnets zooming outward. And then, watching each other carefully, the musicians wound down the piece and ended with "ting-ting-*ting*-ting"—Max on the ride cymbal and Cecil in the treble. The audience leapt to its feet and roared.

It was a truly momentous meeting, and one which kept the jazz world buzzing for days. Everybody was impressed and everybody agreed that *something happened.*

Not long afterward I spoke with Max Roach. "What I think Cecil and I did mainly—we both were familiar with each other's work, and as Stanley Cowell so aptly put it, we co-existed. We didn't rehearse as such—what we did was we sat down and dealt with each other as two human beings and when we found out that we could live with our own attitudes and thoughts about life and things in music and liberty and all the other things that people talk about, we knew that we could deal with each other on stage. And it was pure improvisation, we just dealt from that point of view and we knew from experience that something would happen if we went our own ways but were sensitive to each other at the same time. And I think we co-existed."

As to the technical aspect of the performance, Max said that a lot of people had bad locations acoustically—many on the sides of the orchestra couldn't hear either the drums or piano. "Where I sat on the stage the sound was outasight. Then when I softened down, I couldn't hear myself. Isn't that amazing? That piano is completely overwhelming. And especially the way Cecil plays. He doesn't play light piano.

"We've had offers to travel—people, when they heard about the concert, wanted to know if we would bring it to Paris or to Milano. People in Italy as well as France and Germany were asking if we wanted to come overseas with it. We've already had offers from Japan, Italy and Switzerland for the tapes, without people even hearing them.

"Cecil and I both agree that what we want more than anything else is the kind of visibility—we want people to hear the music, so it's not just a matter of people giving us a lot of money or anything like that. We'd like the people to hear it and just see how they feel about this type of music. This combination takes us into another area—certainly it does that to me. I was with Dizzy last week and he said, 'Now tell me about these duets.'"

Cecil Taylor wouldn't agree to an interview, but sources close to him say that he was just as pleased as Max at the outcome.

Perhaps the tape will be acquired by a major label, and be given the push it deserves. Columbia University has a videotape of the second concert which they have promised to turn over to the two artists.

Many of the young players in jazz uniquely blend the old and new. Players such as Anthony Davis, James Newton, Michael Gregory Jackson and Ricky Ford amalgamate all the styles of jazz—the influences of the beboppers blend into the influences of the free improvisers which blend into the influences of New Orleans style interplay. The results promise to be an exciting mixture as these and other players mature over the next several years. The monumental meeting of two of the stylistic fathers to dozens of these young musicians can only be a good sign for the state of the art of jazz at the dawn of the new decade.

A very good sign. ●

TOSHIKO AKIYOSHI

By Peter Rothbart
AUGUST 1980

Toshiko Akiyoshi is an international phenomenon: a Japanese woman writing in an American art form, for an American band that sells best in Japan. While other name jazz bands tour the United States continuously, Akiyoshi takes her band on tour only occasionally, balancing her schedule between tours and the free time she uses to create new works. She and the band she co-leads with her husband Lew Tabackin are based in Los Angeles, yet her more profitable markets are in the Midwest and eastern United States.

Akiyoshi is consistently at or near the top of critics and listeners polls in the United States; she copped top spot in *Down Beat*'s last Readers Poll (Dec. '79) with her band and as arranger, and placed second to the great Charles Mingus in the composer category. In last year's *DB* Critics Poll, she likewise took two firsts and a second. This year, the Akiyoshi-Tabackin band is again tops with the world's critics. In Japan, their last record, *Farewell*, dedicated to Charles Mingus, received 100 out of a possible 100 points from *Swing Journal*, that country's top jazz magazine.

That Akiyoshi and her band have been able to survive for the past eight years is testimony to the tenacity which is readily perceived when one meets the petite pianist, and to her unwavering demand for excellence. Because her music is so difficult, demands extra rehearsal time, and requires so much doubling in the saxophone section, her musicians are paid high salaries. It's so expensive to take her

band on tour that the best profits on the last four out of five tours were made by airline companies. Nevertheless, the band survives, rehearsing weekly in Los Angeles and doing sound checks when on the road, no matter the logistical difficulties involved.

The band has been touring more frequently in the past few years. It plays in Japan every 18 months. It visited Europe for two days for the first time in 1978 and returned for two weeks in 1979 to play the prestigious Berlin Jazz Festival. The band's increasingly busy schedule placed heavy demands on some musicians with other, more local commitments. Long gone are Dick Spencer, Bobby Shew, Gary Foster and Peter Donald. Although the band has replaced six of its members within the past year, Akiyoshi says, "The band in many ways sounds better than ever."

Akiyoshi has no plans to have the band tour for 40 weeks, explaining, "The main reason we formed the band was to play my music, and my main responsibility is to create music. Lew and I decided we'd like to have a balance between the number of weeks we go out, and leave the rest as free time for myself, to keep creating and do some piano playing, which I've neglected in the past several years. This would also give Lew time to do his pianoless trio."

Akiyoshi's attention to quality and detail has enabled her to create ten high-quality big band albums, and she's proud of them all. To ensure continued control of record quality without the necessity of making artistic concessions, Akiyoshi and Tabackin have just started a record company, Ascent. *Farewell*, previously released on Japanese RCA, and a Tabackin trio record called *Black and Tan Fantasy* will be Ascent's first discs. The band's relationship with U.S. RCA has been ended, to their mutual satisfaction.

"Lew and I are careful about the programming," says Toshiko. "We want to make sure that future albums don't fall from our past levels. The music requires a certain level of musicianship. That's why we don't use many people right out of college. Some younger musicians say, "Don't tell me what to do.' But it has nothing to do with ego—we all have to let the music come out." The concentration required to perform Akiyoshi's music makes the band look almost like a symphony orchestra: there is little unnecessary movement by the musicians.

Akiyoshi's music differs significantly from that of other jazz band composers. Her works often change meter several times. As she explains, "Pulse doesn't mean the same thing as tempo. The pulse should remain the same. This is what should be transmitted to the entire band." Akiyoshi's writing is unpredictable in several aspects. Her accents are often unusually placed, a fact some analysts attribute to her Japanese background. Her forms are often quite extended. Her voicings retain a vertical character that distinguishes them from say, Thad Jones', and she explains that in two situations, given the same lead line and underlying chord structure, she is likely to voice the two examples differently. "It all depends on where the line is coming from and where it's going. I like to write this way. To me, this is music."

While many contemporary writers use a more horizontal or linear writing approach to voicing harmonies (voicing the accented or stressed notes vertically, then simply writing melody notes to link the pitches together), Akiyoshi prefers to voice each note vertically, no matter how fast it goes by. This way, "if it is played slowly, there will still be a beautiful line."

Drawing from a wide range of sources for inspiration, Akiyoshi writes "what I allow myself to hear. I try to put it into actual sound, as accurately as possible. When I write, I start from scratch. I forget the last tune, so each becomes different. All music has a point of view. Circumstances may be different but emotions are experienced by all. My music comes from me, so I hope people can identify with it. We are all the same as the person next door. Human nature remains unchanged, and music should deal with this unchanging human nature. When I listen, it's personal, but the music has a lasting capacity, which I can identify with as I hope others in the future can, too. Hearing is abstract. I don't like to follow systems when I write."

Following this philosophy, some of Akiyoshi's compositions are conceptualized in their entirety, while some develop as she composes. Like many fusion composers. Akiyoshi's compositions are her arrangements; she makes no distinction between the two processes. Some of Akiyoshi's music is inspired by real life. After "Mr. Teng" reflects her happiness with the United States' diplomatic recognition of mainland China. "Kogun" (which means "one who fights alone") is dedicated to the Japanese soldier found in a Philippine jungle over 30 years after World War II.

"Kogun" illustrates a commitment beyond music. "I am a member of society first and a musician second." "Kogun" also represents an important blend of Japanese music with Western instruments. "My father was a student of Noh theater. He was fascinated by it. I'm trying to draw from my heritage and enrich the jazz tradition without changing it. I'm putting into jazz, not just taking out."

Traditional Japanese music is more likely to accompany than tell a story, and relies little on melody, Akiyoshi explains. "The beat if different. It's more circular, arched, rather than an up or downbeat." As she conducts her band, this arched beat is frequently reflected in her movements.

Yet "Kogun" still swings, which Akiyoshi considers vital to jazz. "Jazz is a certain rhythm. It's how you play, not what you play. It's a street music, with a certain earthiness. Swing is a balance between earthiness and being sophisticated."

"Kogun's" successful blend of two seemingly disparate styles is due partly to husband Tabackin's flute ability. His solo and cadenza on "Kogun" are packed with minute sounds, from his subtly sophisticated double-tonguing to his earthy shrieks and quarter-tone smears. "Lew has a French model flute (open-holed) that enables him to do this. He listened to a lot of shakuhachi music. His abilities are so incredible, he can sense the music."

As Akiyoshi points out, "Meeting a good partner is important. After all, Ellington had Strayhorn." While Akiyoshi is expanding structural and harmonic limits with her arrangements. Tabackin is creating a new flute tradition. "Lew respects the saxophone tradition, and sees himself as an extension of that tradition. Yet the flute until recently was a classical instrument without a jazz tradition. Amplification now makes jazz flute possible, so Lew is developing a tradition."

Akiyoshi attributes her success in Japan to several factors. "Competition wasn't as tough as in the United States, so I could rise to the top quicker. The market is so much tighter in this country, and there's so much competition. Most foreign players don't succeed in the U.S. because of the competition. and of course, there was less female competition in Japan. Whenever women competed in a man's world in the United States, they didn't succeed. Those that did became separated from the mainstream and wound up as piano players in the more sophisticated, high-class clubs, such as the East Side Club or the Hickory House in New York. A few, such as Marian McPartland, did succeed."

According to Akiyoshi, part of her success in Japan is due to the practices of recording company executives in that country. Jazz recordings in Japan are marketed much the same way as classical recordings are in the United States. Rather than going for the megabuck superstars who may die musically in a short time, as in the American pop market, Japanese record companies can be satisfied with a smaller return over a longer time. "There's no way to lose money on this band," Akiyoshi explains. "Our monetary outlay in terms of production is moderate, but American companies are not interested in a moderate profit. Jazz musicians are victims of the industry in the U.S. There's no proper exposure or advertising. The Japanese companies are operating more logically, which is better for both of us."

Kendor is publishing many of Akiyoshi's charts and, according to music stores, they are selling well despite the problems inherent in performing Akiyoshi's music on the high school and college level. The woodwind doublings are extensive. For example, Bob Shepherd, whose principal instrument is an alto sax, also plays flute, piccolo, clarinet, alto clarinet and soprano sax. Every player in the sax section plays at least four instruments. With Akiyoshi on piano, the band consists of Lew Tabackin, Dan Higgins, Shepherd, John Gross and Bill Byrne, saxes and other reeds; Buddy Childers, Steve Huffsteder, Larry Ford and Mike Price, trumpets; Hart Smith, Jim Sawyer, Bruce Fowler, Phil Teele, trombones; Steve Houghton, drums; and Bob Bowman, bass. The technical ability this band brings to Toshiko's music is quite rare on any level.

"A jazz band is actually like a small group with a lot of colors," says Akiyoshi, who makes a distinction between big bands and jazz bands. "Big bands used to be the dance bands of the 1930s and forties. Some, like Duke and Basie, went beyond that. Some small groups are very free in terms of tempo; Mingus changed tempos all the time. For another example, Thad Jones is fascinated by soloists; he loves to put the soloist on the spot, like by having the rhythm section lay out unexpectedly. He'd have the rhythm section come in differently every time."

Another distinction Akiyoshi makes is that jazz bands give the soloist more time than the big bands to stretch out. "A quality solo is as important as a quality ensemble section. All great jazz bands have great soloists. College bands are remarkably good in their ensemble playing, but the solos and rhythm sections are the weak points."

Against all odds, Akiyoshi's band and music have survived for eight years and continue to reach more people. When she and Tabackin formed the band in 1973, there was a tremendous amount of skepticism about a Japanese woman writing for a jazz band in Los Angeles. In her own words, "If I had heard this, I'd be skeptical, too. But if the music has conviction, the whole problem will be resolved." ●

JAMES BROWN: ANYTHING LEFT IN PAPA'S BAG?

By Steve Bloom

SEPTEMBER 1980

I'm riding in an elevator at New York's elegant Sherry Netherland Hotel with James Brown, the world-renowned Godfather of Soul. As we descend some 20 floors to the lobby, Brown kibitzes with the operator.

"May I ask you a question, sir?" he begins. "Am I the greatest soul singer to ever stay in this hotel?"

The operator, sensing a perfect opportunity, smiles and drapes his arms around the Godfather's muscular shoulders.

"Pendergrass stayed here, sir," he said, staring directly into Brown's unblinking eyes. "But he couldn't even shine your shoes."

Tyrone Hall

Everyone in the elevator bursts with laughter. Brown, totally ingratiated, shakes the operator's hand and thanks him "very much." As if on cue, the car suddenly lands. Two well-built members of Brown's predominantly male entourage fan out to the left and right, each holding a door. Brown takes the lead and bounces on through. The contingent follows the Godfather of Soul into the lobby.

There is little doubt that James Brown, whose career now spans four decades, is *the* legend of modern black popular music.

There is little doubt, too, that James Brown especially enjoys letting people know all about it. In conversation, he repeatedly compares himself to Elvis Presley, but that's not all. One of his favorite braggadocios goes something like this: "My contention is that there were three B's and now there's four: Beethoven, Bach, Brahms, and now, Brown."

That Brown insists on informing others of his talents and of the inestimable gifts which he has bestowed upon mankind is often laughable; his words, however, are also pointed and usually contain bits of the truth. Certainly if egos were balloons his would be a blimp. Still, James Brown hasn't shined anybody else's shoes since he was a young turk growing up in Georgia. That is, not until the last few years.

There was a time when James Brown records were fixtures on every turntable in every black home across America. A tune called "Please, Please, Please," recorded by the Cincinnati-based King Records, started the ball rolling in 1956. Soul classics like "I Got You (I Feel Good)" (1965), "Papa's Got A Brand New Bag" (1965), and "Cold Sweat" (1966) followed, bringing James Brown to the attention of millions of listeners. He shouted and hollered; he wore sequins and wigs and makeup. Like his peers Little Richard and Chuck Berry, his appearance was that of a rock 'n' roll star.

But there was one difference. Brown's music—and amalgam of gospel testifying, backwoods funk, and ever jazzy innovation that had never been heard before— was a modern twist on rhythm 'n' blues. Though it really was just a stone's throw from early rock, Brown was relegated to second-class status, confined to the chitlin' scene. James Brown didn't go for that at all—instead of touring low pay, funky nightclubs, he wanted a piece of the concert action that rock 'n' rollers took for granted. Since no one was about to steer him in that direction, he grabbed the controls himself.

According to his manager Al Garner, Brown decided to forsake a club engagement he had scheduled for Houston back around 1965. Brown asked Garner, director of a local black radio station, for help in promoting his own Civic Center show. An artist promoting himself was—and still is—relatively unheard of, but Brown felt it was time to test whether or not a black performer could fill a concert arena. "We went to work one month ahead to time," Garner recalls in his native North Carolina accent, "and sure let everyone know about it. Why, we not only sold out the concert (14,500), but even broadcasted it live over my station." This story is only one of many that detail Brown's strong-mindedness when it comes to taking care of business."

Says Polydor vice president Dick Kline, whose career includes a sales stint at King in the late fifties, "Working with James has always been a trip in itself. He's always had his own methods, his own thoughts and his own direction. He's always done everything on his own because he's rarely trusted anyone in the business. I will say one thing about him, though—James Brown is the greatest promoter of James Brown that there ever was."

As of 1980, all Brown's commotion and promotion has done little to revive his sagging sales, James Brown, much to his own disbelief, could no longer sell out Yankee Stadium on any given summer night as he did in the late sixties much less Carnegie Hall, or even the Bottom Line. Disco was something he was not prepared for.

While the Bee Gees and the Doobie Brothers jogged to the bank, the Godfather (who claims "Sex Machine" was the original disco song) continued laying down those infectiously funky tracks on albums titled *Jam/1980's* and *Take a Look at Those Cakes* (both released in 1978).

That these releases were very much in the original funk tradition of James Brown, but still did not produce healthy sales, proved that the market was ever further bottoming out for the waning Godfather of Soul.

By '79, changes had to be made. In some very confidential meetings with Polydor (he signed with them in 1971), Brown was urged—for the first time in his career—to accept the common practice of employing an outside producer. Polydor felt that his technique had been slipping. (Conversely, Brown would say the same about Polydor's promotional work, or lack thereof.) A

studio ace might be able to transform Brown's sound without radically altering it. In what amounted to a major compromise, the Godfather agreed to stand a disco trial with Miami-based producer Brad Shapiro (Wilson Pickett, Millie Jackson) presiding. It was TK Records president Henry Stone, one of Brown's confidantes in the business early on, who negotiated this agreement.

The result was *The Original Disco Man*, both an album and a promotional gimmick. On the surface, Brown was pleased with it especially when the single, "It's Too Funky In Here," momentarily bulleted on the black sales charts. At the time, Brown said of Shapiro, "Brad has the sound we need today—technique. I can do ten times more arrangements than Brad can, and he knows that. But I don't have the sound. So Brad's my right arm. Brad can produce James Brown better that James Brown can produce himself. You cannot take that away from Brad."

But it didn't take long for their romance to ebb. When it came down to recording a second disco-styled project with Shapiro, Brown began to holler. "The problem with Polydor is that they're followers, not leaders," he told me, blasting the label for which he has recorded 19 albums in less than a decade. "They wait for somebody else to do something and by the time they jump in it's all over with. That's what they did with disco. Right now they're not doing anything.

"What the Germans should do," he continued, referring to Polydor's German-owned parent firm, Polygram, "Is give me a label on the side like Gamble and Huff [Philadelphia International, a division of Columbia Records], and then let me go and do what I have to do.

"They delayed me because they wanted to sell disco. Now it's over with. They've sold as many of my old licks as they could and now they want new ones," the Godfather grumbled. "I'm not going to give them no complete albums of funk, they ain't gonna get that no mo'."

"Never again?" I cried.

"No, never."

"Do you mean that we'll never hear the real James Brown again on record?"

"I didn't say that," Brown snapped back. "I said I'll never give you a full album of that 'cause they copy too much. I can only bring out one single at a time. I know what I want to cut, but I'm not going to cut it right now. I made that mistake with

'Groove Machine.' [A song Brown produced and recorded, but which was never released. Another song by the same name then came out, sung by Bohannon. They were both recorded in the same studio, so Brown believes he was robbed.] I should've held it back.

"If I don't record it," he said, chuckling to himself, "then you won't hear it. They may come up with a synthetic, but it won't be James Brown original funk."

Earlier this year, Brown begrudgingly recorded again with Shapiro. What could he really say to Polydor after *The Original Disco Man* posted his most impressive sales stats (175,000) in nearly a decade? But with the follow-up album, *People*, mastered and ready for pressing, Brown took still more potshots.

"It's not funk, but it's good. It's different. It's a new direction, but it's still not James Brown original funk," he pointed out. "It's a very establishment all-funk sound."

Had he not just returned from a tour of Japan, where he recorded his first live concert since "Sex Machine," the Godfather might have had a few more kind words about *People*. But James Brown, has never been noted for his patience. In a telegram to Dick Kline, Brown asked that the live package (two records, though Polydor pleaded for only one) be released in tandem with *People*.

"The live album is unbelievable," he repeated several times. "If Dick Kline and them were smart, they'd release it right now. They'd put 'Regrets' [the single on *People*] and 'Let the Funk Flow' [also on *People*] on it and release it. They wouldn't take time messin' with that other stuff. They're wastin' time with that.

"See, they were committed to the *People* album first, but they're stupid for doing that. They are very stupid for doing that. The people in Europe are smarter than the people in America when it comes to records, 'cause people in Europe release what they hear. Americans release what they are told." Our conversation closed with Brown once again laughing to himself.

Despite Brown's urgings Kline decided to stick with his plan, one which he hopes will raise Brown from the murky mess he is in.

"Since James appeals to a core audience," Kline explained, "the trick is to expand that core. Having a Top 15 hit on the R&B charts with 'Too Funky' has already begun to revitalize his career. I am hoping *People* will further expand that core. Then, with that interest built up, we will go with the live record [planned for release this summer]. James has to trust me now. I'm doing what I think is best for James and at the same time trying to sell records."

Did *The Original Disco Man* and *People* arrive too late, as Brown said, on the disco scene?

"Maybe it was too late, maybe it was too early—who's to know?" Kline replied. "The music business is extremely volatile today. Everything is timing. And, of course, it has to be in the grooves."

James Brown's life has not always, so to speak, been "in the grooves." Born more than 50 years ago in Augusta, Georgia (where he still resides), the son of a gas-station attendant, young James grew up fast. Before the age of ten, he washed cars, picked cotton and shined shoes. Whatever change he could scrape up was added to the family stash that covered the $7 rent for their broken down shack of a home.

"My family was so poor you wouldn't believe it," he remembers. "In the afternoons during the winter I'd walk home by the railroad tracks and pick up pieces of coal left behind by the trains. I'd take that home and we'd use it to keep warm."

Entertainment was a natural path for the enterprising young James to follow. Brown recalls:

"I always loved to dance, especially as a little boy. When I was eight years old I used to go dance for the National Guard soldiers who camped outside of town. They threw nickels and dimes and sometimes even quarters at me."

In 1956, James Brown was "discovered" by Sid Nathan, the owner and founder of King Records. With each hit a new nickname seemed to arrive: first "Soul Brother Number One," then "The Godfather of Soul," and finally, "The Minster of the New New Super Heavy Funk." "Mr. *Please, Please, Please* himself" (as he is most affectionately called by his personal emcee, Mr. Danny Ray) has been plain funkin' down ever since.

Where does that unmistakable James Brown sound come from? Asking Brown is like imploring a magician to explain his tricks. He does acknowledge childhood favorites like Roy Brown, Buddy Johnson and Louis Jordan, but that's usually as far as he's willing to consult his memory.

Otherwise, the Godfather likes to give much of the credit to God.

"He gave me a knowledge and built the antennas in so I can recognize what I should be saying. From a conversation, I can record. Just write something down and I can sing it in tempo. Other people can't do that. I can sit down at a piano and show you so many things it's frightening.

"All that stuff I'm playing, I taught it to them—I did it years ago. That's why when the young acts go into the studio today they say, 'Gimme that James Brown sound.'

"The James Brown sound I didn't learn from nobody. It's from me."

Brown rates his work with the greatest American musical innovations of the twentieth century. He maintains that his music has been so far ahead of its time that he had no choice but to restrict the complexity of the compositions and arrangements. Otherwise, James says, we never could have understood it.

"A lot of times I used to do arrangements and they'd be too good," he thinks back, "so I would take the one that was less precise 'cause I knew the one I was shooting for would've been too sharp. Like when I did 'I Got the Feelin',' I took the very first cut, which was the weakest. And I remember the first time I cut 'I Feel Good'—it was like jazz.

"I went back and made it slower and the sound muddier. I did that on purpose. People were not ready for that sharp sound.

"But every time I came out the box it was gold or platinum 'cause I always cut James Brown," the Godfather continues, relishing each and every thought. "I can cut at four o'clock in the morning. When I get an idea I call everybody to wake up and the engineer rushed right over. I wrote 'Sex Machine' on the back of a placard when we were playing a gig in Nashville. Afterwards, we went right on over to the studio and cut 'Sex Machine' and 'Super Bad.'

"King needed me and depended on me, so they let me do it. It just made them more money after money."

According to Brown's management, he has sold over 50 million records, 44 of which they claim are gold singles. But the Recording Industry Association of America, which certifies gold records, says that Brown has had only *two* gold singles ("Get On The Good Foot, Part 1" in 1972, and "The Payback," in 1974) and

one gold album, *The Payback*. As with many aspects of James Brown's career, the truth is elusive. But the sales discrepancy may be explained by the practice, particularly common among R&B record labels, of under-reporting sales. Whatever the facts, Brown's greatest hits never achieved their expected RIAA certification levels. Brown is dissatisfied with his current, larger label for other reasons.

"See, conglomerates can't afford to take many chances," James explains. "They got to move according to the GNP, Gross National Product, that's what they go by. It's very bad. Try to move in the safety zone, but when you move in the safety zone your profits are very small. That's why it's so hard being an innovator. Big companies don't feel that they can take that big of a risk. But small companies just don't have all that much to lose."

Sweet Georgian Brown paints an almost idyllic picture of his days at King, but he admits it wasn't *all* peaches and cream.

"No matter what," he strains to recall, "every song I ever cut with that strange sound—like 'It's a Mans World'—they said was no good. *Live at the Apollo*—I had to spend my own money to do it. *Prisoner of Love*—they said I couldn't sing ballads. They always said, 'Why sing a song that you've sang all your life?' I said, ''Cause when you do it live it's never the same.'"

For "James Brown the Entertainer" (as he calls himself when dialing strangers on the phone), live performance has always been bread, butter, and lifeline in a very fickle business. When Americans decided to stop listening to him, Brown began accepting countless invitations to travel abroad. The Japanese, Italians, Germans, Mexicans and British and others can be credited with supporting the Godfather during his worst moments of professional distress.

During the seventies, Brown's empire suddenly caved in; not only was his ego blown, but his pockets were empty. Gone were the personal Lear jets, the extravagant expenses, the mansion with a moat in Queens, New York. Also lost were two of his three radio stations, victims to bankruptcy. James Brown, forever the Godfather of Soul, had painfully fallen to earth.

His most recent problem is with the Internal Revenue Service, which is assessing Brown $2.1 million for unpaid taxes covering the years 1975–'77. It has erroneously been reported that Brown has already been indicted for this sum; however, the parties are negotiating and Brown claims to have lost money during this period.

Meanwhile, on the concert trail, things have begun to pick up for the irrepressible Brown. As of May, he began touring the rock club circuit for the first time in his 24-year career. After years of playing to mostly black audiences, it has finally come to his attention that hordes of teenage rock 'n' rollers have been digging James Brown for quite some time. This realization crystallized during spring of 1980 when Brown flew to Chicago to play Reverend Cleophus James in the recently released *The Blues Brothers* movie. There he was greeted with the kind of respect he had not received in the states for years. Says James, "It was deeper than respect: it was love."

I next saw him and his eight man band at one of New York's new wave rock palaces called Irving Plaza, a former Polish meeting hall now disguised as a high-school auditorium. Brown, as always, was most candid.

"I know what this place is and I'm proud of it," he told me. "I'm proud that even though I was acting under instruction with my last two albums the younger people have demanded that James Brown do what he's noted for. They want to hear that again 'cause," he said with emphasis, "it's authentic. They want the real thing—they want it *raw.*

"See, blacks know what I was doing, but they don't know as much as they think they do. They never knew that I was making history then. But you whites know I'm making history because your schools are better. See what I'm saying?

"When someone makes history, it's current until you're reminded that this is history. But like I've said before: everyday I live is another day added to history."

Black, white, purple or green, the fact remains that Brown's two day engagement at Irving Plaza was his most successful appearance in the New York area since he arrived back in town about a year ago. The packed houses danced with the kind of fervor that used to mark ever James Brown and the Famous Flames show. He could've literally pleased them playing all night. ●

WYNTON AND BRANFORD MARSALIS: A COMMON UNDERSTANDING

By A. James Liska
DECEMBER 1982

The year 1982 was the year of Wynton Marsalis—*Down Beat* readers crowned him Jazz Musician of the Year; his debut LP copped Jazz Album of the Year honors; and he was named No. 1 Trumpet (handily defeating Miles in each category). In 1980, the New Orleans-bred brassman first stirred waves of critical praise with Art Blakey's Jazz Messengers; by the summer of '81 (with a CBS contract under his arm), he was honing his chops with the VSOP of Herbie Hancock, Ron Carter, and Tony Williams. By early '82, *Wynton Marsalis* was topping the jazz charts; *Fathers and Sons*—with one side featuring Wynton, brother Branford on sax, and father Ellis on piano—soon followed (both remain charted to this day), as did whistle-stop tours with his own quintet (Wynton, Branford, pianist Kenny Kirkland, bassist Phil Bowler, drummer Jeff Watts). Now, at 21, Wynton is on top, and rapidly rising 22-year-old Branford has been signed by CBS on his own.

A. James Liska: *Let's start by talking about the quintet—the Wynton Marsalis Quintet.*

Branford Marsalis: That's what they call it.

Wynton Marsalis: When he gets his band; it'll be called the Branford Marsalis Quartet.

AJL: *Are you going to play in his band?*

WM: No-o-o-o.

BM: He's barred. Let's face it, when you get a personality as strong as his in a band, particularly playing trumpet and with all the coverage, it would become the Wynton Marsalis Quintet.

AJL: *Even though it would be your band?*

BM: That's what it would be.

AJL: *Is that a reflection on your leadership abilities as well as your personality?*

BM: We're talking from a visual standpoint. When people come to see the band, the whole image would be like if Miles started playing with somebody else's band. You can't picture Miles as a sideman

at any time.

WM: Co-op music very seldom works—the type of music in which everybody has an equal position in deciding the musical direction of the band. I mean, somebody has to be the leader.

BM: Everybody else has to follow.

WM: The thing is though, when you lead a band, you don't lead a band by telling everybody what to do. That's a distortion that I think a lot of people get by watching bands. Nobody has ever had a great band in which they had to tell all the guys what to do. What you do is hire the cats who can play well enough to tell you what to do. But you have to make it seem like you're telling them. It's psychological; you have to be in charge of it, but you don't want to be in charge of it.

AJL: *Then the role of the leader is…*

WM: What I'm saying is that the direction of the band is formed by the band, but it goes through one person: the leader. If you're a leader, you lead naturally, automatically.

AJL: *From the co-op perspective then, don't all-star sessions generally work?*

WM: The don't work as well as an organized band. Sometimes, something exciting can come about. But that's rare because jazz—I hate to use that word—group improvisation is something that has to be developed over years of playing together or, at least, from common understanding. The reason that these all-star things can work so well is that everybody has a common ground. It's when you lump people from all different forms of music together that it sounds like total shit.

BM: Nowadays, sometimes the ego thing is so strong it's like, well, I've actually seen jam sessions where cats would say "I'm not going on the stage first. You play the first solo." As soon as that starts, the music is over. I sat and watched, for over two hours, a battle of egos like that. It was the worst musical experience I ever had. The people were going crazy because there were all these great jazz musicians on the stage. If they only knew what they were listening to and what was really going on. It hurt me, man. I think that's the major problem with all-star things because when you have a group, you have one leader and some followers who maybe can lead but they're followers nonetheless. The position of the follower is always underrated. A band has to have great followers; you can't have five great leaders.

AJL: *The too-many-chiefs, not-enough-Indians syndrome?*

BM: No Indians.

WM: The thing that makes it most intricate is that you have to realize that when you lead a band, you're leading a group of cats that know more about everything they do than you know. That's the one great thing I learned from Art Blakey. He's one of the greatest leaders in the world, and the reason is that he doesn't try to pretend that he knows stuff that he doesn't know. But he's the leader of the band, and when you are in his band,

play just what he could play. But they always knew he was the leader, and you can listen to the records and know he's the leader.

AJL: *Is there a like situation in your own quintet? Are the guys telling you what to do?*

WM: There are certain things that they do that I don't know what it is, that I have to ask about. You know, like, what was that you played? What is that? What chord is that? What voicing? What's the best choice of this? That's what you have to do to learn. The hardest thing about being a leader is that you

Skip Brown

Wynton and Branford Marsalis

you never get the impression that you're leading it. I knew all the time that he was the leader. He didn't have to tell me that. He's that kind of man.

AJL: *And that wasn't ego-inspired?*

WM: His stuff has nothing whatsoever to do with ego, man. He's just a great leader. Of course, he's been doing it for so long. But that's true with a lot of different people. When Miles had the band with Herbie and them, do you think he told them what to do? He was struggling to figure out what *they* were doing. He had never had cats play like that, but he was wise enough to let them decide what was going to happen. He didn't make them

have to lead a group of cats who might know more than you know.

AJL: *Then why are you the leader if you know so little?*

BM: (*Laughing.*) He must know enough.

AJL: *Are you a great follower?*

BM: I'm a great follower.

AJL: *Do you think you'll be a great leader?*

BM: Great leaders were usually great followers. You have to be a follower before you can lead. That's what I've always thought. I'm learning a lot now, particularly economically, you know, business. He's setting the path for me, and I'm not going to have to make the same mistakes and go through the same crap

that he's going through. While he's going through it, I'm sitting back observing, watching everything that they're trying to do to him.

AJL: *Who are they?*

BM: Record companies, agents, managers, the whole works. The hassles with the music, the gigs, riders in additions to contracts.

AJL: *So Wynton deals with it and you have the benefit...*

BM: Sitting around and learning. It's a drag that it had to be like that because all that pressure was thrown on him. People are always asking the classic dumb question: How does it feel to have a brother getting all that attention and blah, blah, blah? They obviously have no idea what all that shit entails. I sit down and watch him doing all of this and say, "Yeah, great...somebody's gotta be in the hot seat. Better him than me."

AJL: *Is Wynton more able to deal with pressures than you?*

BM: He thrives better under pressure than I do. If I had to deal with it, I'd deal with it. But he functions best under pressure. I function best when people leave me the hell alone and I don't have to deal with a lot of crap. If I have to deal with it, I'll deal with it. But, like, he went to the hardest high school to go to.

AJL: *By choice?*

BM: By choice. He could have gone to the middle-of-the-road one like I did. I went to that one which meant I didn't have to study. He went to the hardest one. I'll admit it—I'm the classic lazy cat. I didn't want to be bothered; I didn't want to practice. I just wanted to exist. So I didn't practice. I played in a funk band and had a great time. When it was time to go to college, I went to the easiest one I could go to with the best teacher for music. But I really wasn't serious about music.

But back to the original subject; Wynton

played classical music because someone told him black cats couldn't play classical music. The first time he went out there every one of the oboe players played the notes kind of out of tune, just to throw him off. He thrives best under that kind of stuff. If it were all relaxed and they just said, "Anything you want, man," I think he'd be kind of shaky. When people tell him "No," that's when he's at his best. So all the pressure's on him. Good. When I come around and get my band, there shouldn't be that much pressure.

AJL: *Coming from the same family, being close brothers, how did you end up so different?*

WM: My mother. My mother's a great woman. She treats everybody the same, so we're all different. When you treat everybody the same way and don't tamper with the way you treat them in accordance to their personality, then they act differently. They develop into their own person. Like Branford and me, we're totally different.

BM: Radically different.

AJL: *Yet you appear to be best of friends.*

WM: Well, we have our things.

BM: Appearances can be deceiving.

WM: All my brothers…we grew up living in the same room, you know? He was always my boy, though. Like, I could always talk to him.

AJL: *You two are the closest in age?*

BM: We're 13 months apart.

WM: I always took my other brothers for granted. When Branford went away to college and I was still in high school, that's when I missed him. But we used to argue all the time. We think totally different. Anything I would say, he'd say just the opposite.

AJL: *Just to be obstinate?*

WM: Just to say it.

BM: It wasn't just to say it. It was because I didn't agree.

WM: Nothing I say he agrees with.

BM: Some things I agree with.

AJL: *Musically, did you agree?*

BM: No.

AJL: *Still?*

WM: No.

BM: Know what we agree on? I've thought about this a lot. I think we agree on the final objective. I think the common goal is there, but the route to achieve the common goal is totally different.

WM: Totally.

BM: It's like catching the "E" and the "F" train. They both come from Queens to New York, and they both meet at West 4th Street, but one comes down Sixth Avenue and one comes down Eighth Avenue.

WM: The way I think the shit should be done, he doesn't.

AJL: *How do you work so well together?*

BM: It's simple: he's the leader.

WM: Everybody thinks it's hard because he's my older brother. If we weren't brothers, if he was just another cat, nobody'd think anything of it. People are always going to try to put us together as brothers, and I don't want that. I tell people all the time that the reason Branford's in my band is because I can't find anybody that plays better than him.

AJL: *Are you looking?*

WM: No. (*Laughs.*) But if they come…

BM: Bye-bye me.

WM: I don't have him in the band because he's my brother. I use him because I like the way he plays. Shit is very cut and dried with me: either you can play, or you can't; either you know what you're doing, or you don't. I use him because he's bad. Period.

BM: I've always believed that when you're dealing with certain things, there are businesses and friendships. The two should never meet. The reason we get along so well it that when we play music, it's the Wynton Marsalis Quintet, and I'm in the band. When we're in this house, it's my brother, Wynton.

WM: What you have to realize is that everybody in the band is bad. That's what nobody wants to admit. They'll say "Branford can play" or "Wynton's alright." Everybody in the band is bad. Jeff Watts knows as much as anybody about the music. Kenny Kirkland. Phil Bowler. These cats know about the music. It's not like one cat can play and he towers over everybody else in the band. People think that's how bands run. In this band, all of the cats have the capabilities. And when they do interviews….What about Kenny? Why doesn't he get the publicity? What about Phil? Why doesn't Jeff get interviewed? It's because nobody's said that he's good yet.

AJL: *Where did you find Jeff Watts, the drummer?*

WM: Branford knew him from Boston.

BM: I knew he was bad because nobody liked him. When I heard that, I couldn't wait to hear him.

AJL: *Did you first hear him with a group?*

BM: No. It's hard to get a group in Boston, but we had the privilege of having ensemble rooms; we'd just sit around and have jam sessions, and every time he'd play, everybody would get lost. They couldn't tell where "one" was, and then they'd say, "He's sad. I can't hear 'one'."

WM: He's conceptually bad.

BM: Then we started hanging out and talking.

WM: He knows a lot of shit, man. He has a concept about the music.

AJL: *What about Phil Bowler, the bassist?*

WM: He played with Rahsaan [Roland Kirk] a long time.

AJL: *How did you find him?*

WM: I was playing everybody. Jamil Nasser recommended him. We had tried a lot of different cats. Phil's got great time and that allows Jeff to play what he wants. Plus, he has a good knowledge of harmony and rhythmic-derivational things. He plays interesting ostinatos.

AJL: *Where did you find Kenny Kirkland?*

WM: Everybody knows him. He's one of the baddest cats playing piano today. You just know about him.

AJL: *What's the most difficult thing about keeping your group together?*

WM: Getting gigs. I worked three gigs in May with the band, and those were like one-hour gigs. You've got to gig all of the time, but you can't make money working in the clubs.

AJL: *What about the concert hall situation?*

WM: It hasn't hurt the music because the music in the clubs was dying anyway. It might be picking up now, but it was dying for a long time because the music changed.

AJL: *How so?*

WM: The music was different in the fifties and sixties than it is now. Then you could play popular tunes in the jazz setting and make them sound hip.

AJL: *And now?*

WM: You can't do that now because all of the popular tunes are sad pieces of one-chord shit. Today's pop tunes are sad. Turn on the radio and try to find a pop tune to play with your band. You can't do it. The melodies are static, the chord changes are just the same senseless stuff repeated over and over again. Back then you could get a pop tune, and people were more willing to come out and see the music because it had more popular elements in it. They could more easily identify with it.

AJL: *Have the pop tunes of back then lost their meaning today?*

WM: They haven't lost their meaning, but they're old. You've heard them played so many times by great performers that you don't want to play them again.

AJL: *Any suggestions or solutions?*

WM: I think one of the biggest problems is that nobody wants to do somebody else's song. Everybody thinks that they can write great tunes, and all the public wants is that it sounds different. Music has to be played before it gets old. The music that Ornette Coleman played, that Miles and Trane played in the sixties, some of the stuff that Mingus and Booker Little and Charlie Rouse and these cats were starting to do...that music isn't old because nobody else has ever played it.

AJL: *What happens, what is the reaction, if you do play it?*

WM: People say, "Man, you sound like you're imitating Miles in the sixties," or else, "He sounds like he's imitating Elvin Jones." So what? You just don't come up with something new. You have to play through something. The problem with some of the stuff that all the critics think is innovative is that it sounds like European music—European, avant garde, classical twentieth-century static rhythm music with blues licks in it. And all these cats can say for themselves is "We don't sound like anybody else." That doesn't mean shit. The key is to sound like somebody else, to take what is already there and sound like an extension of that. It's not to not *sound* like that. Music has a tradition that you have to understand before you can move to the next step. But that doesn't mean you have to be a historian.

AJL: *Earlier you expressed an aversion to the word "jazz." Why?*

WM: I don't like it because it's now taken on the context of being everything. Anything is jazz; everything is jazz. Quincy Jones' shit is jazz, David Sanborn...that's

not to cut down Quincy or David. I love funk, it's hip. No problem to it. The thing is, if it'll sell records to call that stuff jazz, they'll call it jazz. They call Miles' stuff jazz. That stuff is not jazz, man. Just because somebody played jazz at one time, that doesn't mean they're still playing it. Branford will agree with me.

BM: (*Laughs.*) No. I don't agree.

WM: The thing is, we all get together and we know that this shit is sad, but we're gonna say it's good, then everybody agrees. Nobody is strong enough to stand up and say, "Wait, this stuff is bullshit." Everybody is afraid to peek out from behind the door and say, "C'mon man." Everybody wants to say everything is cool.

AJL: *Do you have as strong a feeling to maintain the standards?*

BM: Yes. Even stronger in some ways. I just don't talk about it as much. A lot of the music he doesn't like, I like.

AJL: *Like what?*

BM: Like everything.

WM: Like what?

BM: Like Mahavishnu. A lot of the fusion stuff.

WM: I don't dislike that.

BM: It's not that you dislike it, it's that you prefer not to listen to it.

WM: That's true.

AJL: *Do you think you're more open?*

BM: I don't consider it being more open; it's just that he's kind of set in his ways. What I feel strongly about is the way the business has come into the music. Everything has become Los Angeles—everything is great and everything is beautiful. It's kind of tired. Cats come up to me and say: "What do you think of Spyro Gyra?" And I say: "I don't." That's not an insult to Spyro Gyra. I just don't like it when people call it jazz when it's not.

AJL: Any advice for young players?

WM: Avoid roots.

BM: I think the basis of the whole thing is the bass player. The rhythm section is very important. If I've got a sad rhythm section, I'm in trouble.

WM: Listen to the music. High schools all over the country should have programs where the kids can listen to the music. Schools should have the records, and the

students should be required to listen to them all, not just Buddy Rich and Maynard Ferguson. They should listen to Parker and Coltrane and some of the more creative cats. That should be a required thing. Jazz shouldn't be taught like a course. The students should know more than a couple of bebop licks and some progressions.

BM: Never play what you practice; never write down your own solos—a classic waste of time unless you're practicing ear training.

WM: You should learn a solo off a record, but don't transcribe it. It doesn't make sense to transcribe a solo.

BM: You're not learning it then, you're reading it.

WM: And learn a solo to get to what you want to do. You don't learn a solo to play that solo.

BM: What people don't realize is that what a soloist plays is a direct result of what's happening on the bandstand.

WM: You should learn all of the parts—the bass, the piano, the drums—everything.

BM: Right.

WM: Music goes forward. Music doesn't go backwards. Whatever the cats couldn't play before you, you're supposed to play.

BM: There's a huge movement for the perpetuation of ignorance in jazz. Play, that's all. ●

DAVID SANBORN:
THE VOICE OF EMOTION

By Robin Tolleson

MARCH 1983

He goes for the heart—that's for sure. Close your eyes and imagine a tear dripping from the bell of the horn. Or envision the keys blasting off the alto, straining under to torrential sound. Judging from his acceleration in today's musical marketplace, David Sanborn seems to be hitting his mark. A Sanborn contribution to an album may only be three minutes long, but always conjures up a range of feelings, and always leaves a mark.

You're heard the sound. Maybe with James Taylor or David Bowie on your car radio. Maybe watching "Saturday Night Live," where he belted the show's theme out for months, got into more than a few inspired jams, and was featured playing his own material. Or maybe you've been listening to Gil Evans, Stevie Wonder, or Steely Dan. Maybe the guitar freaks have heard him on record with Tommy Bolin and John McLaughlin. It is definitely a measure of the man to see who calls him up.

Sanborn balances a studio career and performing. His seventh solo album, *As We Speak*, hit and held at No. 1 on jazz charts, and Sanborn toured last summer, opening shows for Al Jarreau. Sanborn's band featured bassist Marcus Miller, guitarist Hiram Bullock, drummer Buddy Williams, and Sugar Bear (from the Sam & Dave group) on keyboards. The chart-topping album *Casino Lights* features Sanborn and a host of other Warner Brothers "jazz-stars" at the Montreux, Switzerland fest. I caught Sanborn in his New York apartment, working on his latest project—a film soundtrack. He is scoring *Stelle Sulla Citta* (Stars Above the City), being directed by Massimo Trabaldo Togna. The saxman also learned some Italian so he could make an appearance in the film. "Strangely enough," he laughs, "in the part of a saxophone player." You gotta start somewhere.

Robin Tolleson: *Might I have seen you at the Fillmore auditorium in San Francisco in the sixties with the Paul Butterfield Blues Band?*

David Sanborn: Oh yes, the old Fillmore, and Winterland, and the Carousel. One gig we played, Cream was the opening act, and it was hilarious. Nobody had heard them, so people went, "What is this?"

RT: *How did you get hooked up with Butterfield?*

DS: I grew up in St. Louis, later went to school at Northwestern and at the University of Iowa, and then went to San Francisco in 1967. I knew Phillip Wilson, who was the drummer of Butterfield then, and I ran into him on the street. He said, "Listen, I'm playing with this band, like a blues band with horns, and you've got to hear it." So I went down and checked it out, and played with them. The rest is history.

RT: *Now you're a Grammy winner, for Voyeur.*

DS: Well, it was a minor category, "R&B Instrumental."

RT: *That might seem minor to some people....*

DS: It's nothing to sneeze at.

RT: *Your albums have been charting very well.*

DS: Yeah, the one that's out now was No. 1 on the jazz charts, which is interesting. I think the categories in music are less restrictive; they're less clearly defined than they were before, primarily because people are listening to more different kinds of music—not only the listeners, but the musicians as well. And so you get a lot of cross-influences. In Talking Heads you hear some African music, elements of a lot of other stylistic things that come creeping in, and I think that not only tends to open up the music that's being played, but also the people who are listening to that will be more prone to listen to other kinds of music. If someone who just listens to the Rolling Stones all of a sudden hears a Sonny Rollins solo on a Rolling Stones record, maybe that will pique their interest in who Sonny Rollins is, and maybe lead them to listen to some of his records, or moreover be kind of in-tune to his sound—kind of broken in—and consequently be more open to listen to him.

RT: *It might surprise some people who think of you as a jazz player to see your albums on the rhythm & blues charts as well. But a lot of your background is in R&B, isn't it?*

DS: Well, my early playing experience was in R&B bands in St. Louis....Albert King, and Little Milton, and I think in terms of my musical background, that's what idiomatic form it is...R&B. I tended to listen to jazz later on, I think as any saxophone player would do. I think the pull toward wanting to stretch the limits of your playing automatically leads you into jazz and other kinds of more challenging forms of improvisation; R&B tends to be more an emotional kind of music, perhaps less sophisticated in certain respects, although not any less valid, just that the harmonic and rhythmic sophistication is less than jazz allows.

RT: *The emotion is what sticks out in your solos.*

DS: I take that as a compliment. I think of myself as an emotional player too. Especially in a lot of the contexts that I've been in. You know, the pop context. I've primarily been called in as a soloist, and I think as soloist you respond to whatever your musical surroundings are. I'm a fairly emotional player, so one thing leads to another.

RT: *If you could sing solos, do you think you'd sing the same thing that you would play on sax?*

DS: I was thinking about that very thing the other night, because I was playing something on piano, some chord changes, and I was kind of singing a melody to myself, and I stopped and thought, "Would I play that melody?" And that led me to another conclusion, about one of the problems that I've been having about writing recently. Because I've been writing on piano, what I've been writing is not always conducive to being played melodically on the saxophone. I don't know. I don't think I would play the same notes, but I think it would probably have the same musical and emotional content. But in terms of the notes, I find that in the process of improvising, you end up in places that you didn't expect, and it's what you make out of where you end up. It's kind of like an escape artist. You say, "Whooo, how am I gonna get out of this situation? Ooop, yeah, okay I'll make that A, slap the five, go around the corner, and meet you at the tonic." I think there's a lot of that that goes on in improvisation. Ideally, in the process of growing as a musician, I would like to be able to have what I sing and what I think and what I play be the same thing. And I think probably the gap between those things is less than it was, but certainly it's still there.

RT: *Do you have certain ways to approach solos, such as on a ballad like "Rain on Christmas," or a funkier tune like "Hideaway?"*

DS: "Rain On Christmas" allowed me to play more bebop-oriented lines, within that kind of latin rhythmic feel. The funkier stuff is rhythmically less flexible, and a little more idiomatic, probably. There are things that you can't do, that are out of context in the funk thing. I think there is a kind of language, or vocabulary in funk, just as there is with bebop or any other style or idiom. I think the ones in funk tend to be a little more strict, but that may be in my mind. That may be just because I feel that limitation. I feel really close to R&B, because that's what gets me off playing—to have people dance to it, whether they actually move to it or not, just to involve

Paul Natkin/Photo Reserve

people in it. I think it's a rhythmic fact, a certain kind of rhythmic regularity. But it's not dumb just because it's regular, which is what a lot of jazz musicians incredibly thought. Just because something has a consistent rhythmic motif, that it's simple, or crude. But in actual fact, it's momentum. I mean, African music, which is the source of what we're talking about, is relentlessness, but it doesn't have the structural confines that Western music or popular music has. So just eliminate the structures, make the structures flexible too. Then that doesn't become like a pounding, it's a continuous flow, so you don't even care where "one" is. It's irrelevant.

RT: *You use dynamics a lot when you're soloing.*

DS: Yeah, well I think a lot of people remember me as playing a lot louder and harder-edged than I really play. I don't play that loud, necessarily. I try to use dynamics because that is another element of music and improvising, and melodic creativity. And I'm very conscious of dynamics because I think you shape a line using dynamics—in terms of attack and crescendo, decrescendo, and phrasing, legato, and staccato. I got a lot of my phrasing mannerisms, I think, from Stevie Wonder. When I was working with Stevie from '70 to '72, I picked up a lot of his little turns, and mordents, and appoggiaturas, and all that—things that he did on harmonica. And I think probably Stevie more than anybody else influenced some of the little grace notes—the mannerisms of my playing that I hear a lot of other people imitating when they're trying to sound like; me. Those little "da-de-aa-da," those turns and stuff—I really got from Stevie. It's kind of funny when I

hear it filtered—like Stevie through me, to somebody else. I didn't make it up, nor did Stevie perhaps, but Stevie kind of codified it, and then I just kind of lifted a lot of it from him, because it's very effective.

RT: *You've worked with several vocalists— James Taylor, Paul Simon, Rickie Lee Jones, to name a few. Do you learn from all of them?*

DS: Stevie—that is an influence that I can see a direct connection. I can say specifically "yes" that I picked up certain little mannerisms of his. It's less clear in some of the other people I've worked with. I've been very lucky in my career to have worked with a lot of singer/songwriters, and I think probably more than anything else that's helped my songwriting and general sense of song structure and composition. It's allowed me to hear those people perform their own material night after night, and see how they interpret it from day to day. Just to get that particular insight into their songwriting, the craft that they use in writing. I think it's kind of by osmosis. I just absorb the essence of whatever it is they are, or at least my impression of what their music is. But I do tend to pick up kind of abstract things from people I've worked with. I think I tend to favor James Taylor's kind of song structure, because it's one that's real compatible with mine. Usually when I start out a song, it tends to be loosely structured like a lot of James' songs. Then I'll take it in another direction. But I think about James a lot when I'm writing. He was a big influence on me. And Paul Simon also. Paul is a very methodical, meticulous writer, and his chord movements are very correct and interesting.

RT: *I wanted to ask you if you feel much imitated.*

DS: I do feel imitated, and I'm flattered that people would imitate me. Honestly, outside of some of the more obvious mannerisms of my playing, I don't understand why anybody would want to imitate me. In certain ways I'm not a very innovative player. Maybe my sound and the way I phrase is different or unique— individual—but it's kind of funny in a way. I'm flattered, but it makes me laugh when I hear somebody doing something that's obviously me.

RT: *I hope you're not losing too many sessions because of all the...*

DS: I wonder about that. (*A big laugh.*) Maybe I am, maybe I am. Well, I don't lose much sleep over it.

RT: *You've done quite a bit of playing with the Brecker Brothers.*

DS: I always enjoy playing with them. It's really fun to play in ensembles and stuff, because we respond to each other well. Just the kind of dexterity that they have, especially Michael Brecker, who's one of the most amazing saxophone players I know, on every level, musical or technical. Technically, he's just overwhelming, and it was great for me to be around him. In a certain way he had things that I didn't have, and I had things that he didn't have, because the way we came up was different. He came from a musical family, obviously, and I think he was more schooled, in a sense—at home learning from the piano as a basic frame of reference—whereas I didn't really learn to read until I was in college. I read a little in high school, but not much to speak of. And most of my early playing experience was with R&B bands. I'm not sure what Michael's early experience was, but I think he played more jazz. He's certainly a more accomplished jazz player than I am, or probably ever will be. But we have a mutual respect for each other and the fact that we were different in a lot of ways is why we were so compatible. I think our approach in terms of the emotional aspect of our playing is very similar.

RT: *You've been touring with your own band recently. Do you enjoy the energy of performing live?*

DS: I do, very much. I think it's very necessary. I didn't go on the road for a couple years, and I really started to feel kind of out of it, and isolated. I missed the direct, immediate return of energy that you get playing in front of a live audience. And I think I tended to get a little too careful in playing. Being in the studio, having the opportunity to go back and record yourself leads you to do that perhaps more than you should—and for continuity's sale in terms of just continuing ideas, and some of stamina factors on a purely physical level. I just think it's a necessary part of my life that I overlooked for a while. I try to my life between doing live performing and studio playing not to get too overloaded on either one of those things. I really enjoy working last summer. I had a great band with me.

RT: *Can you describe the music that you are writing for the movie Stelle Sulla Citta?*

DS: Is of romantic, wistful, a little Brazilian in flavor, maybe. Something like one of my albums, *Heart to Heart*. There's a tune on *Lotus Blossom* that was the cornerstone in terms of what the music is like. That's the tone of the music.

RT: *Were you writing the score while you were acting in the film?*

DS: Yes, I was actually. I wrote some of it before I went over there, and also acted some of it while I was there, and am continuing to write it now. I'm going to get a rough cut of the film probably in two weeks, and at that time will finish the soundtrack and record it here. I'm using Steve Vanieri, Warren Bernhardt, and Steve Khan. Not a bad band.

RT: *So you are writing little 15-second interludes and snippets for the film score?*

DS: Yes. That's the part I'm not sure of yet, because I don't have a rough the film, but I will have to write little cues. I'm just not sure what's going to be involved there, what I have to do. But I will have to do that, and I've never done that before. I've got a couple friends who have written for film, and they're going to help me out when I get in trouble, which I hope is not too often.

RT: *On your Hideaway album, you wrote or co-wrote all the tunes except one. I've been disappointed that there weren't more of your tunes on your last two albums.*

DS: I'm really glad to hear you say that, actually, because I've kind of shied away from....I went through a crisis of not really feeling that my tunes were very interesting or valid. and I've recently re-evaluated that stance, and realized that the most effective music I make is my own—interpreting my own material. And that my point of view that it was maybe a little weak, or this or that, is really irrelevant. What really matters is the emotional communication. And that is best communicated through a context that I establish myself. So this next album, I'm going to write or co-write all the songs. I feel a real need to return to that kind of approach that I had on *Hideaway*.

RT: *You have built up a fine supporting cast of players for your albums over the years. Are you going to continue with the same sort of sound on your next album?*

DS: I think so. I'm going to try to distill it. Maybe make it a little more direct. I've tended to write a lot of latin-oriented tunes. I think I have a tendency to gravitate towards that kind of music, I don't know why. But I'm going to try to stretch my limits a little bit. Broaden my horizons as it were, and try to write some different kinds of tunes. I've got about 15 or 20 tunes now that I'm kind of combing through, and seeing what I can get out of them, seeing where they'll lead me. ●

THE KEITH JARRETT INTERVIEW

By Art Lange

JUNE 1984

Ladies and gentlemen, meet Keith Jarrett. You say you already know all there is to know about the pianist/composer/improviser? You've followed him through his reputation-building term with Charles Lloyd in the late-sixties heyday of flower power; his subsequent electric excursions into Fillmore rock psychedelia alongside Miles Davis; his trend-setting solo piano extravaganzas stretching back over a decade; his two distinct yet decisive quartets, one American (Dewey Redman, Charlie Haden, Paul Motian), one Scandinavian (Jan Garbarek, Palle Danielsson, John Christensen); his chamber music experiments from *In the Light*; his spontaneous hymns coaxed from a baroque organ; his composed "concertos" for (variously) piano, flute, saxophone, bass plus orchestra; even his recent return to a stripped-down trio (Jack DeJohnette, Gary Peacock)—and you know just how to categorize him: Jarrett the mystic, Jarrett the Romantic, Jarrett the poseur, Jarrett the Platonist?

You may know all that, but I humbly submit that if you know Keith Jarrett through his music, you know him not at all, for music is sound solely, and sounds can be deceiving. A note reveals nothing about the intent *behind it*—to discern that, you've got to open yourself. If nothing else, the encyclopedic list of activities above suggests a musician of more than a single mind; in fact, Jarrett is a man of contradictions. Some small sense of this *can* be heard in the range of emotions within his music—from the ruthless, slashing, Ornette-ish abandon of the American quartet to the simple, solitary, sweet, and sentimental ballad moments solo; from the gotta testify gospel chord changes to the meditational abstractions focusing on the beauty behind a single sound....

But contradiction goes beyond sound. Though identified closest with spontaneously conceived solo piano concerts, where he seems to go one-on-one with the Muse, Jarrett's still concerned with the well-being of his audience. For the supposed egoist, he's insecure about his technique—so that his switch from solo concerts to classical concertos is a test not only for his audience, but for himself as well.

"Do I contradict myself?/Very well then, I contradict myself/(I am large, I contain multitudes)," Walt Whitman wrote, suggesting that life is based

Teri Bloom

on contradictions. Contradiction inspires concern *and* successes. And contradiction acknowledged admits a struggle with forces possibly larger and more important than we casually care to recognize. Keith Jarrett, in his music and philosophies, is a contradiction. Good for him. Good for us.

Art Lange: *I understand that you are concentrating on performing classical concertos these days, though you've been involved with classical music all your life....*

Keith Jarrett: In the beginning I was trained to become a classical pianist, but it's just now becoming a public focus—actually it's not all that public yet. To develop repertoire takes a lot of years, and I'm mostly working on that now.

AL: *Why have you decided to start performing concertos at this time?*

KJ: It's complex question. It's not a decision as much as a pulling back from a kind of expectancy of freedom in what I've been doing up to now—and I don't mean my own expectancy, I mean the audience's. Their definition of freedom is becoming as limited as it was when, let's say, a solo concert would have been a revolutionary thing to do. So now the audience is thinking that *unless* it's an improvised solo concert, it isn't as much music making as it is in, say, a Mozart piano concerto. I would like to direct them slightly away from that focus—including the fact that solo improvised concerts can go on forever. There's no reason for them to stop, which is a good reason to stop.

In order to hear the recent solo concerts, a listener has had to hear *how* I'm playing the piano, much more than they did during the *Köln Concert* years. Then it was a flurry of ideas coming up within a limited dynamic range; now the dynamic range and how to play the instrument is so much more important in order to hear the concert. So, maybe I can direct a classical audience to improvising and direct a jazz audience to trying to gain a little bit of interest, let's say, to come to grips *with* what that person is doing with his instrument.

AL: *How do you prepare for a notated classical piece? Is it different from the way you prepare for your own music?*

KJ: It's exactly the same as if I were performing my own written music. But if I were going to improvise, then the preparation is reversed. whatever you know about how to prepare for a written piece, you would have to reverse all the instructions for solo concerts. So you can understand why I cannot do both at the same time for very long periods of time. I'd go insane. "What am I doing tonight? Do I have the music? Do I have to have the music?" I have to sit down, for example, in order to play Mozart. Playing Mozart standing up is a contradiction in language. Also it's important for any player to know a lot about that composer, not just look at the notes. That's another parallel to knowing your instrument: knowing about the composer. "We don't want to worry about the composer, let's just play these notes." Well, that doesn't work.

At any rate, the way I prepare for a concerto is the way any concerto player prepares; I think perhaps I'm more fanatical than most because I have much more to lose by not succeeding. No matter what I do, it will probably get written up, whereas in a debut of someone in New York, no one's going to get all upset if he has a bad concert. If I have a bad concert, it's known all over the world.

AL: *So, technically, you practice, whereas in getting set for improvising, you* don't *want to practice because you don't want preconceived things going in.*

KJ: Well, when improvising, you don't know what language you might have to use, or what language might come out that you'd have to be involved with. In other words, you shouldn't even *hear* pianos or be near pianos for a while. It should all be, again, a new sound, from almost a primitive beginning. But with, let's just take Mozart for an example, to even get past what is banal about Mozart's music means you have to understand the language he speaks. To understand that language means you have to know about fortepianos and harpsichords to hear the sound he heard. Once you get into all these things, you start to realize how few people play *Mozart*, you know? Most people play themselves playing Mozart, and the more they ignore that side of things, the more they would be playing their own natural tendencies rather than Mozart's music.

AL: *You're actually talking about another contradiction, because you're immersing yourself—or at least becoming comfortable—with certain aspects of Mozart's style, and "style" is a word that you want to avoid when you improvise.*

KJ: That's right. Well, many improvisers might not think that way. The way I relate to it is that improvisation is really the deepest way to deal with moment-to-moment reality in music. There is no *deeper* way, *personally* deeper. But there is no less depth in working with someone else's music—having found *his* depth becomes exactly the same. And the people who think the two things are different are

going to lose out when they come to listen to one or the other.

AL: *Of the concertos you've played so far, Mozart is the only non-twentieth century composer. Is that because it's harder to get close to Mozart's style because you're chronologically so far removed from it?*

KJ: This choice of how to start the ball rolling was more to do with the audience being able to accept my playing Bartók first, rather than my wanting to play Bartók first. I would have wanted to play Bach, Beethoven first. If it was just like, "What do you want to play today?" I wouldn't say, "Hey, Bartók, man." I would say, "Well, in the situation I'm in what would be the way to open this door?" Number one, the concerto I chose of Bartók's [Concerto No. 2] is one of the hardest piano concertos there is, so from the technical point of view, if I succeed at that, no one's going to fret anymore about whether I can play such and such a piece or not—including me. I mean I have to prove to myself that I can do it. Secondly, from the point of view of the material and how it relates to what I've done up to that time, the shock is less great for the audience. I mean, to go straight into Mozart would have been very difficult.

AL: *Bartók, Barber, Stravinsky, who you've played, all have rhythmic elements that are closer to what a jazz audience is used to hearing than Mozart or Beethoven.*

KJ: That's right; they can be digested. Their language is not that distant from what a jazz listener has heard. In fact, in Stravinsky's case, in Barber's case, they were influenced by a lot of jazz, wrote a lot of seemingly jazz-oriented things. Although in one of his interviews, Stravinsky—of all the people to choose as an example of an influential jazz player—chose Shorty Rogers: "If you listen to Shorty Rogers' phrasing you would find such-and-such a thing."

AL: *If left to your own devices, your own choice, you would have wanted to initially play Bach, Mozart, Beethoven....*

KJ: Well, I only say that because I don't play or think about Bartók very often. However, I always find it healthy to listen to Bach, and often to Beethoven.

AL: *Do you think you'd like to play those pieces in public because they're so far*

divorced from jazz, so you'd personally want to go as far as you can in the other direction?

KJ: Good question. Right, except I have no intention of divorcing myself from jazz, and that's an interesting way of putting that question. I have absolutely no strings that have been untied from anything I have done; I'm just adding maybe a thicker rope, in a way, to all music that I consider, through certain subjective and objective processes, to be important to me. So the question about would I play Bach or Beethoven because of the *difference*—it's really the opposite. I feel that Bach and what I do myself are much *closer* than Bartók is to what I do in the solo concerts. It's the way the music sounds to the listener that makes it seem different. When it gets down to the nitty-gritty, Bach and I are friends, Beethoven and I are friends, Mozart and I are friends sometimes, Bartók and I are friends because we're Hungarian, you know? And on and on. But I know if I went to jail and was allowed to take only one composer's music, I would probably take Bach's music.

AL: *Do you think you feel an affinity for the three you mentioned—Bach, Beethoven, and to a degree, Mozart....*

KJ: I should add Handel in there too....

AL: *...because they were the improvising keyboard artists of their time?*

KJ: I think the music *is* better *because* their relationship to improvising was so strong. I wouldn't say that I like their music because they were all improvisers, but there was something *in* the music, and I would say it is the ecstatic knowledge that comes through in Bach's music and in Beethoven's music. It's the knowledge of the ecstatic state—which means that's why their music conveys so much. [With Bach] almost every time and no matter what state you're in—at least I should speck for myself—there is something coming through, whereas with almost every other composer's music, I need to be in a certain mood to listen to it. So to me that means there's less being communicated. I know that when you're an improviser, a true improviser, you have to be familiar with ecstasy, otherwise you can't connect with music. When you're a composer, you can wait for those moments, you know, whenever. They might not be here today. But when you're an improviser, at 8 o'clock tonight, for example, you have to be so familiar with that state that you can almost bring it on.

AL: *So you do that—you bring the* state *on, but you don't bring on the music that that state leads to.*

KJ: And this is what I can give back to all the composers I play, who I believe were familiar with that state. Within their own language I might be able to give them just a little gift of having understood how tremendous their struggle was with a particular note. Classical players are aware of this process because they're usually studious about everything they do—if they're good—but that doesn't mean they're aware of the *state* as much as, "Oh yes, this phrase means this." If you don't have a relationship with the state that produced the phrase, you can't be as good a player of the music. That's what I hope I can bring.

AL: *So far you've only performed concertos in public. Do you see yourself doing solo classical recitals?*

KJ: Yes I do, but I'm not sure when.

AL: *Do you have any idea yet what music?*

KJ: Not really. I've been working on the Beethoven sonatas for about 13 years now, fairly regularly. I didn't have this studio until several years ago, and before that I didn't practice a hell of a lot because improvising and practicing don't work together.

AL: *I take it you wouldn't consider doing a program of a Bach toccata, a Beethoven sonata, and a Jarrett improvisation.*

KJ: No, probably not. That subject has come up, as you can imagine. An orchestra says, "Would you do this concerto with us and would you improvise in the second half?" No. I feel that is using my music merely as a means of filling out the program.

AL: *You don't feel that it might highlight some of those connections to the audience— you've played Bach and then you play your music so that they could hear some of the things you hear?*

KJ: It certainly would be possible, but it would to too easy. For them *and* for me. Already we're at the point where they want to hear rich ideas related to their favorite solo recordings. They do not want to see that next step, and they won't accept that next step within the context of a solo improvised concert.

I had a interesting interview with the Japanese composer Toru Takemitsu recently. He decided he wanted to interview me for their classical music magazine. He was asking why my solo concerts were slowing down and stopping, and he said something about, "Is it because you don't want to possess the music anymore?" And that was precisely right. The only reason I bring this up is because I don't feel like a composer at this moment at all. And I talk to people about my stopping the solo concerts, and they say, "Oh my god," or "Well maybe you'll be writing something soon." And I tell them, "Wait a minute, you don't understand. This is a *positive* thing that is happening to me." It really is positive, in the sense that anyone who wants to listen to what I'm doing this year has to listen to other people's music, who they may not have a relationship with, and come to terms with whether they can deal with *my* relationship to those people or not. Which is exactly what you do when you're listening well, you know? "What did I like or what didn't I like about it? Was it the piece, or was it the way they played the piece? Or maybe I just don't think he can do this; he shouldn't be doing this." All those things have no application to this point because people assume that if Keith Jarrett's going to play somewhere, he's going to play his own music. Even now if I play a concerto and the audience wants an encore, they want me to improvise.

AL: *So in addition to broadening your own musical experience, you're trying to broaden the listener's range of musical experience as well.*

KJ: My experience has been that when you risk losing a listener, you're either doing something terrible or doing something very important. I've come to terms with when I'm going something terrible—I'm the first person to know it's bad. If I continue to know that, then all I have to do is put those pieces together, and if I'm still risking the listening public, it's got to be a right step, you know? With the exception of pure shock value—anyway, there's no shock left.

AL: *Let's talk about the difference between writing for orchestra and writing for "jazz" quartet. You've had two well-known quartets that you've written for....*

KJ: The hard part of writing for an orchestra is writing for an orchestra. The hard part of the quartet situation is not the writing at all—it is the question of how to make it a personal statement for everyone in the band. So that's a separate thing. In other words, if you take these four people and subtract even one and put a different person in it, the music I would write for *that* group should be different. And if anyone ever does a study on it, they'll see that the American quartet and the Scandinavian group and even the music I wrote for the trio at the Vanguard—I don't know if it will ever get recorded—but you could put them beside each other—and even the string music for Jan—and see how much consideration went into *who* was playing.

AL: *I think they sound very different....*

KJ: Yeah, but a lot of people attribute that to the players. Like they'll say positive or negative things about, "The Swedish band doesn't exert enough pull against Jarrett's free-flowing melodic lines." Or, "Charlie Haden and Paul Motian were always pulling and stretching things, and we think that challenged Jarrett's creativity." But what they're really hearing isn't quite what they're saying. What they're saying is true, but what they're hearing is how considerate I had to be to write for each of those bands. If I wrote the *Belonging* music with Charlie and Paul in the band, they couldn't be pulling in that way. The language wouldn't work. I'd have to stop and say, "Listen, Charlie, you gotta come down on 'one' here." If I wrote chords in a certain manner for Dewey, for example, and he was playing on changes, it would be a whole different sound. By Jan somehow changing his language, and the way the four of us played together, that worked. Someday I'm pretty sure that there'll be some serious studies of a lot of things, and I hope to be alive to see a few of them. (*Laughs.*) Just for fun, to see if it ever really happens. ●

ORNETTE COLEMAN AND PAT METHENY: SONGS OF INNOCENCE AND EXPERIENCE

By Art Lange

JUNE 1986

It's not easy to catch a comet by the tail, but every child has dreamed of doing it. No easier than palpably changing the world we live in for the better—yet some are able to do it, through science, through medicine, through poetry. Inspiring one's fellow man to achieve excellence and individuality through the sheer strength and single-mindedness of one's chosen endeavor is no easy task, but as the poet Robert Browning said, "A man's reach should exceed his grasp, or what's a heaven for?"

I had met and talked to Pat Metheny before this particular interview, and knew of his sincerity and openness. Not having met Ornette Coleman before, I was anxious and eager to make his acquaintance and speak with him. But, as I quickly learned, music is not the end result of Coleman's creativity; it is merely the means through which he aspires to inspire his fellow man. His responses to my questions often suggest the same Zen-like riddles that his music articulates so refreshingly.

Ornette Coleman and Pat Metheny came together earlier this year to document *Song X*, an album of sounds that seeks to, as the pair stated, create its own vocabulary, and the result is fully more than the sum of its quite remarkable parts, a mating of the innocence of experience, and the experience of innocence—songs that can't be named, only felt within the nebulous area where inspiration and imagination turn to creativity.

Art Lange: *Let's start with you, Pat. Where did you first encounter Ornette's music, and how did it affect you?*

Pat Metheny: One reason why I always felt good about growing up in a fairly isolated town is that there was no way to know what was "happening." I was 11, maybe 12, at the time, and in Lee's Summit, MO, where I grew up there was a TG&Y store—a dime store. They had a very small record collection—these were pretty much the only records available in town—and

they had a deal where you could buy three or four records for a dollar. One of Ornette's records happened to be in this batch of records, and I took it home and my instant reaction to it was that I loved it. It completely captured my imagination, and I didn't know that it was "jazz" or what it was. But the nice thing about being a little kid is that you either like something or you don't. Anyway, I responded to it immediately, and started to become a jazz fan about that time through my older brother Mike, who's a trumpet player. I started to get more of Ornette's records and always liked them: in fact, it's funny because by the time I was 13 I got a subscription to *Down Beat* and started to read that there was some kind of controversy about the way that they were playing and I couldn't figure out what they were talking about—I couldn't imagine why people would have a problem with the music, why they couldn't just see that these guys were having a problem with the music, they couldn't just see that these guys were having a blast playing this great music. I also remember that as time went on I'd keep going back to these records, and every time I would hear them they'd sound different—which is something you can't say about too many records—in fact, they *still* sound as *brand new* to me now as they did then.

AL: *Did hearing his music at such an early, impressionable age affect you differently as you grew older and began developing your own style?*

PM: Not in specific ways as much as just the general feeling I got from listening to Ornette and the musicians that played with him: they're playing the music that they felt strongest about with this incredible love and joy about it, without worrying about style, or what was current. It seemed very direct to me, and while, obviously, a large part of the music that I've done over the years stylistically is not close at all, there's always that same feeling I try to play with. For one thing, I'm trying to play whatever I'm going to play with the idea of making a melody. To me, Ornette's

music is about melody. There's a lot more going on besides that, of course, but it's about singing, and talking, and about the shape of the line—and to me it transcends style. It's really purely, and that, more than anything else, has been the inspiration I've drawn from listening to Ornette's music over the years.

AL: *There's an amazing oneness between the two of you on this record, not just in ensemble sound, but in intent, and I think it's because you both are lyrical players, you invent melodies as you improvise instead of playing riffs or soloing on chords.*

Ornette Coleman: Charlie Parker once said how he learned to play bebop based on minor sevenths—standard changes, C minor 7ths, or whatever, where you're working with A minor 7th or B minor 7th—and then you have two-beat changes, or four-beat changes, and when you have two-beat changes, with only two structures of four steps, if you start on the B side and you go to the A side…in other words, that's six whole steps on the one side and six whole steps on the other side—that makes the whole 12 tones. So in all chordal music, there's never been any movement that did not have chords with a whole step—but that whole step always had to lock into a key. Which means that if you take the best fake book in the world and look at all the keys, you'll find that maybe only three or four keys are used in the whole book. So you know what that was, it was ideas placed in a key, not a key placed in ideas.

The guitar is probably the most individual unison sound of all string instruments—I mean, it has a sound of its own no matter how many people play it, and everyone who plays it sounds like an individual unless they're playing clichéd ideas, which has to do with minor thirds and Major thirds. But lots of people play an instrument for position more than for playing what they *hear*, and that has nothing to do with position. Now Pat, he plays with *music*, not with position. When he plays, you don't have to worry about the key or the idea, you just have to worry is what you're playing *something*?

When I was forming Prime Time, the one thing that bothered me was that (in the past) I only played music using two horns and a bass and drums, and I wasn't doing it the best because I was given other things to do. But then James (Blood) Ulmer came to my house one day and studied me, and started playing a line on the guitar, and I found out that not only does a guitar sound like a full orchestra, but when you play a melody on guitar not only does it sound full, but it also sounds like it's moving the melody to another place—and it just happens to sound like that by the guys playing it. And I said, wait a minute—this is the way I hear the saxophone. I don't ever hear the saxophone in a key, or, if I'm playing an idea or a melody, I never hear the idea or the melody on the saxophone—I only hear it because someone had made

Pat Metheny and Ornette Coleman

Andy Freeberg

those melodies sound that way. I take those same notes and play a totally different melody.

So in other words I saw there was a relationship between the alto and the guitar. And when I started playing exactly whatever I'm playing with my band, and it's clear and it's forceful or whatever, and there was not one time when I felt inhibited or limited. And what's exciting to me about this session is even though it's only two horns—or two note instruments, everyone else is rhythm—it sounds like a zillion other things coming besides that. I put on a copy of the tape, and we were playing a song called "Video Games," and

honest to God, I said, "Wait a minute, something is wrong with the tape recorder.…" (*Laughs.*)

AL: *There's 12 people on that song.…*

OC: I said, "I need some batteries." That experience made me realize this idea that I've always had from the day I started to play music: that not only is it alive, but that it's endless and has no ego in it. There's something about creativity that every human being gets an equal s h a r e — a n d

feels as intently as quality of life. Because the quality of life doesn't tell you that you're doing something that you believe is naturally going to allow you to have the experience with your fellow man. And because of the way we grow up to respect each other, and survive, we have built all these images for someone to relate to without allowing them to *participate* in them. For instance, right now you can play any type of music you want, and take it to the audience, and if it's something that's *real* they're going to like it. You don't have to sound like me or Pat, but it is this type of playing that makes people know that's what's important.

PM: That *is* important.

OC: And the one thing that I respect about Pat—not because he's sitting here—is that he has the kind of insight and humanity that he has, and hasn't looked at his success as something that a person gave him: it's something that he actually made happen, and it's still happening. I think it's amazing to find a person with that kind of quality of humanism who wants not to worry about his success, but worry about how well he achieve what he believes. He has my highest respect as an artist and a human being.

AL: *Pat, in addition to playing with Ornette now, you previously worked with Sonny Rollins. Did you approach playing with those two saxists differently?*

PM: Well, they're quite different. This experience with Ornette…for me to say it was the high point of my experience as a musician would be an incredible understatement. You know, playing with Sonny was way up there too, because I've admired him so much, but this wasn't just a record date. We spent about three weeks working, eight hours a day, every day, really *hitting* it, and talking, and really getting to know each other musically and personally.

OC: The feeling I got when I heard the tape.…When John Coltrane decided to play from a strictly spiritual side, as on *Ascension*—he played strictly commercial music before that—and also when I first came to New York, my first band—that same spirit was on that tape, and yet it was *today's* experience. That's what is so fantastic about it. I mean, you hear horns, and ideas, but also something is compelling you to realize that there is something else going on besides what you're hearing, that's causing the things that we are doing to happen. You *hear* that. I haven't heard that in *any* musician in the last 20 years.

I mean, what people call "jazz," or they say, "You've got an electric band, you've got this and that"—they can say anything but it's not what you *have*, it's how you *sound* that's important. Like now, with Prime Time, my band is really into what I'm doing, but sometimes people read so many things and hear so many things that they hold back—and I'm always trying to get my band not to do that. But really, that same quality I've been seeking—the same thing that I heard when I first came to New York in '59, and when I heard Coltrane—is alive right now in '86, and the evidence of that to me is really on this record. Whatever the jazz person needs in this society—which means that you're an individual and you express yourself, whatever it is you feel conviction for—you don't worry about that, you stand on your own. Now that quality to me has been *tamed.* Everybody says, "Well, if I play some minor thirds here and some bebop here, I can get me a gig, and if I put on a green hat and have my ass out, I'll draw some people." (*Laughs.*) All of this has just been camouflage, to hide what the person really wants to do. And all of a sudden you realize you can't (hide it), its either there or it isn't.

That's the one thing that I never really felt bad about. People say, Well, this guy's still far out," or whatever. At least I realize that they didn't believe I was that way because that's how they felt about what I was doing, and I'm still trying....The thing that I really want to achieve in my lifetime is to inspire people to be individuals. That to me is it.

AL: *What brought the two of you together in the first place?*

OC: Well, Charlie Haden told me 10 years ago, "If I can only get you and Pat together; I'd get on my knees." And I said, "Charlie, you know it's gonna happen." And last year, he said he wanted to get us together, and I said, "You tell Pat we're gonna do it this year." Charlie has been the main person to get Pat and I together. The thing about it is I haven't really played a lot with my band, because of the fact that I don't try to get my band to support me, I try to support them. Therefore, when I do get my band going it's really what it is that

I'm actually trying to achieve, and they go with me. I've never felt I've wanted to just go out and try to survive because I had a name or I played. I only wanted to do things that are worthy of doing. And that's the thing I was really reluctant about in the past. Here's a guy who's very successful, and maybe the feeling wouldn't be right if I tried to call him and said, "Man, I want to do this and I want to do that." You know, I'm not even doing it with my own band, and I didn't feel right about that. The only thing I felt right about doing was something *musical* that was worthy of doing.

AL: *And Charlie convinced you....*

OC: Yes, Charlie Haden's something else, and he was right. The thing that was amazing was that when Pat came to New York to start rehearsing. I thought we should use Denardo too, and I'm sure Pat already had the idea for the people he wanted to use. So I said, "Well, let's just try it." So Denardo came over and we rehearsed, and Pat said, "Oh man, we gotta do this," so we want to Texas, and believe me, if you heard the stuff we did in Texas with Denardo and Charlie, you wouldn't believe it was Pat. He played more incredibly than I've ever heard. There's no words for it. And that's what you can do from someone *playing with you.* I mean, I always say that Denardo—not because he's my relative…well, he's really shy, but that night, what he and Pat did—they were playing *so good. (Laughter.)*

PM: Denardo is really something. That was an aspect of this whole project that I had not anticipated at all. I'd always enjoyed Denardo's playing , in particular with Prime Time, but it's hard to appreciate, in a way, the depth of what this thing is until you play with him…

OC: That's true.

PM: …because it's funny, he's got that certain thing drummers have of playing a lot—he's active all the time but he's never in your way. And it's *grooving*, but it's not grooving in the normal way; you can play any tempo, any feel, and it grooves.

OC: And that's the thing that I feel about the growth of how jazz evolved, those types of experiences when someone became aware of it. Like lots of critics say, "So-and-so doesn't swing," or "So-and-so can't do this here," because they're comparing yesterday with tomorrow. But the thing

about it is that when you hear something that makes you feel good, it doesn't matter what style to what it is, it's still having that same *quality*, and that's the thing I've always tried to avoid making a musician feel. I never told Denardo, "I want you to play *ching-ching-ching*," I never told how I wanted him to sound so *I* could sound a certain way. I never told him since he was playing as a kid. That's the same way I realized when you are playing anyone, if they have something to say, the moment you tell them what to do they can't say that anymore; they feel afraid that they're going to lose their job. I've been fired many times because the guy didn't tell me to play and I thought he wanted me to play what I *could* play and then I found out he didn't. (*Laughter.*) He wanted me to play this other thing.

So what I'm saying, with the music that's called jazz, with all the incredible musicians that've played, today there's no image to carry that individual feeling into a mass expression. And there's no reason why: you have maybe 100,00 rock 'n' roll guys—why do you have that, because they're all inspiring? Right? Why couldn't people be inspired to be more creative?

AL: *Has listening to Ornette over the years—as a saxophonist and composer—influenced you as a guitarist, Pat?*

PM: On a number of levels, very much so. One thing about guitar playing in jazz is that very few people have transcended the problem of dynamics, and Ornette is a classic example—he never plays any two notes in a row at the same volume. And to me that's what makes it feel so good. He's a major influence in terms of phrasing—and it's difficult to do that on a guitar, and that's what makes the so-called traditional "jazz guitar sound" not that appealing to al lot of listeners. It's very easy for the guitar to become monodynamic, and in listening to Ornette's playing I definitely got a lot of good lessons of how to make the instrument breathe, so that the phrases fall into a natural *musical* way, not the way they happen to lie on the instrument. I think that a lot of what Ornette plays is not saxophone music, it's music, and that's a quality that *all* instrumentalists should strive for—to transcend the instrument, and as he says, play ideas and sounds and thoughts rather than a pattern on your instrument.

AL: *But at the same time, since the saxophone is an instrument that you have to breathe into to get a sound out of, there are certain limits due to its physical nature, which you don't have on a guitar or piano, that helps define its phrasing; it's like you have to stop and take a breath when you talk.*

OC: In the Western world, whether it's American or European music, everyone uses the same 12 notes. And as people have been able to define their sensitivity through those 2 notes, calling it phrasing or dynamics or whatever, to me what they represented is the equivalent of gravity allowing things in the sky to be where they are in relation to the earth. In other words those notes to me are the true emotional gravity. Which tells me that when you play an instrument, if someone plays a certain note, whether you like it or not, it will move you if the gravity of it is in tune with your emotional state. We are all connected to creation, and we were connected to creation long before finding out we had talent—that came second. We are not creation: we're the talent that's trying to express what creation means, and what effect it has on your nerves, on your emotions. Cyril Scott said that it took Europeans 7,000 years to accept middle C, for them to agree what middle C sounded like, so that the Germans and French and everybody said, "Okay, we're gonna use this as C." And imagine where they were before that. (*Laughter.*) Imagine the musicologists who designed the 12 intervals—when you think of the 12 months, and the 12 tribes of Israel, and all that. That's why I love Buckminster Fuller so much. And all of that means just the components that go into the emotions that creativity passes through you. But that doesn't mean that because they are like that they can only be used one way. Notes are like water—they take the shape of whoever's using them. Your C can make someone cry but someone else's C can make someone laugh. That's the beauty of creation, that we all don't have to be on one line to get the same results.

PM: Taking that one step further is the fact that it has nothing to do with "style." There's too much talk about style—and it's

something that effects us as musicians on such a profound level: that's how you're defined within the musical community, what "style" you play.

OC: When America gets to the point that they won't have to use styles to have people express what they do in a category, then the creativeness in *all* popular music is going to grow. When you think of rock 'n' roll, rhythm 'n' blues, they're using the same notes but they say, "We're playing this, we're playing that." But in Europe, years ago it was just what your name was. If your name was Jim, it was go and listen to Jim—not Jim plays the blues. It was just Jim doing what he's doing. If that was the case in America, we'd all be a lot better. For instance, I never heard anyone say "white music," but I hear everyone say "black music"—and I was black before there was music. That's kind of a drag, and has nothing to do with music.

So what I'm saying is that those styles limit even the person who created the concept. And if the people involved in creative expression had the position that the people in NASA have, their technology, all would be outdated. When you think of the shuttle *Challenger*, it was a shame, those people went up and something happened, but technology is not restricting them. They don't call it style, they call it progress. Here, you take Robert Johnson and someone else who's playing blues, and they're gonna say, "Well, this is a new style," maybe that guy didn't have style then—that was *him*. Someone took that and stylized it and made someone else imitate it and someone kept that alive…in fact, I think that that's one of the most inhuman things to do, to stop growth because you want someone else to be remembered. I was telling someone the other day that Mozart is more alive than some people who are playing who *are* alive, and yet when you saw the movie *Amadeus*, you think he's dead. But Mozart is the most-played composer in the Western world who is deceased—and that's just because of a style, not him. And when it comes to classical music, there are many performers and composers that deserve notice for what they're doing. The points is, we are all victims of the past trying to eliminate the future. And you can't do that. ●

MICHAEL BRECKER: ON IMPULSE
● ● ● ● ● ● ● ● ● ● ● ● ● ● ● ● ● ● ● ●
By Bill Milkowski
JUNE 1987

The man is revered by his peers and idolized by music students who painstakingly pore over transcriptions of his incandescent solos. And they've got plenty of material to draw from. His prodigious output over the past two decades is astounding. As his bio puts it, "His appearance on nearly 400 albums constitutes a virtual pantheon of popular sound."

Michael Brecker's distinctive, emotionally charge tenor sax first made its presence felt worldwide in the context of Dreams, an adventurous fusion outfit he formed in 1970 with older brother Randy on trumpet, Billy Cobham on drums, Will Lee on bass, and John Abercrombie on guitar. They recorded two albums (that still hold up today) for Columbia before disbanding in 1973.

From 1975 to 1980, Michael and Randy team up as The Brecker Brothers, releasing six slick (and very popular) albums on Arista. Steps Ahead was born in 1979 when vibist Michael Mainieri invited Brecker and some friends (keyboardist Don Grolnick, drummer Steve Gadd, bassist Eddie Gomez) down to Brecker's Seventh Avenue South club for some informal gigs. A Japanese producer in the audience liked what he heard, invited the group to play in his country, and the rest is history—three albums on Elektra, personnel changes, a gradual shift in direction toward the electronic side of things, followed by wide acceptance both home and abroad.

And now, at long last, comes Michael's *pièce de résistance*—a dream project on Impulse, his debut as a leader. And check out the company he's keeping: Jack DeJohnette, Charlie Haden, Kenny Kirkland, Pat Metheny. A zillion stars for the sideman alone.

I've long admired Michael Brecker's gutsy tenor voice. I dug his funk 'n' blues chops with the Brecker Brothers (particularly on their 1979 live album, *Heavy Metal Be-Bop*). I was mesmerized by his moody sax on the evocative *Cityscape*, a luscious though overlooked orchestral project written and arranged for him by

Claus Ogerman in 1981 on Warner Bros. I was awed by his application of the Steiner EWI (Electronic Wind Instrument) in concert last year with the touring edition of Steps Ahead (guitarist Mike Stern, drummer Steve Smith, bassist Darryl Jones, vibist Mainieri) and on their last Elektra album, *Magnetic*.

I used to get a kick out of hearing his raspy tenor in the house band on "Saturday Night Live" during the '83–'84 seasons (and seeing his cameo appearance in Eddie Murphy's hilarious "James Brown in a Hot Tub" skit). Hell, I even dug his fiery tenor work on all those cheesy disco albums that Vanguard put out in the mid seventies under the collective name The Players Association. (Sorry, Mike—but don't be embarrassed. We've all got to pay the rent somehow.)

But all of that—the various band projects, the sideman projects, the endless studio sessions with everyone from John Lennon to Martha & The Muffins to James Taylor to Frank Sinatra to Bruce Springsteen—pales in comparison to the heights he hits on this impressive Impulse debut, *Michael Brecker*. With all due respect to his previous efforts, this here is the real deal. It's as if he's waited all his life to make this album. It's that special. Far more than just product, this album is full of passion and soars to peaks of inspiration. It's the crowning achievement in al illustrious career.

From the glorious, gospel-tinged shouts from Michael's horn on the album's opener, "Sea Glass," to the all-out burn of "Syzygy" (with Jack DeJohnette's incredible display of just why he's considered number one), this album surges with energy and daring. And yet it's full of such nuance and subtlety to send chills up your spine. Check out Charlie Haden's playing on the melancholy ballad, "The Cost Of Living," a perfect example of "less is more." As Michael says of Haden's playing on that tune, "Charlie can make me cry with one note. We wanted to use this as a vehicle for him, and I have to say that Charlie's solo here is one of the high points of the album for me."

I talked with Michael about this very personal, very revealing project in the solitude of his loft located in the Chinatown district of Manhattan. Oddly, I found him to be uncommonly shy and unassuming for someone with such a big rep. (And I thought all chopmeisters were

swaggering braggadocios. Oh well, so much for that theory).

Bill Milkowski: *First, tell me about the genesis of the album.*

Michael Brecker: It came about, I guess, from the fact that I felt like I was finally ready to do it. This year I felt ready to make a record under my own name, probably for the first time in my life. I had always shied away from it previously or had worked in collaborative-type efforts, either with my brother Randy or with Michael Mainieri and Peter Erskine. I guess I never really felt that I merited doing an album. I felt afraid to do it, really. But the feeling that I wanted to do something took hold this year, followed by various feelers from different record companies.

So I was approached by Ricky Shultz at Impulse. Initially, it scared me, just the aura of Impulse. Well, not scared me—I was awed by it, in lieu of the rich history of the label—Trane, Sonny Rollins, and everybody.

BM: *And he immediately talked about a jazz record, as opposed to a fusion album?*

MB: Right. We talked about doing a jazz record, which is really what I wanted to do. So I started batting around in my mind certain rhythm sections—people I wanted to play with, who I felt would really create the right musical environment. I had an association with Pat, Charlie, and Jack from years back, beginning with Pat's record *80/81*. We subsequently did a tour, which opened up a door for me. And it's remained opened. I just hadn't really had a chance to pursue that type of playing since then. I guess I hadn't taken quite as far as I wanted. I wanted an opportunity to take it further, particularly with those guys—and with Kenny, whose playing I admire very much.

BM: *Music in which the rhythm section opens up a bit?*

MB: Yes. Where there's a lot of space. It's a way of playing that's really captured by these guys. Where it's open and just seems like the harmonic and rhythmic possibilities are infinite. And there's a warmth that the four of them are able to generate that's very appealing to me. So beyond that feeling, I had to look compositionally at how to structure this, to capture the great talent of these four gentlemen. Their talent at spontaneity and swinging—structure that in a way that wouldn't tie their hands, yet not have it be

like just another free music album. That was the challenge. So I got together with Don Grolnick, who produced the album, and we had a lot of brainstorming sessions. He'd come over every day and we'd write together. And Mike Stern was also taking part in this. We'd just toss ideas around and eventually came up with the tunes.

BM: *It's very different than Steps Ahead, which is about kinetic energy—like being on a roller-coaster that goes from point A to Z, and once you get on you can't get off. But this flows in so many different directions, and everyone in the band seems to be telepathically linked.*

MB: True, very true. Really, all four of them almost transcend their instruments. They play with such musicality and originality that they transcend the difficulty or the limitations of their instruments.

BM: *Is there an intellectual process connected to this quality of openness, like an actor who draws upon method acting techniques to get through a scene?*

MB: Doesn't seem to be with me. It's not an intellectual exercise, although when I'm playing is laying in a way that feels natural. But the emotional part, really, has a life of its own. It's almost like the feelings get in touch with me rather than me getting in touch with them. And it just comes out in the music.

BM: *Many musicians I've talked to over the years have spoken about the music playing them rather than vice versa. Are you interested in that connection between music and spirituality?*

MB: Well, yes I am. And at the risk of sounding pretentious—that feeling that you described is something that I've felt quite often, particularly recently. It sounds kind of pseudo-spiritual, but I feel when I'm really at my best that I'm not really playing at all. It's almost like it takes on a life of its own. And those moments seem to be coming more often now than they used to. It's a very exhilarating feeling but it seems to be something that, at this point, I have no control over. So I just try to move forward—keep up with technique, keep listening, trying to expand and learn, play as much as possible, and just try to have a good attitude. And the rest is really—I don't know. But that does happen.

BM: *Robert Fripp's analogy is "Getting a visit from the Good Fairy." Kind of like group astral projection.*

MB: I can definitely relate to that. It works

the same way with me, depending on the musicians that are playing at the time. For instance, I went out on tour recently with the John Abercrombie Quartet, and we really had some high musical experiences. There were moments where we just—we were so much in tune. It's the same exact thing you're describing. It almost felt like we were being played by some other force.

BM: *I had heard that Pat brought all his hardware to the session, so I was kind of expecting* Son of Song X. *But he plays so subdued on the album, like Jim Hall or Wes Montgomery. And you seem to be flexing your Coltrane muscles. Do I detect a tribute of sorts?*

MB: Pat did bring his Synclavier to the date, but we ended up not finding a need for it. He gets an incredible sound without it, and he plays with such lyricism. He's amazing. As for me, there was an element of tribute in making this album. Just the fact that I had the chance to record on Impulse really means something to me. I didn't take that lightly. That immediately put me in a particular frame of mind. I was tempted to do the techno thing because I've been very wrapped up in learning the EWI and experimenting with it. But I had to separate that. I wanted to really try and capture a mood on this record and stay with it, not to try to throw in everything but the kitchen sink—10 million sampled sounds thrown in just for fun. For me, it was question of less is more, of making an album that would really hold together as a complete statement, which my favorite albums do. And I wanted it to sustain interest, be able to be listened to a lot of times, so you can always hear new things. I really do enjoy the highly techno records on a lot of levels. But I can't listen to them a lot. It's almost like there's no mystery—not a lot left to the imagination. My senses are assaulted sometimes with just this barrage of huge megasounds, which I've been guilty of doing myself. I didn't want to go in that direction on this album—especially not for Impulse.

BM: *How did growing up in Philadelphia affect you?*

MB: Randy and I really didn't play that much together until he went away to school. When he'd come back home, we'd jam and put on some concerts. Meanwhile, I was jamming a lot with Eric Gravitt, a

drummer who played with McCoy Tyner and Weather Report. He was a tremendous influence on me. Eric really turned me on to Trane and McCoy. He taught me a lot about playing. I used to do a lot of that in Philly,

jamming with just tenor and drums. And I'd play a lot of drums myself, reversing the roles just to find out what drummers are comfortable with. In fact, at one point I had decided I was going to become a drummer and seriously study it. I can get around pretty good on the drums. I've studied Elvin's style. But I abandoned the notion of becoming a drummer when I heard Billy Cobham with the Mahavishnu Orchestra. I realized then that I'd better stick to the saxophone. But because of my experience with playing drums in Philadelphia and during the first few years I was living in New York, I'd gained a better understanding of rhythm. So I feel very close to drummers, which is why it was such a great thrill for me to do that free duet thing with Jack at the beginning of "Syzygy." That was very special.

BM: *Did you have a mentor in Philly?*

MB: I studied with Vince Trombetta, who really taught me how to play the saxophone. He was the sax player on "The Mike Douglas Show" for the whole 16-year run of that show. Other than that, I just picked up what I could from hearing people. I used to see Sonny Fortune a lot around Philly. Of course, Coltrane was a tremendous influence. And when I moved to New York in the late sixties I started

hanging around a lot of saxophonists, trying to absorb as much as I could from players like Dave Liebman and Steve Grossman. The whole loft scene was happening then—a lot of jammin' at people's houses. That's really how I slowly learned how to play.

BM: *How did you begin experimenting with electrifying the sax?*

MB: For *Heavy Metal Be-Bop* I was using some electronic things on the tenor. I had been looking for something at the time because I felt that sonority-wise the tenor wasn't able to blend with the rhythm section, which was completely electronic. So I experimented with some electronic outboard devices to put on the tenor, but I didn't really find anything I liked. I found a couple of boxes made by Electro-Harmonix that I thought worked pretty well, but I was never really happy. It never felt right to me. After spending all those years of working on a good saxophone sound and then putting it through a bunch of processors—it felt weird. The sax has such a gorgeous sound. I always felt it cheapened the sound to put a box on it. Eventually, I just gave up on it.

BM: *So now the Steinerphone EWI is the answer to that dilemma.*

MB: Yes, because it's a departure from the saxophone. It's an instrument unto itself. Very different from taking a sax and electrifying it and expecting it to sound good.

BM: How did you meet Nyle Steiner?

MB: I first heard of him through Dave Boroff, a wonderful saxophone player who's now playing in the house band on the Joan Rivers show. He had a working model of the Steinerphone at his house, and he demonstrated it for me. I was impressed but not convinced. I actually called Nyle and asked him if he could make me one. He said yes, and over a year later he sent one to me. I had almost forgotten about it. The instrument has since gone through different stages of development and has recently been purchased by Akai. So the new Akai EWI-1000 should be on the market by the time this article comes out. They'll be very similar to the original, except for a few new features will be added, including programmability.

BM: *When you first got the Steinerphone, did you have to adjust to new fingering positions?*

MB: The fingering positions are basically identical to a saxophone. The main difference being it's touch sensitive, so there's no moving keys, which is hard to adjust to at first because saxophone players are taught to rest their fingers on the keys. But on this, it would activate a sound. So you have to be very careful what you touch. It requires a lot of accuracy both in fingering and in tonguing. The horn is attached to a suitcase-type container with all the electronics, and there's a set of eight rollers on the back of the instrument for making octave leaps. Whatever roller I'm touching determines the octave I'm playing in. So by rolling your thumb, you can make incredibly quick octave leaps. It's really a fascinating instrument. Nyle is a wonderful trumpet player with a wide background in electronics. He's coming from a very musical place, and he's combined his musicality with his electronics background to come up with an extremely musical instrument. [*Note: Steiner also invented what he calls an EVI, or Electronic Valve Instrument, for trumpeters.*]

BM: *What do you particularly like about the EWI?*

MB: The unique thing about Nyle's box is the warmth of the sounds you can get. You can make some gorgeous acoustic-like sounds—alto flute, violin, shakuhachi, a harmonica that sounds like Stevie Wonder. They're organic sounds instead of cold, brittle synthesizer sounds. That's the idea for me. It's got to sound pleasing or I just don't like it. And there's virtually no tracking problems with this instrument. I have this Steinerphone MIDI-ed to an Oberheim Xpander for multiple voicings and to a Yamaha TX7 and an Akai S900 digital sampler. The Steiner box and the Oberheim are actually quicker than the TX7, which has to interpret breath and bending via MIDI. So it takes a while for the note to trigger through that. But otherwise, no tracking problems at all. ●

CHARLIE HADEN: SEARCH FOR FREEDOM

By Howard Mandel

SEPTEMBER 1987

Charlie Haden is a compulsive, though hardly innocent, idealist. He's the champion of the Liberation Music Orchestra (arrangements by Carla Bley), director of the romantically *noir*-ish Quartet West, instigator of the now-dormant Old and New Dreams. Haden at age two was singing and yodeling in regional daily broadcasts of the "Haden Family Radio Show" from small towns in Missouri, Iowa, and Nebraska, is one link between our vanishing rural culture and today's pan-ethnic, improvisatory jazz; at age 50, he's the freely swinging but most secure tether for Ornette Coleman's wildest flights into space, the acoustic guy central to Pat Metheny's highly amplified world, the hard-nosed realist who's prodded the impressionistic pianisms of Keith Jarrett.

Oh yes, Haden plays the bass violin, a 140-year-old amber instrument which he leans into as though the wood whispers a secret message from its core. Sometimes he holds it far away, as a square dance partner *do-si-dos*—sometimes he bends low, as though his bass embraces and comforts *him*, then he plucks at the taut gut strings beneath its bridge to wring out its cries. Haden played bass in mid-fifties West Coast after-hours sessions, a music school dropout immersed in drugs, and played bass when Coleman's iconoclastic quartet stormed New York; he's played bass in Cuba with his Orchestra, and in Los Angeles with the hardcore Minutemen, also opposite Firehouse and his teenage son Joshua's Treacherous Jaywalkers. Charlie's traveled the globe to concertize with Brazilian Egberto Gismonti and Swedish Jan Garbarek, to solo on Gavin Bryar's Adagio for Chamber Orchestra and Bass Violin and Jarrett's "Arbor Zena," to record with Michael Brecker, Henry Butler, Joe Henderson, and Adam Makowicz, to team with Ed Blackwell, Billy Higgins, Paul Motian, and Al Foster, to hang with Scott LaFaro, Paul Bley, Tony Scott, Denny Zeitlin, and Hampton Hawes. He plays bass with a dedication and intensity of

feeling that marks an artist in any medium. If you enroll in California Institute of the Arts, you might attend the classes he teaches as director of jazz studies; if you're in Santa Monica, you might even hear him guest hosting Tom Schnabel's wake-up show, "Morning Becomes Eclectic."

"I do that once or twice a month, whenever I can," says Haden, who loved to perform in his parents' daily program and was starting to cover Nat King Cole's hits on Omaha TV when he caught the mild polio that paralyzed half his face and ended his singing career at 15. "I play music that I think is important for people to hear, as I do in my class sometimes. A Billie Holiday song, or something by a classical composer that I feel close to. Almost everything Bach composed, and special things—mostly adagios—by Ravel, Fauré, Shostakovich, Rachmaninoff, and Mahler. I hardly ever play anything I'm on, but I bring lots of hillbilly music—the Carter Family, Delmore Brothers—and Paul Robeson, Elisabeth Schwarzkopf, French folk songs from the Auvergne."

Eclectic, indeed, but not a surprising range for someone who's curiosity impelled him to borrow his older brother Jim's bass, and improvise by ear with records by Dizzy Gillespie , Lionel Hampton, Stan Kenton, Art Pepper, Shorty Rogers, and the Jazz At The Philharmonic All-Stars. Haden's early, more formal bass training was traumatic for him. Though by his account the teacher was encouraging, he recalls, "I'd never read music I was confronted with reading these notes, the more I felt it didn't have anything to do with what I wanted to do, and that there must be an easier way to do this. Up to that point, music to me was just my ear, and hearing. Putting it out, connecting it with your insides, your brain and heart, and singing. Listening, not thinking about theory or fundamentals. Reading was a shock to me. But I got over it."

Enough to win a scholarship to Oberlin ("I remember a Dave Brubeck album recorded there, that attracted me"), though Haden didn't follow through. After all, he was playing for C&W star Red Foley on a program called "Ozark Jubilee," and getting ego strokes when Nashville cats such as guitarist Hank Garland liked what he did in jams. Learning of West Lake College of Modern Music, a Los Angeles institution, through the pages of *Down Beat*, Haden saved what he earned selling shoes, and left Forsyth, Missouri, for good.

"I found out, as I started to take classes, that it wasn't what I thought it was going to be. There were good teachers there—Dick Grove, for instance, he's got a whole school now. But I started playing gigs at night, so I couldn't make classes in the morning. And I realized I wanted to learn about improvisation, because that was my love. I was learning about it at night, working with good musicians."

Sonny Clark, Hampton Hawes, Frank Morgan, Dexter Gordon, Sonny Criss, Red Mitchell, Les McCann, Art Pepper, Elmo Hope, Gerry Mulligan were all on the scene. Haden developed his technique, it seems through isolated woodshedding. "The same way you develop your mind, your feelings about politics, or about music," he explains. "I never felt I had a choice—all I thought about was playing, first with records, then with musicians. Your sound develops after you ears tell you, 'You're gonna play better if you sound good.' And so you learn how you want the instrument to sound. I loved the bass so much, when I heard Ray Brown play it, or Max Bennett with Kenton's band, it was a real thrill."

But besides the bass' sound, there was something Haden found out he wanted to say. "I was playing all the jazz tunes, Bird's tunes, and the standards in jam sessions, but sometimes I would play a solo and I wanted to not have to play in the chord changes of the song," he admits bashfully.

"Every time I did that, people would get confused. They wouldn't know where I was, and I'd have to play melody to bring them back

Mitchell Seidel

into the song. But I didn't want to play the changes. I kept encountering that, especially as they played the same tunes over and over—you know, 'Stella By Starlight'...."

Haden met then-pianist Don Cherry and drummer Billy Higgins around this time, as well as Paul Bley—"We tried some stuff like free improvisation; he had a signal he'd give when he wanted to play solo piano, so we'd stop." He was told about a player with a white plastic alto who sounded like no one else, and so he recognized Ornette Coleman by his reputation when appeared at the Hague Club, though he was asked to stop after blowing half a chorus.

"His horn looked like a toy, but this cat played sounds that put everybody in another state of mind. The whole sound and direction changed; it was like someone had said, '*This* is the way it should be.' I met Ornette at the next Sunday morning Hillcrest session, and said, 'Man, I really like the way you play.' Ornette said, 'Really?' I said, 'Yeah, I hope we get a chance to play together.' He said, 'Well,

let's go.' I said, 'Now?' We got in his car, a little green and white Studebaker, and drove to his apartment. Opened the door, and you didn't step on the rug, you stepped on music. It was everywhere—on the floor, dressers, bed couch. I unpacked my bass, he picked up a score, put it on the music stand, and said, 'Let's play this tune. I've written out the changes, but you don't have to play the changes. Just play.'"

It was music to Haden's ears. "Ornette told me he worked at a department store, in the freight elevator—that's where he practiced. He told me he didn't have enough work, because wherever he played, they asked him to stop, and when he auditioned for a gig, he never got it. I was thinking how brilliant and beautiful the sound he had was. The intervals he was playing were intervals I'd never heard in my life—and really inspiring to hear, because they went forth with the ideas I was trying to play and hadn't been able to let out. Ornette let them out in a natural way; he wasn't uptight, so I wasn't uptight. I hadn't had any idea what I was doing when I heard this other way of playing, but playing with Ornette it didn't matter. It happened in a natural way, and that was the way it was supposed to be.

"I asked him, 'Do you *want* me to play these changes?' He said, 'Use them as a guide.' *I* really feel that improvisation should be a way that you're not restricted—inspiration shouldn't be restricted. You can be inspired by another composer's chord changes, but if your inspiration goes beyond that, you shouldn't be restricted. So I said to him, 'That's what I really feel. But I always thought I was violating some rules whenever I felt that.' He said, 'Forget it.' I said, 'Great.' Imagine—somebody saying it's alright now! I hadn't slept—it had been an all night jam session—but we played all day long."

Coleman wasn't Haden's sole inspiration—bassist Scott LaFaro roomed with Charlie on his two trips to Los Angeles, practicing from wake-up on, while Haden chased less productive pursuits. "I'd come home and, Scotty would be on the bed, upset, saying, 'I'll never be good enough.' He was a perfectionist, though. I'd tell him how great he was, be wouldn't be satisfied. All the young bass players were trying to play as he did. I always admired his playing very much, even though we expressed ourselves in different ways. I never even knew if he liked playing, until Paul Motian, who was close with Scotty, told me that when they were playing with Bill Evans at the Vanguard and I was with Ornette at the Five Spot, Scotty insisted at intermission that Paul put on his overcoat to hear 'this fantastic bass player who's with Ornette'." Haden beams with boyish pride; his apple cheeks bop higher, and his always-intense eyes brighten.

"I've never really taken jobs I don't want," he conceded. "There *was* a period in New York in the mid sixties, when my family was getting larger—even though I was playing with Tony Scott, Ornette, and Keith, I had to think about extra money. So I joined Radio Registry, made studio sessions, did jingles, practiced electric bass so I could gig on that. But I'd come home depressed, sad, sick, and nauseous. I felt I was perpetuating values, spiritually and musically, I didn't believe in. I felt I was aiding and abetting the enemy. I realized I was miserable, so I decided never to do that again. I've been lucky, able to follow my convictions about playing with people I feel close to. I've met musicians, and I feel close to the way they hear my music and the way they see life—that's how it always happens."

Some of those people are unlikely, and were themselves surprised at Haden's breadth ability. Haden played with Roy Eldridge one night at the Half Note, "And he said, 'How can you play music with both Ornette Coleman and me?'" Haden

recalls. "'Easy,' I said. 'You're both playing beautiful music.' And Roy cracked up!" Haden recorded on Impulse, *The College Concert of Pee Wee Russell and Henry "Red" Allen*; he also worked with Benny Goodman. Even progressive musicians wondered about his associations.

"In '66 I was working with Tony Scott at the Dom, five sets a night, 9 p.m. to 4 a.m. And every night after the first set he'd ask me to sit down with him, have a coffee, then regular as clockwork, Tony would say, 'So what *were* you cats doing with Ornette?'" Few of Coleman's colleagues are so able to analyze his ways.

"It's only that we had a desperate urgency to create something that never was before," explains Haden. "Ornette and I used to talk about making music as though it were something completely new, as though we'd never heard music before. Only a few musicians are inspired in this way. And you know, the more I became sure my mission in this respect, the closer it brought me to my reverence for the chord structure. The inspiration I developed for playing *on* the changes opened up. It's brought me closer to all the possibilities of playing on changes, with renewed energy."

Haden is usually generous with his energy. This summer, besides touring to support his Quartet West debut on the revitalized Verve label (featuring smooth, bluesy saxist Ernie Watts, and arrestingly original pianist Alan Broadbent, and the inimitable Billy Higgins), and working Europe in trio with Joe Henderson and Al Foster, he is preparing the new Liberation Orchestra repertoire: a song for Sandino; a spiritual dedicated to Dr. Martin Luther King, Medgar Evers, and Malcolm X, to be sung by the Harlem Boys Choir; the African National Congress anthem; "Tale of the Tornado" by Cuban composer Silvio Rodriguez. He's scoring an hour-long documentary directed by Academy Award winner Deborah Shaffer, based on the book *Fire from the Mountain: The Making of a Sandinista*, by Omar Cabezas. He hopes to record the adagio Gavin Bryars composed for him, which was performed in England this past summer. He's firm about spending time with his 15-year-old triplet daughters, "so I get to know each

one—Rachel, Petra, and Tanya—as a distinct person." Haden's appearing ever more frequently on other people's dates; there's a trio LP with pianist Fred Hirsch and drummer Joey Baron on Sunnyside, the new Michael Brecker album and an Adam Makowicz date on which Charlie and Dave Holland formed a mutual admiration society.

But Haden's first love—he has no choice—remains personal self-expression, and his musical allegiance—following his responsibility to himself—remains with the man who threw off the bonds on jazz improvisation. Ornette Coleman's return to his "original" quartet on the album *In All Languages*, and to his "legendary" quartet (Blackwell subbing for Higgins) in performance at Town Hall during the JVC festival, is a move Haden's long sought. It was his hope in the seventies that Coleman would play with Old And New Dreams. It was his aim, introducing Coleman to Pat Metheny, to interest Ornette in ensembles besides Prime Time. And at the sold-out, gloriously received JVC Festival concert, Haden says, "I was in heaven, playing with the Quartet. Everything was perfect. The standing ovations when he came onstage, before we played a note. The standing ovations afterwards. I went offstage, and told my girlfriend that she looked so beautiful—that combined with the music made me the happiest guy in the world. I didn't want it to end, I wanted to keep playing. And I said that to Ornette. Ornette said, 'Yeah. We'll keep playing.' I think he's going to keep the Quartet, and Prime Time, and do some other things, too. That's what so beautiful about Ornette: his unpredictability."

What's predictable about Charlie Haden: he'll be playing the bass. ●

STEVE LACY: THE INTERVIEW

By Kevin Whitehead
DECEMBER 1987

Composer and soprano saxophonist Steve Lacy blew into New York from Paris to begin a North American tour with his old pal, pianist Mal Waldron. The previous week he'd been in Holland to observe the Instant Composers Pool's twentieth anniversary; he, Derek Bailey, Anthony Braxton, and George Lewis had helped their Dutch comrades celebrate with some rousing free play. A little while before that, Lacy had been in Italy to accompany silent films by Georges Melies, Buster Keaton, D.W. Griffith, and Fernand Leger.

While in New York, Lacy was reading a biography of T.S. Eliot (who'd pointed out that no artist can work outside "the tradition," because the tradition will stretch to accommodate anything artists do). He's set Herman Melville's last poem to music for a new album; his song cycle *The Way*, a favorite of his, is based on *The Tao* of Lao-Tzu.

Steve Lacy has an eye for visual art, is well-read and well-traveled. (He's lived in Paris since the late sixties). Patiently answering an interviewer's sometimes arcane questions, he has an elegantly aloof air and speaks in an urbane manner, both strikingly reminiscent of Duke Ellington.

Melies, Melville, Lao-Tzu, Duke: Steve Lacy sees culture as a continuum—just as his cosmopolitan music resists easy categorizing.

That new album, *Momentum*, is on RCA/Novus; it's his first new American record in 10 years, not 25 as everyone is claiming. (They've forgotten 1977's *Raps*, on Adelphi.) "It felt like just another record," Lacy says—meaning he attaches no great hopes to *Momentum*, despite its implicitly optimistic title, other than that it will lead to more work for his Paris-based sextet. He hasn't soft-pedaled their sound for mass consumption; it's the usual dourly eerie mix of jazz sonorities, Irene Aebi's art singing, and ping-pong rhythms. (Lacy played ping-pong as a kid; the little crescent scar on his forehead is an old paddle wound).

The opening salvo aside, we tried to concentrate on Lacy in the eighties—his earlier career (including his dixieland apprenticeship and stints with Monk and Cecil Taylor) was neatly synopsized by Lee Jeske in the May '80 *DB*. But Lacy's past and present are interwoven, as hard to separate as his myriad influences.

Kevin Whitehead: *Your 1954 first recordings with Dick Sutton were recently issued. Have you had a chance to listen to them?*

Steve Lacy: I heard a few recently over the radio in France. Wow, what can you say about your youth except it's beautiful? When you're young you can do things that you can't do  later on. There's a certain kind of lightness there that I appreciated; one would like to be that light again 30 years later. But there's also a certain unity through the years, a similar kind of approach, a something that doesn't change. I think the most important thing (about one's style) is the thing that doesn't change. the sound is there, in a way, from the beginning. Or it's not there.

KW: *Your lean, no-vibrato sound was already there; did you adopt it deliberately to avoid sounding like Sidney Bechet?*

SL: Partially, but I wasn't running away from Bechet yet, at that point. It's really a technical solution—an effort not to bullshit. With an instrument like the soprano, you have to do something about the difficulty of control. One way is to cover it up with a vibrato. Another way is to remove the vibrato and come to terms scientifically with it, let it be heard.

KW: Okay, enough history. Can you talk about the process of improvising on your

Hyou Vielz

own tunes? *What goes on in your head when you improvise?*

SL: Each piece is designed to improvise in a slightly different way, to promote a different kind of play. One might have a fixed scale; many have specific scales unique to that piece. Some have a fixed vamp, a rhythm, a dance, a steady beat; some don't. Some have a wide-open part and a completely nailed-down part; some are completely wide-open. there's a variety; in fact the whole idea is not to have a generality, to have things that go in a wide variety of directions.

KW: *On text-settings, do you think about the words while soloing?*

SL: Of course. The text is very important—the composition came from that, and the interpretation, the improvisation, the elaboration, wouldn't be too far from the nature of those words. It couldn't be.

KW: *Are you talking about imagery, or speech rhythms, or both?*

SL: I'm talking about…signification. Story. The story of that piece, the way you tell it. a piece is a thing made in advance so as to be told later.

KW: *Is a solo an equivalent of the story a text tells?*

SL: It's a story of itself. Of you get up there with a saxophone, you play something and then you stop—that was your story. All music is about something. Maybe you couldn't pin it down in words but that's okay. Music is a *thing*, it is a substance.

KW: *Listening to your solos I sometimes get the feeling I'm eavesdropping on someone's mental processes. The soundtrack to you thinking—whew, that's pretty cosmic. Let me put it another way.*

SL: No, I like that, I like that. (*Laughs.*) It is sort of like eavesdropping in a way. In fact, recently in Italy I had a few jobs playing with silent films, and that is a sort of eavesdropping. Watching and trying to accompany something and not get in the way, to be discreet and to help it, is a very, very stealthy position, a very interesting job.

KW: *You often use visual sources for inspiration—as in "Coastline"—and have mentioned the resemblance between your line and a painter's.*

SL: Yes, I've done a whole series of pieces, various kinds of lines, "Coastline" is a painting in a way—it's a line drawing of a particular coastline in Italy that I know very well. It's a way of painting with music something that you see. One of my efforts always has been to make music that's so clear you can see it.

KW: *You've mentioned Paul Klee as a painter you feel affinity for.*

SL: He was the key man for that kind of thing, the master of transmutation of what he saw around him—definitely one of my chief inspirations. I'd like to be that good, but it's difficult; he knew more on a human scale than I'll every know. Joan Miró—there's another one of my favorites. And Marcel Duchamp, who said that you could put anything in a work of art. I really took that to heart, that was a good lesson for me.

KW: *Do you see a piece like "The Duck" as representational in a manner similar to a Klee?*

SL: Well, "The Duck" comes from ducks, from a love of ducks—an observation, and an obsession. You get rid of this obsession musically; so the duck began to get into the music. One of the subjects of saxophone technique is attack, and the duck has an exemplary attack to study—better than most saxophone players. You can learn something about the saxophone from ducks. Also, the piece is something about Ben Webster's technique; he was a high practitioner of attack, he had a million kinds, so this piece was dedicated to him. ["Sadly."] But we played it 'til it died, we played it so much that "The Ducks" died. (*Laughter.*) We buried it in Switzerland.

KW: *Regarding your obsessive devotion to Monk, do you think you could study any great composer and open doors of perception that same way?*

SL: That's an interesting question, because originally that group I had with Roswell [Rudd] in the early sixties was to be not a Monk band but a repertory band; originally we were playing Billy Strayhorn and Kurt Weill, Ellington and Monk. We firmly believed that if you got to the bottom of certain really good pieces, you could get free beyond them. But there was so much, we were getting confused. So we simplified it, decided to play just the Monk tunes.

So the answer is yes, if you really work on some material. but it's really not that simple, because I approached Monk's music like a composer. I wanted to see how it was made, how it worked. Those pieces of his were models for me of jazz composition, [the heads and solos] made a perfect little package that worked like a charm. I'm sure there's a trace of that inspiration in what I write. It's not that I copied his pieces, but tried to understand their principle—to solve the same problems he did in my own way.

I studied many composers in a single-minded way, trying to understand them, but that was a long time ago; Stravinsky, Weill, Schönberg to a certain point. Webern, Harry Partch was another very important one. I saw a work of his in the fifties called "The Bewitched"—total theater with music, dance, song, vibrations, everything. That really staggered me, made me want to do something combining the different arts that way.

KW: *Both you and Partch have a fascination with intervals.*

SL: Well, Stravinsky was the one who pointed the way, how to use and think about them, the importance of intervals. The saxophone is an interval machine, anyway, you can't ignore that. The study of intervals is not too well understood—they're difficult to teach, but that's what's happening. Cecil (Taylor) is the one who opened my mind to all that, really. And of course Monk. And Ellington, too.

KW: *Although you play older material—Monk, Duke, Herbie Nichols—you've never seemed to worry much about being in the tradition.*

SL: Well, jazz has been very good to me. It took me right in; it's never betrayed me, and it can't. It's been a beautiful river that you could just swim in, provided you have the right focus and the right ideals. I think of Earl Hines, Baby Dodds, and Bechet and all those old people, they did so much and what they did was so memorable that it'll keep you warm for the rest of your life,

you know?

I played with Cecil for six years in the fifties, and he used to take a lot of flack about not being in the tradition. He taught me how to fight that particular, somewhat political fight; to do it your own way in spite of what people say. They hold you back as long as they can, but then after awhile they say, well, maybe it's not so bad as I thought.

Certain people proved to me that anything can be done: Klee, Ellington, Duchamp, Ornette Coleman was very important, too. He said if you had a certain amount of space, and something to play, and you wanted to fit that thing in that space, just go ahead and put it in that space; don't worry about bar lines and chord changes and all that. that was a great discovery for us younger players.

KW: *Getting back to the roots, a lot of people have remarked on the relationship between some of your tunes and nursery rhymes.*

SL: Well, nursery rhyme is a convincing structure. I mean, it works. People go on and they sing in the nursery and the kid sings it, this is the beginning of music.

KW: *Did your parents sing you nursery rhymes when you were a kid?*

SL: Hell no. They weren't very musical.

KW: *About free improvising, in free contexts your lines sound like you'd written them as opposed to making up a song on the spot.*

SL: I'm glad it's apparent. Improvisation is part of the music that I compose, in a way. What's made up on the spot and what's prepared should be members of the same family, shouldn't be too different. that was one of the things I learned from Monk. His composing and improvising fit together—the same language, the same values.

When you improvise, certain forms, certain tendencies come forth; they're under your belt, under your fingers. Recently I made a record of saxophone exercises [*Hocus-Pocus*] that are sort of in between what I write and what I play. I could never find soprano saxophone exercises that satisfied me. So I wrote my own, years ago. They're designed to push me, to develop my vocabulary—the kind of thing I tend to play, but a little more difficult.

I had a group in 1966 with Enrico Rava and Johnny Dyani, and Louis Moholo [documented on *The Forest and the Zoo*] and we played completely free music; we dropped the tunes, the rhythm, and the harmony, one by one, until we were completely free of all those things. But after a year, it all started to sound the same—it wasn't free anymore. So we started to structure the free, started to put limits on it. That was the beginning of the whole period that's flowering now—the post-free, the poly-free, controlling what we learned in the sixties revolution. We use that material as an ingredient—but with fences all around it.

To play free in public is dangerous. Unless it's magic, it's just research. I still do it; I work with students that way. Steve Potts and I sometimes do that. But we don't do that in public.

KW: *Would you talk about the virtues of Steve Potts?*

SL: My right hand. He's a lifelong pal, a foil, somebody who will save you from being bad. We play so differently and yet it fits together, I think it's a crime he isn't better known; I know he's one of the greatest alto players in the world, one of the greatest soloists and team players. He should have his own records out.

KW: *Do you feel guilty about monopolizing so much of his time?*

SL: Absolutely. I do.

KW: *Do you try to urge him to step out and do more things on his own?*

SL: No, because he knows what he wants to do, really. I try and urge producers to record him, but so far they haven't. Partnerships like that are a miracle. Other partnerships go on for a year or two, and they're very important also, but not like the thing that I have with (sextet members) Irene Aebi and Steve Potts and Bobby Few and Oliver Johnson. And then there's Mal Waldron, and Gil Evans, and Cecil. These are relationships that go on forever.

I met Irene in Rome in '66. We hooked up, and a very short time later we were experimenting with the voice. It's been 20 years of research and experimentation, fantastic for me because I could study the voice, how it works. I don't know anything else like it in the history of music, such a long collaboration between a composer and a voice and a saxophone., It's an adventure that goes on and on.

KW: *I couldn't picture anyone else singing your pieces now.*

SL: I can, because other people are starting to sing them and they sound quite good, really. An Italian lady, Tiziana Ghiglioni, does a couple. A couple of other people have started to do them, too. But of course they were written for Irene, and she was my model.

The 12-year collaboration with Brion Gysin was another one made in heaven. He supplied me with all these wonderful texts that seemed like they were made for me, made for Irene to sing. His stuff was so easy to work with, so succinct, so wide open to interpretation, it was jazz, right away. I learned a lot from him, and we were all really sad when he died last year. He had his first retrospective, after he died of course, in Paris. They showed all the variety of his work—the paintings, the inventions, the cut-ups, the dream machines. It's only when you see the totality of somebody's work that you understand what they were doing. People are so ahead of their time, so surprising, people don't believe it. Until they're dead. *Then* they believe it.

KW: *Now that you've signed with RCA, are there projects you've wanted to record, but haven't had the chance?*

SL: Quite a few. There's a ballet we did a couple of years ago based on William Burroughs' *Naked Lunch*—text as cut up by Brion Gysin, for the sextet and two voices—and a Samuel Beckett ballet we did that was never recorded. There's a set of 10 Russian songs by nineteenth-century poets, for voice, piano, and saxophone, and some other song cycles. There are two other books of saxophone exercises, big band pieces and things for larger ensembles, a string quartet, a saxophone quartet, French horn music. I do whatever the traffic will bear, but there's always lots more that's waiting in the aging vats. Sometimes something sits in the vat so long, when it comes out it's no longer drinkable, and you have to rewrite it completely.

KW: *Listening to those fifties Cecil Taylor records now, they sound relatively conservative. But then 20 years later nothing sounds like it deserved the kind of furor that it stirred up.*

SL: That's right. You get used to it—the ear develops and [the music] becomes a classic. That's a natural process. New music is for the experts; when it gets a little older it's for everybody. It's like new wine—after it gets a little older, then it's drinkable. ●

ART BLAKEY: CLASS ACTION

By Kevin Whitehead
DECEMBER 1988

Yes sir, I'm gonna stay with the youngsters. When these get too old I'm gonna get some younger ones. Keeps the mind active."—Art Blakey after introducing Horace Silver, Curly Russell, Lou Donaldson, and Clifford Brown—Birdland, February 1954.

Writers say his band's name says it all: The Jazz Messengers. On one level, these Messengers are communicators. "You can't play *down* to the people," Art Blakey says. "You have to play *to* the people." On another level, the Messengers is a prime example of the oral tradition in action: a band where the tricks of the trade are passed down from master to apprentice.

That's the Jazz Messengers everyone knows: the hard-bop finishing school, the post-Kyser college of musical knowledge Nobody in jazz, *nobody* in jazz, *nobody* in jazz has a more impressive list of alumni than Blakey—barely scratching the surface you get Silver, Russell, Donaldson, Brown, Doug Watkins, Spanky DeBrest, Hank Mobley, Ira Sullivan, Benny Golson, Jackie McLean, John Gilmore, Kenny Dorham, Donald Byrd, Lee Morgan, Freddie Hubbard, Woody Shaw, Curtis Fuller, Bobby Timmons, Jymie Merritt, Cedar Walton, John Hicks, Keith Jarrett, Walter Davis Jr., James Williams, Amina Claudine Myers (yep, early '77), Bobby Watson, two Marsalises, Donald Harrison, Terence Blanchard, Wallace Roney, Kenny Garrett, Mulgrew Miller, Benny Green,...you get the idea.

But the stubborn fact you need to confront, pondering Art Blakey as Jazz Godfather, is that he doesn't currently endorse the view of his career we all harp on. He doesn't think the Messengers is a school. "Some people feel that way," Blakey says when the subject is raised, sounding less than convinced. "I don't think about it as a school, I just love to play. I don't try to set myself up as an example, 'cause I'm not a hypocrite. I make mistakes—I make mistakes on the bandstand, and the guys crack up. When I make a booboo I make a loud one," he laughs, "but that's the fun in playing music. You learn." Notice how Blakey turns the academic analogy around—it's a place where *he* gets educated, where *his* needs are fulfilled.

Still, the guys who come through the band learn—ask any of them. And Blakey does have a sense of *noblesse oblige*. "I wish more of the older guys from my generation would keep a group out there. That would help jazz so much. It would help the (younger) guys. But ask Blakey the most important lesson he tries to impart, and his answer is typically modest: "Well, there's no excuse for being late."

The leader famous for giving young musicians a boost became a man early. Born in Pittsburgh in 1919, he was a husband and father by age 15—when he found out that one of the men he knew from the neighborhood was his absent dad. Art Buhaina Blakey is an intensely family-oriented man; he's had seven natural children (including drummer Art Jr., who died of lung cancer in March, at 47) and has adopted seven more. "I look at a kid, he loves me, and I fall in love with him, I'll adopt him. Can't afford it? Can't afford not to, 'cause he needs a parent….I guess that's something psychological, because I was an 'orphan,' I was always by myself, I had nothing to reach back for. I had a good childhood though—everything that happened to me made my character much stronger."

Are the Messengers somehow like children to him? "Hell no. I don't even think of my sons as children—they talk to me like I'm one of the cats, because that's the way I talk to them. I treat musicians like men, I don't care how old they are. When you're 13, you're a man to me." Which doesn't, however, make the Messengers a band of equals. The leader who used to boast that he never fired anybody—that players knew when it was time to move on, or "fired themselves"—will now pull the plug on a musician who second-guesses him, or neglects his ax, or puts his social life before music. Blakey says the business is, finally, "very lucrative," but among musicians the Messengers is known as one the less high-paying gigs. And the boss flies first-class while the band flies coach—he says it gives them a chance to badmouth the leader, a healthy way to let off steam.

Even so, Blakey isn't hurting for hired help. By tradition dating back to the mid fifties, fresh recruits are brought into the band by those moving out—one hears stories of musicians waiting to be referred to Blakey by players waiting to be referred by guys who aren't even in the band yet. The traditional try-out is on a last club set. Blakey prefers to turn over his musicians one at a time. "The way I pick 'em is, when [a new musician] comes in, I see if they can get along together—that the same thing's going on with him that's going on with the rest of the guys. If not, you can't put them in *that* group. You have to wait till you get another group together, who can all work together."

From the late seventies till the mid eighties, turnover was relatively slow: Watson, Wynton Marsalis, Harrison, Blanchard, and tenorist Jean Toussaint put in several-year stints. Now, things move faster. Blakey says when a musician joins on, there's no expectation that the gig will last a certain amount of time. "People don't like to see the same band going around [again and again]. This ain't the Modern Jazz Quartet. I change all the time, 'cause I'm a free spirit. I'm not about to please anybody else. If the cats don't produce, and they're doing the best they can sometimes, then I have to change."

By his own count, Art Blakey has been to Japan 58 times. It was there, he remembers, that the early-sixties Messengers (lionized now but neglected by the stateside press then) were received like royalty. It's a sign of his appreciation that three of his sons are named Kenji, Akira, and Takashi. If Japanese culture has left a mark on Blakey the bandleader, it's on his indirect methodology—the Zen of bandleading, maybe. "Art Blakey never told me what scales to play," Wynton Marsalis told Mitch Seidel in 1981. "He'd tell me stories about Clifford Brown. Art Blakey says if soloists try things that don't work, he doesn't have to mention it. The audience will let them know."

But non-verbal direction begins the first time a fledgling Messenger hits the bandstand. "With other groups," Mulgrew Miller told Gene Kalbacher (*DB* March 1988), "I always felt I needed to direct the rhythm section, pianistically. With my comping I thought I could pull the rhythm section along….But I quickly found out that you can't lead Art. I found that out *fast*." As the drummer says, no matter who's in the band, "It's still going to sound

like Art Blakey. All down the years, the Messengers sound like the Messengers. Got to sound that way because I'm back there directing the traffic."

Blakey's vision as a bandleader starts at the drums—it's by learning to listen to *them* that a musician learns to listen to *him*. Branford Marsalis, 1986: "Art Blakey taught me how to play the drums when I play: rhythm as the incredible source of everything….I understood how time worked when I left his band."

Art Blakey: "By playing drums, I learned the only thing we have to use is dynamics. Use a lot of dynamics." (A pet Blakey peeve is that young drummers neglect their brushes.) Dynamics is the backbone of his celebrated style, with its forceful waves of sound—the long building press rolls, the outbursts or rim clatter, the raising and lowering of a drumhead's pitch with one stick while he strikes it with the other. That attention to making a fluid statement rubs off on his Messengers: the standard line from alumni is that working with the drummer taught them how to structure a solo. But the advice he gives is typically indirect: "I don't tell them what to play, I tell them what *not* to play.

"Don't try to play everything you know in one chorus; don't try to make a career out of one tune. I don't like long solos—long drum solos I especially don't like. When you're playing, and you get to a climax, you stop. You can't build to another climax after you've made one. So you stop, and maybe next tune you'll get another climax. Maybe not. It's only once or twice a month you really get to play, you really feel in your heart what you play. It isn't something you hit every night. So you just play, and try not to drop below a certain level, and maybe once or twice a month you'll go over that—you're feeling good, the audience is throwing them vibes back, there ain't nothing for you to do but blow your brains out, heh, heh. It's beautiful.

"As a drummer, you can't be in competition with a soloist. If a soloist is thinking of something, trying to connect something together, and you make a lot of noise, he'll forget it. Now he's gotta think of something else in a split-second; that makes it very hard." If this seems to contradict Mulgrew Miller's observation about who steers who, Jeff Langford got a handle on the paradox in a 1970 *Jazz Journal* piece on Monk: "[Blakey] can be considered a front-line partner of the pianist, and one of the best, while not deviating from the bop role of a drummer." He leads and supports simultaneously—a marvel easier to hear than explain.

Despite Blakey's close friendship with Monk, and their obvious rapport as players, Monk's overt influence on the Messengers' ensemble sound is scant. What Monk taught Blakey has less to do with association than with attitude. "The whole thing that Monk would teach me is identify: be different, so when people hear you, they know it's you. He always told me, 'Just stay back there and keep knocking in that rhythm section, and sooner or later they'll get into what you're doing.' [So] I always wanted to be an innovator, play stuff that other drummers don't play."

A couple of recent Messengers have worked in more outward—bound settings as well as with Blakey—Donald Harrison with Don Pullen, Robin Eubanks with Dave Holland and Mark Helias. Traditionally, firebrands have trimmed back their excesses to accommodate Blakey's conservative tastes. True, he'd hired John Gilmore when he was on leave from Sun Ra in 1964, but there'd been dissatisfaction on both sides—even if Art still considers Gilmore a great and vastly underrated tenor saxophonist.

"Musicians know the Messengers has a certain standard," the drummer says—they know what he likes and doesn't like, and play accordingly. Still, I remember a spring 1983 Messengers concert for Baltimore's fervently mainstream Left Bank Jazz Society, where altoist Harrison punctuated his phrases with dipped, honked notes, and played searingly vocal zig-zag lines, all with the leader's evident approval. As Blakey's references to a "certain standard" suggests, his distaste for the outside likely stems from the boppers' conviction that the sixties was merely a refuge for scoundrels. (That's certainly how Branford Marsalis sees it.) Harrison got away with it because he took care of business—his semi-abstractions. He obviously wasn't shucking, and he had is own. And now that he's out of the Messengers, he still takes chances. As Harrison has said, "He teaches you…that the important thing is to be true to yourself."

As Art Blakey enters his sixty-ninth year, his hearing is not good. When we spoke at his home in downtown Greenwich Village,

he apologized up-front; the hearing aid he wore needed replacing. (He perspires a lot, and the little buggers get wet, and short out.) He has trouble hearing in conversation—though he talks much like he plays, acting out dialog scenes, doing the participants' voices, modulating his pace and dynamics, and phrasing like the master of time that he is.

Art Blakey doesn't wear a hearing aid on the bandstand—" I play by vibrations, not a hearing aid." He says it worked for Beethoven—but Beethoven wasn't an improviser. I suspect he plays from the shape of a composition as much or more than he does from the shape of a soloist's line: knowing where the punctuation's go, he can fly on automatic.

"In the future, I'll still be out there if I can play with the same kind of fire I have now. But I won't be working as hard because nature takes its course." Blakey and his wife Anne book the Messengers out of an office in the building where they live. He looks forward to a time when they can book other bands as well, getting the music out there and keeping musicians busy, even if he's not on the stand himself.

Blakey has been revered for decades, and so now, inevitably, has fallen due for critical reevaluation. Gene Santoro's potshots in his Miles Davis piece in November's *DB* conveniently synopsize the anti-Blakey view, and its cause. The case against Blakey hinges on his constancy of vision: the Messengers now and the Messengers of 1955 have espoused the same values. Blakey contributes to the neo-con mindset that progress involves only a reinvestigation of the past—that bebop is the music of the future.

Which brings us to the proximate cause of backlash; the sins of the son have been

visited upon the father, the "son" being most every critic's favorite target, Wynton Marsalis, the Messenger's most conspicuous grad. (Not to mention dynasty-maker; his tenure as a Messenger opened the floodgates for all the young Louisianans swamping the jazz scene. Who'd have guessed that Blakey would put New Orleans back on the jazz map?)

Blakey's good press wore off on Marsalis; now Wynton's bad press is rubbing off on Art. Wynton's vision of jazz is insistently narrow, so the insistently hard-boppin' Blakey must be to blame—if you believe parents should be liable for their children's actions after they've left the nest. (Art Blakey, by the way, doesn't monitor the records his alumni have put out: "I don't even listen to my own.") In discussing Marsalis' shortcomings, Gene knocks Blakey to praise Miles. Methinks he's got it all backwards. Marsalis' lack of tolerance for diversity, his imperfect view of history, and the nagging suspicion observers get—that he thinks his audience is somehow not quite good enough for his music—have less to do with boss Blakey than with idol Miles, whose (best) music he worships. (You know how abrasive Wynton's interviews are. Miles has shot his mouth off so for decades. Davis' October 1988 *DB* interview—with his putdowns of McCoy Tyner, curt dismissal of the great Jimmy Garrison, and attribution of Jimmy Giuffre's "Four Brothers" to Ralph Burns—is merely the latest in a series.)

Hell yes, Art Blakey remains fiercely committed to hard—bop, while his contemporary Max Roach explores a wide variety of playing situations—though you'll recall that Blakey experimented with percussion choirs in the fifties, only to find that other drummers weren't ready. Blakey long ago settled into a format in which he feels comfortable, and given that he's one of the originators of the soul-cookin', hard-boppin' genre, who's to complain? It's not like he says everyone has to play that way. The most productive graduates of the Blakey school, like Bobby Watson and Donald Harrison, have expanded their musical horizons after leaving the band, instead of acting like Blakey's esthetic was all there is. Branford Marsalis, despite his maddening reluctance to find his own style, shows much the same open-minded attitude toward playing situations.

The difference between Art Blakey and Wynton and Miles—who belittle alternative points of view—is that they tend to sound an awful lot like know-it-alls, which is not Art Blakey's problem. When Blakey says he doesn't see the Messengers as a school because he makes mistakes, too, he's not being coy.

The key to understanding Art Blakey's contributions is to think of the Messengers not as a college, but as a classroom: a place where a musician might pick up three or 15 or 30 credits, but not all 120. A musician goes to Blakey to learn about dynamics, pace, and energy conservation, to learn how to discover something new in the same material—"Blues March" and "Moanin'," every night—through repetition (much the way Steve Lacy does, come to think of it—Lacy being a Zen jazzman in a different way). A musician does not go to Blakey to study extended forms, polytonality, post-structuralism, or pointillism. But there are other classrooms—such as those run by drummers Tony Williams and Jack DeJohnette. Like, say, Wayne Shorter (who worked for Blakey and Miles Davis), modern Messengers apprentice with other masters, too—like Kenny Garrett with Miles, or Lonnie Plaxico with DeJohnette, or Wallace Roney, Mulgrew Miller, and Billy Pierce with Tony Williams.

Art Blakey has shown generations of musicians so much—nobody in jazz, *nobody* in jazz, *nobody* in jazz has a more impressive list of alumni. But he's not presumptuous enough to think that what they learn from him is all they need to know. ●

TONY WILLIAMS: STILL, THE RHYTHM MAGICIAN

By John Ephland
MAY 1989

I wouldn't change anything that I've done because it's all brought me to where I am. And where I am is a good place to be."

Perhaps more than any drummer over the past 30 years, Tony Williams has epitomized that incessant drive towards newness of expression on his chosen instrument. For him, change has been a necessary and vital ingredient to his evolution as an artist, whether it has come through the music of Art Blakey and Max Roach, or from playing with such key figures as Sam Rivers, Gil Evans, Eric Dolphy, Jackie McLean, and Cecil Taylor.

But it was his six-year tenure with Miles Davis, beginning in 1963, that set him apart forever in the annals of jazz drumming. With cohorts Ron Carter and Herbie Hancock, Williams completed one of the greatest rhythm sections of all time. It was with Davis that his new vision for drumming was showcased; lightning-fast cymbal work, displaced accents, polyrhythmic irregularities that served as drum solos as well as rhythmic accompaniment, and a bullet snare working in tandem with a sizzling hi-hat and jabbing bass drum. Williams helped to disconnect drumming from its timekeeping role (akin to Kenny Clarke's innovation 25 years earlier), emphasizing meterless percussive sounds over a steady beat. With the Davis quintet, which also included Wayne Shorter, Williams greased the wheels that turned an exceptional band into one that became known for, among other things, their uncanny ability to listen and dialog with one another. Perhaps most significant, Tony Williams was the percussive bridge for Davis as he moved his music beyond acoustic jazz into the various realms of electronic funk and fusion. Pioneering colleagues they were.

And since he has continued to play in a variety of musical contexts, The Tony Williams School of Drumming, as a matter of course, has included as part of its curriculum the realization "that drumming is more important than style." This becomes very apparent when one considers his immediate forays into alternative post-sixties jazz. His musical conceptions included explosive rock-rhythms and helped to set the standards for seventies jazz fusion with an assortment of new sounds; all of which involved electric music with, at one time or another, such key figures as John McLaughlin, Larry Young, Jack Bruce, and Allan Holdsworth.

As the seventies began to wind down, and into the early eighties, Williams reemerged in more trad-jazz settings—playing and recording with the celebrated VSOP quintets (Miles' mid-sixties band minus Miles plus Freddie Hubbard or Wynton Marsalis), with Hank Jones and Ron Carter as a trio, and with Sonny Rollins. In 1985, he appeared in the movie *'Round Midnight*, playing alongside such jazz greats as Dexter Gordon and his fellow Davis alums as well as contributing to the soundtrack recording.

Also in '85, Williams formed a new straightahead jazz quintet that has proven to be an excellent forum for his ongoing writing and production talents in addition to his ever-growing drum work. The band has gone on to record three well-received albums and has toured worldwide on a number of occasions. Except for the change at bass of Bob Hurst for Charnett Moffett, the lineup remains Mulgrew Miller on piano, trumpeter Wallace Roney, and Billy Pierce on saxophones.

Looking rather dapper, Mr. Williams dropped hints of future excursions into the unknown—to places probably just as discontinuous as previous musical dwellings. They were hints that may prove to be windows onto other musical vistas only he knows the looks of, for now.

John Ephland: *What was it that steered you in the direction to play the drums?*

Tony Williams: What do you mean? Drums…it's a great instrument. My father would take me with him to all these different engagements that he had. So, I was just drawn to the drums. I would sit in the audience when I was a kid and just watch the drummer. And I'd look at the drummer doin' what he did, and I remember the feeling I had, which was, "If *he* can do that, I know *I* can do that."

JE: *That's something you can't teach somebody.*

TW: No, that's just something you know. Children are like that. They don't fear; they don't have the experience to fear things. So, when I was nine, I asked my dad one night if I could sit in with the band. And so, the first time I played the drums was in front of an audience.

JE: *You made important connections with Sam Rivers and Jackie McLean. Tell me about your experiences with them.*

TW: What happened was, Alan Dawson—the only person I took [private] lessons from, basically for reading—was teaching at Berklee. I was too young to go there, and never did, actually.

JE: *How long a period of time was that?*

TW: On and off for about a year, year-and-a-half. So, there was a club that he played at, the Mt. Auburn Club 47 in Boston, in Cambridge. My dad brought me out to the club and asked him to listen to me. Alan would let me, as part of his show, sit in on a couple of tunes each night. Then a guy named Leroy Fallana, a piano player asked me to join his band. I was about 14 or 15. He hired me, Sam Rivers, and a bass player named Jimmy Towles.

JE: *What kind of music did you play?*

TW: It was basically straightahead stuff. Leroy was more of a soul, kind of Horace Silver-type of piano player. That was when I started to go around Boston by myself. I didn't need my dad to take me around

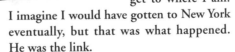

Mitchell Seidel

anymore. I started playin' dates, playin' casuals and things like that. Then around '62—to leap, 'cause there were a lot of things happening—I had been playing in a club called Connelly's, as part of a house rhythm section; a club where they would hire a name horn player to come in from New York for a week. He would play with the house rhythm section. So this one week, Jackie McLean came to Boston. We played the weekend and during the week. He started liking the way I played and invited me to come back to New York with him. When he asked me, I said, "Yeah sure, I'd love to, but you'll have to ask my mom." He came over, and said he would look out for me. She said it was okay. I lived in his house in New York for a couple of months. That was something I had wanted to do for a long time. I mean, I was dyin' to get out of Boston and get to New York. My mom's involvement and Jackie's kindness to my family really helped. I was 16 at the time. So, Jackie was the reason for me to really get to where I am. I imagine I would have gotten to New York eventually, but that was what happened. He was the link.

JE: *But prior to this point, you were doing some interesting things with Sam Rivers. Tell me about that.*

TW: When we had a band with Sam, we were doing a lot of Third Stream, which meant at the time a combination of jazz players playing avant-garde music. This was the late fifties, early sixties. We were playing with this chamber group [The Boston Improvisational Ensemble], doing things in the afternoons where they had

cards and numbers and you're playing to time, watches, and big clocks; playing behind poetry, all kinds of stuff. But I was also playing with trios and cocktail parties, having to do the regular kinds of things— sorority and fraternity parties. One time I played a fraternity party that was supposed to be a beach party, but it was the dead of winter; so it was indoors, in the downstairs area of the house, and they brought in all this sawdust to simulate sand on the beach. So I'm sitting there with my drums and there's the sawdust, and everytime I hit the bass drum it slides 'cause there's all this sawdust on a wood floor. (*Laughs.*)

JE: *What were the conditions around which you moved to New York and were eventually asked to join Miles' band?*

TW: I guess I'd been in New York about four or five months, working with Jackie; we were playing different things around New York and Brooklyn. We played a concert at some hall in midtown Manhattan, and Miles came in with Philly Joe Jones…and that's where he heard me. I think Jackie had been talking to Miles and maybe he had mentioned that he had a new band and said, "Come hear the band." A month later, I got a call from Grachan Moncur, the trombone player; his girlfriend at the time was the secretary for Miles' lawyer, and they were looking for me. And so, I pick up the phone and Grachan says, "Did Miles call you today? He's lookin' for you." And I said, "Yeah, sure. Right. Give me a break." He responded, "No, really. Hang up the phone. He's trying to get in touch with you. He's in California, man." So we get off the phone and Miles ends up calling from California, and he wanted to know could we get together when he got back— he'd be back in a couple of weeks. And, I was more than happy, because at the time, Miles was my biggest influence musically. I was just in love with his music, his bands.

When I was in Boston—to get back a bit—in 1960, '61, he came to Boston, and a year earlier I had met Jimmy Cobb. So when they came to town, it was my first time to see Miles Davis' band. It was the band with Hank Mobley and Wynton Kelly, Paul Chambers, and Jimmy. And so, when they did come, I asked Jimmy if I could sit in with Miles, being my usual pest again. (Laughs.) And he said, "You'll have to ask Miles." So, having no fear, being still basically a child, I ran up on stage after the set through the curtains to the back, and caught Miles as he was goin' somewhere. And I said, "Miles," I mean, "Mr. Davis, can I sit in with your band? I already asked Jimmy." And Miles turned around and said, "Go back, sit down, and listen." So that was the first time I met Miles.

JE: *At the same time, you were starting to put out some albums as a leader.*

TW: My first record was in '64. It was the first record that Blue Note had ever made of free, avant-garde music. I think they wanted me to make a record. I wanted to make a record, and by that time I guess, because I was so adamant about what I wanted to do, they were willing to take the chance.

JE: *You wanted to play free music, not the straightahead stuff?*

TW: Yeah. I mean, what's been important to me is to show diversity in different things, and to show different colors of things. I mean, if I'm working with a band, it sounds one way; and then I'm recording with other people and it sounds another way, then why not—if I get the chance to do something of my own—do a third thing? That makes sense to me. That's logical because it gives me a chance to, number one, show that I can do that, and secondly, it brings a fresh sound to the ear of people who have heard me do the other two things.

JE: *And it was consistent with some of the music you'd done before.*

TW: Right, before that. And, you know, when I was in Boston, playin' with Sam, one of the things that really opened my ears was the first time I heard Ornette Coleman. That first record I heard—I think it was *Change of the Century*—was just unbelievable, the impact it made on me. This was about 1959, 1960.

JE: *So it planted a seed?*

TW: Yeah. That music was the way to go, for me, at that time.

JE: *It seems to be a trademark of Miles' bands over the years to let his drummers have a real strong personality. What was it like when you started playing with him? Did he guide you in your drumming?*

TW: He didn't say anything. I mean, he hired me because of the way I sounded; so what was there to say?

JE: *And you appreciated the fact that he didn't tell you what to play?*

TW: No, I didn't think about it. At the time I didn't notice it.

JE: *You just played as if it were your own band?*

TW: No, I played what I thought was most appropriate. And that's what I always do. I mean, if I play with Blossom Dearie, and she's singing, I'm playing behind her; I'm not playing behind, you know, Wayne Shorter. I always try to play what's appropriate for the situation.

JE: *If anybody's paid any attention to you, they know that.*

TW: Right. If you pay attention, you know that I can sound very different depending on who I'm playing with; which is what I like to do.

JE: *Which is different, wouldn't you say, than someone from the Max Roach or Art Blakey school; or the Philly Joe Jones school?*

TW: Yeah. If you're gone pick just one style of playing and you can only play that way, that's what you want to do....I don't discourage that; but I think that drumming is more important than style. When I've given lessons or clinics, I try to emphasize that learning how to play the drums is more important than having your own style; really knowing what the drums can do and the scope and range of the instrument is more important. You know the reason I play the way I do is because when I first started playing, all I ever wanted to do was to *sound* like Max Roach, was to *sound* like Art Blakey, was to *sound* like Philly Joe Jones, was to *sound* like Louis Hayes, was to *sound* like Jimmy Cobb, was to *sound* like Roy Haynes. I really wanted to figure out why they sounded the way they did. I wasn't interested in my own style. So, I set about playing like these guys religiously, and playing their style because it was just such a wonderful, magical experience. I don't see that kind of wonder in others. I get guys comin' up to me—they just got a drum set, they've been playin' maybe four years—and they want their own style. They want to be expressive. I say, "Well, then, if you want to be expressive, you gotta find out what the instrument will do. And to do that, you gotta go back and find out and get an idea of what's already been done."

That's what the instrument's all about. It's the *instrument* that's more important, the quality and the magic of the instrument are more important than you are. That's one phrase I always use. You know, people use the instrument to make themselves look good. they just want to be able to tell some girl, "I'm a drummer." So anyway, it wasn't as if Miles was letting me do something. Like I said, I knew all his music, I knew every track off all his records. So, on the first date that we played, we went up and played a live date with no rehearsal; he just got the band together—Ron, George Coleman, Herbie, and myself—and we went up to, I think it was, Boden College in upstate New York, and we just stomped off the first tune....That was May of '63. I think the first tune was "Walkin'." And after that first set, Miles came off stage and gave me a huge hug...didn't say anything. I'll never forget that.

JE: *What did you learn from playing with Miles?*

TW: Well, I think basically, the things that I learned from Miles were all in the social area. (Laughs.) One of the things that is most obvious, if you've ever been in a band like Miles', is the way he lets things develop. See, the thing is, if he hires people who are really good, that's what he wants them to be; he wants them to be as good as they are and get better. Most people—I've noticed in other musicians who will remain nameless but are famous—will hire a guy that's really good, but they get upset if the *audience* thinks that they're really good. They don't see it the other way, where if the guy is getting great applause and he's making the audience happy, that reflects on the bandleader. They see it some other kind of way, some weird way, like they're being pushed aside or something, they're threatened, or competition or something. And that's the beauty, one of the wonderful things about Miles in that he *wants* those people, he hires you and gets good combinations of musicians together so that they can make this music which then again reflects on him, his judgment.

JE: *Going a bit further, your interest in rock rhythms, as you began your departure from Miles' band, caused me to think about some of your early influences. What was it that drew you to rock music, and how come jazz got in there before you could become a rhythm & blues or blues drummer?*

TW: Good question. The reason is that because in 1954 and '55, the only interesting things about playing music were in jazz. Jazz was more adventurous. In 1954, you had The Everly Brothers, who I loved, Frankie Lymon & The Teenagers;

you had Elvis, you had all these kinds of things in the pop world. But, there were no *Bands*. Drumming was not something that was *exciting* in that kind of music.

JE: *But wasn't the beat becoming more pronounced?*

TW: No, the beat was *not* becoming more pronounced. What I'm saying is, if I wanted to be a drummer, if I wanted to *play* music, I looked to where they were *playing* music; and that was the music of jazz, where guys are actually playing the drums and not just playing beats. Playing beats is one thing; that's not drumming. So, I'm coming home from school and listening to "American Bandstand" just like all the rest of the kids in my class. But there's no *drumming* going on. So, the way for me to get into music is to listen to this other music, where there's some interesting drumming going on. Plus, the music my father had around the house was of Count Basie, Gene Ammons, that kind of music. So, by the time the late sixties come along, the middle sixties, there's this music happening where the drums are really startin' to really *pound*.

JE: *Who were some of the people playing then that caught your interest?*

TW: The two biggest groups, I thought, were Cream and Jimi Hendrix's band. But before that, I was in love with The Beatles. I was a real Beatle fanatic. When I was with Miles, I had an apartment in New York with a Beatles poster up on my wall. When you walked in the front door, it was staring you right in the face....And in '65, I told Miles, "Miles, we oughtta do a tour with the Beatles; we oughtta open up for them." He said, "What?" We were still wearing suits and ties to these gigs, and I'm telling him, we oughtta be playin' with the Beatles. So anyway, the energy of the music is happening, but it's rock 'n' roll. See, like soul music....

JE: *Like Motown?*

TW: Yeah, like Motown. The songs were great, but it's still [*demonstrates a more fixed beat*]. In rock & roll, the guys are goin' [*demonstrates a more explosive percussive sound*]. You know, they're crashin' cymbals and so forth. But in funk and soul, it's still [*demonstrates that more measured beat*]. So, because I'm a drummer, I'm attracted more to the power kind of drumming, and the emotional kind of drumming ●

BENNY CARTER: A LEGEND IN PROCESS

By Mitchell Seidel

DECEMBER 1989

atchel Paige once said, "Don't look back. Something may be gaining on you." At 82, Benny Carter isn't looking back. But it doesn't matter, because nobody's even close.

After a long career in music, it seems odd for Carter not to reflect. The man whose musical skills earned him the nickname "The King" more than half a century ago and who went on to become one of Hollywood's most versatile arranger/composers has covered a lot of ground, both in score paper and show leather. One explanation is that most of his thoughts on that career were presented by the late Morroe and Edward Berger and James Patrick in the 1982 bio *Benny Carter: A Life in American Music*. Another is that Carter has too many irons in the fire to dwell on the past.

"People always ask me about the good old days. My good old days are here and now," he is quoted in the newly released documentary film, *Benny Carter: Symphony in Riffs*.

Recent recordings on the MusicMasters label with an all-star saxophone ensemble and The American Jazz Orchestra have rekindled interest in Carter's arranging skills, and this year he took the top spot in the *Down Beat* International Critics Poll in that category. His alto saxophone playing, if anything, has improved over the last 30 years, with Carter remaining as contemporary as ever. Chops permitting, he even plays a little trumpet on club dates.

In addition to lecturing at colleges and performing, the last few years have been spent laurel-gathering, with Carter humbly, if reluctantly, being honored as an "elder statesman" of jazz wherever he plays. Japanese tours are now common for Carter, and he collects frequent-flyer credits as often as he gets royalty checks. In addition, Carter and Morroe Berger—a longtime friend—will be remembered by an Institute of Jazz Studies at Rutgers Morroe Berger-Benny Carter Jazz Research fund, designed to provide grants to jazz scholars to study at the Institute, to publish the results in the Institute's "Annual Review of Jazz Studies," and to lecture at the university. Carter celebrated his eighty-second birthday on stage at Alice Tully Hall at New York's Lincoln Center, and followed that up two weeks later with a performance at the Chicago Jazz Festival, featuring works from his landmark 1961 album *Further Definitions*.

That recording occurred in the middle of Carter's career of writing music for films and television, and early in a period that saw few recordings issued under his own name. By the early 1970s, Carter's career took a turn back toward performing publicly and recording albums.

Ironically, the Hollywood work that Carter walked away from a few years ago doesn't exist anymore.

"They're not doing the work that they were doing years ago when they had those large orchestras in all of the studios, and so much independent stuff is going on; and from what I hear, they're doing these one-man things with synthesizers," says Carter, adding that he's so far removed from that line of work, all of his information about it now is secondhand.

"I've been out of it for quite some time. The last thing I did for film was probably something for an animated film, which I did about three or four years ago, and since then I've done nothing. I've been more concerned with my performance, and particularly concerned with keeping away from deadlines, which, at this point, I do not welcome," he explains.

"They call 40 guys in the studio at 8 o'clock in the morning. You can't call up and say, 'Gee, I won't have it ready until tomorrow.' You know, it means it's got to be there. There's no excuses, no putting it off; no postponements. No cancellations, unless it happens to be yours, after you do that once," he says, chuckling.

"A lot of times you take on more than you can really chew, because there will be something at the last minute. You get a little greedy, you figure you can do it. And you *can* do it, if you stay up all night for four nights running; you know what I mean. That's what I think is one thing that happened to Oliver Nelson. That's what the people who were close to him tell me. He got so popular at Universal that he couldn't say no. He'd get through conducting one picture, then he'd go right to the projection room to see it."

The Hollywood of Benny Carter was one where films produced songs that went on to become standards, while on the East Coast, Broadway was equally productive.

A fluent tunesmith, Carter's songbook includes such diverse entries as "When Lights Are Low," "Cow Cow Boogie," and "Evening Start." While they don't write songs like that anymore, Carter still does.

"Broadway isn't what it was. There is no Tin Pan Alley anymore," says Carter. "I think that's kind of like an era that has passed. There are still tunes that become standards that are written today, but when we think of the vehicles for which those things were written, those were all written for situations for theater. 'We need a song for this spot in the show and for this particular singer.' It's something that was fashioned just for that. I don't know, are there any shows from which great songs have come in the last 20 years? Maybe a few good songs from films."

Citing "Laura" by David Raksin and "The Shadow of Your Smile" by Johnny Mandel as superior examples of film music, Carter says they come to mind because "they're well-constructed and unusually lovely. But then, those tunes are well over 20 years old."

Carter's composing and arranging are as distinctive in his alto saxophone playing, a sound that was forged alongside such contemporaries as Coleman Hawkins and Roy Eldridge. When asked if the young musicians of today don't seem to have voices as distinctive as those of Carter's youth, he hesitates in gentlemanly fashion lest he be perceived of serving a salad of moldy figs and sour grapes.

"You mean individuality. Yeah, that's what I miss, too. Because the younger players, there're so many clones around today. Nobody sounds like themselves," he says.

In teaching at colleges, often, after hearing students play briefly, Carter will simply say, "Now play a nice melody"; an obvious reflection of his tastes in playing and composing. Melody is something he finds frequently missing in younger musicians' performances.

"Very oftentimes when they start out playing, they say, 'Let's play such and such a tune,' and they start out improvising from the word go. By the time they play three or four choruses, the listening audience doesn't necessarily even know what the tune is they're playing, unless it's been pre-announced. And maybe some people can recognize chord changes; but today, so many of the chords are the same—so many of the same chords are in different tunes."

Carter, though, feels there are a great number of talented

Mitchell Seidel

young players on the scene today and declines strong comment on the theory that students spend too much time playing Charlie Parker and John Coltrane solos note for note, only to use the next seven years "unlearning" what they were taught.

"I'm not a reviewer, I'm not a critic, so don't get me into that," Carter responds. "Coleman Hawkins, to me, was a great creator because he had no prior influences. From what you know historically, who was there before him on his instrument? But then again, when Parker came along, he still had something full-blown of his own. I don't know if he got anything from me or from Willie Smith or from Johnny Hodges or from anybody. He came on the scene with something quite different."

Could the lack of widespread mass communications have had an influence on that earlier generation, forcing them to find their own voices?

"Absolutely, absolutely," Carter replied. "You didn't have those great influences of those role models."

Ironically, trying to get an opinion from Carter on future trends in music also sends him back a generation.

"Who knows what's going to spring forth? And from where? I always think back to 1928, when I first heard Art Tatum. Just sort of out of the blue, really," says Carter. "There'd been Fats Wallers and J.P. Johnsons and Willie 'The Lion' Smith and people like that with that great stride piano. And then along comes an Art Tatum with something vastly different and much more advanced harmonically and technically. But where did he get it from, I wonder? I don't know. These things do happen like that."

When it comes to trends in modern music, Carter takes his usual diplomatic tack, stepping around toes instead of on them. His most intent listening is done while behind the wheel of his Rolls Royce while tooling around Hollywood, which would make you wonder what his driving record is like.

"The listening that I'm able to do is when I'm in the car, because at home I cannot find the time. Unless, in rare instances, I can just listen and do nothing else," he says. "I listen to a lot of people and work available today. But I won't mention any names, because if I do, immediately when you leave I'll say, 'Oh gee, I should have mentioned so-and-so.'

"There are a lot of young arrangers doing very interesting things. Yes there are a lot," he said. "There is a lot of interesting music being played and a lot of the experimental stuff is very interesting. And a lot of it, of course, is very uninteresting and unpretentious. But a lot of it is very valid, very good.

"I can't elucidate that too clearly. These things, of course, are very personal, you know. Very subjective," Carter says, adding that his tastes encompass a wide range of styles.

"I like some funk. I like some rock & roll. I like fusion. Of course, to begin with, jazz is fusion. What does the word 'fusion' itself mean? Well, they claim that jazz was that, you know. From the European harmonic thing and the African drums, field hollers, and all that—that's fusion when it comes together."

Carter does recall being very impressed by Lester Bowie's Brass Fantasy and its spirited recording of "I Only Have Eyes For You."

"Oh yeah, you can mention that I love that. I think [it was] the freshness of it. I know it's sort of the old New Orleans feeling, but to me that was new, almost. It was a good, great, honest feeling. I think, the music is more important if it says something to you, if it moves you somewhat. I don't care how many notes are played. It sounds as though they were

happy and having fun with it."

The work that distracts Carter from listening to music at home is his own composing. The Harrison Engle and Lucille Ostrow one-hour documentary film about his life offers a brief example of what it's like to be a fly on the wall, showing Carter almost effortlessly crafting a tune while humming quietly to himself. That oversimplifies matters somewhat. Operating something like a novelist, Carter jots down ideas as they hit him, whether that means relaxing at home or racing along in a Japanese bullet train.

Central City Sketches, a Carter jazz suite, premiered at an American Jazz Orchestra concert in New York in 1987. He is currently working on a Japan suite based on his frequent visits to the Far East.

As a result of all these notes, "I've got a lot of bits and pieces about, fragments." When actually sitting down to write a piece, "first you pull out a piece of score paper and you sit and look at the blank page for a long time," Carter laughs. "And then finally an idea will come to you. The hardest thing is always getting that first note down. No, seriously, I'd had it on my mind for quite some time and I've got some thematic material already mapped out. And I've got some stuff already written."

But when he's really stuck for an idea, those piles don't really help, he says; explaining that you "just sit down and fool around at the piano. And then sometimes, I just get away from the piano, to the kitchen table, just do it there. Don't try to pull anything out of the piano if it won't

come. Leave it. Forget it, just go away from it."

Preparations for a recent Japanese tour had Carter getting his scoring juices flowing by settling in at his copyist's office, particularly because it has no piano. "When I go to his office, the copyist is breathing down my neck. You have to continue. And it's quiet there, because nobody else is doing anything. There are about five or six guys sitting at different desks, but they're just writing."

It went the same way with Carter's latest album, a saxophone ensemble effort called *Over the Rainbow*. Faced with 45 minutes left before entering the studio with Herb Geller, Jimmy Heath, Frank Wess, Joe Temperley, Richard Wyands, Milt Hinton, and Ronnie Bedford, Carter put the finishing touches on the score while simultaneously chatting with producer Ed Berger.

The saxophone ensemble format is not new to Carter, his work in it going back to the thirties. But it is one in which he is rarely recorded these days, the most recent such American work being 1966's *Additions to Further Definitions*.

Benny Carter's life has been one that has touched at least three generations of musicians and nearly encompasses the history of jazz. Peers ranging from Wynton Marsalis to Dizzy Gillespie feted him at Lincoln Center, a few steps from where Carter was raised in New York's San Juan Hill neighborhood. Carter was perhaps prescient of the birthday cake that was soon to splatter over his gray suit; or more likely, sincerely overwhelmed by the standing ovation when he said, "Whether it's a long life or a short life, moments like this are rare." ●

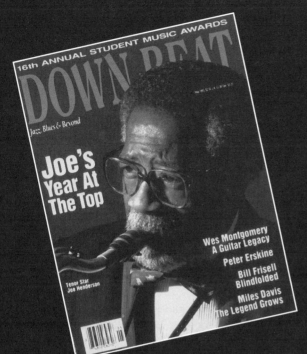

THE 1990s

INTRODUCTION

By Frank Alkyer

As jazz entered the 1990s, "What is jazz?" became more than the simple question for the meekly curious. It became a rallying cry for musicians who couldn't bear to sit in the same ideological room with each other, let alone play on the same bandstand.

The ability of jazz artists to absorb and incorporate everything from world beat and classical music to rap and rock continued to prove the resilience of jazz as a living, growing art form. In some quarters, though, musicians felt the "jazz-is-everything" movement had gone too far. A return to jazz purity championed by trumpeter Wynton Marsalis in the 1980s blossomed into a full-fledged movement of its own: and neo-conservativism was born. At the other end of the spectrum, Kenny G, Najee, and radio-friendly smooth jazz gave the upwardly mobile something to relax to while leaving hard-core jazz fans and musicians sucking lemons.

It was into this atmosphere that I became the editorial director of *Down Beat* magazine. Jazz had developed into a far-reaching umbrella covering a variety of music, much of which sounded nothing like any tune Satchmo would have ever played.

But a number of battle lines were being drawn. Wynton Marsalis and Miles Davis barreled headlong into a feud wherein the young trumpeter committed jazz heresy by contending that Miles had turned his back not only on his audiences, but also on jazz itself, by playing fusion. Marsalis' comments created an avalanche of letters and foreshadowed that he would be the center of many a debate over the direction jazz would take.

Miles, for his part, was winding down. He had become godlike, filling festivals around the world with fans who wanted just a scent of his haunting tone and to hear just a few choice grooves from his band of mostly incredible electrified soloists.

But his crowning achievement in the nineties would be to return to the past and the arrangements of the late Gil Evans. It was something he said he'd never do. For 30 years, he refused. But in 1991, Quincy Jones finally convinced Miles that now was the time to reminisce a little. It happened at the Montreux Jazz Festival, with Quincy directing an all-star big band. While recordings and videos of the date show an orchestra that was under-rehearsed at times and a Miles Davis that needed the backup of young trumpeter Wallace Roney to handle difficult passages, Miles' presence and his glorious tone on such classics as "My Ship," "Boplicity," and "Summertime" proved to be pure magic.

A few short months later, Miles died.

But jazz is a continuum. While there would be no replacing Miles Davis, others received their opportunities to shine in the spotlight he vacated—none more impressive than veteran tenor saxophonist Joe Henderson.

Henderson was the underground hero of thousands of musicians, but not a household name. Then he was signed to Verve records in 1992 and recorded one of the decade's most lasting theme albums—*Lush Life*, a tribute to the music of Billy Strayhorn.

He was an instant hit after more than 30 years on the road. *Lush Life* went to number one on the jazz charts, Henderson's face appeared on the cover of *Down Beat* twice in the span of 13 months, and he won Album of the Year, Artist of the Year, and Tenor Saxophonist of the Year honors in two consecutive *Down Beat* Critics and Readers polls—something no other artist has done.

While Joe Henderson ruled, new stars rose. Trumpeter Roy Hargrove put together one of the hardest-swinging young bands of the decade. Tenor saxophonist Joshua Redman (son of Dewey Redman) went from being a Harvard political science student to *Down Beat*'s Jazz Artist of the Year in less than 36 months. Steve Coleman and Greg Osby, members of the Brooklyn's M-BASE music collective, jammed with experimental abandon. Vocalist Cassandra Wilson, another M-BASE-er, became a star with the release of the beautiful *Blue Light 'til Dawn*.

There were disappointments. There are always disappointments—the greatest, to me, being the death of Dizzy Gillespie. Around the offices of *Down Beat*, I remember Miles' death being a somber day, as if we lost a guiding light. When Dizzy Gillespie passed away in 1992, we felt as though we lost a guiding light who also happened to be our favorite uncle. In our tribute issue (April 1993), we selected a cover photo that showed a benevolent Dizzy. His face both smiling and melancholy, yet reassuring as if to say, "Everything's going to be all right." We debated, long and hard, what headline should go on the cover, but none seemed to measure up. Finally, Jack Maher, *Down Beat*'s president, took one look at it and said, "You don't need copy. The photo speaks for itself." He was right.

Along with Dizzy and Miles, the first half of the nineties witnessed the passing of such great artists as Sun Ra, Stan Getz, Red Rodney, Joe Pass, Sonny Sharrock, Ed Blackwell, Andy Kirk, Clifford Jordan, Frank Zappa, Walter Davis, Jr., Henry Mancini, and former *Down Beat* writer Leonard Feather.

Other disappointments centered around jazz on television. In 1990, "Night Music," the most eclectic and hip music show to ever appear on network television, ended a short-lived run. Hosted by David Sanborn, "Night Music" dared to mix jazz, pop, rap, world beat, and avant-garde artists together in a way never before imagined. It was highly creative and, thus, doomed to mass-audience failure.

We had much more hope in 1993, when Branford Marsalis began to lead one of the finest jazz bands in the nation as the house band on "The Tonight Show with Jay Leno." Leno had taken over for television legend Johnny Carson, and Branford replaced Doc Severinsen. In the beginning, the band was adventurous, bringing jazz to the masses and introducing them to a host of our most beloved artists. But hopes of a new jazz revolution evaporated, the casualty of ratings wars that cut into the band's playing time and forced them to play less jazz and more pop.

On the up side, Black Entertainment Television proposed a 24-hour cable-jazz channel called *BET on Jazz*. At this writing the channel's launch was still pending following several delays.

In case you missed it, the discussion to this point has focused mainly on the young and the legendary, which turned out to be an unsettling theme of the early nineties. Record labels appeared possessed to sign younger and younger artists to their rosters *or* elder statesmen whose marquee power could spell record sales. Somewhat lost were those "middle-aged" artists who were guilty only of being the wrong age at the wrong time. Bass player Ron Carter led a vocal contingent of "40-something" and "50-something" musicians, routinely bashing recording-industry executives for their shortsightedness.

Even so, artists such as Arturo Sandoval, John Scofield, Bobby Watson, Victor Lewis, Joe Lovano, Muhal Richard Abrams, Henry Threadgill, David Murray, and a host of others established themselves as important players in the future of jazz.

But the largest story in jazz for the 1990s centered around taking the music "uptown."

For starters, when Bill Clinton became president, the entire nation knew they had elected a frustrated saxophone player. But Clinton did more than just noodle his tenor on "The Arsenio Hall Show." He and his administration showed new respect for jazz as well as all music and arts. Early in his term, Clinton hosted a high-profile, all-star jazz jam on the White House lawn, the first time since the Carter administration that jazz received such a presidential reception.

"We need a musician in the White House because arts fundings have been suffering," said tenorman Illinois Jacquet during the event. "Here's a man who can do something about it. It's so important to have a president that's involved in music personally."

Indeed, the new administration's stance on music and the arts changed drastically from the Bush years—virtually overnight.

While the Bush administration completely discounted music and the arts as important facets of a well-rounded education, the Clinton administration embraced the concept and included it in national educational goals.

At the same time, the nation's top classical concert venues also began taking a more careful look at jazz. Ever since the first jazz concert at Carnegie Hall in 1938 and Norman Granz's famed Jazz at the Philharmonic tours, jazz had flirted with classical music palaces. For jazz, these venues offered the music legitimacy as "America's Classical Music." For classical venues, jazz provided more variety in programming and the possibility of a box office boost.

But, in April 1991, the Lincoln Center for the Performing Arts went beyond such flirtations by creating a permanent Department of Jazz, with Wynton Marsalis acting as its first artistic director. Without question, this was an important moment for jazz, but it would also become the source for bitter disagreement. From the outset, Marsalis and his associates clearly put his stamp on programming, with an emphasis on masters such as Jelly Roll Morton, Duke Ellington, and Louis Armstrong. In less than two years, critics of the program charged racism (because no tributes to white jazz greats had been programmed), age-ism (because of a foolish attempt to fire any musician in the band over 30), cronyism, and that Jazz at Lincoln Center (JALC) was ignoring the contributions of many other musical cornerstones such as the avant garde. Rarely in jazz history has the dialog over programming been quite so spicy.

Articles on JALC's growing pains and missteps became the fodder of many critics and musicians in New York and across the nation, with its accomplishments seemingly overshadowed. Still, the JALC, as of this writing, is flourishing, as are programs at Carnegie Hall and the Smithsonian Institution. The great hope is that, from the fiery debate over what should be programmed, other departments of jazz will sprout and fill the voids.

As *Down Beat* celebrated its sixtieth anniversary, the magazine, too, took some criticism. Early in the decade, *Down Beat's* cover began sporting the tag line "Jazz,

Blues & Beyond." "Beyond" was adopted to keep the magazine from being trapped in the "What-is-Jazz?" debate. It was taken directly from Duke Ellington, who often described music and musicians as "beyond category...."

In 1990 and 1991 we took it a bit too far beyond, with cover articles on Lyle Lovett, Living Colour, and Lou Reed. Just a few letters from our readers put *Down Beat* back on course.

Still, some critics weren't satisfied. In a cover article on *Down Beat's* sixtieth anniversary in the *Chicago Tribune Magazine*, writer Howard Reich wrote, "...*Down Beat* hasn't fully come to terms with its own mission. Its subtitle, 'Jazz, Blues and Beyond' suggests no clear definition of where its coverage starts and stops."

Down Beat wears that criticism as a badge of honor. For 60 years, the editors and publishers of this magazine have come into the office each morning seeking the best that jazz has to offer. Many times it's straightahead and swinging; sometimes it's beautifully classical, avant garde, fusionary, or free; and on the rarest of occasions, it's the beginning of this music's next wondrous revolution. And that search is the essence of jazz.

Long live the revolution. Long live *Down Beat*! ●

FRANK ALKYER joined *Down Beat* in 1989 as editorial director. Two years later he was also named associate publisher and continues to serve the magazine in both capacities. Prior to joining *Down Beat*, Alkyer served as a newspaper journalist, covering everything from music and arts to politics and even the art of growing extremely large vegetables.

HERBIE HANCOCK AND QUINCY JONES: TALKIN' 'BOUT THE MUSIC OF THESE TIMES

By Josef Woodard

JANUARY 1990

When *Down Beat* thought to pair up Herbie Hancock and Quincy Jones for the kickoff issue of a new year and a new decade, we didn't know quite how fortuitous the match was. Symbolically, here are two West Coast-based veterans of the jazz and pop wars (not to mention film music), still very much in active duty. As emblems of the present, past and future, they function as both father time and the baby ringing in the new as they wax nostalgic about the old.

Hancock, born in 1940, and Jones, born in 1933 (both in Chicago, although Jones grew up in Seattle), have a lot of songs left in their fiddles, a lot of heads to turn and controversies to ignite. Are they jazz artists? Are they erstwhile jazzers who have cashed in and settled comfortably in Hollywood? Or are they—as both would have it—beboppers by breeding, answering honestly to the call of music, by whatever name it comes?

There's no pat answer. Suffice to say, both boast a sound, creative muscle tone and have the capacity to deliver music of substance—and marketability.

Work-wise, too, Hancock and Jones have recently joined forces, again. Hancock was part of the who's who cast of musical characters on Jones's first solo album in almost a decade, tellingly entitled *Back on the Block.* There is an eerie synchronicity in the fall air the day the interview takes place. Talking by the pool, they discover that the release date of both Jones' *Back on the Block* and *Harlem Nights*—the Eddie Murphy film which Hancock scored—is the same day, Nov. 16.

On Halloween, it's a beautiful Southern Californian day in the neighborhood, the neighborhood of Bel Air, that is. Jones' lavish but unpretentious hilltop house, previously owned by Julio Iglesias, is armed with a stunning view.

Josef Woodard: *Let's start by touching on your connection together. Where have you crossed paths in the past?*

Quincy Jones: With Herbie? My God. When we first worked together, you must have been what, 21 years old? I think it was in '64, when we did *Mirage.*

Herbie Hancock: But I think I met you in '61, when I was 21. Probably at Birdland.

QJ: You used to give Donald Byrd a hard time about being 30. "Ah, that's ancient, man."

HH: (*Laughs.*) We always have this thing, see, we tease each other about age. The funny thing is, I'll be 50 next year, and when you get around that point up to about 60, it's all the same.

QJ: It's all the same, and there's a psychological countdown. You wonder, "How many more do I have?" You appreciate each one. After my brain operation [an aneurysm in 1974], it really focused me. It meant that I enjoyed every day.

JW: *Did that also motivate you creatively?*

QJ: Absolutely, because you can't take it for granted that you're going to get another shot. You can't say, "I'll do it next time." You better do it now. When I had that operation, the first thing I realized was, "Damn, I've got so many dreams that I haven't even touched yet This is it?" I thought that was it. That was 15 years ago. That's pretty scary and it makes you apply another kind of biological time clock on things. I never take anything for granted anymore, relationships and things you feel for people.

My doctor says to me, "When you're staying up at night, if you're dissatisfied with the end result, then it's destructive. If it's satisfying and rewarding and you're happy with the end result, it does absolutely nothing wrong to you." It's a funny phenomenon.

We do brutal hours, man. Herbie just came through it, too. But if it comes out in the end and you're happy and there's a smile, your whole soul gets healed. It really does—it heals itself. We really beat our bodies up, you know. It's ridiculous.

The Color Purple almost put me in my grave. It was like holding onto the tail of a 747. And then, on top of that, we had to mess with the music, too. The production was a mind-boggler—10 trillion details to deal with everyday.

JW: *You've both worked under inherently tight deadlines to do film scores. Herbie, you only had three weeks to finish the score for* Harlem Nights. *Does that force both of you to rise to the challenge?*

QJ: Absolutely. It's the only thing that will force you to rise to the challenge. Otherwise, you procrastinate. The worse thing they could do is to tell Herbie, "You just take your time. Whenever you get it just like you want it, that's when you turn it in."

He wouldn't hit it until the week before they put it out. If they gave you three years to work on an album, you'd be working the last two months.

HH: If I didn't have some kind of deadline, I wouldn't write a note. I find all kinds of excuses not to do it. When I have to produce something, I tell myself, "The next idea that comes out—I don't care what it is—I'm using it." The very last thing I had to do, it was a cue they threw at me at the end. I told them, "Look, I'm going to do that last. You've got no business adding another piece of music with all the other stuff." It was the last day. I had been up all night again and I'm supposed to be at the studio in 15 minutes. I remembered that there was one piece that I had recorded an alternate introduction for and we didn't know where to stick it. So I said, "I'm using it."

I played it back and it wasn't long enough. So I just played another piece of music for the front of the scene, and it worked. Then I took that other piece of music and butt-spliced it....

QJ: Worked like a charm?

HH: Yeah. I looked at it and saw about five different things get hit with expressions and cuts and everything, so I wrote it exactly for that scene.

QJ: That's when God walks in the room.

JW: *Film score deadlines are one thing—a hard-and-fast situation. How do you go about making your own project, such as you just have. Do you have to make a self-*

Cory Graves

Herbie Hancock and Quincy Jones

imposed deadline?

QJ: To even pay attention, yes. This went past a self-imposed deadline. It's almost nine—going on 10 years—late. That's ridiculous. That makes even Stevie [Wonder] look like a swifty. But you know, I got sidetracked with a lot of other things that really couldn't be put back. We did *Thriller* and then *Color Purple*. I started my album and then the picture just ran over it. We did that and *We Are the World* and *Bad*.

I didn't go to the beach on this, really. Other things just took priority over what was happening. It's okay. Everything has its own time. The records that I've made I'm really happy with. Maybe they're supposed to simmer a little bit. Like some greens. It's a long simmer, though.

HH: Yeah. (*Laughs.*) You probably wouldn't have made the same record.

QJ: No doubt about it, Herbie. All the living and everything that happened went into it. It was a very heavy decade.

HH: From everything you've told me, it sounds like a summary album in a way.

QJ: It's all the roots. Dizzy and Miles were my answer to the Rolling Stones and the Beatles. To see Dizzy and Miles—who have never played together on a record—and Ella and Sarah—who have probably never sung together on a record, was like a fairy tale. James Moody—I started with James Moody when I was 19. I used to write for him. I survived off him. He used to give me $12 a week to write for his

band. All of it seems like that was the way it was supposed to be.

JW: *Was that the intention, to touch on a broad spectrum of music, or did it just keep growing?*

QJ: No, it just came out like that. It had been so long since I'd made a record that I really went for definitiveness in every category. It worked out like that. I was also very interested in pulling the different generation's fans together. That's why Kool Moe Dee and Big Daddy Kane are introducing Ella, Sarah, Dizzy and Miles Davis.

There's a correlation between bebop and hip-hop. I can't put my finger on it, but I feel there's a real natural alliance, for many reasons. Right down to colloquialisms. We called each other "homeboy" in the old days. Like beboppers, they play for each other and rappers rap for each other. There are a lot of correlations and similarities there. My son's heavily into rap and hip-hop: He's a dancer. So it all felt real natural.

HH: The great thing about Q is that he can relate to all of those different genres and different ages without any pretension, because it's natural. (*To Jones:*) You have to do it that way, because that's the way you are. You're all those things.

QJ: It's what we learned, Herbie. You're the same way. You want to taste the whole menu. Other guys are saying, "No, you can't do this. No man, you gotta play acoustic instruments" and all that bullshit. I don't even want to hear about that. If Bach were alive today, he would be all over the synthesizer, because of the extension of our vocabulary. That's all it is. It doesn't replace a real string section or anything else. It's just an extension and it enhances and enlarges our vocabulary.

I want to come through these 25,000 days having experienced all of it, man. I don't just want this tiny little cubbyhole over here and can't get out of it. Herbie's

always been like that. People jump all over you for it, but who cares? He'll still wear out anybody that sits down next to him in any category. Herbie don't have to worry about that.

JW: *Dance music has been a fixture in your music for years, Herbie. Future Shock, for instance, was a real turning point for you and the R&B world at large.*

QJ: Oh, long before that.

HH: I'm into phase two. I made a big decision back in 1973. I came to a realization about myself. I'm the kind of guy who had always preached about equality in music and that you shouldn't put this type of music over that type, that music is not a sport and that idiom cannot be the measure of good or bad. You can only look at the works in that idiom. The only thing you can really say is, "I like it," or, "I don't." One man's wheat is another man's poison. I preached all of that, but, at that point in my life, I started to realize that I drew lines myself.

One thing was, I loved hearing Sly Stone. If he would have said, "Come and sit in," I would have done it. But, for me to actually do that, it was no-no-no-no. It was like, "I'll do that on your stage, in your setting, but in my setting, I don't want to do that." But then I really looked at myself and said, "Wait a minute, who are you? What are you saying? What was all of this stuff about that you'd been saying before?" So I sat back, reexamined myself, and realized that I was just as guilty as the people I had condemned.

I said to myself, "Obviously, you like jazz, but you obviously like funk and R&B." When I was a kid, I listened to it and then got away from it. I became kind of a jazz snob when I noticed that all the coolest kids—the ones who seemed more mature—in high school were all listening to jazz. Everybody else was running around silly listening to pop and R&B. But then James Brown got me back listening to it. But I was only *listening* to it.

Anyway, I decided that I wanted to try it myself. I looked at it from a lot of different angles. I said, "You might lose all the audience that you've gained up to this point and you might not even gain a new one." But I said, "I have no choice. I have to do it."

Headhunters was *supposed* to be a funk album. As it started to evolve, I heard that it wasn't a funk album; but, whatever it was becoming, I liked the way it was headed. So I said, "Whatever this is, let's just do it." So we did it.

QJ: We started out with the eclectic thing from the very beginning, back in Seattle. When I was 14 years old and Ray Charles was 16, our average night went like this: We played from seven to 10 at a real pristine Seattle tennis club, the white coats and ties, roomful of roses, we'd accompany to dinner music, dying inside. Between Ray and Bumps Blackwell's band and our band, we had every job in town, you know.

From 10 to about one o'clock, we'd go play the black clubs: the Black and Tan, the Rocking Chair, and the Washington Educational Social Club—which is a funny name, funkiest club in the world. We'd play for strippers and comedians and play all the Eddie Cleanhead Vinson and Roy Milton stuff, all that R&B. It was a vocal group. Then, at about 1:30 or 2 a.m., everybody got rid of their gigs and we went to the Elks Club to play hardcore bebop all night long. That was it, didn't get paid a quarter. That's where we all would go at the end of the night—Cecil Young, Gerald Brashear and Ray Charles. Anybody coming in from out of town, like Jimmy Cleveland, Jerome Richardson, even Eric Dolphy would come by. Bebop was it, that was the love.

But we had to do everything—schottisches [Scottish dances], funk, R&B, pop music, bebop, "Clair de Lune," everything. So it was an eclectic background in the beginning, also with school bands and marches. I was into R&B before I was into bebop—or at least simultaneously. We were real hip then. It was pitiful how hip we were then. We were trying to make these schottisches and everything else sound like bebop, and I remember Ray Charles said one night, "Every music has its own soul. Be true to it." I never forgot that. Its own pure soul. It doesn't need to have something imposed on it. That was a big lesson.

So it feels absolutely normal to be eclectic and, whatever criticisms there might be about it, it doesn't phase me.

HH: The other thing is that, you're aware of the essences of the different kinds of music. So when you combine them, you're still maintaining what Ray was talking about.

QJ: Right, the essence and integrity of where the music comes from without violating it. You don't have to violate it. Our music is really based on hybrid music. One great thing about jazz is that its very essence is like osmosis. It absorbs and eats everything in its path—dances, marches, Stravinsky, country music, everything. That's why it's so rich and that's why when someone wants to go find something fresh, it's always there.

HH: You know, I don't think I could have done the things I've done in pop music—and I'm sure you'd say the same thing—if we had not had our foundation in jazz.

QJ: Absolutely. It's like a classical music training. It's just in your mind and your thinking. You're never so rigid as to say, "Hey, you played a sharp ninth instead of a flatted ninth there. You can't do that." Just go with the sharp ninth or whatever you've got going. That's almost like a philosophy of life, about the way you deal with life. Do you flow with the punches or do you have a rigid preconceived idea of where you want to go and get stuck in it? It opens your head up so that you can be lucid about whatever happens. Roll with it, be resilient.

HH: I know that sometimes jazz musicians may have a tendency to be rigid about their own set of rules, but I feel fortunate that, even though I was that way at a certain time, because of circumstances, there was a point where I was able to get out of that. I look at people who seem to be stuck with those rules and I think, "Well, I'm glad I'm not there." (*Laughs.*)

QJ: You don't grow, getting stuck in one thing. Miles is the same way. He's already done that. Herbie, we came out of that school.

Back in 1953, it was a big turning point, playing clubs with Lionel Hampton. We knew what it was like to have people love your music and be into it, because we'd already experienced that. It was kind of unnatural to aim at being disliked, you know. You had to work at it. I don't know if you went through this, Herbie, but we also had the attitude of kidding about "they ain't playing shit." The whole attitude was that, if you wanted to, you could be commercial like that (*snaps his fingers*), which is another joke. It doesn't work that way if it's not sincere.

HH: Even today, they think that.

QJ: They say, "If we play three chords, it will be commercial." That's a myth. I still think that sincerity is the most important component. It has to be something you believe in.

HH: In that regard, one part of my experience is with the guitarist Wah Wah Watson. He's a rhythm guitar player, not really a soloist. When I first hired him to play in my band, we played this one tune each night that he would solo on. He would play the same solo every night, because that was the way he was taught. His training was to perfect one way of doing something.

He didn't have a lot of things to draw on, either. What amazed me was that, every night, he'd play the same solo the same way, but every night, it sounded like it was the first time he ever played it. It was fresh everytime. And I didn't know how to do that, because jazz doesn't teach you that. I said, "I've got to learn that."

He would just play two or three things and the audience would immediately remember and respond to that. I could play rings around this guy, play all over the place, and that little statement that he would make would get incredible acknowledgment every night. I wasn't playing rings around him. I was just playing a lot of notes around him. It really taught me a lesson about what music is about and the value of the direction I was going in at the time.

QJ: That's another point, Herbie. Starting out as a bebopper—and I wear that banner with pride—is also a statement that you are aware of the latest thing that's gone on up to the moment. To *stay* there is to almost contradict that statement. If you stay there, it's just the opposite of what you're proud of. The latest word in terms of vernacular or colloquialisms or musical phrases, the latest lick, the latest figure on "All God's Children Got Rhythm"…you were right on top of the latest thing that was happening. But that's not the latest thing right now.

So it's a matter of being a part of an aura of an awareness. You don't have to work at that. You just get up every day and constantly move, it will happen automatically.

When you talk about pop music, you have to realize that in the thirties, pop music was Duke Ellington and Count Basie. That was pop, dance music. It had other elements in there, too, but it was pop music. They were equivalent to the Rolling Stones.

HH: Any music from that root was jazz, and rock 'n' roll came from that same root. So if somebody hadn't imposed other terminology, rock 'n' roll would have been jazz, too.

QJ: The first electric guitar players were around in 1939. Then, in 1953, a guy came to us just before we went to Europe with Hamp. Monk Montgomery was playing bass with us and Leo Fender said to him, "Why don't you try this for awhile." Nobody knew what the hell it was and the critics were saying, "Hamp doesn't have a bass player. What's wrong?" It was the Fender bass. We made records with that with Art Farmer and Clifford [Brown].

The electric guitar and the Fender bass were the cornerstones of rock 'n' roll. When electric bass came along, that's when the focus in the rhythm section changed. They came from a jazz foundation, but those were the two cornerstones that made it possible for rock 'n' roll to happen. It's always fascinated me, especially being there when we picked the first one up. Then we had to conceive of the bass part's function in the rhythm section.

I remember when Miles did things leading up to *Bitches Brew*, he played trumpet almost like a percussive instrument while all the action happened in the rhythm section. The roles shifted. Before, they used to keep time for the instruments to dance around: the rhythm section danced and they had to keep almost a percussion-type presence.

HH: This reminds me of when Wayne Shorter wrote "Nefertiti." We were in the recording studio and Wayne brought it in. We were trying to learn the song. Miles gave me a part. Miles was trying to play the melody and Wayne was sort of following behind. Wayne could have just played it, but he wanted to see Miles interpretation of it. The rhythm section was working on it and we would play it over and over again while they'd play the melody.

Finally, I said to Miles, "Listen, Miles, the melody is so beautiful, how would it be if the horns basically played the melody and the rhythm section actually evolved? He said (*in a gruff whisper*), "Okay." That's what we did. ●

HARRY CONNICK, JR.: WHEN HARRY MET STARDOM

By Michael Bourne

MARCH 1990

It oughtta be a movie. Something dangerous from the forties. Very *noir*.

It's about this District Attorney in New Orleans. He's tough, a crusader. He's sworn to bust crime on Bourbon Street. But there's a troubled look on his face, and at his desk he's looking at a photo. It's him with a child playing piano. And as some blues resound, the camera walks through the smoke of a jazz joint. Someone dances for a table of gawking gangsters, and on the bandstand, as an old black clarinetist blows a mean chorus, the camera stops at the piano.

There's a white kid playing, his eyes closed, enraptured by the music. And in spite of the cigarette and the demimonde around him, it's obvious he's an innocent. Just then, a whistle! It's a raid! Cops everywhere! Over at the bar, a whore jumps aside, pushing away a drunken hand snatching at nylons. And a pusher drops a white packet but slams into angry, blue beef. And the kid looks up, frightened. There, standing at the eye of the storm, gunshots and screaming all around him, is the D.A.—his father.

"It wasn't as bad as all that," said young New Orleans entertainer Harry Connick, Jr. Now a destined star of the nineties as a pianist and singer with three albums on Columbia (the newest, his best-selling soundtrack from the movie *When Harry Met Sally…*), and on screen as an actor in the forthcoming World War II movie *Memphis Belle*, and on tour with his trio or his orchestra playing sold-out concerts and crooning to babes young and old, and ga-ga as if he's Sinatra rejuvenated, Harry first gigged on Bourbon Street when all of 13— and when his father was indeed the District Attorney. Only, the scene wasn't so…cinematic.

"It was quite unusual and looks strange now, but then it was just a gig. There were really no gangsters, but a lot of prostitutes were hanging around and a lot of dope pushers. My father came down there to clean up the prostitution and to bust a big heroin ring and he successfully completed that. I'd be playing down there and he'd be down there at the same time. He'd stick his head into the club just to make sure I was alright. I was surrounded by nice, older guys who'd never let anything happen to me anyway."

What? No temptations? No fallen angels offering to show the kid the joys of manhood? Not even a raid?

"A raid is nothing like 25 policemen bust in with rifles and shout, 'Stick 'em up!' A raid is seeing a prostitute or an act going on, handcuffing them, and putting them on a bus until the bus is full. That's a raid. It was never 'Oh Daddy, don't shoot!'"

Harry was five in 1973 when his father was first elected, beating Jim Garrison, the D.A. who'd become famous when he'd accused the Warren Commission of covering up a conspiracy to assassinate JFK. "I wasn't aware until last year when my daddy explained how corrupt it was before he got there." And if one righteous parent wasn't enough, Anita Connick, his mother, was a judge as politically determined as his father. When she was dying of cancer, she beat seven men for the judgeship.

But, really? No troubles for young Harry? No hookers and Hurricanes? If not the melodramatic scenario, at least some youthful foolishness?

"When you have a dad who's a D.A. and a mom who's a judge, you don't go around smoking pot and getting drunk. I stayed clean, not only for my health's sake but for the sake of their political careers."

And when his father was first sworn in, June (as Junior is called by his family) realized his own true calling.

"My mother said, 'I want Harry, Jr., to play "The Star-Spangled Banner" at the ceremony.' My father said, 'I have the biggest speech of my life to give today! I don't have a piano!' She was a proud mother. She said, 'I want him to play!' So my daddy called up a friend who had a warehouse with a piano and a flat-bed truck. I played and I remember hearing the crowd applaud. I wanted to continue to play but my daddy shoved me out of the way and said, 'Look, this is my day, not yours!' But that sound generated my interest to continue to play. I've always wanted to hear that applause. To me, that's what a lot of it is all about."

He'd played the piano as if from the womb. "I don't know where I got it from. There were no outstanding musicians in my family. I've always just played. It's been a part of my life as long as I can remember. The first time I touched a piano, I knew it was what I wanted to do."

Harry's cousin Georgia was his first teacher. "She taught me what middle C was." And eventually he worked with many others, in particular, two legends of New Orleans piano, James Booker and Ellis Marsalis, father of the remarkable Marsalis brothers, Wynton, Branford, and Delfeayo. "I've known the Marsalis family a very long time. Me and Delfeayo played basketball together. I remember hearing Wynton and Branford playing with Ellis in the seventies when I was a child."

At nine, Harry joined the union, first recording two albums featuring his impression of Louis Armstrong. Harry was enrolled at the New Orleans Center for the Creative Arts—but was already working professionally. He first gigged, at 13, at the Dixieland joint the Famous Door. "There'd be 16 hours of music seven days a week. I played just about every club there is. I played jazz, rap, funk, fusion, dixieland. I played classical recitals." Though his instrumental style nowadays hearkens to the masters of jazz piano, especially Thelonious Monk, Duke Ellington and the energetically entertaining Erroll Garner, jazz was not, early on, his delight.

"I was a teenager in the seventies and I don't think any teenager, unless he's an introvert, will listen to music that's not popular. I wanted to be popular, so I'd do Stevie Wonder imitations. I'd do the Bee Gees, Donna Summer, Michael Jackson. It wasn't until I'd moved up to New York when I was 18 that I started playing the piano seriously. I'd listen to Chick Corea

and Herbie Hancock, the Return to Forever albums and *Thrust*, and I was impressed by those records. But then I started playing the piano seriously. I started listening to Monk—and I hated Monk. I hated Duke. I hated Erroll Garner. I said, 'Why can't I do this? Why can't I play like Monk? It sounds so easy!' That's when I discarded Chick and Herbie—because I could play like them. I'm not denying their talents. I think they're wonderful players—but I'm still saying, 'Why can't I play like *Monk*?'"

Harry became a jazz classicist, excited by Earl Hines and Fats Waller, the stride of James P. Johnson, the boogie woogie of Meade Lux Lewis, Albert Ammons, Pete Johnson, the pianistic

William Coupon

phantasmagoria of Art Tatum—"all of the people who really *played* the piano!" Elements of all of them resound in Harry's playing. And as a singer, he also listened back to classic crooners—Russ Colombo, Bob Eberle, Dick Haymes, and especially Frank Sinatra. He's already being called, in his way with ballads and his appeal as an entertainer, the *next* Sinatra.

"Tony Bennett said that, and that was a high compliment. Sinatra is my favorite. He's the greatest singer in the world. He's initiated things that had never been done before him. Nobody ever changed lyrics in a song before like him. No one could slide

on the notes like him. No one ever extended phrases, like for 25 seconds without breathing, before he did. Nobody ever used a microphone like he did. No one had ever been that popular and changed fashion like he did. No one had ever won an Oscar, being a musician, like he did. No one had ever been 74 years old on the Lou Rawls telethon a while ago and completely made untrue what people say, that he can't sing anymore. He sang 'Luck Be A Lady' and completely trashed everyone else on that show!"

Tony Bennett, likewise a singer Harry appreciates, praised Harry after his sensational stand in January 1989 at The Algonquin, the chic-beyond-chic cabaret of New York—a professional leap that was quite quantum.

He'd settled in New York in 1985 and gigged around—a church in the Bronx, weddings, the Empire Diner, other piano joints. Wynton Marsalis encouraged George Butler to sign him with Columbia and Delfeayo Marsalis produced the eponymous 1987 release *Harry Connick, Jr.* He dedicated the album to his mother and recorded "On The Sunny Side Of The Street" in the spirit of James Booker. Ellis Marsalis was also honored, and Harry's original called "E" is the only trio—with bassist Reginald Veal and drummer Herlin Riley, regulars now with Wynton's band. All of the other music, including "I Mean You" by Monk, features Harry's duets with Ron Carter.

Kevin Blanq, another New Orleans friend and the son of Harry's classical teacher, Betty Blanq, produced his second Columbia release, *20*—his age at the time. Marion Cowings worked with Harry on his singing debut—that is, as a grownup. It's almost all solo and is all standards, most written generations before Harry was alive, from "Avalon" to masterworks of Irving Berlin, Harold Arlen, Hoagy Carmichael, and "Don't Get Around Much Anymore" by Ellington, the latter with bassist Robert Hurst, Carmen McRae and Dr. John also guesting.

Yet, even with two albums, Harry Connick, Jr., was not a name to reckon with. Not yet. "The Algonquin is a cabaret, and I don't want to be a cabaret musician, but it's a room that would get me a lot of attention, and it surely did. January 1989 was when my career started." Nobody was certain what to expect. Nobody but Harry. "They said they'd get me the guy who wrote *Sugar Babies* to write some patter. I said, 'I don't need no patter!' They said they'd give me songs. I said, 'I don't need any songs. I'll do it myself.' They were scared to death."

More than half the audience opening night were critics—and Harry was annoyed they weren't reacting like a *real* audience. "I was wondering why I wasn't getting much applause. Press people don't clap. I said, 'What the hell's wrong with you people? Come on, now! I'm from New Orleans and I want to hear some applause!'" They were nonetheless charmed, said so in review after review, and all of the 36 shows sold out.

Soon thereafter Harry sold out a concert at Lincoln Center so fast he didn't have a ticket for his father. Harry even showed up in Liz Smith's gossip column after he'd played a birthday party for cabaret superstar Peter Allen, a friend he's now recorded with. He'd also played a Ted Kennedy party and a variety of all-star shows. Harry Connick, Jr., was almost…*there.*

But some supposed breaks turned into breaks of his spirit. Harry played "The Tonight Show" in 1988 and was angered when they rejected him playing solo. "They said Doc Severinsen's band plays loud and going to solo piano is gonna be anti-climactic. I said, 'I'm from New Orleans. I play loud!'" They then, after already booking him, wanted Harry to audition just before the broadcast. He'd auditioned for "The Tonight Show" years before, when he was a prodigy of nine, and Harry remembers being hurt. "I played 'Sophisticated Lady' and Doc Severinsen said, 'Get away, kid!' He was an adult and could've acted like an adult."

Harry, now an adult, was stuck with a bassist from the band. "I was incredibly nervous and right before the curtain goes up, the first time I'll perform for 30 million people, Freddie DeCordova pats me on the shoulder and says, 'Don't screw up, kid!' That made me feel just *great!* I cracked the first note." Harry sang "I Can't Give You Anything But Love," and wowed the audience—but vowed never to return. "They've insulted me twice!"

It was much the same, being pissed,

when he played "Late Night with David Letterman" to promote the Algonquin. "I had a number all worked out to do with Paul Shaffer, and he said, 'That sounds too lounge act, too much like Duke Ellington.' I'd never heard Duke Ellington and 'lounge act' in the same sentence before. I was so miserably insulted by that, I said to myself, 'I don't want to play a duet with you.' So during rehearsal, I played just fierce piano to make him scared. He's great for that show but he ain't no piano player!" Harry eventually played solo, some boogie woogie as requested by the show, some stride for himself, and then sang "Shake, Rattle And Roll"—but it wasn't satisfying, not for the audience, not for Harry.

"I don't like those shows. You play one song and that's supposed to represent what you do. But I don't do one thing. I sing ballads and swing songs. I play stride and boogie woogie. I play New Orleans. I tap dance. If I could play five songs…."

Harry won't have to return to TV, not after the success of his soundtrack to *When Harry Met Sally….* Bobby Colomby at CBS talked director Rob Reiner into working with Harry. "Don't ask me why, but Rob took this unknown jazz musician and said, 'Do my movie.' I said, 'I'd love to do it but I have to play jazz.' Listen to the opening theme, the instrumental of 'It Had To Be You'—that's jazz. It's like 'Paris Blues' by Duke, even though it's not on that level—but it's real jazz. Rob is a great director and he's got balls. He said he wanted this and that's what he did."

Billy Crystal and Meg Ryan inexorably fell in love to the classic New York love songs of the Gershwins, Rodgers and Hart, Vernon Duke and Duke Ellington. Louis Armstrong, Ella Fitzgerald, Ray Charles, Bing Crosby and Frank Sinatra all sing in the movie, but on the soundtrack album, it's all Harry. "They, or their estates, didn't want to part of the album, and I ended up doing all the songs. It's the biggest break of my life."

Harry's album sold 200,000 in a month, headed for gold, and quadrupled sales for *20.* He was also featured on two videos from the movie, singing "It Had To Be You" and "Don't Get Around Much Anymore" all around Manhattan and looking so *mah-velous.* He's classically photogenic, a clothes horse with a Hollywood face and that trademark pompadour. And with the movie, plus the momentum from the Algonquin, Harry

leaped from 300-seat rooms to 3,000-seat halls, often with nineties-style bobby-soxers swooning.

"I don't mean to be chauvinistic, but young girls love to be sung to. I do concerts in San Francisco, Seattle, Minneapolis, and 15 to 20 rows are all young girls. They throw flowers! It's like a rock concert. I come out backstage after an hour and there's still 200 people out there in the cold waiting for autographs. I try to be cool, but inside I'm jumping for joy. I can't believe this is happening, not just for me but for the music. Of course I want the money. Of course I want the attention. But jazz is becoming popular again! Wynton started it, and Branford, and I'm continuing it. And it's not that Lite-FM jazz. It's the real thing!"

Harry looks back to Armstrong and Ellington, jazz greats who also entertained, and aspires to do likewise. "Some jazz musicians seem to feel that the audience doesn't matter, that only music matters. But the audience absolutely 100 percent matters, and every performer wants a full house. Some people think entertaining is wrong, but the reason we get on stage is we have big egos and we want to play music in front of a crowd. I'm not ashamed to admit that. I watched Lionel Hampton play and you can see when he smiles that old school coming out. In the forties and fifties, jazz musicians entertained. In the sixties, rock 'n' roll entertained and jazz stopped entertaining. In the seventies, jazz got very obscure. In the eighties, jazz was dead and rock was #1. Jazz was absolutely nothing until Wynton Marsalis came along and pretty much brought it out of obscurity. He made it possible for me and every other young jazz musician who's making it today."

Harry Connick, Jr., is making it today—and there's more to come. He's just finished acting in a movie, *Memphis Belle,* filmed in England. David Puttman produced, Michael Caton-Jones directed, and Harry stars. "Memphis Belle was the first B-17 to fly 25 missions over Germany without getting blown up. I played a guy from New Orleans who sings a little and plays the piano, so it wasn't that difficult to settle into the character. But the technique of working with a director, working with the camera, finding your mark and trying to portray a character that was authentic to that time, that was difficult. My character was based on a guy from Yonkers, Johnny

Quinlan, who was the tail-gunner. All of the crew except him came over to England and had dinner with us and told us the stories. That was the most rewarding experience of all of it."

He expects he'll act again on screen soon—for Harry, it's more fun than work. There's talk that he'll play Bobby Darin, a singer he's often considered to be similar to, in a bio. And he'll have a song on another soundtrack, the Warren Beatty blockbuster, *Dick Tracy*. He's already turned away several offers to star on Broadway—a revival of *Pal Joey*, a stage adaptation of *An American in Paris*. "I'd love to do it, but for Broadway, you have to be on the road and by the time I got to New York, I'd be sick of it, the same thing night after night. One day I will. It's a challenge to me, but now is not the right time."

What he'll do in the meantime is travel with his trio, with bassist Ben Wolfe and drummer Shannon Powell, or his 30-piece orchestra. "They call it 'When Harry Met *When Harry Met Sally*,' but I call it Harry Connick, Jr., trying to sing in tune in front of an orchestra. People don't know, but that's hard work." He'll record twice this year, a trio album and an album of songs, most of the songs his own. And at 22, he's only just beginning.

So, with all this success, the inevitable covers of *People* and *GQ*, the girls, the money, the gossip, the inevitable blather of critics outraged that's he's so young and cocksure, there's an obvious question: What's to stop Harry Connick, Jr., from pumpkin-ing, from turning into just another phenomenon of show biz, just another sensation of the moment, just another asshole?

"I'm good at what I do, but 50, 60 years ago, Duke Ellington did stuff I can't do. How can I be conceited if I'm not mastering what I do? I have no doubt about my talent, but I just don't rank up there with the people I respect. I might become a jerk one day. But right now, as far as I can see, until I become great at what I do, I have no reason to be that. And even if I become great, I have no reason to be that. I have a big family, 45 cousins. They'll keep an eye on me. They'll kill me if I get uppity!" ●

By Howard Mandel
APRIL 1991

Drummer Roy Haynes has kept the tempo of the times for Luis Russell's Savoy Ballroom band, Lester Young, Charlie Parker, and Sarah Vaughan in her prime, John Coltrane and the earliest jazz-rock of Gary Burton, Chick Corea's standards trio, and Pat Metheny on his *Question and Answer* tour and album. Venturing from his home in Freeport, Long Island, to pick up a Grammy, lead a quintet at Condon's or pay paternal attention to his trumpeter/son Graham's career, Haynes is a lively presence and much in demand for his abilities to spark soloists and unite ensembles. He's had previous Blindfold Tests, and was given no information about the music played—but he needs a new needle and cartridge, if not a turntable. Hearing one channel of stereo, he still knew players young and old almost immediately.

1 JONATHAN "JO" JONES. "I Want To Be Happy" (from *The Main Man*, Pablo). Jones, brushes on drums; Roy Eldridge, Harry Edison, trumpets; Vic Dickenson, trombone; Eddie Davis, tenor sax; Sam Jones, bass; Freddie Green, guitar; Tommy Flanagan, piano. Recorded 1976.

Is that one of my favorite players playing brushes? (*Hums along with Jones' break.*) That's Jonathan, right? What year was this made? I knew from the start, but I wanted to listen to it all the way through. I laid one brush on his heart at the funeral—I got permission to do that. He was my idol. When the Basie band would come to Boston in the early forties, I had no school that week. People have said I looked like him; Dorothy Donegan told me recently, "You look more like Jonathan every day."

His touch and some of the licks he played—as he would say, he invented the high-hat. And the way he played a cymbal! He was the first drummer I heard intentionally turn the beat around—others may have done it earlier, but he was the first I heard. Jo Jones gets five stars, anyhow.

2 PANAMA FRANCIS AND THE SAVOY SULTANS. "Clap Hands, Here Comes Charlie" (from *Panama Francis and The Savoy Sultans*, Classic Jazz). Francis, drums, leader, arranger; Francis Williams, Irv Stokes, trumpets; Norris Turney, Howard Johnson, George Kelly, reeds; Red Richards, piano; John Smith, guitar; Bill Pemberton, bass.

The new Savoy Sultans? Panama Francis—his solo is just an edge faster than the band's tempo, which is normal. He knows, he played with Lucky Millinder, Cab Calloway, too, I think; he was one of the big band drummers of the forties.

"Clap Hands, Here Comes Charlie"—Basie used to feature Jo doing that. You didn't think I'd get Panama Francis? I respect everybody. Three stars.

3 BEN WEBSTER. "Spang" (from *The Big Three*, Doctor Jazz). Sid Catlett, drums; Ben Webster, tenor sax; Idrees Sulieman, trumpet; Tony Scott, clarinet; Argonne Thornton (Sadik Hakim), piano; Bill DeArango, guitar; John Simmons, bass.

Ben Websterish; that's not Tony Scott, is it? The feeling on the drums is Sid Catlett's. I knew him—drove him home to Harlem in my first automobile. Sid was a tall, graceful, warm guy—I never saw him get angry. I love his drumming, but I'd have preferred to hear something he did with Lester Young, trading fours.

You might say he's dropping bombs—I'd say he's making accents. It's not what he did, it's how he did it. Sticks *or* brushes, he had an amazing bag of tricks. Just the way he made rim shots....Neither he nor Jonathan played rudimental drums, which intrigued me in itself. This isn't a five-star record, but Sid Catlett was one of the greatest drummers there ever was; five stars for Sid.

4 ED BLACKWELL, DON CHERRY. "Mutron," "Bemsha Swing" (from *El Corazon*, ECM). Blackwell, drums; Cherry, organ, pocket trumpet.

Sounds a little avant-gardish, like the guys who played with Ornette Coleman—Cherry and Blackwell. Yeah? Hey, I'm great at this. I could feel something from that,

Mitchell Seidel

could tell even if Blackwell's not playing cymbal, even before Don played the horn. I like how they played with Ornette; I like Billy Higgins, too. It's a different approach—not a style, not a sound, but an approach to the instrument, the way it was hit, the feeling from the drums. Blackwell has that New Orleans concept, *plus.* Five stars for that— and five for me knowing them.

5 MARVIN "SMITTY" SMITH. "Just Have Fun" (from *Keeper of the Drums,* Concord). Smith, drums, composer; Ralph Moore, tenor sax; Wallace Roney, trumpet; Robin Eubanks, trombone; Steve Coleman, alto sax; Lonnie Plaxico, bass; Mulgrew Miller, piano.

Ralph Moore—I find him for my band, and all of a sudden he's the hottest tenor player around. Smitty. I got that 'cause I'm listening—the critics don't know the depth of Roy Haynes! Smitty's playing, it's there on the record—yeah! He knows it, and he grows all the time; he's a good musician. Nice hands. Cool. Five stars. ●

MILES DAVIS: MILES PLAYS GIL AT MONTREUX

By Bill Milkowski

OCTOBER 1991

He has said "Time After Time" that he would never again tread on old musical ground, that it was against his "Human Nature" to go backward and play music from the past.

Well, miracles do happen.

It started with a fax from Montreux Jazz Festival founder Claude Nobs to the late Gil Evans' widow, Anita, saying that Quincy Jones had this marvelous idea. He wanted to recreate live *Sketches of Spain,* the classic Miles Davis album arranged and orchestrated by Evans. The catch? Quincy wanted Miles, in person, to play it as part of the festival's 25th anniversary.

"When Quincy first called me, I said, 'Of course we'd like to do it, but I can't imagine Miles doing it,'" said Anita, who provided some of Gil's original charts for the project. "'You don't have a problem here, you just gotta talk Miles Davis into it.' And Quincy said, 'I already have. I used love. I've been on him. I told him it would be my dream come true to do it.'"

With that, a miracle was conceived, nurtured and born. Miles, for the first time, accepted the challenge to go back more than 30 years and perform the arrangements of Gil Evans from not only *Sketches of Spain,* but also from *Birth of the Cool, Miles Ahead,* and *Porgy & Bess.*

Billed as "L'Evenement" (the Event), the festival ground buzzed with anticipation. Could Miles, the renegade of the cutting edge, turn back time? Could he leave his funk and fusion trappings backstage and, for one fine evening, embrace these classic scores? After all these years, did he still have the chops to put his muted touch on complicated Gil Evans arrangements?

"I called up Quincy after the first rehearsal and said, 'You know, we really gotta get Miles,'" said arranger Gil Goldstein, who transcribed a great deal of the material. "Then I started to get nervous about Miles being able to play all of this stuff without coming to a rehearsal, because it's a hell of a lot of music. It's like classical music. You have to play it with the

orchestra."

Miles didn't attend rehearsals in New York, where a combination of the Gil Evans Orchestra and the George Gruntz Concert Jazz Band met to prepare for the gig. He opted to catch up with the band at Montreux.

"But, I did bring the music to his house before he left, just so he could start looking at it," Goldstein said. "The first rehearsal in Montreux was full of confusion. A million things were still up in the air as far as details of what was really gonna happen. People were uptight about various business issues. It was just a kind of nervous not-knowing-what-was-going-to-happen environment. Quincy showed up at 2 p.m. That was the first time we had actually met face to face.

"By 11 p.m., Miles showed up. It was unbelievable, just the perfect entry for Miles Davis. We were rehearsing 'Boplicity' [*from Birth of the Cool*] and he just kind of walked in right at the first phrase, sat down, and started taking out his horn."

The next evening, Miles received a hero's welcome as he made his way to the Casino stage and took his place before the 45-piece ensemble. With Quincy conducting, they opened with the lush, lightly swinging "Boplicity." And, from the first notes, all doubts were erased. The crowd was transported to jazz heaven.

One of the most enraptured listeners in the house was Quincy himself, who conducted the piece with obvious glee, smiling like a child on Christmas morning. After the number, he remarked to the crowd, "This is a great way to feel 17 again."

The sight of Miles Davis performing this classical material from the 1950s was like watching Muhammad Ali climb back into the ring with his jab intact. For jazz purists, it was a monumental comeback, a welcome return to the fold after years of jiving and vamping. Miles showed up and delivered the goods, blowing with the kind of confidence, soulful phrasing and dramatic power that few critics thought he still had in him.

IN SEARCH OF...

No one said it would be easy, but no one expected piecing together the charts for *Miles Plays Gil* to be as difficult as it was, either.

"Initially, nobody could find the music," said Anita Evans, Gil Evans' widow. "Gil always told me that the scores were over at Miles' house in New York. But when Cicely [Tyson, one of Miles' ex-wives] sold that house, only she knew where the stuff in the basement went. Miles said as far as he knew, Cicely had the music. But Quincy called her and she said she didn't. Finally, [Gil's sons] Noah and Miles started digging up some of Gil's old stuff that hadn't seen the light of day in 30 years. And, what they came up with were rough sketches of the charts, things that Gil had worked on before completing the official score for the record. Most of it was on score paper…incredibly precious stuff, like Gil's brain on a piece of paper. So, I sent those to Quincy and he looked them over. At this point, Gil Goldstein became very important to the project in helping Quincy make sense of Gil's charts."

"Finding those rough sketches of Gil's charts was like finding the Dead Sea Scrolls of jazz," Goldstein remarked. "It freaked me out when I saw them. No real complete scores, but really historical kinds of sketches on music paper. It was just unbelievably fascinating to see this stuff and have it in your hands.

"I already had full scores for 'Blues for Pablo' and 'Springsville,' which Gil had given me when I took some quasi-lessons with him when he was still here. So, I had a head start on those two.

The rest I had to just fill in the blanks by looking at these sketches and going back and listening to the records.

"In the end, I had to basically re-orchestrate a lot of it, so what we played is not the actual orchestration that is on the record. I had to make some educated guesses to fill in the blanks, but I was just gratified that it was all sounding like Gil and giving this general impression of those charts."

Goldstein may have been proud to work on the project, but he promptly placed credit for it success on the shoulders of two others.

"[Miles] really nailed the stuff," he said. "It took him a little while to warm up to the music and slide back into it, and doing it like, really, nobody else can do. Especially the stuff like 'My Ship.' It's just like…forget about it. Nobody can play that ballad like Miles.

"I also thought that Quincy was amazing," Goldstein added. "I just dig the fact that he can hang with Madonna and Michael Jackson and still be the total fan of this music. And, his love of this music filters into whatever he does. Really, he is the only person who could've pulled this thing together—the only one who could've encouraged Miles to do it and just have the persistence and vision to see it through. And, he really brought a lot of ideas to the thing. He went through the scores and really refined the stuff with a fine-toothed comb. I think as much as the guys were playing for Gil and Miles, they were playing for Quincy, too."

—Bill Milkowski

Sitting up-front alongside Miles were soloists Wallace Roney on trumpet and Kenny Garrett on alto saxophone. Roney functioned as a kind of safety net, occasionally doubling Miles' parts. This not only relieved Miles of any pressure of having to cut the difficult passages single-handedly, it also freed him up to take greater liberties with the melodies through his own adventurous phrasing.

The Miles magic was very much intact throughout the *Miles Ahead* medley. His seductive, muted trumpet work on "Springsville" and "My Ship" caused audible sighs from the audience and had Roney shaking his head in disbelief. The tone was captivating, unmistakably Miles; the lines characterized by masterful restraint, uncanny use of space, and a kind of sly, behind-the-beat phrasing on ballads that once caused Gil Evans to call him "a sensational singer of songs."

Miles' skillful timing was especially apparent on the title cut from *Miles Ahead*, which also featured a flowing, boppish alto solo from Garrett. On "Blues For Pablo," Miles engaged in spirited open-horn exchanges with Roney, who, throughout the program, would glance over at his hero with the eyes of a rookie watching Babe Ruth.

The idea of having Roney shadow Miles came up spontaneously during the first day of rehearsals at Montreux. "Miles didn't show up and we needed somebody to play his part," said Goldstein. "At first, we were going to have [trombonist] Benny Bailey do it, but at the last minute we gave it to Wallace Roney, who was one of the trumpets in George Gruntz' band. So, Wallace was up there playing Miles' part when Miles finally walked in during 'Boplicity.' Wallace just kind of stayed up there and started playing unison lines and trading solos with Miles.

"It was a great experience for him, and I think Miles really dug playing with him. And, I don't think that anybody could've done it as good as Wallace did in terms of just having real courtesy and respect and still play his ass off. He had to walk a kind of fine line between being a brat and being totally respectful. And, I think he was both."

But onstage, others were playing their asses off, too. Mike Richmond supplied a formidable bass presence, anchoring the pieces along with Grady Tate, whose brushwork on "My Ship" was sublime. Kenwood Dennard took over the drum chair on "Gone" from *Porgy & Bess* and kicked the band into high gear, inspiring some fiery eights between Miles, Roney and Garrett.

Miles dug deep on "Summertime," another muted-trumpet vehicle for the maestro, buoyed by a cushion of oboes and alto flutes. Delmar Brown added an earthy edge here with some lively, syncopated keyboard comping. Garrett responded with his finest solo of the

Hyou Vielz

evening, blowing more horn than he's ever had a chance to play in the context of Miles' electric band. Garrett also contributed some strong alto work on "Here Come De Honey Man," though Miles seemed indifferent to this serenely melodic piece, virtually laying out and relying on Roney to cover his parts.

The evening closed dramatically with two pieces from *Sketches of Spain*. With glasses in place, Miles diligently read the charts down, navigating his way through "Pan Piper" (which, unfortunately, was marred by a sharp E string on Carlos Benavent's electric bass) and culminating beautifully with the flamenco-flavored "Solea."

The next day, a group gathered to watch the videotape of "L'Evenement" at Claude

Nobs' chalet in the mountains. Members of the orchestra stood in awe of the aching tone, the vocal expression, the sheer power and unpredictable choices that Miles made throughout the evening. If a videotape of this performance is ever made available, a lot of skeptics are going to have to eat their words. (Memo to Messrs. Wynton Marsalis and Stanley Crouch: Dinner is served.)

"It was really a struggle sometimes getting all of the diverse realities together for this," said Anita Evans. "It just seemed unbelievable that it could happen. Every year for the past 25 years somebody would call up and ask Gil if they would get together and do it again. Depending on what year, either Gil would refuse or Miles would refuse. So, I had long ago gotten over the thought that I could possibly ever hear that happen. Gil was always thinking about the future or what he was doing next. He didn't want to look back. Miles had the same attitude. And, after all, some of this paper hadn't been unfolded in 34 years.

"So, you can imagine, it must have been scary for [Miles], not that he would ever admit it. But he braved it out, he showed up, and the music was beautiful. All the elements were set into place, then Miles came in and did what he does...those magical tones and colors, his masterful sense of time and space. He just breathed his Miles Davisness at the right moment while the orchestra played the stuff. I'm still floating over how beautiful it sounded."

Perhaps trumpet veteran Lew Soloff put it more succinctly: "That's one soulful motherf**ker."

In character, Miles didn't speak after the show, but his feelings about the music were captured in more ways than through his playing. "To me, one of the nicest things of the whole experience happened on the last rehearsal," Goldstein said. "I kind of walked over to Miles to give him some changes I had written out, and he was just standing there listening to the band rehearse *Sketches*, and he said, 'Nobody will ever write like that again.' It was obvious that he loves Gil's writing, but it was just nice to hear him say it again." ●

STEVE COLEMAN AND BRANFORD MARSALIS: GANG OF TWO

By Bill Milkowski
JANUARY 1992

The posters were splashed all over town: "Branford Marsalis with very special guests Steve Coleman and his Five Elements. Don't miss this explosive sax showdown. Five extraordinary performances only!"

While it wasn't exactly a cutting contest on the order of Flip Phillips and Lester Young in one of their classic Jazz at the Philharmonic battles, the two did mix it up a little bit during their week-long engagement at the Joyce Theater last fall, a prestigious concert hall in the Chelsea section of Manhattan that ordinarily showcases up-and-coming dance companies.

Coleman and his Five Elements ensemble opened with an electrified, rhythmically charged set, serving as a visceral counterpart to the acoustic intimacy of Branford's trio (with bassist Robert Hurst and drummer Jeff Watts). Steve exuded a funky Brooklyn street vibe with basketball shoes and colorful, loose-fitting garb. Branford dressed strictly *GQ*. Coleman danced openly to the groove, his unbound enthusiasm at times causing him to leap off the ground, à la Pete Townshend. Branford played it cool.

Seemingly polar opposites—one an instigator on the cutting edge, the other in the neo-classicist camp—beneath the surface, the two saxophonists have much in common, not the least of which is a wicked sense of humor and their mutual disdain for critics. The engagement at the Joyce gave audiences a chance to hear for themselves what they have in common musically. We spoke to both saxophonists backstage just minutes before their final night together.

Down Beat: *This billing sort of implies the two of you are kindred spirits.*

Branford Marsalis: Is that true, Steve? No, not us, man.

Steve Coleman: We supposed to hate each other.

BM: You know, he's with the M-BASE clan, and I'm with the neo-classicists. (*Laughs.*) The two shall never mix, man.

DB: *I didn't know that a neo-classicist could play on a Gang Starr record.*

BM: Oh, that's right. I forgot about that. (*Laughs.*) Uh…that was an aberration, man. Don't mind that.

SC: On that stuff, he doesn't care. Gang Starr, Sting, Grateful Dead, all that shit. He doesn't care. That's what that's about. (*Laughs.*)

DB: *A neo-classicist with no conscience.*

BM: (*Laughs.*) Yeah, an eye on the market always, babe. The truth is, I dig Steve Coleman and have for a long time. I first heard him on one of the early Five Elements records. This was right after I came to town in '82. I was real scared when I first got to New York. You know, this was supposed to be the place where all the bad motherf**kers are. Then I hear 'em, and I wasn't scared no more.

SC: (*Laughs.*) Well, I remember a friend of mine said, "Have you heard Wynton's brother?" I said, "What brother?" So I went to this place called Possible 20 to check this guy out. You were playing alto then, weren't you?

BM: No, that's when I first started playing tenor. That was my first week.

DB: *Can you remember your impression of Branford then?*

SC: I thought he could play. The thing is, when you first hear cats when they first come to town…when I listen to people I listen for not only what they're doing but the potential of what they might become. At that time, I was pretty young, he was pretty young. I could hear what his basic influences were but I really didn't get a good listen to him until I heard him later with Blakey and a little after that with Wynton. I heard you with Blakey on alto [check out Blakey's *Keystone 3* on Concord Jazz]. Man, I saw this funny video of you with Blakey. You were playing these hybrid, funk-bop licks. Just watching y'all was funny. I mean, Wynton was a little, skinny kid. And you had all this big hair.

BM: It was never big, but I just never got it cut…just a lot of out-of-shape hair. But it looked great with a tuxedo.

SC: That hairstyle was coming out of the seventies, that whole period. It was before

he got his Magic Johnson look.

BM: I prefer the term "neo-classicist" look. (*Laughs.*) But what was very apparent to me when I first came to town was a lot of the people I met in New York were primarily concerned with the perpetuation of their own egos. And the thing that struck me about Steve was that he was about the music. Everybody thought he played "out" at the time, I guess. But when I heard Steve play, the first thing that came to my mind was Charlie Parker. And critics that were hearing you playing Five Elements shit, they never dug the cross reference. They never heard Bird. They couldn't really hear where that shit was coming from so they wrote all this bullshit about obtuse meters and all this other nonsense. So when I did *Scenes of the City* in 1983, for that [Charles] Mingus track, I said I wanted to get Steve Coleman. And all these people said, "Steve Coleman??!! That cat?!" And I said, "That's right, Steve Coleman."

DB: *You obviously didn't have a problem with the way he played.*

BM: None whatsoever. See, most people that I know can't hear. They have good memories. They memorize sounds or records like how you memorize a photograph. But they can't hear for shit.

SC: You talking about audiences or musicians?

BM: Both. And critics, too. Like for instance, when I was in Wynton's band I

was playing like Wayne [Shorter]. And the writers said, "He plays very much like Wayne." So then I go on a gig and start playing verbatim Sonny Rollins solos and these writers would say, "Wow, man, I hear a lot of Wayne in your playing."

SC: (*Laughs.*) See, most jazz musicians and critics have this thing about whether you can play changes or not. Ain't that right? It's like, "Can he play? Can he play *changes*?" You heard that shit all your life, right? Cats be saying, "He can't play no changes." That kind of thing. I know what they mean…I understand, basically. But I always thought one of the most important things was not changes, but phrasing. I

really notice a big difference in the phrasing of cats who checked out Bird and transcribed his solos and whatever…just went through a whole thing with Bird. And with Branford, I heard it immediately the first time I heard him play. And, to me, it's not about whether you can play the shit verbatim or not. It's about hearing a certain lineage in a cat's playing, in his phrasing, his form, how he gets in and out of things, his sense of balance in the music. You can hear all that in the music. And you can hear a big difference in different people's playing because of that. A lot of cats who come straight out of Albert Ayler, they're gonna have a different sense of balance and resolution and phrasing and everything than a person who comes out of Newk [Rollins] or Bird.

BM: The bottom line is, jazz has an underlying logic that can't be denied. I started reading *Down Beat* in the seventies, and in interviews that I read, there had been those people who constantly tried to pretend as though the lineage didn't exist. They always used the coinage "new" as in "the new sound," as if previous generations had no cumulative influence on this new music. I was a history major in college and I never once heard a history teacher say that in order for us to progress as a nation we must destroy the past. Nor were historians ever labeled neo-classicists. But it seems in jazz there's an obsession with new vs. good. It seems like new is much

Branford Marsalis and Steve Coleman

more important than being good, and I don't agree.

DB: *Isn't that more about marketing?*

BM: I'm talking about interviews…critics, musicians themselves, the way they refer to the music. The fact is, as I once said in an interview, there's freedom in structure. There's really no freedom in what they call freedom. If a cat is playing a certain style of music and that's the only style of music that he can play, then he's not free. He doesn't choose to play avant garde or whatever they call it…open-sky music, all these f**ked-up names. He ain't got no choice. He has to play that because that's the only thing he can play. That's not freedom; that's slavery.

SC: It's like only knowing one way to get to your house and you don't have any other way to get there. If that way is blocked off, then you can't go home.

BM: And you have a slew of musicians who are getting tumultuous amounts of credit, and they only know one way to their home. And they make fun of people who know five or six ways instead of trying to learn other ways. Well, most of them don't have the musical ability to learn five or six ways.

SC: It's hard, too, because once you start getting known for something, that's when it becomes even harder to learn something else. Because you're getting all this hype now and you have to live up to this big image, you know what I mean? And then, you can't admit that you don't know anything. When nobody knows you, it's much easier to learn, I feel.

BM: But then the question they throw at you is, "Why are you even bothering to learn that? You

Teri Bloom

should be trying to develop your own sound." But I am developing my own sound. By learning all this other stuff, I will eventually get my own sound. Sonny Rollins and Wayne Shorter and Herbie [Hancock] and Ron [Carter]…they all told me the same shit.

SC: Getting back to when I first heard you: Around that time, I read this thing you said in an interview about originality. You said, "I'm too young, I got time to get my own sound. By the time I'm 30, I'll have my own sound." And then recently, I talked to somebody…not one of your fans.…

BM: One of my dear friends. (*Laughs.*)

SC: (*Laughs.*) Yeah, right. And he was

saying, "Well, I read this article where Branford Marsalis said that he was gonna get his own sound, and I don't feel like he's done that." But I feel like I hear a big difference between your playing then and your playing now. And it's not…you know, critics look for this…I don't know what they look for, but they're always wrong.

BM: Most of 'em can't hear, first of all.

SC: But I'm sitting here listening to him this week, and I'm hearing a lot of shit…there's a depth there, a certain kind of detail that was never there before. And it's funny because I hear some of that same thing that I heard in your early stuff and in my own early recordings that I hear in some of the younger guys today.

BM: It's because we are signing record contracts much earlier than the previous generation. So we are expected to play with the technical fluidity and melodic innovation of people in their early 30s when we're still in our early 20s.

SC: Well, I don't wanna name names, but there's a whole lot of young cats out there…some of them are getting

recognized right now but they really don't have any experience, they haven't played with anybody and they're getting this kind of hype heaped on 'em now. And I just hope it doesn't stop them from learning, because it has a tendency to just squash that whole growing process.

BM: Well, that's really up to them. It's like the thing you can never do…I feel there's a lot of hyperbole that influences reality. Like if somebody's gonna do an interview and tell some writer that I'm the saddest motherf**ker that's come down the pike…if I believe that shit, that is also my problem. I think that every artist of every kind in any idiom, be it a writer or a musician or a dancer, *you* have to know when you're good and when you suck. You have to get into yourself and you have to do what you have to do to improve. So all of the other stuff is all peripheral. It doesn't even matter, anyway.

DB: *So you must feel satisfied about your new trio record [*The Beautyful Ones Are Not Yet Born*]. It's like an incremental leap from the first three records you did.*

BM: Oh, hell yeah. And I expected it to be this way. It's just been a logical progression. I turned 30 right when *Crazy People Music* hit. Not like 30 is a magical number, but around here…29, 30, 31…something happens. There's a point at which, with all deference to the people you love and respect, you have to say, "I don't want to play like them anymore." And for me, the big step was saying, "I can't stand playing standards." And I know that would come one day.

SC: You knew that would come one day?

BM: Hell yeah, it's bound to come if you gonna play anything worth a damn. You know what I mean? Like Bird and them did to the standards what we'll never be able to do to the standards. So the only thing we can do is do our thing, you know? I mean, there are certain standards I don't mind playing, and most of them have never really been standards…Monk tunes, Wayne Shorter tunes, Herbie tunes, shit like that. But standards in general, man…I'm like…that's why when we did *Trio Jeepy* and it was considered like this landmark record, it was very amusing to me. Because *Trio Jeepy* was a record…I had to do a record before I went out on tour with Sting. *Royal Garden Blues* was disastrous because I did it after Sting's tour, and I need at least six to eight months to get my jazz chops back. And that would've meant a two-year lapse again. So I recorded *Trio Jeepy* right before I went on Sting's tour. I didn't have a band, so I called up Milt [Hinton] and we went into the studio [with Jeff Watts] and we did some standards. And it was called this really modern-day landmark, but really we just went in and had a jam session, essentially.

DB: *It sounded like it.*

BM: You know, that's what it was. And people were saying, "This is great!" But that wasn't my idea of a great record at all.

DB: *Mine either.*

BM: Good. I'm glad you agree.

DB: *But this new one is my idea of a great record.*

BM: Yeah, it is. This is what I would've done as far back as '87, except one thing that is often overlooked in terms of development is personnel. Don't nobody play the drums like Jeff Watts. And very few play the bass like Bob Hurst. But neither one of them was available in '87. So I had to go with what was available…not trying to be mean to the cats I was playing with at the time, because they're great musicians. I mean, Lewis Nash and Delbert Felix are definitely great musicians. But *Random Abstract* was a compromise record. Because when we started rehearsing, I brought out all of this material that wound up being a part of *Crazy People Music*, and it couldn't be played, so I had to shelve it.

SC: And it's also about the rapport you have with Jeff and Bob. 'Cause that's what I'm hearing.

BM: It's an intellectual rapport, though. I had a great personal relationship with Delbert and Lewis, but we didn't have the kind of intellectual relationship that can really make the music take off. There are very few people I can have that kind of relationship with, though. The shit is all about music for me. And that's what I love about Steve. It's all about music for Steve. Steve is one of the few musicians I can talk to where when we talk we don't have to deal with each other's ego. We have a conversation. I don't have to say…like if Steve is playing next to whoever and I say, "Yeah, man, that motherf**ker played a great solo," I don't have to dance around and go, "Yeah, and *you* sounded great, too." We can just talk. If Jeff is playing some bad shit on a tune, I can say, "Hey man, Tain was *playin'* that shit." And if the shit I played was sad, he don't have to say, "Man, that sounded really good." We don't

have to deal with any of that pampering-egos stuff. We can talk about Bird or talk about Sly Stone or James Brown or whatever the f**k you wanna talk about, and it never has to become a debate on personal taste. Like, if I ain't into the shit, I ain't into it, and it ain't no thing. With everybody else, it's a thing. You have to like the person that they like or you're somehow indicting them.

SC: A lot of times in interviews, interviewers try to get you to go at each other. One guy did an interview with me once and wanted me to come down on Kenny G. And I mean, Kenny G's music is not my favorite type of music, true. But I'm not gonna sit there and rag the cat, because I got better things to do. Kenny G should be allowed to play anything he wants. It makes no difference what I like and what I don't like. And they try to underscore this thing between me and Branford. I mean, it's obvious that we have different tastes, just by listening to us play.…

BM: But then again we don't.

SC: What they miss is the connection. I really think it's maybe because what you said before. They can't hear.

BM: Oh, they can't, man. I mean, the shit they be writing!

SC: I think that when I started my band, I could've told interviewers anything about my influences or whatever, and they would've believed me.

BM: I shoulda said, "I'm a bad motherf**ker." And at least two or three people would've wrote that I was.

SC: Some of the early gigs I got…I remember one time, I went to this punk-rock place and I asked the cat for a gig. Cat say, "What kind of music do you play?" I say, "What kind of music do you have here?" He tells me they book punk rock, so I say, "That's what we play." I gave him a tape, and the next day he says, "Well, sounds great. There's one tune in here that sounds a little bit like jazz, but the rest of it sounds good." And that was it. We just went in and played it the way we played it. And the only reason I did that was because I knew club owners, for the most part, can't hear.

BM: That's right.

SC: Same with critics. If I tell them I'm influenced by music from Siberia or whatever, they'll write that shit down and then the next interviewer will copy that

and it goes on and on. That shit has happened to me. People have called me up and said, "Well, I don't know much about you so could you send me some materials, some interviews." So they copy from those interviews to write their interview. You know what I mean? Or sometimes you'll say something and people will make mistakes. Geri Allen did something in one of her interviews where she said M-BASE meant "Basic Array of Structured Experimentation"…she f**ked up the last word and said "Experimentation" instead of "Extemporations." And I saw that same mistake in 20 interviews after that, just from that one time she said it wrong. Which, to me, just proved that cats get other interviews and copy the shit down. They have no idea themselves what's going on.

BM: I had one interview in *Down Beat* [Nov. '89] where I made a reference to Nicolas Slonimsky's *Thesaurus of Scales and Melodic Patterns*, and it came out as "Leo Straminski"! Then some guy sends me a letter saying, "You oaf! It's not Straminski, it's Slonimsky." Well, no shit, but I didn't say that.

DB: *Sounds like lazy-writer syndrome…too many critics doing the equivalent of learning on the bandstand.*

BM: All I know is, the first person who ever decided to describe music with all adverbs should be shot in his ass.

SC: (*Gales of laughter.*)

BM: I have yet to hear a "thundering drum" or a "lachrymose saxophone." I'm still waiting to hear that shit. I mean, you know, it worked in Walter Mitty, but I haven't seen it work since. I have yet to see onomatopoeia be effective in describing any kind of artistic performance.

SC: And you have to understand that most critics and writers…they're usually cats who tried to be musicians and didn't make it, so they turn to some music-related job.

DB: *Branford, has playing in a trio liberated you in a sense?*

BM: Well, it's always been easy for me to play in a trio setting. I've never had that problem. It's really strange to me that every time you say trio, people say, "Man, you must've been terrified."

SC: I don't get that either, man. What is that about?

BM: I think somebody must've told them 20 years ago that it was terrifying to be in a trio setting.

SC: I didn't get that. Even when I was

reading about Rollins and shit, I still didn't get it. I think a lot of musicians who aren't good musicians think that you need a piano in order to make music. But Branford can go up there and play solo and make it work.

BM: I don't know about all *that* shit. (*Laughs.*) *You* get up there and do that.

SC: But you know what I'm saying. They think that if the piano leaves, you can't hear no more, it just gets like some kind of "out" shit.

BM: Well, most musicians…that's the way they are. They hang on that piano for dear life, boy. For me, the thing was, I used to sing to myself. That's how I learned songs. That's how I knew when I could play a song. If I couldn't internalize the song, then I couldn't play it. Like, I could just learn the scales for "Giant Steps" and play it in a passable fashion. But for me, I was very insistent on being able to play melody on songs. And I've always known if I could sing the song in my head, I could play the melody on my horn. If I couldn't hear the changes go by in my head, I wouldn't play it. So all those songs, I can here the shit in my head. And if I can do that, then the piano's right here (*points to his head*).

SC: And you can get to a certain point where you hear the whole band in your head…the bass, the drums, everything. And that's the difference between playing music and faking it. There's a lot of guys, for example, who can't even keep a form straight. They'll play and go to the bridge and generally get lost on normal shit, you know? And a lot of that's because when they practice alone they don't hear that whole thing in their head. Or else they just practice licks completely divorced from any kind of context.

BM: I think the biggest problem with playing music in the United States is that, you know…the United States societal norms are defined by Western European civilization. And the majority of American musical culture was developed by African Americans, who have a completely different aural sensibility. That's a-u-r-a-l, not o-r-a-l. But anyway, that's where the school problem comes in. Because, from the Western vantage point, everything is written down, everything is understood through the literal text. Whereas, for the African sensibility, the tradition is passed down orally. There's a dichotomy there, there's a problem there. Because when you talk to cats at clinics about the way shit

sounds, they immediately raise their hand and start asking about chord scales. And you know how I feel? I say, f**k chord scales, because it's only a theory. It doesn't exist. I mean, we can burn all the sheet music right now and the only thing that that means is we wouldn't have a chance to butcher Mozart's music. Because Mozart's dead, we don't know how the shit was supposed to sound. Mozart wrote down the shit that he heard in his head, but there are people that are teaching where they make you think that Mozart wrote what he wrote because he could write music. But there are ways of knowing, man, that supersede writing. Louis Armstrong couldn't read music. Didn't seem to hurt him none. I think that a lot of times in the educational environment, when it comes to jazz, it's just tough…everybody that's teaching the music was brought up to believe in the Western European philosophy. And in America, it's a combination of the two, but the oral tradition is never really highlighted. They don't talk about it, it's never really brought into focus. It's all theory, chord scales, theory, chords scales. "This is what Bird played." It's never like *why* did Bird play this? And the why is the most important question to mankind.

SC: They don't know why.

BM: I mean, World War I started in 19-whatever…14, 19, 11, whatever that shit was…who cares when? The question is why? Why did it start? What were the ramifications of this? That's the shit that, when I listen to music, I ask myself. Why did Bird play what he played? What are the musical ramifications of him playing this exactly the way he played it? And that's something that a chord-scale book can never teach you. I think that it is the logic of music in general that slips by most people. Education is almost a deterrent, sometimes. And I'm not putting down education, because I was musically educated. I can read and all that shit, but I say f**k that because the way that it's taught is an overwhelming deterrent for a lot of people who play jazz. What do you think, Steve?

SC: I always say that about Western education.

BM: You supposed to disagree with me, man. ●

JOE HENDERSON: THE SOUND THAT LAUNCHED A THOUSAND HORNS

· · · · · · · · · · · · · · · · · · · ·

By Michael Bourne
MARCH 1992

He's not Pres-like or Bird-like, not Trane-ish or Newk-ish. None of the stylistic adjectives so convenient for critics work for tenor saxist Joe Henderson. It's evident he's listened to the greats, to Lester Young, Charlie Parker, John Coltrane, Sonny Rollins—to them and all the others he's enjoyed. But he doesn't play like them, doesn't *sound* like them. Joe Henderson is a master, and, like the greats, unique.

When he came along in the sixties, jazz was happening every which way, from mainstream and avant to blues, rock and then some, and *everything* that was happening, he played. Henderson's saxophone became a Triton's horn and transformed the music, whatever the style, whatever the groove, into himself. And he's no different (or, really, always different) today. There's no "typical" Joe Henderson album, and every solo is, like the soloist, original and unusual, thoughtful, and always from the heart.

"I think playing the saxophone is what I'm supposed to be doing on this planet," says Joe Henderson. "We all have to do *something*. I play the saxophone. It's the best way I know that I can make the largest number of people happy and get for myself the largest amount of happiness."

Joe was born April 24, 1937, in Lima, Ohio. When he was nine he was tested for musical aptitude. "I wanted to play drums. I'd be making drums out of my mother's pie pans. But they said I'd gotten a high enough score that I could play anything, and they gave me a saxophone. It was a C melody. I played that about six months and went to the tenor. I was kind of born on the tenor."

Even before he played, Joe was fascinated by his brother's jazz records. "I listened to Lester Young, Flip Phillips, Stan Getz, Charlie Parker, all the people associated with Jazz at the Philharmonic. This stuff went into my ears early on, so when I started to play the saxophone I had in my mind an idea of how that instrument was supposed to sound. I also heard the rhythm 'n' blues saxophone players when they came through my hometown."

Soon he was playing dances and learning melodies with his friends. "I think of playing music on the bandstand like an actor relates to a role. I've always wanted to be the best interpreter the world has ever seen. Where a precocious youngster gets an idea like that is beyond me, but somehow improvisation set in on me pretty early, probably before I knew what improvisation was, really. I've always tried to recreate melodies even better than the composers who wrote them. I've always tried to come up with something that never even occurred to them. This is the challenge: not to rearrange the intentions of the composers but to stay within the parameters of what the composers have in mind and be creative and imaginative and meaningful."

One melody that's become almost as much Henderson's as the composer's is "Ask Me Now" by Thelonious Monk. He's recorded it often, each performance an odyssey of sounds and feelings.

"I play it 75 percent of the time because I like it and the other 25 percent because it's demanded that I play it. I sometimes have to play it twice a night, even three times. That tune just laid around for a while. Monk did an incredible job on it, but other than Monk I don't think I heard anyone play it before I recorded it. It's a great tune, very simple. There are some melodies that just stand by themselves. Gershwin was that kind of writer. You don't even have to improvise. You don't have to do anything but play the melody and people will be pleased. One of the songs like that is 'Lush Life.' That's for me the most beautiful tune ever written. It's even more profound knowing that Billy Strayhorn wrote it, words *and* music, when he was 17 or 18. How does an 18-year-old arrive at that point of feeling, that *depth?*"

Lush Life is the title of Henderson's new album of Strayhorn's music. "Musicians have to plant some trees—and *re*-plant some trees to extend the life of these good things. Billy Strayhorn was one of the people whose talent should be known. Duke Ellington knew about him, so that says something. There are still a lot of people who haven't heard Strayhorn's music, but if I can do something to enable them to become aware of Strayhorn's genius I'd feel great about that."

Lush Life is the first of several projects he'll

Hyou Vielz

record for Verve. Don Sickler worked with Henderson selecting and arranging some of Strayhorn's classics and, with Polygram Jazz Vice President Richard Seidel, produced the album. Henderson plays "Lush Life" alone, and, on the other songs, he's joined for duets to quintets by four of the brightest young players around: pianist Stephen Scott, bassist Christian McBride, drummer Gregory Hutchinson, and trumpeter Wynton Marsalis. That the interplay of generations is respectful, inspirational and affectionate is obvious.

"I think this was part of it, to present some of the youngsters with one of the more established voices. This is the natural way that it happens. This is the way it happened for me. I wouldn't have met the people I met if it hadn't been for Kenny Dorham, Horace Silver, Miles Davis, people I've been on the bandstand with. They introduced me to their audience. We have to do things like this. When older musicians like me find people who can continue the tradition, we have to create ways to bring these people to the fore."

Henderson came to the fore in the sixties. He'd studied for a year at Kentucky State, then four years at Wayne State in Detroit, where he often gigged alongside Yusef Lateef, Barry Harris, Hugh Lawson, and Donald Byrd. He was drafted in 1960 and played bass in a military show that traveled the world. While touring in 1961 he met and played with Bud Powell and Kenny Clarke in Paris. Once he was discharged in 1962 he settled in New York, where so many of his friends from Detroit were already regulars and where trumpeter Kenny Dorham became a brother. "Kenny Dorham was one of the most important creators in New York, and he's damn near a name you don't hear anymore. That's a shame. How can you overlook a diamond in the rough like him? There haven't been that many people who have that much on the ball creatively as Kenny Dorham."

Henderson's first professional recording was Dorham's album *Una Mas*, the first of many albums he recorded through the sixties as a sideman or a leader for Blue Note. This was the classic time of Blue Note, and what's most remarkable is the *variety* of music Henderson played, from the grooves of Lee Morgan's *The Sidewinder* to the avant sounds of Andrew Hill's *Point of Departure*. Whatever was happening musically, Joe Henderson was a natural.

"That's part of what I wanted to do early on—be the best interpreter I could possibly be. I wanted to interpret Andrew Hill's music better than he could write it, the same with Duke Pearson and Horace Silver. I'd study and try to find ways of being imaginative and interesting for this music without changing the music around. I didn't want to make Horace Silver's music different from what he had in mind. I wanted to make it even *more* of what he had in mind."

He joined the Horace Silver band for several years and fronted a big band with Kenny Dorham—music he'll recreate and record this year at Lincoln Center. He worked with Blood, Sweat & Tears for a minute in 1969 but quit to work with Miles Davis. "Miles, Wayne Shorter and I were the only constants in the band. I never knew who was going to show up. There'd be a different drummer every night—Tony Williams, Jack DeJohnette, Billy Cobham. Ron Carter would play one night, next night Miroslav Vitous or Eddie Gomez. Chick Corea would play one night, next night Herbie Hancock. It never settled. We played all around but never recorded. This was previous to everyone having Walkman recorders. Miles had a great sense of humor. I couldn't stop laughing. I'd be on the bandstand and I'd remember something he said in the car to the gig, and right in the middle of a phrase I'd crack up!"

Henderson's worked more and more as a leader ever since, and recorded many albums, like *Lush Life*, with particular ideals. He recorded "concept" albums like *The Elements* with Alice Coltrane and was among the first to experiment with the new sounds of synthesizers. He composed tunes like "Power to the People" with a more *social* point of view. "I got politically involved in a musical way. Especially in the sixties, when people were trying to affect a cure for the ills that have beset this country for such a long time, I thought I'd use the music to convey some of my thoughts. I'd think of a title like 'Black Narcissus,' and then put the music together. I'd try to create a nice melody, but at the same time, when people heard it on the radio, a title like 'Afro-Centric' or 'Power to the People' made a statement."

Words have always inspired Joe Henderson. "I try to create ideas in a musical way the same as writers try to create images with words. I use the mechanics of writing in playing solos. I use quotations. I use commas, semicolons. Pepper Adams turned me on to a writer, Henry Robinson. He wrote a sentence that

spanned three or four pages before the period came. And it wasn't a stream of consciousness that went on and on and on. He was stopping, pausing in places with hyphens, brackets around things. He kept moving from left to right with this thought. I can remember in Detroit trying to do that, trying to play the longest meaningful phrase that I could possibly play before I took the obvious breath."

Henderson names Truman Capote, Norman Mailer, Herman Hesse, and the Bible among the favorites. "I think the creative faculties are the same whether you're a musician, a writer, a painter. I can appreciate a painter as if he were a musician playing a phrase with a stroke, the way he'll match two colors together the same as I'll match two tones together.

He tells a story uniquely as a soloist and composer, and he's inspired many musicians through the years. But what sometimes bothers Henderson is when others imitate his strokes and his colors but don't name the source. He heard a popular tenor saxist a while ago and was staggered. "I heard eight bars at a time that I know I worked out. I can tell you when I worked the music out. I can show you the music when I was putting it together. But when guys like this do an interview they don't acknowledge me. I'm not about to be bitter about this, but I've always felt good about acknowledging people who've had something to do with what I'm about. I've played the ideas of other people—Lester Young, Charlie Parker, John Coltrane, Sonny Rollins, Lee Konitz, Stan Getz— and I mention these guys whenever I do an interview. But there are players who are putting stuff out as if it's their music and *they* didn't create it. I did."

He's nonetheless happy these days and amused about some of the excitement about *Lush Life*, that the new album, like every new album from Joe Henderson, feels like a *comeback*. "I have by no means vanished from the scene. I've never stopped playing. I'm very much at home in the trenches. I'm right out there on the front line. That's where I exist. I've been inspired joining the family at Polygram in a way I haven't been inspired in a long time. I'm gonna get busy and do what I'm supposed to do." ●

By John McDonough
DECEMBER 1992

SONNY ROLLINS: SONNY'S SIDE OF THE STREET

Is this going to be another negative, punch-Sonny-Rollins-in-the-eye article for *Down Beat*?" the man asked with weary resignation as he plopped into a den chair. "Well, I agreed to do it. I know how it's going to come out anyway. So go ahead, ask me. I'm ready."

It was a telephone interview. I imagined Sonny Rollins sitting there in his Hudson River Valley country home north of Rhinebeck, New York; sitting there in a nimbus of ennui waiting to be prodded and poked with an assortment of those unpleasant, blunt instruments we journalists call questions.

His wife Lucille had answered the phone and handed it to her husband. "This sure is going to be a mighty short interview," she thought as she walked out the door, got into her car, and drove off on some mid-morning errands. Maybe she even pitied the poor schnook on the other end of the line a bit. She was surprised—actually "astonished," she admitted later—to return in an hour and a half and find the conversation still pumping along and probing the merits of cowboy actor Ken Maynard, "B" westerns and actress Joan Leslie.

How Sonny Rollins got down from *Down Beat* to Joan Leslie within 90 minutes is the subject of this modest tale at hand. He took the scenic route, by and large, along the little roads of conversation not always traveled in the music interviews. The kind that demand a little improvisation. But Rollins knows about that, doesn't he? The talk avoided the long and familiar chronological expressways that wind past more than 40 years of various "sabbaticals," crises, triumphs and what have you. All that's been well mapped in insightful essays by such career cartographers as Gary Giddins, Francis Davis, Bob Blumenthal (in his booklet accompanying the new seven-CD Prestige set, *The Complete Prestige Recordings*) and

Charles Blanca in his book *Sonny Rollins: The Journey of a Jazzman.*

So, the assumption in this article will be that no reader needs to be instructed on any of this; or on Rollins' immensity and influence as a tenor saxophonist, an influence that may in the aggregate dwarf that of his one-time contemporary, the late John Coltrane. With all this as given, then, back to *Down Beat*.

"I find it petty," he groused on. "I find the things it says about great musicians petty. It tries to denigrate people with these John Simon-type reviews. I guess that's what pays off, though. Writers have to write this type of piece to become famous. I know that's the way it goes. I also know you won't print any of this." [Thus insuring that every word would get printed. Rollins is no media amateur.]

In the twenties, I reminded him, H.L. Mencken liked to say of his fellow journalists that it was their duty "to comfort the afflicted and afflict the comfortable." To which Rollins replied that no jazz musician is ever comfortable.

"There are those celebrities who are comfortable," he admitted; "movie stars and rock musicians. But jazz musicians are not movie stars. Knowing what it takes to play jazz, and live the jazz life, I would disagree with any writer who assumed that the jazz musician in this society is comfortable, and thus fair game for attack. I know *Down Beat*'s been pretty hard on me recently, which I suppose is a kind of badge of honor. Maybe now that Miles is dead, they figure they have me to kick around. I'm not saying I'm beyond criticism. That's not where I'm coming from. I'm my biggest critic. I know when I'm not sounding good before *Down Beat* or anyone else tells me so. But I object to *Down Beat* for what I've seen it do to other musicians." He didn't offer a bill of particulars; his wife, whom he met in 1956 and who stills hates the word "gig," reads the articles and reviews, only occasionally passing one along to him. But then he said this:

"I think that the jazz business is fragile enough. It's a real art, and it should be boosted. That's how I feel."

Ah ha, now it was clear. Of course! That's exactly how he *should* feel. He's a jazz musician. Naturally he identifies with the world that has defined him. A more disinterested third person, however, might have looked at the two of us—musician and writer—and seen it another way. How little these writers often know about the reality of the world they cover, he might say; and how little musicians understand that writers have nothing if not their independence. They must resist the temptation to be liked by the famous subjects they hobnob with by becoming "boosters."

Whichever side you might favor in this gentlemen's disagreement, one fact is immutable: Rollins, like all the finest jazz artists, will be remembered by his recordings, not his press clippings or reviews, in this magazine or any other. Through many label associations, he has always taken his recordings very seriously. Differences between labels? "Mainly whether they pay me my royalties," he said. "Some pay, some don't." Over the decades, he has worked with the most astute jazz producers in the industry—Bob Weinstock, Ira Gitler, Orrin Keepnews, Norman Granz, George Avakian, and Bob Thiele. In recent years, his wife has held that function. All have been astute enough to let him produce himself. "The creative decisions on arrangements and material were always mine. That's why I don't think whether the producer was George or Orrin was ever particularly material in terms of the final product. They may disagree, but that's the way I see it."

Even his 1962–'64 period with a major non-jazz label, RCA, presented no pressures to "expand his audience." "The contract at RCA," he said, "was a big contract at the time and called for a certain amount of product within a certain period. It was stricter in terms of what had to be done—three records a year, maybe. It was very high-profile. Paul Desmond was signed, too. But they took us both on our own terms. They didn't expect me to sell like Elvis Presley, and they didn't pay me like Elvis Presley, either. But there was no interference."

Rollins says he rarely gives much thought to his record sales or calculates ways to boost them. To him they are almost a peripheral concern, serving more a publicity than an income function. "I've been recording for many years and get certain royalties from my compositions and record sales," he explains. "But I couldn't live on that sum. Most of my income comes from live performances. If I break my arm or can't play, I'm out of luck. That's how close to the edge a jazz musician lives."

Happily Rollins gets princely concert fees, which he deserves and which help keep that "edge" rounded down to something more like a gently sloping hill. Although he won't discuss fees, he reportedly received more than $20,000 for one 50-minute set at the recent Chicago Jazz Festival. Rollins knows his full value and doesn't quibble or give anything away. He would not consider, for instance, permitting National Public Radio to air his Chicago Jazz Festival appearance on the network. Yet, he is one of the relatively few jazz artists today who can maintain an active concert schedule within the United States. Most have to trot the globe to find a steady concert circuit. He plays almost no clubs anymore. And the preferred bookings are the ones where he doesn't have to share the bill, says wife Lucille.

Although the albums he turns out every year and a half or so don't generate great cash windfalls, they keep his profile high in the marketplace. That, in turn, produces the awareness, the interest and the personal-appearance bookings that generate the real money. In this, he is no different than any other aging music legend. Neither Frank Sinatra nor the Rolling Stones have been able to generate important record sales lately; Sinatra seems to have given up, in fact. Yet, on the road they mint money. On the jazz world's smaller fiscal scale, the same is true of Rollins. "You have to record to stay famous, to keep your name out there," he says. "Albums are more a publicity thing in a lot of ways."

They're also a record of his musical career. And history—and his place in it—is something he's keenly alert to. Maybe this is why he is said to have such mixed feelings about the whole recording process. If it's not my best, I don't want it preserved, seems to be the standing policy. That way there's no danger of anything slipping out.

When something does, Rollins is not a happy man. A French RCA collection of alternate takes from the sixties, for instance, came out this year on a Bluebird CD (*Alternatives*). Orrin Keepnews' album notes will provide the details for anyone who wishes to inquire. But they are of little consolation to Rollins.

"I feel it's an invasion of my prerogative to decide how I want to be represented on records," he said. "I used to go ballistic over these things. Now I realize it's done a lot. All kinds of performances are subject to this sort of thing [including radio broadcasts]. But if I don't like the way I sound, I don't want the world to hear it more than once. It's an issue of privacy almost." It's also something that only the most important musicians experience, artists whose work is considered so vital that even the scraps have value. It's the ultimate honor. "I understand that," he says. "But I'm a musician. Music is my living. I have to control the product I produce."

If Rollins is conscious of history, he still finds it hard to see himself as an historical figure. Most of the leading young players of jazz today never knew a world in which Sonny Rollins was not a star—just as Rollins never knew a world in which Armstrong or Ellington were not stars. In their eyes, Rollins is Ellington. "Yes," he grants, "but it's impossible for me to look at myself as these young people might. I think of myself as I always have. The good thing is that when I play somewhere I don't have to fight for acceptance. The bad part is I have to produce at a standard I set for myself 30 or 40 years ago. You can't go stink up the joint just because you're supposed to be great. But I can't be sucked in by the fact that some people may think I'm an icon. That would be as ridiculous as taking all the bad things writers write seriously. My own assessments are the most important. They're also the harshest, but that's for me to live with."

Still, when Rollins plays "Oleo" or "St. Thomas" and hears that wave of recognition roll across an audience, he feels good about it. "I want to communicate, even though I basically play for myself," he admits. "When I can reach an audience, I feel as if I've persuaded them to come into my camp and accept what I am. You have to be careful not to let that tempt you either to phone in a performance or to become solicitous of the crowd. That's why I stopped playing at one time. The pressure I felt from the audience made me want to do something for them I wasn't able to do."

If an audience doesn't recognize one of Rollins' own pieces, such as "Oleo," they'll certainly recognize familiar melodies like "Tennessee Waltz," which he turned into an aria at this year's Chicago Jazz Festival. No jazz musician, of course, plays such an unexpected repertoire. The hippest in his audiences, who can't resist sneering at Irving Berlin, have always preferred to regard this Rollins

Ken Franckling

trademark as part of some imagined sardonic side to his personality. They think he's kidding. But the joke's on them. He seems almost offended when someone refers to pieces like "There's No Business Like Show Business" or "I'm An Old Cowhand" as corn. He certainly never condescends to them in performance. These songs are rooted in memories of his childhood, in some cases. Maybe he even remembers Benny Goodman and Gene Krupa's "The Last Roundup," circa 1935. In any case, he can bring a child's excitement and straightforwardness to them.

Rollins gives the impression of being a pessimist. Sometimes it's more than an impression. When he speaks of the world's future, it's often with a conditional "if." He seems discouraged by the state of the environment, the government, the media. "I'm concerned about the state of the world," he says grimly, "but I'm also too sophisticated to read newspapers or watch TV and think I'm being seriously informed." He recommends Bill McKibbon's recent book, *The Age of Missing Information*, to friends. It puts everything in perspective, he says. "Things are happening that nobody is seeing. Don't miss it."

So he retreats to the things he trusts most: his home, his family, his friends. And, oh yes, his old movies. There's a wonderfully healthy innocence in this passionate affection he holds for "the stuff that dreams are made of." "They're the best thing on TV," he insists. "They're television's one redeeming virtue." At home he's probably more likely to leaf through a movie book or watch a film than listen to music. His video shelf, like his repertoire, is packed with the greats: John Huston's *The Maltese Falcon*, Marlene Dietrich in Sternberg's *The Blue Angel*, Humphrey Bogart in *Casablanca*, and W.C. Fields' *The Bank Dick*.

"I like those older black & white ones particularly," he confesses. "In fact, the ones I really look for are the B-pictures, especially westerns. I grew up on guys like Ken Maynard, Hoot Gibson, Buck Jones, Bob Steele and Johnnie Mack Brown.

"There're a few musicals I've been trying to find, too. I'd love to get *The Sky's the Limit*. That's the one in which [Fred] Astaire introduced 'My Shining Hour' and 'One for My Baby' in 1942—a great Harold Arlen score. Joan Leslie was the young ingenue at the time. She was beautiful."

The interview had been going on about 80 minutes by the time we got to Ken Maynard and Joan Leslie. Lucille Rollins was back from her errands by now, and it seemed we'd covered enough. "Should I have my wife read this when it comes out?" he said. "Or should we just pretend it never happened?"

I was noncommittal. But if anyone can get Sonny Rollins a copy of *The Sky's the Limit*, let him know. And when you do, tell him *Down Beat* asked you to do it. ●

DAVID MURRAY: SO MUCH MUSIC, SO LITTLE TIME

By Bill Milkowski

JANUARY 1993

A prolific composer, a frequent collaborator and relentless road warrior, reedman David Murray is eager to place his distinctive horn in as many contexts as possible. And he has had the luxury, unlike some of his peers, to document many of his ideas on record. Currently, Murray records for Columbia/DIW but also has an association with Bob Thiele's Red Baron label and has had an ongoing relationship with Giovanni Bonandrini, the Black Saint label head who championed Murray's cause throughout the eighties.

The man's output is staggering. Even Murray himself has had a hard time keeping up with which ones are coming out on what label and which ones remain on the shelf. Last year saw two excellent releases on DIW in *Special Quartet* (with Elvin Jones, McCoy Tyner and Fred Hopkins) and *Shakill's Warrior* (with Don Pullen, Stanley Franks and Andrew Cyrille). Around the same time, Thiele released *Black and Black* (with Roy Haynes, Kirk Lightsey, Santi DeBriano, and Marcus Belgrave). Yet another Murray offering was his superb big-band release on DIW with Butch Morris conducting and featuring a cast of "overlooked all-stars" from New York.

A restlessly creative spirit, Murray is back with another deluge of releases in the coming year; again, no two are alike. On the DIW horizon, in no particular order, are *David Murray Quartet Plus One*, with special guest Branford Marsalis; a kinetic duet with waves-of-energy drummer Milford Graves, appropriately titled *The Real Deal*; a recording of Bobby Bradford's heartfelt tribute to John Carter, the gorgeous *Have You Seen Sideman?* suite featuring the late, great Ed Blackwell on drums; a suite for Picasso with his octet; and another big-band recording with Butch Morris and company that he insists is better than the previous one.

Other upcoming recordings on unspecified labels include *The Baltic Suite* with an ensemble of German and Scandinavian musicians, another duet recording with pianist Dave Burrell, and a special project showcasing bass-clarinet playing exclusively. Meanwhile, Thiele is releasing *MX*, a musical tribute to Malcolm X, under the Murray banner for Red Baron. Plus, there's a new killer World Saxophone Quartet album on its way from Elektra Nonesuch featuring vocalist Fontella "Rescue Me" Bass and pianist Amina Claudine Meyers.

Murray is able to juggle all these projects because he doesn't get bogged down with the non-musical aspects of the business. He just continues to steamroll ahead, working and composing and recording, picking up momentum in his career as he hits age 38.

He was on his way to the airport immediately following this interview. Today, Istanbul for a gig with some Turkish percussionists, tomorrow Hamburg with the Baltic Ensemble. Have horn will travel. So little time, so much music to make.

"I would like to be able to play with everyone who plays jazz…everyone who plays any kind of music," says the tenor titan. "By the time I die, I would like to be able to play with any musician on the planet and know something about what they do as well as they know about what I do. I think that's the process that Duke Ellington went through in his lifetime. He learned a little bit from every culture, and he reflected that in is suites about different cultures."

Murray's own recent interest in suites (*The Baltic Suite*, Bradford's *Have You Seen Sideman?*, and *Picasso Suite*, inspired by and orchestrated from a 1948 solo by Coleman Hawkins that he dedicated to Pablo Picasso) seems to be partially motivated by an awareness of marketing strategy.

"Suites seem to be the thing of the day, I guess," he reasons. "Most record companies want some kind of angle. So rather than going at the angle of mixing up musicians who would never, ever play with one another, to me, it's better to go at the angle of having the music performed in a suite. It keeps the music from being trite. In the eighties I was getting tired and weary of producers wanting to throw me in with people who didn't have anything to do with jazz. The last thing they would want would be a jazz drummer. I couldn't understand it, and a lot of those dates were terrible. I did some of them just to make some money, but my heart wasn't quite into it. It was some type of fusion, I guess you'd call it. Some of it was electric. But it just never gelled to me.

"The only guy who I was really able to gel with who did that kind of stuff was Kip Hanrahan. I worked on his project, *Conjure* [on Pangaea], and we also did a tour with Billy Bang, Little Jimmy Scott and Ishmael Reed. That was most satisfying. For something that's in that mode, that's probably about the best there is, I would think.

Searching for the source of his mid-eighties discontent, I wondered aloud if he had problems with the electric, harmolodic approach of James Blood Ulmer and Jamaaladeen Tacuma in their Music Revelation Ensemble.

"Oh, I love playing with Blood because he has a concept. Playing with him is always exhilarating because Blood is the best at what he does. Jamaaladeen is also the best at what he does. I have no problems there. The electric thing doesn't bother me as long as somebody's got a concept. I'll always be attracted to a cat who's got a concept. Milford Graves is one of those guys that has his own concept. As long as a person has something that he's developed that really depicts what he thinks about all the time…when a person has a concept, you can hear the agony, you can hear the blissfulness, you can hear everything. In Milford's playing you can hear Africa, you can hear Brazil, you can hear everything. You can see the whole world in somebody's playing if they have a concept. It's the same with Blood Ulmer, the same with Craig Harris, same with Dave Burrell and Billy Bang. These are people who really have a concept.

"And I have a concept, but it took me a long time to really develop it. When I came to New York in 1975, I was studying everybody, probably sounding like them. Like any younger player who wants to sound good, you have to study others, you're not just gonna come upon it all by yourself. Not unless you're Charlie Parker or somebody. They threw away the mold when he died. So you've gotta study people to be good. It's like, you can't be a great writer without acknowledging the great works. You just can't get around James Joyce, you can't get around Ralph Ellison, you can't get around Albert Murray, you can't get around Chaucer. You can't get around these people. You don't just come up with a concept all on your own, because they didn't either.

"But as far as being a saxophone player, I probably developed my own sound when I got to be 27 or 28. And I encourage my students around the world to keep trying to develop their own sound because that's their ticket to success. A sound is like a signature, to quote Cecil Taylor."

Murray laments the fact that certain seasoned musicians who *have* developed their own sound and *do* have a concept have been largely ignored by the recording industry and overlooked by the music media.

"There's so many good musicians out here, so many good jazz musicians in New York, that to focus on just a few, to me, is just obscene. It doesn't make any sense. And even if I thought in that vein, if I may be one of the chosen ones, for me it's no good because I didn't come here to be a scapegoat of any kind. I'm in love with the art of jazz. And there's a lot of players, man, that are being overlooked.

"It's a shame," he continues. "I hate to see great musicians in their latter years being frustrated. These kind of frustrations seem to be dictated by certain powers-that-be in the jazz world. And those are the kinds of things that I would like to see corrected. One of these days…if things don't get fixed correctly, I don't know what I'm gonna do. Maybe I need to be a producer or something…try to record these people myself. Because it ain't right

that these cats have not gotten their due."

I mention Carter Jefferson, he comes back with Bobby Bradford, Rasul Siddik, Hugh Ragin, Craig Harris,…"I could make a list, man. Look, there's a lot of people out here who really can play. And not just in that particular genre but in other genres, too. There's a lot of bop

David Gahr

players that haven't got their due that are being pushed aside for the younger generation of kids that seem to pose at being bebop players. You got Dizzy Reece, for one. He's a great player who is one of the pioneers. I mean, he played with Bird, man. Why isn't he trumpeted out here? Does he have to be 85 years old like Doc Cheatham to start getting a little play? You know, there's a lot of guys, man, and if I start naming them we'll be here all day. On every instrument there are great, great players being ignored. I just don't understand it.

"Jazz has never been the kind of business when you get old you get pushed aside. Most musicians play until they die. Clifford Jordan is sick now, but I always thought he should've had a much bigger

push than he got. There's a tenor saxophone player over in Europe named Andy Hamilton. He's like the Lester Young or Ben Webster of England. I've done a recording with him called *Silvershine* [World Circuit]. Man, he's a great player, and he's been overlooked, even by the English. So there's a lot of great players that are out there. All over the world."

Murray also maintains that some of the best new music being composed today goes unrecorded. "There's a lot of people out here doing good writing and arranging these days. Baikida Carroll's music that he dedicated to John Carter is beautiful. And, of course, Bobby Bradford's suite for John is gorgeous. Anthony Davis and James Newton are doing some beautiful things. Craig Harris is coming on like Mozart or somebody. He's got a wealth of music inside him…and on paper, as does Leroy Jenkins. So it's time for the record companies to wake up and start recording all this music that's just sitting around."

When I mention that it's very commendable of him to bring some of these players to the attention of people through performances and recordings with his octet and big band, Murray is quick to point out, "Look, the tides could be turned, and I could be playing in their big band. And if they ask me, I certainly will because I respect these players. I'm not here to be a star show. I'm not here for that. I just wanna be one of the cats who can play."

At the time of this interview, Murray was eagerly anticipating a December guest appearance with the American Jazz Orchestra at Cooper Union in New York. "Gary Giddins called me up for that, and it was really nice that he did because I always wanted to play with that orchestra. It was nice to be able to play with them because I'll probably never get the opportunity to play with this orchestra they have at Lincoln Center, with Wynton Marsalis and all his cousins and all their dogs and cats, family and generations."

Hmm…touched a nerve, or what?

When I suggest that a recent engagement at the Village Vanguard is one example of how he's gained mainstream acceptance since the eighties, David snaps, "Oh, I was playing at the Vanguard when it meant something to play at the Vanguard.

When Max Gordon was alive I think it meant a lot more to play at the Vanguard, because his tastes were very rigid in a certain way, but in a positive way. First of all, you had to be good to play at the Vanguard. And he didn't go for no nonsense. I just remember him coming up to me and saying, 'Keep playing the ballads. Keep playing the ballads. That fast stuff I don't like. Play some ballads.' And I thought about it. He had a point. It's just like he's part of the old guard, and he's gone now. I dug Max.

"And his wife [Lorraine]…she's a little more flexible in terms of the choice of music she brings in. But at the same time, when it was difficult to get into the Vanguard, I was already playing there. Not like today…darn near anybody plays at the Vanguard. It doesn't have to fit the mold of the old Max Gordon Vanguard, which in a way is good because time must move on. But at the same time, I feel like I've been there a little longer. I've had more experience playing that gig than a lot of players do. So if somebody now tells me they're playing at the Vanguard, it's not like 12 years ago when they'd tell me they're playing at the Vanguard. It's a little more flexible now. He would bring people in to play who he respected, nothing more, nothing less.

"I also play at Condon's in town, and I might even go back into Sweet Basil. The Blue Note has already told me that my music is too…they associate me with a certain crowd…avant-garde musicians or something. I always thought that avant garde was a painting style of a certain period. I never knew that it applied to music."

His wife, Ming Smith Murray, a fine-arts photographer whose work has graced several Black Saint covers, is seated with us in the Columbia conference room. She pulls out a copy of her latest project, *A Ming Breakfast: Grits and Scrambled Moments*. It's a book full of evocative black & white portraits of jazz musicians, including Sun Ra, Betty Carter, Babs Gonzales and David Murray, with captions by writer Albert Murray and a foreword by director Gordon Parks. "We're in business together," says David, looking at his wife with obvious pride. "This book will be for sale in stores and everywhere I am. We're gonna be selling them off the bandstand."

And with that, he glances at his watch and announces his desire to head to the airport. Istanbul is waiting…and then on to Hamburg, followed by Lincoln, Nebraska, for a duet concert with percussionist Kahil El'Zabar, then a week with his quartet in Canada, followed by the American Jazz Orchestra gig in New York.

Constant motion, constant growth.

"Yeah, I'm busy. I like to stay busy…stay alive. I'll continue to keep creating. That's the main focus for me. There's a lot of people out there that play the same stuff over and over. But I'm constantly kicking myself, trying to make myself change and do something different, so I won't become bored with my own self. So right now, writing fills that void. The more I write, the more strange the music sounds, and the more strange my playing gets. After a certain point, it gets less strange, then the next thing I know it becomes part of my concept. But you have to go through that period of strangeness and assuredness to get to something that's normal or kosher enough for people's palate."

Connecting with listeners, then, seems to be on Murray's agenda for the nineties. And collaboration just might be the key. "You have to be a little more flexible if you want to survive financially playing jazz. That's something I need to do very much, is survive financially. And I have to have my feet in different camps to do that."

As he rises to leave, he adds, "I can play with anybody…hopefully, I can. I'd like to play with the Philharmonic. I'd like to be a soloist with them one day. That's probably impossible, but I would be all ears for that. I'd like to play at Bill Clinton's Inaugural Ball. I try not to put any boundaries on myself. When you say 'can't,' you usually mean 'won't.' My mother and father always taught me there's nothing you can't do if you have God behind you and if you put your heart into it. Eleanor Roosevelt said, 'The things that you cannot do are the things that you should do.' And, to me, that meant a lot. Because things that are difficult are things that are gonna be more satisfying once you accomplish them. I feel like that."

Look for Murray to sit in with some philharmonic at some point in the future…maybe at the Inaugural Ball for Clinton's second term. ●

SUN RA: ORBITING WITH SUN

By John Diliberto
FEBRUARY 1993

S hards of sound scatter across the concert hall. Blips and bleeps, squiggles and snarls spew out from stage right, where a short, portly figure dressed in iridescent robes turns knobs and throws switches, orchestrating a sonic collision of satellites and asteroids. Suddenly, he turns from his Moog synthesizer and begins spinning around bodily, wiping the backs of his hands across a Fender Rhodes piano.

These are some early moments of electric jazz, courtesy of the Columbus of space music, Sun Ra.

Sun Ra!

The name resonates out of the tombs of ancient Egypt. But somewhere, Sun God took a turn into the taverns of Chicago and the nightlife of jazz. It's been just about 40 years since Sun Ra formed the Arkestra in Chicago after leaving the big band of Fletcher Henderson. He began cloaking strange new sounds in a mythology from the rings of Saturn, leading his own big band in a vortex of swing, electronics, bebop, the avant garde, R&B and a maze of cosmic metaphysics. In that time, he's maintained a stable of musicians who have toured relentlessly and released more than 200 albums on labels as small as El Saturn and as large as A&M. Musicians passing through his group have singed the fringe of the avant garde, including John Coltrane, Pharoah Sanders, Sunny Murray and Julian Priester.

You'd think that this *Down Beat* Hall of Famer and winner of the Big Band category in the '92 Critics Poll would be treasured as an institution of jazz, held up alongside Bird and Basie, Duke and Miles. With literally thousands of compositions, it seems like Wynton Marsalis and the Lincoln Center Jazz Orchestra would be dedicating programs to him. But despite appearances on "Saturday Night Live" and the cover of *Rolling Stone*, accolades from the mainstream have eluded Sun Ra. "In America, and lot of people don't know about me because most musicians try to be famous or make lots of money or get booking agents and all that," he says with little self-effacement. "But I wouldn't fit into some places because a lot of people in America are out of it, you know?"

That may be, but there's been no dearth of Sun Ra albums or performances throughout the United States and Europe, where they headline festivals and sell out concert halls with the consistency, if not the audience size, of the Grateful Dead.

But these are not the best of times for Sun Ra and his Arkestra. The celestial being from Saturn has become a victim of some earth-bound infirmities. Sun Ra is approximately 80 years old (his birth date was always speculative), having suffered a stroke in 1990, and two more since. The most recent occurred this past October, days before we were scheduled for our interview. Once a robust, rotund figure who danced across the stage, waving his robed arms to direct his Arkestra, he's now carried to his keyboard in a wheelchair, his face wooden, his hand movement minimal. Yet he still plays, and some Arkestra members claim he sounds better than ever.

And Sun Ra isn't the only one with problems as this ancient clan closes in on 40 years together. Over the years, members such as trumpeter Hobart Dotson, bassist Ronnie Boykins, wind player Eloe Omoe, and, most recently, saxophonist Pat Patrick, have left the planet, to use the Ra vernacular. Longtime vocalist June Tyson died November 24 after battling breast cancer. Influential tenor titan John Gilmore suffers tooth maladies and hasn't fully recovered from pneumonia.

The Arkestra has never had an easy time of it. For the last 20 years or so they've lived hand to mouth, occupying a run-down row house in Philadelphia—not the most elegant way to travel the spaceways.

But Sun Ra has been stretching the boundaries of jazz the way Einstein bent the laws of physics. Building on a foundation of swing from his days with the Fletcher Henderson Orchestra in the early 1950s, Ra used Henderson, Count Basie and Duke Ellington as launching pads for his often-electronic new music. Ra, whose self-aggrandizing personality makes him frugal with compliments, is effusive when he speaks of Henderson.

"When I arrived on the planet, I always liked music that was together, and that was the most together music I ever heard," he says. "He was the one behind Bessie Smith and Ethel Waters, schooling them, playing for them. He was just an innovator, a creator you might say, someone who was interested in the precision and discipline of being able to put things together and coordinate it with taste, with mastership [sic] and all that."

But Sun Ra was already a disciple of bop by the time Henderson died in 1952, and that's what his first group, the Herman "Sonny" Blount trio, started playing. But by the mid fifties, a bop band was nothing new, and Sun Ra discovered a hook that set him apart. With his producer, Alton Abraham, he was folding the Bible, Egyptian mythology, black spiritualism, and science fiction into a unique and convoluted cosmology. He took on the name Sun Ra, and, with costumes lifted

Michael Lavine

from a Chicago Opera performance of *Madame Butterfly*, he began the Arkestra. He ended his life as Herman Sonny Blount, proclaiming himself a citizen of the universe, born on Saturn, and preaching of the space age.

"He was playing a lot of standard tunes with the trio," recalls saxophonist John Gilmore. "We weren't playing a whole lot of his arrangements, mostly standards. About six months later we were playing this number, 'Saturn,' and I heard it. For the first time I heard it, and I knew that I wasn't just up there playing. I thought, 'God, this cat is somethin' else.' I could hear those intervals."

It's not easy for everyone to get aboard the Ra spacecruiser. Overly serious jazz fans are put off by the carnival atmosphere of a Ra performance. More traditional audiences think Ra is making nothing but noise, a "keening dissonance," according to *The New York Times* in 1961. But a quick listen to any of the Evidence reissues, e.g., *Holiday for Soul Dance*, *Supersonic Jazz*, and *We Travel the Spaceways*, reveals the roots and traditions of Sun Ra's sound, as well as the beginnings of what would be called free-jazz. (Other titles are available on Delmark, hat ART, Black Saint, ESP, and Rounder.)

Arkestra performances are free-flowing affairs that might start with saxophonist Marshall Allen playing an African kora, segue into Fletcher Henderson's "Big John Special," slide into Ra crooning "East Of The Sun, West Of The Moon," and careen into a free-for-all of horns blowing at the precipice of infinity.

"Sun Ra has the biggest book I've seen in my life," exclaims saxophonist Noel Scott, who has been with the Arkestra since 1979. "Marshall [Allen] has four suitcases full of music. Ra has three arrangements of almost any standard that you name, be it 'Old Black Magic' or 'I Didn't Know What Time It Was.' He has four arrangements of 'But Not for Me.'"

Ra doesn't call out the tunes in concert.

He just starts playing, and eventually a lead emerges as the band scrambles through sheaves of paper, pulling sheet music off the floor, tying to find the right tune. "He doesn't sit in the dressing room and run off the tunes we're going to play," says saxophonist Allen, who's been with the band since 1958. "When he gets to the audience, that's when he decides. The way he calls them is to just play the intro, and off we go. Sometimes you don't have time to find your music, so you better know your part well enough."

"Sometimes it sounds like the intro to 'But Not for Me,' then he goes into 'Yesterdays,'" laughs Scott. "Sometimes he changes his mind. It's a competition between the reed and brass sections to see who would catch a tune first."

He adds, "And heaven forbid you make a mistake and pick the wrong song."

"The music is like a journey," says Ra, speaking slowly from his hospital bed, "and they have to have a map."

But Sun Ra says that map is only a guide. "It's like a journey, but you're on the road, and you have to do what you have to do for the changes of scenery, changes of feelings," he says. "You have to be ready for those potholes in the road."

That may account for the Arkestra's penchant for free improvisation. Even in recent years, when Ra's sets have been dominated by standards from Fletcher Henderson, Jelly Roll Morton and George Gershwin, the band always takes an opportunity to blast off.

Allen is at his best in these sections, hammering his alto keys like pistons with lines scrawling across the consciousness in a blur of sound. "The way Sun Ra does it, you're creating at the same time," says Allen. "If everybody's in tune, everybody's clicking, you're on the vibration."

"Sometimes, none of it's written 'cause everybody's coming from intuition," adds Gilmore.

"It's all discipline, working and discipline," says Ra, who once said that everything they do on stage is completely planned. "Music is a language, a conversation, and they have to keep talking the same language and dialect."

Ra used to rehearse the Arkestra every day in the cramped living room of his row house. His keyboards were stacked at one end while the Arkestra piled in amongst the frayed furniture and garish, surreal paintings of aliens and Egyptian symbology. Now, while he still hits the stage with 12 or more pieces, most of them are pickup musicians from each location. The current core band is just Ra, reed players Allen, Gilmore, James Jackson and bassist Tyrone Hill.

As an avatar of the space age, Ra needed instruments that reflected the new technology. Almost from the beginning, he played unusual electronic keyboards at a time when even the Fender Rhodes wasn't used in jazz. "People didn't know what was happening, they didn't know it was electronic," says Gilmore. The origins of these instruments are as lost in the mists of time as the Pyramids of Egypt. The Solovox was an early keyboard instrument made by Hammond that emulated the sustained sounds of strings. You can hear it intertwining with the violin of Stuff Smith on Ra's earliest sides from 1956, released last year as part of *Sound Sun Pleasure* (Evidence).

The Clavioline was another techno-relic with its eerie, theremin-like sound gracing *The Magic City* (Impulse!). The funky, clavinet sounds of the Rok-si-chord dominated *Night of the Purple Moon* (El Saturn). Ra also got some gentle, ethereal whispers from his electric celesta, heard to beautiful effect on an album called *Impressions of Patches of Blue* (MGM), a set of duets by Ra and vibraphonist Walt Dickerson. "I still have it [the celesta]," says Ra, "but it's too fragile to take out." (None of these titles are currently available.)

However, it's the Moog synthesizer for which Sun Ra is still best known, launching astral epics like *Space Probe* (El Saturn) and "Out In Space" from *It's After the End of the World* (MPS). "I'm fascinated by the sounds," says Ra in his soft, Southern drawl, still present from his former life in Alabama. "I can do things with synthesizers. If I wanted to get the feeling of thunder, it's there. If I want the feeling of space, it's there. You could do it maybe with a piano, too, but the point of it is that with a synthesizer I can not only play the melody, but I can play the rhythm, and then I can pull something down that I never heard before. That's important to me because music's my food, and I need to hear me some different sounds. I don't want to eat the same food everyday, I don't want to hear the same sounds everyday. That's why I have a band. They get some strange sounds out of the instruments. I don't need no electronics. I can make a band sound like an electronic band, without electricity. I can do that."

Sometimes, his band *has* been electronic. In the early eighties, the horn section was as likely to step up playing Electronic Valve Instruments (EVIs) as reeds. Designed by Nyle Steiner, they were manufactured by the Crumar company in Italy, and subsequently by Akai. With trumpet-style valves and a wheel that allowed you to bend notes and jump through seven octaves, it was a space-age clarion call for the band. "It had a great sound," says Allen. "You just blow in it lightly, and you can slur and trill."

But it was difficult to manipulate. "A lot of guys had trouble playing the keys and turning the knob at the same time," admits Allen, who still plays it occasionally.

Not even state-of-the-art technology can escape the pull of Ra's mysticism. Most musicians may think they're plugging in for electricity, but Sun Ra knows they're really plugging into the spirit world. "If some of my instruments go out, the electronic instruments, that's when I reach over into the spirit thing and play all the instruments," Ra proclaims. "Although they use their hands, I play them. I just let them tap in on my spirit. That may be too far-out for some people at this particular point."

No doubt it is. Ra's keyboard pyrotechnics have been toned down in recent years. He's gone through instruments such as the Crumar synthesizers in the early 1980s, then used several Casio models, but now he relies on a Yamaha SY22, mostly for piano and organ sounds. Electronics are almost absent from more recent albums such as *Blue Delight* and *Purple Night* (both A&M).

Despite his ill health, he still speaks confidently of the future and says he's going on the road as soon as he leaves the hospital. "I need a change of scenery," says Sun Ra, who is into his fourth decade of altering the musical landscape for the rest of us. ●

MARIO BAUZA AND ARTURO SANDOVAL: CUBANO BOPPER AND THE MAMBO KING

By Larry Birnbaum

JUNE 1993

Enid Farber

Arturo Sandoval and Mario Bauza

"This kind of reunion doesn't happen every day," says Mario Bauza, between generous helpings of shrimp with black beans and rice at Victor's Cafe 52 in midtown Manhattan, a mecca for New York's Cuban community. "We're having a beautiful luncheon, and the atmosphere is just right. And Victor just got through giving Arturo Sandoval and Mario Bauza two cigars from Cuba—free."

Strange as it might seem, Bauza, the 82-year-old patriarch of Afro-Cuban jazz, and Sandoval, the 43-year-old émigré trumpet wizard, never heard of each other until Dizzy Gillespie visited Havana on a 1977 jazz cruise. Even in the U.S., Bauza was overshadowed by his brother-in-law Machito, whose mambo orchestra he directed for 35 years, while a U.S. embargo kept Sandoval and his records out of this country until a brief détente brought him to New York with the Cuban supergroup Irakere in 1978.

Bauza had known both Armando Romeu and his uncle Antonio Maria Romeu, who took Mario—then a teenaged clarinetist with the Havana Philharmonic—on his first trip to New York to record with his society band. Soon Bauza was back in the Big Apple, first as an alto saxophonist with Noble Sissle's orchestra and later as lead trumpeter and musical director of Chick Webb's big band, where he discovered Ella Fitzgerald. After brief stints with Don Redman and Fletcher Henderson, he joined Cab Calloway, bringing Gillespie into the band. Leaving Calloway in 1940 to help organize the Machito orchestra, he composed "Tanga," considered to be the first true Latin-jazz hybrid.

But it wasn't until after Machito's death in 1984 that Bauza's place in history began to be acknowledged. He formed his own big band and recorded with Machito's sister and former vocalist Graciela, but drew only a middling response until he gave an 80th birthday concert at New York's Symphony Space in 1991. German producer Götz Wörner was in the audience and signed Bauza to his Messidor label; the resulting album, with vocalist Rudy Calzado, featured a five-part suite based on "Tanga," arranged by Chico O'Farrill. The *Tanga* album won unanimous raves, and Bauza triumphantly toured the U.S. and Europe with his band; his new Messidor album, with Calzado and Graciela, is called *My Time Is Now.*

As for Sandoval, his latest release, *Dream Come True*, features an orchestra arranged and conducted by Michel Legrand. He's already looking ahead to his next project, a classical album with the London Symphony that will include his own trumpet concerto along with material by Hummel, Telemann, Vivaldi, and Leopold Mozart.

Lunching at Victor's, Bauza and Sandoval traded jibes and reminiscences over cups of steaming espresso.

Larry Birnbaum: *When did you two meet?*
Mario Bauza: The first time Irakere came to New York. They played a concert in Carnegie Hall, and that's where I met him. And then they recorded for Columbia, and I went to the recording session.
Arturo Sandoval: We met in July '78.
MB: The only guy in that band I knew before was Paquito D'Rivera. His father brought him to New York, and I accompanied Paquito in New York and in Puerto Rico. Paquito was about 15 years old, played a little soprano. His father, Tito, was a good friend of mine in Cuba, from way back.
LB: *So you already knew about Irakere?*
MB: Oh, yeah. I'd been listening to the records. Bebo Valdez, the father of [Irakere pianist and leader] Chucho Valdez, was a good friend of mine. Bebo lives in Stockholm; he's another great musician. He used to be Armando Romeu's piano player at the Tropicana.
LB: *But Arturo, you didn't know about Mario?*
AS: Before I met Dizzy, no. They didn't play nobody's records who left Cuba. They said if they live in the States, they represent the enemy. And they used to say that jazz is the music of the imperialists. I met Mario through Dizzy, because Dizzy was the first guy to talk to me about him. Dizzy went to Cuba for the first time in 1977, and he told me about Mario then. The admiration and respect that Dizzy felt for Mario is something that just a few people know. Actually, he called him "Papa." He'd say, "This is my dad, in music and in life."
MB: Dizzy said to me, "I heard a trumpet player in Cuba I want you to meet." I said, "What are you talking about, Dizzy? Cuba doesn't produce good trumpet players." He said, "Mario, you never heard a trumpet player that's got so many octaves on the horn. I want you to hear this guy." So when Arturo came to New York, I went to the concert. Diz said, "What did I tell you?" And I said, "You're right. He's the greatest."

...I met Dizzy when he was with the Teddy Hill orchestra and I was with Chick Webb. He said, "Get me in your band," but Chick didn't want him. He was too progressive. So when I got in Cab Calloway's band, I said, "Don't worry, I'm going to get you in there. I'm going to send you to the Cotton Club in my place. You've got to get there 15 minutes before the show, so they can't call nobody else. Just play your stuff easy, and don't overdo anything." When I got back, Cab said, "What happened to you?" I said, "Well, I had a cold. How's the man?" He said, "You know, he ain't bad." Dizzy was a hell of a man, but he was crazy. He was my roommate. I'd say, "Dizzy, please put the light out. Let's sleep, man. We've got five shows tomorrow." We used to do five, six shows a day in the theaters. Sometimes Calloway would call a rehearsal at six in the morning, and at a quarter to six he'd be sitting on the stage with a baton, waiting. Six o'clock—boom!

AS: It's amazing how musicians complain about a job now, when we have to play three sets.

MB: We went on tour with the Mills Brothers—six shows every night for two weeks. The first show was at nine o'clock in the morning, and the last one was at midnight. You'd finish around two o'clock. I used to feel like I had nails in my chops. I said, first chance I get, I ain't going to play trumpet no more. Those were the good old days, though.

AS: Is that the advice you're giving me, that I should get away from the trumpet?

MB: That was when I was playing my old trumpet that I gave you. You had to fix it.

AS: Oh yeah. We fixed it, and I played it and everything. They got it working.

MB: That trumpet is over 200 years old. It used to belong to Max Schlossberg.

LB: *Who was he?*

AS: Max Schlossberg was a classical trumpet player, one of the greatest ever. He wrote a wonderful book, too. Everybody practiced and learned from his book.

MB: And then they gave the trumpet to Toscanini's first-trumpet player. Then he gave it to his nephew, who played with the Chicago Symphony, and his nephew gave it to me. He said, "Mario, when you don't want it no more, return it to the family."

AS: And Mario gave it to me—to fix it, play it, keep it, and ruin it.

LB: *Have you two ever played together?*

MB: No.

AS: I played with your band here in New York, at the Village Gate.

MB: That's right. We played at Roseland, too.

AS: You forget, but I don't forget.

MB: I don't forget nothing. I remember, you played your head off. The people went crazy.

AS: Mario has been very busy lately. Mario, watch out, man. Don't work so hard. Take it a little easy. Look what happened to Dizzy.

MB: Dizzy used to make at least 40 weeks a year on the road.

AS: He was working too much. He never stopped.

LB: *Arturo, did you hear jazz when you were growing up in Cuba?*

AS: When I was a kid, never. There was no way in Artemisa, my home town. Even now, the people there don't know about jazz. The only thing I used to hear was traditional Cuban music, what we call *son*, which is played by a septet with a trumpet and bongos. But one day, a trumpet player there said, "Hey, you should listen to this." He had a Dizzy and Charlie Parker record from 1946, with Cozy Cole on drums, Milt Jackson on vibes, Slam Stewart on bass. Oh, man! I said, "This is so weird. I don't understand nothing about what they're trying to play." But that changed my mind completely. And I'm still trying to find out what they were doing.

MB: You know how I met Charlie Parker? Norman Granz heard the Machito orchestra, and he said, "I want to record this band." So he brought Charlie Parker to the rehearsal. I said, "I ain't got no music for you, because practically everything we play is with vocalists for people to dance." He said, "Never mind. Play whatever you got." So I played "Mango Mangue" by Gilberto Valdez, and he said, "I'll play that." I said, "But this is a vocal arrangement." He said, "All you've got to do is give me the cue and tell the singer I'm going to play." He went through the tune one time and said, "We're going to record that right now." I said, "This guy's a genius."

AS: No doubt about it.

LB: *(To Arturo.) But you did play with Armando Romeu, one of the best jazz musicians in Cuba.*

AS: Armando, and Mario, too, and Ruben, I met all the brothers.

MB: I got Armando his first job and the Montmartre.

AS: Armando is still in Cuba, teaching. He's one of the most intelligent men I've met in my entire life. One time he talked to Frank Emilio, a very fine piano player in Cuba who's blind. He said, "Frank, why don't you play the Gershwin piano concerto in F?" Frank said, "I would like to, but it's very difficult to play it by ear." Armando said, "I'm going to write it for you in braille." And he learned the system in a matter of weeks and wrote the concerto in braille, just for him. He's an amazing musician.

MB: He's a good tenor player.

AS: He was a good saxophone player, but I never heard him play. When I met him he was just doing arrangements and conducting. I played with him at the Tropicana in the early sixties.

MB: His father was the conductor of the navy band, his brother Mario is a hell of a piano player, and his sister was a piano teacher.

AS: The best in the country—Zenaida. Chucho Valdez studied with her.

MB: And his uncle, Antonio Maria Romeu, was the guy who I came here with.

AS: He had one of the best orchestras in Cuba.

MB: I came here to record with him in 1926.

AS: 1926? My mother was born in 1926.

MB: I went to Harlem and heard all those bands, and I fell in love with jazz. I couldn't stay because I was too young to get a passport. But when I turned 18 I came back here to live.

LB: *And then Don Azpiazu recorded "The Peanut Vendor" with Antonio Machin singing and El Chino Lara on trumpet.*

MB: That's how I came to play trumpet. When Lara went back to Cuba with Don Azpiazu, Machin was recording for Victor with a quartet, but he couldn't find no trumpet player here to play Cuban music. I told him, "If you buy me a trumpet, I'll play that stuff." He said, "Mario, you ain't no trumpet player." I said, "You buy me one and I'll play it." He said, "I've got to record in 15 days." I said, "That's all I need to get some chops." And then I fell in love with the trumpet. I wanted to be like Louis Armstrong; I knew all his solos. That's how I got into the Savoy with the Missourians, and that's where Chick Webb heard me. He taught me a whole lot of things, more than anybody. To me he was the best jazz leader in the country. He was a heck of a drummer, too. Krupa and Buddy Rich used to come to hear him. He came from Baltimore with a washboard; that was his drum.

AS: I feel embarrassed to talk after Mario, because he's part of the history, and he met all those people and was part of all those things. And I never met any of those great guys—only Dizzy. But when I came from Artemisa to go to music school, I met a clarinet player named Roberto Sanchez, and I asked him, "Who is a good trumpet player here in Havana?" And he said, "There's a guy you should know named Luis Escalante, because he plays everything well. He is the first-trumpet in the National Symphony Orchestra, he plays jazz, and he plays Cuban music." I never forgot that, and it has been my goal all my life to play as many things as I can. I don't want any sign on me that says "jazz" or "salsa" or "blues." I'm a musician, man.

MB: Musicians today don't think much about the public. Everybody tries to see how many notes they can play—but it's what you do with the notes. That's the thing they've got to learn. Arturo played "Body And Soul" one night at the Blue Note with Dizzy, and the things he did with that tune! The first time people heard "Body And Soul" is when Coleman Hawkins came from England and recorded it. He was a poet of the saxophone. That man was something else—a guy with pace, a guy with swing, a guy with everything. He used to sit down and play piano.

AS: I read that Miles [Davis] came to Dizzy asking for lessons, and Dizzy said, "Learn some piano; and when you're familiar with the keyboard, come back." And now I recommend to all my students to learn some piano, because you understand the music a lot better. But Dizzy made me feel so embarrassed, because he asked me many times for lessons. I'd say, "Oh, Diz, please," and he'd say, "Come on, man." So I would give him some exercises and advice about embouchure and things, and he would come back and say, "You know, man, that worked." Nobody can give Dizzy advice about music, but he asked me about technique, because he didn't have any classical training. Number one, he didn't need it, and number two, he never had the chance. But it was incredible how he looked like a young kid trying to learn something, paying attention to everything you said.

MB: We lost a hell of a man, a hell of a musician, a hell of a human being. He had a full life, but we've got to face destiny sooner or later. Myself, I don't want to go, but if it comes, I've got to go. This morning I read in the paper that Billy Eckstine passed away, another one of my friends. When Dizzy first started, Billy was starting, and Miles Davis and Charlie Shavers. We were a bunch of kids trying to make it. We were all together, and every one of us found a way and made it, and left something for the young generation to talk and learn about. And I hope that this will be a great lesson to the young generation, and that they will try to create something. Create—Don't copy no more—because they're copying the ones who already made it. Those people didn't get there by copying; they got there by creating. Everybody wants to be [John] Coltrane; but Coltrane was a creator. Don't try to be Coltrane; try to be yourself. Dizzy was Dizzy, and he made it. That's what I tell all the young generation. And that's good advice. ●

LESTER BOWIE AND GREG OSBY: JAZZ REBELS

By Kevin Whitehead
AUGUST 1993

Y ou've got to have several irons in the fire," Lester Bowie told Greg Osby years ago, "and my irons are my different bands." The trumpeter with the all-star sextet the Leaders and with the Art Ensemble of Chicago—touring this year with bluesmen or chamber orchestra added—also leads the funky Brass Fantasy (still playing Michael Jackson covers) and Organ Ensemble, and last year recorded six tracks with pop star David Bowie ("A nice cat, straightahead and professional"). Lester's life is good; we met at his big, airy home in Brooklyn's Clinton Hill, where he's lived 14 years. During our session, Bowie smoked a fine Cuban cigar Bill Cosby gave him—these days he's also cultivating a Cosbyesque mumble—and freely needled a certain trumpet-playing nemesis.

Like Bowie, alto and soprano saxophonist Greg Osby came up in St. Louis, but his manner is more subdued; he chooses his words more carefully. He, too, has his many irons, however, at a time when conservatives want to drum free-thinkers like him and Lester out of jazz. Osby and buddy Steve Coleman have started two record labels, Rebel-X and Funk Mob. Two recent Osby albums suggest his range: *3D Lifestyles*, a jazz musician's rap record hip enough for hip-hoppers, and Strata Institute's *Transmigration* (DIW/Columbia), where Greg, Coleman, and Von Freeman jam on Mancini and James Moody tunes. A personification of eighties jazz's Brooklyn rebels, Osby now lives outside Philadelphia.

The musicians set the direction of their conversation with little interference from me. Some opinions expressed will raise controversy. For example, other musicians hold similar views about Wynton Marsalis' stewardship of Jazz at Lincoln Center, and the frosty ways Young Lions deal with more liberal musicians; they just don't discuss them on the record. Self-sufficiency

frees Bowie and Osby to say what they please. They have nothing to lose.

Greg Osby: I got the call to play with Lester Bowie's big band when I first came to town [in 1983]. Lester is one of the cats that inspired me to pursue an individual voice in the music. I was playing with Jon Faddis at the time, and the whole direction of that was what [Hamiet] Bluiett calls "Model-T Music." Playing with Lester's group—and close inspection of his history—showed me that his approach was more appealing than continuing to regurgitate everybody else's ideas.

When me and Steve Coleman started M-BASE, it was a bunch of people getting together and talking, but we didn't have anything established. Lester would say, "So what is that? Whatchyall gonna do for yourselves?" (*Weakly:*) "We'll try....We're gonna do...." He said, "I got all this stuff set up, I can play with this band, that band, Brass Fantasy, the Leaders." That struck a chord: You could create a workbase, diversify your skills, using the same core of people—an umbrella structure, like the AACM combined with George Clinton's Parliament-Funkadelic. As opposed to working with the same group all the time, putting out the same kind of records. That's the most boring pursuit I could ever imagine. Because not only are you uninspired, but your audience can anticipate what your stuff is gonna sound like.

Lester Bowie: When you're not really into the music, you get bored, and you transmit that boredom quick. It comes out your horn. Cats who confine themselves to one area, they're limiting themselves. They think they're playing, and they ain't playing.

GO: They stunt their growth. I grew so fast when I had a chance to sub with the World Saxophone Quartet, and play with Craig Harris, Julius Hemphill, David Murray's big band and octet. That was a lot more challenging than playing some show tunes.

LB: Jazz is so difficult. A lot of people think once they've learned these licks they can get up and play them for the rest of their life. But that's not being truthful to the music 'cause it's not developing. Cats you hear that don't make no mistakes? They ain't trying to do nothing. Everything they hear is on the mark, but they've played it so many times.

GO: The beauty of it is regrouping from a mistake. Some of the baddest stuff that's been thought was accidental.

LB: That's right. So I've built a whole career out of making mistakes!

Kevin Whitehead: *Greg, isn't it arrogant to project your own style before proving you've mastered the styles of past giants?*

GO: See, that's where the confusion is. Because these people that we hold in so much esteem were inventors in their own time. Charlie Parker didn't make his mark by continuing to sound like Lester Young. Without your own sound, you couldn't even hang out!

LB: That used to be a thing. You could be good, but even local cats wouldn't regard you as hip unless you had your own personal phrasing and sound. That was a prerequisite. Now they try to turn it inside out, make the least developed the most developed. You do have to go through the music of the past, to learn how to play; but once you do that, that's it. Because jazz is not some academic exercise.

When Wynton got out there, I couldn't believe it. He's supposed to be the *Down Beat*, hip, jazz, Leonard Feather-type motherf**ker. Here's this cat, obviously, obviously—everybody *knows* this cat ain't got it. But they keep on pressing: (*Scholarly voice.*) "He's got the technique, and any day he's gonna come up with the astounding new development...." Believe me, it ain't gonna happen. How long did it take Lee Morgan to play something of his own, or Clifford [Brown], or Booker Little? Wynton's a good musician, but he's been totally miscast. No way in the world is he the King of Jazz, the King of Trumpet.

KW: *Are you saying he doesn't have a great and moving command of what Rex Stewart and Cootie Williams were doing?*

LB: He's not that kind of a cat, that's what I'm saying. You can't feel an emotional attachment because he's not playing *him*. But he can be the King of the *Classical* Trumpet Players, because of his knowledge of jazz and harmony, because (*laughing*) there's no way that he can express hisself. He could completely revolutionize classical trumpet without a doubt. Get classical musicians to improvise, the way they used to. Then he'd be somebody I could respect.

KW: *Wynton has a big job at Lincoln Center, they give him $20,000 commissions, he writes these long suites that are glowingly reviewed in the national press. How can you say he doesn't have it?*

LB: He's got the money. But I feel sorry for him.

GO: This isn't a tirade against him or the institution he represents or anything like that. These are just observations. When things are misappropriated, I have to address it myself. He's a good brother, he's cool, and everything; but his dogma, his rantings, some of those things are unforgivable.

LB: Why is it that these sorts of responsibilities are pressed on a negative person? He even accused Miles [Davis] of treason. Because Miles played a Cyndi Lauper tune ["Time After Time"]? In the fifties, "Surrey with the Fringe on Top" was on the Hit Parade. That's part of the thing, to be contemporary, to express yourself. Wynton's trying to tamper with the music's development, and I see some kind of evil overlay on that.

GO: Unwittingly, people like that become a pawn, they become an agent for those who would like to suppress creative intent.

KW: *Greg, Jon Faddis and Red Rodney already did the rap thing. So why are you jumping on the bandwagon now?*

GO: No, they haven't done the rap thing. I lived in Brooklyn for most of 10 years, I've collaborated with a lot of the rap artists. You can't just jump on that bandwagon and expect to (*laughs at the prospect*) enhance that sensibility. This is a project that I've wanted to do for some time. It's only currently that I've gotten the support and financial backing. I met a lot of resistance, up until I delivered something tangible.

LB: That's what I like about what Greg is doing—he's into the vibe, the rhythms of what's going on out here now. Playing "Bye Bye Blackbird" or sounding like Duke Ellington, that's got nothing to do with where we're coming from. That's the foundation, we got to do the rest of the house. With jazz, it's not so much what you play as how you play it. It's not something you put into the repertoire, it's a living, breathing, young, baby music.

KW: (*Mock-exasperated.*) *"Jazz is America's*

Judi Schiller

classical music." We have to put it into the concert hall to get respect.

LB: I agree with you. Love to see Jazz at Lincoln Center—it should have been there years ago. Every city should have a jazz orchestra with a budget equal to the philharmonic's. But don't negate the other things that are happening, don't stunt the growth of the music. We're not gonna sacrifice the music to get into the concert hall.

GO: These people have to expand their tolerance of other branches in the tree. These are all facets coming from the same root source. I consider what I'm doing, what Lester's been doing, to be truer to jazz's historical motive than playing works reminiscent of other times, another climate.

LB: I think Americans are ready for some jazz now, seriously. They're so bored, they haven't heard the music in so long. On tour with the Leaders, the first 30 minutes of every concert would be totally improvised, really advanced, and it was accepted well: "Good! Yeah! It's here! At last! Something different!" So [cultural institutions] should fund our composers, too: Anthony Braxton, Muhal [Richard Abrams], Roscoe [Mitchell], those AACM cats were writing some advanced things years ago.

GO: Seriously, seriously.

LB: It's not a simple music anymore. So it does belong in the concert hall. But it also belongs in the street, on the farm, it needs equal access everywhere, the same as country 'n' western, rap, anything. Because jazz is all of these. Cat's sitting back scared, "I won't play in that rhythm, I don't play country 'n' western. That ain't jazz." I say, later for them. Jazz is hip-hop, dixieland, anything the people playing it want it to be. "Man, don't listen to that Argentinean shit, it might influence you." C'mon. baby! Influence me!

If it wasn't for Greg and [Organ

Nobody's getting rich, but everybody makes damn near enough to pay their rent for that year. And I tell them this has got to be just one of their projects, so everybody in the band's got three or four bands. We keep working, and we look out for each other.

GO: I've talked to Lester only two or three times about the business of music and the business of self-promotion, but those were some of the key conversations of my career, that catapulted me to the next level. A lot of the older cats were reluctant to share any insight with me at all. I guess they figured, "He just rolled into town and is touring the world with Jon Faddis. You haven't paid your dues," whatever dues are. A due is whatever you do. Do what you wanna do.

LB: Dues is just life: love, tragedy, happiness. It's not about how long you've lived, it's about the emotional attachment.

GO: It's sad when somebody who classifies themselves as a creative artist doesn't allow everyday occurrences and new alliances to influence their music. There's a lot of people who experience a lot of things—tragedy, triumph, all this kind of stuff—that their documented works don't reflect.

LB: We got to get the music back to when musicians had a ball playing music,

have to tell them that. A lot of people attend these lectures at schools and colleges: "Come to New York, blah blah," and they build it up into this grandiose…

KW: *I'm gonna bring my horn down to the Vanguard and sit in…*

GO: …and get a contract. They're like that!

LB: Realistically, you have to develop your network. That involves a lot of things. It involves going places. Say you go to Paris, go over and make some noise for awhile; you come back here, now you got two places to play. Go to a third place, a fourth place, you start developing your audience. Regardless of whether you get a review in *Down Beat*, they're gonna want to hear what you sound like year in and year out.

KW: *And if you stop performing up to your standard, the word's gonna get around.*

LB: Yeah, but then people will pay to see what you've deteriorated to!

KW: *Do you feel sympathy for younger musicians who think they have to do things in a certain way, that they don't have many options?*

LB: I feel so sorry for them boys. Some of them are ruining their careers. Like poor [Wallace] Roney. He's a good musician, he can play, but he pretends he's Miles reincarnated or something. He's got to look like him. There was a time I wanted to be like Miles, too—that was part of being hip. But you don't keep on doing it for the rest of your life.

KW: *Besides James Carter, are there any young players you're encouraged by?*

LB: (*To microphone, with cupped hands.*) "Nicholas Payton! I want you to be a man! Don't listen to all that bullshit, just continue to develop yourself! Don't let nobody tell you to stop, or you're great, or you're not that hip. Please!"

KW: *Greg, any younger players you'd single out?*

GO: Joshua Redman. He's pretty open-minded, as long as he doesn't let his big contract and all the attention infest his mind. Ravi Coltrane, he just needs to be a little more assertive. Antoine Roney, Wallace's brother.

LB: Plays saxophone? He don't look like Wayne Shorter does he? ●

Lester Bowie and Greg Osby

Ensemble saxophonist] James Carter, I'd damn near have given up hope. I thought all the young cats were turning posers and shit. Developing this music is not about how much technique you have. No one has given Don Cherry his creative due. He's not a great trumpet technician, but he is one hell of a musician. He loosened all of us up, set us free.

Americans often look for the easy way out, and they get misinformation. These young guys don't know any better. They've just been to school, and they don't really have an idea what it's like out here yet. It's not just learning some songs; we have to learn how to live and exchange information as people. "Man, how do you do this? I need some help with this, give me some advice." So we can survive in the industry. I got about 30 musicians in my employ.

hanging out, and talking. Now we got cats looking funny at each other. When I was coming up, I got to hang out with some great cats, who treated me like a brother: Blue Mitchell, Lou Donaldson, Tommy Turrentine, Kenny Dorham, Marcus Belgrave, Johnny Coles. They weren't looking at me funny, they were telling me the truth. Cats who act halfway funny ain't nearly on that level.

GO: When I came to town, I was going out to the clubs, trying to find out who the cats were who were dealing, my supposed peer group. And I got a lot of resistance. I'd come up to cats I knew from Berklee or Howard on the gig: "Hey, that's some nice stuff you're doing man, what's happening?" "Aw man, that's just some stuff I'm trying to hear, y'know?" The brush-off. "Man, I'm kind of busy now."

When you talk to young people, you

ANTHONY BRAXTON: OF SCIENCE AND SINATRA

By John Corbett

APRIL 1994

No other figure so handily condenses the hopes and fears of contemporary musical discourse as composer/multiple-reedman Anthony Braxton. Since emerging in the mid sixties, he's been a veritable lightning rod for writers, holding out for some the great non-white hope of musical progress and exploration, at the same time drawing from others vitriolic and dismissive attacks for "over-intellectualization" and treacherous mergers of jazz with contemporary classical music. "I read in *Coda* magazine that our music was a poor example of Webern," he wrote in 1969, in liner notes that were never used for his important solo album *For Alto*. "The jazz musicians say it is not jazz and the classical musicians say it is not classical."

Can you think of another post-sixties musician associated with the avant garde who has *three* full-length studies in print? Graham Lock's 1988 book *Forces in Motion* has now been followed by Ronald Radano's *New Musical Figurations* and a book in German by writer/bassist Peter Niklas Wilson. If you add a forthcoming tome by scholar/trombonist Mike Heffley (who, like Wilson, has also recorded with Braxton) and throw in Braxton's own *Tri-Axium Writings* and *Composition Notebooks*, not to mention liner notes by Braxton and a list of journalists long enough to fill his incessant output of discs with verbiage, you begin to get the picture. What's refreshing, if not surprising, is the fact that there's so little redundancy in these studies—a clear testament to the breadth, depth and richness of Braxton's sound world.

"For me, this is a kind of validation of the path I've taken in my work," he says on the phone from Wesleyan University in Middletown, Conn., where he is currently chairman of the Department of Music. "I have felt from the very beginning that the dynamic implications of the restructural

musics from the sixties time cycle, what I call the 'sixth restructural cycle' musics, were important; and that the seventh restructural response from musicians like myself and the AACM, but also including musicians like Frederic Rzewski, David Behrman, Pauline Oliveros, was legitimate. I'd like to hope that the spectrum of writing will give future students of music an opportunity to consider some of the breakthroughs from, say, the last 27 years, in my case.

"I think the interest in my work goes back to the fact that I have, at every point, tried to document how my processes have evolved. And finally, we find ourselves having to justify what happened in the last 30 years because we're confronted with a power structure that says nothing existed, everything stopped, or everything went crazy after 1960, when Coltrane did *Ascension*, or whatever. In the case of my work, I can talk to you about what happened. I can tell you how I started with it and how I proceeded with it, like it or not. It's evolved in a consistent way, and I can show how it's related to other things. So my work has become, or maybe will become, one of the ways to look around some of these dynamic arguments and start looking for how these experiences might relate to the future. Whatever the merits or demerits of my work, I was always *trying* to do something. I might have blown it, but at least I've documented it in a way where there'll be a lot to read about!"

Most recently, and strangely, Braxton was used by writer Tom Piazza in a *New York Times* piece concerning jazz at Lincoln Center. "I was surprised to see my work again being used in the spectacle-diversion games of the marketplace and media," he admits. "It is fashionable now to put down Wynton Marsalis or Stanley Crouch, but in fact I find myself thinking, 'I will *distance* myself from this.' I used to say I was a jazz musician, and all jazz musicians said, 'No, you're not.' So I thought about it, and said, 'Wait a minute, if I say that I'm a classical

musician, then I can do whatever I want, *including* play jazz! If I say I'm a jazz musician, then I have to play jazz "correctly".'

"All of this is part of what the jazz world has become, what jazz journalism has become, what the jazz recording complex has become. An attempt to enshrine blackness and jazz exoticism and contain it within one definition-space runs contrary to the total progression of the music. So now there's suddenly a controversy at Lincoln Center. Why, if I were president of Lincoln Center, I would choose the musicians *I* liked myself. My disagreements with those guys have more to do with…how can I put it, I find their use of the phenomenon of 'balance' to be profoundly *creative*," he says with uncharacteristic sarcasm.

Braxton sees this all presaging what he calls a "techno-minstrel period." "The new minstrel era is being manifested, in my opinion, by the images portrayed on television, also by a concept of 'blackness' that would be open to the kind of manipulation that is historically consistent. By chopping off the innovation of the music, you have chopped off anything to grow from. If bebop and dixieland are it, that's great, but that's a Eurocentric idea, anyway."

He laughs hard, then sobers a bit. "You can put this in your article if you want to get me shot, but what the heck: The African-American intellectual community from the sixties/seventies time cycle has now embraced Eurocentricity on a level that boggles the mind. Remember now, I'm called the 'white negro.' Nobody wants to use those terms, but I'm supposed to be the embodiment of that which has not been black, when in fact I never gave one inch of my beliefs or experiences. What is this notion that you can corral blackness? That's a marketplace notion. You can be sure that when you start hearing arguments about what is properly black we're moving toward another spectacle and diversion cycle and a narrowing of possibilities. But you show me one person in the last 30 years who has grown up in America and who hasn't had to confront MTV, Bruce Springsteen or my man Frank Sinatra."

In specific, Braxton suggests looking at four current tendencies: "One, the African-American community is no longer gonna be able to hide behind the concept of bogey-man, and as we begin to look into the next thousand years we aren't going to be able to blame the Europeans for every problem on the planet. Two, the concept of marketplace alignment that we see in this period, which has happened before with the early New Orleans period, would seek to, in many cases, build an idea of 'blackness' that would be more limiting than equal to the processes Jelly Roll Morton was talking about. I'm seeing New Orleans used in this time period to crush the composite aspirations of the music. How unfortunate! Three, I think, if you're an African-American, this is a great time to have a *comedy TV show*. Four, we're going to find ourselves forced to look at America in terms of where we are and where we'd like to be as we get ready to move out into the new millennium—I feel that our diversity is part of our strength. I align myself with the people who respect Frank Sinatra, even if they don't want to give him four or five stars! There's no reason to disrespect the guy, he is one of our masters."

That's right, Braxton's a big fan of Ol' Blue Eyes…and the whole Rat Pack. And Barbra Streisand (particularly her version of "Who's Afraid Of The Big Bad Wolf?"). And Johnny Mathis. And Tony Bennett and Nat King Cole. "I have been warming up of late," he 'fesses, "to Natalie Cole, as well. That's one of the wonderful areas

given to us, the American song-form tradition. I'm trying to get tickets to see Sinatra when he comes to Connecticut. I'd do anything to see my man! He's an old guy, he sings like an old guy, but he's a great master who's

Hyou Vielz

come to his old and senile period, and I want to hear it! I'll love every moment. It's past perfect pitch, past all of that. It's got heavy life-experience!

"The music that pushed my button was more than a word 'jazz.' It was individuals who were approaching the music in a certain way, with a certain set of value systems and intentions, a certain honesty and humility. There was respect for similarities and differences." It's in the flow of this broadminded tradition that Braxton

situates himself, placing a high premium on the ethic of innovation and ecumenicalism that perhaps was once more fully associated with jazz. "Nowadays, when you say 'jazz' it's like going to a dixieland festival, there's a way to play and you better not step outside of that or it's not jazz. They've closed off the definitions in a way that's laughable. I'm not jazz, but I'm what jazz *used to be*! When the 'ism' is more important than the 'is,' you have jazz. And…swing it, baby!"

Of course, Braxton's distancing himself from the jazz arguments hasn't exactly made him central to "new music," either. "I've had to build an involvement in the cracks, because no definition camp wanted to respect me as a person, as an African-American, as an American. The classical guys were never interested in me. 'A black guy with a saxophone—are you kidding? Give me a break!'" Without the official recognition of these camps, in the tradition of maverick loners like Harry Partch and John Cage, Braxton has pursued the development of his panoramic, highly personal approach to composition and performance.

Over the last 10 years, he has been working diligently on a theoretico-poetical musical model based on a science-fictive city/state metaphor, replete with storytelling based on a set of characters—check the liner notes to New Albion's *Composition 165* and hat ART's *2 Compositions (Ensemble) 1989/91* for examples of Braxton's stories. These pieces synthesize many aspects of his work, combining his preoccupations with science (which appeared early on, in the erector-set-like schematic titles of his seventies works), ritual and mythology, humor and humanism. He likens the extensive territory in these fantasy lands to Plato's *Republic*. "In my system I will be able to discuss the philosophical implications of the various arguments in the *Tri-Axium Writings*, and at the same time, as far as the 3-D components of that information, give the kindly traveling musician the possibility to move in that space with all kinds of worked-out, choreographed, sequential materials that can be re-targeted inside of that experience."

In October, at the Contemporary Improvised Music Festival in Den Haag, Holland, I had the pleasure of seeing Frederic Rzewski perform Braxton's "Composition 171," for piano and narration, which took the audience on a didactic tour (narrated by an uncostumed Rzewski as a mounted tourist guide, though missing the slide-projected maps and prompters which were called for in the score) through regions that were at once musical and geographical. Braxton's "Composition 174" (for four percussionists), recently performed at Arizona State, "demonstrates a similar logic, in that a group of mountaineers will be scaling a mountain—in fact, they will be demonstrating *gradient* logic interactive components, and as such will be demonstrating the theoretical and poetic implications of my system."

Braxton's poetics, stories and science references might beg the question: What does his music sound like? It's so wide you can't get around it, of course: jagged and smooth, disparate and unified, consonant and dissonant, abstract and down-to-earth, able to leap from Lou Donaldson to Karlheinz Stockhausen in a single bound. As a way in, you might start with his solo music, which has grown considerably since 1968. Where his early solos isolated particular aspects or techniques, Braxton now blends them in search of undiscovered timbral possibilities. For instance, "No. 170c (+77d+99f)" (subtitled "Ojuwain's

Pep Talk," in reference to one of his fantasy characters), from *Wesleyan (12 Alto Solos) 1992*, integrates forced, high squeaks with key-pad slapping and a ghostly parallel line of growled vocalizations. These, he says, will eventually constitute fully scripted vocals to be "spoken in tongues" while simultaneously playing the sax.

Looking ahead, Braxton is excited about the future, stimulated by a recent demonstration of artificial sonic environments by composers Morton Subotnick and Joan LaBarbara. "The act of experiencing music won't be so much about putting a CD on, as much as taking advantage of new processes in technology. CD-ROM is just the beginning, I feel. One aspect I hope to arrive at would be akin to a sonic *Jurassic Park*, a three-dimensional composite state that will invite the traveling listener, musician, experiencer to visit 12 states of geometric identities, within each state a type of people, 12 states of language components, imagery components, gesture components. We have arrived in the future," he says, echoing a proclamation from Sun Ra. "We are now in the post-future, and only the jazz musicians are arguing about 'How High The Moon'."

With all of his wide-eyed enthusiasm for the future, Braxton remains entranced and involved in a variety of traditions. At times, he unquestionably plays jazz (he just finished a record of Charlie Parker tunes with Dutch pianist Misha Mengelberg,

tenor saxophonist Ari Brown, trumpeter Paul Smoker, bassist Joe Fonda, and drummer Pheeroan Ak Laff), though that doesn't necessarily make him a "jazz musician." He'd rather not be hemmed in by those definitions, and it only seems right to respect that wish. Still, in a way, Braxton considers himself a traditionalist (he *has* released two records called *Standards* and two called *In the Tradition*). "They're using tradition to kill the tradition. When you stop to think about it, what's all the controversy about? I've kept my nose on the grindstone about the tradition. I might have been wrong when I thought the kids would be dancing to my music and I'd have $5 million by 1970. But with the exception of that, it was a sound career move!"

As this comment brings us to the end of our phone conversation, I read to Braxton from the *For Alto* notes that he forgot he wrote back in '69. "If this record doesn't sell a million copies I will be very disappointed. Already I am making room on my mantle for a gold record and I am going to have parties and I am preparing an acceptance speech." At this, the nearly 50-year-old laughs his sparkly, wonderful, slightly loony laugh. "That's perfect! I was ready for the *big time*! Beautiful life. I've had a strange career, but I must say, music has made the difference. Tell 'em, in the nineties kids will be dancing to Braxton. We'll all make a billion!" ●

INDEX